PSYCHOLOGISTS' DESK REFERENCE

PSYCHOLOGISTS' DESK REFERENCE

Editors

Gerald P. Koocher

John C. Norcross

Sam S. Hill III

New York • Oxford • Oxford University Press • 1998

Oxford University Press

Oxford   New York
Athens   Auckland   Bangkok   Bogota   Bombay
Buenos Aires   Calcutta   Cape Town   Dar es Salaam
Delhi   Florence   Hong Kong   Istanbul   Karachi
Kuala Lumpur   Madras   Madrid   Melbourne
Mexico City   Nairobi   Paris   Singapore
Taipei   Tokyo   Toronto   Warsaw

and associated companies in
Berlin   Ibadan

Published by Oxford University Press, Inc.
198 Madison Avenue, New York, New York 10016

Oxford is a registered trademark of Oxford University Press

Library of Congress Cataloging-in-Publication Data

Psychologists' desk reference / Gerald P. Koocher,
John C. Norcross, Sam S. Hill.
p.   cm.
Includes index.
ISBN 0-19-511186-9
1. Clinical psychology—Handbooks, manuals, etc.   I. Koocher, Gerald P.
II. Norcross, John C., 1957– .   III. Hill, Sam S.
RC467.2.P78   1998
616.89—dc21   98-5781

3 5 7 9 8 6 4 2

Printed in the United States of America
on acid-free paper

We dedicate this volume to
Robin C. Koocher
Nancy A. Caldwell
and
Betty Ann Pratt Hill

PREFACE

The *Psychologists' Desk Reference* is intended as an authoritative and indispensable companion of mental health practitioners of all theoretical orientations and professional disciplines. This volume organizes and presents key guides and essential information that clinicians, from practicum students to seasoned practitioners, want on their desks. It contains diagnostic codes, test information, report checklists, practice guidelines, treatment principles, ethics refreshers, legal regulations, special population materials, professional resources, practice management tips, and related data that all clinicians need at their fingertips. When asked what the *Psychologists' Desk Reference* includes, we reply, "Everything essential but the tissue box." When asked who should purchase it, we reply, "Every clinician."

A brief history of the *Psychologists' Desk Reference* will place it in context and explain our optimistic expectations for its use. This volume is the product of several years of sequential research and development. In 1994 we sent letters to directors of psychology training programs requesting their thoughts on the contents of such a desk reference. Many ideas were offered in response. In 1995 we surveyed members of the American Psychological Association's (APA) Division 12. Over 500 clinical psychologists responded to the question, "All clinicians seem to have a file in which they place useful checklists, guidelines, and summaries, such as mental status exam questions, suicide risk checklists, and so forth. If you had such a collection at your desk, what topics would you want in it?" In addition to providing hundreds of nominations and a healthy consensus on the desirable contents, the vast majority of the Division 12 respondents agreed that a *Psychologists' Desk Reference* would be both a very practical and a very popular manual for the practicing clinician. During the past two years, we have inventoried the desk contents of several colleagues. We have also formally and informally interviewed dozens of practitioners regarding their preferences for a functional desk reference. In sum, the project began with an ambitious idea, was sharpened by program directors' responses, was strengthened by thoughtful nominations of clinical psychologists across the nation, and was shaped by field observations and collegial feedback.

Two recurring themes of our research and development were that the *Psychologists' Desk*

Reference should be compact and user-friendly. Our fellow practitioners told us in no uncertain terms that the volume should be comprehensive but concise and focused. As a consequence, all 125 contributions are concisely written, designed as summaries or thumbnail guides. We chose only authors who possessed special expertise in particular subject areas and who manifested an ability to synthesize the material in 10 manuscript pages or less. The text is a combination of narrative, numbered or bulleted points, tables, and checklists. The chapter titles are succinct and descriptive. The references accompanying each contribution are not intended as an exhaustive listing but rather as documentation of key sources and recommendations for additional reading.

Multiple features of the *Psychologists' Desk Reference* contribute to its ease of use. These entail

- A detailed table of contents
- A coherent organization into eight parts, in which chapters are arranged both chronologically (according to how treatment or consultation would proceed) and topically
- Cross references within contributions to related chapters in the book
- Running heads that identify the part number and title on the left-hand page and the chapter number and title on the right-hand page

- A comprehensive index at the end of the book

This volume is the culmination of lengthy labors and multitudinous contributions; in the best sense of the term, it has been a "group effort." Although we are, of course, ultimately responsible for the book, we genuinely hope the *Psychologists' Desk Reference* does justice to all of those who have assisted us. From its inception, Joan Bossert, editor extraordinaire at Oxford University Press, nurtured the book. In selecting the contents, directors of training programs, members of the APA's Division of Clinical Psychology, dozens of colleagues, and the editorial board of Oxford Textbooks in Clinical Psychology provided invaluable assistance. More than 100 authors participated generously and adhered to a challenging writing format. Not to be outdone, our spouses and children endured our absences and preoccupations with grace. Finally, we acknowledge each other for the collaborative spirit and the interpersonal pleasures of coediting this volume.

Gerald P. Koocher, Ph.D.
Boston, Massachusetts

John C. Norcross, Ph.D.
Scranton, Pennsylvania

Sam S. Hill III, Psy.D.
Corpus Christi, Texas

CONTENTS

CONTRIBUTORS

Gerald P. Koocher, Ph.D., is chief of psychology at Boston's Children's Hospital and Judge Baker Children's Center. He also serves as associate professor of psychology and executive director of the Linda Pollin Institute at Harvard Medical School. A diplomate of the American Board of Professional Psychology in clinical, health, and forensic psychology, Dr. Koocher is former editor of the *Journal of Pediatric Psychology* and *Clinical Psychologist*. He serves on the editorial boards of several scholarly journals and currently edits the journal *Ethics and Behavior*. A past president of the Massachusetts and New England Psychological Associations as well as three divisions of the American Psychological Association (APA), he is currently a member of the Board of Directors and Treasurer of the APA. He is author or coauthor of more than 100 articles and chapters, in addition to 8 books. His book (with Patricia Keith-Spiegel) *Ethics in Psychology: Professional Standards and Cases* is the best-selling textbook in its field. He has won research grant support from federal and foundation sources totaling more than $2 million. Gerry lives in Brookline, Massachusetts, with his wife, daughter, and an assortment of vociferous psittacines.

John C. Norcross, Ph.D., is professor of psychology and former chair of the department at the University of Scranton and a clinical psychologist in part-time independent practice. Author of more than 125 scholarly articles, Dr. Norcross has written or edited 10 books, the most recent being the fourth edition of *Systems of Psychotherapy: A Transtheoretical Analysis* (with James Prochaska), *An Insider's Guide to Graduate Programs in Clinical and Counseling Psychology* (with Michael Sayette and Tracy Mayne), *Changing for Good* (with James Prochaska and Carlo DiClemente), and *Handbook of Psychotherapy Integration* (with Marvin Goldfried). He has served on the editorial boards of a dozen journals and as a clinical and research consultant to a variety of organizations, including the National Institute of Mental Health. He has also received numerous awards, such as fellow status in professional associations, the Krasner Memorial Award from the American Psychological Association's Division of Psychotherapy, and the Pennsylvania Professor of the Year from the Carnegie Foundation. John lives, works, and plays in the northern Pocono Mountains with his wife, two children, and deranged weimaraner.

Sam S. Hill III, Psy.D., is associate professor of psychology at Texas A & M University–Corpus Christi, where he teaches and coordinates graduate study in psychology. Dr. Hill is also a clinical psychologist in part-time practice of pediatric psychology at the Driscoll Children's Hospital in Corpus Christi, where he is assistant director of medical education for psychology. He serves as director of the Division for the Psychological Study of Diverse Populations of the Texas Psychological Association, as well as chair of the Multicultural Affairs Committee of the American Psychological Association's Division of Psychotherapy. Dr. Hill conducts and reviews research on the psychological aspects of pediatric oncology. Sam lives in Corpus Christi with his wife, three children, and their best friends Schatzie and Gus, the family dachshunds.

Arwa Aamiry, Ph.D.
Graduate Student, Department of Clinical Psychology, University of Florida, Gainesville, FL

Stuart A. Anfang, M.D.
Staff Psychiatrist, Baystate Medical Center, Springfield, MA
Assistant Professor of Psychiatry, Tufts University School of Medicine, Boston, MA

Paul S. Appelbaum, M.D.
A. F. Zeleznik Distinguished Professor and Chair, Department of Psychiatry, University of Massachusetts Medical School, Worcester, MA

Jeannie Baker, M.A., L.P.A.
Associate Clinical Psychologist, Driscoll Children's Hospital, Corpus Christi, TX

Robert W. Baker, M.D.
Associate Professor of Psychiatry, University of Mississippi Medical School, Jackson, MS

Joseph K. Belanoff, M.D.
Acting Assistant Professor of Psychiatry, Stanford University School of Medicine, Stanford, CA
Director of Residency Education, Palo Alto VA Hospital, Palo Alto, CA

Bruce E. Bennett, Ph.D.
Executive Director, American Psychological Association Insurance Trust, Washington, DC

Jane Holmes Bernstein, Ph.D.
Director, Neuropsychology Program, Department of Psychiatry, Children's Hospital, Boston, MA
Assistant Clinical Professor of Psychology, Harvard Medical School, Boston, MA

Larry E. Beutler, Ph.D., ABPP
Professor, Departments of Education and Psychology, University of California, Santa Barbara, CA

Joseph Biederman, M.D.
Director, Joint Program in Pediatric Psychopharmacology Clinic, McLean and Massachusetts General Hospitals, Boston, MA
Professor of Psychiatry, Harvard Medical School, Boston, MA

Bruce Bongar, Ph.D., ABPP
Professor, Pacific Graduate School of Psychology, Palo Alto, CA
Consulting Professor of Psychiatry and the Behavioral Sciences, Stanford University School of Medicine, Stanford, CA

Randy Borum, Psy.D., ABPP
Department of Psychiatry and Behavioral Sciences, Duke University Medical Center, Durham, NC

Barry Bricklin, Ph.D., ABPP
President, Bricklin Associates, Wayne, PA
Adjunct Associate Professor, Institute for Graduate Clinical Psychology, Widener University, Chester, PA

Stanley L. Brodsky, Ph.D.
Professor, Department of Psychology, University of Alabama, Tuscaloosa, AL

Pamela Brouillard, Psy.D.
Assistant Professor of Psychology, Texas A & M University, Corpus Christi, TX

Laura S. Brown, Ph.D.
Independent Practice, Seattle, WA

Simon H. Budman, Ph.D.
President, Innovative Training Systems, Newton, MA
Assistant Professor of Psychology, Harvard Medical School, Boston, MA

Robin A. Buhrke, Ph.D.
Coordinator of Lesbian, Gay, and Bisexual Services, Counseling and Psychological Services
Assistant Clinical Professor in Psychiatry and Behavioral Sciences, Duke University, Durham, NC

James N. Butcher, Ph.D.
Professor of Psychology, University of Minnesota, Minneapolis, MN

Esther Calzada, B.A.
Graduate Student in Clinical and Health Psychology, University of Florida, Gainesville, FL

Dorothy W. Cantor, Psy.D.
Independent Practice, Westfield, NJ

Michael P. Carey, Ph.D.
Professor of Psychology, Syracuse University, Syracuse, NY

Kara Cattani-Thompson, B.S.
Doctoral Student in Clinical Psychology, Florida State University, Tallahassee, FL

Dianne L. Chambless, Ph.D.
William Leon Wylie Professor of Psychology, University of North Carolina, Chapel Hill, NC

Jeremy A. Chiles, B.S.
Doctoral Candidate in Clinical Psychology, Brigham Young University, Provo, UT

John F. Clarkin, Ph.D.
Professor of Psychology, Cornell University Medical College, New York Hospital, White Plains, NY

Jennifer S. Clifford, B.S.
Graduate Student in Psychology,
    Villanova University, Villanova, PA

Phebe Cramer, Ph.D.
Professor of Psychology, Williams College,
    Williamstown, MA

Roger D. Davis, Ph.D.
Institute for Advanced Studies in Personology and
    Psychopathology, Coral Gables, FL

Charles DeBattista, D.M.H., M.D.
Department of Psychiatry and Behavioral Sciences,
    Stanford University School of Medicine,
    Stanford, CA

Carlo C. DiClemente, Ph.D.
Professor and Chair, Department of Psychology,
    University of Maryland, Baltimore County,
    Baltimore, MD

Joyce S. Dorado, Ph.D.
Department of Psychiatry, University of Califor-
    nia, Los Angeles, School of Medicine and
    Harbor-UCLA Medical Center, Torrance, CA

Sheila M. Eyberg, Ph.D., ABPP
Professor of Clinical and Health Psychology,
    University of Florida, Gainesville, FL

David Faust, Ph.D.
Department of Psychology, University of Rhode
    Island, Kingston, RI

William F. Fluck, Jr., Ph.D.
Postdoctoral Fellow, National Center for PTSD, VA
    Medical Center, Boston, MA
Fellow in Psychiatry, Boston University School of
    Medicine, Boston, MA

Pamela A. Foelsch, Ph.D.
Instructor of Psychology,
Cornell University Medical College, New York
    Hospital, White Plains, NY

Kenneth France, Ph.D.
Professor of Psychology, Shippensburg University,
    Shippensburg, PA
Franco Psychological Associates, Carlisle, PA

Margaret Gatz, Ph.D.
Professor of Psychology, University of Southern
    California, Los Angeles, CA

Samuel Z. Goldhaber, M.D.
Staff Cardiologist, Brigham and Women's Hospital,
    Boston, MA
Associate Professor of Medicine, Harvard Medical
    School, Boston, MA

Stuart M. Goldman, M.D.
Director of Psychiatric Education and Diagnostic
    Services, Children's Hospital, Boston, MA
Assistant Professor of Psychiatry, Harvard Medical
    School, Boston, MA

Juan Carlos Gonzalez, Ph.D.
Children's Psychiatric Center, Miami, FL

Carol D. Goodheart, Ed.D.
Independent Practice, PsychHealth, P.A.,
    Highland Park, NJ

Betty N. Gordon, Ph.D.
Research Associate Professor, University of North
    Carolina, Chapel Hill, NC

John R. Graham, Ph.D.
Professor of Psychology, Kent State University,
    Kent, OH

Roger L. Greene, Ph.D.
Professor and Director of Clinical Training
    Pacific Graduate School of Psychology,
    Palo Alto, CA

Kathryn E. Gustafson, Ph.D.
Assistant Professor of Medical Psychology,
    Duke University, Durham, NC

James D. Guy, Jr., Ph.D., ABPP
Dean and Professor, Graduate School of
    Psychology, Fuller Theological Seminary,
    Pasadena, CA
Independent Practice, Pasadena, CA

Douglas C. Haldeman, Ph.D.
Independent Practice, Seattle, WA
Assistant Clinical Professor of Psychology,
    University of Washington, Seattle, WA

Eric A. Harris, J.D., Ed.D.
Risk Management Consultant, American
    Psychological Association Insurance Trust,
    Washington, DC

Susan Heitler, Ph.D.
Adjunct Faculty, University of Denver,
    Graduate School of Professional Psychology,
    Denver, CO

Thomas P. Hogan, Ph.D.
Professor of Psychology and Director, Assessment
    and Institutional Research Office, University of
    Scranton, Scranton, PA

Lê X. Hy, Ph.D.
Center for Multicultural Human Services, Falls
    Church, VA
George Mason University, Fairfax, VA

Ronn Johnson, Ph.D.
Associate Professor and Director of Training,
    University of San Diego, San Diego, CA
Co-Investigator, Center for Research on Child and
    Adolescent Mental Health Services, Children's
    Hospital and Health Center, San Diego, CA

Arthur E. Jongsma, Jr., Ph.D.
Director, Psychological Consultants,
    Grand Rapids, MI

Betsy Kammerer, Ph.D.
Staff Neuropsychiatrist, Department of Psychiatry,
    Children's Hospital, Boston, MA
Instructor in Psychology, Harvard Medical School,
    Boston, MA

Rhonda S. Karg, B.S.
Doctoral Student in Clinical Psychology,
    Auburn University, Auburn, AL

Terence M. Keane, Ph.D.
Chief, Psychology Service, VA Medical Center,
    Boston, MA
Vice Chairman, Department of Psychiatry, Boston
    University School of Medicine, and Director of
    National Center for Post Traumatic Stress Dis-
    order, Boston, MA

Patricia Keith-Spiegel, Ph.D.
Voran Honors Distinguished Professor of Social
    and Behavioral Sciences, Ball State University,
    Muncie, IN

Shelli R. Kesler, B.S.
Doctoral Candidate in Clinical Psychology,
    Brigham Young University, Provo, UT

Bob G. Knight, Ph.D.
Merle H. Bensinger Associate Professor, Andrus
    Gerontology Center, University of Southern
    California, Los Angeles, CA

Mireika Kobayashi, B.S.
Research Assistant, Department of
    Psychology, University of Scranton,
    Scranton, PA

Manferd D. Koch, Ph.D.
Professor of Psychology,
    Texas A&M University, Corpus Christi, TX

Stuart L. Koman, Ph.D.
Psychological Consultant, Winchester, MA

Kathryn Kuehnle, Ph.D.
Adjunct Assistant Professor, Department of Mental
    Health Law and Policy, Louis de la Parte Florida
    Mental Health Institute, University of South
    Florida, Tampa, FL

Michael J. Lambert, Ph.D.
Professor of Psychology, Brigham Young
    University, Provo, UT

Arnold A. Lazarus, Ph.D., ABPP
Distinguished Professor Emeritus, Graduate School
    of Applied and Professional Psychology, Rutgers
    University, New Brunswick, NJ
President, Center for Multimodal Psychological
    Services, Princeton, NJ

Clifford N. Lazarus, Ph.D.
Director, Comprehensive Psychological Services,
    Princeton, NJ
Clinical Director, Center for Multimodal Psycho-
    logical Services, Princeton, NJ

Jay L. Lebow, Ph.D., ABPP
Director of Research, Chicago Center for Family
    Health, Chicago, IL
Clinical Associate Professor, Department of Psychi-
    atry and Behavioral Sciences, University of
    Chicago, Chicago, IL

Ronald F. Levant, Ed.D., ABPP
Dean and Professor, Center for Psychological
    Studies, Nova Southeastern University,
    Fort Lauderdale, FL

Karen Levine, Ph.D.
Children's Hospital, Spaulding Rehabilitation
    Hospital, and Harvard Medical School,
    Boston, MA

Paul D. Lipsitt, LL.B., Ph.D., ABPP
Lecturer on Psychology, Department of
    Psychiatry, Harvard Medical School,
    Boston, MA
Senior Supervisor and Clinical Associate,
    Student Mental Health Center, Boston
    University, Boston, MA

Ray William London, Ph.D., ABPP, ABPH
C.E.O., London Associates International, London
    Research Ltd., Tustin, CA

Joseph LoPiccolo, Ph.D.
Professor of Psychology, University of Missouri,
    Columbia, MO
Director of Psychological Services, Sexual Medicine
    Center of Missouri, Columbia, MO

James L. Lukefahr, M.D.
Associate Professor of Pediatrics,
    University of Texas Medical Branch,
    Galveston, TX

Don-David Lusterman, Ph.D., ABPP
Independent Practice, Baldwin, NY

G. Alan Marlatt, Ph.D.
Professor of Psychology and Director, Addictive
    Behaviors Research Center, University of Wash-
    ington, Seattle, WA

Geoffrey R. McKee, Ph.D., ABPP
Chief Psychologist, Forensic Psychiatry
    Division, William S. Hall Psychiatric Institute,
    Columbia, SC

Theodore Millon, Ph.D., D.Sc.
Visiting Professor, Harvard Medical School,
    Boston, MA
Dean, Institute for Advanced Studies in Personol-
    ogy and Psychopathology, Coral Gables, FL

Theresa B. Moyers, Ph.D.
Veterans Affairs Medical Center,
    Albuquerque, NM

Aaron Nelson, Ph.D.
Director of Neuropsychology, Brigham and
    Women's Hospital, Boston, MA
Instructor in Psychology, Harvard Medical School,
    Boston, MA

Margaret O'Connor, Ph.D.
Director of Neuropsychology, Behavioral Neurol-
    ogy Unit, Beth Israel Deaconess Medical Center,
    Boston, MA
Assistant Professor of Psychology, Harvard Medical
    School, Boston, MA

Brian J. O'Leary, B.S.
Research Assistant, Department of Psychology,
    University of Scranton, Scranton, PA

Elaine Orabona, Ph.D.
Major, U.S. Air Force, Keesler AFB Medical Center,
    Biloxi, MS

Irene S. Pollin, M.S.W.
President, Linda Pollin Foundation, Chevy
    Chase, MD
Lecturer in Psychiatry, Harvard Medical School,
    Boston, MA

Kenneth S. Pope, Ph.D., ABPP
Independent Practice, Norwalk, CT

Penny Prather, Ph.D.
Staff Neuropsychologist, Department of Psy-
    chiatry, Children's Hospital, Boston, MA
Instructor in Psychology, Harvard Medical School,
    Boston, MA

James O. Prochaska, Ph.D.
Professor of Psychology and Director of the Cancer
    Prevention Research Center, University of
    Rhode Island, Kingston, RI

Vianey R. Reinhardt, M.A.
Doctoral Student in Clinical Psychology, Univer-
    sity of North Texas, Denton, TX

Robert J. Resnick, Ph.D., ABPP
Dominion Behavioral Healthcare, Richmond, VA
Randolph-Macon College, Ashland, VA

Celiane Rey-Casserly, Ph.D., ABPP
Staff Neuropsychologist, Department of Psy-
    chiatry, Children's Hospital, Boston MA
Instructor in Psychology, Harvard Medical School,
    Boston, MA

Barry A. Ritzler, Ph.D., ABPP
Psychology Department, Long Island University,
    Brooklyn, NY

Lisa J. Roberts, M.A.
Department of Psychology, University of Wash-
    ington, Seattle, WA

Richard Rogers, Ph.D., ABPP
Professor of Psychology, University of North Texas,
    Denton, TX

Alice K. Rubenstein, Ed.D.
Monroe Psychotherapy and Consultation Center,
    Pittsford, NY

Karen J. Saywitz, Ph.D.
Associate Professor, UCLA School of Medicine, Los
    Angeles, CA
Director, Child and Adolescent Psychology, Harbor-
    UCLA Medical Center, Torrance, CA

Charles E. Schaefer, Ph.D.
Professor of Psychology and Director of the Center
    for Psychological Services, Fairleigh Dickinson
    University, Hackensack, NJ

Alan F. Schatzberg, M.D.
Professor of Psychiatry and Behavioral Sciences,
    Stanford University School of Medicine,
    Stanford, CA

Gary Richard Schoener, B.A.
Executive Director, Walk-In Counseling Center,
    Minneapolis, MN

Carolyn S. Schroeder, Ph.D.
Chapel Hill Pediatric Psychology, Chapel Hill, NC
Research Professor of Psychology, University of
    North Carolina, Chapel Hill, NC

David L. Shapiro, Ph.D., ABPP
Chief Psychologist, Maryland Penitentiary, Balti-
    more, MD
Faculty Associate, Johns Hopkins University School
    of Continuing Studies, Baltimore, MD

Thomas P. Smith, M.A., C.A.G.S.
Psychologist, University of Scranton Counseling Center, Scranton, PA

Linda C. Sobell, Ph.D., ABPP
Professor, Center for Psychological Studies, Nova Southeastern University, Fort Lauderdale, FL

Mark B. Sobell, Ph.D., ABPP
Professor, Center for Psychological Studies, Nova Southeastern University, Fort Lauderdale, FL

Thomas J. Spencer, M.D.
Assistant Director, Pediatric Psychopharmacology Clinic, Massachusetts General Hospital, Boston, MA
Assistant Professor of Psychiatry, Harvard Medical School, Boston, MA

Len Sperry, M.D., Ph.D.
Department of Psychiatry, Medical College of Wisconsin, Milwaukee, WI

Brett N. Steenbarger, Ph.D.
Assistant Professor and Director of Student Counseling, Department of Psychiatry and Behavioral Sciences, State University of New York Health Center, Syracuse, NY

Richard M. Suinn, Ph.D., ABPP
Professor of Psychology, Colorado State University, Fort Collins, CO

Robert J. Thompson, Jr., Ph.D., ABPP
Dean of Undergraduate Affairs and Professor of Medical Psychology, Duke University, Durham, NC

Paula T. Trzepacz, M.D.
Professor of Psychiatry and Neurology, University of Mississippi Medical School, Jackson, MS

Leon VandeCreek, Ph.D., ABPP
Dean, School of Professional Psychology, Wright State University, Dayton, OH

Lynn M. Van Male, M.A.
Doctoral Candidate, Department of Psychology, University of Missouri, Columbia, MO

R. Enrrique Varela, M.S.
Clinical Child Psychology Program, University of Kansas, Lawrence, KS

Melba J. T. Vasquez, Ph.D., ABPP
Executive Director, Vasquez & Associates Mental Health Services, Austin, TX

David A. Vermeersch, B.S.
Doctoral Candidate in Clinical Psychology, Brigham Young University, Provo, UT

Eric M. Vernberg, Ph.D.
Associate Professor, Clinical Child Psychology Program, University of Kansas, Lawrence, KS

Janice Ware, Ph.D.
Director, Pediatric Psychology, Division of General Pediatrics, Children's Hospital and Instructor in Psychology, Harvard Medical School, Boston, MA

Irving B. Weiner, Ph.D., ABPP
Professor of Psychology and Behavioral Medicine, University of South Florida, Tampa, FL

Arthur N. Wiens, Ph.D., ABPP
Professor of Medical Psychology, Oregon Health Sciences University, Portland, OR

Timothy E. Wilens, M.D.
Director of Substance Abuse Services, Pediatric Psychopharmacology Clinic, Massachusetts General Hospital, Boston, MA
Associate Professor of Psychiatry, Harvard Medical School, Boston, MA

Oliver B. Williams, Ph.D.
Research Associate, Department of Education, University of California, Santa Barbara, CA

Susan L. Williams-Quinlan, Ph.D.
Counseling Center Director and Assistant Professor of Psychology, University of Scranton, Scranton, PA

Jennifer Kate Henley Woody, M.S.
School Psychologist, Millard Public Schools, Millard, NE

Robert Henley Woody, Ph.D., J.D., ABPP
Professor, Department of Psychology, University of Nebraska, Omaha, NE

Victor J. Yalom, Ph.D.
Independent Practice, San Francisco, CA

Edward L. Zuckerman, Ph.D.
Armbrust, PA

PART I
Assessment and Diagnosis

1 LIFETIME PREVALENCE OF MENTAL DISORDERS IN THE GENERAL POPULATION

Brian J. O'Leary & John C. Norcross

The following table presents the approximate lifetime prevalence rates of mental disorders in the general population of the United States. These rates will obviously vary as a result of the different sample compositions, diagnostic criteria, and assessment methods employed in each study. Three data sources are presented: the National Comorbidity Study (NCS; Kessler et al., 1994); the fourth edition of the *Diagnostic and Statistical Manual of Mental Disorders* (*DSM-IV*; American Psychiatric Association, 1994); and the NIMH Epidemiological Catchment Area (ECA) study (Robins & Reiger, 1991).

The NCS reports prevalence rates of mental disorders from a national probability sample of noninstitutionalized civilians across the 48 continental states and uses *DSM-III-R* diagnostic criteria. The *DSM-IV* extracts its prevalence rates from various epidemiological and clinical studies reported in the literature. The ECA bases its prevalence rates on structured interviews of more than 20,000 American adults in five cities across the United States and uses *DSM-III* criteria. In those disorders where a gender predominance has been established, separate prevalence rates are provided for men and women.

TABLE 1. Lifetime Prevalence of Mental Disorders in the General Population

Disorder	NCS	*DSM-IV*	ECA
Adjustment disorders		5.0–20.0%	
Agoraphobia w/out panic disorder	5.3% overall 3.5% of men 7.0% of women		

(continued)

3

TABLE 1. Lifetime Prevalence of Mental Disorders in the General Population (*continued*)

Disorder	NCS	*DSM-IV*	ECA
Alcohol abuse	9.4% overall 12.5% of men 6.4% of women	7.0%	
Alcohol dependence	14.1% overall 20.1% of men 8.2% of women	14.0%	13.8% overall 23.8% of men 4.6% of women
Alzheimer's		2.0–4.0% age 65 and over	
Amphetamine dependence/abuse		2.0%	
Anorexia nervosa		0.5–1.0% of women	
Antisocial personality disorder	3.5% overall 5.8% of men 1.2% of women	3.0% of men 1.0% of women	2.6% overall 4.5% of men 0.08% of women
Attention-deficit/hyperactivity disorder		3.0–5.0% of school-age children	
Autism		0.02–0.05%	
Bipolar I disorder		0.4–1.6%	
Bipolar II disorder		0.5%	
Borderline personality disorder		2.0%	
Bulimia nervosa		1.0–3.0% of women	
Conduct disorder		6.0–16.0% of boys 2.0–9.0% of girls	
Conversion disorder		0.01–0.3%	
Cyclothymic disorder		3.0–5.0%	
Delirium		20.0% over age 65 in general medical hospitals	
Delusional disorder		0.03%	
Dementia		3.0% with severe cognitive impairment 20.0% over age 85	
Dissociative fugue		0.2%	
Dissociative identity disorder		subject of controversy	
Drug abuse	4.4% overall 5.4% of men 3.5% of women		
Drug dependence	7.5% overall 9.2% of men 5.9% of women		6.2% overall 7.7% of men 4.8% of women
Dysthymic disorder	6.4% overall 4.8% of men 8.0% of women	6.0%	3.3% overall 2.2% of men 4.1% of women
Encopresis		1.0% of 5-year-olds	
Enuresis		7.0% of 5-year-old boys 3.0% of 5-year-old girls 3.0% of 10-year-old boys 2.0% of 10-year-old girls	
Gender identity disorder		0.003% of men 0.001% of women[a]	
Generalized anxiety disorder	5.1% overall 3.6% of men 6.6% of women	5.0%	5.8% overall 4.5% of men 6.8% of women
Histrionic personality disorder		2.0–3.0%	
Kleptomania		<5.0% of identified shoplifters	
Learning disorders		2.0–10.0% 5.0% of students in public schools	
Major depressive disorder	17.1% overall 12.7% of men 21.3% of women	5.0–12.0% of men 10.0–25.0% of women	6.4% overall 3.6% of men 8.7% of women

TABLE 1. Lifetime Prevalence of Mental Disorders in the General Population (*continued*)

Disorder	NCS	DSM-IV	ECA
Manic episode	1.6% overall 1.6% of men 1.7% of women		0.8% overall 0.7% of men 0.9% of women
Mental retardation		1.0%	
Narcissistic personality disorder		<1.0%	
Narcolepsy		0.02–0.16%	
Nonaffective psychosis (also see schizophrenia)[b]	0.7% overall 0.6% of men 0.8% of women		
Obsessive-compulsive disorder		2.5%	2.6% overall 2.0% of men 3.0% of women
Obsessive-compulsive personality disorder		1.0%	
Opioid dependence/abuse		0.7%	
Oppositional defiant disorder		2.0–16.0%	
Panic disorder	3.5% overall 2.0% of men 5.0% of women	1.5–3.5%	1.6% overall 1.0% of men 2.1% of women
Paranoid personality disorder		0.5–2.5%	
Pathological gambling		1.0–3.0%	
Phobia (general)			14.3% overall 10.0% of men 17.4% of women
Posttraumatic stress disorder		1.0–14.0%	
Schizophrenia (also see nonaffective psychosis)		0.5–1.0%	1.5% overall 1.2% of men 1.7% of women
Schizophreniform disorder		0.2%	
Schizotypal personality disorder		3.0%	
Sedative, hypnotic, or anxiolytic dependence/abuse		1.2%	
Selective mutism		<1.0%	
Separation anxiety disorder		4.0% of children	
Simple/specific phobia (also see phobia [general])	11.3% overall 6.7% of men 15.7% of women	10.0–11.3%	
Sleep terror episodes		1.0–6.0% of children 1.0% of adults	
Sleepwalking disorder		1.0–5.0% of children 1.0–7.0% of adults	
Social phobia	13.3% overall 11.1% of men 15.5% of women	3.0–13.0%	
Somatization disorder		2.0% of women 0.2% of men	0.1% overall 0.02% of men 0.23% of women
Stuttering		1.0% of prepubertal children 0.8% of adolescents	
Tourette's disorder		0.04–0.05%	
Trichotillomania		1.0–2.0% of college samples	

[a]Information obtained from a survey conducted in smaller European countries.
[b]Includes schizophrenia, schizophreniform disorder, schizoaffective disorder, delusional disorder, and atypical psychosis.

References & Readings

American Psychiatric Association (1994). *Diagnostic and statistical manual of mental disorders* (4th ed.). Washington, DC: American Psychiatric Association.

Dohrenwend, B. P., Dohrenwend, B. S., Gould, M. S., Link, B., Neugebauer, R., & Wunch-Hitzig, R. (1980). *Mental illness in the United States: Epidemiological estimates.* New York: Praeger.

Kessler, R. C., McGonagle, K. A., Zhao, S., Nelson, C. B., Hughes, M., Eshleman, S., Wittchen, H. U., & Kendler, K. S. (1994). Lifetime and 12-month prevalence of *DSM-III-R* psychiatric disorders in the United States: Results from the National Comorbidity Study. *Archives of General Psychiatry, 51,* 8–19.

President's Commission on Mental Health (1978). *Report to the President from the President's Commission on Mental Health.* Washington, DC.

Reiger, D. A., Myers, J. K., Kramer, M., Robins, L. N., Blazer, D. G., Hough, R. L., Eaton, W. W., & Loche, B. Z. (1984). The NIMH Epidemiologic Catchment Area program. *Archives of General Psychiatry, 41,* 934–941.

Robins, L. N., Helzer, J. E., Weissman, M. M., Orvaschel, H., Gruenberg, E., Burke, J. D., Jr., & Reiger, D. A. (1984). Lifetime prevalences of specific psychiatric disorders in three sites. *Archives of General Psychiatry, 41,* 949–958.

Robins, L. N., & Reiger, D. A. (Eds.) (1991). *Psychiatric disorders in America: The Epidemiological Catchment Area study.* New York: Free Press.

Related Topics

Chapter 20, "*DSM-IV* Multiaxial System"

2 MENTAL STATUS EXAMINATION

Robert W. Baker & Paula T. Trzepacz

In conjunction with history taking, mental status examination (MSE) provides the database for psychiatric assessment and differential diagnosis. It comprises the observed and objective portion of the evaluation, along with results of laboratory and radiological testing. Although the MSE is part of a thorough physical examination, it is usually more comprehensive when performed by a psychiatrist than when performed by other physicians. Except for the cognitive and language portions of the MSE, which usually are administered in a structured fashion, much of the MSE is semistructured, and information is obtained throughout an interview.

The following material describes a standard format for documenting the MSE, along with some advice for its performance. During assessments for follow-up, only particular portions of the MSE may be emphasized. This outline for the MSE has six sections and is derived from our textbook, *The Psychiatric Mental Status Examination.*

APPEARANCE, ATTITUDE, AND ACTIVITY

Appearance is ascertained by direct observation of physical characteristics. The following items should be considered:

• *Level of consciousness:* Normally patients are attentive and respond to stimuli; when this is not the case, the examiner may try to rouse the patient, such as by speaking loudly or shaking the patient's arm. "Hyperarousal" or "hypervigilance" is sometimes seen, such as in mania or stimulant intoxication. A decreased level of consciousness can be described in rough order of increasing severity with the following terms: drowsy, lethargic, obtunded, stuporous, comatose.

- *Apparent age* is judged by vigor, mode of dress, mannerisms, and condition of hair and skin.
- *Position/posture* records where the patient is (e.g., in bed, on a chair, or on the floor) and pertinent abnormalities, such as the "waxy flexibility" of catatonia or the use of leather restraints.
- *Attire/grooming* is reported in nonjudgmental, descriptive terms, such as casually dressed, neat, clean, meticulously groomed, unshaven, disheveled, clothing torn, mismatched socks.
- *Abnormal physical traits* are noted, such as skin lesions or tattoos, body odor, sweating, amputations, Down's syndrome facies.
- *Eye contact* can be described as "good" or "poor" or is described quantitatively (e.g., "made normal eye contact about half of the time").

Attitude describes the patient's approach to the interview:

- Degree and type of *cooperativeness:* Useful terms are cooperative/uncooperative, friendly, open, hostile, guarded, suspicious, or regressed.
- *Resistance,* if any, is noted here, such as "He refused to answer any questions about his family." Resistance may be nonverbal, such as avoiding eye contact, muteness, or fist shaking.

Activity describes physical movement. Five aspects to consider are as follows:

- *Voluntary movement* and its intensity: Increased movement is described directly ("He was pacing/fidgety/restless") or is labeled "psychomotor agitation." Decreased movement is localized (e.g., paresis or masked facies) or general, known as bradykinesia or (especially if mentation also is slowed or delayed) psychomotor retardation.
- *Involuntary movements* are observed at rest, during motion, and, if relevant, with provocative maneuvers, such as having the patient stand with eyes closed and arms outstretched. Tremors are regular or rhythmic. Resting tremor improves during action, whereas intention tremor is worst during the most demanding phase of an action. Chorea is sudden and irregular, while athetoid movements are irregular and writhing. Dystonias are sustained, like a muscle spasm.
- *Automatic movements* may appear spontaneously during partial seizures. Common examples are chewing, lip smacking, or clumsy limb movements. Movements may be more complex, such as walking or pulling at buttons, but purposeful action is not characteristic of automatism. Typically the patient has decreased alertness during automatic movement; if repetitive, automatisms usually are stereotyped, that is, the same movement is repeated.
- *Tics* are sudden, stereotyped, brief, abrupt, and sometimes (temporarily) consciously mitigated or suppressed. They may increase if topic matter is stressful. Most noticeable are facial tics, but other body areas can be affected, and tics can be verbal utterances, such as in Tourette's disorder.
- *Compulsions* may be reported by the patient or observed by the examiner. Screen by asking about repeated or undesired activities. Patients should recognize that the behavior is unreasonable, but they may become anxious if the action is resisted. Common compulsions include hand washing or checking (locks, stove, wallet, etc.).

MOOD AND AFFECT

Mood is a person's predominant feeling state at a given time. It is judged primarily by self-report but also by observation throughout the interview. Individuals with "alexithymia" have diminished awareness and inability to describe their mood state; nonverbal expression is inhibited. Listed below are six categories of mood states that are used to describe the predominant mood:

- *Normal:* calm, euthymic, pleasant, unremarkable.
- *Angry:* belligerent, frustrated, hostile, irritable, sullen.
- *Euphoric:* cheerful, elated, happy.
- *Apathetic:* bland, dull.
- *Dysphoric:* despondent, distraught, hopeless, overwhelmed, sad.
- *Apprehensive:* anxious, fearful, frightened, panicky, tense, worried.

Affect describes external manifestations of a person's emotional state. Unlike mood, description of affect is entirely objective, and affect is usually variable over the course of an interview, whereas mood usually is sustained for relatively longer periods. The following parameters of affect can be recorded:

- *Type* of affect: Types of affect seen during the interview are reported, using the same list of terms outlined for mood above.
- *Intensity* of affect: When increased, affect is described as "heightened" or "exaggerated"; reduced is "blunted"; no emotional expression is "flat" (flat affect has no intensity, range, or mobility).
- *Reactivity* of affect is assessed in the response to emotional cues from the examiner. Normally the examiner should see reaction to very subtle cues, such as smiling or commiserating.
- *Range* of affect is measured in the variety of emotions expressed during an interview. Inability to express both happy and negative feelings is "restricted" affective range.
- *Appropriateness* or congruence of affect is monitored by comparing emotional expression to the subject matter. For example, the examiner should expect a frightened appearance when anyone is describing being pursued or poisoned by the CIA.
- *Mobility* is the changeability of affect. Rapidly changing affect, especially if precipitous and unprovoked, is "labile" or "volatile."

Slowness in change of affective expression can be called "constricted" or "phlegmatic" affect; unchanging affect is "fixed" or "immobile."

SPEECH AND LANGUAGE

Careful examination can differentiate types of aphasia (demonstrated in Figure 4.2 and Table 4.2 of Trzepacz and Baker, 1993) or other language disorders. Major psychiatric disorders (e.g., mania) can affect speech or language. Eight speech and language parameters should be considered:

- *Fluency* is the initiation and flow of speech in conversation; its description is based on the smoothness of the speech rather than its communicativeness. Fluency is assessed in spontaneous speech, its initiation and maintenance, pauses between words, use of connectors, and grammatical correctness. Abnormalities include nonfluent aphasia, scanning, stuttering, and cluttering.
- *Comprehension:* Spoken and written comprehension is tested by increasingly complex commands (such as "open your mouth" and "touch your right ear with your left hand"). Deafness, paresis, or apraxia may falsely suggest impaired comprehension.
- *Repetition:* Tested by asking the patient to repeat words and phrases.
- *Naming:* Assessed by confronting with an object or picture and asking the patient for the name. Other approaches include requesting the patient to generate a list of words starting with a given letter or testing in nonvisual modalities (e.g., naming a small object by touch alone).
- *Writing:* Assessed by giving dictation and also by requesting spontaneous composition.
- *Reading:* Assessed by requesting patient to read aloud (visual impairment should be excluded).
- *Prosody:* Assessed by monitoring intonation, rate, rhythm, and musicality of speech and relationship of intonation to content of speech. With deficient prosody, speech is monotonous. Prosody underlies much of the emotional expressiveness of speech, such as sarcasm (consider the different ways to say

"you're *really* smart"). Abnormally fast or slow speech is recorded here. Irrespective of rate, speech that is persistently difficult to interrupt is "pressured."

- *Quality of speech:* Assessed in pitch, volume, articulation, and amount. Articulation is tested with phrases like "no ifs, ands, or buts." Dysarthrias reduce clarity. Manics often speak loudly, and depressed individuals may speak softly, with prolonged latency and reduced spontaneity.

THOUGHT PROCESS, THOUGHT CONTENT, AND PERCEPTION

Thought process (or "form") is assessed in spontaneous communication and in answers to questions throughout the interview. This part of the MSE is objective in that it is based on observation only, but it requires significant reflection and judgment by the clinician, such as "How clear was the communication?"; "Was I frequently confused by the patient?"; "Did he jump from subject to subject, or keep returning to one subject?"; "Did words or ideas keep coming 'out of the blue'?" The following two elements should be included in the MSE report:

- *Connectedness* of thought is how logically or smoothly statements and ideas flow from each other and how relevant answers are to questions. Decreased connectedness is described (in terms for increasing severity) as tangentiality, loosening of associations, or word salad. Circumstantiality is talking around a subject. Flight of ideas is quick and frequent tangentiality.
- *Peculiar thought processes:* neologisms, perseveration, clanging, or blocking.

Thought content also is described. Spontaneous speech is important, especially in identifying predominant themes, but it is helpful to specifically inquire about the following:

- *Delusions* may be clear-cut and spontaneously divulged or may appear only on questioning. For example, when persecutory psychosis is suspected, gentle probes such as "How safe do you feel?"; "How are people treating you?"; or "Do strangers seem to be noticing you?" may be revealing. Reality testing similarly can be assessed: "How certain are you of that?"; "What do you think is the reason for that?"; or "Do you think it could have been a coincidence?" Behavioral impact determines the severity or dangerousness of delusions. The type of delusion is recorded, such as persecutory, grandiose, referential, somatic, religious, or nihilistic.
- *Overvalued ideas* are illogical or objectively false beliefs, but compared with delusions they are held less tenaciously or with better recognition that they may be wrong.
- *Obsessions* are undesired and unpleasant ("ego-dystonic"); at times difficult to distinguish from delusions, obsessions are recognized by the patient as unreasonable or unwarranted. Ask about any ideas or thoughts that keep repeating; specifically query for common obsessions like losing control, doing something dangerous or embarrassing, or being contaminated by germs.
- *Rumination* is persistent mulling over of an unpleasant thought or theme.
- *Preoccupation* is an unduly prominent recurrent topic that is not a delusion or an obsession.
- *Suicidal ideation* may be expressed spontaneously; if not, probe directly by asking about thoughts of death and indirectly by discussing future plans. Questions about suicidality include "Have you thought about dying?"; "Would you be better off/happier/more comfortable dead?"; "Would you like to die?"; "Have you thought about killing yourself?"; "Are you going to kill yourself?" Other potentially relevant information includes intent, past suicidality, steps taken to settle affairs, means for suicide, alternatives to suicide, barriers to suicide, and so on.
- *Other violent ideas:* Self-harm ideation may be less severe than suicidality, such as laceration, mutilation, or intentional neglect. Ideation of violence to others can be of varying urgency and intensity (e.g., "I'd like to punch him" versus "I'd like to shoot him"). Some important issues are identification of a specific intended victim, availability of a weapon, and barriers to violent action.

- *Phobias:* Agoraphobia, social phobia, and relevant simple phobias are recorded here if the patient manifests such symptoms while being observed by the examiner.

Perceptual abnormalities:

- *Hallucinations* may be of any sensory modality, but auditory hallucinations are most characteristic of primary psychiatric illness. Helpful inquiries include asking whether people are talking about the patient, the patient hears voices without seeing anyone, or there has been communication from God or spirits. Auditory hallucinations may be behaviorally evident if the patient appears to talk to the unseen. Voices that talk to each other or make running commentary on the patient's behavior are particularly severe, but perhaps most important is the impact of hallucinations on behavior (e.g., obeying "command" hallucinations that require violence). Hallucinations of a visual, olfactory, tactile, or gustatory nature further raise suspicion of an identifiable organic etiology.
- *Other perceptual abnormalities* include illusions, derealization, depersonalization, déjà vu, and so on.

COGNITION

This section of the MSE describes higher cortical functions, such as the ability to use intellect, reason, attentiveness, logic, and memory. It is an important part of most screening exams and many follow-up exams, especially when neuropsychiatric dysfunction is likely. Some examination may be indirect, such as evaluating memory by discussion of past conversations, names of medicines, or last week's football game. Cognitive functions can be categorized into a number of main areas. Definitions vary, however, for different types of declarative memory. MSE usually does not include testing of procedural memory. Testing each of the following areas is a reasonable screen for cognitive impairment.

- *Orientation:* Orientation to time, place, and person usually are assessed.

- *Attention and concentration:* Attentiveness or distractibility can be monitored in the interview itself or formally tested. Digit span is a measure of attention. Tests of concentration include backward recitation of months or weekdays, spelling backward, or serial subtraction.
- *Registration:* The capacity to immediately repeat a very short list of information, such as three to five words.
- *Short-term memory:* Memory over the course of a few minutes. It can be saturated and is not permanent. A common approach is testing recollection of three unrelated items after two to three minutes. More detailed approaches include story recall, word list learning tasks, or testing other modalities such as visual memory.
- *Long-term memory:* More permanent memory stores that cannot be saturated. May be recent, such as days or weeks ago, or remote, such as years or decades ago. "Episodic" memory is personal and time-tagged; a corroborative source is needed to exclude confabulation. "Semantic" memory tests general information, such as names of recent presidents.
- *Visuoconstructional ability:* Visuospatial abilities are necessary for everyday functions like driving or preparing a meal. Drawing or copying figures, such as a cube, intersecting pentagons, a clock, or a map of the state or country, or making a puzzle can test this function.
- *Executive functions:* These are higher level cognitive functions that include abstracting ability. Abstraction can be assessed in the interview through general conversation or by formal testing. For example, cognitively concrete individuals may respond literally to questions such as "What brought you to the hospital?" Formal testing includes identifying similarities between pairs of objects (e.g., table/chair, orange/apple, painting/poem) or meanings of well-known proverbs.

INSIGHT AND JUDGMENT

Insight is awareness of internal and external realities. For the MSE, assess the patient's recognition of illness, how it impacts other people, and the role of treatment.

Assessment of *judgment* considers the ability to weigh different aspects of an issue. The examiner can discuss important past choices (marriage, work, retirement, big purchases) and recent choices (e.g., how did the patient come to clinical attention?) to demonstrate the degree of judgment used by the patient in decision making. Traditional tests for judgment (e.g., "What would you do if you found a stamped, unmailed envelope on the street?") are relatively insensitive.

Insight and judgment are impacted by *defense mechanisms*. These are less frequently cited in mental status reports than in the past, but, if included, they belong here. One categorization of defense mechanisms is mature types—altruism, humor, sublimation, suppression; neurotic types—repression, displacement, dissociation, reaction formation, intellectualization; immature types—splitting, externalization, idealization, projection, acting out; psychotic types—denial, distortion.

References & Readings

American Psychiatric Association (1994). *Diagnostic and statistical manual of mental disorders* (4th ed.). Washington, DC: American Psychiatric Association.

Campbell, R. J. (1989). *Psychiatric dictionary* (6th ed.). New York: Oxford University Press.

Cutting, J. (1990). *The right cerebral hemisphere and psychiatric disorders.* New York: Oxford University Press.

Kaplan, H. I., & Sadock, B. J. (1995). Psychiatric report, and typical signs and symptoms of psychiatric illness. In H. I. Kaplan & B. J. Sadock (Eds.), *Comprehensive textbook of psychiatry* (6th ed., pp. 531–544). Baltimore: Williams and Wilkins.

Strauss, G. D. (1995). The psychiatric interview, history, and mental status examination. In H. I. Kaplan & B. J. Sadock (Eds.), *Comprehensive textbook of psychiatry* (6th ed., pp. 521–531). Baltimore: Williams and Wilkins.

Trzepacz, P. T., & Baker, R. W. (1993). *The psychiatric mental status examination.* New York: Oxford University Press.

Vaillant, G. E. (1977). *Adaptation to life: How the best and brightest come of age.* Boston: Little, Brown.

Related Topics

Chapter 3, "Improving Diagnostic and Clinical Interviewing"

Chapter 6, "Increasing the Accuracy of Clinical Judgment (and Thereby Treatment Effectiveness)"

3   IMPROVING DIAGNOSTIC AND CLINICAL INTERVIEWING

Rhonda S. Karg & Arthur N. Wiens

The purposes of clinical interviews are to gather information about the patient and his or her problems that is unavailable from other sources, to establish a relationship with the patient that will facilitate assessment and treatment, to provide the patient with an understanding of his or her pathological behavior, and to support and direct the patient in his or her search for relief. Toward these goals, the following list describes empirically supported and clinically tested guidelines to improve the efficacy and efficiency of diagnostic and clinical interviews.

1. *Prepare for the initial interview:* Before the initial meeting, carefully review the referral request and other available data. Clients become understandably annoyed at being asked for information contained in the record and frequently feel slighted by the interviewer who did not take the time to review the file. In a similar vein, interview preparation should involve becoming well informed regarding the problem areas presented by the patient, such as chemical dependence, attention-deficit/hyperactivity disorder, or depression (Wiens & Tindall, 1995).

2. *Determine the purpose of the interview:* Before proceeding with an interview, the clinician should have a clear understanding of what he or she desires to accomplish in the interview. Ask yourself: What are the objectives of this interview? For example, is it for making a diagnosis, planning treatment, initiating psychotherapy, or all three? In other cases, the interview will accomplish more detailed objectives. For example, should the patient be considered incompetent? Should this suicidal patient be released from the hospital?

3. *Clarify the purpose and parameters of the interview to the client:* Present the rationale for interviewing the patient. The intent is to give the patient a "set" or an expectation of what will occur during the interview and why this time is important to both patient and interviewer. For example, it is useful to describe the amount of available time, the type of questions, the limits of privileged information, and to whom the interview findings may be reported. Monumental misunderstandings can occur when clinician and client are not "on the same page."

4. *Conceptualize the interview as a collaborative enterprise:* The etymology of *diagnosis* denotes a relational meaning. Derived from the Latin *assidere*, the term means "to sit beside" —a metaphor for the way we should think about and conduct interviews. "To sit beside" conjures up images of team learning, working together, discussing, building, and collaborating (Braskamp & Ory, 1994).

5. *Truly hear what the interviewee has to say:* In clinical practice, patients often express their appreciation that someone was willing to hear them out. Let patients tell their entire story in their own ways and words. The importance of listening can hardly be overemphasized (Wiens & Tindall, 1995).

6. *Use structured interviews:* By ensuring adequate coverage of critical areas of functioning and by standardizing the interview, structured interviews enhance diagnostic reliability and interview validity (Rogers, 1995; Wiens, 1990). These include the Structured Clinical Interview for the *DSM-IV* (SCID) and the MINI SCID (the computerized format), the Structured Clinical Interview for the *DSM-IV* Dissociative Disorders (SCID-D), the Schedule for Affective Disorders and Schizophrenia (SADS), and the World Health Organization–sponsored Composite International Diagnostic Interview (CIDI; Endicott & Spitzer, 1978; First, Spitzer, Gibbon, & Williams, 1995).

7. *Encourage the client to describe complaints in concrete behavioral terms:* Clients will often describe their symptoms in vague, general terms ("It's my nerves"). To get around this limitation, use interview strategies to pinpoint behaviors, for example, by asking such questions as "Can you give me an example?" or "How do you think and feel when your nerves act up?" or "Tell me what a typical day for you is like." Also, probe for the three dimensions of problematic behavior: frequency (how often?), duration (how long?), and intensity (how severe?).

8. *Complement the interview with other assessment methods:* The comprehensiveness and validity of an interview are enhanced by the use of psychological testing, behavioral or situational observations, and family or social reports. In fact, research consistently demonstrates that objective psychological testing (especially actuarially driven) should be used in practically all diagnostic interviews (Dawes, Faust, & Meehl, 1989; Sawyer, 1966).

9. *Identify the antecedents and consequences of problem behaviors:* In the behavioral tradition, antecedents include any preceding environmental variables that maintain, strengthen, or weaken the problem behaviors. In examining antecedents, be particularly interested in what conditions occur before the problem behavior that make the behavior less likely or more likely to occur. Similarly, attempt to identify both internal and external events that either strengthen the problem behavior or weaken it. Consider six sources of consequences: affective, somatic, behavioral, cognitive, contextual, and relational (Cormier & Cormier, 1991).

10. *Differentiate between skill and motivation:* Traditional interviews frequently confuse a person's skill and motivation. Ask: Is this behavior within the person's repertoire? In other words, does the person have the skills to carry through with the assigned task? Or is it a motivational deficit? Is the person sufficiently motivated? What are the person's reinforcers? While interrelated, skill and motivation have differing clinical implications and thus should be clearly delineated.

11. *Obtain base rates of behaviors:* Base rates should guide, in part, the prediction of behaviors and the establishment of diagnostic decisions. Acquire some knowledge of the base rates of certain client characteristics in your professional setting. For example, what is the base rate of patients committing suicide on your ward? Collect data through examining previous records or perhaps through comparison with data from related settings. In the long run, considering base rates is likely to improve your clinical decision making (Finn & Kamphuis, 1995).

12. *Avoid expectations and biases:* "We see what we expect to see." Expectations tend to influence both our information-gathering procedures and our perceptions. As described by Meehl (1977), examples of such biases include a tendency to perceive people very unlike ourselves as being sick (the "sick-sick fallacy"), denying the diagnostic significance of an event because it has also happened to us (the "me-too fallacy"), and the idea that understanding a patient's beliefs or behaviors strips them of their significance (the "understanding-it-makes-it-normal fallacy"). Furthermore, our natural tendency is to search for supporting evidence for our expectations. Again, we suggest using base rates and other objective means to help avoid biases and expectations.

13. *Use a disconfirmation strategy:* To be efficient and accurate, we should employ a disconfirmation strategy. What in this protocol disputes evidence for, say, schizophrenia? Avoid the confirmation strategy of searching the entire database to confirm a hunch while ignoring discrepant data. Instead, hunt for information that will disprove initial impressions.

14. *Counter the fundamental attribution error:* This recurrent error occurs when the clinician attributes a client's disorder primarily to dispositional or intrapsychic factors, without giving serious consideration to environmental or situational determinants. Making a multiaxial diagnosis, particularly Axis IV (Psychosocial and Environmental Problems), may reduce the chance of the fundamental attribution error, but additional concern is warranted.

15. *Combine testing and interview data mechanistically:* As discovered by Sawyer (1966), the clinical interview alone was found to be the least accurate method of judgment. The best predictions (or judgment methods) are those that statistically combine test data and clinical interview data. As a result, judgments relying solely on the mental status examination should be avoided.

16. *Delay reaching decisions while the interview is being conducted:* Research has generally shown that the most accurate clinical decision makers tend to arrive at their conclusions later than do less accurate clinicians (Elstein, Shulman, & Sprafka, 1978; Sandifer, Hordern, & Green, 1970). The clinical implication of these findings is to reserve your diagnostic judgments until after the interview has been completed so that you are less susceptible to bias.

17. *Consider the alternatives:* Another debiasing strategy is to make yourself think about alternatives after you have generated an initial impression (Arkes, 1981). If we find ourselves unable to generate alternatives, it is time to seek consultations with colleagues.

18. *Provide a proper termination:* Anticipate the termination of the interview and prepare the client accordingly. Point out when time is running short (usually 5–10 minutes prior to ending the interview). One can combine this forewarning with eliciting the patient's reactions to the interview and asking if there is any additional topic he or she would like to discuss before ending. Two of our favorite closing queries: "I've asked you dozens of questions. Now, what questions do you have for me?" and "Is there anything else about your life or experiences that we haven't touched upon, at least briefly?"

References & Readings

Arkes, H. R. (1981). Impediments to accurate clinical judgment and possible ways to minimize their impact. *Journal of Consulting and Clinical Psychology, 49*, 323–330.

Braskamp, L. A., & Ory, J. C. (1994). *Assessing faculty work: Enhancing individual and institutional performance.* San Francisco: Jossey-Bass.

Cormier, W. H., & Cormier, L. S. (1991). *Interviewing strategies for helpers* (3rd ed.). Pacific Grove, CA: Brooks/Cole.

Dawes, R. M., Faust, D., & Meehl, P. E. (1989). Clinical versus actuarial judgment. *Science, 243,* 1668–1674.

Elstein, A. S., Shulman, A. S., & Sprafka, S. A. (1978). *Medical problem solving: An analysis of clinical reasoning.* Cambridge, MA: Harvard University Press.

Endicott, J., & Spitzer, R. L. (1978). A diagnostic interview: The Schedule for Affective Disorders and Schizophrenia. *Archives of General Psychiatry, 35,* 837–844.

Finn, S. E., & Kamphuis, J. H. (1995). What a clinician needs to know about base rates. In J. N. Butcher (Ed.), *Clinical personality assessment* (pp. 224–235). New York: Oxford University Press.

First, M. B., Spitzer, R. L., Gibbon, M., & Williams, J. B. W. (1995). The Structured Clinical Interview for *DSM-III-R* Personality Disorders II (SCID-II): II. Multi-site test-retest reliability study. *Journal of Personality Disorders, 9,* 92–104.

Meehl, P. E. (1977). Why I do not attend case conferences. In P. E. Meehl (Ed.), *Psychodiagnosis: Selected papers* (pp. 225–302). New York: Norton.

Rogers, R. (1995). *Diagnostic and structured interviewing.* Odessa, FL: Psychological Assessment Resources.

Sandifer, M. G., Hordern, A., & Green, L. M. (1970). The psychiatric interview: The impact of the first three minutes. *American Journal of Psychiatry, 126,* 968–973.

Sawyer, J. (1966). Measurement *and* prediction, clinical *and* statistical. *Psychological Bulletin, 66,* 178–200.

Strauss, G. D. (1995). The psychiatric interview, history, and mental status examination. In H. I. Kaplan & B. J. Sadock (Eds.), *Comprehensive textbook of psychiatry* (6th ed., pp. 521–531). Baltimore: Williams and Wilkins.

Wiens, A. N. (1990). Structured clinical interviews for adults. In G. Goldstein & M. Hersen (Eds.), *Handbook of psychological assessment* (pp. 324–340). Elmsford, NY: Pergamon Press.

Wiens, A. N., & Tindall, A. G. (1995). Interviewing. In L. Heiden & M. Hersen (Eds.), *Introduction to clinical psychology* (pp. 173–190). New York: Plenum Press.

Related Topics

4 CLINICAL PURPOSES OF THE MULTIMODAL LIFE HISTORY INVENTORY

Arnold A. Lazarus & Clifford N. Lazarus

Arnold Lazarus in Wolpe and Lazarus (1966) wrote: "Anamnestic interviews may be considerably shortened with literate individuals by asking them to complete, at their leisure, a Life History Questionnaire. . . . Using the completed questionnaire as a guide, patient and therapist may quite rapidly obtain a comprehensive picture of the patient's past experiences and current status" (p. 26). One of the first Life History Questionnaires that Arnold Lazarus compiled appeared in Wolpe and Lazarus (1966, pp. 165–169). Five years later, the initial Life History Questionnaire had been revised and considerably amplified and was published in 1971 (Lazarus, 1971, pp. 239–251). A new version, one that had benefited from further field testing, appeared in 1981 (Lazarus, 1981, pp. 239–251). Prepared in collaboration with Clifford N. Lazarus, the most recent version, now referred to as the Multimodal Life History Inventory, appeared in 1997 (Lazarus, 1997, pp. 127–142). This 15-page inventory is copyrighted and sold by Research Press, 2612 North Mattis Avenue, Champaign, IL 61821.

The use of the Multimodal Life History Inventory facilitates treatment by

- encouraging clients to focus on specific problems, their sources, and attempted solutions;
- providing focal antecedents, presenting problems, and relevant historical data; and
- generating a valuable perspective regarding a client's style and treatment expectations.

Basically, the inventory provides a therapeutic "road map" that aids in clinical decision making by helping patients, and hence therapists, identify a wide range of potentially salient problems within all the major spheres of biopsychosocial functioning. Typically, the Multimodal Life History Inventory is handed to patients at the end of the initial interview, and they are asked to fill it out and bring it with them to their second session. Seriously disturbed (e.g., deluded, deeply depressed, highly agitated) clients will obviously not be expected to comply, but most psychiatric patients who are reasonably literate will find the exercise useful for speeding up routine history taking, thus readily providing the therapist with significant data to generate a viable treatment plan. For individuals who cannot or will not complete it, the inventory may be used as a guide during the sessions to obtain a thorough overview of the client's background—early development, family interactions, and educational, sexual, occupational, and other experiences.

Clients are advised not to try to complete the inventory in a single sitting but to space it out over several days. When the completed form is received, the therapist peruses it in his or her own time, making notations and queries that are discussed during the next and perhaps subsequent sessions. Items that have been omitted also become grist for the mill.

We tend to read through the brief section "Expectations Regarding Therapy" before anything else because it gives clues to the patient's expectations, as well as the type of therapeutic style and cadence to which he or she may best respond. For example, a client who sees therapy as an opportunity to ventilate and to be heard by a good listener will require a different treatment trajectory than one who expects to be coached and reeducated. We also zero in on the 15 questions at the end of the section entitled "Thoughts" that appear as a 5-point rating scale on the inventory. This section immediately alerts the therapist to dysfunctional thoughts and irrational ideas the client may harbor.

We instruct clients to omit their names, addresses, or any other identifying information if this will lead them to answer the inventory more honestly and completely.

We now present the items that constitute the inventory. The actual forms, of course, are laid out differently, with adequate space for different answers and room for clients to elaborate should they so desire.

Multimodal Life History Inventory

The purpose of this inventory is to obtain a comprehensive picture of your background. In psychotherapy records are necessary since they permit a more thorough dealing with one's problems. By completing these questions as fully and as accurately as you can, you will facilitate your therapeutic program. You are requested to answer these routine questions in your own time instead of using up your actual consulting time (please feel free to use extra sheets if you need additional answer space).

It is understandable that you might be concerned about what happens to the information about you because much or all of this information is highly personal. Case records are strictly confidential.

General Information

Name:
Address:
Telephone numbers: Day, Evening
Age:
Occupation:
Sex:
Date of birth:
Place of birth:
Religion:
Height:
Weight:
Does your weight fluctuate?
If yes, by how much?
Do you have a family physician?
Name of family physician:
Telephone number:
By whom were you referred?
Marital status:

Remarried? How many times?
With whom do you live?
What sort of work are you doing now?
Does your present work satisfy you?
If no, please explain:
What kind of jobs have you held in the past?
Have you been in therapy before or received any professional assistance for your problems?
Have you ever been hospitalized for psychological/psychiatric problems? If yes, when and where?
Have you ever attempted suicide?
Does any member of your family suffer from an "emotional" or "mental" disorder?
Has any relative attempted or committed suicide?

Personal and Social History

Father:
Name:

Age:
Occupation:

Health:

If deceased, give his age at time of death:

How old were you at the time?

Cause of death:

Mother:

Name:

Age:

Occupation:

Health:

If deceased, give her age at time of death:

How old were you at the time?

Cause of death:

Siblings:

Age(s) of brother(s):

Age(s) of sister(s):

Any significant details about siblings:

If you were not brought up by your parents, who raised you and between what years?

Give a description of your father's (or father substitute's) personality and his attitude toward you (past and present):

Give a description of your mother's (or mother substitute's) personality and her attitude toward you (past and present):

In what ways were you disciplined or punished by your parents?

Give an impression of your home atmosphere (i.e., the home in which you grew up). Mention state of compatibility between parents and between children.

Were you able to confide in your parents? Basically, did you feel loved and respected by your parents?

If you have a stepparent, give your age when your parent remarried:

Has anyone (parents, relatives, friends) ever interfered in your marriage, occupation, etc.?

Scholastic strengths: Scholastic weaknesses:

What was the last grade completed (or highest degree)?

Check any of the following that applied during your childhood/adolescence: Happy childhood; Unhappy childhood; Emotional/behavior problems; Legal trouble; Death in family; Medical problems; Ignored; Not enough friends; Sexually abused; School problems; Severely bullied or teased; Financial problems; Eating disorder; Strong religious convictions; Drug use; Used alcohol; Severely punished

Description of Presenting Problems

State in your own words the nature of your main problems:

Please estimate the severity of your problem(s): Mildly upsetting; Moderately upsetting; Very severe; Extremely severe; Totally incapacitating

When did your problems begin?

What seems to worsen your problems?

What have you tried that has been helpful?

How satisfied are you with your life as a whole these days? Not satisfied 1 2 3 4 5 6 7 Very satisfied

How would you rate your overall level of tension during the past month? Relaxed 1 2 3 4 5 6 7 Tense

Expectations Regarding Therapy

In a few words, what do you think therapy is all about?

How long do you think your therapy should last?

What personal qualities do you think the ideal therapist should possess?

(continued)

Modality Analysis of Current Problems

The following section is designed to help you describe your current problems in greater detail and to identify problems that might otherwise go unnoticed. This will enable us to design a comprehensive treatment program and tailor it to your specific needs. The following section is organized according to the seven modalities of Behaviors, Feelings, Physical sensations, Images, Thoughts, Interpersonal relationships, and Biological factors.

Behaviors

Check any of the following behaviors that often apply to you:
Overeat; Loss of control; Phobic avoidance; Crying; Take drugs; Suicidal attempts; Spend too much money; Outbursts of temper; Unassertive; Compulsions; Can't keep a job; Odd behavior; Smoke; Insomnia; Drink too much; Withdrawal; Take too many risks; Work too hard; Nervous tics; Lazy; Procrastination; Concentration difficulties; Eating problems; Impulsive reactions; Sleep disturbance; Aggressive behavior; Others:
What are some special talents or skills that you feel proud of?
What would you like to start doing?
What would you like to stop doing?
How is your free time spent?
What kind of hobbies or leisure activities do you enjoy or find relaxing?
Do you have trouble relaxing or enjoying weekends and vacations? If yes, please explain:
If you could have any two wishes, what would they be?

Feelings

Check any of the following feelings that often apply to you:
Angry; Fearful; Happy; Hopeful; Bored; Optimistic; Annoyed; Panicky; Conflicted; Helpless; Restless; Tense; Sad; Energetic; Shameful; Relaxed; Lonely; Depressed; Envious; Regretful; Jealous; Contented; Anxious; Guilty; Hopeless; Unhappy; Excited; Others:
List your five main fears:
What are some positive feelings you have experienced recently?
When are you most likely to lose control of your feelings?
Describe any situations that make you feel calm or relaxed:

Physical sensations

Check any of the following physical sensations that often apply to you:
Abdominal pain; Bowel disturbances; Hear things; Pain or burning with urination; Tingling; Watery eyes; Menstrual difficulties; Numbness; Flushes; Headaches; Stomach trouble; Nausea; Dizziness; Tics; Skin problems; Palpitations; Fa-

tigue; Dry mouth; Muscle spasms; Twitches; Burning or itching skin; Tension; Backpain; Chest pains; Sexual disturbances; Tremors; Rapid heartbeat; Unable to relax; Fainting spells; Don't like to be touched; Blackouts; Excessive sweating; Visual disturbances; Hearing problems; Others:

What sensations are pleasant for you? Unpleasant for you?

Images

Check any of the following that apply to you. I picture myself:

Being happy; Being talked about; Being trapped; Being hurt; Being aggressive; Being laughed at; Not coping; Being helpless; Being promiscuous; Succeeding; Hurting others; Losing control; Being in charge; Being followed; Failing; Others:

I have:

Pleasant sexual images; Seduction images; Unpleasant childhood images; Images of being loved; Negative body image; Unpleasant sexual images; Lonely images; Others:

Describe a very pleasant image, mental picture, or fantasy:

Describe a very unpleasant image, mental picture, or fantasy:

Describe your image of a completely "safe place":

Describe any persistent or disturbing images that interfere with your daily functioning:

How often do you have nightmares?

Thoughts

Check each of the following that you might use to describe yourself:

Intelligent; Confident; A nobody; Inadequate; Useless; Confused; Worthwhile; Evil; Ambitious; Sensitive; Crazy; Worthless; Ugly; Stupid; Can't make decisions; Morally degenerate; Naive; Suicidal ideas; Loyal; Considerate; Trustworthy; Deviant; Full of regrets; Unattractive; Honest; Incompetent; Concentration difficulties; Memory problems; Attractive; Persevering; Deviant; Good sense of humor; Horrible thoughts; Hard working; Unlovable; Conflicted; Undesirable; Lazy; Untrustworthy; Dishonest; Others:

What do you consider to be your craziest thought or idea?

Are you bothered by thoughts that occur over and over again? If yes, what are these thoughts?

What worries do you have that may negatively affect your mood or behavior?

On each of the following items, please circle the number that most accurately reflects your opinions:

[On the actual inventory, this appears as a scale ranging from "1" Strongly Disagree to a "5" Strongly Agree.] I should not make mistakes; I should be good at everything I do; When I do not know something, I should pretend that I do; I should not disclose personal information; I am a victim of circumstances; My life is controlled by outside forces; Other people are happier than I am; It is very im-

(continued)

portant to please other people; Play it safe, don't take any risks; I don't deserve to be happy; If I ignore my problems, they will disappear; It is my responsibility to make other people happy; I should strive for perfection; Basically, there are two ways of doing things—the right way and the wrong way; I should never be upset.

Interpersonal relationships

Do you make friends easily? Do you keep them?

Did you date much during high school? College?

Were you ever bullied or severely teased?

Describe any relationship that gives you: Joy; Grief

Rate the degree to which you generally feel relaxed and comfortable in social situations:

Very relaxed 1 2 3 4 5 6 7 Very anxious

Do you have one or more friends with whom you feel comfortable sharing your most private thoughts?

Marriage (or a committed relationship)

How long did you know your spouse before your engagement?

How long were you engaged before you got married?

How long have you been married?

What is your spouse's age? His/her occupation?

Describe your spouse's personality:

What do you like most about your spouse?

What do you like least about your spouse?

What factors detract from your marital satisfaction?

How satisfied are you with your marriage?

How do you get along with your partner's friends and family?

How many children do you have?

Please give their names and ages:

Do any of your children present special problems? If yes, please describe:

Any significant details about a previous marriage(s)? Sexual relationships?

Describe your parents' attitude toward sex. Was sex discussed in your home?

When and how did you derive your knowledge of sex?

When did you first become aware of your own sexual impulses?

Have you ever experienced any anxiety or guilt arising out of sex or masturbation?

Relevant details regarding your first or subsequent sexual experiences?

Is your present sex life satisfactory? If no, please explain:

Provide information about any significant homosexual reactions or relationships:

Are there any problems in your relationships with people at work? If yes, please describe:

Please complete the following:

One of the ways people hurt me is; I could shock you by; My spouse (or boyfriend/girlfriend) would describe me as; My best friend thinks I am; People who dislike me

Are you currently troubled by any past rejections or loss of a love relationship?

Biological factors

Do you have any current concerns about your physical health?

List any medications you are currently taking:

Do you eat three well-balanced meals each day?

Do you get regular physical exercise? If yes, what type and how often?

Please list any significant medical problems that apply to you or to members of your family:

Please describe any surgery you have had (give dates):

Please describe any physical handicap(s) you have:

Menstrual history

Age at first period:

Were you informed? Did it come as a shock?

Are you regular? Duration: Do you have pain?

Do your periods affect your moods? Date of last period:

Check any of the following that apply to you:

Muscle weakness; Tranquilizers; Diuretics; Diet pills; Marijuana; Hormones; Sleeping pills; Aspirin; Cocaine; Pain killers; Narcotics; Stimulants; Hallucinogens (e.g., LSD); Laxatives; Cigarettes; Tobacco (specify); Coffee; Alcohol; Birth control pills; Vitamins; Undereat; Overeat; Eat junk foods; Diarrhea; Constipation; Gas; Indigestion; Nausea; Vomiting; Heartburn; Dizziness; Palpitations; Fatigue; Allergies; High blood pressure; Chest pain; Shortness of breath; Insomnia; Sleep too much; Fitful sleep; Early morning awakening; Earaches; Headaches; Backaches; Bruise or bleed easily; Weight problems; Others:

Structural Profile

[On the actual inventory, clients are asked to rate the following items on a 7-point scale.]

Behaviors: Some people may be described as "doers"   they are action oriented, they like to busy themselves, get things done, take on various projects. How much of a doer are you?

Feelings: Some people are very emotional and may or may not express it. How emotional are you? How deeply do you feel things? How passionate are you?

Physical sensations: Some people attach a lot of value to sensory experiences, such as sex, food, music, art, and other "sensory delights." Others are very much aware of minor aches, pains, and discomforts. How "tuned in" to your sensations are you?

Mental images: How much fantasy or daydreaming do you engage in? This is separate from thinking or planning. This is "thinking in pictures," visualizing real or imagined experiences, letting your mind roam. How much are you into imagery?

Thoughts: Some people are very analytical and like to plan things. They like to reason things through. How much of a "thinker" and "planner" are you?

Interpersonal relationships: How important are other people to you? This is your self-rating as a social being. How important are close friendships to you, the tendency to gravitate toward people, the desire for intimacy? The opposite of this is being a "loner."

(continued)

Biological factors: Are you healthy and health conscious? Do you avoid bad habits like smoking, too much alcohol, drinking a lot of coffee, overeating, and so on? Do you exercise regularly, get enough sleep, avoid junk foods, and generally take care of your body?

Please describe any significant childhood (or other) memories and experiences you think your therapist should be aware of.

References & Readings

Lazarus, A. A. (1971). *Behavior therapy and beyond.* New York: McGraw-Hill.
Lazarus, A. A. (1981). *The practice of multimodal therapy.* New York: McGraw-Hill.
Lazarus, A. A. (1997). *Brief but comprehensive psychotherapy.* New York: Springer.
Wolpe, J., & Lazarus, A. A. (1966). *Behavior therapy techniques.* Oxford: Pergamon Press.

Related Topics

Chapter 2, "Mental Status Examination"
Chapter 3, "Improving Diagnostic and Clinical Interviewing"
Chapter 6, "Increasing the Accuracy of Clinical Judgment (and Thereby Treatment Effectiveness)"

5   KEY PRINCIPLES IN THE ASSESSMENT OF PSYCHOTHERAPY OUTCOME

Michael J. Lambert & Kara Cattani-Thompson

The assessment of psychotherapy outcome is an important endeavor. The information obtained enables the clinician to objectively examine the degree of change experienced by the client. In addition, such information generates quality assurance data surrounding the effectiveness of psychotherapy, providing practitioners with an additional data source for tracking patient progress and making clinical decisions. The decision regarding how to go about assessing outcome is a serious matter that may impact both the individual patient and future policy decisions.

Because client problems are inherently complex and unique at least in some respects to each individual, multiple assessment methods are frequently employed. This approach is a way of capturing the complexity of human functioning and change. However, the question of which instruments and methods to use in assessing change still remains. The following guidelines for choosing instruments are presented in an attempt to facilitate the selection of potentially useful measures by the practicing clinician. It should be kept in mind that instruments and methods that are particularly useful for diagnostic purposes and treatment planning are unsuitable for the purpose of measuring patient change.

- *Consider the content areas covered by the instrument:* The three broad areas to be assessed are the subjective state of the client (intrapersonal functioning, including behavior, affect, and cognition), the state of the client's intimate relationships (interpersonal functioning), and, more broadly, the state of the individual's participation in the community (social role performance). The degree to which an instrument measures intrapsychic attributes of the client versus characteristics of the client's interpersonal world may affect its utility to the clinician. Empirically, the results of outcome studies are more impressive when content is measured across all three content areas.
- *Change should be measured from multiple perspectives:* In an ideal study of change, all the parties involved who have information about client change might be represented. Potential sources of information include *client self-report, therapist rating,* a *trained observer,* a *significant other,* and/or *societal or institutional records.* Measurement in psychotherapy is strongly affected by the biases of those providing the data (e.g., Farrell, Curran, Zwick, & Monti, 1983). It is important to realize that the results of studies can be misunderstood and/or misrepresented when the effects of different perspectives (on the level of change reported) are not appreciated.
- *The methods used to collect outcome data can impact the final index of change:* Lambert, Ogles, and Masters (1992) describe four categories of methods or "technologies." These are global ratings (including measures of client satisfaction); description (specific symptom indexes); observation (behavioral counts); and status (physiological

and institutional measures). There are both advantages and disadvantages to using a particular technology as well as a particular source of information. In general, more specific technologies, as opposed to those that are global, yield more objective reports of change because they focus the raters' attention on the status of specific symptoms and signs rather than on the general outcome of therapy. The careful clinician will weigh the costs and benefits of obtaining outcome information from different sources using a variety of methodologies before determining which instruments are the most practical. The interested reader should consult Ogles, Lambert, and Masters (1996, Tables 3-2, 3-3) for a helpful consideration of the costs and benefits associated with each method used to collect data.
- *Consider the issue of temporality in measuring outcomes:* Temporality is another dimension on which assessment methods vary (Lambert et al., 1992). The issue here regards the extent to which the instrument attempts to measure a stable, traitlike characteristic or a more unstable, statelike characteristic.
- *Be aware of the advantages and disadvantages of tailoring the change criteria to each individual in therapy:* This approach has been advocated as a technique that is more responsive to the needs of the clinician and general clinical practice. The therapist is able to assess change from an idiographic and multifaceted approach, which is consistent with the wide range of problems presented by individuals (e.g., Persons, 1991). However, the clinician should be aware of the limitations inherent in individualized outcome assessment. These include, but are not limited to, the following: individual goals cannot be viewed as much more than poorly defined subjective decisions by the patient or clinician; units of change derived from individually tailored goals are unequal and therefore not comparable across clients; and different goals will respond differentially to the influence of psychotherapy.
- *The use of standardized outcome assessment scales overcomes the limitations of in-*

dividualized scales but comes at another expense: Standardized measures allow for comparison of a client's score with a sample of "normals," the pretest scores of other patients, and the posttest scores of other patients, as well as comparisons with widely accepted standards of improvement. Unfortunately, the gains in practical utility presented by this technique come at a certain expense. Information about the client's unique problems and concerns, within the context of a more generalized disorder, is lost.

- *The ideal approach is probably to supplement assessments based on individualized scales with standardized clinical rating scales:* Numerous standardized scales for measuring patient outcome exist. Comprehensive reviews of many of these instruments are available to the interested reader (e.g., Maruish, 1994; Ogles et al., 1996).

- *Look for clinically meaningful change:* While an important standard for most research is to report treatment results in terms of statistical significance, these findings may be of limited value to the practitioner. Outcome assessment will demonstrate practical value to practitioners when the clinical relevance of the findings and the impact of the treatment on individual clients is clearly established. Methods have been developed to set standards for clinically meaningful patient change (Jacobson, Follette, & Revenstorf, 1986; Jacobson & Truax, 1991). The clinical significance methodology provides for the calculation of two specific statistical indexes: a cutoff point between normal and dysfunctional samples and an evaluation of the reliability of the change score. These indexes provide the practitioner with specific guidelines for interpreting patient change. Many existing measures provide such guidelines. When they are not available, however, the clinician should consult the work of Jacobson for the formulas for establishing cutoff scores, as well as a reliable change index.

- *Consider other practical and unobtrusive ways of gauging the effectiveness of treatments:* As public policy continues to demand increased accountability among service orga-

nizations, there is a push for data to demonstrate that high-quality and efficient services are being offered to the consumer. In these instances, unobtrusive measures of client change (e.g., days on the job before and after treatment) may be useful and practical measures of client change.

- *Consult reviews of suitable instruments:* Such reviews can be found in a variety of source books, a sampling of which is included in "References and Readings."

References & Readings

Farrell, A. D., Curran, J. P., Zwick, W. R., & Monti, P. M. (1983). Generalizability and discriminant validity of anxiety and social skills ratings in two populations. *Behavioral Assessment, 6*, 1–14.

Fischer, J., & Corcoran, K. (1994). *Measures for clinical practice* (2nd ed., Vols. 1 & 2). New York: Free Press.

Jacobson, N. S., Follette, W. C., & Revenstorf, D. (1986). Toward a standard definition of clinically significant change. *Behavior Therapy, 17*, 308–311.

Jacobson, N. S., & Truax, P. (1991). Clinical significance: A statistical approach to defining meaningful change in psychotherapy research. *Journal of Consulting and Clinical Psychology, 59*, 12–19.

Lambert, M. J., Ogles, B. M., & Masters, K. S. (1992). Choosing outcome assessment devices: An organizational and conceptual scheme. *Journal of Counseling and Development, 70*, 527–532.

Maruish, M. E. (Ed.) (1994). *The use of psychological testing for treatment planning and outcome assessment.* Hillsdale, NJ: Lawrence Erlbaum.

Ogles, B. M., Lambert, M. J., & Masters, K. S. (1996). *Assessing outcome in clinical practice.* New York: Allyn and Bacon.

Persons, J. B. (1991). Psychotherapy outcome studies do not accurately represent current models of psychotherapy: A proposed remedy. *American Psychologist, 46*, 99–106.

Sederer, L. I., & Dickey, B. (1996). *Outcomes assessment in clinical practice.* Baltimore: Williams and Wilkins.

Strupp, H. H., Horowitz, L. M., & Lambert, M. J. (Eds.) (1997). *Outcome assessment: A core battery approach for anxiety, mood, and personal-*

ity disorders. Washington, DC: American Psychological Association.

Vibbert, S., & Youngs, M. T. (Eds.) (1995). *The 1996 behavioral outcomes and guidelines sourcebook.* New York: Faulkner and Gray.

Related Topics

Chapter 46, "Empirically Validated Treatments"
Chapter 47, "Thumbnail Systematic Assessment and Treatment Matching"

INCREASING THE ACCURACY OF CLINICAL JUDGMENT

6

(and Thereby Treatment Effectiveness)

David Faust

Increased predictive accuracy improves clinical practice. This is not only because patients may seek guidance about the likelihood of various outcomes (e.g., "Am I in a relationship with a future?") but also because intervention usually presumes prediction. Our interventions are guided by our expectations (predictions) of their effects and effectiveness. After all, we would not say, "Let's try this, although I don't have the slightest idea how well it's going to work, and who cares anyway, because what's going to happen next is of no concern," but rather, "I think what's most likely to help is . . ." Similarly, therapeutic interpretation is guided by predicted impact or what is expected to benefit the patient.

There is much useful knowledge and methodology for increasing predictive accuracy, although, unfortunately, this information usually is not provided in the training of mental health professionals (see Faust, 1984; Faust & Willis, in press; Meehl, 1973; Dawes, 1988). A few of the more important principles are conveyed in the "rules of thumb" that follow.

GO WITH THE MORE FREQUENT EVENT

Principle

Assume the evidence points about equally toward two alternatives, and that the potential disadvantages of misidentifying both conditions or outcomes are about the same. Under such circumstances, you should guess that the more frequent of the two conditions is present. To the extent the frequency of the two conditions or outcomes varies, such a strategy will enhance predictive accuracy. In fact, not uncommonly, the frequency of an event (i.e., the base rate) is the single most predictive variable or useful piece of information.

Illustration

To illustrate, suppose that Alzheimer's disease occurs about 10 times more often than Pick's disease and that the manifestations of these disorders, at least initially, are often very similar. If one guesses Alzheimer's disease every time, one will be correct about 9 in 10 times. For example, if, across a series of 100 cases, there are 91 cases of Alzheimer's disease and 9 cases of Pick's disease, and if one guesses Alzheimer's every time, one will achieve a 91% accuracy rate.

Elaboration

This guide, as narrowly stated above, assumes that evidence points about equally in the direction of two conditions and that there are roughly equal costs and benefits for both types of correct and incorrect judgments (i.e., correctly identifying Condition A versus missing Condition A; correctly identifying Condition B versus missing Condition B). Of course, such relatively clean examples are not that common, and often there is an imbalance across one or both of these dimensions. This does not negate the underlying principle, that is, that frequency data or base rates are often among the most important guides to decision making, but it does call for adjustments.

Suppose, for example, that a set of signs indicate posttraumatic stress disorder (PTSD) versus major depression (MD) at a 2:1 ratio, but that in the setting of application MD occurs four times more often than PTSD. Under such circumstances, most individuals with the sign will still have MD. One can think of this as the 4:1 ratio (or base rate) in favor of MD more than offsetting the 2:1 ratio (the sign) in favor of PTSD. It is simply a matter of one indicator pointing to MD and the other to PTSD, with the former indicator being a more powerful or accurate one. However, there is a partial offset of the 4:1 ratio, and the base rate will not be as strong an indicator of MD as it would be were the sign neutral or not indicative of the alternative diagnosis. The point is that deviations from clean examples change the operating characteristics, although not the underlying principles, and call for certain steps to determine, for example, shifts in the relative probabilities of alternative outcomes.

These adjustments can be difficult to make impressionistically, especially as the differences among alternatives become less extreme. Fortunately, exact determinations can be made using relatively simple formalisms (see Meehl & Rosen, 1973). Steps can also be taken to deal with gaps in information about frequencies or base rates and to consider utilities or the costs and benefits of different types of correct and incorrect decisions (see Faust & Nurcombe, 1989).

Summary of the First Principle

In summary, the frequency of a condition or event is often among the most useful, if not the single best, predictor of that event or outcome. The extreme case illustrates this point: If something never occurs or always occurs, knowing this alone would lead to 100% predictive accuracy. Indeed, as events become more or less frequent or more or less frequent than one another, greater and greater predictive accuracy can be achieved by playing the base rates, that is, guessing the event that is less frequent will not occur or the event that is more frequent will occur. Under such circumstances, the rate of accurate decisions can increase 10-fold or more by utilizing base rates versus contrary diagnostic or predictive signs or indicators, even those that, in conditions of equal frequency, perform reasonably well.

INCLUDING A BAD PREDICTOR IS USUALLY MUCH WORSE THAN EXCLUDING A GOOD PREDICTOR

Principle

For technical reasons to be described, mistakenly including a weak or invalid variable in the predictive mix usually does considerably more harm than mistakenly overlooking or disregarding a good predictor. Therefore, in most situations, especially when other predictors of known value are available, if in doubt, exclude rather than include; in other words, avoid incorporating additional variables into the decision process.

Explanation of Principle

Clinicians are commonly advised to integrate most or all the data, a strategy that flows from mistaken beliefs about validity and is almost sure to *decrease* overall accuracy. The misconception is that validity is cumulative, and hence the more (data or predictors) the better. It is not uncommon, for example, for authors to call for the integration of dozens, if not hundreds, of test scores and data points. Were validity strictly cumulative, then, if one could identify 15 predictors that each accounted for 10% of the variance, their combination would account for 150% of the variance! This does not hold because predictors are often redundant or overlap with each other. Consequently, they are not carving out unique pieces of the predictive pie but are re-covering the same ground. To illustrate, if we are trying to obtain a proper physical description of a person and measure the person's weight first in pounds and then in kilograms, the second measurement really adds nothing new. We have only measured the same dimension twice. Similarly, two depression inventories may both measure roughly the same thing.

Starting with the first predictor (and for purposes of this discussion bypassing the issue of reliability), additional predictors are valuable to the extent they are *both* valid and non-redundant. In many domains in clinical psychology, once one combines about three to five of the most valid and independent variables, adding a new variable often does little or nothing to increase predictive accuracy, even if it has a very respectable level of validity (owing to its redundancy). However, combining or integrating a weaker or invalid variable cannot help matters and will often decrease judgmental accuracy.

Suppose, for example, that sexual abuse has not occurred and that the three best predictors of possible abuse are negative. Three other variables, which, unfortunately and unbeknownst to the clinician, are really weak or poor predictors, indicate otherwise. Obviously, a correct conclusion might be overturned, and in the long run, the inclusion of weak or invalid variables will have a detrimental overall affect.

Further Elaboration

Precisely determining alterations in predictive accuracy as variables are combined in different ways or are added or subtracted is very difficult to do via observation or experientially. For example, even an astute observer is rather unlikely to get it just right when subjectively "calculating" the figure for shared variance or redundancy across two variables. Proper development of decision procedures through formal research includes analysis of predictive accuracy, level of redundancy, and the impact of adding new variables to the predictive mix. This is clearly a situation in which human ingenuity, via the development of scientific and analytic methods, has gone a long way toward solving tasks that place unrealistic demands on the unaided human mind, much like the telescope has extended human senses.

Also contrary to common belief, the exact weighting of variables is often of much lesser importance than selecting which variables to use and which to exclude. Indeed, in many situations, weighting the relevant variables equally results in the same, or about the same, predictive accuracy as optimal weighting, and the "optimal" weights derived in one situation are often relatively unstable across other situations anyway, reducing their potential advantages (Dawes, 1979; Dawes & Corrigan, 1974; Dawes, Faust, & Meehl, 1989). All these considerations lead to the same prescription: Identify (preferably through well-conducted research) the limited set of variables that are most valid and nonredundant and then be conservative, that is, worry much more about adding questionable variables to the mix than overlooking additional valid variables.

TO REDUCE RISK OF A BAD OUTCOME, START WITH THE *LEAST* LIKELY EVENT IN THE CHAIN OR SET

Principle and Explanation

When a set of events *all* must occur for something bad to happen, the greatest proportionate reduction in risk occurs when one lowers the probability of the *least* likely link. Consider the following example. Suppose two things, Event A and Event B must take place for a bad outcome to occur. Suppose that the probability of Event A is .20 and of Event B is .90, making the probability of the outcome $.20 \times .90 = .18$. Now suppose for practical reasons that you can intervene with either A or B but not both, perhaps because of limited time or resources. Suppose further that you can decrease the probability of either of the variables by .10.

In attempting to reduce risk, intuition usually leads one to focus first on the segment of the chain that appears most likely to occur. For example, if we are trying to avoid a suicide attempt, we might direct most of our efforts toward the most probable event (e.g., access to a means). However, it is instructive to examine the consequences of this strategy using the hypothetical figures stated above. If I reduce Event B by .10, or from .90 to .80, the result is $.20 \times .80 = .16$, or a minimal reduction in risk. In contrast, if I decrease A by .10, or from .20 to .10, the result is $.10 \times .90 = .09$; that is, I have cut the risk in half.

The results or proportionate impact can be even more dramatic as the probability of the least likely event decreases below that stated in the hypothetical, especially when these probabilities start out rather low. For example, assume that the probability of A is now .06 and that B is still at .90, and that we could reduce either A or B by .05. Before intervention, we start at $.06 \times .90 = .054$. If we reduce B by .05, the result is $.06 \times .85 = .051$; but if we reduce A by .05, the result is $.01 \times .90 = .009$. By intervening in the right place, rather than achieving a very minor decrease in risk, we have reduced it almost sixfold, or from about 1 in 18 to about 1 in 100. The obverse also holds and tends to align more closely with intuition; that is, when one wants a positive outcome to occur, all other things being equal, bolster the least likely link in the chain.

Cautionary Note

It is of utmost importance to recognize that this principle of risk reduction assumes that all events in the set must occur for the event to occur. (Technically, it is better to use the term *set* rather than *chain* because no particular sequence needs to be assumed.) Also, as with base rates, the conditions stated here (i.e., all other things being equal) often will not hold, and adjustments will have to be made (e.g., What if I can reduce A, the less frequent event, by .10 and

B by .20?). However, the mathematics are usually simple because one need only multiply the probabilities of each relevant variable by the others (i.e., $A \times B \times C$, etc.). The main point is that the tendency to focus time and effort on the most likely event is often misdirected and opposite to the more effective approach.

BEFORE DECIDING, GENERATE REASONS TO DECIDE OTHERWISE

Principle and Explanation

The simple exercise of generating reasons to decide otherwise or of actively considering or bringing to mind contrary evidence tends to counter a number of problematic judgment tendencies. For one, once individuals formulate hypotheses or tentative conclusions, they tend to look for possible confirming evidence more so than contrary evidence, or, given a certain mental set, supportive evidence may be more salient or noticeable. This may skew the evidence that is gathered or considered in favor of supportive evidence, resulting in premature termination of data collection, erroneous conclusions, and overconfidence. Active attempts to recognize and consider contrary evidence tend to rebalance the scales.

Further Explanation

Given the variability of human behavior over time and place, as well as error in our measuring devices, a plausible but false, or mainly false, conclusion will often still find considerable supportive evidence. For example, if one concludes that the patient has more than expectable levels of interpersonal conflict, when the patient actually is a little better than average on this score, thorough probing of his or her history ought to uncover many instances in which interpersonal conflicts occurred. If alternative or contrary evidence becomes more salient, the false initial impression may be overturned.

Confidence that is unduly inflated by the tendency to focus on one side of the coin, or evidence consistent with one's conclusions, can lead to many secondary, damaging judgment practices. For example, when one is more confident than is justified, there is a tendency (a) to make overly extreme or risky predictions ("I know he won't commit murder when on parole"); (b) to fail to gather important sources of information (because one feels one already knows); and (c) to not learn or implement the many useful methods that scientific research and work in decision making, such as those discussed in this chapter, have uncovered.

References & Readings

Arkes, H. R. (1981). Impediments to accurate clinical judgment and possible ways to minimize their impact. *Journal of Consulting and Clinical Psychology, 49,* 323–330.

Dawes, R. M. (1979). The robust beauty of improper linear models in decision making. *American Psychologist, 34,* 571–582.

Dawes, R. M. (1988). *Rational choice in an uncertain world.* New York: Harcourt Brace Jovanovich.

Dawes, R. M., & Corrigan, B. (1974). Linear models in decision making. *Psychological Bulletin, 81,* 95–106.

Dawes, R. M., Faust, D., & Meehl, P. E. (1989). Clinical versus actuarial judgment. *Science, 243,* 1668–1674.

Faust, D. (1984). *The limits of scientific reasoning.* Minneapolis: University of Minnesota Press.

Faust, D., & Nurcombe, B. (1989). Improving the accuracy of clinical judgment. *Psychiatry, 52,* 197–208.

Faust, D., & Willis, W. G. (in press). *Counterintuitive imperatives: A guide to improving clinical assessment and care by predicting more accurately.* Boston: Allyn and Bacon.

Meehl, P. E. (1973). *Psychodiagnosis: Selected papers.* Minneapolis: University of Minnesota Press.

Meehl, P. E., & Rosen, A. (1973). Antecedent probability and the efficiency of psychometric signs, patterns, and cutting scores. In P. E. Meehl, *Psychodiagnosis: Selected papers* (pp. 32–62). Minneapolis: University of Minnesota Press.

Slovic, P., Fischhoff, B., & Lichtenstein, S. (1982). Facts versus fears: Understanding perceived risk. In D. Kahneman, P. Slovic, & A. Tversky (Eds.), *Judgment under uncertainty: Heuristics and biases* (pp. 463–489). New York: Cambridge University Press.

Related Topics

7 ADULT NEUROPSYCHOLOGICAL ASSESSMENT

Aaron Nelson & Margaret O'Connor

GENERAL CONSIDERATIONS

Fundamental Assumptions of Clinical Neuropsychological Assessment

1. It is possible to make valid inferences regarding the integrity of the brain through the observation of behavior. Such inferences require a firm grasp of brain-behavior relationships and characteristic neurobehavioral syndromes.

2. Observable behavior is frequently the most sensitive manifestation of brain pathology.

3. Observable behavior, including "test behavior," is a reflection of the interaction between the domains of person and environment; variables from each domain must be assessed in order to arrive at an understanding of the clinical significance of a given behavior.
4. A neuropsychological test is simply one means of eliciting a sample of behavior, under standardized conditions, which is then to be observed and analyzed.
5. Test performance and "real-life" behavior are imperfectly correlated. Proceed with caution in using test data to predict behavior.
6. Most behaviors are multifactorial and depend on a complex interplay of cognitive, perceptual, emotional, and environmental factors.
7. Most neuropsychological tests are multifactorial and depend on a confluence of cognitive and perceptual functions for their performance.
8. As with any psychological intervention, the neuropsychological evaluation should proceed in a sensitive manner and with explicit communications regarding the use of clinical information.
9. A dynamic developmental life span perspective is critical in the evaluation of each patient.
10. All behavior should be viewed within a sociocultural context.

Uses of Neuropsychological Assessment

1. Neuropsychological assessment is indicated for questions of differential diagnosis and prognosis.
2. Neuropsychological assessment should be considered in the setting of a deterioration in neuropsychological status or when there is a history of neurological disease, injury, or developmental abnormality affecting cerebral functions.
3. Neuropsychological assessment is used to clarify the significance of known or suspected pathology for "real-life" functioning in day-to-day activities, relationships, education, and work.

4. Neuropsychological assessment provides information relevant to management, rehabilitation, and treatment planning for identified cognitive problems.
5. Baseline (pretreatment) status and measurement of treatment response (medication, neurosurgery, behavioral intervention, electroconvulsive therapy) can be monitored with serial neuropsychological testing.
6. Neuropsychological consultation is frequently critical in determination of legal/forensic issues, including need for guardianship, neuropsychological damages, criminal responsibility, and competence to stand trial.
7. Neuropsychological research investigations enhance the understanding of brain-behavior relationships and neurobehavioral syndromes. These studies are of tremendous value to the understanding of neurological disease and normal brain function.

Approach to Neuropsychological Evaluation

1. Evaluation should be individually tailored to each patient.
2. Test data are viewed from both qualitative and quantitative perspectives.
3. Assessment proceeds in a hypothesis testing manner. Tests are selected to answer specific questions, some of which emerge during the evaluation process.
4. Standardized tests can be modified to test limits and produce richer qualitative data.
5. Task performance is analyzed to determine component processes, with the goal of identification of dissociations between such processes.

CLINICAL METHOD

Referral Question

The chief complaint and presenting problems are reviewed to produce a clear description of their onset and course, as well as information regarding the medical and social context in which the problem(s) emerged. The patient's overall understanding of his or her current circumstances and the reason for the consultation are sought.

History

Information is obtained from a variety of sources, including the patient's self-report, observations of family members or close friends, medical records, and prior evaluations from academic or work situations. Information is obtained regarding the following:

1. Developmental background, including circumstances of gestation, birth/delivery, acquisition of developmental milestones, and early socialization skills
2. Social development, including major autobiographical events and relationships (a three-generational genogram is highly useful in gaining relevant family information)
3. Past medical history, including illnesses, injuries, surgeries, medications, hospitalizations, substance abuse, and relevant familial medical history
4. Psychiatric history, including hospitalizations, medications, and outpatient treatment
5. Educational background, including early school experiences and academic performance during high school, college, postgraduate study, and other educational and technical training
6. Vocational history, including work performance, work satisfaction, and relationships with supervisors and coworkers
7. Recreational interests and hobbies

Behavioral Observation

Physical appearance is inspected, including symmetry of gross anatomic features, facial expression, manner of dress, and attention to personal hygiene. The patient is asked specific questions regarding unusual sensory or motor symptoms. Affect and mood are assessed with respect to range and modulation of felt/expressed emotions and their congruence with concurrent ideation and the contemporaneous situation. Interpersonal comportment is assessed in the context of the interview. Does the patient's behavior reflect a normal awareness of self and other in interaction? The patient's motivation and compliance with examination requests, instructions, and test procedures are observed with respect to the validity of test findings.

Domains of Neuropsychological Function

A sufficiently broad range of neuropsychological functions is evaluated using tests and other assessment techniques.

1. *General intellectual ability:* Intelligence encompasses a broad array of capacities, many of which are not directly assessed in the traditional clinical setting. The estimate of general intellectual ability is based on both formal assessment methods and a survey of demographic factors and life accomplishments. Particular care must be exercised in the evaluation of patients from varying educational and sociocultural backgrounds. In cases of known or suspected impairment, premorbid ability is surmised from performance on measures presumed less sensitive to cerebral dysfunction (i.e., vocabulary), so-called best performance methods, educational/professional accomplishment, avocational interests and pursuits, and demographic variables. The level of general ability provides a reference point from which to view performance on other measures.
2. *Sensation and perception:* It is important to establish to what degree primary sensation and perception are intact prior to initiation of testing. Significant impairment of sensory function (auditory, visual, kinesthetic) is usually obvious and points to a need for specialized assessment procedures. Unusual or abnormal gustatory and olfactory experiences should be sought through direct questioning. Simple auditory function can be assessed by finger-rub stimuli to each ear. Vision is examined with tests of acuity, tracking, scanning, depth perception, color perception, and attention/neglect for visual field quadrants. Kinesthetic perception is assessed with tests of graphesthesia and stereognosis. Double simultaneous stimulation

can be used in auditory, visual, and kinesthetic modalities to determine whether hemiextinction occurs.

3. *Motor functions:* Naturalistic observations of the patient's gait and upper and lower extremity coordination are an important part of the motor examination. Hand preference should be assessed through either direct inquiry or a formal handedness questionnaire. Motor speed, dexterity, and programming are tested with timed tasks, some of which involve repetition of a specific motor act (e.g., finger tapping, peg placement) and others of which involve more complex movements (e.g., finger sequencing, sequential hand positions). Manual grasp strength can be assessed with a hand dynamometer. Various forms of verbally guided movement or praxis are examined.

4. *Attention/concentration:* The capacity to selectively maintain and shift attentional focus forms the basis of all cognitive activity. Evaluation of attention includes observations of a broad array of interrelated behaviors. General level of arousal or alertness is determined through clinical observation. An appraisal is made of the extent to which environmental or diurnal factors modify arousal. Attentional functions are assessed in both auditory/acoustic and visual modalities. Attention span is measured by determining the number of unrelated "bits" of information that can be held on line at a given moment in time. Sustained attention is assessed with tests that require the patient to maintain focused attention over longer periods. Selective attention is measured with tasks requiring the patient to shift focus from one event to another. Resistance to interference is assessed with tasks requiring the patient to inhibit overlearned responses or other distractions that could undermine a desired response.

5. *Learning and memory:* The assessment of memory function is perhaps the most complex endeavor of the neuropsychological examination. Memory is assessed with respect to time of initial exposure (anterograde vs. retrograde), modality of presentation (acoustic vs. visual), material (linguistic vs. fig-

ural), and locus of reference (personal vs. nonpersonal). The evaluation of memory should include measures that allow the neuropsychologist to parse out the component processes (encoding, consolidation, retrieval) entailed in the acquisition and later recall of information. To this end, measures are used to assess performance with respect to length of interval between exposure and demand for recall (none vs. short vs. long delay) and extent of facilitation required to demonstrate retention (free recall vs. recognition). The assessment of retrograde memory function poses a special problem insofar as it is difficult to know with certainty what information was contained at one time in the remote memory of a particular patient. Although a number of formal tests can be used for this purpose, we also assess this aspect through asking for personal information that presumably is or had been well known at one time by the patient (e.g., names of family members, places of prior employment).

6. *Language:* Language is the medium through which much of the neuropsychological examination is accomplished. Language function is assessed both opportunistically, as during the interview, and via formal test instruments. Conversational speech is observed with respect to fluency, articulation, and prosody. The patient's capacity to respond to interview questions and test instructions provides an informal index of receptive language ability or comprehension. Visual confrontation naming is carefully assessed so that word-finding problems and paraphasic errors may be elicited. Repetition is measured with phrases of varying length and phonemic complexity. Auditory comprehension is evaluated by asking the patient questions that vary in length and grammatical complexity. Reading measures include identification of individual letters, common words, irregularly spelled words, and nonwords, as well as measures of reading speed and comprehension. Spelling can be assessed in both visual and auditory modalities. A narrative handwriting sample can be obtained by instructing the patient to describe a standard stimulus scene.

7. *Visuospatial functions:* After basic visuo-perceptual status is established, the assessment of visuospatial function commences with the evaluation of the spatial distribution of visual attention. Visual neglect is examined by way of tasks entailing scanning across all quadrants of visual space. Left/right orientation can be assessed by having the patient point to specific body parts on himself or herself or the examiner. Topographic orientation can be tested in most patients by instructing them to indicate well-known locales on a blank map. Graphic reproduction of designs and assembly of patterns using sticks, blocks, or other media are used to assess visual organization and constructional abilities.

8. *Executive functions:* Executive functions comprise the capacity of the patient to produce cognitive behavior in a planned, organized, and situationally responsive manner. The assessment of executive functions is accomplished in an ongoing fashion through observation of the patient's approach to all types of tests and via his or her comportment within the consultation. Although few tests assess these functions directly or specifically, the clinician looks for evidence of flexibility versus perseveration, initiation versus abulia, self-awareness versus obliviousness, planfulness versus impulsivity, and capacity to assume an abstract attitude versus concreteness.

9. *Psychological factors and emotion:* Standardized measures of mood, personality, and psychopathology can be used to explore the role of these issues in the patient's presentation and diagnosis. It is important to note, however, that neurological and other medical conditions can skew performance on certain personality tests; hence, interpretation must take this into account through the use of "correction" methods where available and in exercising caution in drawing diagnostic conclusions.

Diagnostic Formulation

Data from the history, observation, and testing of the patient are analyzed collectively to pro-duce a concise understanding of the patient's symptoms and neuropsychological diagnosis. A configuration of abilities and limitations is developed and used both diagnostically and as a framework for the elucidation of goals for treatment. When possible, the diagnostic formulation should identify the neuropathological factors giving rise to the patient's clinical presentation, including underlying anatomy and disease process.

Recommendations and Feedback

Consultation concludes with feedback, in which findings and recommendations are reviewed with relevant individuals (e.g., referring physician, patient, family, treatment team members). A variety of treatment plans may be advised, including pharmacological intervention, psychiatric consultation, psychotherapy, vocational guidance, and cognitive-behavioral remediation. Recommendations should be pragmatic and individually tailored to each patient's specific needs. Strategies for optimizing performance in personal, educational, and occupational spheres are identified and discussed in lay language that the patient and family member can comprehend. Where possible, specific behaviorally based suggestions are made for remediation of identified problems. Further clinical evaluations and other neurodiagnostic procedures are suggested when appropriate in order to provide more information relevant to differential diagnosis, response to treatment, and functional status over time. Appropriate neuropsychological follow-up is also arranged.

References & Readings

Feinberg, T., & Farrah, M. (Eds.) (1997). *Behavioral neurology and neuropsychology.* New York: McGraw-Hill.

Heilman, K., & Valenstein, E. (Eds.) (1993). *Clinical neuropsychology* (3rd ed.). New York: Oxford University Press.

Kaplan, E. (1983). Process and achievement revisited. In S. Wapner & B. Kaplan (Eds.), *Toward a holistic developmental psychology* (pp. 143–156). Hillsdale, NJ: Erlbaum.

Kaplan, E. (1988). A process approach to neuropsychological assessment. In T. Boll & B. Bryant (Eds.), *Clinical neuropsychology and brain function: Research, measurement, and practice*. Washington, DC: American Psychological Association.

Kolb, B., & Wishaw, I. Q. (Eds.) (1990). *Fundamentals of human neuropsychology* (3rd ed.). New York: Freeman.

Lezak, M. (1995). *Neuropsychological assessment* (3rd ed.). New York: Oxford University Press.

Mesulam, M. M. (Ed.) (1985). *Principles of behavioral neurology*. Philadelphia: F. A. Davis.

Spreen, O., & Strauss, E. (1991). *A compendium of neuropsychological tests: Administration, norms, and commentary*. New York: Oxford University Press.

Walsh, K. W. (1987). *Neuropsychology: A clinical approach* (2nd ed.). Edinburgh: Churchill Livingstone.

Walsh, K. W. (1992). Some gnomes worth knowing. *Clinical Neuropsychologist, 6*, 119–133.

Related Topics

Chapter 2, "Mental Status Examination"

Chapter 8, "Developmental Neuropsychological Assessment"

Chapter 9, "Attention-Deficit/Hyperactivity Disorder Through the Life Span"

8   DEVELOPMENTAL NEUROPSYCHOLOGICAL ASSESSMENT

Jane Holmes Bernstein, Betsy Kammerer, Penny Prather, & Celiane Rey-Casserly

FUNDAMENTAL ASSUMPTIONS OF NEUROPSYCHOLOGICAL (NP) ASSESSMENT OF CHILDREN

- Clinical assessment in neuropsychology, as in psychology, involves extracting diagnostic meaning from an individual's history, from direct and indirect observations of behavior, and from performance on targeted tests.
- NP assessment requires analysis of both neurological and psychological (behavioral) variables. Observed behavior is a function of the interaction of the brain with the environment.

- The practice of neuropsychology is based on knowledge of the brain as a necessary, but not sufficient, substrate for behavior relationships. Its goal is to explicate brain-behavior relationships. Neuropsychology is not defined by a set of tests, no matter how extensive or well organized the cognitive domains tapped by the tests.
- The goal of NP assessment is better adjustment to all aspects of real life.
- Children are not small adults. Comprehensive assessment models for children must incorporate development in their analysis of behavior. Models of relatively static, modu-

lar adult behavioral function should be applied to children with extreme caution.

- The practice of neuropsychology requires formal and rigorous training of the clinician.

ASSUMPTIONS OF DEVELOPMENTAL ANALYSIS

- Development implies a dynamic interaction between an organism and its environment. The principles at the core of a developmental NP analysis of behavior are those of the developmental sciences: structure, context, process, and experience.
- In the developing child the contribution of the "brain" to observed behavior cannot be meaningfully assessed without reference to the child's developmental course, maturational status, immediate environment, and wider sociocultural context.
- Knowledge of normal development and its variation is a prerequisite for all developmental analysis.
- A disturbance of the brain at any point in time is necessarily incorporated into the subsequent developmental course. Both neurological and behavioral development will proceed in a different fashion around the new brain organization.
- The timing of an insult will have differential impact on behavioral outcome as a function of the developmental status of the disrupted brain system at the time of the insult.
- The behaviors or "symptoms" that prompt referral are neither random nor universal but reflect the expected competencies of the child at a given stage, that is, the same underlying neuropsychological problem will be manifest in different ways at different points in development.

INDICATIONS FOR NP ASSESSMENT

- In contrast to adults, children undergo frequent psychological and/or educational testing. "Overtesting" is thus of serious concern. Referral questions should be carefully reviewed. NP consultation, rather than comprehensive NP assessment, should be considered where appropriate.
- NP assessment is indicated when behavioral change is seen in the context of changed central nervous system (CNS) status. It should be considered when a child unexpectedly fails to meet environmental demands in either academic or psychosocial contexts, and/or when psychological, psychiatric, psychoeducational, or multidisciplinary assessment does not provide an adequate explanation for presenting behavior or sufficient information to guide intervention planning.
- NP assessment is indicated (a) when behavioral change is seen in the context of known or suspected neurological disorders; known or suspected systemic disorders with impact on the CNS; treatment regimens with potentially deleterious impact on CNS status; degenerative, metabolic, or specific genetic disorders; and disorders associated with structural CNS abnormalities; (b) to clarify the relationship of behavioral change to specific medical/neurological diagnoses or to specific neural substrates; (c) to provide a baseline profile to monitor recovery, effects of treatment, and/or the impact of developmental change on behavioral function; (d) to provide ongoing monitoring of neurobehavioral status in the context of developmental change, recovery, and/or treatment — particularly in the case of specific injury and/or medical or surgical intervention (e.g., epilepsy surgery, medication trials or changes, radiation therapy) and in the context of medications use; and (e) for clinical research in neurological, psychiatric, and psychological populations.
- NP services are provided in the form of (a) comprehensive individual assessments (outpatient); (b) consultation — to educational, psychiatric, social work, medicine, and rehabilitation professionals — including review of records, analysis of behavioral data, interpretation of neurological data in the behavioral arena, application of neurologically relevant information to everyday settings (home, school), and assistance in diagnostic formulation and intervention strategies;

(c) inpatient assessment or consultation to localize function (seizures), monitor behavioral change in the intraoperative setting, and document behavioral functioning in psychiatric patients; and (d) forensic evaluation to provide a comprehensive description of developmental status, cognitive functioning, academic achievement, and psychosocial adjustment and to address future risks/needs in forensic situations.

DIAGNOSTIC STRATEGY

- Diagnosis in neuropsychology is not a function of test performance. It is the result of a formal assessment strategy that is ideally formulated as an experiment with an N of 1, theoretically driven, with hypotheses that are systematically tested and with a design and methodology that include appropriate controls for variability and bias.
- The diagnostic strategy not only should address the referral questions but also should be framed within the biopsychosocial context of the child's life. It should incorporate adaptive competence, emotional well-being, and functional processing style, as well as cognitive and academic ability structures. Its goal is to promote optimal psychosocial and intellectual development.
- The diagnostic strategy must integrate the "vertical" dimension of development with the "horizontal" dimension of the child's current neurobehavioral repertoire.
- Relevant diagnostic data are derived from the individual's history, direct and "indirect" observations of behavior, and performance on psychological tests.
- The diagnostic formulation is the basis for referencing the child's profile to categories of neurological, psychological, and/or educational disorders.
- Diagnostic categories can be framed in terms of neuropsychological or neurodevelopmental variables, specific psychological (cognitive, perceptual, information processing) factors, primary academic deficits, and/or specific nosological schemes (*DSM-IV*).

- The diagnostic formulation is the basis for determination of *risk* (prediction of future response to expectable challenges, both psychosocial and intellectual) and for the design and implementation of the *overall management strategy* that addresses the pattern of risks faced by *this* child in *this* family with *this* history, *this* profile of skills, and *these* goals (both short- and long-term).

BEHAVIORAL DOMAINS

- In NP assessment, behavioral domains rather than test performance are the units of analysis.
- Behavioral domains tapped can be organized in a number of ways—and labeled differently by clinicians with differing theoretical perspectives. What they have in common, however, is that they are sufficiently wide-ranging to address both the behavioral repertoire of the individual being assessed and the referral question(s).
- Domains include regulatory and exploratory *executive capacities* (arousal, attention, mood, affect, emotion, reasoning, planning, decision making, monitoring, initiating, sustaining, inhibiting, and shifting abilities; *skills and knowledge bases* (sensory and perceptual processing in [primarily] visual and auditory modalities, motor capacities, communicative competence, social cognition, linguistic processing, speech functions, spatial cognition); and *achievement* (academic skills, adaptive functioning, social comportment, societal adjustment).

SOURCES OF DATA

- The history is typically obtained from interviews of the child, parent(s)/guardian(s), teacher(s), psychologist, and physician; from medical/educational records; and from questionnaires. The goal of the history is to determine the *child's heritage* (genetic, medical, socioeconomic, cultural, educational) derived from the family history and to assess the *child's ability to take advantage of this heritage* (the child's developmental, medical, psychological, and educational history). The history also provides important information on the attributions given by others as to the nature and source of the child's presenting difficulties.

- Observational data are derived from examination of the child's appearance and behavior, from information obtained from questionnaires and interviews, completed by people familiar with the child in nonclinical contexts, from direct observation of the child-parent interaction during the clinical interview, from analysis of the examiner-child dyad, and from observation of the child's behavior and problem-solving style under specific performance demands (including both specific tests and the activities of the natural environment).
- Tests provide *psychometric* data relating level of performance to age peers; *behavioral* data on behaviors elicited under different problem-solving demands and problem-solving strategies for reaching solutions; and *task analysis* data such as information regarding complexity of task demands, allocation of resources, systemic relationships in task/situation.

THE USE OF PSYCHOLOGICAL TESTS

- Psychological tests have limitations with respect to NP assessment. They provide interchild rating and cognitive profiling. Used alone, they cannot model the neural substrate or explicate childhood neuropathology.
- No test measures just one thing. All behavior, including test responses, is the result of a complex interaction of executive, cognitive, and perceptual variables, motor and sensory capacities, and emotional factors.
- Tests provide samples of observed behavior under structured conditions; they complement, but do not substitute for, observations (direct or elicited) of the child in the natural environment.

- Test performance varies in response to contextual variables, including the nature of the test setting, rapport with the clinician, age of the child, test format/materials, and test construction/scoring criteria. No test can be rendered so "objective" that the interaction between child and examiner is eliminated as an important source of diagnostic information.
- Psychological tests are designed to tap specific aspects of behavioral function. They are constructed according to sound psychometric principles, administered rigorously, and scored according to standard guidelines. Their normative data should be up to date, reliable, valid, and appropriate in terms of age and/or cultural or language group for the population under study.
- NP assessment protocols require a core of population-based standardized psychological test instruments. These typically include a measure of general mental/cognitive abilities, appropriate to the child's age and general competency, which serves to "anchor" the clinician by referencing this child's performance to that of other children of the same age. It also provides a context of general ability against which specific neuropsychologically relevant skills and weaknesses can be evaluated.
- Additional tests are then selected to address the full range of behavioral domains and to provide more detailed analysis of specific psychological processes. These may have population-based or research-based norms. The latter typically have less extensive normative bases but can target specific skills more precisely.

COMMUNICATION OF FINDINGS

- Communication of findings is undertaken by means of a written report and an informing session. These are complementary: the informing session provides a forum for discussion of the findings and their meaning, as well as an opportunity for parents to discuss and reframe their understanding of the child; the report provides details of the assessment process, the scores derived from standardized measures, the diagnostic formulation, and the management and recommendations.

- The goal of the report and informing session is to educate the child, parents/guardians, and teachers/other professionals about the nature of children's neurobehavioral development in general; to explain how brain-behavior relationships in children are examined in the evaluation; to "normalize" this child's NP performance by situating it in the larger context of neurobehavioral development; to relate observed behaviors to the specific medical/neurological condition (where relevant); and to demonstrate the relationship of the diagnostic formulation to the management plan proposed.

- The written report should present a clear statement of the referral question(s); summarize relevant history, observations, and test findings organized so that the weight of the findings is clear; integrate the findings into a clear diagnostic statement (not a list of what the child "can" and "cannot" do); discuss the relationship of the diagnostic formulation to the child's real-world functioning; address the referral question specifically; reference the findings to the medical/neurological condition where relevant (noting specifically when data are, or are not, consistent with a known disorder and locus); identify areas of concern (risks) based on or referenced to the diagnostic statement; and outline the management plan and recommendations to maximize the child's functioning in the real-world contexts of family, play, and school.

- The management plan should provide general educational information about neurobehavioral development in children; relate this child's performance to that of other children (with and without a similar diagnosis); and provide detailed information about this child's individual style, expectable risks (both short- and long-term), and educational and psychosocial/emotional needs. It should address medical and psychological health, as well as both academic/vocational and psychosocial development and achievement. It should incorporate both general and specific recomendations for promoting optimal adjustment.

- Recommendations should respond to the specific risks that the child faces now and in the future; be tailored to different contexts as necessary; provide general guidelines for maximizing behavior in both social and academic contexts; foster specific cognitive, social, and academic skills; and address psychosocial development and emotional well-being.

References & Readings

Baron, I. S., Fennell, E., & Voeller, K. S. (1996). *Pediatric neuropsychology in the medical setting*. New York: Oxford University Press.

Bernstein, J. H., & Waber, D. P. (1990). Developmental neuropsychological assessment: The systemic approach. In A. A. Boulton, G. B. Baker, & M. M. Hiscock (Eds.), *Neuromethods: Vol. 17. Neuropsychology* (pp. 331–371). Clifton, NJ: Humana Press.

Dennis, M. (1989). Assessing the neuropsychological abilities of children and adolescents for personal injury litigation. *Clinical Neuropsychologist, 3*, 203–229.

Pennington, B. F. (1991). *Diagnosing learning disorders*. New York: Guilford Press.

Rapin, I., & Segalowitz, S. J. (Eds.) (1992). *Handbook of neuropsychology: Vol. 6. Child neuropsychology*. Amsterdam: Elsevier.

Reynolds, C. R., & Fletcher-Janzen, E. (Eds.) (1989). *Handbook of clinical child neuropsychology*. New York: Plenum Press.

Rourke, B. P., Fisk, J., & Strang, J. D. (1986). *Neuropsychological assessment of children*. New York: Guilford Press.

Taylor, H. G. (1988). Neuropsychological testing: Relevance of assessing children's learning disabilities. *Journal of Consulting and Clinical Psychology, 56*, 795–800.

Related Topics

9 ATTENTION-DEFICIT/ HYPERACTIVITY DISORDER THROUGH THE LIFE SPAN

Robert J. Resnick

Attention-deficit/hyperactivity disorder (ADHD) is the most frequent reason children access health care. On average there are two children with ADHD in every classroom. This disorder is not outgrown in adolescence, and up to 70% of children so diagnosed will have discernible symptoms into adulthood. It is estimated that 3–5% of children and 2–5 million adults have symptoms of ADHD. Boys outnumber girls by about 4 to 1, and they may present in different ways: boys tend to be more externalizing and aggressive, whereas girls tend to be more internalizing, showing more difficulties with emotion and much less assertiveness. ADHD is not caused by poor parenting, diet, excess sugar, or inadequate schools, but all of these may exacerbate the ADHD behaviors.

According to the *DSM-IV* (1994), the two primary symptom clusters are inattention and impulsivity and hyperactivity. The diagnostic rubrics are attention-deficit/hyperactivity disorder: predominantly inattentive type (note there is no hyperactivity of significance); attention-deficit/hyperactivity disorder: predominantly hyperactive-impulsive type; attention-deficit/hyperactivity disorder: combined type (incorporating both clusters); and attention-deficit/hyperactivity disorder: not otherwise specified, for individuals who exhibit symptoms of ADHD but do not meet full criteria. For adolescents and adults who currently have symptoms but no longer meet full criteria, the notation "in partial remission" should be added. Onset of symptoms occurs before age 7, lasts at least 6 months, and is observed in more than one setting (e.g., home, school, church, work, neighborhood, day care). Symptoms must be at an age-inappropriate level, with significant impairment in social, occupational, or academic functioning.

Appropriate "rule outs" need to be considered because they can present as ADHD. In children and adolescents, mood disorders, anxiety, autism and other developmental disorders, intellectual retardation, learning disabilities, hearing loss, and poor vision can mask as ADHD. Similarly, seizure disorders (especially brief but frequent seizures known as "absence" and petit mal) need to be considered as well. Because of the nature of the symptoms, conduct disorders and oppositional defiant disorders are a common comorbid condition. Similarly, many children will carry a dual diagnosis of ADHD and learning disabilities; some will be learning disabled because of the ADHD, and in others the learning disability is a parallel process.

The former type of learning disability shows much more improvement with treatment of the ADHD than the latter. With adults, depressive disorders as well as bipolar disorders can present as ADHD. Anxiety disorders, schizophrenia, borderline and schizotypal personality disorders, intellectual retardation, and learning disabilities may also mask as ADHD. It would be unusual for an adult to have had a seizure undiagnosed since childhood. Academic and vocational underachievement, multiple marriages, and problems in social relationships should raise the question of ADHD. Disorganization, problems handling everyday stress, moodiness, and hair-trigger temper, usually with quick offset, all can be related to ADHD. In both adolescents and adults, alcohol and substance abuse are not unusual cofindings.

THE EVALUATION

- *History:* A rigorous psychological, developmental, and social history must be taken. Include employment and educational history for adults.
- *School records:* A complete copy of school records, including report cards, achievement tests, teacher/school commentaries, and special services/special education testing along with individualized educational plans (IEPs), should be obtained. These provide an invaluable view of the person over time in school. For older children, look for a downward spiral of grades, especially starting in third or fourth grade.
- *Teacher ratings:* Teacher rating scales are helpful at baseline and treatment points. They are commercially available.
- *Parent ratings:* Parents should fill out ratings separately because they, like teachers, frequently have different thresholds of tolerance for the child's behavior.
- *Computerized assessments:* These measure inattention, distractibility, and impulsivity. Continuous performance tests (CPTs) are the most common and are commercially available (e.g., Conner's Continuous Performance Test).
- *Mental status exam:* Observe the person for ADHD symptoms and behaviors while ruling out other diagnoses by appropriate questioning/observation.

TREATMENT

School-Age Children

- Thorough explanation to parents and child of the nature of ADHD, including etiology, treatment, and outcome. Significant under-

standing of ADHD by family and child is imperative.
- School-based behavioral strategies to ensure homework, class work, and school participation are at an acceptable level. Strategies are also aimed at increasing compliance (on task) and decreasing inappropriate and frequently aggressive behaviors. Referral to the school system for special education screening and evaluation may be necessary so that the ADHD child can be identified as qualifying for special education services. Academic tutoring may also be necessary.
- Home-based behavioral interventions similar to the end points in school (i.e., ensuring completion and turning in of all schoolwork); additional intervention around household chores, siblings, and play/recreation. The goal again is to increase compliance with rules in the household and community. Parental skills training may be necessary.
- Stimulant medication is most often, and appropriately, used in conjunction with the above strategies. Other pharmacological agents can be used as well (i.e., antidepressants).
- Individual therapy around issues of ADHD and/or comorbid features. Therapy may be intermittent over the course of time.
- Connect family to local, state, and national parents' support group, such as Children and Adults with Attention Deficit Disorder (CHADD) and Attention Deficit Disorders Association (ADDA).
- Bibliotherapy for child and parents. Connect them to ADD Warehouse (800-233-9273) for free catalog.

Adults

- Thorough explanation of the life course of the ADHD to adult and significant other.
- Cognitive and behavioral interventions at home and at work to decrease disorganization, inattention, and distractibility.
- Use of prompts such as *Voice It*, a personal audio-reminder, and/or organizers such as the *Franklin Planner*.
- Focused trial on stimulant medication or other pharmacological agents.

- Individual psychotherapy as needed for issues around ADHD and/or other comorbid conditions.
- Marital/couples psychotherapy focusing on the relationship and ways of coping with ADHD within that relationship.
- Bibliotherapy to augment understanding, intervention skills, and interpersonal relationships (e.g., Katie Kelly and Peggy Ramundo's *You Mean I'm Not Lazy Stupid or Crazy*, and Lynn Weiss's *Attention Deficit Disorders in Adulthood: Practical Help for Sufferers and Their Spouses*). Connect the person to the ADD Warehouse for a catalog.
- Provide information about CHADD and/or ADDA.

A number of federal statutes have a bearing on treatment of ADHD and therefore on the outcome. A school-age population with ADHD can be affected by Section 504 of the Rehabilitation Act of 1973 and the Individuals With Disabilities Education Act of 1990 (IDEA), which was reauthorized in 1997. Both can require specific interventions when a school-age person has been identified as having ADHD. A person at any age with ADHD may have legal standing under the Americans with Disabilities Act (ADA) of 1990 if education or employment as a "major life activity" is "substantially limited."

References & Readings

American Psychiatric Association (1994). *Diagnostic and statistical manual of mental disorders* (4th ed.). Washington, DC: American Psychiatric Association.

Barkley, R. (1990). *Attention-deficit hyperactivity disorder: A handbook for diagnosis and treatment*. New York: Guilford Press.

Barkley, R. (1995). *Taking charge of ADHD: The complete authoritative guide for parents*. New York: Guilford Press.

Ingersoll, B., & Goldstein, S. (1993). *Attention deficit disorder and learning disabilities*. New York: Doubleday.

Resnick, R., & McKvoy, K. (1994). *Attention deficit/hyperactivity disorder: Abstracts of the psychological and behavioral literature, 1967–1994*. Washington, DC: American Psychological Association.

Spencer, T., Biederman, J., Wilens, T., Harding, M., O'Donnell, D., & Griffin, B. (1996). Pharmacotherapy of attention-deficit hyperactivity disorder across the life cycle. *Journal of the American Academy of Child and Adolescent Psychiatry, 35,* 409–432.

Wender, P. (1995). *Attention-deficit hyperactivity disorder in adults*. New York: Oxford University Press.

10   ASSESSMENT OF SUICIDAL RISK

Kenneth S. Pope & Melba J. T. Vasquez

Evaluating suicidal risk is one of the most challenging aspects of clinical work, in part because it is literally a life-or-death matter. False positives and false negatives are frequent because of such issues as suicide's low base rate (Pope, Butcher, & Seelen, 1993). The following list, adapted from Pope and Vasquez (1991), is meant to highlight some factors that are widely accepted as significantly associated with suicide attempts. Awareness of such factors as they emerge from the research and clinical literature may be helpful in assessing suicidal risk.

Among the essential qualifications are the following. First, space limitations mandate mentioning these factors in a very general way. There may be many exceptions to the trends noted here, and various factors may interact with one another. The purpose is solely to call attention to some areas that clinicians should be aware of in assessing risk. Second, this list is merely a snapshot of some current trends. Emerging research continues to correct false assumptions and refine our understandings, as well as reflect changes. For example, there are indications of an increase in the suicide rate for women, bringing it closer to that for men. Third, this list is by no means comprehensive. It only provides examples of some of the kinds of factors statistically associated with suicide attempts or completed suicides. Fourth, this list is meant to increase awareness of factors empirically associated with suicidal risk, but it should never be used in an unthinking, mechanical manner. Awareness of such factors can serve as an important aspect of—but never a substitute for—a careful, informed, comprehensive evaluation of suicidal risk.

1. *Direct verbal warning:* A direct statement of intention to commit suicide often precedes a suicide attempt. Such statements deserve careful attention and adequately comprehensive exploration. It is crucial to resist the temptation to reflexively dismiss such warnings as "a hysterical bid for attention," "a borderline manipulation," "a clear expression of negative transference," "an attempt to provoke the therapist," or "yet another grab for power in the interpersonal struggle with the therapist." It is possible that the statement may reflect issues other than an actual increase in suicidal risk, but such a working hypothesis should be set forth only after a respectful, careful, open-minded evaluation.

2. *Plan:* The presence of a plan frequently re-

flects an increased suicidal risk. The more specific, detailed, lethal, and feasible the plan, the more likely it may be that the person will attempt suicide.

3. *Past attempts:* The research suggests that most completed suicides have been preceded by a prior attempt. Schneidman (1976) found that the clients with the greatest suicidal rate were those who had entered into treatment with a history of at least one attempt.

4. *Indirect statements and behavioral signs:* People planning to end their lives may communicate their intent indirectly through their words and actions, for example, talking about "going away," speculating on what death would be like, giving away their most valued possessions, wondering aloud what it might be like to attend their own funeral, or acquiring lethal instruments.

5. *Depression:* As might be expected, the research suggests that the suicide rate for those with clinical depression is much higher—perhaps as much as 20 times greater—than the suicide rate for the general population.

6. *Hopelessness:* The sense of hopelessness appears to be closely associated with suicidal intent (see, e.g., Kazdin, 1983; Petrie & Chamberlain, 1983; Wetzel, 1976).

7. *Intoxication:* The research suggests that many suicides are associated with alcohol as a contributing factor; an even greater number may be associated with the presence of alcohol (without clear indication of its contribution to the suicidal process and lethal outcome).

8. *Special clinical populations:* Some clinical populations such as clients who have been sexually involved with a prior therapist (Pope, 1994), who are survivors of incest (Pope & Brown, 1996), or who have been victims of torture (Pope & Garcia-Peltoniemi, 1991) may be at increased risk for suicide.

9. *Sex:* The suicide rate for men tends to be about 3 times that for women. (For youths, the rate is closer to 5:1.) The rate of suicide attempts for women is about 3 times that for men.

10. *Age:* The risk for suicide tends to increase over the adult life cycle. Attempts by older people are much more likely to be lethal. The ratio of attempts to completed suicides for those up to age 65 is about 7:1 but is 2:1 for those over 65.

11. *Race:* Generally in the United States, Whites tend to have one of the highest suicide rates.

12. *Religion:* Suicide rates among Protestants tend to be higher than those among Jews and Catholics.

13. *Living alone:* The research suggests that suicidal risk tends to be reduced if someone is not living alone; it is reduced more if he or she is living with a spouse and even further if there are children.

14. *Bereavement:* Brunch, Barraclough, Nelson, and Sainsbury (1971) found that 50% of those in their sample who had committed suicide had lost their mothers within the last 3 years (compared with a 20% rate among controls matched for age, sex, marital status, and geographic location). Furthermore, 22% of the suicides, compared with only 9% of the controls, had experienced the loss of their father within the past 5 years. Krupnick's (1984) review of studies revealed a link between childhood bereavement and suicide attempts in adult life, perhaps doubling the risk for depressives who had lost a parent compared with depressives who had not experienced the death of a parent. Klerman and Clayton (1984; see also Beutler, 1985) found that suicide rates are higher among the widowed than the married (especially among elderly men) and that, among women, the suicide rate is not as high for widows as for the divorced or separated.

15. *Unemployment:* Unemployment tends to increase the risk for suicide.

16. *Health status:* The research suggests that illness and somatic complaints tend to be associated with increased suicidal risk, as are disturbances in patterns of sleeping and eating. Clinicians who are helping people with AIDS, for example, need to be sensitive to this risk (Pope & Morin, 1990).

17. *Impulsivity:* Those with poor impulse con-

trol are at increased risk for taking their own lives (see, e.g., Patsiokas, Clum, & Luscumb, 1979).

18. *Rigid thinking:* Suicidal individuals often display a rigid, all-or-none way of thinking (see, e.g., Neuringer, 1964). A typical statement might be: "If I don't find work within the next week, then the only real alternative is suicide."

19. *Stressful events:* Excessive numbers of undesirable events with negative outcomes have been associated with increased suicidal risk (Cohen-Sandler, Berman, & King, 1982; Isherwood, Adam, & Hornblow, 1982). Some types of recent events may place clients at extremely high risk. For example, Ellis, Atkeson, and Calhoun (1982) found that 52% of their sample of multiple-incident victims of sexual assault had attempted suicide.

20. *Release from hospitalization:* Some clinicians use voluntary or involuntary hospitalization to address severe suicidal risk. However, even when it has been determined that a person may safely leave the hospital setting, suicidal risk cannot be ignored. Research suggests that suicidal risk may increase—sometimes sharply—when a person leaves the hospital, for example, for a family visit, during a weekend pass, or at discharge.

References & Readings

Beutler, L. E. (1985). Loss and anticipated death: Risk factors in depression. In H. H. Goldman & S. E. Goldston (Eds.), *Preventing stress-related psychiatric disorders* (pp. 177–194). Rockville, MD: National Institute of Mental Health.

Brunch, J., Barraclough, B., Nelson, M., & Sainsbury, P. (1971). Suicide following death of parents. *Social Psychiatry, 6,* 193–199.

Cohen-Sandler, R., Berman, A. L., & King, R. A. (1982). Life stress and symptomatology: Determinants of suicidal behavior in children. *Journal of the American Academy of Child Psychiatry, 21,* 178–186.

Ellis, E. M., Atkeson, B. M., & Calhoun, K. S. (1982). An examination of differences between multiple- and single-incident victims of multiple sexual assault. *Journal of Abnormal Psychology, 91,* 221–224.

Isherwood, J., Adam, K. S., & Hornblow, A. R. (1982). Life event stress, psychosocial factors, suicide attempt, and auto-accident proclivity. *Journal of Psychosomatic Research, 26,* 371–383.

Kazdin, A. E. (1983). Hopelessness, depression, and suicidal intent among psychiatrically disturbed inpatient children. *Journal of Consulting and Clinical Psychology, 51,* 504–510.

Klerman, G. L., & Clayton, P. (1984). Epidemiologic perspectives on the health consequences of bereavement. In M. Osterweis, G. Solomon, & M. Green (Eds.), *Bereavement: Reactions, consequences, and care* (pp. 15–44). Washington, DC: National Academy Press.

Krupnick, J. L. (1984). Bereavement during childhood and adolescence. In M. Osterweis, F. Solomon, & M. Green (Eds.), *Bereavement: Reactions, consequences, and care* (pp. 99–141). Washington, DC: National Academy Press.

Neuringer, C. (1964). Rigid thinking in suicidal individuals. *Journal of Consulting Psychology, 28,* 54–58.

Patsiokas, A. T., Clum, G. A., & Luscumb, R. L. (1979). Cognitive characteristics of suicidal attempters. *Journal of Consulting and Clinical Psychology, 47,* 478–484.

Petrie, K., & Chamberlain, K. (1983). Hopelessness and social desirability as moderator variables in predicting suicidal behavior. *Journal of Consulting and Clinical Psychology, 51,* 485–487.

Pope, K. S. (1994). *Sexual involvement with therapists: Patient assessment, subsequent therapy, forensics.* Washington, DC: American Psychological Association.

Pope K. S., & Brown, L. S. (1996). *Recovered memories of abuse: Assessment, therapy, forensics.* Washington, DC: American Psychological Association.

Pope, K. S., Butcher, J. N., & Seelen, J. (1993). *The MMPI, MMPI-2, and MMPI-A in court: A practical guide for expert witnesses and attorneys.* Washington, DC: American Psychological Association.

Pope, K. S., & Garcia-Peltoniemi, R. E. (1991). Responding to victims of torture: Clinical issues, professional responsibilities, and useful resources. *Professional Psychology: Research and Practice, 22,* 269–276.

Pope, K. S., & Morin, S. F. (1990). AIDS and HIV infection update: New research, ethical responsibilities, evolving legal frameworks, and published resources. *Independent Practitioner, 10,* 43–53.

Pope, K. S., & Vasquez, M. J. T. (1991). *Ethics in psychotherapy and counseling.* San Francisco: Jossey-Bass.

Schneidman, E. (1976). *Suicidology: Contemporary developments.* New York: Grune and Stratton.

Wetzel, R. (1976). Hopelessness, depression, and suicide intent. *Archives of General Psychiatry, 33,* 1069–1073.

Related Topics

Chapter 62, "Treatment and Management of the Suicidal Patient"

11   CLINICAL ASSESSMENT OF DEFENSE MECHANISMS

Phebe Cramer

The methods available for the assessment of defense mechanisms may be grouped into two large categories: self-report and observer report. Self-report measures are based on what the individual being assessed reports about his or her own behavior. Generally, this information is obtained from self-administered questionnaires or from other prepared formats, in which the person is asked to report on his or her usual, or most likely, behavior in differing circumstances. Observer-report measures are based on the opinion of experts who have observed the individual being assessed. This observation may take the form of an interview, or it may involve the interpretation of a projective test that has been administered to the individual.

SELF-REPORT MEASURES

The most frequently used self-report measures of defense mechanisms are the Defense Mechanism Inventory, the Defense Style Questionnaire, the Life Style Index, and the Coping and Defending Scales. These measures share the same general strengths and weaknesses. Strengths include ease of test administration, possibility of group administration, standard response format, objective scoring of keyed responses that can be readily quantified, and the existence of normative data to evaluate individual responses. Unfortunately, these strengths are also the source of certain weaknesses. Information obtained is restricted to the questions asked; other potentially relevant material is not revealed. However, the primary weakness shared by all self-report measures is a logical one: Is it logically possible for persons to self-report on a mental mechanism that, by definition, occurs outside of their awareness? Proponents of self-report defense measures have tried to address this issue, but it remains a problem with this approach to defense assessment. Further, even if a person is *able* to self-report on use of defenses, there is still the question of whether the individual is *willing* to report this use, depending on the social desirability of the behavior. Additional strengths and weaknesses of each individual measure are discussed below.

The Defense Mechanism Inventory

Developed by Gleser and Ihilevich (1969), the Defense Mechanism Inventory (DMI) assesses the use of five defense mechanisms: Turning Against the Self, Turning Against the Object (includes displacement and identification with the aggressor), Projection, Reversal (includes negation, denial, reaction formation, and regression), and Principalization (includes intellectualization, isolation, and rationalization). The inventory consists of 10 stories, each of which describes a potentially conflictual situation. Following each story, possible reactions are described for actual behavior, fantasy behavior, thought, and affect. For each of these four categories, a reaction representing each of the five defenses is provided. The person being assessed is asked, for each category, which reaction would be most representative (scored 2) and which least representative (scored 0) for himself or herself. The maximum score for any defense is thus 80 (4 categories × 10 stories × score of 2). Since only one defense may be selected as most representative from each behavior category, it is not possible to have a high score on all five defenses. The summed defense scores may then be plotted on a preprinted profile to determine standard scores. Norms are available for males and females from college and general adult populations.

Although the DMI is easily administered, the test taker must be able to differentiate between overt behavior, fantasy, thought, and affect. Scoring is objective; a template may be placed over the response sheet and responses summed for each defense. Scores may then be plotted on a profile that automatically provides normative information. Weaknesses include the clustering together of different defenses into the composites of Reversal and Principalization, and the status of Turning Against the Object as a defense is questionable.

Psychometrically, the five defense scales show adequate reliability. Evidence for validity of the scales is mixed; Reversal and Turning Against the Self are the only scales to clearly relate to criteria in the manner expected. Further, there is a strong intercorrelation between several of the scales, and the conflict situations described may not be relevant to the experience of some individuals taking the test. An extensive review of this measure appears in Cramer (1991).

The Defense Style Questionnaire

The Defense Style Questionnaire (DSQ; Bond, 1986) assesses 20 different defenses, which are grouped into three defense style categories: Immature (includes projection, passive aggression, acting out, omnipotence, isolation, splitting, regression, and denial); Neurotic (includes reaction formation, undoing, inhibition, withdrawal, idealization, and pseudoaltruism); and Mature (includes suppression, task orientation, anticipation, sublimation, and humor). The questionnaire consists of 88 items, responded to on a 9-point Likert scale to indicate the degree to which the behavior described in the item is characteristic of the test taker.

Specific advantages of this measure include the use of factor analysis to select the test items that best represent the defenses being assessed and the fact that the defenses assessed are chosen to be consistent with the glossary of defense mechanisms listed in the *DSM-III-R* (American Psychiatric Association, 1987). Psychometrically, many of the individual defense scales have low reliability, but both internal consistency and retest stability are reasonably good for the three defense styles. Evidence for validity of the defense styles is found in studies demonstrating the expected relationships with ego strength, ego level, and psychopathology (see Bond, 1986).

The Life Style Index

The Life Style Index (LSI; Conte & Plutchik, 1993; Plutchik, Kellerman, & Conte, 1979) assesses the use of eight defense mechanisms: denial, displacement, projection, reaction formation, regression/acting out, repression (includes isolation and introjection), compensation (includes identification and fantasy), and intellectualization (includes sublimation, undoing, and rationalization). Much of the development of this measure was based on a 138-item version of the questionnaire, although a 97-item version is currently in use. Respondents answer each item "usually true" or "usually not true."

Psychometric studies show variable reliability: internal consistency is low for some defense scales (e.g., displacement, intellectualization) but adequate for others (e.g., reaction formation, projection). Evidence for validity has been examined within the authors' theory of emotion and psychopathology. Within this framework, defense scores were generally found to relate in predicted ways to self-esteem, anxiety, and pathology.

In addition to the advantage of the fixed question-response format is the association of this approach to defense measurement with a theory of emotion. Specific disadvantages are the restriction of response to a binary yes-no format and the clustering together into a single scale of defense mechanisms that are conceptually quite different. For example, sublimation is typically considered a "successful" defense (Fenichel, 1945), while undoing and rationalization involve cognitive distortions; likewise, the clustering of repression, isolation, and introjection into one scale combines defenses with quite different defining characteristics. A further question at this point is whether the current 97-item version will demonstrate the same predictive validity as the original LSI scales.

The Coping and Defending Scales

The Coping and Defending Scales (CDS) were developed by Joffe and Naditch (in Haan, 1977), following the models of Haan and Kroeber (Haan, 1977) that related coping and defense processes to basic ego functions. The CDS consists of 10 defense scales: denial, displacement, doubt, intellectualization, isolation, projection, rationalization, reaction formation, regression, and repression. The items on most scales are derived from the California Psychological Inventory (CPI) and are criterion-keyed, with the criterion being interview-based ratings of the use of these defenses. This feature makes the CDS critically different from the other self-report measures. The items, while having been demonstrated to statistically differentiate between high and low users of each defense, do not bear any obvious relation to the defense itself. This feature enables these scales to avoid the characteristic problem of the other self-report defense scales; it is not obvious to the test taker that the questions are related to the use of defenses. Questions are answered true or false; defense scores are calculated by adding up the number of scale items marked in the criterion direction. For each sex, different items and different numbers of items make up the same-named defense scales; that is, the items constituting the projection scale for males are not necessarily identical to those constituting the projection scale for females. Norms for community adults and undergraduates are available (Haan, 1977).

Psychometrically, no information is available regarding internal consistency reliability. Evidence for retest reliability is mixed, with some scales being adequate and others showing low reliability. Estimates of validity are also quite varied; some of the validity coefficients are unacceptably low, and this varies by gender.

The specific advantage of this approach is that it avoids the logical difficulty involved in asking persons to report on their own use of defenses. Also, using the CPI items to obtain information about defenses simultaneously provides information regarding other dimensions of personality. Insufficient and/or unsatisfactory information regarding the reliability and validity of the scales is an obvious disadvantage.

OBSERVER-REPORT MEASURES

Observer-report measures may be based on clinical interviews (e.g., the Defense Mechanism Rating Scales), on Rorschach protocols (e.g., the Lerner Defense Scale, the Rorschach Defense Scale), or on Thematic Apperception Test (TAT) stories (the Defense Mechanism Manual). These measures share a number of strengths and weaknesses. An important strength is the presence of an open-ended response format, which allows individuals to exhibit, without arbitrary constraints, their typical way of reacting to anxiety- or stress-producing situations. In contrast to self-report measures, responses are not limited by a specific set of predetermined questions and response alternatives. Further, the open-ended

nature of the response format does not alert the individual that a particular aspect of behavior is being studied; although problems of social desirability are not eliminated, attempts to create a good impression may be judged as a manifestation of a defense mechanism. On the other hand, the very openness of the response process contributes to a major weakness of observer-report measures—namely, that the determination of the use of defense mechanisms is largely dependent on the clinical skill of the observer, with all of the attendant problems of subjectivity, possible bias, and the potential for disagreement among observers about the interpretation of any particular response. Detailed rules for coding responses help to reduce these problems. Also, when a permanent record is available from videotapes, audiotapes, or transcriptions, it is possible to systematically review the behavior being rated and to make use of multiple raters to obtain consensus ratings.

The Defense Mechanism Rating Scales

The Defense Mechanism Rating Scales (DMRS; Perry, Kardos, & Pagano, 1993) were designed to identify the use of 28 different defense mechanisms, based on the observation of a person's behavior in an interview. The observation may be made in situ, or it may be based on a videotape and/or transcript of the interview. Using a specially designed manual, the observer is provided with a description of each defense, a description of how the defense functions, and an explanation of how to differentiate among similar defenses. The interview may be rated to yield qualitative information (was this defense used?) or quantitative data. In the latter case, each occurrence of the defense during the interview is noted and summed; the final quantitative score is based on the number of times a particular defense is rated, divided by the total number of instances of all defenses. In addition, defenses have been clustered into seven categories, representing increasing defense maturity. The seven levels of maturity, from lowest to highest, and their associated defenses are Level 1 (action level): acting out, hypochondriasis, and passive aggression; Level 2 (major image-distorting level; borderline): splitting and projective identification; Level 3 (disavowal level): denial, projection, and rationalization; Level 4 (minor image-distorting level): devaluation, idealization, reaction formation, and displacement; Level 5 (neurotic level): repression, dissociation, reaction formation, and displacement; Level 6 (obsessional level): intellectualization, isolation of affect, and undoing; and Level 7 (high adaptive): affiliation, altruism, anticipation, humor, self-assertion, self-observation, sublimation, and suppression. To obtain an Overall Defense Maturity score, the occurrence of each defense is multiplied by its numerical weight, based on this 7-point hierarchy; the weighted average of all the defenses rated from the interview provides the Overall Maturity score.

Psychometric evidence for the interrater reliability of the individual defense scales shows considerable variability, with some scales showing very little agreement among raters. The interrater reliability for the Overall Defense Maturity scores (Levels 1–7) is somewhat better. One-week retest reliability was high. Evidence for validity is seen in the positive relation of the lower-level defense scales to impairment in psychosocial functioning and in the positive correlation between DMRS Level 1 scores and the DSQ maladaptive, immature defense style. However, other levels of the DMRS did not relate to the DSQ. Further, DMRS defenses were not found to be related to psychiatric diagnosis.

Advantages of this approach include the careful attention that has been given to the training of raters; also, the rating measure has been revised several times in an attempt to improve both reliability and validity. Nevertheless, the interrater reliability for the individual defense scales is rather low. The reliability for the composite, seven-level scales is adequate, but one may question whether many of the behaviors measured at Level 7 (e.g., affiliation, self-assertion, self-observation) should be considered defense mechanisms. More information on the validity of both the individual and level defense scales is clearly needed.

The Lerner Defense Scale and Rorschach Defense Scale

The Lerner Defense Scale (LDS; Lerner & Lerner, 1980) and the Rorschach Defense Scale (RDS; Cooper, Perry, & Arnow, 1988) are both designed to assess the use of defenses from Rorschach responses. They differ in that the LDS is based on Kernberg's object relations theory and considers only Rorschach "human" responses, while the RDS is based on Kohut's developmental arrest theory and scores all responses given, human and otherwise. In addition, the LDS focuses on primitive, borderline defenses (denial, splitting, devaluation, idealization, and projective identification), while the RDS includes a wider variety of defenses (in addition to the above, intellectualization, isolation, omnipotence, projection, rationalization, reaction formation, and repression).

Interrater reliability has been found to be quite high for the LDS but somewhat lower for the RDS. For the latter, grouping the scales into neurotic, borderline, and psychotic defenses produced a small improvement in interrater reliability. Evidence for validity of the LDS is based primarily on its demonstrated ability to distinguish patients with a borderline personality disorder (BPD) from those with other diagnoses. While certain of the RDS scales have been shown to correlate with similar BPD scales, scores on the RDS defense scales do not discriminate BPD patients from either antisocial or bipolar disorders. A comparison of the success of the LDS and the RDS in predicting diagnosis indicated that both measures differentiated hospitalized borderline patients from neurotics and schizophrenics, but only the LDS differentiated schizophrenics from neurotics and outpatient borderlines. On the other hand, only the RDS differentiated between inpatient and outpatient borderlines.

In addition to the differences in discriminatory power, similarly named defense scales of the two measures are not highly correlated. Further, the scales within the LDS are strongly intercorrelated; this problem is not found with the RDS. Further, an evaluation of a number of studies using the LDS suggested that the idealization scale was measuring an adaptive capacity rather than a primitive defense.

The Defense Mechanism Manual

The Defense Mechanism Manual approach to defense evaluation is based on the coding of TAT stories (Cramer, 1991). A detailed manual provides guidance for the assessment of three defenses: denial, projection, and identification. For each defense, seven components are defined, representing different aspects of the defense; each component is scored as many times as it occurs in each story, and the scores for each defense are summed over all stories.

Multiple studies have found adequate interrater reliability for all three defenses with children, adolescents, adults, and psychiatric patients. The validity of the coding approach has been demonstrated through observational studies of children, adolescents, adults, and psychiatric patients, in which defense mechanism scores differentiated between age-groups or were related to psychiatric psychopathology in ways predicted by theory (e.g., Cramer & Blatt, 1990). Validity has also been demonstrated through experimental studies, in which the use of defenses changed in ways predicted, as a result of the experimental manipulation.

Advantages of this approach include the fact that the assessment may be carried out individually or in groups, using a written version of the TAT; it is not necessary for a highly skilled person to administer the test. Stimulus cards may be selected to represent individual areas of suspected conflict for the individual being assessed. Another advantage is that the assessment method is clearly tied to a theory of defense mechanism development, and the approach may be used with persons of all ages. An additional advantage of this approach, not found with the other methods, is the experimental validation of the measure. Disadvantages include the time required to train coders, the inevitable subjectivity involved in the use of projective approaches, and the fact that the coding scheme assesses only three defenses.

References & Readings

American Psychiatric Association (1987). *Diagnostic and statistical manual of mental disorders* (3rd ed., rev.). Washington, DC: American Psychiatric Association.

Bond, M. (1986). Defense Style Questionnaire. In G. E. Vaillant (Ed.), *Empirical studies of ego mechanisms of defense* (pp. 146–152). Washington, DC: American Psychiatric Press.

Conte, H. R., & Plutchik, R. (1993). The measurement of ego defenses in clinical research. In U. Hentschel, G. J. W. Smith, W. Ehlers, & J. G. Draguns (Eds.), *The concept of defense mechanisms in contemporary psychology* (pp. 275–289). New York: Springer-Verlag.

Cooper, S. H., Perry, J. C., & Arnow, D. (1988). An empirical approach to the study of defense mechanisms: I. Reliability and preliminary validity of the Rorschach Defense Scales. *Journal of Personality Assessment, 52,* 187–203.

Cramer, P. (1991). *The development of defense mechanisms: Theory, assessment, and research.* New York: Springer-Verlag.

Cramer, P., & Blatt, S. J. (1990). Use of the TAT to measure change in defense mechanisms following intensive psychotherapy. *Journal of Personality Assessment, 54,* 236–251.

Fenichel, O. (1945). *The psychoanalytic theory of neurosis.* New York: Norton.

Gleser, G. C., & Ihilevich, D. (1969). An objective instrument for measuring defense mechanisms. *Journal of Consulting and Clinical Psychology, 33,* 51–60.

Haan, N. (1977). *Coping and defending.* New York: Academic Press.

Ihilevich, D., & Gleser, G. C. (1986). *Defense mechanisms: Their classification, correlates, and measurement with the Defense Mechanisms Inventory.* Owosso, MI: DMI Associates.

Lerner, P. M., & Lerner, H. D. (1980). Rorschach assessment of primitive defenses in borderline personality structure. In J. S. Kwawer, H. Lerner, P. Lerner, & A. Sugarman (Eds.), *Borderline phenomena and the Rorschach test* (pp. 257–274). New York: International Universities Press.

Perry, J. C., Kardos, M. E., & Pagano, C. J. (1993). The study of defenses in psychotherapy using the Defense Mechanism Rating Scales (DMRS). In U. Hentschel, G. J. W. Smith, W. Ehlers, & J. G. Draguns (Eds.), *The concept of defense mechanisms in contemporary psychology* (pp. 122–132). New York: Springer-Verlag.

Plutchik, R., Kellerman, H., & Conte, H. R. (1979). A structural theory of ego defense and emotions. In C. E. Izard (Ed.), *Emotions in personality and psychopathology* (pp. 229–257). New York: Plenum Press.

Vaillant, G. E. (1977). *Adaptation to life.* Boston: Little, Brown.

Vaillant, G. E. (1992). *Ego mechanisms of defense: A guide for clinicians and researchers.* Washington, DC: American Psychiatric Press.

Vaillant, G. E. (1993). *The wisdom of the ego.* Cambridge, MA: Harvard University Press.

Related Topics

12 EGO STRENGTH AND EGO DEVELOPMENT

Assessment and Clinical Application

Lê X. Hy

DEFINING EGO STRENGTH

Ego strength is the competence that one develops to deal with one's own impulse and the environment to achieve a goal. The goal may be to satisfy one's own impulse, or it may be something more complex. The term *ego* is commonly associated with psychoanalysis, although Freud did not use this Latin word. Dealing with oneself and the environment is part of many behaviors and thus is important in many psychological theories. The word *strength* sounds unidimensional, but even a generally strong person may still have mental illness. Thus a measure of ego strength should detect various strengths and weaknesses, which together form different styles or types. In a diagnosis and treatment plan, it may be more important to identify the types of strengths and weaknesses than to measure an overall competence.

THE EGO STRENGTH SCALE

It is uncertain what the popular Ego Strength Scale (*Es*) measures. In 1953, Frank Barron chose 68 items from the Minnesota Multiphasic Personality Inventory (MMPI) based on their contents to predict the positive response to psychotherapy, but the scale has not done that (Last, 1980). In the MMPI-2 the scale lost 16 items, so it is now even more uncertain what the scale measures. Unfortunately, *Es* has frequently been used as the criterion to test other measures of ego strength, probably because of its name and ease of use.

High *Es* scores may point to the following characteristics: high stress tolerance, lack of chronic psychological problems, emotional stability, less prejudice, self-confidence, intelligence, resourcefulness, acceptance by others, determination, and tolerance of confrontation in therapy (Butcher & Williams, 1992, p. 172). Duckworth and Anderson (1995) suggested the following interpretation of the *Es* based on its T score: <35: subject has poor self-concept, is helpless and unable to carry out good intention, thus requires ego building before dealing with problem; 35–45: subject has poor self-concept; 45–60: subject is strong enough to deal with life's stresses and minor setbacks though less confident than the average college student; >60: typical of college student, subject is resilient and responds well to treatment but resists treatment of emotional problems subject does not recognize.

THE RORSCHACH

The Rorschach has been another popular way to measure ego strength, although there is disagreement on what set of variables to use. The Rorschach Prognostic Rating Scale (RPRS), proposed by Klopfer and associates to measure adjustment potential, was the most popular. Garwood (1977) reviewed 13 RPRS studies and found that "the RPRS predicts therapeutic outcome for a wide variety of patient populations and therapeutic techniques including behavior modification." On the other hand, Last (1980) cited evidence that discrete Rorschach variables may predict therapeutic outcome even better than Klopfer's full scale. Currently there is no consensus on what variables or combination to use (some candidates have been *M, FM, S, FC, CF, X+%, F+%, Lambda, D, A+, m, Sh,* and *FL*).

Clinicians may be more interested in ego weakness or adjustment difficulties rather than ego strength, and a different set of Rorschach variables can be used to measure this. Weiner (1995) suggested *Mp-* in *Dd* locations, *(H), Hd,* and *(Hd)*. Perry and Viglione (1991) derived an Ego Impairment Index from a complex combination of their Good:Poor Human Experience variable (based on a special coding of human responses) with depressed content, Sum FQ–, and W SUM 6.

SOME OTHER SCALES

There are a number of less popular ego strength scales. Pascal and Suttell constructed an index based on the Bender Gestalt, reasoning that accurate drawing of geometric figures represents adequate response to the environment. Cattell extracted a source trait from the 16 Personality Factor (16PF). Bellak constructed the Global Ego Strength Scale to measure different ego functions. Some other scales are based on various scoring of the Thematic Apperception Test. There has been some research using these measures but not enough to validate their constructs or show their clinical utility. Correlations of various ego strength measures have not been higher than chance. Last (1980) provided a concise review of all the tests mentioned so far, and not much has changed since then (except for the shorter *Es* scale in MMPI-2).

THE WASHINGTON UNIVERSITY SENTENCE COMPLETION TEST

Paradoxically, a number of clinicians have found much clinical utility in the Washington University Sentence Completion Test (WUSCT), constructed by a psychometrician, Jane Loevinger, who denies any expertise in psychotherapy. The test aims to measure both the path of human development and personality types. It has one main factor, but woven into this central factor are a number of characteristics that peak at different times during the course of development, resulting in eight detectable levels: Impulsive, Self-protective, Conformist, Self-aware, Conscientious, Individualistic, Autonomous, and Integrated. The construct was not derived from psychoanalytic theory. The test has favorable psychometric properties (Loevinger, in press) and has been used in a variety of settings in different countries and different languages, including a number of longitudinal studies.

The WUSCT is a simple and standardized paper-and-pencil test, with 36 items on two sheets of paper. It is available free of charge and can be administered to a group. The rating manual has complete instructions and exercises to train raters. The recent revision (Hy & Loevinger, 1996; Loevinger, in press) has made the test easier to use in a number of ways: the forms for men and women are closely compatible; the two pages can be used as two short forms, although the full test is much preferred; the test forms can be photocopied directly from the book for better standardization; the rating categories are updated, divided into simple themes, and printed on oversized pages so raters can scan them quickly; a computer can be used to automate part of the rating procedure; and suggestions are provided on how to use the test in languages other than English. Even so, it takes time to learn how to use the test and rate the responses. Careful attempts to develop a multiple-choice version have failed.

The scale is not intended to measure adjustment or mental health, and people at all levels of ego development have shown different psychological problems. Yet the scale allows an overall context (including such characteristics as impulse control, interpersonal mode, and conscious preoccupations) to understand complex interactions among variables that may result in psychological problems. For example, adolescents at both the Conformist and pre-Conformist (Impulsive or Self-protective) levels may attempt suicide but for different reasons: Conformists are self-blaming, depressed, and concerned about being lost or abandoned; pre-Conformists are defiant, angry, and revengeful. A number of studies also show a relationship between the WUSCT and all the variables in the Defense Mechanism Inventory (for more on this test, see chapter 11). The test has also been used to study depression, sexual activities, pain management, conceptions of psychotherapy, creativity, parental control, adolescent autonomy, eating disorders, and so on (Westenberg, Blasi, & Cohn, 1997). Another common clinical use of the test is to discuss with clients in the first therapy sessions their responses to 36 different topics, which may indicate some problems, insights, or hypotheses.

MEASURES OF PARTICULAR DIMENSIONS

Many people have suggested breaking the construct of ego strength into numerous components that can be measured separately, possibly without abandoning an overall measure. Several theorists, such as Haan and Bellak, have attempted to build such a set of constructs. Meanwhile the term *ego strength* is invoked casually in all types of situations, often without being measured. One temporary solution is to clarify the term and to see if a more focused construct can be used instead. Robinson, Shaver, and Wrightsman (1991) have reviewed a dozen or more measures for each of the following constructs: subjective well-being, self-esteem, shyness, loneliness, alienation, interpersonal trust, locus of control, authoritarianism, androgyny, and values. Their list was, of course, not exhaustive.

SUMMARY

Ego strength is an important construct for diagnosis, treatment planning, and outcome assessment. Barron's *Es* does not measure ego strength as such. Different Rorschach variables measure response to psychotherapy, which is only a part of ego strength, and it is unclear which variables do this best. WUSCT measuring the central trait of ego development predicts defenses but not mental health; it can provide a context for explaining behavior and starting psychotherapy. Other measures have not been researched thoroughly. Constructs related to and narrower than ego strength should also be considered.

References & Readings

Butcher, J. N., & Williams, C. L. (1992). *Essentials of MMPI-2 and MMPI-A interpretation*. Minneapolis: University of Minnesota Press.

Duckworth, J. C., & Anderson, W. P. (1995). *MMPI & MMPI-2 interpretation manual for counselors and clinicians* (4th ed.). Briston, PA: Accelerated Development.

Garwood, J. (1977). A guide to research on the Rorschach Prognostic Rating Scale. *Journal of Personality Assessment, 41*, 117–119.

Hy, L. X., & Loevinger, J. (1996). *Measuring ego development* (2nd ed.). Mahwah, NJ: Erlbaum.

Last, U. (1980). Ego strength. In R. H. Woody (Ed.), *Encyclopedia of clinical assessment* (pp. 341–349). San Francisco: Jossey-Bass.

Loevinger, J. (Ed.) (in press). *Technical foundations for measuring ego development*. Mahwah, NJ: Erlbaum.

Perry, W., & Viglione, D. J., Jr. (1991). The Ego Impairment Index as a predictor of outcome in melancholic depressed patients treated with tricyclic antidepressants. *Journal of Personality Assessment, 56,* 487–501.

Robinson, J. P., Shaver, P. R., & Wrightsman, L. S. (Eds.) (1991). *Measures of personality and social psychological attitudes*. San Diego, CA: Academic Press.

Weiner, I. B. (1995). Variable selection in Rorschach research. In J. E. Exner Jr. (Ed.), *Issues and methods in Rorschach research*. Mahwah, NJ: Erlbaum.

Westenberg, P. M., Blasi, A., & Cohn, L. D. (Eds.) (1997). *Personality development: Theoretical, empirical, and clinical investigations of Loevinger's conception of ego development*. Mahwah, NJ: Erlbaum.

Related Topics

Chapter 11, "Clinical Assessment of Defense Mechanisms"

Chapter 14, "Conceptualization and Assessment of Secondary Gain"

13 ASSESSMENT OF MALINGERING ON PSYCHOLOGICAL MEASURES

A Synopsis

Richard Rogers

Psychologists vary considerably in their understanding of malingering and their sophistication at its detection. The standard definition of malingering is the deliberate fabrication or gross exaggeration of psychological or physical symptoms for some external goal (American Psychiatric Association, 1994). Critical decision points include (a) the deliberateness of the presentation (e.g., somatoform disorder vs. malingering); (b) the magnitude of the dissimulation (e.g., minor embellishment vs. gross exaggeration); and (c) the identification of the goal and its primary source (e.g., internal vs. external). Rogers (1997) provides a comprehensive resource for addressing these issues.

The focus of this synopsis is twofold. First, I address common misconceptions about malingering that are likely to influence professional practice. Second, I distill the empirical literature relative to the clinical detection of malingering. This distillation is necessarily selective and concentrates on the more robust clinical indicators for feigned mental disorders and cognitive impairment.

COMMON MISCONCEPTIONS

• *Because malingering is very infrequent, it should not be a cause of diagnostic concern:*

Survey data strongly question the premise of this fallacy. Two extensive surveys yielded almost identical estimates that accounted for an appreciable percentage of assessment cases (7.4% and 7.8%). Even if the premise were true, psychologists should not equate infrequency with inconsequentiality. As an analogue, suicide attempts are very rare in certain clinical populations, but no responsible psychologist would argue against their examination.

• *Because malingering is a global response style, it is easy to detect:* This premise is easily assailable. Psychological practice with veteran populations, for example, provides ample evidence of how some malingerers become very targeted in their dissimulation. The implicit message of this misconception is that malingering is relatively easy to detect because of its obviousness. At least with feigned cognitive deficits, the available literature suggests that many simulators remain undetected unless specific measures of malingering are employed (for a review, see Rogers, Harrell, & Liff, 1993).

• *If psychologists pay attention to DSM-IV indices, they are likely to be effective at identifying malingerers:* This viewpoint disregards the nature of *DSM-IV* indices. Unlike inclusion criteria found with most disorders, these indices are intended merely to raise the index of suspicion. Moreover, the only available data suggest that the use of these indices may result in a false-positive rate of about 80%. In addition, the *DSM-IV* emphasis on criminality (i.e., medicolegal evaluation and antisocial personality disorder) is largely unwarranted (see Rogers, 1990) and may lead to misclassifications in both forensic (false-positives) and nonforensic (false-negatives) cases.

• *Inconsistencies are the hallmark of malingerers:* Although inconsistencies are found among many malingerers, the equating of inconsistencies with malingering is a grievous error. For example, research on the MMPI-2 has demonstrated convincingly that inconsistent profiles may result from psychosis, inability to attend, or inadequate comprehension (Greene, 1997). Data from structured interviewing (Structured Interview of Reported Symptoms [SIRS]; Rogers, Bagby, & Dickens, 1992) further illustrates this point. Although malingerers tend to be inconsistent in their symptom presentation, a substantial minority of the clinical population is also inconsistent. Depending on the prevalence rate for malingering in a particular setting, an individual with an inconsistent presentation may have a greater likelihood of being a genuinely disordered patient than a malingerer.

• *Mental illness and malingering are mutually exclusive:* Most psychologists are not likely to openly embrace this false dichotomy. However, many clinical evaluations appear to be concluded once malingering is determined. I also suspect that the establishment of a bona fide disorder reduces the scrutiny given to the genuineness of other presented symptoms. Unquestionably, neither malingering nor mental illness offers any natural immunity to the other.

• *Deceptive persons are likely to be malingerers:* The mislogic of "if you lie, you will malinger" is readily apparent. While malingerers are deceptive persons, the obverse is not necessarily true. The sustained effort involved in successful feigning, the stigmatization of mental disorders, and the often severe penalties for detection are likely to militate against widespread malingering. Moreover, Ford, King, and Hollender (1988) cogently describe the numerous genuine disorders for which deception is commonplace.

ASSESSMENT OF FEIGNED MENTAL DISORDERS

The assessment of feigned psychopathology involves the use of well-validated measures in a multimethod evaluation. Although a number of brief self-report measures have recently been published, these measures lack the discriminability and extensive cross-validation for their use in the determination of malingering (see Smith, 1997); however, they may serve a useful screening function. The two best established measures are the MMPI-2 and the SIRS. Each will be summarized separately.

Meta-analyses of the MMPI (Berry, Baer, & Harris, 1991) and the MMPI-2 (Rogers, Sewell, & Salekin, 1994) underscore their general usefulness in the evaluation of feigning and the marked variability in optimum cutting scores. For example, Rogers et al. (1994) found cutting scores for F that ranged from 9 to 30. The following guidelines are proposed.

1. Is the profile consistent? A random or inconsistent profile likely will be indistinguishable from a feigned profile on fake-bad indicators. One benchmark is to exclude profiles with VRIN > 14.
2. Are the standard validity indicators extremely elevated? Psychologists should have greater confidence in scores that exceed all or nearly all studies in a meta-analysis. As a benchmark of malingering, is $F > 30$ or $F-K > 25$?
3. If standard indicators are elevated but not to an extreme level, are specialized indicators extremely elevated? For persons faking global impairment or psychosis, F and $F-K$ appear to be remarkably robust. For more focal feigning of nonpsychotic disorders, the results are much less clear. As a benchmark of malingering, is $Dsr2 > 28$ or $O-S > 190$?
4. Caution should be exercised in applying these results to minority populations. For instance, nonclinical populations (African Americans and Hispanic Americans) score higher on F than their Anglo-American counterparts.

The SIRS is a structured interview that has been extensively validated with clinical, community, and correctional samples. Unlike the numerous cutting scores generated for multiscale inventories, the SIRS has employed standard cutting scores throughout its development and validation. Its results combine data from both simulation and known-groups comparisons. Guidelines (see Rogers et al., 1992; Rogers, 1997) for its use are straightforward.

- *Any SIRS scale in the definite feigning range:* Any extreme elevations on the primary scales designate feigning and have a negligible false-positive rate (1.0%).
- *Three or more scales in the probable feigning range:* The most robust measure of feigning is the combination of markedly elevated primary scales; again, the false-positive rate appears to be very small (< 3.0%).
- *Total SIRS score (all scores except Repeated Inquiries):* In indeterminant cases, a summation of endorsed items represents a supplementary criterion; Rogers et al. (1992) found no false positives.

Further research is needed on the use of the SIRS with adolescents and persons with neuropsychological impairment. As clearly articulated in the test manual (Rogers et al., 1992), the SIRS is designed to assess the feigning of psychopathology and mental disorders; different strategies are needed with persons faking cognitive impairment.

ASSESSMENT OF FEIGNED COGNITIVE IMPAIRMENT

Unlike simulated mental disorders, feigned cognitive impairment does not require the complex generation of believable symptoms and associated features with concomitant data on the onset and course of the simulated disorder. Rather, persons who malinger intellectual or neuropsychological impairment must simply put forward a suboptimal effort with an appearance of sincerity. Because of the disparateness between types of malingering, different strategies are recommended for its detection. As an important caution, the MMPI-2 is frequently recommended in neuropsychological consults where malingering is suspected; however, it is unlikely to be effective in detecting markedly suboptimal performances on cognitive tasks. Nonetheless, the MMPI-2 may be useful in those cases of global malingering when feigning encompasses both psychopathology and cognitive functioning.

Rogers et al. (1993) summarized detection strategies for feigned cognitive impairment. Significantly, most strategies are useful in screening for feigned impairment but not for making the actual determination. The detection strategies include the following.

- *Floor effect:* Some malingerers fail on exceptionally simple questions that even very impaired persons are able to answer correctly. For example, "Who is older, a mother or her child?" The most common use of the floor-effect strategy is found in the presentation of Rey's 15-Item Memory Test that has only modest sensitivity.
- *Performance curve:* Many malingerers do not take into account item difficulty. While they fail more difficult than easy items, the decline based on item difficulty is generally more gradual than found with genuine patients. Frederick and Foster (1991) have successfully applied this strategy to a modified version of the Test of Nonverbal Intelligence (TONI). It has also been successfully applied to Ravens Progressive Matrices.
- *Symptom validity testing (SVT):* Pankratz (1988) championed this method for the detection of feigned sensory or memory deficits through the presentation of a large number of trials. Based on probability, some malingering cases can be identified based on performance worse than chance. The best validated measure for this purpose is the Portland Digit Recognition Test (PDRT; Binder, 1993). More recent efforts to establish performance *below expectations* versus *below chance* are worthwhile but lack the certitude of below-chance results.
- *Magnitude of error:* Some malingerers are theorized to make very atypical mistakes, in terms of either gross errors or near misses, akin to the Ganser syndrome. Although this may prove fruitful for further research, empirical data are lacking on the efficacy of this strategy.
- *Psychological sequelae:* An important issue is the effectiveness of persons feigning cognitive impairment at describing both decrements to their daily functioning and psychological symptoms that are likely to arise from their purported impairment. Recent research would suggest that untrained persons are likely to recognize symptoms associated with postconcussion syndrome and

mild brain injury. What remains to be investigated is whether such persons can accurately depict psychological sequelae (e.g., depression and anxiety) that frequently follow such injuries.
- *Inconsistent or atypical presentations:* Many clinicians believe that variable performance or an atypical pattern of test scores signifies malingering. Many factors argue against any facile conclusions: (a) No cutting scores are established for making this determination; (b) patients with neuropsychological impairment often have variable performances; and (c) personality changes, as a result of brain injury, are likely to affect performance.

Determinations of malingering are complex, multimethod evaluations. Conclusions should never be based on a single symptom, scale, or measure. When data are inconclusive but suggestive of feigning, the response style may be described as "inconsistent" or "unreliable." To misclassify a genuine patient as a malingerer may have devastating consequences to that individual's future treatment, financial well-being, and legal status. To misclassify a malingerer as a genuine patient may have grave consequences for other concerned parties (e.g., insurance companies, employers, or the criminal justice system). Psychologists shoulder a heavy responsibility to minimize both types of misclassification in their assessment of malingering. They must base their findings on a comprehensive evaluation that utilizes specific measures that are well validated for malingering and related response styles.

References & Readings

American Psychiatric Association (1994). *Diagnostic and statistical manual of mental disorders* (4th ed.). Washington, DC: American Psychiatric Association.

Berry, D. T. R., Baer, R. A., & Harris, M. J. (1991). Detection of malingering on the MMPI: A meta-analysis. *Clinical Psychology Review, 11,* 585–598.

Berry, D. T. R., Wetter, M. W., & Baer, R. A. (1995). Assessment of malingering. In J. N. Butcher (Ed.), *Clinical personality assessment: Practi-*

cal approaches (pp. 236–248). New York: Oxford University Press.

Binder, L. M. (1993). Assessment of malingering after mild head trauma with the Portland Digit Recognition Test. *Journal of Clinical and Experimental Neuropsychology, 15,* 170–183.

Ford, C. V., King, B. H., & Hollender, M. H. (1988). Lies and liars: Psychiatric aspects of prevarication. *American Journal of Psychiatry, 145,* 554–562.

Frederick, R. I., & Foster, H. G. (1991). Multiple measures of malingering on a forced-choice test of cognitive ability. *Psychological Assessment: A Journal of Clinical and Consulting Psychology, 3,* 596–602.

Greene, R. L. (1997). Assessment of malingering and defensiveness by multiscale personality inventories. In R. Rogers (Ed.), *Clinical assessment of malingering and deception* (2nd ed., pp. 169–207). New York: Guilford Press.

Pankratz, L. (1988). Malingering on intellectual and neuropsychological measures. In R. Rogers (Ed.), *Clinical assessment of malingering and deception* (pp. 169–192). New York: Guilford Press.

Rogers, R. (1990). Models of feigned mental illness. *Professional Psychology, 21,* 182–188.

Rogers, R. (Ed.) (1997). *Clinical assessment of malingering and deception* (2nd ed.). New York: Guilford Press.

Rogers, R., Bagby, R. M., & Dickens, S. E. (1992).

Structured Interview of Reported Symptoms (SIRS) and professional manual. Odessa, FL: Psychological Assessment Resources.

Rogers, R., Harrell, E. H., & Liff, C. D. (1993). Feigning neuropsychological impairment: A critical review of methodological and clinical considerations. *Clinical Psychology Review, 13,* 255–274.

Rogers, R., Sewell, K. W., & Goldstein, A. (1994). Explanatory models of malingering: A prototypical analysis. *Law and Human Behavior, 18,* 543–552.

Rogers, R., Sewell, K. W., & Salekin, R. (1994). A meta-analysis of malingering on the MMPI-2. *Assessment, 1,* 227–237.

Schretlen, D. J. (1988). The use of psychological tests to identify malingered symptoms of mental disorder. *Clinical Psychology Review, 8,* 457–476.

Smith, G. (1997). Assessment of malingering with self-report instruments. In R. Rogers (Ed.), *Clinical assessment of malingering and deception* (2nd ed., pp. 351–370). New York: Guilford Press.

Related Topics

Chapter 11, "Clinical Assessment of Defense Mechanisms"

Chapter 14, "Conceptualization and Assessment of Secondary Gain"

14 CONCEPTUALIZATION AND ASSESSMENT OF SECONDARY GAIN

Richard Rogers & Vianey R. Reinhardt

Unpublicized controversies surround the professional understanding and clinical assessment of secondary gain across diverse populations.

Originally, Freud postulated that genuine disorders (e.g., hysteria) may be complicated by both intrapsychic and environmental factors that contribute to the persistence of the disorder and the subsequent thwarting of treatment efforts. From these dynamic origins, widely divergent constructs of secondary gain (see Fishbain, Rosomoff, Cutler, & Rosomoff, 1995) have been articulated that encompass behavioral and forensic perspectives. In this chapter we delineate these multifarious conceptualizations and subsequently examine the assessment of secondary gain in clinical practice.

CONCEPTUALIZATIONS OF SECONDARY GAIN

The following distillation summarizes the divergent models of secondary gain, along with relevant examples of each model's clinical application.

1. The *psychodynamic* model postulates a disabling somatoform or other disorder as precipitating secondary gain. Primary gain is the patient's protection from psychic trauma; secondary gain is motivated by a maintenance of this protection and the satisfaction of psychic needs derived from incapacitation.

- Motivation for secondary gain: gratification of previously unmet needs, dependency, masochism, protection against further traumatization, identity as a patient, and support for narcissistic structure.
- Focus of clinical attention: primarily on the individual's intrapsychic needs and defenses.

In explaining hypochondriacal reactions, Busse (1986) articulated the essence of secondary gain from a dynamic viewpoint. Incapacitation largely exempts an individual from social expectations and subsequent failures. Adoption of a sick role provides a socially acceptable escape from threatening circumstances and personal inadequacies. According to Cabbage and Thomas (1989), Freud was the first to articulate the strong and persistent identity issues in which the disability becomes consonant with a "disabled" self-image. Treatment probably will address the patient's dependency needs and enlist family support to minimize the enmeshment found with secondary gain.

2. The *behavioral* model assumes that illness behavior, like all behavior, responds to salient contingencies within the environment. Although secondary gain is conceptualized as a consequence of a genuine disorder, no primary gain is formulated.

- Motivation for secondary gain: avoidance of negative stimuli, psychosocial reinforcers of maladaptive behaviors, overfocus on illness behavior, and use of poor coping strategies.
- Focus of clinical attention: predominantly on health care professionals and significant others in order to modify current reinforcers to decrease maladaptive illness behavior.

From a behavioral perspective, Miller and Dworkin (1977) reported that even organic symptoms (e.g., tachycardia and certain visceral responses) may be "learned because they are instrumental in achieving some rewarding goal" (p. 1278). In such cases, the psychologist must interrupt this reinforcement and provide other, more acceptable reinforcers. In this regard, Dickes (1974) described the treatment of 16 inpatients with conversion disorders by removing all social reinforcers for illness and providing systematic reinforcement of symptom improvement. Initially, patients were isolated and placed on complete bed rest without any visitors or other forms of stimulation. With symptom improvement, privileges were introduced gradually. Reinforcement patterns often extend beyond family and friends; social and health care agencies frequently provide sustained financial incentives for maintaining the disabled role (Lamb & Rogawski, 1978). For example, Social Security programs may reinforce and shape recipients' self-perceptions as disabled and dysfunctional. In addition, the provision of benefits may diminish motivation for rehabilitation and eventual recovery.

3. The *forensic* model posits an explicit legal incentive for secondary gain. Unlike psychodynamic and behavioral models, the forensic model typically emphasizes the intentional selection of secondary-gain behaviors, sometimes in the absence of any genuine disorder.

- Motivation for secondary gain: deliberate acquisition of one or two highly desired objectives, such as avoidance of criminal prosecution or gaining unwarranted financial compensation.
- Focus of clinical attention: chiefly on the individual, often with confrontation of conscious and sustained efforts to manipulate the legal system.

Using a forensic paradigm, Weissman (1990) delineated the various influences on patients' self-reporting. Pending litigation with protracted hearings and implicit questions of the patients' credibility may increase frustration and influence their presentations. Psychologists must differentiate blatant efforts of malingering from secondary gain, which is typically characterized by an admixture of conscious and unconscious motives. Beyond the thoughtful writings of Weissman, however, the term *secondary gain* is also used in forensic contexts to refer to essentially manipulative acts that are deliberately accomplished for increased attention, special services, or some external incentive. Often pejorative, the term is utilized in forensic evaluations to describe attempted deception of psychologists and potentially criminal acts via perjury and fraud

RECENT CONCEPTUALIZATIONS OF SECONDARY GAIN

Radley and Green (1987) provide a thoughtful overview of persons' adjustment to chronic illness as one of four modalities: accommodation (modification of life goals to include the illness), secondary gain (withdrawal from usual social roles and pursuit of other rewarding goals), active denial (attempt to retain original goals and minimize impairment), and resignation (loss of social roles and being overwhelmed by illness). Beyond accommodation, each modality reflects a potential maladjustment that may complicate a patient's recovery. In preliminary data, males with high socioeconomic status (SES) evidenced more accommodation and secondary gain, whereas males with low SES had more active denial. Radley and Green offer

health care professionals a valuable paradigm for understanding secondary gain in the broader context of adjustment/maladjustment to chronic illness.

In the assessment of pain patients, Bayer (1985) found traditional explanations of secondary gain to be less than compelling. In most patients misrepresenting their pain and resulting disability, he found that the monetary gains and social reinforcers were insufficient by themselves to explain persistent secondary gain. Instead, he proposed cognitive dissonance as a more convincing and compelling explanation. According to cognitive dissonance theory, persons experiencing negative affect will focus on consonant information and disregard dissonant information. Regarding somatoform disorders, Bayer posited a two-part process. Initially, inducements to exaggerate illness behavior are rewarded promptly. Subsequently, patients will attend to and interpret ambiguous internal stimuli as disabling symptoms (e.g., pain and other physical complaints), consistent with the reinforced self-perceptions. In this model, the misrepresented or exaggerated symptoms evolve into truly experienced symptoms, based on ambiguous cues.

ASSESSMENT OF SECONDARY GAIN

1. *Be careful in using the term.* The greatest concern is that psychologists will apply the concept of secondary gain in a nonstringent and potentially pejorative manner. Without an articulated model, secondary gain can become shorthand for "uncooperative," "manipulative," "demanding," "treatment-resistant," or "fraudulent." Even with a clearly articulated position on the part of the evaluating psychologist, other health care professionals may be susceptible to the negative characterizations associated with secondary gain. Therefore, we caution psychologists to avoid using the term *secondary gain*, except in specialized clinical settings where a consensual meaning is established and treatment implications are clearly understood.

2. *Never employ backward reasoning.* Rogers (1997) argues strongly against the use of backward reasoning in attempting to establish response styles. Simply because potentially strong incentives (e.g., financial rewards or escape from intolerable circumstances) exist, we cannot assume willy-nilly that these incentives determined the patients' previous behavior and response style. As previously noted by Radley and Green (1987), some patients may deny and minimize impairment, despite obvious incentives to the contrary. Incalculable harm can be caused to patients by invoking this mislogic regarding secondary gain. The following example illustrates an unsubstantiated inference.

Established fact:
　The patient is receiving $4,000 per month in disability insurance and is freed from a high-pressure position.
Clinical observation:
　The patient continues to be preoccupied with his or her impairment.
Unwarranted inference:
　The patient is motivated by secondary gain to maintain his or her "sick role."

3. *Avoid clinical inferences based on the potential for secondary gain.* The facile equation of *potential* for secondary gain with the *determination* of secondary gain must be avoided. Even very large rewards do not preclude genuine impairment. Psychologists are left with the difficult challenge of determining the patient's motivation.

4. *Acknowledge the limitations of assessment methods.* Systematic methods for the assessment of secondary gain are not well validated. The following is a distillation of available methods.

- Radley and Green (1987) provide a 20-item structured interview on adjustment to illness, with 5 nonpejorative questions regarding secondary gain embedded in its format. Although not constituting a formal scale, this interview format is recommended as one systematic method of evaluating secondary gain.
- McIntosh, Melles, and Hall (1995) provide sample questions on barriers to reha-

bilitation. Unfortunately, the two specific questions regarding secondary gain equate the potential for secondary gain with its determination. The questions address only the magnitude and length of compensation. This approach is not recommended.

- Larson, Busby, Wilson, Medora, and Allgood (1994) examined the concept of secondary gain in vocational assessments on the Career Decision Diagnostic Assessment (CDDA; Bansberg & Sklare, 1986). They used secondary gain to refer to the conscious or unconscious motivation for delaying career decisions. Because of its atypical definition (i.e., motivation to delay career decisions) and vocational focus, the CDDA is inapplicable to most clinical settings.

5. *Address the following questions in clinical assessment.*

- Does the patient receive benefits or services as a result of his or her impairment? The answer is almost invariably "yes" in cases referred for psychological assessment. Some psychologists attempt to use the magnitude of the benefits and services as an indicator of secondary-gain potential. Inconsequential benefits and services are unlikely, by definition, to provide sufficient motivation for secondary gain. This observation, however, begs the question of what constitutes secondary gain for different patients: the sick role, avoidance of responsibility, self-punishment for moral turpitude, financial gain, or provision of a different environment.
- Does every patient have his or her price? An implicit and cynical assumption of some psychologists is that every person and every patient can be "bought." This assumption falters on two grounds. First, many patients in extreme circumstances (e.g., felony cases with overwhelming evidence against them) do not attempt to use mental disorders for secondary gain. Second, patients with genuine and catastrophic impairment are unlikely to have any incentive for secondary gain.

- Is the patient aware of his or her incentives for continued impairment? Most patients will be cognizant of any tangible benefits (e.g., disability insurance or avoidance of an unpleasant job) of their impaired status. Their awareness of social or personal benefits possibly accruing from their disabilities is less clear. Awareness and intentionality are not necessarily related; persons may be aware of certain maladaptive behaviors (e.g., somatic complaints during family arguments) without making conscious choices to engage in them. To complicate matters further, dynamic proponents may argue that the overt behaviors are conscious but the underlying motivation is not (see Rogers, Bagby, & Vincent, 1994).
- Is the problem of secondary gain with the patient or the patient's family? The focal point for this question is the psychologist's model of secondary gain. From a dynamic model, the emphasis is on the patient's dependency needs and defenses. From an adjustment perspective à la Radley and Green, the patient's adaptation to illness is emphasized in conjunction with social roles. From a behavioral perspective, familial and interpersonal elements of secondary gain, particularly social reinforcers, are accentuated.
- Is secondary gain a viable construct in this professional setting? At best, secondary gain is an ambiguous psychological construct that is invoked in different health care settings to address important but disparate clinical issues. At worst, secondary gain is a pernicious concept that sabotages a patient's status as a patient and impugns his or her integrity. In most clinical cases, more useful and less pejorative descriptions are readily available.

From an assessment perspective, secondary gain is fraught with difficulty. Psychologists must avoid any facile conjectures that equate the potential for secondary gain with its determination. Cynicism and countertransference issues often confound the accurate assessment of secondary gain. Our understanding of secondary gain is complicated by the important yet enigmatic constructs surrounding its assessment: intentionality, unconscious motives, and adoption of a "sick role." In specialized settings (e.g., psychodynamic treatment of somatoform disorders or behavioral treatment of chronic illness), secondary gain may have sufficient currency to warrant its continued use. Beyond these specialized settings, we advise psychologists to adopt simpler clinical descriptions without the conceptual baggage and negativity that surround secondary gain.

References & Readings

Bansberg, B., & Sklare, J. (1986). *The Career Decision Diagnostic Assessment*. Monterey, CA: CTB/McGraw-Hill.

Bayer, T. L. (1985). Weaving a tangled web: The psychology of deception and self-deception in psychogenic pain. *Social Sciences and Medicine, 20*, 517–527.

Busse, E. W. (1986). Treating hypochondriasis in the elderly. *Generations, 10*, 30–33.

Cabbage, M. F., & Thomas, K. R. (1989). Freud and disability. *Rehabilitation Psychology, 34*, 161–173.

Dickes, R. A. (1974). Brief therapy of conversion reactions: An in-hospital technique. *American Journal of Psychiatry, 131*, 584–586.

Fishbain, D. A., Rosomoff, H. L., Cutler, R. B., & Rosomoff, R. S. (1995). Secondary gain concept: A review of the scientific literature. *Clinical Journal of Pain, 11*, 6–21.

Lamb, H. R., & Rogawski, A. S. (1978). Supplemental security income and the sick role. *American Journal of Psychiatry, 135*, 1221–1224.

Larson, J. H., Busby, D. M., Wilson, S., Medora, N., & Allgood, S. (1994). The multidimensional assessment of career decision problems: The Career Decision Diagnostic Assessment. *Journal of Counseling and Development, 72*, 323–328.

McIntosh, G., Melles, T., & Hall, H. (1995). Guidelines for the identification of barriers to rehabilitation of back injuries. *Journal of Occupational Rehabilitation, 5*, 195–201.

Miller, N. E., & Dworkin, B. R. (1977). Effects of learning on visceral functions: Biofeedback. *New England Journal of Medicine, 296*, 1274–1278.

Radley, A., & Green, R. (1987). Illness as adjustment: A methodology and conceptual framework. *Sociology of Health and Illness, 9,* 179–207.

Rogers, R. (Ed.) (1997). *Clinical assessment of malingering and deception* (2nd ed.). New York: Guilford Press.

Rogers, R., Bagby, R. M., & Vincent, A. (1994). Factitious disorders with predominantly psychological signs and symptoms: A conundrum for forensic experts. *Journal of Psychiatry and Law, 22,* 99–106.

Weissman, H. N. (1990). Distortions and deceptions in self-presentation: Effects of protracted litigation in personal injury cases. *Behavioral Sciences and the Law, 8,* 67–74.

Related Topics

15   IDENTIFICATION AND ASSESSMENT OF ALCOHOL PROBLEMS

Linda C. Sobell & Mark B. Sobell

A well-formulated assessment is fundamental to successful treatment planning. The following discussion is intended to help clinicians better identify, assess, and treat individuals with alcohol problems. This brief overview is relevant not only for clinicians treating clients with primary alcohol problems but also for those treating clients with an alcohol use disorder who also have a primary or secondary psychiatric disorder.

1. *Setting clients at ease:* Because there is a social stigma related to having an alcohol problem, making the first call to a treatment program can be highly stressful. Similarly, arriving for the first appointment can provoke considerable anxiety. Individuals who are thinking of changing their drinking have probably made a decision to seek treatment only after careful consideration and with some degree of ambivalence. For these reasons, it is very important for therapists and interviewers working with individuals with alcohol problems to do what all

good clinicians do—set the client at ease by establishing rapport and being empathetic and supportive. Because clients are often asked to complete several assessment instruments, it is important to gain their cooperation by explaining the nature of each instrument, why it is being used, and what feedback, if any, they might expect from the instrument. Early discussion of how long treatment will take and what treatment will entail will also help establish a good therapeutic relationship that will gain the client's trust and cooperation. One way to help ensure that accurate information is gathered is to tell clients that what is discussed in treatment is confidential and to explain the conditions under which confidentiality would have to be broken.

2. *Choosing assessment instruments/measures:* When choosing an assessment instrument, clinicians should consider the following questions: (a) What purpose will it serve (e.g., screening, diagnosis, triage, treatment planning, goal setting, monitoring, evaluating treatment)? (b) Is it clinically useful (i.e., Will it help a clinician develop a better course of treatment?)? (c) Is it user-friendly for clients (e.g., easy to complete, relevant)? (d) How long does it take to administer and score, and over what time interval can information be collected (e.g., one month, one year)? (e) What costs are involved, if any?

3. *Value of an assessment:* Good assessments have several clinical benefits: (a) They can serve as the basis for treatment planning and goal setting (e.g., determining intensity of treatment; focusing on motivation or action; matching clients to treatments; identifying high-risk triggers for use); (b) they can help in formulating diagnoses; (c) the results can be used to give clients feedback or advice about their past drinking and related behaviors; such advice can enhance or strengthen motivation for change (Miller & Rollnick, 1991; Sobell et al., 1996); and (d) because assessments are dynamic and ongoing throughout treatment, they can determine whether treatment is working (e.g., self-monitoring of alcohol use during treatment) and, if not, what the next step should be to modify the course of treatment (i.e., stepped care; Sobell & Sobell, in press).

4. *Alcohol problem severity:* When evaluating a client's use of alcohol, it is important to assess problem severity because such information is relevant to goal setting and treatment planning (Sobell & Sobell, 1996). Problem severity can be viewed as lying on a continuum ranging from mild (e.g., problem drinkers) to severe (e.g., chronic alcohol abuse). Table 1 lists two measures (AUDIT, SADD) that can be used to evaluate problem severity.

5. *Alcohol abusers' self-reports are generally accurate:* Clinicians must rely on their clients' self-reports for a considerable amount of assessment and treatment planning information. Contrary to folklore, several studies have shown that alcohol abusers' self-reports are generally accurate if they are interviewed when (a) alcohol-free, (b) given assurances of confidentiality, and (c) in a clinical or research setting (Sobell, Toneatto, & Sobell, 1994). When individuals with alcohol problems have been drinking, however, their self-reports may

not be accurate. In this regard, a portable breath alcohol tester can be used to determine whether a person is under the influence of alcohol (Sobell et al., 1994), and if so, the assessment should be rescheduled.

6. *Key measures in assessing alcohol use and abuse:* There is no shortage of instruments, scales, and questionnaires for assessing individuals with alcohol problems (for a review and sample copies of instruments, see Allen & Columbus, 1995). For a clinician the key question is "What will I learn from the instrument/measure that I will not otherwise know from a routine clinical interview?" To assist clinicians in assessing a person's alcohol use and related problems, a listing of one or two key measures in each of several areas and a brief description of the measures are presented in Table 1. These instruments were selected according to the following criteria: (a) is user-friendly, (b) requires minimal time and resources, (c) is psychometrically sound, and (d) if possible, provides meaningful feedback to clients.

7. *Interviewing style:* Interviewing style is very important to obtaining accurate information about an individual's alcohol use (Miller & Rollnick, 1991; Sobell et al., 1994). The way questions are asked can also affect a client's answers. The following are important considerations when conducting assessments with individuals who might have alcohol problems.

- *Empathy:* Empathy helps clinicians gain the acceptance and trust of clients and is associated with decreased client resistance and improved outcomes. A key way of expressing empathy is *reflective listening*, in which the therapist forms a reasonable guess about what the client has said and shares it with the client. Reflective listening is intended to minimize resistance.
- *Periodic summary:* Frequent summarizing throughout the interview allows a therapist to synthesize the information gathered and solicit a client's feedback about the accuracy of the therapist's understanding.
- *Flexibility:* When a clinician senses that a client finds the interview threatening, is

TABLE 1. Key Measures for Assessing Alcohol Use and Related Problems

Area	Measure and Brief Description
Adverse consequences of use/problem severity	*Alcohol Use Disorders Identification Test (AUDIT):* This is a 10-item, self-administered questionnaire addressing past and recent alcohol consumption and alcohol-related problems; it identifies high-risk drinkers, as well as those experiencing consequences.[a, b]
	Short Alcohol Dependence Data (SADD): This is a 15-item, self-administered questionnaire assessing psychosocial consequences and dependence symptoms related to recent alcohol use; problem severity scores can aid in making decisions about drinking goals and treatment intensity.[a, b]
Alcohol use	*Timeline Followback (TLFB; for alcohol use before treatment):* Using memory aids, individuals are asked to recall their estimated daily drinking for intervals ranging from 7 to 360 days; the TLFB can be used in treatment as an advice-feedback tool to analyze clients' drinking and to increase their motivation to change.[a, b]
	Self-monitoring (for alcohol use during treatment): This measure requires clients to record aspects of their alcohol use or urges (e.g., amount, frequency, mood, consequences); it has several clinical advantages including identifying situations that pose a high risk of excessive drinking and providing feedback about changes in drinking.[a, b]
Drug use other than alcohol	*Drug Use History Questionnaire (DUHQ):* This captures lifetime and recent information (e.g., years used, route of administration, year last used, frequency of use) about the use of different drugs.[b, c]
	Drug Abuse Screening Test (DAST-10): This is a 10-item, self-administered measure of drug use consequences in the past 12 months; it assesses the severity of drug problems.[b, d]
Tobacco use	*Time to the First Cigarette:* A single question—"How many minutes upon waking until the first cigarette is smoked?"—is strongly predictive of nicotine dependence.[b]
Cognitive functioning	*Trails A and B:* This is a brief, sensitive, and nonspecific screening test for assessing probable signs of organic brain dysfunction that may be related to severe alcohol problems.[b, e]
	Mini Mental Status Exam: This is a standardized 8-item questionnaire for assessing current cognitive functioning.[e]
High-risk triggers for use	*Situational Confidence Questionnaire (SCQ):* This assesses situational self-efficacy, that is, how confident clients are at the present time that they will be able to resist the urge to drink heavily in 39 situations (fee for use); because relapse rates are extremely high, assessment of high-risk situations for alcohol use is important.[a, b]
	Brief SCQ-8: This is a variant of the SCQ that asks about 8 major categories of relapse (assesses alcohol or drug use situations; no fee; easy to score).[f]
Motivation/readiness to change	*Decisional Balance Exercise:* This is a brief exercise that asks clients to evaluate their perceptions of the costs and benefits of continuing to drink problematically versus changing; it is intended to make more salient the costs and benefits of changing and to identify obstacles to change.[f]
	Readiness to Change Questionnaire (RTCQ): This is a 12-item questionnaire that can be used to identify readiness to change; the scale has only recently been extended to clients in treatment.[f]
Psychiatric comorbidity	*Depression Anxiety Stress Scales (DASS):* These are 3 self-report scales (14 items each) designed to measure the negative emotional states of depression, anxiety, and stress; items are rated on 4-point scales indicating the extent to which they were experienced in the past week.[g]
	Symptom Checklist 90-R (SCL-90-R): This is a 90-item self-report questionnaire that reflects psychiatric symptoms that occurred in the past week; items are rated on 5-point scales of discomfort; the SCL-90-R takes about 15 minutes to complete and has been widely used as an outcome measure in psychotherapy; 3 global scores of distress can be derived, as well as scores for 9 primary symptom dimensions (e.g., somatization, depression, anxiety, anger, paranoid ideation, psychoticism); this instrument reflects patterns of psychological distress currently being experienced by clients.[h]

Note: Information and reviews about and/or copies of the measures/instruments can be found in the footnoted publication after each measure.

[a]Allen & Columbus, 1995. [d]Skinner, 1982. [g]Lovibond & Lovibond, 1995.
[b]Sobell, Sobell, & Toneatto, 1994. [e]Lesak, 1995. [h]Seidner & Kilpatrick, 1988.
[c]Sobell, Kwan, & Sobell, 1995. [f]Sobell et al., 1996.

ambivalent, or is reluctant to discuss issues, it is important to "roll with resistance" by using reflective listening rather than confronting the resistance directly. It is also important to emphasize to clients that it is their choice whether a matter will be discussed.

• *Confrontation:* Confrontation and arguments should be avoided whenever possible because confrontational strategies can be counterproductive. Miller, Benefield, & Tonigan (1993), for example, found that alcohol abusers randomly assigned to confrontational counseling had higher levels of resistance, drank more during treatment, and had poorer outcomes than clients assigned to motivational counseling.

• *Labeling:* Clients are generally reluctant to be labeled as "alcoholic." This especially applies to individuals whose problems are not severe. Labeling should be avoided because it has no clinical advantages and because it has been associated with alcohol abusers' delaying or avoiding entry into treatment (Sobell, Sobell, & Toneatto, 1992). Asking about an individual's alcohol use in the past year and any concerns he or she may have is more likely to get a client to engage in an open dialogue about drinking than asking, "How many years have you had an alcohol problem?" or "How long have you been an alcoholic?"

• *Terminology:* Explaining the meaning of key terms to clients is an important part of the interviewing process. Clinicians need to know how to properly ask questions in relation to the following terms: blackouts, delirium tremens (DTs), morning drinking, and cirrhosis. All these terms reflect the severity of the disorder, but their meaning can be easily misunderstood (reviewed in Sobell et al., 1994). For example, DTs, which must include actual delirium, are often confused with minor withdrawal symptoms (e.g., psychomotor agitation). Similarly, the term *morning drinking*, which refers to drinking upon waking to avoid withdrawal symptoms, is different than drinking before noon while on a fishing trip. Morning drinking and DTs are significant be-

cause they are associated with severe dependence on alcohol.

8. *Measures complementary to self-reports:* There has been a tendency to view biochemical measures such as liver function and urinalysis and collateral (e.g., friends or family) reports as superior to a client's report of his or her drinking. However, several major comparative evaluations have revealed problems with biochemical measures and collateral reports (reviewed in Maisto & Connors, 1992; Sobell et al., 1994). Consequently, at the present time, biological markers and collateral reports should be seen as complementing rather than replacing self-reports of alcohol use.

9. *Psychiatric comorbidity:* Psychiatric comorbidity among alcohol abusers has been well documented (Ross, Glaser, & Germanson, 1988). Because of the high prevalence of psychiatric comorbidity among alcohol abusers (rates range from 7% to 75%), diagnostic formulations involve a two-step process: document the extent and nature of the alcohol problem and establish whether other psychiatric disorders are present; if so, determine whether the alcohol use disorder is primary or secondary. Because of the lack of empirical guidelines about how to treat alcohol abusers who have other clinical disorders (Smyth, 1996), decisions about treating alcohol and psychiatric problems simultaneously or sequentially need to be made on a case-by-case basis.

10. *Comorbidity of other drug problems, including nicotine:* For alcohol abusers who use or abuse other drugs, including nicotine, it is important to gather a profile of their psychoactive substance use (e.g., see DUHQ in Table 1). Also, drug use patterns may change over the course of treatment (e.g., decreased alcohol use, increased smoking; decreased alcohol use, increased cannabis use). Three issues are important when assessing alcohol abusers who use other drugs: (a) pharmacological synergism (i.e., a multiplicative effect of similarly acting drugs taken concurrently); (b) cross-tolerance (i.e., decreased effect of a drug due to previous or current heavy use of pharmacologically similar drugs); and (c) cigarette use (80–90% of alcohol abusers report having at some time smoked cigarettes; Sobell, Sobell, & Kozlowski, 1995). Finally, because it appears that continued smoking may serve as a trigger for relapse for alcohol abusers attempting to change their drinking (Sobell, Sobell, & Kozlowski, 1995), the smoking behavior of alcohol abusers should be a part of the assessment and treatment planning process.

11. *Motivation for change:* An important assessment issue is the need to evaluate a client's motivation for and commitment to change. Motivation can be conceptualized as a state of readiness to change that may fluctuate over time and can be influenced by several variables, including the therapist's behavior and treatment procedures. For a thorough description of motivational interviewing, see Miller and Rollnick (1991). Table 1 lists a measure (RTCQ) that can be used to assess readiness for change and an exercise (Decisional Balance) that can be used to enhance or strengthen motivation for change. The most important issue regarding motivation is that treatment of clients who are assessed as weakly committed to changing their drinking should initially focus on increasing their motivation rather than on methods for achieving change. Use of a motivational interviewing style can be helpful for increasing clients' motivation.

12. *Base conclusions on a convergence of information:* While alcohol abusers' self-reports are generally accurate if gathered under the conditions noted earlier, a small proportion of reports will be inaccurate. To deal with this potential problem, it is advisable to obtain information from several sources when possible (e.g., psychological tests, family, friends, probation officers, medical records, biochemical tests). Clinicians who base their conclusions on a convergence of information can have increased confidence in their assessments (Sobell et al., 1994).

A careful and continuing assessment is an important part of the treatment process for individuals with alcohol problems. Accurate evaluation of alcohol problems and other concurrent disorders is integral to the assessment process, and a good assessment is critical to the development of meaningful treatment plans. Assessment instruments and procedures should be user-friendly and relevant to treatment planning. Various interviewing strategies can be used to enhance the accuracy of information obtained from clients and to increase clients' motivation for change.

References & Readings

Allen, J. P., & Columbus, M. (1995). *Assessing alcohol problems: A guide for clinicians and researchers.* Rockville, MD: National Institute on Alcohol Abuse and Alcoholism.

Annis, H. M., & Davis, C. S. (1988). Assessment of expectancies. In D. M. Donovan & G. A. Marlatt (Eds.), *Assessment of addictive behaviors* (pp. 84–111). New York: Guilford Press.

Derogatis, L. R. (1983). *SCL-90 revised version manual-1.* Baltimore: Johns Hopkins University School of Medicine.

Lesak, M. D. (1995). *Neuropsychological assessment* (3rd ed.). New York: Oxford University Press.

Lovibond, P. F., & Lovibond, S. H. (1995). The structure of negative emotional states: Comparison of the Depression Anxiety Stress Scales (DASS) with the Beck Depression and Anxiety Inventories. *Behaviour Research and Therapy, 33,* 335–343.

Maisto, S. A., & Connors, G. J. (1992). Using subject and collateral reports to measure alcohol consumption. In R. Z. Litten & J. Allen (Eds.), *Measuring alcohol consumption: Psychosocial and biological methods* (pp. 73–96). Totowa, NJ: Humana Press.

Miller, W. R., Benefield, R. G., & Tonigan, J. S. (1993). Enhancing motivation for change in problem drinking: A controlled comparison of two therapist styles. *Journal of Consulting and Clinical Psychology, 61,* 455–461.

Miller, W. R., & Rollnick, S. (1991). *Motivational interviewing: Preparing people to change addictive behavior.* New York: Guilford Press.

Ross, H. E., Glaser, F. B., & Germanson, T. (1988). The prevalence of psychiatric disorders in patients with alcohol and other drug problems. *Archives of General Psychiatry, 45,* 1023–1031.

Seidner, A. L., & Kilpatrick, D. G. (1988). Derpgatis symptom checklist 90-R. In M. Hersen & A. S. Bellack (Eds.), *Dictionary of behavioral assessment techniques* (pp. 174–175). Elmsford, N.Y.: Pergamon.

Skinner, H. A. (1982). The drug abuse screening test. *Addictive Behaviors, 7,* 363–371.

Smyth, N. J. (1996). Motivating persons with dual disorders: A stage approach. *Families in Society: The Journal of Contemporary Human Services, 77,* 605–614.

Sobell, L. C., Cunningham, J. C., Sobell, M. B., Agrawal, S., Gavin, D. R., Leo, G. I., & Singh,

K. N. (1996). Fostering self-change among problem drinkers: A proactive community intervention. *Addictive Behaviors, 21,* 817–833.

Sobell, L. C., Kwan, E., & Sobell, M. B. (1995). Reliability of a Drug History Questionnaire (DHQ). *Addictive Behaviors, 20,* 233–241.

Sobell, L. C., Sobell, M. B., & Toneatto, T. (1992). Recovery from alcohol problems without treatment. In N. Heather, W. R. Miller, & J. Greeley (Eds.), *Self-control and the addictive behaviours* (pp. 198–242). New York: Maxwell Macmillan.

Sobell, L. C., Toneatto, T., & Sobell, M. B. (1994). Behavioral assessment and treatment planning for alcohol, tobacco, and other drug problems: Current status with an emphasis on clinical applications. *Behavior Therapy, 25,* 533–580.

Sobell, M. B., & Sobell, L. C. (1996). *Problem drinkers: Guided self-change treatment.* New York: Guilford Press.

Sobell, M. B., & Sobell, L. C. (in press). Stepped care for alcohol problems: An efficient method for planning and delivering clinical services. In J. A. Tucker, D. A. Donovan, & G. A. Marlatt (Eds.), *Changing addictive behavior.* New York: Guilford Press.

Sobell, M. B., Sobell, L. C., & Kozlowski, L. T. (1995). Dual recoveries from alcohol and smoking problems. In J. B. Fertig & J. A. Allen (Eds.), *Alcohol and tobacco: From basic science to clinical practice* (NIAAA Research Monograph No. 30) (pp. 207–224). Rockville, MD: National Institute on Alcohol Abuse and Alcoholism.

Related Topics

16 POSTTRAUMATIC STRESS DISORDER IN ADULTS

William F. Flack, Jr. & Terence M. Keane

WHAT IS POSTTRAUMATIC STRESS DISORDER?

Posttraumatic stress disorder (PTSD) is a complex biopsychosocial disorder caused by exposure to one or more traumatic events, accompanied by an extreme fear reaction, and characterized by a subsequent, heterogeneous set of dysfunctional behaviors, thoughts, and feelings. The standard criteria for diagnosing PTSD, as contained in the *DSM-IV* (American Psychiatric Association, 1994), are as follows:

- *Criterion A:* The person has been exposed to a traumatic event in which both of the following were present: (a) The person experienced, witnessed, or was confronted with an event or events that involved actual or threatened death or serious injury or a threat to the physical integrity of self or others; (b) the person's response involved intense fear, helplessness, or horror (in children, this may be expressed instead by disorganized or agitated behavior).

- *Criterion B:* The traumatic event is persistently *reexperienced* in one (or more) of the following ways: (a) recurrent and intrusive distressing recollections of the event, including images, thoughts, or perceptions (in young children, repetitive play may occur in which themes or aspects of the trauma are expressed); (b) recurrent distressing dreams of the event (in children, there may be frightening dreams without recognizable content); (c) acting or feeling as if the traumatic event were recurring (includes a sense of reliving the experience, illusions, hallucinations, and dissociative flashback episodes, including those that occur on awakening or when intoxicated; in young children, trauma-specific reenactment may occur); (d) intense psychological distress at exposure to internal or external cues that symbolize or resemble an aspect of the traumatic event; (e) physiological reactivity on exposure to internal or external cues that symbolize or resemble an aspect of the traumatic event.

- *Criterion C:* Persistent *avoidance* of stimuli associated with the trauma and *numbing* of general responsiveness (not present before the trauma), as indicated by three (or more) of the following: (a) efforts to avoid thoughts, feelings, or conversations associated with the trauma; (b) efforts to avoid activities, places, or people that arouse recollections of the trauma; (c) inability to recall an important aspect of the trauma; (d) markedly diminished interest or participation in significant activities; (e) feeling of detachment or estrangement from others; (f) restricted range of affect (e.g., unable to have loving feelings); (g) sense of a foreshortened future (e.g., does not expect to have a career, marriage, children, or a normal life span).
- *Criterion D:* Persistent symptoms of increased *arousal* (not present before the trauma), as indicated by two (or more) of the following: (a) difficulty falling or staying asleep; (b) irritability or outbursts of anger; (c) difficulty concentrating; (d) hypervigilance; (e) exaggerated startle response.
- *Criterion E:* Duration of the disturbance (symptoms in Criteria B, C, and D) is more than 1 month.
- *Criterion F:* The disturbance causes clinically significant distress or impairment in social, occupational, or other important areas of functioning.

In addition, the disorder is considered to be "acute" if the duration of symptoms is less than 3 months, "chronic" if 3 months or more, and "with delayed onset" if the symptoms begin at least 6 months after the traumatic event.

PTSD is commonly accompanied by other psychological disturbances, most often depression, alcohol use and abuse, drug use and abuse, panic and other anxiety disorders, and changes in personality. Additional features often associated with PTSD include suicidal behavior, interpersonal dysfunction, deficits in coping skills, and somatic complaints.

PREVALENCE, RISK, COURSE, AND OUTCOME

Although the results of epidemiological studies (e.g., Kessler, Sonnega, Bromet, Hughes, & Nelson, 1995) indicate that PTSD is not rare, not everyone who is exposed to traumatic events develops the disorder. Prevalence rates of PTSD in the general population are estimated to be 5–10% (see Litz & Roemer, 1996), making this disorder relatively common as compared with other psychiatric conditions. The prevalence rate rises in groups of individuals who have been exposed to extremely stressful events, such as combat, natural disasters, and sexual assault (e.g., Resnick, Kilpatrick, Best, & Kramer, 1992).

A constellation of diverse factors puts individuals at greater than normal risk for developing PTSD. In general, it appears that more frequent, severe, and chronic traumatic events are associated with more chronic disorder. Additional potential risk factors include poor premorbid coping capacity, existing psychological conditions, prior trauma history, and unsupportive and unstable living environment and interpersonal interactions. The course and outcome of PTSD seem to be highly variable, ranging from immediate onset and chronic duration to delays in onset of months or years and phasic waxing and waning of symptoms.

ASSESSMENT

A number of clinical instruments are available for the assessment of PTSD (see Wilson & Keane, 1997). Scales for PTSD have been developed from standard paper-and-pencil measures such as the Minnesota Multiphasic Personality Inventory-2 and the Symptom Checklist-90.

Other self-report instruments have been constructed specifically for assessing PTSD, including the Mississippi Scale for Combat-Related PTSD, the PTSD Checklist, the PTSD Diagnostic Scale, the Impact of Event Scale-Revised, and the PTSD Symptom Scale–Self Report.

Although self-report instruments are often useful for the purpose of rapid, low-cost clinical screening, accuracy of diagnosis (both of PTSD and of frequently associated conditions) is increased by the use of multiple, converging methods. Structured clinical interviews provide another source of diagnostic information. The Structured Clinical Interview for the *DSM-IV* can be used to assess the full range of Axis I disorders. The Clinician-Administered PTSD Scale for the *DSM-IV* is a structured interview designed specifically for the assessment of PTSD.

The comprehensive clinical assessment of PTSD should include an evaluation of trauma across the life span. Instruments that are useful for this purpose are the Potential Stressful Events Interview and the Traumatic Stress Schedule. Ethnocultural considerations are also important in the assessment of PTSD, given the likelihood that members of different groups may understand and respond to traumatic events in significantly different ways (Marsella, Friedman, Gerrity, & Scurfield, 1996). Finally, psychophysiological assessment is sometimes useful for complex cases in which a differential diagnosis requires further data for clarification.

TREATMENT

Psychotherapeutic options for treating PTSD include psychodynamic approaches (e.g., Herman, 1992) and cognitive-behavioral ones (e.g., Foa, Olasov-Rothbaum, Riggs, & Murdock, 1991; Keane, 1995; Resick & Schnicke, 1992), as well as psychopharmacological interventions (Friedman, 1989). Talk-based therapies can be conducted in individual or group contexts or both. Group treatments for PTSD are becoming increasingly popular, driven in part by the current economics of health care, although controlled outcome data supporting the efficacy of group treatments are lacking. At present, the weight of the evidence argues in favor of exposure-based treatments, although more systematic, head-to-head comparisons of the efficacy of different therapeutic techniques and modalities need to be conducted.

One comprehensive approach in which exposure-based treatment is an option is the cognitive-behavioral therapy program developed by Keane (1995). In this approach, targets of intervention are determined by the current phase of disorder and, thus, by the most pressing clinical concerns. Typically, patients are guided through a series of interventions, starting with emotional and behavioral stabilization and proceeding with psychoeducation (about trauma, PTSD, and the impact of PTSD on significant others), stress management, focus on the trauma (the phase in which exposure-based interventions are used), relapse prevention, and follow-up aftercare.

Cognitive processing therapy (Resick & Schnicke, 1992) has been developed to treat the victims of sexual assault. It is characterized by a combination of psychoeducation, exposure therapy, and cognitive restructuring. The latter component includes specific emphases on beliefs about safety, trust, power, esteem, and intimacy. Eye movement desensitization and reprocessing (Shapiro, 1995) is another recent approach to the treatment of PTSD, in which the element of therapeutic exposure appears to be central.

Psychopharmacological interventions are frequently employed in treating PTSD. Recent studies of the selective serotonin reuptake inhibitors (SSRIs) provide promise for ameliorating some symptoms of the disorder. Other studies utilizing different medications have not found much systematic success. Friedman (1989) has urged clinicians to use psychopharmacological methods judiciously, providing medications that directly treat those symptoms, whether affective- or anxiety-based, that are prominent in the case at hand.

References & Readings

American Psychiatric Association (1994). *Diagnostic and statistical manual of mental disorders* (4th ed.). Washington, DC: American Psychiatric Association.

Davidson, J. R. T., & Foa, E. B. (Eds.) (1993). *Post-traumatic stress disorder: DSM-IV and beyond*. Washington, DC: American Psychiatric Press.

Foa, E. B., Olasov-Rothbaum, B., Riggs, D. S., & Murdock, T. B. (1991). Treatment of post-traumatic stress disorder in rape victims: A comparison between cognitive-behavioral procedures and counseling. *Journal of Consulting and Clinical Psychology, 59*, 715–723.

Friedman, M. J. (1989). Toward a rational pharmacotherapy for posttraumatic stress disorder: An interim report. *American Journal of Psychiatry, 145*, 281–285.

Herman, J. L. (1992). *Trauma and recovery*. New York: Basic Books.

Keane, T. M. (1995). The role of exposure therapy in the psychological treatment of PTSD. *National Center for PTSD (NCP) Clinical Quarterly, 5*, 1–6.

Kessler, R. C., Sonnega, A., Bromet, E., Hughes, M., & Nelson, C. B. (1995). Posttraumatic stress disorder in the National Comorbidity Survey. *Archives of General Psychiatry, 52*, 1048–1060.

Litz, B. T., & Roemer, L. (1996). Post-traumatic stress disorder: An overview. *Clinical Psychology and Psychotherapy, 3*, 153–168.

Marsella, A. J., Friedman, M. J., Gerrity, E. T., & Scurfield, R. M. (Eds.) (1996). *Ethnocultural aspects of posttraumatic stress disorder: Is-sues, research, and clinical applications*. Washington, DC: American Psychological Association.

Resick, P. A., & Schnicke, M. K. (1992). Cognitive processing therapy for sexual assault victims. *Journal of Consulting and Clinical Psychology, 60*, 748–756.

Resnick, H. S., Kilpatrick, D. G., Best, C. L., & Kramer, T. L. (1992). Vulnerability-stress factors in development of posttraumatic stress disorder. *Journal of Nervous and Mental Disease, 180*, 424–430.

Shapiro, F. (1995). *Eye movement desensitization and reprocessing*. New York: Guilford Press.

Van der Kolk, B. A., McFarlane, A. C., & Weisaeth, L. (Eds.) (1996). *Traumatic stress: The effects of overwhelming experience on mind, body, and society*. New York: Guilford Press.

Wilson, J. P., & Keane, T. M. (Eds.) (1997). *Assessing psychological trauma and PTSD*. New York: Guilford Press.

Wilson, J. P., & Raphael, B. (Eds.) (1993). *International handbook of traumatic stress syndromes*. New York: Plenum Press.

Related Topics

17   MEASURES OF ACCULTURATION

Juan Carlos Gonzalez

The importance of cultural awareness and respect in the provision of psychological services to individuals from other countries or subcultures has been clearly outlined in the *APA Guidelines for Providers of Psychological Services to Ethnic, Linguistic, and Culturally Diverse Populations* (American Psychological Association, 1990). Acculturation is highlighted in these guidelines as one of the factors that all psychologists should be familiar with when working with individuals from nonmajority groups. The ability to differentiate between psychopathology and the effects of acculturative stress is essential for psychologists who assess and treat individuals from different cultures.

DEFINITION

Acculturation is the stressful and complex process that individuals undergo in adjusting to a new culture. A useful structure of four distinct acculturation styles is commonly used to help categorize and understand an individual's response to this difficult adaptational process (Berry, 1984):

- *Assimilation:* Embracing the characteristics of the majority culture while rejecting the characteristics of the culture of origin.
- *Integration:* Embracing the majority culture while maintaining a strong culture-of-origin identity.
- *Rejection:* Maintaining own culture while rejecting both assimilation and integration.
- *Deculturation:* Eventual rejection of both the majority culture and the culture of origin.

NEGATIVE EFFECTS OF ACCULTURATIVE STRESS

The process of acculturation has been hypothesized to lead to a deterioration in physical, social, and emotional well-being (Berry, Kim, Minde, & Mok, 1987). Elevations in anxiety, depression, identity confusion, and somatic complaints have been associated with elevated levels of acculturative stress (Williams & Berry, 1991). Psychologists assess the individual's acculturation experience in order to ascertain how this stressful process may contribute to the presenting symptomatology. In general, individuals who are able to find a balance between the majority culture and their own tend to exhibit fewer negative consequences (Berry et al., 1987; Pawliuk et al., 1996; Szapocznik, Kurtines, & Fernandez, 1980). However, multiple variables (i.e., race, education, language proficiency, reason for immigration, premorbid adjustment) often serve to ameliorate or exacerbate the effects of acculturation.

BRIEF LINGUISTIC MEASURES OF ACCULTURATION

Psychologists practicing in clinical settings may find brief linguistic measures of acculturation particularly useful for determining an individual's general level of acculturation. The proponents of these circumscribed measures have argued persuasively that language usage and proficiency may serve as accurate estimates of overall acculturation (Epstein, Botvin, Dusenbury, Diaz, & Kerner, 1996; Marin & Marin, 1991; Marin, Sabogal, Marin, Otero-Sabogal, & Perez-Stable, 1987). Although research regarding these brief strategies has focused primarily on Hispanic adolescents, it is likely that the general findings may apply to other groups. In general, individuals from non-English-speaking groups who report using their native language in all or most interpersonal settings are less likely to be significantly assimilated or integrated into the majority culture. The following multiple-choice questions may be useful in helping to determine linguistic acculturation (suggested answer choices adapted from Epstein et al., 1996, are only English, mostly English, English and my native language, mostly my native language, only my native language):

- What language do you usually use with your (parents, children, spouse, friends)?
- In what language do you (think, dream, describe emotional experiences)?
- In what language do you (listen to the radio, watch TV, read)?

SELF-REPORT OF ACCULTURATION AND ACCULTURATIVE STRESS

Another useful strategy in clinical settings is to simply ask about the individual's perception of his or her own degree of acculturation and the stressors associated with this adaptational process. Allow the individual to educate you about his or her culture of origin, as well as goals, wishes, and fears concerning the new environment.

- What has the process of adapting to a new environment (i.e., language, diet, culture, rules, expectations) been like for the individual?
- What is the individual's perception of the benefits and risks of embracing the majority culture?
- How does the individual define his or her own cultural, linguistic, and/or ethnic identity in relation to the majority culture?

STANDARDIZED MEASURES OF ACCULTURATION

Most measures of acculturation have been designed by researchers studying the acculturation process. The following encompasses a small sampling of the measures available for assessing acculturation in various nonmajority groups. These measures are available directly from the authors.

- The *Acculturation Rating Scale for Mexican Americans-II* (ARSMA-II) (Cuellar, Arnold, & Maldonado, 1995) is a behavioral measure designed to yield five levels of acculturation (from a very Mexican orientation to very assimilated or Anglicized). It also has two subscales that measure the individual's orientation toward Anglo culture and toward Mexican culture.
- The *Bicultural Involvement Scale* (Szapocznik, Kurtines, & Fernandez, 1980) is designed to assess general cultural involvement (i.e., comfort with majority language, preference for recreational activities). This scale was originally used with Cuban-Americans, but it may easily be adapted for use with other groups (Pawliuk et al., 1996).
- The *Brief Acculturation Scale for Hispanics* (Norris, Ford, & Bova, 1996) is a four-item linguistic measure of acculturation for Hispanics.
- The *Minority-Majority Relations Survey* (Sodowsky, Lai, & Plake, 1991) is a 38-item questionnaire designed to assess the attitudes of Hispanics and Asians along three subscales: perceived prejudice, language usage, and acculturation.
- The *Suinn-Lew Asian Self-Identity Accul-*

turation Scale (Suinn, Ahuna, & Khoo, 1992) is a 21-item questionnaire that focuses on attitudes, identity, language, friendships, behaviors, and geographic background. It is used to rate individuals along an acculturation continuum (low acculturation to high acculturation) and in terms of being "Asian-identified" or "Western-identified."

ADDITIONAL RESOURCES

Comprehensive information regarding the process of acculturation for various nonmajority groups can be found in the *Gale Encyclopedia of Multicultural America* (Vecoli & Galens, 1995). Additional measures of acculturation may be found by using the frequently updated ERIC/AE Test Locator service on the Internet (http://ericae2.educ.cua.edu/testcol.htm), as well as by consulting the psychological research literature.

References & Readings

American Psychological Association (1990). *APA guidelines for providers of psychological services to ethnic, linguistic, and culturally diverse populations.* Washington, DC: American Psychological Association. Also found at http://www.apa.org/pi/guide.html.

Berry, J. W. (1984). Multicultural policy in Canada: A sociopsychological analysis. *Canadian Journal of Behavioral Sciences, 16*(4), 353–370.

Berry, J. W., Kim, U., Minde, T., & Mok, M. (1987). Comparative studies of acculturative stress. *International Migration Review, 21*, 19, 491–511.

Cuellar, I., Arnold, B., & Maldonado, R. (1995). Acculturation Rating Scale for Mexican Americans-II: A revision of the original ARSMA scale. *Hispanic Journal of Behavioral Sciences, 17*, 275–304.

Epstein, J. A., Botvin, G. J., Dusenbury, L., Diaz, T., & Kerner, J. (1996). Validation of an acculturation measure for Hispanic adolescents. *Psychological Reports, 76*, 1075–1079.

Marin, G., & Marin, B. V. (1991). *Research with Hispanic populations* (Applied Social Research Methods Series, Vol. 23). Newbury Park, CA: Sage.

Marin, G., Sabogal, R., Marin, B. V., Otero-Sabogal,

R., & Perez-Stable, E. J. (1987). Development of a short acculturation scale for Hispanics. *Hispanic Journal of Behavioral Sciences, 9,* 183–205.

Norris, A. E., Ford, K., & Bova, C. A. (1996). Psychometrics of a brief acculturation scale for Hispanics in a probability sample of urban Hispanic adolescents and young adults. *Hispanic Journal of Behavioral Sciences, 18,* 29–38.

Pawliuk, N., Grizenko, N., Chan-Yip, A., Gantous, P., Mathew, J., & Nguyen, D. (1996). Acculturation style and psychological functioning in children of immigrants. *American Journal of Orthopsychiatry, 66,* 111–121.

Sodowsky, G. R., Lai, E. W., & Plake, B. S. (1991). Moderating effects of sociocultural variables on acculturation attitudes of Hispanics and Asian Americans. *Journal of Counseling and Development, 70,* 194–204.

Suinn, R., Ahuna, C., & Khoo, G. (1992). The Suinn-Lew Asian Self-Identity Acculturation Scale: Concurrent and factorial validation. *Educational and Psychological Measurement, 52,* 1041–1046.

Szapocznik, J., Kurtines, W. M., & Fernandez, T. (1980). Bicultural involvement and adjustment in Hispanic-American youths. *International Journal of Intercultural Relations, 4,* 353–365.

Vecoli, R. J., & Galens, J. (Eds.) (1995). *Gale Encyclopedia of Multicultural America* (2 vols.). Detroit: St. James Press.

Williams, C. L., & Berry, J. W. (1991). Primary prevention of acculturative stress among refugees: Application of psychological theory and practice. *American Psychologist, 46,* 632–641.

Related Topics

Chapter 23, "Clinical Assessment of Ethnic Minority Children Using the *DSM-IV*"

18   INTERVIEWING PARENTS

Carolyn S. Schroeder & Betty N. Gordon

Parents are usually the primary referral source when a child is brought to the attention of a mental health professional. They have a unique knowledge and understanding of the child and thus are an integral part of the assessment and treatment process. During the initial interview with the parent(s), the information-gathering process begins, essential preliminary clinical decisions are made, and the parents become engaged in a collaborative working relationship with the therapist. A successful parent interview will ultimately determine treatment goals and their priority and will ensure that parents will cooperate in carrying out these goals.

Parent interviews can be structured or unstructured. Both methods have advantages and disadvantages. Structured interviews involve a prearranged set of questions to be asked in sequential order that usually focus on gathering information about a specific problem behavior. Although providing a more standardized format, structured interviews generally give more global information about the existence of a disorder rather than specific details about a particular child, family, or peer group that are needed for planning an intervention program. An unstructured interview, on the other hand, allows the clinician more freedom to explore the nature and context of a particular problem, as well as the opportunity to investigate potential contributing factors, such as stimuli that may elicit the problem behaviors. Moreover, this type of interview allows the clinician to begin to delineate acceptable behavioral alternatives, as well as other potential problem areas for the child or family. Unstructured interviews, however, assume that the interviewer has the necessary knowledge about the nature of the specific presenting problem to guide the content and process of the interview (Mash & Terdal, 1988).

Given the limited psychometric support for structured interviews and the uniqueness of each child, family, and environment, we think the unstructured interview has more advantages than disadvantages over the structured interview format. Thus, this discussion will focus on unstructured parent interviews. The reader is referred to Edelbrock and Costello (1988) for a review of available structured parent interviews.

One format for gathering and organizing information using an unstructured interview is called the Comprehensive Assessment-to-Intervention System (CAIS; Schroeder & Gordon, 1991). The CAIS focuses on the specifics of the behavior of concern and the characteristics of the child, family, and environment that potentially influence the behavior. It helps the interviewer decide which questions need to be asked and ensures that essential information is gathered quickly and efficiently (Schroeder & Gordon, 1991).

SETTING THE STAGE

Prior to interviewing parents, it is helpful to have them complete a general questionnaire about the child and family (see Schroeder & Gordon, 1991, for an example), as well as a rating scale that screens for problem behavior and compares the child's behavior to a normative sample. Examples of useful behavior rating scales are the Child Behavior Checklist (Achenbach & Edelbrock, 1983), the Parenting Stress Index (Abidin, 1990), the Eyberg Child Behavior Inventory (Eyberg & Ross, 1978), and the Conners Parent Rating Scale (Goyette, Conners, & Ulrich, 1978). Each parent should be asked to complete the selected behavior rating scale; if they are separated or divorced, each

should be asked to complete a general parent questionnaire. The information gained from the completed questionnaires permits the clinician to generate preliminary hypotheses about the nature and causes of the problem, as well as to plan for and focus the parent interview.

It is important to include both parents in the initial interview if they both are actively involved in the child's life. If they are unable or unwilling to participate in a joint interview, an attempt should be made to interview them separately, even if this is done by telephone. Each parent brings his or her own perspective on the problem and also will provide the clinician with information about his or her willingness to support the child's treatment. We routinely include preschool children in the initial parent interview, with age-appropriate toys and activities provided to keep the child occupied. Although some clinicians may find this difficult, we have discovered that the information being discussed is rarely new to the child. Moreover, the opportunity to observe the child and the parent-child interaction firsthand far outweighs any disadvantages. If necessary, later interviews can be conducted with the parents alone, to go over more sensitive information or to receive information or provide information to the parents without the distraction of a particularly disruptive child. Parents of school-age children are typically interviewed alone, before the child is seen; parents of adolescents are first seen with the adolescent present or absent, depending on the nature of the problem.

Interviewing parents is an interactive process that sets the tone for future intervention efforts. To promote collaboration, it is important for the interviewer to create an atmosphere that puts the parents at ease in discussing their child's problems and gives them some sense of optimism that the child's or family's life can improve as a result of professional help. Characteristics of a good interviewer can contribute to a positive tone. These include warmth, empathy, a sensitive and nonjudgmental approach that respects others' feelings and cultures, and an ability to keep the interview moving along in a smooth, purposeful fashion (Kanfer, Eyberg, & Krahn, 1992). The ability to listen also is an essential skill. Listening helps parents focus on the problem, and reflecting or paraphrasing lets the parents know that they have been heard (Morganstern, 1988). Recognizing the parents' distress as they discuss areas of concern encourages them to share their fears and beliefs about the problem(s).

It is helpful to begin the interview by briefly summarizing what is already known about the situation and explaining the purpose of the interview (i.e., to get a better understanding of their concerns in order to help determine what, if any, intervention is necessary). This gives parents some initial information on what is expected of them, as well as on what they can expect from the interviewer. Further, it helps them start talking about their concerns. Whereas it is important to get a thorough understanding of the nature and context of the problematic behavior, it is not possible or advisable to assess everything in the child's or family's background. Background information is important, but the goal is to be selective in pursuing a particular topic. It should also be remembered that working with children almost always involves an ongoing relationship with the parents; if a relevant area is missed initially, it is very likely to be discussed in future meetings. Problems with parent interviews include inaccurate recall, conflicting perceptions of the child between parents, and a tendency to describe the child in unrealistically positive and precocious terms (Kanfer et al., 1992). Parents also may describe their child's behavior in excessively negative terms when they are under personal stress (e.g., marital discord, depression). Focusing on the current situation—that is, current behavior, current child management techniques, and current family strengths and weaknesses—can help increase the reliability of parental reports.

COMPREHENSIVE ASSESSMENT-TO-INTERVENTION SYSTEM

The following is a logical and systematic guide to assuring that information in important areas is gathered. The information does not have to be obtained in any particular order, and although it may be gathered during the parent interview, a variety of other sources and methods could be used (e.g., parent or teacher questionnaires, psychometric testing, observation of parent-child interaction). The CAIS is very useful for complex cases, but it also provides a framework to assist the clinician in quickly gathering essential information for brief assessment cases.

Clarifying the Referral Question

Although the need to clarify the referral question seems obvious, its importance cannot be overemphasized. After the parent has described the problem, the clinician should be certain that he or she and the parent are thinking about the same problem. This can be done by simply reflecting what the parent has said: "It sounds like you are concerned about your child refusing to go to school, as well as the different ways you and your husband are handling the situation." This gives the parent the opportunity to restate his or her concerns until there is a mutual understanding of the concerns that are to be addressed.

Determining the Social Context

A child is referred because someone is concerned. This does not necessarily mean that the child needs treatment or that the child's behavior is the problem. The clinician should ask: Who is concerned about the child? Why is this person concerned? Why is this person concerned now as opposed to some other time? The parents' affect in describing the problems is also significant. Are they overwhelmed, anxious, depressed, or nonchalant? Two mothers, for example, describe their 3-year-old daughters as being anxious and fearful. One mother is calm, in control of herself, and using good judgment in attempting to deal with the problem. The other mother, however, is extremely upset, fearful, and unable to view the problem objectively. Each of these parents presents a different focus for the assessment/intervention process.

The family's sociocultural characteristics can play an important role in the planning and implementation of a treatment program (Garcia Coll & Meyer, 1993). Questions such as the following can help the clinician get a better understanding of the parent's perspective: What do you think has caused your child's problem? Why do you think it started when it did? How does the problem affect you or your child? How severe do you feel your child's problem is? Do you expect it will have a short- or long-term course? What kind of treatment do you think your child should receive? Who can help with the treatment? What are the most important results that you hope your child will receive from treatment? What is your greatest fear about your child (Garcia Coll & Meyer, 1993)? Asking the parents about their expectations, hopes, and fears in coming to a mental health professional helps in both gathering and interpreting the material, especially if the clinician's recommendations are contrary to the parents' expectations or confirm their worst fears. This information also can help the clinician develop a treatment program that is sensitive to sociocultural influences.

Assessing General Areas

Information about the characteristics of the child and the family is important in putting problems or concerns in perspective and determining the resources the family has or will need to carry out a successful intervention plan. Asking parents to briefly describe a typical day for their child (when he or she gets up; the morning, daily, and evening routines; when he or she goes to bed, etc.) usually gives a great deal of information about how the family and child functions, their stresses and limitations, and, in general, the context in which they live. The following general areas are important to assess:

• *Developmental status:* Knowledge of the child's developmental status (physical/motor, cognitive, language, social, personality/emotional, psychosexual) allows the clinician to evaluate the child's behavior in comparison with that of other children of the same age or developmental level. Behavior that may be considered a significant problem at one stage in development or at one age may be

quite normal at another. The job of the clinician is to judge whether the behavior of concern is less or more than one would expect of any child at that age and in that environment. A 3-year-old who wets the bed, for example, may be considered "normal" for that age, whereas a 10-year-old who wets the bed is viewed as having a significant problem. Behavior also changes over the course of development, and some problem behaviors change in the appropriate or desired direction without intervention. Thus, the time at which a behavior occurs in a child's life is as important as the behavior itself. Furthermore, knowledge of early development is important when assessing children in the preschool years, since this is a critical time for identification of and intervention in developmental problems.

• *Characteristics of parents and extended family:* Although it is difficult to identify causal mechanisms in the development of childhood disorders, and equally difficult to delineate the specific factors contributing to or mediating outcome, the child development and child clinical literature does provide evidence for certain parent characteristics and parenting practices that facilitate development, as well as those that make the child more vulnerable (Schroeder & Gordon, 1991). Forehand, King, Peed, and Yoder (1975), for example, found that low parental tolerance, high expectations for child behavior, marital stress, and family problems influenced parents' perception of their child's behavior. Similarly, Wahler's (1980) work shows that a mother's perception of her child's behavior is highly correlated with the type of environmental interactions (positive or coercive) she has just experienced. Thus, the perspective of the referring person must be taken into account. The referring person may lack information about child development in general, may have emotional problems, or may be experiencing stress, all of which can distort his or her perception of the child's behavior. In addition, parenting styles, techniques, and models; marital status; and the presence of psychopathology in parents and other family members are especially important areas to assess, as are sibling relationships and the availability and use of social support.

- *Environment:* Recent stressful life events, socioeconomic status, and subculture norms and values can provide important information about the problems the child is experiencing and the intervention strategies that may be most helpful. The child's environment provides the setting conditions for the behavior and in some cases may be a more appropriate focus for intervention than the behavior itself. The setting conditions can include very specific antecedents to the behavior (repeated commands, teasing, criticism, or hunger), socioeconomic status, or major events such as parental divorce, a death in the family, a chronic illness, or an impending move.

- *Consequences of the behavior:* Information in this area includes the ways in which the parents are currently handling the behavior problem; the techniques that have been tried in the past and the "payoff" for the child; the impact of the problem behavior on the child, parents, and environment; and the prognosis with and without treatment. Lack of careful assessment of these factors usually leads to parents' responding to suggestions by saying, "Yes, but we've tried that and it doesn't work."

- *Medical/health status:* This area should include information on the family's history of medical/genetic problems, chronic illnesses of the child, current health and medications, prenatal history, and early development. Much of this information can be gathered in a general parent questionnaire with specific areas of concern followed up in the interview.

Assessing Specific Areas

In addition to the general areas already mentioned, it is important to gather information on the specific behaviors or concerns, including (a) the persistence of the behavior (how long has it been going on?); (b) changes in behavior (is it getting worse?); (c) severity (is the behavior very intense or dangerous or low-level but "annoying"?); (d) frequency (has the behavior occurred only once or twice or many times?); (e) situation specificity (does the behavior occur only at home or in a variety of settings?); and (f) the type of problem (is the problem a discrete behavior or a set of diffuse problems?).

Determining the Effects of the Problem

It is important to note who is suffering from the referral problem(s). It may be that the child's behavior is bothering one parent but not the other or is annoying to the teacher but is not a problem for the parents. In other cases, although the behavior may be interfering with some aspect of the child's development, it may not be seen as a problem to the parents or other adults and without intervention may lead to a poor outcome for the child. For example, a learning disability may not be seen as a problem for the parents, but the child is likely to suffer negative consequences in school and in future opportunities.

Determining Areas for Intervention

After assessing each of these areas, the clinician should have a good idea about the nature of the problem and should know what additional information is needed to conceptualize the problem. It should be possible at this time to formulate plans for further assessment and/or intervention strategies. Although it is not possible to answer every question and/or to intervene effectively in every situation, intervention strategies follow naturally from the assessment, if the child's development and behavior and the emotional, physical, and sociocultural context in which he or she lives have been examined systematically. For example, interventions in the *developmental area* could include (a) teaching new responses; (b) providing appropriate stimulation; or (c) increasing or decreasing specific behaviors. In the *parental area*, one could (a) teach new parenting techniques; (b) focus on the emotional atmosphere in the home or school; (c) treat (or refer for treatment) marital problems or parent psychopathology; or (d) change parental expectations, attitudes, or beliefs. *Environmental* interventions might involve (a) changing the specific cues that elicit inappropriate behavior or prevent appropriate behavior from occurring; (b) focusing on the emotional atmosphere in the home by helping parents build support networks and deal with the stresses of daily life; (c) helping the child/family cope with life events such as a death; or (d) changing the physical environment where the problem behavior most often occurs. Focusing intervention on the *consequences of the behavior* might involve (a) changing the responses of the parents; (b) changing the responses of other significant adults such as teachers; or (c) changing the behavior of the child by focusing on a more appropriate payoff for the child (e.g., providing reinforcers). Intervening in the *medical/health* area may involve (a) referral for treatment of the cause of the problem (e.g., persistent ear infections) or (b) treating the effect of the problem (e.g., teaching relaxation skills to a child with cerebral palsy).

CLOSING THE INTERVIEW

Time should be allowed at the end of the initial parent interview to summarize and integrate the information gathered. This lets the parents know that their concerns have been accurately heard and gives them feedback on the clinician's initial conceptualization of the problem. An explanation should be given for any additional information that is needed (e.g., school visit, behavioral rating scales, psychometric testing of the child, child interviews, further interviews with the parents, observations of parent-child interactions, medical evaluation) and how this information will be gathered. If possible, potential treatment strategies should be discussed, as well as the estimated length of time and cost for that treatment. While it might not be possible to give all this information without further assessment, it is important that the parents have some understanding of the clinician's thoughts regarding treatment and a sense of hope that something can be done to help them and their child (Morganstern, 1988). Early in the interview, the clinician should have asked about the parents' expectations, and

at the end of the interview, their expectations can be discussed in relation to the gathered information. A collaborative relationship with parents is developed by sharing information with them and allowing them choices in how to proceed. Asking the parents what they think (or feel) about what they have heard and engaging them in the process of setting treatment goals encourage them to be part of this process and maximize the chances that they will support the child's treatment.

References & Readings

Abidin, R. R. (1990). *Parenting Stress Index manual* (3rd ed.). Charlottesville, VA: Pediatric Psychology Press.

Achenbach, T. M., & Edelbrock, C. (1983). *Manual for the Child Behavior Checklist and Revised Child Behavior Profile.* Burlington, VT: University Associates in Psychiatry.

Bellack, A. S., & Hersen, M. (Eds.) (1988). *Behavioral assessment: A practical handbook.* Elmsford, NY: Pergamon Press.

Edelbrock, C., & Costello, A. J. (1988). Structured psychiatric interviews for children. In M. Rutter, A. H. Tuma, & H. D. Lann (Eds.), *Assessment and diagnosis in child psychopathology* (pp. 87–112). New York: Guilford Press.

Eyberg, S. M., & Ross, A. W. (1978). Assessment of child behavior problems: The validation of a new inventory. *Journal of Clinical Child Psychology, 7,* 113–116.

Forehand, R. L., King, H. E., Peed, S., & Yoder, P. (1975). Mother-child interactions: Comparisons of a non-compliant clinic group and non-clinic group. *Behaviour Research and Therapy, 13,* 79–84.

Garcia Coll, C. T., & Meyer, E. C. (1993). The sociocultural context of infant development. In C. H. Zeanah Jr. (Ed.), *Handbook of infant mental health* (pp. 56–70). New York: Guilford Press.

Goyette, C. H., Conners, C. K., & Ulrich, R. F. (1978). Normative data on the revised Conners Parent and Teacher Rating Scales. *Journal of Abnormal Child Psychology, 6,* 221–236.

Kanfer, F., Eyberg, S. M., & Krahn, G. L. (1992). Interviewing strategies in child assessment. In C. E. Walker & M. C. Roberts (Eds.), *Handbook of clinical child psychology* (2nd ed., pp. 49–62). New York: Wiley.

Mash, E. J., & Terdal, L. G. (1988). Behavioral assessment of child and family disturbance. In E. J. Mash & L. G. Terdal (Eds.), *Behavioral assessment of childhood disorders: Selected core problems* (2nd ed., pp. 3–68). New York: Guilford Press.

Morganstern, K. P. (1988). Behavioral interviewing. In A. S. Bellack & M. Hersen (Eds.), *Behavioral assessment: A practical handbook* (pp. 86–118). Elmsford, NY: Pergamon Press.

Schroeder, C. S., & Gordon, B. N. (1991). *Assessment and treatment of childhood problems: A clinician's guide.* New York: Guilford Press.

Wahler, R. G. (1980). The insular mother: Her problems in parent-child treatment. *Journal of Applied Behavior Analysis, 13,* 207–219.

Wixted, J. T. (1988). Assessment of child behavior problems. In A. S. Bellack & M. Hersen (Eds.), *Behavioral assessment: A practical guidebook* (pp. 578–608). Elmsford, NY: Pergamon Press.

Related Topics

19 MEDICAL EVALUATION OF CHILDREN WITH BEHAVIORAL OR DEVELOPMENTAL DISORDERS

James L. Lukefahr

This chapter is designed to familiarize the psychologist with the diagnostic medical evaluation of children with disordered development or behavior. The three components of a comprehensive medical evaluation (*history, physical examination,* and *laboratory evaluation*) will be described, with emphasis on those considerations pertinent to children with behavioral or developmental disorders.

MEDICAL HISTORY

Birth History

• *Prenatal factors: Prematurity* (birth prior to 37 weeks of gestation) and *low birth weight* are risk factors for developmental and cognitive delays, as well as for some behavior disorders, such as attention-deficit/hyperactivity disorder (ADHD). *Intrauterine growth retardation* (IUGR), also referred to as *small for gestational age,* refers to conditions that impair fetal growth, so that birth size is disproportionately small for the gestational age. IUGR is a particularly important risk factor because its presence indicates significant toxic, nutritional, or infectious insult to the developing fetus. A partial list of causes of IUGR is shown in Table 1.

For example, congenital infection with *cytomegalovirus* (CMV) affects 1% of U.S. newborns (about 40,000 infants every year). Although most of these newborns are asymptomatic, 6% have severe disease evident at

TABLE 1. Common Causes of Intrauterine Growth Retardation

Fetal

Chromosomal disorders (e.g., Down syndrome [trisomy 21], trisomies 18 or 13)
Chronic fetal infection (e.g., human immunodeficiency virus [HIV], cytomegalovirus [CMV], syphilis)
Severe congenital anomalies or syndrome complexes
Radiation injury
Multiple gestation

Placental

Decreased placental size
Placental infection or tumor
Twin-to-twin transfusion

Maternal

Hypertension or preeclampsia
Renal disease
Hypoxemia (chronic lung or cardiac disease)
Malnutrition or anemia
Drugs (e.g., tobacco, alcohol, cocaine, narcotics)

birth with IUGR, psychomotor retardation, microcephaly, and multiple organ involvement. Another 14% of CMV-infected infants do not have obvious disease at birth but are later found to have sensorineural hearing loss (making CMV infection the most common noninherited cause of deafness).

• *Perinatal factors: Complications during labor and delivery* appear to cause developmental and learning disabilities less often than previously believed. However, very premature infants and infants with severe perinatal complications remain at risk if they sustain episodes of hypoxemia or intracerebral hemorrhage. Advances in neonatal intensive care have diminished the impact of *respiratory distress syndrome* (or *hyaline membrane disease*) on later development for most premature infants.

Neonatal jaundice (hyperbilirubinemia) is an extremely common condition, reported to affect as many as 60% of all infants. Developmental sequelae appear to occur only in those infants who experience extremely high serum bilirubin levels or (more often) when the jaundice is a result of a severe perinatal illness.

Complete Past Medical History

• *Chronic severe illnesses:* Children with chronic illnesses such as diabetes mellitus, seizure disorders, and asthma often have concurrent behavioral and developmental problems. For example, children with severe *congenital heart disease* often experience developmental delays due to the cerebral effects of chronic hypoxemia. Similarly, severe *chronic renal disease* may also cause cognitive or developmental compromise as a result of growth failure and high levels of circulating toxic metabolic products. Children with *cancer* may have cognitive impairments due to either the malignancy itself or the toxic effects of the cancer treatment. Severe *seizure disorders* are often associated with brain lesions or malformation syndromes with developmental and cognitive implications.

Children with chronic illnesses frequently experience concurrent behavioral problems. For example, small children with severe asthma may experience separational difficulties as a result of parental overprotection. Adolescents with diabetes or epilepsy often rebel against their dependency on medical treatment regimens and refuse to comply with prescribed therapy—frequently resulting in serious complications.

• *Recurrent illnesses:* Children with recurrent otitis media during the first few years of life may sustain speech and language delays due to prolonged periods of decreased hearing. Frequent episodes of asthma may affect physical and social development by inhibiting normal childhood activities.

• *Family history:* The clinician should inquire about heritable conditions known to occur within the family. Examples of congenital familial conditions with developmental consequences include *tuberous sclerosis*, which is often associated with severe seizures and mental retardation, and *fragile X syndrome*, the most common cause of mental retardation in boys. Acquired conditions can also have familial occurrence patterns. *Thyroid disease, collagen-vascular disease* (e.g., systemic lupus or juvenile rheumatoid arthritis), and *inflammatory bowel disease* (e.g.,

TABLE 2. The HEADSSS Psychosocial Interview Technique

H	Home environment (e.g., relations with parents and siblings)
E	Education/employment (e.g., school performance)
A	Activities (e.g., sports participation, after-school activity, peer relations)
D	Drug, alcohol, or tobacco use
S	Sexuality (e.g., is the patient sexually active; does he/she use condoms or contraception)
S	Suicide risk or symptoms of depression or other mental disorder
S	"Savagery" (e.g., violence or abuse in home environment or in neighborhood)

Crohn's disease) commonly cluster within families. These may first present with changes in behavior or school performance, or with chronic pain that initially may appear to be functional in nature.

- *Social history:* Physicians recognize the importance of psychosocial factors in disease states and are accustomed to exploring these concerns with parents of young children. Direct discussion of psychosocial issues with older children and adolescents during a single medical encounter is often more difficult. A brief structured interview technique, commonly utilized with adolescents, is the *HEADSSS interview,* summarized in Table 2.

PHYSICAL EXAMINATION

Growth Parameters

Many chronic developmental and somatic disorders are accompanied by disordered physical growth, and physicians routinely maintain *standardized growth charts* for their child patients. These growth charts allow comparison of children's length or height, weight, and head circumference to national norms for those growth parameters and are reproduced in Figure 1. A child with any growth parameter less than the 5th percentile for age (or greater than the 95th percentile) should undergo thorough medical evaluation. *Head circumference* is particularly important in evaluating developmentally delayed children, since this growth parameter is closely correlated with brain growth.

General Physical Examination

- *Vital signs:* Temperature, pulse, blood pressure, and respiratory rate.
- *Head:* Malformations of the skull, external ears, and other structures (often the most visible signs of major malformation syndromes). Microcephaly, small palpebral fissures, and short, flat upper lips are the classic physical findings of *fetal alcohol syndrome.*
- *Eyes, ears, nose, and throat:* Abnormalities of the iris, pupil, lens, or retina; middle-ear fluid or tympanic membrane abnormality; malformations of the nose and throat (such as cleft or high arched palate).
- *Neck:* Enlargement of the thyroid gland (goiter) or lymph nodes.
- *Chest:* Malformations of the chest wall; heart murmur or other evidence of cardiac malformation; lung abnormalities.
- *Abdomen:* Enlarged liver, spleen, or kidneys (associated with congenital infection or metabolic disorders); abnormal masses; cachexia or obesity.
- *Back:* Evidence of spina bifida or scoliosis.
- *Genitalia and anus:* Malformations of sexual organs or perineum; testicular enlargement (common in fragile X syndrome).
- *Extremities:* Signs of limb malformation; decreased or asymmetrical muscle mass.
- *Skin:* Pigmentation abnormalities, such as the café au lait spots of neurofibromatosis, ash-leaf spots of tuberous sclerosis, hyperpigmentation of incontinentia pigmenti, and *acanthosis nigricans* associated with type II diabetes.
- *Neurological examination:* Neurological examination is a critical element in the evaluation of children with behavioral or developmental disorders. It includes cranial nerve function, tendon reflexes, muscle tone, muscle strength, cerebellar function (such as stereognosis and proprioception), gait abnormalities, and presence of persistent or abnormal infantile reflexes (such as the startle and glabellar reflexes).

Vision and Hearing Testing

Accurate assessment of visual and auditory function should be performed in all children

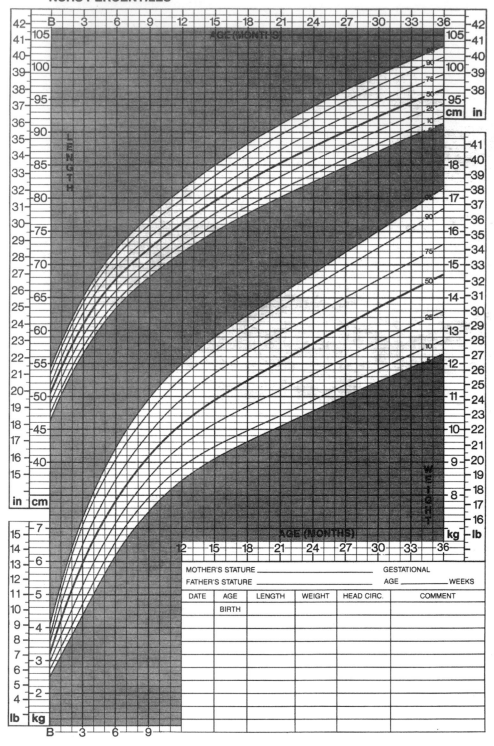

FIGURE 1A. NCHS Standardized Childhood Growth Charts:
Infant Boys—Length and Weight (Reprinted with permission of Ross Products Division,
Abbott Laboratories, Columbus, OH 43216, from "NCHS Growth Charts," © 1982 Ross
Products Division, Abbott Laboratories.)

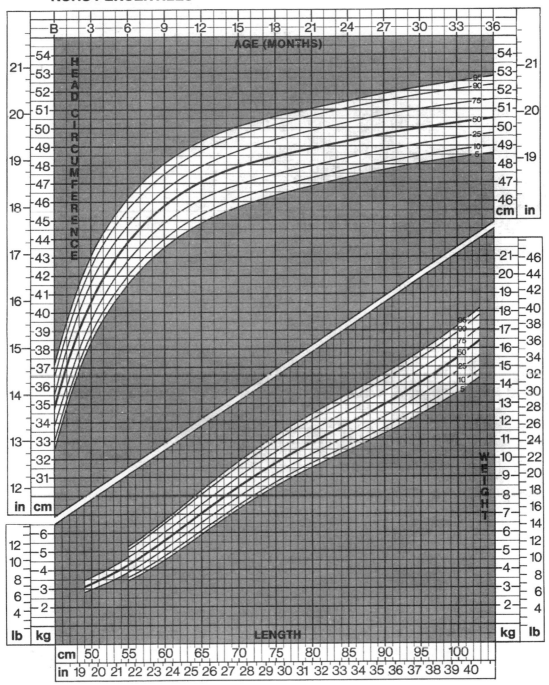

FIGURE 1B. NCHS Standardized Childhood Growth Charts: Infant Boys—Head Circumference and Weight-for-Length

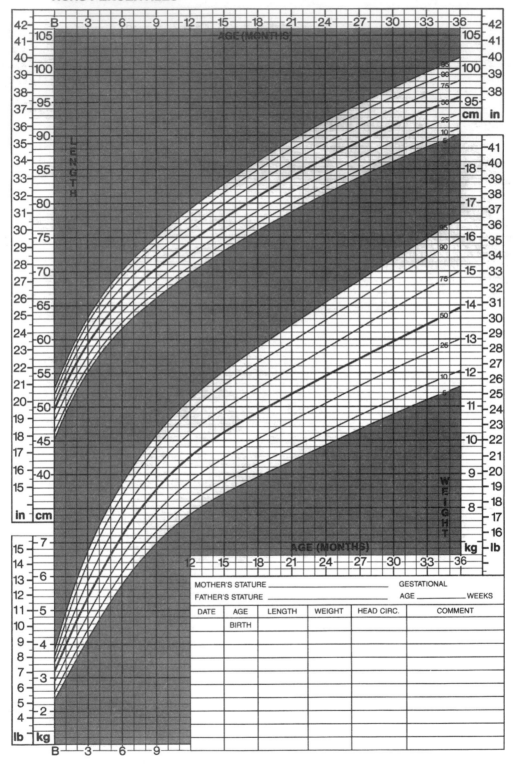

FIGURE 1C. NCHS Standardized Childhood Growth Charts:
Infant Girls—Length and Weight

84

GIRLS: BIRTH TO 36 MONTHS
PHYSICAL GROWTH
NCHS PERCENTILES

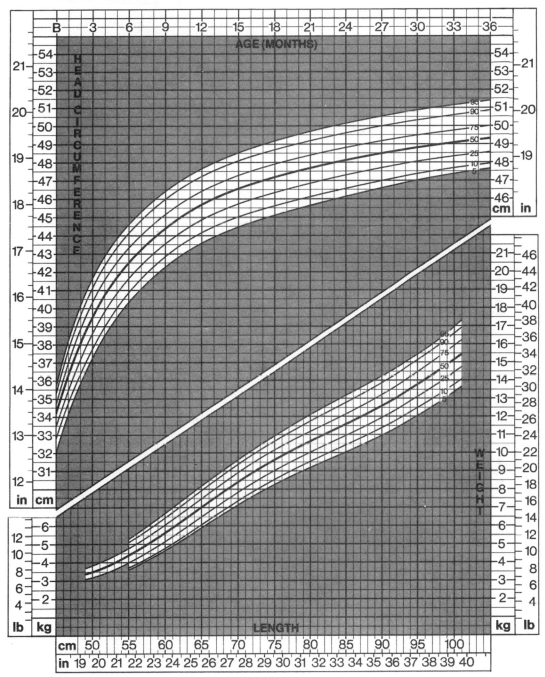

FIGURE 1D. NCHS Standardized Childhood Growth Charts:
Infant Girls—Head Circumference and Weight-for-Length

BOYS: 2 TO 18 YEARS
PHYSICAL GROWTH
NCHS PERCENTILES

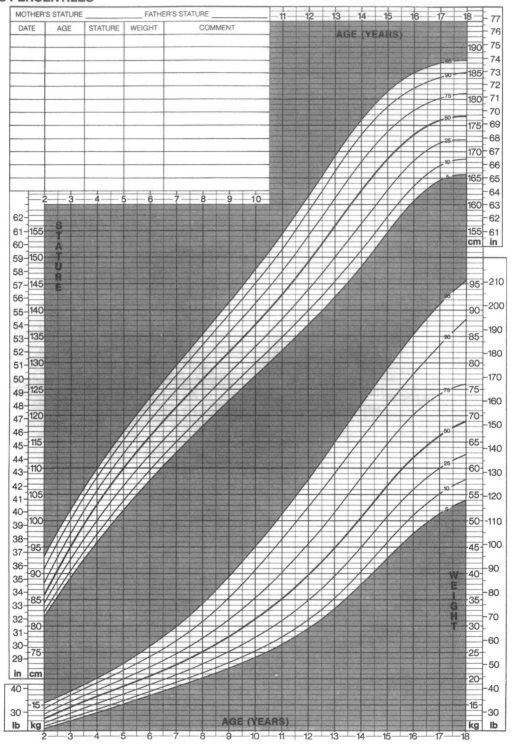

FIGURE 1E. NCHS Standardized Childhood Growth Charts:
Boys—Height and Weight

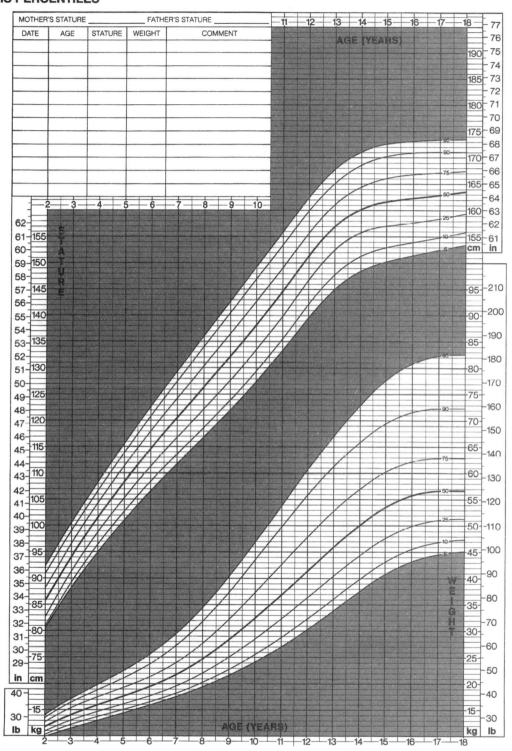

GIRLS: 2 TO 18 YEARS
PHYSICAL GROWTH
NCHS PERCENTILES

FIGURE 1F. NCHS Standardized Childhood Growth Charts:
Girls—Height and Weight

with behavioral or developmental disorders. Several technologies, such as auditory and visual brain stem evoked potentials, are now available that allow such testing even in newborns or children with severe communication impairment.

LABORATORY TESTS AND
IMAGING PROCEDURES

Table 3 provides a partial listing of laboratory tests commonly obtained during evaluation of children with developmental or behavioral disorders. Developmental disorders presenting in early infancy are usually more severe and often warrant extensive evaluation for metabolic disorders or congenital infection. Studies aimed at detecting infectious agents that may cause fetal injury and subsequent developmental delay include *urine for CMV culture* and *serum antibody titers* for congenital infection by organisms such as toxoplasmosis and syphilis. *Skull and extremity X rays* are often obtained to detect metabolic or infectious damage to skeletal structures. *Computed tomography* (CT) or *magnetic resonance imaging* (MRI) of the brain may be ordered to identify congenital malformations. *Chromosome determination* (karyotype) is ordered if a major malformation syndrome (e.g., Down syndrome or Turner syndrome) is suspected.

Laboratory evaluation of behavior disorders and learning disabilities presenting later in childhood is usually not as extensive. In the typical case, where a child has a long and relatively stable symptomatology with a diagnosis such as reading disability or ADHD, laboratory evaluation is usually not helpful. However, a child who was previously thriving and over a short time begins to do poorly in school is more likely to have a treatable medical condition. *Electroencephalography* (EEG) should be performed if a child's abnormal behaviors show a

TABLE 3. Selected Laboratory Tests and Their Indications in Evaluating Behavioral or Developmental Disorders

Laboratory Test	Indication
Alpha-fetoprotein, serum	Abnormal in maternal serum or fetal amniotic fluid in Down syndrome and neural tube defects
Amino or organic acids, serum or urine	Elevated in some congenital metabolic diseases
Ammonia, blood	Elevated in some congenital metabolic diseases
Antinuclear antibody (ANA), serum	Elevated in collagen-vascular diseases (e.g., systemic lupus erythematosus)
Bilirubin, serum	Elevated in neonatal jaundice and in liver disease
Chromosome evaluation (karyotype)	Abnormal in many major malformation syndromes (e.g., Down syndrome, trisomy 18)
Creatinine, serum	Elevated in chronic renal diseases
DNA for fragile X syndrome	Detection of fragile X syndrome
Electrolytes, serum	Abnormal in some congenital metabolic diseases
Erythrocyte sedimentation rate (ESR), blood	Elevated in chronic inflammatory diseases, such as systemic lupus erythematosus and Crohn's disease
Gamma-glutamyltransferase (GGT), serum	Elevated in chronic liver disease
Glucose, blood or serum	Abnormal in diabetes mellitus and in some inborn errors of metabolism
Glycosylated hemoglobin (hemoglobin A1C), serum	Elevated in diabetes mellitus with undertreatment or poor compliance with treatment
Hemoglobin electrophoresis, blood	Detects abnormal hemoglobin types, such as in sickle-cell disease
Lead, blood	Elevated in chronic lead exposure
Thyroid function tests (thyroxine, triiodothyronine, thyroid-stimulating hormone, T4, T3, TSH), serum	Used to detect abnormal thyroid function
Transaminases (AST, ALT, SGOT, SGPT), serum	Elevated in acute or chronic liver disease
Urea nitrogen (BUN), serum	Elevated in acute or chronic renal disease

discrete episodic pattern that may represent seizure activity. Otherwise, the EEG is not routinely indicated for the evaluation of learning and behavior problems. *Thyroid function tests* may be indicated, particularly in girls with recent changes in cognitive performance or if there is a family history of thyroid disease.

References & Readings

Behrman, R. E., Kliegman, R. M., & Arvin, A. M. (1996). *Nelson textbook of pediatrics* (15th ed.). Philadelphia: Saunders.

Bithoney, W. G., Dubowitz, H., & Egan, H. (1992). Failure to thrive/growth deficiency. *Pediatrics in Review, 13,* 453–460.

Goldenring, J. M., & Cohen, E. (1988). Getting into adolescent heads. *Contemporary Pediatrics, 5*(7), 3–14.

Hack, M., Taylor, H. G., Klein, N., et al. (1994). School-age outcomes in children with birth weights under 750g. *New England Journal of Medicine, 331,* 753–759.

Hanshaw, J. B. (1995). Cytomegalovirus infections. *Pediatrics in Review, 16,* 43–48.

Jones, K. L. (1997). *Smith's recognizable patterns of human malformation* (5th ed.). Philadelphia: Saunders.

Kuban, K. C. K., & Leviton, A. (1994). Cerebral palsy. *New England Journal of Medicine, 330,* 188–195.

Roberts, M. C. (Ed.) (1995). *Handbook of pediatric psychology* (2nd ed.). New York: Guilford Press.

Turk, J. (1995). Fragile X syndrome. *Archives of Diseases in Childhood, 72,* 3–5.

Related Topics

20   *DSM-IV* MULTIAXIAL SYSTEM

Axis I	Clinical Disorders
	Other Conditions That May Be a Focus of Clinical Attention
Axis II	Personality Disorders
	Mental Retardation
Axis III	General Medical Conditions
Axis IV	Psychosocial and Environmental Problems
Axis V	Global Assessment of Functioning

AXIS IV: PSYCHOSOCIAL AND ENVIRONMENTAL PROBLEMS

Problems with primary support group
Problems related to the social environment
Educational problems
Occupational problems
Housing problems
Economic problems
Problems with access to health services
Problems related to interaction with legal system/crime
Other psychosocial and environmental problems

DSM-IV CLASSIFICATION

Disorders Usually First Diagnosed in Infancy, Childhood, or Adolescence

Mental Retardation
   Note: These are coded on Axis II.

317	Mild Mental Retardation
318.0	Moderate Mental Retardation
318.1	Severe Mental Retardation
318.2	Profound Mental Retardation
319	Mental Retardation, Severity Unspecified

Learning Disorders

315.00	Reading Disorder
315.1	Mathematics Disorder
315.2	Disorder of Written Expression
315.9	Learning Disorder NOS

Motor Skills Disorder

315.4	Developmental Coordination Disorder

Communication Disorders

315.31	Expressive Language Disorder
315.31	Mixed Receptive-Expressive Language Disorder
315.39	Phonological Disorder
307.0	Stuttering
307.9	Communication Disorder NOS

Pervasive Developmental Disorders

299.00	Autistic Disorder
299.80	Rett's Disorder
299.10	Childhood Disintegrative Disorder
299.80	Asperger's Disorder
299.80	Pervasive Developmental Disorder NOS

Attention-Deficit and Disruptive Behavior Disorders

314.xx	Attention-Deficit/Hyperactivity Disorder
.01	Combined Type
.00	Predominantly Inattentive Type
.01	Predominantly Hyperactive-Impulsive Type
314.9	Attention-Deficit/Hyperactivity Disorder NOS
312.8	Conduct Disorder
313.81	Oppositional Defiant Disorder
312.9	Disruptive Behavior Disorder NOS

Feeding and Eating Disorders of Infancy or Early Childhood

307.52	Pica
307.53	Rumination Disorder
307.59	Feeding Disorder of Infancy or Early Childhood

Tic Disorders

307.23	Tourette's Disorder
307.22	Chronic Motor or Vocal Tic Disorder
307.21	Transient Tic Disorder
307.20	Tic Disorder NOS

Elimination Disorders

787.6	Encopresis With Constipation and Overflow Incontinence
307.7	Encopresis Without Constipation and Overflow Incontinence
307.6	Enuresis (Not Due to a General Medical Condition)

Other Disorders of Infancy, Childhood, or Adolescence

309.21	Separation Anxiety Disorder
313.23	Selective Mutism
313.89	Reactive Attachment Disorder of Infancy or Early Childhood
307.3	Stereotypic Movement Disorder
313.9	Disorder of Infancy, Childhood, or Adolescence NOS

Delirium, Dementia, and Amnestic and Other Cognitive Disorders

Delirium

293.0	Delirium Due to . . . [*Indicate General Medical Condition*]
——.—	Substance Intoxication Delirium (*refer to Substance-Related Disorders for substance-specific codes*)
——.—	Substance Withdrawal Delirium (*refer to Substance-Related Disorders for substance-specific codes*)
——.—	Delirium Due to Multiple Etiologies (*code each of the specific etiologies*)
780.09	Delirium NOS

Dementia

290.xx Dementia of the Alzheimer's Type, With Early Onset (*also code 331.0 Alzheimer's disease on Axis III*)

.10 Uncomplicated
.11 With Delirium
.12 With Delusions
.13 With Depressed Mood

290.xx Dementia of the Alzheimer's Type, With Late Onset (*also code 331.0 Alzheimer's disease on Axis III*)

.0 Uncomplicated
.3 With Delirium
.20 With Delusions
.21 With Depressed Mood

290.xx Vascular Dementia

.40 Uncomplicated
.41 With Delirium
.42 With Delusions
.43 With Depressed Mood

294.9 Dementia Due to HIV Disease (*also code 043.1 HIV infection affecting central nervous system*)

294.1 Dementia Due to Head Trauma (*also code 854.00 head injury on Axis III*)

294.1 Dementia Due to Parkinson's Disease (*also code 332.0 Parkinson's disease on Axis III*)

294.1 Dementia Due to Huntington's Disease (*also code 333.4 Huntington's disease on Axis III*)

290.10 Dementia Due to Pick's Disease (*also code 331.1 Pick's disease on Axis III*)

290.10 Dementia Due to Creutzfeldt-Jakob Disease (*also code 046.1 Creutzfeldt-Jakob disease on Axis III*)

294.1 Dementia Due to . . . [*Indicate the General Medical Condition not listed above*] (*also code the general medical condition on Axis III*)

——.—— Substance-Induced Persisting Dementia (*refer to Substance-Related Disorders for substance-specific codes*)

——.—— Dementia Due to Multiple Etiologies (*code each of the specific etiologies*)

294.8 Dementia NOS

Amnestic Disorders

294.0 Amnestic Disorder Due to . . . [*Indicate General Medical Condition*]

——.—— Substance-Induced Persisting Amnestic Disorder (*refer to Substance-Related Disorders for substance-specific codes*)

294.8 Amnestic Disorder NOS

Other Cognitive Disorders

294.9 Cognitive Disorder NOS

Mental Disorders Due to a General Medical Condition Not Elsewhere Classified

293.89 Catatonic Disorder Due to . . . [*Indicate General Medical Condition*]

310.1 Personality Change Due to . . . [*Indicate General Medical Condition*]

293.9 Mental Disorder NOS Due to . . . [*Indicate General Medical Condition*]

Substance-Related Disorders

Alcohol-Related Disorders

Alcohol Use Disorders

303.90 Alcohol Dependence
305.00 Alcohol Abuse

Alcohol-Induced Disorders

303.00 Alcohol Intoxication
291.8 Alcohol Withdrawal
291.0 Alcohol Intoxication Delirium
291.0 Alcohol Withdrawal Delirium
291.2 Alcohol-Induced Persisting Dementia
291.1 Alcohol-Induced Persisting Amnestic Disorder

291.x   Alcohol-Induced Psychotic
         Disorder
  .5   With Delusions
  .3   With Hallucinations
291.8   Alcohol-Induced Mood
         Disorder
291.8   Alcohol-Induced Anxiety
         Disorder
291.8   Alcohol-Induced Sexual
         Dysfunction
291.8   Alcohol-Induced Sleep
         Disorder
291.9   Alcohol-Related Disorder NOS

Amphetamine (or Amphetaminelike)-Related Disorders

Amphetamine Use Disorders
304.40   Amphetamine Dependence
305.70   Amphetamine Abuse

Amphetamine-Induced Disorders
292.89   Amphetamine Intoxication
292.0   Amphetamine Withdrawal
292.81   Amphetamine Intoxication
         Delirium
292.xx   Amphetamine-Induced Psychotic
         Disorder
  .11   With Delusions
  .12   With Hallucinations
292.84   Amphetamine-Induced Mood
         Disorder
292.89   Amphetamine-Induced Anxiety
         Disorder
292.89   Amphetamine-Induced Sexual
         Dysfunction
292.89   Amphetamine-Induced Sleep
         Disorder
292.9   Amphetamine-Related Disorder
         NOS

Caffeine-Related Disorders

Caffeine-Induced Disorders
305.90   Caffeine Intoxication
292.89   Caffeine-Induced Anxiety
         Disorder
292.89   Caffeine-Induced Sleep Disorder
292.9   Caffeine-Related Disorder NOS

Cannabis-Related Disorders

Cannabis Use Disorders
304.30   Cannabis Dependence
305.20   Cannabis Abuse

Cannabis-Induced Disorders
292.89   Cannabis Intoxication
292.81   Cannabis Intoxication Delirium
292.xx   Cannabis-Induced Psychotic
         Disorder
  .11   With Delusions
  .12   With Hallucinations
292.89   Cannabis-Induced Anxiety
         Disorder
292.9   Cannabis-Related Disorder NOS

Cocaine-Related Disorders

Cocaine Use Disorders
304.20   Cocaine Dependence
305.60   Cocaine Abuse

Cocaine-Induced Disorders
292.89   Cocaine Intoxication
292.0   Cocaine Withdrawal
292.81   Cocaine Intoxication Delirium
292.xx   Cocaine-Induced Psychotic
         Disorder
  .11   With Delusions
  .12   With Hallucinations
292.84   Cocaine-Induced Mood Disorder
292.89   Cocaine-Induced Anxiety
         Disorder
292.89   Cocaine-Induced Sexual
         Dysfunction
292.89   Cocaine-Induced Sleep Disorder
292.9   Cocaine-Related Disorder NOS

Hallucinogen-Related Disorders

Hallucinogen Use Disorders
301.50   Hallucinogen Dependence
301.30   Hallucinogen Abuse

Hallucinogen-Induced Disorders
292.89   Hallucinogen Intoxication
292.89   Hallucinogen Persisting Percep-
         tion Disorder (Flashbacks)

292.81   Hallucinogen Intoxication
           Delirium
292.xx   Hallucinogen-Induced Psychotic
           Disorder
   .11   With Delusions
   .12   With Hallucinations
292.84   Hallucinogen-Induced Mood
           Disorder
292.89   Hallucinogen-Induced Anxiety
           Disorder
292.9   Hallucinogen-Related Disorder
           NOS

Inhalant-Related Disorders

Inhalant Use Disorders
304.60   Inhalant Dependence
305.90   Inhalant Abuse

Inhalant-Induced Disorders
292.89   Inhalant Intoxication
292.81   Inhalant Intoxication Delirium
292.82   Inhalant-Induced Persisting
           Dementia
292.xx   Inhalant-Induced Psychotic
           Disorder
   .11   With Delusions
   .12   With Hallucinations
292.84   Inhalant-Induced Mood Disorder
292.89   Inhalant-Induced Anxiety
           Disorder
292.9   Inhalant-Related Disorder NOS

Nicotine-Related Disorders

Nicotine Use Disorder
305.10   Nicotine Dependence

Nicotine-Induced Disorder
292.0   Nicotine Withdrawal
292.9   Nicotine-Related Disorder NOS

Opioid-Related Disorders

Opioid Use Disorders
304.00   Opioid Dependence
305.50   Opioid Abuse

Opioid-Induced Disorders
292.89   Opioid Intoxication

292.0   Opioid Withdrawal
292.81   Opioid Intoxication Delirium
292.xx   Opioid-Induced Psychotic
           Disorder
   .11   With Delusions
   .12   With Hallucinations
292.84   Opioid-Induced Mood
           Disorder
292.89   Opioid-Induced Sexual
           Dysfunction
292.89   Opioid-Induced Sleep Disorder
292.9   Opioid-Related Disorder NOS

Phencyclidine (or Phencyclidinelike)-Related Disorders

Phencyclidine Use Disorders
304.90   Phencyclidine Dependence
305.90   Phencyclidine Abuse

Phencyclidine-Induced Disorders
292.89   Phencyclidine Intoxication
292.81   Phencyclidine Intoxication
           Delirium
292.xx   Phencyclidine-Induced Psychotic
           Disorder
   .11   With Delusions
   .12   With Hallucinations
292.84   Phencyclidine-Induced Mood
           Disorder
292.89   Phencyclidine-Induced Anxiety
           Disorder
292.9   Phencyclidine-Related Disorder
           NOS

Sedative-, Hypnotic-, or Anxiolytic-Related Disorders

Sedative, Hypnotic, or Anxiolytic Use Disorders
304.10   Sedative, Hypnotic, or Anxiolytic
           Dependence

Sedative-, Hypnotic-, or Anxiolytic-Induced Disorders
292.89   Sedative, Hypnotic, or Anxiolytic
           Intoxication
292.0   Sedative, Hypnotic, or Anxiolytic
           Withdrawal
292.81   Sedative, Hypnotic, or Anxiolytic
           Intoxication Delirium

292.81   Sedative, Hypnotic, or Anxiolytic Withdrawal Delirium
292.82   Sedative-, Hypnotic-, or Anxiolytic-Induced Persisting Dementia
292.83   Sedative-, Hypnotic-, or Anxiolytic-Induced Persisting Amnestic Disorder
292.xx   Sedative-, Hypnotic-, or Anxiolytic-Induced Psychotic Disorder
   .11   With Delusions
   .12   With Hallucinations
292.84   Sedative-, Hypnotic-, or Anxiolytic-Induced Mood Disorder
292.89   Sedative-, Hypnotic-, or Anxiolytic-Induced Anxiety Disorder
292.89   Sedative-, Hypnotic-, or Anxiolytic-Induced Sexual Dysfunction
292.89   Sedative-, Hypnotic-, or Anxiolytic-Induced Sleep Disorder
292.9   Sedative-, Hypnotic-, or Anxiolytic-Related Disorder NOS

Polysubstance-Related Disorder
304.80   Polysubstance Dependence

Other (or Unknown) Substance-Related Disorders

Other (or Unknown) Substance Use Disorders
304.90   Other (or Unknown) Substance Dependence
305.90   Other (or Unknown) Substance Abuse

Other (or Unknown) Substance-Induced Disorders
292.89   Other (or Unknown) Substance Intoxication
292.0   Other (or Unknown) Substance Withdrawal
292.81   Other (or Unknown) Substance-Induced Delirium
292.82   Other (or Unknown) Substance-Induced Persisting Dementia
292.83   Other (or Unknown) Substance-Induced Persisting Amnestic Disorder
292.xx   Other (or Unknown) Substance-Induced Psychotic Disorder

   .11   With Delusions
   .12   With Hallucinations
292.84   Other (or Unknown) Substance-Induced Mood Disorder
292.89   Other (or Unknown) Substance-Induced Anxiety Disorder
292.89   Other (or Unknown) Substance-Induced Sexual Dysfunction
292.89   Other (or Unknown) Substance-Induced Sleep Disorder
292.9   Other (or Unknown) Substance-Related Disorder NOS

Schizophrenia and Other Psychotic Disorders

295.xx   Schizophrenia
   .30   Paranoid Type
   .10   Disorganized Type
   .20   Catatonic Type
   .90   Undifferentiated Type
   .60   Residual Type
295.40   Schizophreniform Disorder
295.70   Schizoaffective Disorder
295.71   Delusional Disorder
298.8   Brief Psychotic Disorder
297.3   Shared Psychotic Disorder
293.xx   Psychotic Disorder Due to . . . [*Indicate General Medical Condition*]
   .81   With Delusions
   .82   With Hallucinations
——.——   Substance-Induced Psychotic Disorder (*refer to Substance-Related Disorders for substance-specific codes*)
298.9   Psychotic Disorder NOS

Mood Disorders

Code current state of Major Depressive Disorder or Bipolar Disorder in fifth digit:
   1 = Mild
   2 = Moderate
   3 = Severe Without Psychotic Features
   4 = Severe With Psychotic Features
   5 = In Partial Remission
   6 = In Full Remission
   0 = Unspecified

Depressive Disorders
296.xx	Major Depressive Disorder
.2x	Single Episode
.3x	Recurrent
300.4	Dysthymic Disorder
311	Depressive Disorder NOS

Bipolar Disorders
296.xx	Bipolar I Disorder
.0x	Single Manic Episode
.40	Most Recent Episode Hypomanic
.4x	Most Recent Episode Manic
.6x	Most Recent Episode Mixed
.5x	Most Recent Episode Depressed
.7	Most Recent Episode Unspecified
296.89	Bipolar II Disorder
301.13	Cyclothymic Disorder
296.80	Bipolar Disorder NOS
293.83	Mood Disorder Due to . . . [*Indicate General Medical Condition*]
——.—	Substance-Induced Mood Disorder (*refer to Substance-Related Disorders for substance-specific codes*)
296.90	Mood Disorder NOS

Anxiety Disorders

300.01	Panic Disorder Without Agoraphobia
300.21	Panic Disorder With Agoraphobia
300.22	Agoraphobia Without History of Panic Disorder
300.29	Specific Phobia
300.23	Social Phobia
300.3	Obsessive-Compulsive Disorder
309.81	Posttraumatic Stress Disorder
308.3	Acute Stress Disorder
300.02	Generalized Anxiety Disorder
293.89	Anxiety Disorder Due to . . . [*Indicate General Medical Condition*]
——.—	Substance-Induced Anxiety Disorder (*refer to Substance-Related Disorders for substance-specific codes*)
300.00	Anxiety Disorder NOS

Somatoform Disorders

300.81	Somatization Disorder
300.81	Undifferentiated Somatoform Disorder
300.11	Conversion Disorder
307.xx	Pain Disorder
.80	Associated With Psychological Factors
.98	Associated With Both Psychological Factors and a General Medical Condition
300.7	Hypochondriasis
300.7	Body Dysmorphic Disorder
300.81	Somatoform Disorder NOS

Factitious Disorders

300.xx	Factitious Disorder
.16	With Predominantly Psychological Signs and Symptoms
.19	With Predominantly Physical Signs and Symptoms
.19	With Combined Psychological Signs and Symptoms
300.19	Factitious Disorder NOS

Dissociative Disorders

300.12	Dissociative Amnesia
300.13	Dissociative Fugue
300.14	Dissociative Identity Disorder
300.6	Depersonalization Disorder
300.15	Dissociative Disorder NOS

Sex and Gender Identity Disorders

Sexual Dysfunctions

Sexual Desire Disorders
| 302.71 | Hypoactive Sexual Desire Disorder |
| 302.79 | Sexual Aversion Disorder |

Sexual Arousal Disorders
| 302.72 | Female Sexual Arousal Disorder |
| 302.72 | Male Erectile Disorder |

Orgasmic Disorders
| 302.73 | Female Orgasmic Disorder |

302.74   Male Orgasmic Disorder
302.75   Premature Ejaculation

Sexual Pain Disorders
302.76   Dyspareunia (Not Due to a General Medical Condition)
306.51   Vaginismus (Not Due to a General Medical Condition)

Sexual Dysfunction Due to a General Medical Condition
625.8   Female Hypoactive Sexual Desire Disorder Due to . . . [*Indicate the General Medical Condition*]
608.89   Male Hypoactive Sexual Desire Disorder Due to . . . [*Indicate the General Medical Condition*]
607.84   Male Erectile Disorder Due to . . . [*Indicate the General Medical Condition*]
625.0   Female Dyspareunia Due to . . . [*Indicate the General Medical Condition*]
608.89   Male Dyspareunia Due to . . . [*Indicate the General Medical Condition*]
625.8   Other Female Sexual Dysfunction Due to . . . [*Indicate the General Medical Condition*]
608.89   Other Male Sexual Dysfunction Due to . . . [*Indicate the General Medical Condition*]
——.—   Substance-Induced Sexual Dysfunction (*refer to Substance-Related Disorders for substance-specific codes*)
302.70   Sexual Dysfunction NOS

Paraphilias
302.4   Exhibitionism
302.81   Fetishism
302.89   Frotteurism
302.2   Pedophilia
302.83   Sexual Masochism
302.84   Sexual Sadism
302.3   Transvestic Fetishism
302.82   Voyeurism
302.9   Paraphilia NOS

Gender Identity Disorders
302.xx   Gender Identity Disorder
.6   In Children
.85   In Adolescents or Adults
302.6   Gender Identity Disorder NOS
302.9   Sexual Disorder NOS

Eating Disorders

307.1   Anorexia Nervosa
307.51   Bulimia Nervosa
307.50   Eating Disorder NOS

Sleep Disorders

Primary Sleep Disorders

Dyssomnias
307.42   Primary Insomnia
307.44   Primary Hypersomnia
347   Narcolepsy
780.59   Breathing-Related Sleep Disorder
307.45   Circadian Rhythm Sleep Disorder
307.47   Dyssomnia NOS

Parasomnias
307.47   Nightmare Disorder
307.46   Sleep Terror Disorder
307.46   Sleepwalking Disorder
307.47   Parasomnia NOS

Sleep Disorders Related to Another Mental Disorder
307.42   Insomnia Related to . . . [*Indicate the Axis I or Axis II Disorder*]
307.44   Hypersomnia Related to . . . [*Indicate the Axis I or Axis II Disorder*]

Other Sleep Disorders
780.xx   Sleep Disorder Due to . . . [*Indicate the General Medical Condition*]
.52   Insomnia Type
.54   Hypersomnia Type
.59   Parasomnia Type
.59   Mixed Type

——.—   Substance-Induced Sleep Disorder (*refer to Substance-Related Disorders for substance-specific codes*)

Impulse-Control Disorders Not Elsewhere Classified

312.34   Intermittent Explosive Disorder
312.32   Kleptomania
312.33   Pyromania
312.31   Pathological Gambling
312.39   Trichotillomania
312.30   Impulse-Control Disorder NOS

Adjustment Disorders

309.xx   Adjustment Disorder
.0   With Depressed Mood
.24   With Anxiety
.28   With Mixed Anxiety and Depressed Mood
.3   With Disturbance of Conduct
.4   With Mixed Disturbance of Emotions and Conduct
.9   Unspecified

Personality Disorders

Note: These are coded on Axis II.
301.0   Paranoid Personality Disorder
301.20   Schizoid Personality Disorder
301.22   Schizotypal Personality Disorder
301.7   Antisocial Personality Disorder
301.83   Borderline Personality Disorder
301.50   Histrionic Personality Disorder
301.81   Narcissistic Personality Disorder
301.82   Avoidant Personality Disorder
301.6   Dependent Personality Disorder
301.4   Obsessive-Compulsive Personality Disorder
301.9   Personality Disorder NOS

Other Conditions That May Be a Focus of Clinical Attention

Psychological Factors Affecting Medical Condition
316   . . . [*Specified Psychological Factor*] Affecting . . . [*Indicate the General Medical Condition*] Choose name based on nature of factors: Mental Disorder Affecting Medical Condition; Psychological Symptoms Affecting Medical Condition; Personality Traits or Coping Style Affecting Medical Condition; Maladaptive Health Behaviors Affecting Medical Condition; Stress-Related Physiological Response Affecting Medical Condition; Other or Unspecified Psychological Factors Affecting Medical Condition

Medication-Induced Movement Disorders
332.1   Neuroleptic-Induced Parkinsonism
333.92   Neuroleptic Malignant Syndrome
333.7   Neuroleptic-Induced Acute Dystonia
333.99   Neuroleptic-Induced Acute Akathisia
333.82   Neuroleptic-Induced Tardive Dyskinesia
333.1   Medication-Induced Postural Tremor
333.90   Medication-Induced Movement Disorder NOS

Medication-Induced Disorder
995.2   Adverse Effects of Medication NOS

Relational Problems
V61.9   Relational Problem Related to a Mental Disorder or General Medical Condition
V61.20   Parent-Child Relational Problem
V61.1   Partner Relational Problem
V61.8   Sibling Relational Problem
V62.81   Relational Problem NOS

Problems Related to Abuse or Neglect
V61.21   Physical Abuse of Child (*code 995.5 if focus of attention is on victim*)

V61.21   Sexual Abuse of Child (*code 995.5 if focus of attention is on victim*)

V61.21   Neglect of Child (*code 995.5 if focus of attention is on victim*)

V61.1   Physical Abuse of Adult (*code 995.81 if focus of attention is on victim*)

V61.1   Sexual Abuse of Adult (*code 995.81 if focus of attention is on victim*)

Additional Conditions That May Be a Focus of Clinical Attention

V15.81   Noncompliance With Treatment

V65.2   Malingering

V71.01   Adult Antisocial Behavior

V71.02   Child or Adolescent Antisocial Behavior

V62.89   Borderline Intellectual Functioning (*Note: This is coded on Axis II.*)

780.9   Age-Related Cognitive Decline

V62.82   Bereavement

V62.3   Academic Problem

V62.2   Occupational Problem

313.82   Identity Problem

V62.89   Religious or Spiritual Problem

V62.4   Acculturation Problem

V62.89   Phase of Life Problem

Additional Codes

300.9   Unspecified Mental Disorder (nonpsychotic)

V71.09   No Diagnosis or Condition on Axis I

799.9   Diagnosis or Condition Deferred on Axis I

V71.09   No Diagnosis on Axis II

799.9   Diagnosis Deferred on Axis II

Source: American Psychiatric Association, *Diagnostic and Statistical Manual of Mental Disorders* (4th ed.) (Washington, DC: American Psychiatric Association, 1994). Reprinted with permission.

Related Topics

Chapter 21, "Axis V: Global Assessment of Functioning (GAF) Scale"

Chapter 22, "Child and Adolescent Diagnosis With *DSM-IV*"

Chapter 23, "Clinical Assessment of Ethnic Minority Children Using the *DSM-IV*"

AXIS V

21 *Global Assessment of Functioning (GAF) Scale*

Consider psychological, social, and occupational functioning on a hypothetical continuum of mental health illness. Do not include impairment in functioning due to physical (or environmental) limitations.

Code

91–100 Superior functioning in a wide range of activities, life's problems never seem to get out of hand, is sought out by others because of his or her many positive qualities. No symptoms.

81–90 Absent or minimal symptoms (e.g., mild anxiety before an exam), good functioning in all areas, interested and involved in a wide range of activities, socially effective, generally satisfied with life, no more than everyday problems or concerns (e.g., an occasional argument with family members).

71–80 If symptoms are present, they are transient and expectable reactions to psychosocial stressors (e.g., difficulty concentrating after family argument); no more than slight impairment in social, occupational, or school functioning (e.g., temporarily falling behind in schoolwork).

61–70 Some mild symptoms (e.g., depressed mood and mild insomnia) or some difficulty in social, occupational, or school functioning (e.g., occasional truancy or theft within the household), but generally functioning pretty well, has some meaningful interpersonal relationships.

51–60 Moderate symptoms (e.g., flat affect and circumstantial speech, occasional panic attacks) or moderate difficulty in social, occupational, or school functioning (e.g., few friends, conflicts with peers or coworkers).

41–50 Serious symptoms (e.g., suicidal ideation, severe obsessional rituals, frequent shoplifting) or any serious impairment in social, occupational, or school functioning (e.g., no friends, unable to keep a job).

31–40 Some impairment in reality testing or communication (e.g., speech is at times illogical, obscure, or irrelevant) or major impairment in several areas, such as work or school, family relations, judgment, thinking, or mood (e.g., depressed man avoids friends, neglects family, and is unable to work; child frequently beats up younger children, is defiant at home, and is failing at school).

21–30 Behavior is considerably influenced by delusions or hallucinations or serious impairment in communication or judgment (e.g., sometimes incoherent, acts grossly inappropriate, suicidal preoccupation) or inability to function in almost all areas (e.g., stays in bed all day; no job, home, or friends).

11–20 Some danger of hurting self or others (e.g., suicide attempts without clear expectation of death, frequently violent, manic excitement) or occasionally fails to maintain minimal personal hygiene (e.g., smears feces) or gross impairment in communication (e.g., largely incoherent or mute).

1–10 Persistent danger of severely hurting self or others (e.g., recurrent violence) or persistent inability to maintain minimal personal hygiene or serious suicidal act with clear expectation of death.

0 Inadequate information.

Source: American Psychiatric Association, *Diagnostic and Statistical Manual of Mental Disorders* (4th ed.) (Washington, DC: American Psychiatric Association, 1994). Reprinted with permission.

Related Topics

Chapter 20, "*DSM-IV* Multiaxial System"
Chapter 22, "Child and Adolescent Diagnosis With *DSM-IV*"
Chapter 23, "Clinical Assessment of Ethnic Minority Children Using the *DSM-IV*"

22 CHILD AND ADOLESCENT DIAGNOSIS WITH *DSM-IV*

Stuart M. Goldman

The fourth edition of the *Diagnostic and Statistical Manual of Mental Disorders (DSM-IV)* follows the approach to diagnosis established by *DSM-III* and *DSM-IIIR* of an atheoretical, descriptive assessment based primarily on history. It provides a five-axis system of evaluation, each of which covers a different realm of information.

- Axis I refers to the majority of the primary psychiatric disorders.
- Axis II refers to personality disorders and mental retardation.
- Axis III covers general medical conditions.
- Axis IV provides a scale of psychosocial stressors from 1 (none) to 6 (catastrophic).
- Axis V details, utilizing the Global Assessment Scale of Functioning, the patient's level of functioning on a scale of 1 (worst) to 100 (best).

This multiaxial, multidimensional system enhances the clinician's capacity for assessment, planning, and prognosis. In addition to its clinical utility, it was designed to be interrater reliable, compatible with *ICD-9CM*, and consistent with and suitable for research studies.

In practice, most clinicians want a practical and succinct approach to arrive at a working *DSM-IV* diagnosis. It must include both childhood and general diagnosis, since almost all diagnoses are applicable to a child or adolescent population. To this end, we have developed an easy-to-use schema utilizing four questions to arrive rapidly at a working diagnosis, which then must be confirmed against the full *DSM* criteria.

1. Where is the problem primarily located?

If it is within the child (such as attention-deficit/hyperactivity disorder [ADHD]), continue with the next set of questions.

If it is not within the child, is it between the parent and the child? *V-codes.*

In the parent? Consider *adjustment disorders* for the child and a *primary diagnosis* for the parent.

Between the child and the school? Consider a *systems-based etiology* and intervention.

2. Is the problem reactive to an identifiable stressor or event?

No: Move on to Question 3.

Yes: The child has either an *adjustment disorder* or *posttraumatic stress disorder (PTSD)*.

Did the event include actual or threatened serious injury or death with intense affects?

No: Move on to *adjustment disorder.*

Yes: What has been the duration (Question 4)?

Less than 1 month? *Acute stress disorder.*

More than 1 month? Is there reexperiencing, avoidance, or numbing and increased arousal? Yes: *PTSD* (all three must be present).

No: *Adjustment disorder*, which is modified by the affected area (Question 3) to include disturbance of mood (anxiety, depression), conduct, or mixed.

3. What basic area or areas are affected?
As one gathers history, are the primary

symptoms behavioral, mood, body parts or functions, disconnection, multiple/pan, or externally induced? This refers to the predominant areas of concern as one is undertaking the diagnostic evaluation. Each area, when answered in the affirmative, leads to a short decision tree culminating in *DSM-IV* diagnosis. There may be more than one area of significant concern, leading to several diagnoses. When there are concerns in almost every area, the multiple/pan category should be considered first.

Behavioral disorders are characterized by either an inability or an unwillingness to behave and/or follow social or societal rules.

Does the child appear to deliberately misbehave?

Yes: Does he or she break societal rules (things that would lead to arrest in adults)? Likely *conduct disorder.*

Yes: Breaks mostly social rules (hard, unpleasant to manage or get along with)? Likely *oppositional defiant disorder.*

No: Is the child inattentive, hyperactive, or impulsive? Likely *ADHD.*

If the child is hyperactive, inattentive, impulsive, and deliberately misbehaves, likely both *ADHD* and either *oppositional defiant* or *conduct disorder.*

Mood disorders are characterized by a predominance of unpleasant or inappropriate moods and may include anxiety, depression, mania, irritability, or some combination. They must be sufficiently intense to cause some dysfunction. Each leads to a symptom-focused decision tree.

Which affect is primarily involved?

Anxiety?

Is the child anxious in almost all ways? *Generalized anxiety disorder.*

If specific, is it fear of being away from family/home? *Separation anxiety disorder.*

Fear or difficulty being in places? *Agoraphobia.*

Fear with multiple incapacitating somatic symptoms? *Panic attacks.*

Anxiety with unremitting worries or persistent useless behaviors? *Obsessive-compulsive disorder.*

Fear of a certain circumscribed thing? *Simple phobia* reflecting the specific item.

Depression (may present as sadness, irritability)?

Is this a clinically significant depression with dysphoria, isolation, boredom, or irritability?

No: Return to other categories.

Yes: What is the duration of symptoms?

Greater than 1 year, with disruption of functioning? Likely *dysthymic disorder.*

Greater than 2 weeks, with major somatic symptoms (sleep, weight, concentration) and/or suicidal elements (ideation, plan, attempts)? Likely *major depressive disorder.*

Elements of both? *Dysthymic and major depressive disorder.*

Have there been periods of elation, increased activity, racing thoughts, out-of-control actions?

No: *Unipolar major depression.*

Yes: Mild? Likely *cyclothymia.* Severe? *Manic-depressive disorder.*

Body part or function disorders are characterized by specific troubles in carrying out a daily bodily function or by complaints about a specific body part or parts.

Is there a body part or function that the clinical difficulties center upon?

No: Return to schema.

Yes: Name the part or dysfunction, and the disorder follows.

Does the trouble center on eating?

Too little: *Anorexia nervosa.*

Too much: *Bulimia nervosa.*

Not food: *Pica.*

Regurgitation: *Rumination disorder.*

Bowel or bladder problems (specify if never controlled [primary] versus regression [secondary])?

Bladder: *Enuresis.*

Bowel: *Encoporesis.*

Unwanted movements or sounds?

Less than a year? *Transient tic disorder.*

More than a year?

Muscles: *Motor tic.*

Sounds: *Vocal tic.*

Both: *Tourette's syndrome.*

Sleep problems?

Dramatic awakening with morning memories? *Nightmares.*

Dramatic awakening without morning memories? Likely *night terrors.*

Genitalia, gender complaints?

With complaints or confusion about physical parts, roles, and so on: *Gender identity dx.*

Complaints about other body parts?

One part not working: *Conversion disorder.*

Many things (13) not working: *Somatoform disorder.*

Parts working but very worried: *Hypochondriasis.*

Language trouble?

Input: *Receptive language.*

Output: *Expressive.*

Both: *Mixed.*

Decreased output but normal capability: *Selective mutism.*

Learning trouble?

Specific area? *Reading, writing, math.*

General cognition?

Mild to profound retardation on Axis II.

Disconnection disorders appear around a discontinuity in sense of self or in functioning that is not deliberate on the part of the patient. They are relatively uncommon and should raise the suspicion of abuse or maltreatment.

Many selves? *Multiple personality.*

Travel? (How did I get here? Where am I?) *Fugue disorder.*

Forgetting? *Amnestic disorder.*

Unreal? *Depersonalization disorder.*

Multiple or pan disorders present with major disruptions in all spheres of the patient's functioning, including school, home, peers, and self. Generally patients' impairments are quite obvious, even if their diagnosis is not.

Has the child's ability to interact with others been the major area of concern since early childhood?

No: Continue below.

Yes: Is language capacity mostly spared?

No: Likely *autism* (must consider other diagnoses, such as major language disorders).

Yes: Probably *Asperger's syndrome.*

Has the child been related but developed major dysfunctioning with odd or bizarre behaviors?

No: Continue below.

Yes: There is bizarre or odd behavior, but there is affective component. Probably *childhood schizophrenia.*

Yes: Is there a major ongoing component of depression or of elation, increased activity, or irritability?

Yes: Depression? Probably *major depressive disorder* (possibly with psychotic features).

Yes: Elation, activity, and so on, or a combination of depression and elation? *Manic-depressive disorder.*

Does the child have marked shifts in his or her level of functioning dependent upon the context?

No: Return to earlier on the decision tree.

Yes: Possibly *borderline character of childhood* Axis II (trouble with relationships, rage, identity concerns/confusion, self-destructive, all in a shifting framework of functioning).

Externally induced disorders are caused by an external substance such as alcohol, marijuana, tobacco, or cocaine. Each of these disorders is diagnosed by a significant involvement with the substance in question and then named accordingly. Although they are far more common in adolescents, they are seen in younger children as well. They are commonly seen as comorbid disorders with a wide range of other psychiatric diagnoses.

Is there substantial involvement with a substance?

> Yes: Give the child a *substance disorder* (naming the substance in question).

4. Are the symptoms in question longstanding and ego-syntonic? If yes, then consider the relevant Axis II diagnosis.

SUMMARY

The schema just described is designed to help clinicians in a time- and energy-sensitive manner to focus their diagnostic efforts and come to a probable *DSM-IV* diagnosis. Each diagnosis should be confirmed by applying the full *DSM-IV* criteria. The diagnosis must then be placed in the context of a multidimensional formulation to ensure that an optimal treatment plan is implemented.

References & Readings

American Psychiatric Association (1994). *Diagnostic and statistical manual of mental disorders* (4th ed.). Washington, DC: American Psychiatric Association.

Beitman, B., & Godried, M. (1989). The movement toward integration of the psychotherapies. *American Journal of Psychiatry, 146,* 138–147.

Goodman, A. (1991). Organic unity theory: The mind:body revisited. *American Journal of Psychiatry, 148,* 553–563.

Sperry, L., Gedeman, J., et al. (1992). *Psychiatric case formulations.* Washington, DC: American Psychiatric Association.

Weiner, J. M. (1997). Diagnostic classification in *DSM-IV*. In J. Weiner (Ed.), *Textbook of child and adolescent psychiatry.* Washington, DC: American Psychiatric Association.

23 CLINICAL ASSESSMENT OF ETHNIC MINORITY CHILDREN USING THE *DSM-IV*

Ronn Johnson

The *Diagnostic and Statistical Manual of Mental Disorders* (*DSM-IV*; American Psychiatric Association, 1994) is the primary clinical reference tool used in the psychodiagnostic process with children. It contains information relevant for making diagnoses across ethnoracial groups. Yet, while the inclusion of cultural factors within the *DSM-IV* is a noteworthy development in psychiatric nosology, it represents a somewhat tension-filled milestone. On one level, the more extensive coverage of culture within the *DSM-IV* than was the case in previous editions of the *Diagnostic and Statistical Manual* signals long-awaited recognition of the need to consider ethnoracial factors in the diagnostic process. The American Psychological Association has emphasized the relevance of culture by developing a set of guidelines for psychological practice with culturally diverse populations, for example, addressing the cultural issues in the "Ethical Principles of Psychologists and Code of Conduct" (APA, 1992). Attention to cultural issues is also a guiding principle in determining APA accreditation for all clinical, counseling, and school psychology training programs. In spite of such professional attention, there is still concern about how culture is being integrated into the diagnostic classification of mental illness.

The *DSM-IV's* cultural infusion occurs in a disjointed, uneven manner. Some argue that it is beyond the scope of the *DSM-IV* to completely establish the role of culture within the diagnostic process. Despite the lengthy debates that could occur in this area, it is important to recognize and examine three central issues related to the use of the *DSM-IV* with ethnic minority children:

1. Culture must be viewed as a relevant factor when diagnosing mental illness in children, but the *DSM-IV* does not provide enough guidance in how to integrate cultural influences with diagnostic questions.
2. The differences in the cultural competencies of clinicians working with ethnic minority children are often reflected in their diagnostic skills. While it is obvious that ethnoracial factors are important for clinical work, only within the past decade have they emerged as a significant topic within mainstream training programs.
3. Since cultural factors influence the way ethnic minority children present themselves (e.g., patterns of cultural characteristics associated with behavior or shared meanings), it is the objective of this article to introduce some of the cultural elements that are often relevant to the diagnosis of ethnic minority children.

The goal is to provide a starting place for clinicians as they perform diagnostic work using the *DSM-IV* with ethnic minority children. Because all ethnic groups cannot be considered here individually, some ethnoracial African American and Hispanic children will be used as illustrative examples, but it is hoped that the guidelines presented here will serve as a conceptual diagnostic framework when working with any ethnic minority children. It is important to recognize that cultural factors associated with African American and Hispanic children are different from those presented by children of other ethnic minority groups, and that the examples provided here do not exhaust the content base necessary for working effectively with African American and Hispanic children.

- By definition, culture generally refers to the meanings held by members of a particular group. This includes their worldview, beliefs, ethics, values, norms of conduct, and so forth. These meanings must be accounted for when formulating a diagnostic impression with ethnic minority children or the diagnosis will be invalid (Johnson, 1993).
- The clinician is the largest source of error in the reliability and validity of *DSM-IV* diagnosis with ethnic minority children. Three factors associated with that error are discussed below.
- The clinician must competently assess the child's level of acculturation and the child's transition distress from the home culture to another cultural experience. *Transition distress* refers to a child's reluctance or struggle to successfully move from one activity or setting to another. To do so, the clinician must (minimally) establish credibility (Sue & Sue, 1990) with the child as well as with the adult caretakers and must conduct an appropriate interview addressing these issues.
- The clinician must accept the client's language, socioeconomic status, and attitude toward mental health treatment as irrelevant to any psychopathology diagnosis that is to be established.
- The clinician must also remain supremely aware of his or her impact on the inter-

viewee. There is some indication that less obvious and unintentional discrimination by a clinician can affect the assessment data presented by ethnic minority patients.

- The use of assessment tools to measure acculturation should be considered.

- The clinician must collect a culturally relevant history that includes an assessment of the child's racial identity. An informed examination of all the cultural influences on the child's identity may not be readily observable by the clinician, and some issues of racial identity development may contribute to a negative reaction to the clinician by the child. One preferred method of determining a child's racial identity development involves studying the various racial identity models (e.g., Cross, 1991; Ponterotto, 1988). Unfortunately, this approach relies too heavily on the competencies the clinician brings to the diagnostic process.

- The more mainstream the clinician's own cultural identification, the more likely is the clinician to overlook certain salient cultural frameworks. In this case, cultural sensitivity is not synonymous with cross-cultural competency. Cross-cultural training and requisite supervision are highly recommended for the clinician involved with an ethnic minority child.

- Finally, the clinician's knowledge of ethnoracial oppression and rejection may offer a critical insight into the patient's response to the diagnostic process. For example, African Americans have historically been the targets of undesirable attributes or stereotypes (e.g., low intelligence, sexual prowess, criminal behaviors). African Americans also carry into the diagnostic process significant experiences of exploitation, discrimination, and generally bad treatment. Consequently, many children are taught by adult caretakers to be wary of their disclosures to mainstream clinicians. That is, part of the cultural will passed from generation to generation is aimed at protecting children from hostility.

It is only logical to presume those children's cultural expectations and experiences may cloud a clinician's ability to diagnose accurately, so knowledge of those expectations and experiences is critical. One way a mainstream clinician may learn more about ethnoracial oppression and rejection involves reading history and devoting part of the clinical interview to discussing the topic of racism experiences.

TREATMENT PLANNING

In a cautionary statement, the *DSM-IV* warns clinicians that the manual is not intended to encompass all mental health conditions. Unfortunately, there is no such warning that information available from the *DSM-IV* may be irrelevant for the development of treatment plans for ethnic minority children. Historically, the *DSM* has been ripe for ethnocentric criticisms. Many of its diagnostic criteria have limited cross-cultural utility, and diagnosis with the *DSM-IV* is too dependent on clinicians who are not adequately cross-culturally trained. In addition, tools or methods typically used to arrive at a *DSM* diagnosis for ethnic minority children are inappropriate (Berry, Poortinga, Segall, & Dasen, 1992).

Johnson (1993) points out the restricted clinical utility of certain diagnostic categories with these children (e.g., conduct disorder, oppositional disorder, and posttraumatic stress disorder). For example, there is an undesirable tendency for the *DSM-IV* to be overly inclusive (i.e., yield increased false-positive diagnoses). This characteristic is likely to produce a more damaging effect on ethnic minority children. For example, under conduct disorder the psychologist is strongly encouraged to consider a child's "reaction to the immediate social context." Despite this *DSM-IV* warning, some ethnic minority children displaying externalizing behaviors related to poverty or exposure to violence may be inappropriately labeled as having a conduct disorder. Anderson (1991) demonstrates that stress is underdiagnosed in some of these ethnoracial populations.

The most common mental disorders of childhood and adolescence listed in the *DSM-IV* include adjustment disorders, behavior disorders, attention-deficit/hyperactivity disorder, oppositional defiant disorder, conduct disorder, depressive disorders, anxiety disorders, substance-related disorders, and eating disorders.

One of the strengths of the *DSM-IV* is the fact that it is empirically based. It was developed in conjunction with the World Health Organization's publication of the 10th edition of the *International Classification of Diseases (ICD-10)*. It is at least minimally sensitive to culturally relevant issues and represents a considerable improvement over the *DSM-III-R* in terms of cultural factors. Cultural considerations are now mentioned in a significant manner, in contrast to the scant allusion made to culture in the introductory sections of the *DSM-III-R*. In the *DSM-IV* the criteria for many disorders are accompanied by descriptive sections on culture, age, and gender, reflecting an understanding of mental disorders in a context broader than their symptoms.

Extending this thinking, the clinician can take the following steps to use the *DSM-IV* more effectively with ethnic minority children:

1. Clinicians should become as familiar as possible with the sections that specifically address childhood diagnostic issues. The *DSM-IV*'s classification of disorders usually diagnosed in infancy, childhood, and adolescence is based on empirical findings and is developmentally relevant. For example, mental retardation, attention-deficit/hyperactivity disorder to stereotypic movement disorder, and other childhood-onset disorders may occur within the context of poverty, racial trauma, generational differences, immigration stress, and acculturation (Johnson, 1993), though they are not caused by cultural factors.

2. Clinicians must recognize that cultural conditions can have an impact on the presentation of these disorders. For example, an African American foster child was diagnosed as having oppositional defiant disorder, but it was never disclosed that he had experienced several episodes on a school bus in which he was racially taunted by other riders.

3. Understanding of acculturation problems is key when an ethnic minority child comes to the attention of the psychologist. Acculturation reflects the extent to which ethnic minority children completely release, modify, and retain aspects of both their home environment and the mainstream culture (Locke, 1992). Acculturation may occur in at least two ways. External acculturation may be assessed through behavioral patterns (e.g., dress, language use). Internal acculturation involves the extent to which children articulate their experiences according to the home culture versus the more mainstream culture. There may in fact be no reportable difference. In this case, the child may feel less compelled to display a prescribed set of behaviors just to accommodate to the mainstream. On the other hand, some children feel a need to display different sets of behavior due to some discomfort or other reasons. Diagnostically, the way the child presents under either of these conditions influences the clinical picture as assessed by the psychologist.

4. The clinician should also recognize that diagnostically relevant behaviors might be cloaked by the stage of racial identity development. This may be important with biracial children who can have a more dichotomous racial identity. Some empirical evidence suggests that biracial children move through racial identity development in different ways than children from more racially homogeneous backgrounds.

5. The *DSM-IV*'s 10 appendixes should be utilized fully. While Appendix I's outline for cultural formulation and glossary of culture-bound syndromes examination appear most relevant to the issues being addressed here, each appendix has the potential to influence the effective use of the *DSM-IV* with ethnic minority children. These appendixes require the clinician to take a proactive stance in viewing culture as a factor in the diagnostic process.

For example, Appendix A presents decision trees for six diagnostic categories. The decision tree framework allows the culturally skilled clinician to inject culturally relevant questions at appropriate decision points before arriving at a diagnosis. One of the question points for clarifying an anxiety diagnosis, for instance, regards anxiety concerning attachment figures with the onset in childhood. Some Hispanic girls are brought up to rely on and value a close-knit family. In their case, it is culturally appropriate to experience some distress when placed in situations away from the immediate family (e.g., distant sleep-over or leaving home to attend college). The culturally informed clinician will question whether the distress represents a true anxiety disorder or more simply a culturally appropriate response to separation. Appendix I describes cultural influences on pathology and defines culturally based syndromes. It also presents cultural issues salient to diagnosis (e.g., cultural identity, cultural explanations of the individual's illness) and encourages the clinician to generate narrative summaries for these same categories. The brevity of this section might erroneously lead some clinicians to believe there is little to know regarding cultural issues, but the intent of this appendix is clearly the opposite. It makes passing mention of indigenous clinicians' capability of formulating their own diagnostic systems for some of the more commonly occurring North American idioms of distress (e.g., anorexia nervosa, dissociative disorders). Johnson (1993) has shown that some single-entity disorders (e.g., posttraumatic stress disorder) may be sorted into several subcategories, such as racial trauma or racial encounter distress disorder. Other extensions of Appendix I include consideration of certain ethnoracial factors such as cultural will in assigning a global adaptive functioning rating on Axis V.

The *DSM-IV*'s attempt to be culturally appropriate makes it reasonably responsive to practical clinical issues while allowing room for culturally competent practice. This article was guided by the belief that cultural patterns affect the presentation of psychopathology and the diagnostic process. A culturally relevant diagnosis is at the heart of effective therapeutic interventions and outcome assessment. Communication between clinicians is enhanced when

practitioners can share treatment information that includes cultural nuances.

A culturally competent clinician needs to identify clearly the subtle interactions between the child, the clinician, and the *DSM-IV* in order to yield the most useful clinical assessment. It is worth noting that some practitioners have misgivings or serious doubts about the presumptions within the *DSM-IV*. Others might argue the need to extend the *DSM-IV* axes to include identification of cultural and gender factors. Here, the clinician is challenged to more fully understand the behavior of children from diverse backgrounds.

References & Readings

American Psychiatric Association (1987). *Diagnostic and statistical manual of mental disorders* (3rd ed., rev.). Washington, DC: American Psychiatric Association.

American Psychiatric Association (1994). *Diagnostic and statistical manual of mental disorders* (4th ed.). Washington, DC: American Psychiatric Association.

American Psychological Association (1992). Ethical principles of psychologists and code of conduct. *American Psychologist, 47,* 1597–1611.

Anderson, L. P. (1991). Acculturative stress: A theory of relevance to Black Americans. *Clinical Psychology Review, 11,* 685–702.

Berry, J. W., Poortinga, Y. H., Segall, M. H., & Dasen, P. R. (1992). *Cross-cultural psychology: Research and applications.* Cambridge, England: Cambridge University Press.

Cross, W. E. (1991). *Shades of Black: Diversity in African-American identity.* Philadelphia: Temple University Press.

Hardiman, R. (1982). *White identity development: A process oriented model for describing the racial conscious of White Americans.* Unpublished doctoral dissertation, University of Massachusetts, Amherst.

Helms, J. E. (1984). Toward a theoretical explanation of the effects of race on counseling: A Black and White model. *Counseling Psychologist, 12,* 153–165.

Johnson, R. (1993). Clinical issues in the use of the *DSM-III-R* with African American children: A diagnostic paradigm. *Journal of Black Psychology, 19,* 447–460.

Locke, D. C. (1992). *Increasing multi cultural un-*

derstanding.: A comprehensive model. Newbury Park, CA: Sage.

Ponterotto, J. G. (1988). Racial consciousness development among White counselor trainees: A
stage model. Journal of Multicultural Counseling and Development, 16, 146–156.

Sue, D. W., & Sue, D. (1990). Counseling the culturally different: Theory and practice (2nd ed.).
New York: Wiley.

World Health Organization (1992). International classification of diseases and related health problems
(10th ed.). Geneva: World Health Organization.

Related Topics

Chapter 18, "Interviewing Parents"
Chapter 19, "Medical Evaluation of Children With
    Behavioral or Developmental Disorders"
Chapter 22, "Child and Adolescent Diagnosis With
    DSM-IV"

24 NORMAL MEDICAL LABORATORY VALUES AND MEASUREMENT CONVERSIONS

Gerald P. Koocher & Samuel Z. Goldhaber

Although conversion data provided here are fairly standard, it is important to note that normal biological and chemical values differ across hospitals and laboratories as a function of the methods, reagents, and equipment used. The data presented here represent an overview from several sources and should not be regarded as absolute. When interpreting specific results, contact personnel at the lab in question to ascertain their normal ranges for the test in question.

TABLE 1. Temperature Conversions: Fahrenheit = ⅝ (Centigrade) + 32; Centigrade = ⅝ (Fahrenheit − 32)

Fahrenheit	Centigrade
95.0	35.0
96.8	36.0
98.6	37.0
100.0	37.8
100.4	38.0
101.0	38.3
102.0	38.9
102.2	39.0
103.0	39.4
104.0	40.0

TABLE 2. Units of Measurement Conversions

1 kg = 2.204 lb
22 lb = 10 kg
1 lb = 16 oz = 0.454 kg or 454 g
1 oz = 29.57 ml
1 tsp = 5 ml
1 tbsp = 15 ml
1 in = 2.54 cm
1 cm = 0.394 in
1 ft = 30.48 cm
1 yd = 91.44 cm
1 m = 1.093 yd
1 m = 3.28 ft
1 mile = 1669.3 m
1 km = 1093.6 yd

TABLE 3. Prefixes Denoting Decimal Factors

Prefix	Factor	Prefix	Factor
mega	10^6	milli	10^{-3}
kilo	10^3	micro	10^{-6}
hecto	10^2	nano	10^{-9}
deka	10^1	pico	10^{-12}
deci	10^{-1}	femto	10^{-15}
centi	10^{-2}		

TABLE 4. Normal Lab Values

Chemistries	Adult Values	Pediatric Values		
Sodium	134–146 mEq/L	Term, 132–142 mEq/L		
		Child, 135–146 mEq/L		
Potassium	3.5–5.1 mEq/L	Term, 3.8–6.1 mEq/L		
		> 1 month, 3.5–5.1 mEq/L		
Chloride	92–109 mEq/L	95–108 mEq/L		
Bicarbonate	24–31 mEq/L			
BUN (blood urea nitrogen)	8–25 mg/dl	5–25 mg/dl		
Creatinine	< 1.5 mg/dl	0.7–1.7 mg/dl		
Glucose	55–115 mg/dl	Term, 32–100 mg/dl		
		> 2 weeks, 60–110 mg/dl		
Calcium	8.0–10.5 mg/dl	Term, 7.2–12.0 mg/dl		
		> 1 year, 7.8–11.0 mg/dl		
Phosphorus	2.6–4.6 mg/dl			
Uric acid	2.4–7.5 mg/dl	3.0–7.0 mg/dl		
Total protein	5.6–8.4 g/dl			
Albumin	3.4–5.4 g/dl	3.8–5.6 g/dl		
Total bilirubin	0.2–1.5 mg/dl	Total Bilirubin	Premature	Term
		1 day	< 8–9	<6
		2 days	<12	<9
		1 week	<15	<10
		2–4 weeks	<10–12	<6
Direct bilirubin	0.0–0.3 mg/dl	< 0.2 mg/dl		
SGOT, AST (serum glutamic oxaloacetate, aminotransferase)	0–40 U/L	Term, 25–125 U/L		
		Infant, 20–60 U/L		
		Child, 10–40 U/L		
SGPT, ALT (alanine aminotransferase, serum glutamic pyruvate transaminase)	0–40 U/L			
LDH (lactic dehydrogenase)	50–240 U/L	Term, 150–600 U/L		
		< 1 year, 140–350 U/L		
		Child, 140–280 U/L		
CK (creatine kinase)	5–200 U/L			
CK MB (CK-myocardial band)	< 3–5%			
Cholesterol	< 200 mg/dl			
LDL cholesterol (low-density lipoprotein)	< 130 mg/dl			
HDL cholesterol (high-density lipoprotein)	> 35–40 mg/dl			
Triglycerides	30–135 mg/dl			
Amylase	60–180 U/L			
Lipase	4–25 U/L			
Magnesium	1.6–3.0 mg/dl	1.5–2.1 mg/dl		

(continued)

TABLE 4. Normal Lab Values (*continued*)

Chemistries	Adult Values	Pediatric Values
GGTP (gamma-glutamyl transpeptidase)	10–50 U/L	
PSA (prostate-specific antigen)	< 4.0 ng/ml	
Osmolarity	274–296 mOsm/kg	274–296 mOsm/kg
Iron	50–160 µg/dl	
TIBC (total iron-binding capacity)	240–425 µg/dl	
Iron % sat	20–55%	
Ferritin	30–250 ng/ml	
Anion gap	8–12 mEq/L	10–14 mEq/L
Vitamin B_{12}	200–1,000 pg/ml	
Folate	5–12 ng/ml	
Ammonia	< 45 µg/dl	
Lactate	4–16 mg/dl	
Aluminum	4–10 µg/L	
Copper	90–200 µg/dl	
Zinc	50–150 µg/dl	50–160 µg/dl
APF (alpha-fetoprotein)	< 25 ng/ml	
CEA (carcinoembryonic antigen)	< 2.5 ng/ml	
CEA, smoker	< 5.0 ng/ml	

Hematology

Hgb (hemoglobin)	Males, 14–18 g/dl	
	Females, 12–16 g/dl	
		Term, 13–20 g/dl
		1–4 days, 14–22 g/dl
		2 weeks, 13–20 g/dl
		1 month, 11–18 g/dl
		2 months, 10–15 g/dl
		6 months, 10–14 g/dl
		1 year, 10–13 g/dl
		2–8 years, 11–14 g/dl
Hematocrit	Males, 40–52%	
	Females, 37–47%	
		Term, 40–58%
		1–4 days, 45–60%
		2 weeks, 40–58%
		1 month, 32–54%
		2 months, 28–44%
		6 months, 30–42%
		1 year, 32–40%
		2–8 years, 33–40%
RBC (red blood cell [density])	Males, $4.8–6.0 \times 10^6/mm^3$	
	Females, $4.1–5.5 \times 10^6/mm^3$	
MCV (mean corpuscular volume)	Males, 80–90 fl	
	Females, 80–100 fl	
MCH (mean corpuscular hemoglobin)	27–32 pg	
MCHC (mean corpuscular hemoglobin concentration)	32–36%	
Hgb A_{1c} (hemoglobin A_{1c})	3–5%	
WBC (white blood cells)	5,000–10,000/µl	Term, 8–30 $(10^3/mm^3)$
		1–3 days, 9–32 $(10^3/mm^3)$
		2–4 weeks, 4–20 $(10^3/mm^3)$
		2 months, 5–20 $(10^3/mm^3)$
		6 months, 6–18 $(10^3/mm^3)$

TABLE 4. Normal Lab Values (*continued*)

Chemistries	Adult Values	Pediatric Values
		1 year, 5–18 ($10^3/mm^3$)
		2–8 years, 5–15 ($10^3/mm^3$)
Segs	40–60%	
Bands	0–5%	
Lymph	20–40%	
Mono	4–8%	
Eos	1–3%	
Baso	0–1%	
Platelets	150–400 × $10^3/\mu l$	150–357 × $10^3/\mu l$
Haptoglobin	100–250 mg/dl	
ESR (eosinophil sed rate)	Males, < 10 mm/hr	
	Females, < 20 mm/hr	
Retic Count	0.5–2.0%	Term, 3–8%
		2 days, 2–4%
		1 month, 0.3–1.6%
		6 years, 0.5–1.3%
PT (prothrombin time)	11–13 s	11–14 s
PTT (partial prothrombin time)	25–35 s	21–35 s
Bleeding time	< 5–6 min	
Thrombin time	10–14 s	
Fibrinogen	200–400 mg/dl	150–375 mg/dl
Lymphocyte (differential)		
Total T, CD3	60–87%	
Total T/mm³	630–3,170	
B cell	1–25%	
Suppr, CD8	10–40%	
Suppr/mm³	240–1,200	
Helper, CD4	30–50%	
Helper/mm³	390–1,770	
H:S, CD4/CD8	0.8–3.0	

ABGs (arterial blood gasses)

pH	7.35–7.45	Birth, 7.32–7.45
		1 day, 7.27–7.44
		2 days, 7.36–7.44
		1 month, 7.35–7.45
$PaCO_2$	35–45 mmHg	Birth, 25–45 mmHg
		> 2 months, 30–45 mmHg
PaO_2	80–100 mmHg	Birth, 65–80 mmHg
		Infant, 70–100 mmHg
		Child, 85–105 mmHg
HCO_3	22–28 mEq/L	
O_2, saturation, artery	95–98%	
O_2, saturation, vein	60–85%	

Endocrinology

T4 RIA (thyroxine radioiodine uptake)	5.0–12.0 μg/dl	
T3 uptake (thyrotropin)	22–36%	
Free T4 (thyroxine)	0.8–2.2 ng/dl	
T3 (thyrotropin)	75–200 ng/dl	
TSH (thyroid-stimulating hormone)	0.3–5.0 μIU/ml	
Aldosterone, supine	3–12 ng/dl	
Aldosterone, upright	5–25 ng/dl	

(*continued*)

TABLE 4. Normal Lab Values (*continued*)

Chemistries	Adult Values	Pediatric Values
Calcitonin	< 75 pg/ml	
Cortisol	6–24 μg/dl, A.M.	
	2–10 μg/dl, P.M.	
Gastrin	0–200 pg/ml	
Growth hormone	1–10 ng/ml	
Pepsinogen	25–100 mg/ml	
Prolactin	Males, 0–5 ng/ml	
	Females, 0–20 ng/ml	
PTH (parathyroid homone)	10–60 pg/ml	
BHCG (beta human chorionic		
gonadotropin, nonpregnant)	< 5 mlU/ml	
0–2 weeks	0–250 mlU/ml	
2–4 weeks	100–5,000 mlU/ml	
1–2 months	4,000–200,000 mlU/ml	
2–3 months	8,000–100,000 mlU/ml	
2nd trimester	4,000–75,000 mlU/ml	
3rd trimester	1,000–50,000 mlU/ml	

Urine

Albumin	20–100 mg/day	
Amylase	< 20 U/hr	
Calcium	< 300 mg/day	
Creatinine	0.75–1.5 g/day	
Creatinine clearance	80–140 ml/min	
Glucose	< 300 mg/day	
Osmolarity	250–1,000 mOsm/L	
Phosphorous	0.5–1.3 g/day	
Potassium	25–115 mEq/day	
Protein	10–200 mg/day	
Sodium	50–250 mEq/day	
Total volume	720–1,800 ml/day	
Urea nitrogen	10–20 g/day	
Uric acid	50–700 mg/day	
Specific gravity	1.002–1.030	

Cerebral spinal fluid

Protein	10–45 mg/dl	Preterm, 60–150 mg/dl
		Newborn, 20–170 mg/dl
		> 1 year, 5–45 mg/dl
Glucose	40–80 mg/dl	Preterm, 24–75 mg/dl
		Newborn, 34–119 mg/dl
		> 1 year, 40–80 mg/dl
Pressure	60–180 mmH$_2$O	Newborn, 70–120 mmH$_2$O
		Child, 70–180 mmH$_2$O
Leukocytes, total	< 5/mm^3	
Leukocites, differential		
Lymph	60–75%	
Mono	25–50%	
Neutro	1–3%	
Cell count	0–5 lymphs/HPF	Preterm, 0–25 WBC/mm^3; < 35% polys
		Newborn, 0–25 WBC/mm^3; < 35% polys
		> 2–4 weeks, 0–5 WBC/mm^3; 0% polys

Toxicology

Ethanol		
Normal	< 0.005% (5 mg/dl)	

TABLE 4. Normal Lab Values (*continued*)

Chemistries	Adult Values	Pediatric Values
Intoxicated	0.1–0.4%	
Stuporous	0.4–0.5%	
Coma	> 0.5%	
Mercury, urine	< 100 µg/24 hr, normal	
CoHgb (carbon monoxide hemoglobin)		
Nonsmokers	0–2.5%	
Smokers	2–5%	
Toxic	>20%	
Lead	0–40 µg/dl, normal	< 10 ug/dl
Lead, urine	< 100 µg/24 hr, normal	

TABLE 5. Pediatric Normal Values (Subject to Individual Patient's Circumstances)

Values	Preterm	Term	3 Months	6 Months	9 Months	1 Year	1–1.5 Years	2 Years
Weight in kilograms	< 3	3–4	5–6	7	8–9	10	11	12
Pulse rate	130–160	120–150	120–140	120–140	120–140	120–140	110–135	110–130
Blood pressure (systolic)	45–60	60–70	60–100	65–120	70–120	70–120	70–125	75–125
Respiratory rate	40–60	30–60	30–50	25–35	23–33	20–30	20–30	20–28

TABLE 5. Pediatric Normal Values (*continued*)

Values	3 Years	4 Years	5 Years	6 Years	8 Years	10 Years	12 Years	14 Years
Weight in kilograms	14–15	16–17	18	20	24–25	30–32	40	45
Pulse rate	100–120	95–115	90–110	90–110	80–100	75–95	70–90	60–90
Blood pressure (systolic)	75–125	80–125	80–125	85–120	90–120	90–125	95–130	110–130
Respiratory rate	20–28	20–28	20–25	20–25	16–24	16–24	16–24	15–20

References & Readings

Barkin, R. M. (Ed.) (1992). *Pediatric emergency medicine: Concepts and clinical practice.* St. Louis: Mosby.

Bennett, J. C., & Plum, F. (1996). *Cecil textbook of medicine.* Philadelphia: Saunders.

Henry, J. B. (1991). *Clinical diagnosis and management by laboratory methods.* Philadelphia: Saunders.

Hoekelman, R. A., Friedman, S. B., Nelson, N. M., Seidel, H. M., Weitzman, M. D. (Eds.) (1997). *Primary pediatric care.* St. Louis: Mosby.

Isselbacher, K. J., Braunwald, E., Wilson, J. D., Martin, J. B., Fauci, A. S., & Kasper, D. L. (Eds.) (1994). *Harrison's principles of internal medicine.* New York: McGraw-Hill.

Lee, G. R., Bithell, T. C., Foerster, J., Athens, J. W., & Lukens, J. N. (1993). *Wintrobe's clinical hematology.* Malverne, PA: Lea and Febiger.

Stein, J. H. (Ed.) (1990). *Internal medicine.* Boston: Little, Brown.

Related Topics

PART II
Psychological Testing

25 CLINICAL SCALES OF THE MMPI-2

John R. Graham

This chapter summarizes each Minnesota Multiphasic Personality Inventory-2 (MMPI-2) clinical scale in terms of the dimensions assessed by the scale. Descriptive material on persons who have particularly high or low scale scores is given in chapter 28. Summary information is based on previously reported data for the clinical scales of the original MMPI and consideration of new data concerning extra-test correlates of the MMPI-2 clinical scales, which are basically the same as in the original MMPI. A few items were deleted from the original test as outdated or because the content was deemed objectionable (e.g., those having to do with religious beliefs or bowel and bladder function). Other items were modified slightly to modernize them, eliminate sexist references, or improve readability.

SCALE 1 (HYPOCHONDRIASIS)

- Scale 1 originally was developed to identify patients manifesting symptoms associated with hypochondriasis. The syndrome is characterized by preoccupation with the body and concomitant fears of illness and disease. Although such fears usually are not delusional in nature, they tend to be quite persistent. One item was deleted because of objectionable content, reducing Scale 1 from 33 items in the original MMPI to 32 items in the MMPI-2.

- Scale 1 seems to be the most homogeneous and unidimensional in the MMPI-2. All the items deal with somatic concerns or with general physical competence. Factor analysis indicates that much of the variance in Scale 1 is accounted for by a single factor, characterized by the denial of good health and reporting a variety of somatic symptoms. Patients with bona fide physical problems typically show somewhat elevated T scores on Scale 1 (approximately 60). Elderly individuals tend to produce Scale 1 scores that are slightly more elevated than those of adults in general, probably reflecting declining health associated with aging.

SCALE 2 (DEPRESSION)

- Scale 2 originally was developed to assess symptomatic depression. The primary characteristics of depression are poor morale, lack of hope in the future, and a general dissatisfaction with one's life situation. Of the 60 items originally in Scale 2, a total of 57 were retained in the MMPI-2. Many of the items in the scale deal with aspects of depression such as denial of happiness and personal worth, psychomotor retardation, withdrawal, and lack of interest in one's surroundings. Other items in the scale cover a variety of symptoms and behaviors, including somatic complaints, worry or tension, denial of hostile impulses, and difficulty in controlling one's own thought processes.

- Scale 2 is an excellent index of people's discomfort and dissatisfaction with their life situations. Whereas highly elevated scores on this scale suggest clinical depression, more moderate scores tend to be indicative of a general attitude or lifestyle characterized by poor morale and lack of involvement.

- Scale 2 scores are related to age, with elderly persons scoring approximately 5–10 T-score points higher than the mean for the total MMPI-2 normative sample. Some individuals who have recently been hospitalized or incarcerated tend to show moderate elevations on Scale 2 that reflect dissatisfaction with current circumstances rather than clinical depression.

SCALE 3 (HYSTERIA)

- This scale was developed to identify patients who were utilizing hysterical reactions to stress situations. The hysterical syndrome is characterized by involuntary psychogenic loss or disorder of function.

- All 60 items in the original version of Scale 3 were retained in MMPI-2. Some of the items deal with a general denial of physical health and a variety of rather specific somatic complaints, including heart or chest pain, nausea and vomiting, fitful sleep, and headaches.

Another group of items involves a general denial of psychological or emotional problems and of discomfort in social situations. Although these two clusters of items are reasonably independent in normal people, those utilizing hysterical defenses seem to score high on both clusters.

- Scale 3 scores are related to intellectual ability, with brighter persons scoring higher. In addition, high raw scores are much more common among women than among men in both normal and psychiatric populations.

- It is important to take into account the level of scores on Scale 3. Whereas marked elevations (T > 80) suggest a pathological condition characterized by classical hysterical symptoms, moderate levels are associated with characteristics that are consistent with hysterical disorders but do not include the classical hysterical symptoms. As with Scale 1, patients with bona fide medical problems for whom there is no indication of psychological components to the conditions tend to obtain T scores of about 60 on this scale.

SCALE 4 (PSYCHOPATHIC DEVIATE)

- Scale 4 was developed to identify patients diagnosed as having a psychopathic personality, asocial or amoral type. Whereas persons in the original criterion group were characterized in their everyday behavior by such delinquent acts as lying, stealing, sexual promiscuity, excessive drinking, and the like, no major criminal types were included. All 50 of the items in the original scale were maintained in MMPI-2. The items cover a wide array of topics, including absence of satisfaction in life, family problems, delinquency, sexual problems, and difficulties with authorities. Interestingly, the keyed responses include both admissions of social maladjustment and assertions of social poise and confidence.

- Scores on Scale 4 tend to be related to age, with younger people scoring slightly higher than older people. In the MMPI-2 normative samples, Whites and Asian Americans scored somewhat lower on Scale 4 (5–10 T-score points) than did African Americans, Native Americans, and Hispanics.

- One way of conceptualizing what Scale 4 assesses is to think of it as a measure of rebelliousness, with higher scores indicating rebellion and lower scores indicating acceptance of authority and the status quo. The highest scorers on the scale rebel by acting out in antisocial and criminal ways; moderately high scorers may be rebellious but may express the rebellion in more socially acceptable ways; and low scorers are apt to be overly conventional and accepting of authority.

SCALE 5 (MASCULINITY-FEMININITY)

- Scale 5 originally was developed by Hathaway and McKinley to identify homosexual invert males. The test authors identified only a very small number of items that differentiated homosexual from heterosexual men. Thus, items were added to the scale if they differentiated between normal men and women in the standardization sample. Items from an earlier interest test were also added to the scale. Although Hathaway and McKinley considered this scale preliminary, it has come to be used routinely in its original form.
- The test authors attempted, without success, to develop a corresponding scale for identifying "sexual inversion" in women. As a result, Scale 5 has been used for both men and women. Fifty-two of the items are keyed in the same direction for both genders, whereas 4 items, all dealing with frankly sexual content, are keyed in opposite directions for men and women. After obtaining raw scores, T-score conversions are reversed for the sexes so that a high raw score for men automatically is transformed by means of the profile sheet itself into a high T score, whereas a high raw score for women is transformed into a low T score. The result is that high T scores for both genders are indicative of deviation from one's own gender.
- In the MMPI-2, 56 of the 60 items in the

original Scale 5 were maintained. Although a few of the items in Scale 5 have clear sexual content, most items are not sexual in nature, instead covering a diversity of topics, including work and recreational interests, worries and fears, excessive sensitivity, and family relationships.

- Although MMPI Scale 5 scores were strongly related to the individual's amount of formal education, the relationship is much more modest in the MMPI-2. More highly educated men tend to obtain slightly higher Scale 5 T scores than do less educated men. More highly educated women tend to obtain slightly lower Scale 5 T scores than do less educated women. These differences probably reflect the broader interest patterns of more educated men and women and are not large enough to necessitate different Scale 5 interpretations for persons with differing levels of education.

SCALE 6 (PARANOIA)

- Scale 6 originally was developed to identify patients who were judged to have paranoid symptoms such as ideas of reference, feelings of persecution, grandiose self-concepts, suspiciousness, excessive sensitivity, and rigid opinions and attitudes. Although the scale was considered preliminary because of problems in cross-validation, it was retained because it produced relatively few false positives. Persons who score high on this scale usually have paranoid symptoms. However, some patients with clearly paranoid symptoms are able to achieve average scores on Scale 6.
- All 40 of the items in the original scale were maintained in the MMPI-2. Although some of the items in the scale deal with frankly psychotic behaviors (e.g., excessive suspiciousness, ideas of reference, delusions of persecution, grandiosity), many items cover such diverse topics as sensitivity, cynicism, asocial behavior, excessive moral virtue, and complaints about other people. It is possible to obtain a T score greater than 65 on this

scale without endorsing any of the clearly psychotic items.

SCALE 7 (PSYCHASTHENIA)

- Scale 7 originally was developed to measure the general symptomatic pattern labeled *psychasthenia*. Although this diagnostic label is not used commonly today, it was popular when the scale was developed. Among currently popular diagnostic categories, the obsessive-compulsive disorder probably is closest to the original meaning of the psychasthenia label. Such persons have thinking characterized by excessive doubts, compulsions, obsessions, and unreasonable fears. This symptom pattern was much more common among outpatients than among hospitalized patients, so the number of cases available for scale construction was small.
- All 48 items in the original scale were maintained in the MMPI-2. They cover a variety of symptoms and behaviors. Many of the items deal with uncontrollable or obsessive thoughts, feelings of fear and/or anxiety, and doubts about one's own ability. Unhappiness, physical complaints, and difficulties in concentration also are represented in the scale.

SCALE 8 (SCHIZOPHRENIA)

- Scale 8 was developed to identify patients diagnosed as schizophrenic. This category included a heterogeneous group of disorders characterized by disturbances of thinking, mood, and behavior. Misinterpretations of reality, delusions, and hallucinations may be present. Ambivalent or constricted emotional responsiveness is common. Behavior may be withdrawn, aggressive, or bizarre.
- All 78 of the items in the original scale were maintained in the MMPI-2. Some of the items deal with such frankly psychotic symptoms as bizarre mentation, peculiarities of perception, delusions of persecution, and hallucinations. Other topics covered include social alienation, poor family relationships, sexual concerns, difficulties in impulse control and concentration, and fears, worries, and dissatisfactions.
- Scores on Scale 8 are related to age and race. College students often obtain T scores in a range of 50–60, perhaps reflecting the developmental turmoil associated with that period in life. African Americans, Native Americans, and Hispanics in the MMPI-2 normative sample scored higher (approximately 10 T-score points) than Whites. The elevated scores for members of ethnic minority groups do not necessarily suggest greater psychopathology. They may simply be indicative of the feelings of alienation and social estrangement sometimes experienced by minority group members.
- Some elevations of Scale 8 can be accounted for by persons who are reporting a large number of unusual experiences, feelings, and perceptions related to the use of prescription and nonprescription drugs, especially amphetamines. Also, some persons with disorders such as epilepsy, stroke, or closed-head injury endorse sensory and cognitive items, leading to high scores on Scale 8.

SCALE 9 (HYPOMANIA)

- Scale 9 originally was developed to identify psychiatric patients manifesting hypomanic symptoms. Hypomania is characterized by elevated mood, accelerated speech and motor activity, irritability, flight of ideas, and brief periods of depression.
- All 46 items in the original scale were maintained in the MMPI-2. Some of the items deal specifically with features of hypomanic disturbance (e.g., activity level, excitability, irritability, grandiosity). Other items cover topics such as family relationships, moral values and attitudes, and physical or bodily concerns. No single dimension accounts for much of the variance in scores, and most of the sources of variance represented in the scale are not duplicated in other clinical scales.

- Scores on Scale 9 are related to age and race. Younger people (e.g., college students) typically obtain scores in a T-score range of 50–60. For elderly people, Scale 9 T scores below 50 are common. African Americans, Native Americans, and Hispanics in the MMPI-2 normative samples scored somewhat higher (5–10 T-score points) than Whites.
- Scale 9 can be viewed as a measure of psychological and physical energy, with high scorers having excessive energy. When Scale 9 scores are high, one expects that characteristics suggested by other aspects of the profile will be acted out. For example, high scores on Scale 4 suggest asocial or antisocial tendencies. If Scale 9 is elevated along with Scale 4, these tendencies are more likely to be expressed overtly in behavior.

SCALE 0 (SOCIAL INTROVERSION)

- Scale 0 was designed to assess a person's tendency to withdraw from social contacts and responsibilities. Items were selected by contrasting high and low scorers on the Social Introversion-Extroversion Scale of the Minnesota T-S-E Inventory. Only women were used to develop the scale, but its use has been extended to men as well.
- All but 1 of the 70 items in the original scale remain in the MMPI-2. The items are of two general types: one group deals with social participation, whereas the other group deals with general neurotic maladjustment and self-depreciation. High scores can be obtained by endorsing either kind of item or both.

- Scores on Scale 0 are quite stable over extended periods.

References & Readings

Ben-Porath, Y. S., Graham, J. R., Hall, G. N., Hirschman, R. D., & Zaragoza, M. S. (Eds.) (1995). *Forensic applications of the MMPI-2*. Thousand Oaks, CA: Sage.

Butcher, J. N. (1989). *Minnesota Multiphasic Personality Inventory-2, user's guide, the Minnesota Report: Adult clinical system*. Minneapolis: National Computer Systems.

Butcher, J. N., Dahlstrom, W. G., Graham, J. R., Tellegen, A., & Kaemmer, B. (1989). *Minnesota Multiphasic Personality Inventory (MMPI-2): Manual for administration and scoring*. Minneapolis: University of Minnesota Press.

Butcher, J. N., & Williams, C. L. (1992). *Essentials of MMPI-2 and MMPI-A interpretation*. Minneapolis: University of Minnesota Press.

Duckworth, J. C., & Anderson, W. P. (1995). *MMPI and MMPI-2: Interpretation manual for counselors and clinicians* (4th ed.). Bristol, PA: Accelerated Development.

Graham, J. R. (1990). *MMPI-2: Assessing personality and psychopathology*. New York: Oxford University Press.

Graham, J. R., Ben-Porath, Y. S., & McNulty, J. L. (in press). *MMPI-2 correlates for outpatient mental health settings*. Minneapolis: University of Minnesota Press.

Greene, R. L. (1991). *The MMPI-2/MMPI: An interpretive manual*. Boston: Allyn and Bacon.

Related Topics

26 ASSESSING MMPI-2 PROFILE VALIDITY

James N. Butcher

The most important step in the Minnesota Multiphasic Personality Inventory-2 (MMPI-2) profile interpretation is the initial one of determining whether the profile contains valid, useful, and relevant information about the client's personality and clinical problems. A number of indices are available on the MMPI-2 to aid the clinician in determining whether the client's item responses provide key personality information or are simply reflecting response sets or deceptive motivational patterns to fend off the assessor as to the client's true feelings and motivations. This brief introduction to assessing MMPI-2 profile validity will provide the following: a summary of each of the useful response indices contained on the MMPI-2; a strategy for evaluating the validity indices; and key references for the information presented.

RESPONSE INDICES

Cannot Say Score

This index is not a scale but simply the number of omitted items in the record and is used as an index of cooperativeness. If the item omissions are at the end of the booklet (beyond item 370), the validity and clinical scales may be interpreted, but the supplemental and MMPI-2 Content Scales should not be interpreted. The content of omitted items often provides interesting information about the client's problems. If the individual has omitted more than 10 items, the MMPI-2 scales should be evaluated to determine the percentage of omitted items that appear on a particular scale. For example, a

large number of items could appear on a particular scale, thereby reducing its value as a personality measure. If the person has omitted more than 30 items, the response record is probably insufficient for interpretation, particularly if the omissions fall within the first 370 items.

The L Scale

The L Scale is a measure of cooperativeness and willingness to endorse faults or problems. Individuals who score high on this scale (T > 60) are presenting an overly favorable picture of themselves. If the L score is greater than 65, the individual is claiming virtue not found among people in general. The L Scale is particularly valuable in situations like personnel screening or forensic cases because many individuals being assessed in these settings try to put their best foot forward and present themselves as "better" adjusted than they really are.

The K Scale

The K Scale was developed as a measure of test defensiveness and as a correction for the tendency to deny problems. The profiles of persons who are defensive on the MMPI-2 are adjusted to offset their reluctance to endorse problems by correcting for the defensiveness. Five MMPI scales are corrected by adding a determined amount of the K score to the scale scores of *Hs, Pd, Pt, Sc,* and *Ma*. The K Scale appeared to operate for MMPI-2 normative subjects much as it did for the original MMPI subjects. Consequently, the K weights originally derived by Meehl were maintained in the MMPI-2. In the MMPI-2, both K corrected and non-K corrected profiles can be obtained for psychologists interested in using non-K corrected scores.

The S Scale or Superlative Self-Description Scale

The S Scale is an empirical measure developed by contrasting individuals who took the MMPI-2 in an employment selection situation from the normative sample. Applicants are usually defensive when they are assessed in an employment screening context. Even well-educated individuals who are applying for a highly desirable job tend to approach the MMPI-2 items with a cognitive set to convince the assessment psychologist that they have a sound mind, high responsibility, strong moral values, and great capacity to work effectively with others. In their efforts to perform well on personality evaluation, applicants tend to deny psychological symptoms, aggressively disclaim moral flaws, and assert that they are responsible people who get along extremely well with others and have the ability to compromise in interpersonal situations for the good of safety. In addition, they report being responsible and optimistic about the future, and they assert that they have a degree of good adjustment that most normals do not. In sum, they present themselves in a superlative manner, claiming to be superior in terms of their mental health and morality. The five subscales contained on the S Scale are described as follows: Beliefs in Human Goodness; Serenity; Contentment with Life; Patience/Denial of Irritability and Anger; and Denial of Moral Flaws.

The F Scale

The F Scale is an infrequency scale that is sensitive to extreme or exaggerated problem endorsement. The items on this scale are very rare or bizarre symptoms. Individuals who endorse a lot of these items tend to exaggerate symptoms on the MMPI-2. High F responding is frequently obtained by individuals with a set to convince professionals that they need to have psychological services. This motivational pattern is also found among individuals with a need to claim problems in order to influence the court in forensic cases. High-ranging F scores can raise several possible interpretations: The profile could be invalid because the client became confused or disoriented or got mixed up in responding. The F Scale is also elevated in random response records. High F scores are also found among clients who are malingering or producing exaggerated responding in order to falsely claim mental illness.

The $F_{(B)}$ Scale

The $F_{(B)}$ Scale, or Back F Scale, was developed for the revised version of the MMPI to detect possible deviant responding to items located toward the end of the item pool. Some subjects may modify their approach to the items partway through the item pool and answer in a random or unselective manner. Since the items on the F Scale occur earlier in the test, before item number 370, the F Scale will not detect deviant response patterns occurring later in the booklet. The 40-item $F_{(B)}$ Scale was developed following the same method as for the original F Scale, that is, by including items that had low endorsement percentages in the normal population. Suggested interpretations of the $F_{(B)}$ Scale include the following considerations: If the F Scale is above T = 90, no additional interpretation of $F_{(B)}$ is indicated, since the clinical and validity scales are invalid by F Scale criteria; if the T score of the F Scale is valid, that is, below a T = 89, and the $F_{(B)}$ is below T = 70, then a valid response approach is indicated throughout the booklet and no additional interpretation is needed; or if the T score of the F Scale is valid, that is, below a T = 89, and the $F_{(B)}$ is above a T = 90 (that is, if the original F Scale is valid and the individual has dissimulated on the later part of the booklet), then an interpretation of $F_{(B)}$ is needed. In this case, interpretation of the clinical and validity scales is possible; however, interpretation of scales such as the Content Scales, which require valid response to the later appearing items, needs to be deferred.

The $F_{(P)}$ Scale

The Psychopathology Infrequency Scale $F_{(P)}$ was developed by Arbisi and Ben-Porath (1995) to assess infrequent responding in psychiatric settings. This scale is valuable in appraising the tendency for some people to exaggerate mental health symptoms in the context of patients with genuine psychological disorder. A high score on $F_{(P)}$, for example, above a T score of 80, indicates that the individual is endorsing more bizarre item content than even inpatient psychiatric cases endorse.

TRIN and VRIN

Two inconsistency scales for determining profile validity have been included in the MMPI-2. These scales are based on the analysis of the individual's response to the items in a consistent or inconsistent manner. The first scale, True Response Inconsistency (TRIN), is made up of 20 pairs of items in which a combination of 2 true or 2 false responses is semantically inconsistent—for example, a pair of items that contain content that cannot logically be answered in the same direction if the subject is responding consistently to the content.

TRIN can aid in the interpretation of scores on L and K, since the former is made up entirely of items that are keyed false and the latter is made up of items all but one of which is keyed false. Thus, an individual who inconsistently responds "false" to MMPI-2 pairs of items that contain opposite content will have elevated scores on Scales L and K that do not reflect intentional misrepresentation or defensiveness. An individual whose TRIN score indicates inconsistent "true" responding will have deflated scores on L and K that do not reflect a particularly honest response pattern or lack of ego resources.

The Variable Response Inconsistency (VRIN) scale may be used to help interpret a high score on F. VRIN is made up of 49 pairs of (true-false; false-true; true-true; false-false) patterns. The scale is scored by summing the number of inconsistent responses. A high F in conjunction with a low to moderate VRIN score rules out the possibility that the F score reflects random responding.

Two Obsolete Traditional Measures

Two measures, popular with the original MMPI, are not recommended for interpreting in MMPI-2: the F-K Index (though sensitive to dissimulation) and the so-called subtle-obvious items. First, the F-K Index does not appear to provide much additional information beyond what is provided by the F Scale alone. The F-K Index, in which F is higher than K, tends to be superfluous and does not add any interpretive power beyond F alone. The F-K Index in which K is greater than F (sometimes suggested as a measure to assess "fake good" profiles) has not worked out well in practice and is not recommended for clinical use because too many valid and interpretable protocols are rejected by this index.

Second, the subtle-obvious items are essentially chance items. They are not related to the criteria for the scales (Weed, Ben-Porath, & Butcher, 1990) and do not provide an index of invalidity. The subtle scales have been eliminated from official MMPI-2 scoring services and are not recommended for use in clinical decisions.

VALIDITY ASSESSMENT GUIDELINES

The following guidelines or strategies are recommended for determining the interpretability of profiles:

Clues to non–content oriented responding
- High Cannot Say's (≥ 10)
  Noncompliance
- Preponderance of T or F
  Careless or devious omissions
- VRIN greater than 80
  Inconsistency
- TRIN greater than 80
  "Yea-saying" or "Nay-saying" (depending on whether the score is TRIN [T] or TRIN [F])

Indicants of defensive self-presentation
1. Overly positive self-presentation, leading to a somewhat attenuated record, if any, of these conditions, is present.

- Cannot Say between 5 and 29
- L over 60 but less than 65
- K over 60 but less than 69
- S over 65

2. Likely invalid MMPI-2 because of test defensiveness if any of the following conditions are present:
   - Cannot Say greater than 30
   - L greater than 66
   - K greater than 70
   - S greater than 70

Indicators of exaggerated responding and malingering of symptoms

1. Excessive symptom claiming
   - F (infrequency) greater than 90
   - $F_{(B)}$ greater than 90
   - $F_{(P)}$ greater than 80
2. Possibly exaggerated-invalid range
   - F greater than 100
   - $F_{(B)}$ greater than 10
   - $F_{(P)}$ greater than 90
3. Likely malingering
   - F greater than 109, with VRIN less than or equal to 79
   - $F_{(B)}$ greater than 109, with VRIN less than or equal to 79
   - VRIN less than 79, with VRIN less than or equal to 79
   - $F_{(P)}$ greater than 100, with VRIN less than or equal to 79

References & Readings

Arbisi, P., & Ben-Porath, Y. S. (1995). An MMPI-2 infrequency scale for use with psychopathological populations: The Infrequency-Psychopathology Scale, $F_{(P)}$. *Psychological Assessment, 7*, 424–431.

Baer, R. A., Wetter, M. W., & Berry, D. T. (1992). Detection of underreporting of psychopathology on the MMPI: A meta-analysis. *Clinical Psychology Review, 12*, 509–525.

Baer, R. A., Wetter, M. W., Nichols, D., Greene, R., & Berry, D. T. (1995). Sensitivity of MMPI-2 validity scales to underreporting of symptoms. *Psychological Assessment, 7*, 419–423.

Berry, D. T., Baer, R. A., & Harris, M. J. (1991). Detection of malingering on the MMPI: A meta-analysis. *Clinical Psychology Review, 11*, 585–591.

Berry, D. T., Wetter, M. W., Baer, R. A., Larsen, L.,

Clark, C., & Monroe, K. (1992). MMPI-2 random responding indices: Validation using a self-report methodology. *Psychological Assessment: A Journal of Consulting and Clinical Psychology, 4*, 340–345.

Berry, D. T., Wetter, M. W., Baer, R. A., Widiger, T. A., Sumpter, J. C., Reynolds, S. K., & Hallam, R. A. (1991). Detection of random responding on the MMPI-2: Utility of F, Back F, and VRIN scales. *Psychological Assessment: A Journal of Consulting and Clinical Psychology, 3*, 418–423.

Berry, D. T. R., Wetter, M. W., Baer, R., Youngjohn, J. R., Gass, C., Lamb, D. G., Franzen, M., MacInnes, W. D., & Bucholz, D. (1995). Over-reporting of closed-head injury symptoms on the MMPI-2. *Psychological Assessment, 7*, 517–523.

Butcher, J. N., & Han, K. (1995). Development of an MMPI-2 scale to assess the presentation of self in a superlative manner: The S Scale. In J. N. Butcher & C. D. Spielberger (Eds.), *Advances in personality assessment* (Vol. 10, pp. 25–50). Hillsdale, NJ: LEA Press.

Graham, J. R., Watts, D., & Timbrook, R. (1991). Detecting fake-good and fake-bad MMPI-2 profiles. *Journal of Personality Assessment, 57*, 264–277.

Lim, J., & Butcher, J. N. (1996). Detection of faking on the MMPI-2: Differentiation between faking-bad, denial, and claiming extreme virtue. *Journal of Personality Assessment, 67*, 1–26.

Schretlen, D. (1988). The use of psychological tests to identify malingered symptoms of mental disorder. *Clinical Psychology Review, 8*, 451–476.

Timbrook, R. E., Graham, J. R., Keiller, S. W., & Watts, D. (1993). Comparison of the Wiener-Harmon subtle-obvious scales and the standard validity scales in detecting valid and invalid MMPI-2 profiles. *Psychological Assessment, 5*, 53–61.

Weed, N., Ben-Porath, Y. S., & Butcher, J. N. (1990). Failure of the Weiner-Harmon MMPI subtle scales as predictors of psychopathology and as validity indicators. *Psychological Assessment, 2*, 281–283.

Wetter, M. W., Baer, R. A., Berry, D. T., Robison, L. H., & Sumpter, J. (1993). MMPI-2 profiles of motivated fakers given specific symptom information. *Psychological Assessment, 5*, 317–323.

Wetter, W., Baer, R. A., Berry, D. T., Smith, G. T., & Larsen, L. (1992). Sensitivity of MMPI-2 validity scales to random responding and malingering. *Psychological Assessment, 4*, 369–374.

27 EMPIRICAL INTERPRETATION OF THE MMPI-2 CODETYPES

James N. Butcher

The Minnesota Multiphasic Personality Inventory (MMPI) is the most widely researched and extensively used objective instrument in clinical assessment (Butcher & Rouse, 1996; Lubin, Larsen, & Matarazzo, 1984). Following its initial publication in 1940, the MMPI came to be employed across a wide variety of clinical, academic, military, industrial, and forensic settings. The initial test developers, Hathaway and McKinley, followed an empirical scale construction strategy by finding items that separated groups of individuals with known psychiatric problems, such as anxiety or depression, from "normals" (Hathaway & McKinley, 1940).

The original MMPI underwent a substantial revision and redevelopment during the 1980s, and the MMPI-2 was published for use with adults in 1989 and for adolescents (the MMPI-A) in 1992. The modern versions of the instrument were standardized on contemporary, representative samples of individuals in the United States. The resulting instruments, with their expanded range of scales, have demonstrated strong psychometric properties similar to those of their predecessor (Butcher & Williams, 1992) and have now replaced the original MMPI for assessment in mental health settings.

Although portions of the test remained the same, several changes were made during the revision, such as the omission of items with objectionable content and rewording of items that were out of date. The traditional validity and clinical scales were retained for the revised versions in order to maintain continuity with the original MMPI—that is, L (Lie), F (Infrequency), K (Defensiveness), 1 (Hypochondriasis), 2 (Depression), 3 (Hysteria), 4 (Psychopathic Deviate), 5 (Masculinity/Femininity), 6 (Paranoia), 7 (Psychasthenia), 8 (Schizophrenia), 9 (Mania), and 0 (Social Introversion). In addition, a number of new validity measures were developed for the revised forms (i.e., True Response Inconsistency [TRIN] and Variable Response Inconsistency [VRIN]). In addition to the traditional clinical scales, an important new set of scales, the MMPI-2 (Butcher, Graham, Williams, & Ben-Porath, 1990) and MMPI-A Content Scales, was published (Williams, Butcher, Ben-Porath, & Graham, 1992). These scales were derived according to a rational-empirical scale construction strategy to provide several measures of specific clinical problems.

Since the MMPI-2 revision, there have been numerous studies to examine whether the extensive literature on the use of the original MMPI can be generalized to the revised instruments (Archer, Griffin, & Aiduk, 1995). The psychometric properties of the MMPI-2 and MMPI-A scales have been found to be comparable to those of the clinical scales for the original MMPI. Test-retest coefficients were of a similar magnitude (Butcher, Dahlstrom, Graham, Tellegen, & Kaemmer, 1989). Results from validity studies on the MMPI-2 and MMPI-A to date have been very promising (Ben-Porath, Butcher, & Graham, 1991; Williams & Butcher, 1989a, 1989b).

The extensive objective information available for each of the MMPI-2 patterns makes interpretation of the test relatively straightforward. Empirical scale interpretation with the MMPI-2 works as follows: An individual taking the MMPI-2 answers a series of true-false questions, which are scored according to objective rules. The scores are assigned T-score values on different scales (e.g., Scale 1 = Hypochondriasis; Scale 2 = Depression); profiles are then drawn to allow for easy comparison to normals. When a new case is obtained with profiles that resemble known patient groups, that is, that match a particular prototype, the empirical descriptors (referred to as *scale correlates*) are generated to provide an indication of that individual's psychological adjustment problems. That is, when a particular pattern is obtained by an individual, the interpreter simply refers to the established behaviors and personality factors established for it. These established behavior patterns can be *automatically* applied whenever the scores are obtained.

The scale scores have been extensively researched, and a number of resources, known as codebooks or "cookbooks," have accumulated to provide a rich catalog of personality descriptors that have been empirically shown to be associated with various scale patterns. This objective strategy makes it possible for individual test protocols to be effectively interpreted by electronic computer (Butcher, 1995). Automated interpretation, that is, interpreting MMPI profiles using actuarial tables, was initially shown by Meehl (1954) to be a more powerful strategy than clinical interpretation. He convincingly demonstrated that clinical predictions based on automatic combination of actuarial data for MMPI codetypes were more accurate than those based on "clinical" or intuitive interpretation strategies.

A number of empirical studies followed Meehl's recommendations for developing an actuarial "cookbook" as an aid to stringent test interpretation. The empirical research on MMPI profile patterns that followed during the 1960s and 1970s has established a broad interpretive base for many of the common MMPI codetypes found in clinical settings (Gilberstadt & Duker, 1965; Marks, Seeman, & Haller, 1974). Meehl's compelling argument on the strength of the actuarial method and the empirical demonstration that such mechanically generated predictions were highly accurate influenced a number of investigators to develop "actuarial tables" for personality description using MMPI scales and profile codes.

A codetype is defined by the highest elevated scale or groupings of clinical scales in the profile and their rank order in terms of elevation. Most of the empirical research on MMPI codetypes has included only the basic clinical scales *Hs, D, Hy, Pd, Pa, Pt, Sc,* and *Ma.* Research-based behavioral descriptions associated with codetypes can be confidently applied to individuals whose profiles match the codetype. The *Single Point Code,* or "profile spike," occurs when a single clinical scale is elevated in the critical range, that is, above a T score of 65. The *Two-Point Codetype,* one of the most frequently researched profile codes, occurs when two clinical scales, such as *D* and *Pt,* are elevated above a T = 65. This codetype would be defined as a two-point code of 2-7/7-2. The *Three-Point Code,* prominent in several research populations, occurs when three clinical scales are elevated in the profile. For example, clinical elevations on scales *D, Pd,* and *Pt* produce a three-point code of 2-4-7, a profile type often found in drug and alcohol treatment programs. A few *Four-Point Codes* have been researched, for example, the 1-2-3-4 codetype in medical settings.

Two general rules are followed to determine whether a particular profile pattern meets the requirements of a reliable codetype: First, the profile should be clearly defined; that is, if the profile code is at least five points greater than the next scale in the profile, the codetype is likely to be the same on MMPI or on MMPI-2 norms and likely to be a good prototypal match. In general, Graham, Smith, and Schwartz (1986) recommend exercising caution in applying traditional MMPI behavioral correlates for a given codetype if the MMPI profile does not possess clear codetype definition or a clear elevation above the next scale in the profile. Graham, Timbrook, Ben-Porath, and Butcher (1991) demonstrated that MMPI-2 codes were quite congruent with MMPI profile codes when codetype definition was maintained. Over 90% of the profiles with a five-point profile code definition will have the same codetype on MMPI-2 as with the original MMPI. Second, when there has been sufficient research on the behavioral descriptions for the code (e.g., 2-7-8 codetype), there would likely be a sufficient empirical base to provide reliable information about the client. If a codetype is an infrequent one (with a relatively small database such as with the 2-9/9-2 profile code), then a scale-by-scale interpretation strategy should be followed. With the MMPI-2, as with the original MMPI, empirical descriptors are sparse for some codetypes. Not enough codetypes have been empirically studied and described across a broad range of settings to classify the range of profiles that clinicians can obtain.

How likely are MMPI-2 profile codes to remain stable over time, for example, if the client is retested at a later date? First, as a general rule, MMPI scales tend to have high test-retest stability. Test-retest correlations for various groups have been reported to range from moderate to high, depending on the population studied and the retest interval. Even test-retest correlations over very long intervals, for example, over 30 years (Leon, Gillum, Gillum, & Gouze, 1979), are quite high, with some scales (i.e., *Si*) showing correlations as high as .73.

Several studies of MMPI profile stability have been conducted. Graham et al. (1986) reported that the percentages of people with the same high-point, low-point, and two-point code showed only modest congruence on retest.

They noted, however, that codetypes with more extreme scores, and those that were well defined by a substantial point separation between scale scores in the codetype from those not included in the code, tended to be similar at retest. The greatest codetype agreement at retest was obtained for profiles having a 10-point T-score spread between the codetype. However, high congruence was obtained at retest if the codetype was even 5 points higher than the next scale in the profile.

ILLUSTRATION OF THE 2-7/7-2 PROFILE CODE

The 2-7/7-2 profile code is defined by having two scales (Scale 2, or Depression, and Scale 7, or Psychasthenia) elevated above a T score of 65 and appearing as the highest two clinical scales in the profile. The following summary would likely be found to apply with the client producing the 2-7/7-2 code:

Symptomatic Pattern
Individuals with this profile code appear anxious, tense, nervous, and depressed. They report feeling unhappy and sad and tend to worry to excess. They feel vulnerable to real and imagined threat and typically anticipate problems before they occur—often overreacting to minor stress as though it is a major catastrophe. They usually report somatic symptoms such as fatigue, exhaustion, tiredness, weight loss, slow personal tempo, slowed speech, and retarded thought processes. They tend to brood and ruminate a great deal.

These persons may have high expectations for themselves and others and show a strong need for achievement and recognition for accomplishments. They may feel guilty when their goals are not met. These individuals typically have perfectionistic attitudes and a conscientious life history. They may be excessively religious or extremely moralistic.

Personality Characteristics
Individuals with this pattern appear docile and passive-dependent in relationships. They report problems in being assertive. They usually show a capacity for forming deep, emotional ties and tend to lean on people to an excessive degree. They tend to solicit

nurturance from others. Feelings of inadequacy, insecurity, and inferiority are long term issues. They tend to be intropunitive in dealing with feelings of aggression.

Predictions and Dispositions
Individuals with this profile code are usually diagnosed as depressive, obsessive-compulsive, or anxiety disordered. They are usually motivated for psychotherapy and tend to remain in therapy longer than other patients. They tend to be somewhat pessimistic about overcoming problems and are indecisive and rigid in their thinking. This negative mind set is likely to interfere with their problem-solving ability. However, they usually improve in treatment. (Butcher & Williams, 1992)

The empirically based MMPI-2 correlates have considerable robustness when applied to new samples—even across other languages and cultural groups. The MMPI-2, if adapted carefully to new cultures, can provide important information on psychopathology about patients in diverse clinical settings. The MMPI-2 appears to work similarly in a wide variety of countries. The original MMPI was widely translated, with over 140 translations in 46 countries (Butcher & Pancheri, 1976), and the MMPI-2 has undergone a number of foreign-language translations since it was published in 1989. Butcher (1996) conducted an extensive cross-national MMPI-2 research program detailing the clinical and research use of the MMPI-2 across a large number of countries.

The MMPI-2 empirical descriptors apply well across international boundaries even when applied by an electronic computer. A recent study by Butcher et al. (in press) found that patients from several countries were described with a high degree of accuracy by computer-based reports generated from U.S. norms and descriptors derived from American based research. This research provided support for the generalization validity of MMPI-2 correlates in cross-cultural contexts.

References & Readings

Archer, R. P., Griffin, R., & Aiduk, R. (1995). Clinical correlates for ten common code types. *Journal of Personality Assessment, 65,* 391–408.

Ben-Porath, Y. S., Butcher, J. N., & Graham, J. R. (1991). Contribution of the MMPI-2 scales to the differential diagnosis of schizophrenia and major depression. *Psychological Assessment: A Journal of Consulting and Clinical Psychology, 3,* 634–640.

Butcher, J. N. (1995). Clinical use of computer-based personality test reports. In J. N. Butcher (Ed.), *Clinical personality assessment: Practical approaches.* New York: Oxford University Press.

Butcher, J. N. (Ed.) (1996). *International adaptations of the MMPI-2: Research and clinical applications.* Minneapolis: University of Minnesota Press.

Butcher, J. N., Berah, E., Ellertsen, B., Miach, P., Lim, J., Nezami, E., Pancheri, P., Derksen, J., & Almagor, M. (in press). Objective personality assessment: Computer-based MMPI-2 interpretation in international clinical settings. In C. Belar (Ed.), *Comprehensive clinical psychology: Sociocultural and individual differences.* New York: Elsevier.

Butcher, J. N., Dahlstrom, W. G., Graham, J. R., Tellegen, A., & Kaemmer, B. (1989). *Minnesota Multiphasic Personality Inventory-2 (MMPI-2): Manual for administration and scoring.* Minneapolis: University of Minnesota Press.

Butcher, J. N., Graham, J. R., Williams, C. L., & Ben-Porath, Y. S. (1990). *Development and use of the MMPI-2 content scales.* Minneapolis: University of Minnesota Press.

Butcher, J. N., & Pancheri, P. (1976). *Handbook of cross-national MMPI research.* Minneapolis: University of Minnesota Press.

Butcher, J. N., & Rouse, S. V. (1996). Personality: Individual differences and clinical assessment. *Annual Review of Psychology, 47,* 87–111.

Butcher, J. N., & Williams, C. L. (1992). *Essentials of MMPI-2 and MMPI-A interpretation.* Minneapolis: University of Minnesota Press.

Butcher, J. N., Williams, C. L., Graham, J. R., Archer, R. P., Tellegen, A., & Ben-Porath, Y. (1992). *MMPI-A (Minnesota Multiphasic Personality Inventory-Adolescent): Manual for administration, scoring, and interpretation.* Minneapolis: University of Minnesota Press.

Gilberstadt, H., & Duker, J. (1965). *A handbook for clinical and actuarial MMPI interpretation.* Philadelphia: Saunders.

Graham, J. R., Smith, R., & Schwartz, G. (1986). Stability of MMPI configurations for psychiatric inpatients. *Journal of Consulting and Clinical Psychology, 54,* 375–380.

Graham, J. R., Timbrook, R., Ben-Porath, Y. S., &

Butcher, J. N. (1991). Code-type congruence between MMPI and MMPI-2: Separating fact from artifact. *Journal of Personality Assessment, 57,* 205–215.

Hathaway, S. R., & McKinley, J. C. (1940). A multiphasic personality schedule (Minnesota) I: Construction of the schedule. *Journal of Psychology, 10,* 249–254.

Leon, G., Gillum, B., Gillum, R., & Gouze, M. (1979). Personality stability and change over a thirty-year period: Middle age to old age. *Journal of Consulting and Clinical Psychology, 47,* 517–524.

Lubin, B., Larsen, R. M., & Matarazzo, J. (1984). Patterns of psychological test usage in the United States, 1935–1982. *American Psychologist, 39,* 451–454.

Marks, P. A., Seeman, W., & Haller, D. L. (1974). *The actuarial use of the MMPI with adolescents and adults.* Baltimore: Williams and Wilkins.

Meehl, P. E. (1954). *Clinical versus statistical prediction: A theoretical analysis and a review of the evidence.* Minneapolis: University of Minnesota Press.

Williams, C. L., & Butcher, J. N. (1989a). An MMPI study of adolescents: I. Empirical validity of the standard scales. *Psychological Assessment: A Journal of Consulting and Clinical Psychology, 1,* 251–259.

Williams, C. L., & Butcher, J. N. (1989b). An MMPI study of adolescents: II. Verification and limitations of code type classification. *Psychological Assessment: A Journal of Consulting and Clinical Psychology, 1,* 260–265.

Williams, C. L., Butcher, J. N., Ben-Porath, Y. S., & Graham, J. R. (1992). *MMPI-A content scales: Assessing psychopathology in adolescents.* Minneapolis: University of Minnesota Press.

Related Topics

Chapter 25, "Clinical Scales of the MMPI-2"
Chapter 26, "Assessing MMPI-2 Profile Validity"
Chapter 28, "Characteristics of High and Low Scores on the MMPI-2 Clinical Scales"
Chapter 29, "Using the MMPI-2 in Assessing Alcohol or Drug Abuse"

28 CHARACTERISTICS OF HIGH AND LOW SCORES ON THE MMPI-2 CLINICAL SCALES

John R. Graham

These descriptions of high and low scores on each clinical scale of the Minnesota Multiphasic Personality Inventory-2 (MMPI-2) are based on examination of previously reported data for the original MMPI and new data concerning the MMPI-2.

DEFINITIONS

• The definition of a high score on a clinical scale has varied considerably in the literature and from one scale to another. Some consider MMPI-2 T scores above 65 as "high." Others have defined high scores as the upper quartile in a distribution or as several T-score levels on each scale. Another approach identifies the highest scale in the profile (high point) as significant irrespective of its T-score value. The most usual practice is to consider T scores above 65 as high scores.

- Low scores also have been defined in different ways, sometimes as T scores below 40 and other times as scores in the lowest quartile of a distribution. This latter approach has led to scores well above the mean being considered as low scores. In contrast with high scores, limited information is available in the literature concerning the meaning of low scores. The most usual practice is to consider T scores below 40 as low scores.

GENERAL PRINCIPLES

- Some original MMPI data support the notion that low scores on a particular scale indicate the absence of problems and symptoms characteristic of high scorers on that scale. Other data have suggested that low scores on some scales are associated with problems and negative characteristics. Still other data have been interpreted as indicating that both high and low scores on some scales indicate similar problems and negative characteristics.

- It is clear that low scores on the MMPI-2 convey important information but not as important as high scores. In nonclinical settings, low scores are associated with fewer than average symptoms and problems and above-average adjustment. There is little basis for interpreting low scores on the clinical scales as indicating problems and negative characteristics in nonclinical samples.

- Based on the empirical data concerning the meaning of low scores on the MMPI and MMPI-2, a very conservative approach to interpretation of low scores on the MMPI-2 clinical scales is recommended. In nonclinical settings (e.g., personnel selection), low scores in a valid protocol should be interpreted as indicating more positive adjustment than high or average scores. However,

if the validity scales indicate that the test was completed in a defensive manner, low scores should not be interpreted at all. In clinical settings, it is recommended that low scores on the clinical scales not be interpreted. The exceptions are Scales 5 and 0, for which some limited inferences can be made about low scorers (see below).

- In general, T scores greater than 65 are considered high, although inferences about persons with scores at different levels are presented for some scales. Note that the T-score levels noted are somewhat arbitrary and that clinical judgment is critical in deciding which inferences should be applied to scores at or near the cutoff scores described. Not every inference presented will apply to every person who has a T score at that level.

- In general, greater confidence should be placed in inferences based on more extreme scores, with all inferences treated as hypotheses to be considered in the context of other available information about the person.

INTERPRETATION OF HIGH SCORES ON SCALE 1

- For persons with extremely high scores on Scale 1 (T > 80), dramatic and sometimes bizarre somatic concerns should be suspected. If Scale 3 also is elevated, the possibility of a conversion disorder should be considered. If Scale 8 is very elevated along with Scale 1, somatic delusions may be present.

- Persons with more moderate elevations on Scale 1 (T = 60–80) tend to have generally vague, nonspecific complaints. When specific symptoms are elicited, they tend to be epigastric in nature. Chronic weakness, lack of energy, and sleep disturbance also tend to be characteristic of high scorers. As stated above, medical patients with bona fide physical problems generally obtain T scores of about 60 on this scale. When medical patients produce T scores much above 60, one should suspect a strong psychological component to the illness. Moderately high scores on Scale 1 tend to be associated with diagnoses such as somatoform disorders, somatoform pain disorders, anxiety disorders, and depressive disorders. Acting-out behavior is rare among high Scale 1 scorers.

- High Scale 1 scorers (T > 60) in both psychiatric and nonpsychiatric samples tend to be characterized by a rather distinctive set of personality attributes. They are likely to be selfish, self-centered, and narcissistic. Their outlook toward life tends to be pessimistic, defeatist, and cynical. They are generally dissatisfied and unhappy and are likely to make those around them miserable. They complain a great deal and communicate in a whiny manner. They are demanding of others and are very critical of what others do, although they are likely to express hostility in rather indirect ways. High scorers on Scale 1 often are described as dull, unenthusiastic, unambitious, and lacking ease in oral expression.

- High scorers generally do not exhibit much manifest anxiety, and in general they do not show signs of major incapacity. Rather, they appear to be functioning at a reduced level of efficiency. Problems are much more likely to be long-standing than situational or transient.

- Extremely high and moderately high scorers typically see themselves as physically ill, and they seek medical explanations and treatment for their symptoms. They tend to lack insight concerning the causes of their somatic symptoms, and they resist psychological interpretations. These tendencies, coupled with their generally cynical outlook, suggest that these individuals are not very good candidates for psychotherapy or counseling. They tend to be highly critical of their psychotherapists and to terminate therapy if the therapist is perceived as suggesting psychological reasons for their symptoms or as not giving them enough support and attention.

INTERPRETATION OF HIGH SCORES ON SCALE 2

- High scorers on Scale 2 (particularly if the T scores exceed 70) often display depressive symptoms. They may report feeling depressed, blue, unhappy, or dysphoric. They tend to be quite pessimistic about the future in general and more specifically about the likelihood of overcoming their problems and making a better adjustment. They often talk about committing suicide. Self-depreciation and guilt feelings are common. Behavioral manifestations may include lack of energy, refusal to speak, crying, and psychomotor retardation. Patients with such high scores often receive depressive diagnoses.

- Other symptoms of high scorers include physical complaints, bad dreams, weakness, fatigue or loss of energy, agitation, tension, and fearfulness. They also are described as irritable, high-strung, and prone to worry and fretting. They may have a sense of dread that something bad is about to happen to them.

- High scorers also show a marked lack of self-confidence. They report feelings of uselessness and inability to function in a variety of situations. They act helpless and give up easily when faced with stress. They see themselves as having failed to achieve adequately in school and at their jobs.

- High scorers tend to be described as introverted, shy, retiring, timid, seclusive, and secretive. A lifestyle characterized by withdrawal and lack of intimate involvement with other people is common. These individuals also tend to be aloof and to maintain psychological distance from other people. They may feel that others do not care about them, and their feelings are easily hurt. They often have a severely restricted range of interests and may withdraw from activities in which they previously participated. They are very cautious and conventional in their activities, and they are not very creative in problem solving.

- High scorers may have great difficulty in making even simple decisions and may feel overwhelmed when faced with major life decisions such as vocational choice or marriage. They tend to be very overcontrolled and to deny their own impulses. They are likely to avoid unpleasantness and tend to make concessions in order to avoid confrontations.

- Because high Scale 2 scores are suggestive of great personal distress, they suggest a good prognosis for psychotherapy or counseling. There is some evidence, however, that high scorers may tend to terminate treatment prematurely when the immediate crisis passes.

INTERPRETATION OF HIGH SCORES ON SCALE 3

- Marked elevations on Scale 3 (T > 80) suggest persons who react to stress and avoid responsibility by developing physical symptoms. The symptoms usually do not fit the pattern of known organic disorders, often including, in some combination, headaches, stomach discomfort, chest pains, weakness, and tachycardia. Nevertheless, such persons may be symptom free most of the time, but when they are under stress, symptoms may appear suddenly and are likely to disappear just as abruptly after the stress subsides.
- Except for the physical symptoms, high scorers may tend to be relatively free of other symptoms. Although they sometimes describe themselves as prone to worry, lacking energy and feeling worn out, and having sleep disturbances, they are not likely to report severe anxiety, tension, or depression. Hallucinations, delusions, and suspiciousness are rare. The most frequent diagnoses for high Scale 3 scorers among psychiatric patients are conversion disorder and psychogenic pain disorder.
- A salient feature of the day-to-day functioning of high scorers is a marked lack of insight concerning the possible underlying causes of their symptoms. In addition, they show little insight concerning their own motives and feelings.
- High scorers are often described as extremely immature psychologically and at times even childish or infantile. They are self-centered, narcissistic, and egocentric, and they expect a great deal of attention and affection from others. They often use indirect and devious means to get the attention and affection they crave. When others do not

respond appropriately, they may become hostile and resentful, but these feelings are likely to be denied and not expressed openly or directly.

- High Scale 3 scorers tend to be emotionally involved, friendly, talkative, enthusiastic, and alert. Although affectional and attention needs drive them into social interactions, their relationships tend to be superficial and immature. They are involved with people primarily because of what they can get from them, rather than out of sincere interest.
- Because of their needs for acceptance and affection, high scorers may initially be quite enthusiastic about counseling and psychotherapy. However, they may view themselves as having medical problems and want to be treated medically. They are slow to gain insight into underlying causes of their behavior, and they resist psychological interpretations. If therapists insist on examining psychological causes of symptoms, premature termination of therapy is likely. High Scale 3 scorers may be willing to talk about problems in their lives as long as they are not conceptualized as causing or contributing to their symptoms. These individuals often respond well to direct advice and suggestion.
- When high Scale 3 scorers become involved in therapy, they discuss worry about failure in school or work, marital unhappiness, lack of acceptance by their social groups, and problems with authority figures. Histories may include a rejecting father to whom females reacted with somatic complaints and males with rebellion and overt hostility.

INTERPRETATION OF HIGH SCORES ON SCALE 4

- Extremely high scores (T > 75) on Scale 4 tend to be associated with difficulty incorporating the values and standards of society. Such high scorers are likely to engage in a variety of asocial, antisocial, and even criminal behaviors. These behaviors may include lying, cheating, stealing, sexual acting out, and excessive use of alcohol and/or other drugs.

- High scorers on Scale 4 tend to be rebellious toward authority figures and often are in conflict with authorities. They often have stormy relationships with families, and family members tend to blame others for their difficulties. Underachievement in school, poor work history, and marital problems are also characteristic of high scorers.

- High scorers are highly impulsive persons who strive for immediate gratification. They often do not plan their behavior, and they act without considering the consequences. They are very impatient and have limited frustration tolerance. Their behavior may involve poor judgment and considerable risk taking. They tend not to profit from experiences and may find themselves in the same difficulties repeatedly.

- High scorers on Scale 4 are described by others as immature and childish. They are narcissistic, self-centered, selfish, and egocentric, and their behavior often is ostentatious and exhibitionistic. They are insensitive to the needs and feelings of other people and are interested in others in terms of how they can be used. Although they tend to be seen as likable and generally create good first impressions, their relationships often are shallow and superficial. This may be due in part to rejection on the part of the people they mistreat, but it also seems to reflect their inability to form warm attachments with others.

- In addition, high Scale 4 scorers typically are extroverted and outgoing. They are talkative, active, adventurous, energetic, and spontaneous. They are viewed by others as intelligent and self-confident. Although they have a wide range of interests and may become involved in many activities, they lack definite goals and clear direction.

- High scorers tend to be hostile and aggressive. They are resentful, rebellious, antagonistic, and refractory. Their attitude is characterized by sarcasm and cynicism. Both men and women with high Scale 4 scores may act in aggressive ways, but women are likely to express aggression in more passive, indirect ways. Often there does not appear to be any guilt associated with the aggressive behavior. Whereas high scorers may feign guilt and remorse when their behaviors get them into trouble, such responses typically are short-lived, disappearing when the immediate crisis passes.

- Although high scorers typically are not seen as being overwhelmed by emotional turmoil, at times they may admit feeling sad, fearful, or worried about the future. They may experience absence of deep emotional response, which may produce feelings of emptiness and boredom. Among psychiatric patients, high scorers tend to receive personality disorder diagnoses, with antisocial personality disorder or passive-aggressive personality disorder occurring most frequently.

- Because of their verbal facility, outgoing manner, and apparent intellectual resources, high scorers on Scale 4 are often perceived as good candidates for psychotherapy or counseling. Unfortunately, the prognosis for change is poor. Although these individuals may agree to treatment to avoid something more unpleasant (e.g., jail or divorce), they generally are unable to accept responsibility for their own problems and tend to terminate treatment as soon as possible. In therapy they often intellectualize excessively and blame others for their difficulties.

INTERPRETATION OF SCORES ON SCALE 5

- Very high scores on Scale 5 (T > 65) for men and women suggest the possibility of sexual concerns and problems. These may be associated with homoerotic trends or homosexual behavior, but they also can center around sexual problems and behaviors of other kinds.

- High scores (T > 60) for men on Scale 5 indicate a lack of stereotypical masculine interests. These individuals tend to have aesthetic and artistic interests and are likely to participate in housekeeping and child-rearing activities to a greater extent than most men.

- High scores on Scale 5 are very uncommon among women. When encountered, they generally indicate rejection of traditional female roles. Women with high Scale 5 scores are interested in sports, hobbies, and other activities that tend to be stereotypically more masculine than feminine.

- Men who score low on Scale 5 are presenting themselves as extremely masculine. They have stereotypically masculine preferences in work, hobbies, and other activities.
- Women who score low on Scale 5 have many stereotypically feminine interests. They are likely to derive satisfaction from their roles as spouses and mothers. They may be traditionally feminine or may have adopted a more androgynous lifestyle.

INTERPRETATION OF HIGH SCORES
ON SCALE 6

- Persons whose Scale 6 T scores are above 70, especially when Scale 6 also is the highest scale in the profile, may exhibit frankly psychotic behavior. Their thinking may be disturbed, including delusions of persecution or grandeur. Ideas of reference also are common. These individuals may feel mistreated and picked on; they may be angry and resentful; and they may harbor grudges. Projection is a common defense mechanism. Among psychiatric patients, diagnoses of schizophrenia or paranoid disorders are most frequent.
- When Scale 6 T scores range from 60 to 70, blatant psychotic symptoms are not as common. However, persons with scores within this range are characterized by a variety of traits and behaviors suggesting a paranoid predisposition. They tend to be excessively sensitive and overly responsive to the opinions of others. They believe they are getting a raw deal out of life and tend to rationalize and blame others for their difficulties. Also, they are suspicious and guarded and commonly exhibit hostility, resentment, and an argumentative manner. They tend to be very moralistic and rigid in their opinions and attitudes. Rationality is likely to be greatly overemphasized.
- Women who score in the 60–70 T-score range describe sadness, withdrawal, and anxiety and are seen by others as emotionally labile and moody.
- Prognosis for psychotherapy is poor because these people do not like to talk about emotional problems and are likely to rationalize most of the time. They have great difficulty in establishing rapport with therapists. In therapy, they are likely to reveal hostility and resentment toward family members.

INTERPRETATION OF HIGH SCORES
ON SCALE 7

- Scale 7 is a good index of psychological turmoil and discomfort, with higher scorers experiencing greater turmoil. High scorers tend to be very anxious, tense, and agitated. They worry a great deal, even over small problems, and are fearful and apprehensive. They are high-strung and jumpy, report difficulties in concentrating, and often receive anxiety disorder diagnoses.
- High scorers tend to be highly introspective and sometimes report fears that they are losing their minds. Obsessive thinking, compulsive and ritualistic behavior, and ruminations, often centering around feelings of insecurity and inferiority, are common among very high scorers. These persons lack self-confidence; are self-critical, self-conscious, and self-degrading; and are plagued by self-doubts. They tend to be very rigid and moralistic and to have high standards of behavior and performance for themselves and others. They are likely to be quite perfectionistic and conscientious, experiencing guilt feelings about not living up to their own standards or depression about falling short of goals.
- In general, high scorers are neat, orderly, organized, and meticulous. They are persistent and reliable but lack ingenuity and originality in their approach to problems. They are seen by others as dull and formal and as having great difficulty in making decisions. In addition, they are likely to distort the importance of problems and to be overreactive in stressful situations.

- High scorers tend to be shy and do not interact well socially. They are described as hard to get to know, and they worry a great deal about popularity and social acceptance. Other people see them as sentimental, peaceable, softhearted, trustful, sensitive, and kind. Other adjectives used to describe them include dependent, unassertive, and immature.
- Some high scorers on Scale 7 express physical complaints centering around the heart or the gastrointestinal or genitourinary system. Complaints of fatigue, exhaustion, insomnia, and bad dreams are common.
- Although high scorers may be motivated to seek therapy because they feel so uncomfortable and miserable, they are not very responsive to brief psychotherapy or counseling. In spite of some insight into their problems, they tend to rationalize and intellectualize a great deal. They often are resistant to interpretations and may express much hostility toward the therapist. However, they tend to remain in therapy longer than most patients and may show slow but steady progress. Problems presented in therapy may include difficulties with authority figures, poor work or study habits, or concern about homosexual impulses.

INTERPRETATION OF HIGH SCORES
ON SCALE 8

- Although one should be cautious about assigning a diagnosis of schizophrenia on the basis of only the score on Scale 8, T scores in a range of 75–90 suggest the possibility of a psychotic disorder. Confusion, disorganization, and disorientation may be present. Unusual thoughts or attitudes, perhaps even delusional in nature, hallucinations, and extremely poor judgment may be evident.
- Extreme scores (T > 90) usually are not produced by psychotic individuals; they more likely indicate an individual in acute psychological turmoil or a less disturbed person who is endorsing many deviant items as a cry for help. However, some recently hospitalized psychiatric patients obtain high scores on Scale 8, accurately reflecting severe psychopathology.
- High scores on Scale 8 may suggest a schizoid lifestyle. Such people tend to feel isolated, alienated, misunderstood, and unaccepted by their peers. They are withdrawn, reclusive, secretive, and inaccessible and may avoid dealing with people and with new situations. They are described by others as shy, aloof, and uninvolved.
- High scorers experience a great deal of apprehension and generalized anxiety, and they often report having bad dreams. They may feel sad or blue. They may feel very resentful, hostile, and aggressive, but they are unable to express such feelings. A typical response to stress is withdrawal into daydreams and fantasies, and some people may have a difficult time separating reality and fantasy.
- High scorers may be plagued by self-doubts. They feel inferior, incompetent, and dissatisfied. They give up easily when confronted with problem situations. Sexual preoccupation and sex role confusion are common. The behavior of such persons often is characterized by others as nonconforming, unusual, unconventional, and eccentric. Physical complaints may be present, and these usually are vague and long-standing.
- High scorers may at times be stubborn, moody, and opinionated. At other times they are seen as generous, peaceable, and sentimental. Other adjectives used to describe high scorers include immature, impulsive, adventurous, sharp-witted, conscientious, and high-strung. Although they may have a wide range of interests and may be creative and imaginative in approaching problems, their goals generally are abstract and vague. They seem to lack basic information required for problem solving.
- The prognosis for psychotherapy is not good because of the long-standing nature of high scorers' problems and their reluctance to relate in a meaningful way to the therapist. However, high scorers tend to stay in therapy longer than most patients and eventually may come to trust the therapist. Medical consultation to evaluate the appropriateness of medication may be indicated.

INTERPRETATION OF HIGH SCORES
ON SCALE 9

- Extreme elevations (T > 80) on Scale 9 may suggest a manic episode. Patients with such scores are likely to show excessive, purposeless activity and accelerated speech; they may have hallucinations and/or delusions of grandeur; and they are emotionally labile. Some confusion may be present, and flight of ideas is common.
- Persons with more moderate elevations are not likely to exhibit frank psychotic symptoms but have a definite tendency toward overactivity and unrealistic self-appraisal. They are energetic and talkative, and they prefer action to thought. They have a wide range of interests and are likely to have many projects going at once. However, they do not use energy wisely and often do not see projects through to completion. They may be creative, enterprising, and ingenious, but they have little interest in routine or details. Such persons become bored and restless easily and have low frustration tolerance. They have great difficulty inhibiting impulsivity, and periodic episodes of irritability, hostility, and aggressive outbursts are common. Unrealistic and unqualified optimism is also characteristic of high scorers. They seem to think that nothing is impossible, and they have grandiose aspirations. They also have an exaggerated appraisal of their own self-worth and self-importance and are not able to see their own limitations. High scorers have a greater than average likelihood of using nonprescription drugs and getting into trouble with the law.
- High scorers are very outgoing, sociable, and gregarious. They enjoy other people and generally create good first impressions. They impress others as being friendly, pleasant, enthusiastic, poised, and self-confident. They often try to dominate other people. Their relationships are usually quite superficial, and as others get to know them better, they become aware of their manipulations, deceptions, and unreliability.
- In spite of an outward picture of confidence and poise, high scorers are likely to harbor feelings of dissatisfaction about what they are getting out of life. They may feel upset, tense, nervous, anxious, and agitated, and they describe themselves as prone to worry. Periodic episodes of depression may occur.
- In psychotherapy, high scorers often report negative feelings toward domineering parents, difficulties in school or at work, and a variety of delinquent behaviors. They resist interpretations, are irregular in their attendance, and are likely to terminate therapy prematurely. They engage in a great deal of intellectualization and may repeat problems in a stereotyped manner. They do not become dependent on the therapist, who may be a target for hostility and aggression.

INTERPRETATION OF SCORES
ON SCALE 0

- The most salient characteristic of high scorers on Scale 0 is social introversion. These persons are very insecure and uncomfortable in social situations, tending to be shy, reserved, timid, and retiring. They feel more comfortable when alone or with a few close friends, and they do not participate in many social activities. They may be especially uncomfortable around members of the opposite sex.
- High scorers lack self-confidence and tend to be self-effacing. They are hard to get to know and are described by others as cold and distant. They are sensitive to what others think of them and are likely to be troubled by their lack of involvement with other people. They are overcontrolled and are unlikely to display feelings directly. They are submissive, compliant, and overly accepting of authority.
- High scorers are also described as serious and having a slow personal tempo. Although they are reliable and dependable, their approach to problems tends to be cautious, conventional, and unoriginal. They give up easily and are somewhat rigid and inflexible in their attitudes and opinions. They also have great difficulty in making even minor decisions. They seem to enjoy their work and get pleasure from personal achievement.

- High scorers tend to worry, to be irritable, and to feel anxious. They are described by others as moody. Guilt feelings and episodes of depression may occur. Such persons lack energy and do not have many interests.
- Low scorers on Scale 0 tend to be sociable and extroverted. They are outgoing, gregarious, friendly, and talkative. They have a strong need to be around other people, and they mix well socially. They are seen by others as verbally fluent, expressive, active, energetic, and vigorous. They are interested in power, status, and recognition, and they tend to seek out competitive situations.
- Low scores on Scale 0 are indicative of persons who are sociable, extroverted, outgoing, gregarious, friendly, and talkative; who have a strong need to be around other people; who mix well; and who are seen as expressive and verbally fluent.

References & Readings

Butcher, J. N. (1989). *Minnesota Multiphasic Personality Inventory-2, user's guide, the Minnesota Report: Adult clinical system*. Minneapolis: National Computer Systems.

Butcher, J. N., Dahlstrom, W. G., Graham, J. R., Tellegen, A., & Kaemmer, B. (1989). *Minnesota Multiphasic Personality Inventory (MMPI-2): Manual for administration and scoring*. Minneapolis: University of Minnesota Press.

Butcher, J. N., & Williams, C. L. (1992). *Essentials of MMPI-2 and MMPI-A interpretation*. Minneapolis: University of Minnesota Press.

Duckworth, J. C., & Anderson, W. P. (1995). *MMPI and MMPI-2: Interpretation manual for counselors and clinicians* (4th ed.). Bristol, PA: Accelerated Development.

Graham, J. R. (1990). *MMPI-2: Assessing personality and psychopathology*. New York: Oxford University Press.

Graham, J. R., Ben-Porath, Y. S., & McNulty, J. L. (in press). Empirical correlates of low scores on MMPI-2 scales in an out-patient mental health setting. *Psychological Assessment*.

Graham, J. R., Ben-Porath, Y. S., & McNulty, J. L. (in press). *MMPI-2 correlates for outpatient mental health settings*. Minneapolis: University of Minnesota Press.

Graham J. R., & McCord, G. (1985). Interpretation of moderately elevated MMPI scores for normal subjects. *Journal of Personality Assessment, 49*, 477–484.

Greene, R. L. (1991). *The MMPI-2/MMPI: An interpretive manual*. Boston: Allyn and Bacon.

Keiller, S. W., & Graham, J. R. (1993). The meaning of low scores on MMPI-2 clinical scales of normal subjects. *Journal of Personality Assessment, 61*, 211–223.

Related Topics

29   USING THE MMPI-2 IN ASSESSING ALCOHOL OR DRUG ABUSE

Roger L. Greene

The use of any form of psychological assessment of alcohol or drug abuse has been hampered by the traditional bias in the field against any form of assessment, which has stated more or less explicitly that once a person stops drinking or drugging, his or her other problems will go away. Clinicians also must consider a number of potential issues in alcohol or drug abuse and their potential impact on the Minnesota Multiphasic Personality Inventory-2 (MMPI-2): whether the person uses substances constantly, only on weekends, or during binges; gender differences in substance abuse and the consequences of substance abuse (Galanter, 1996); the type of substance(s) used, as well as whether the person uses only one substance or multiple substances; whether the person uses substances only by himself or herself, withdraws and isolates as the result of the use of substances, uses only in social contexts, or exhibits some combination of these behaviors; how the person is entering treatment, since it may be voluntarily or because of the "encouragement" of the legal system, employer, or spouse; and finally, the person's socioeconomic class and education. All these issues and factors can have significant effects on both how the person responds to and the interpretations made of the MMPI-2.

The primary dilemma regarding the timing of administering the MMPI-2 is that early assessment can provide information that is crucial for effective treatment planning, but administration too soon after admission may be distorted by the consequences of toxicity or withdrawal. Clinicians who treat alcoholics and other substance-dependent patients are well aware of the need to delay the administration of the MMPI-2 when the patient who enters the treatment program is still suffering from the toxic effects of withdrawal. Despite the awareness of the need to delay assessment to allow for detoxification and withdrawal, clear guidelines for the optimal time to administer the MMPI-2 are lacking. Recommendations regarding the optimal time for testing may vary depending on such factors as the drug abused by the patient, the severity and length of the abuse, the person's age and general health status, and so on. As a rule of thumb, clinicians should wait approximately 7–10 days following detoxification before administering the MMPI-2. In all cases, measures of consistency of item endorsement (Variable Response Inconsistency Scale) need to be reviewed carefully to ensure that the person has responded to the items appropriately.

SCREENING WITH THE MMPI-2

The importance of screening for substance abuse problems cannot be overestimated when it is considered that the lifetime prevalence for substance abuse disorders in adult men approaches 16% and that at least 20% of adults who visit a physician have had an alcohol problem at some time. Similar concerns arise in clinical settings, where prevalence for substance abuse has been estimated to range from 12% to 30%. Clinicians frequently fail to recognize that the patient's symptoms may reflect substance abuse or dependence rather than, or in addition to, psychiatric symptomatology (Jacobson, 1989).

The MMPI-2 has three scales that can be used to screen for substance abuse problems. The MacAndrew Alcoholism Scale-Revised (MAC-R) has been a standard in the field for a number of years, and most clinicians are familiar with it. The Addiction Admission Scale (AAS), a 13 item scale, differs significantly from the MAC-R in that it focuses on simple denial or acknowledgment of substance abuse problems. The Addiction Potential Scale (APS), a 39-item scale, was designed to identify personality features and lifestyle patterns that are related to alcohol and drug abuse.

The MAC-R identifies White men who have a propensity to use substances, with 70–75% hit rates and false negatives around 20% (Greene & Garvin, 1988). Data on adolescents and White women who use substances are less reliable because of limited research. There are substantial gender effects on the MAC-R, with women scoring approximately 2 points lower than men, and significant effects of the type of setting in which the MMPI-2 is administered. When White men who use substances must be discriminated from other psychiatric patients, hit rates decrease and the percentage of false positives increases. When patients have comorbid disorders, these discriminations become even more difficult. Finally, the MAC-R should be used very cautiously with Black men because of the extremely low hit rates and high percentages of false positives in psychiatric samples. It is unclear whether similar problems occur in other ethnic groups and with Black women because there is no research on which to make any conclusions. Gottesman and Prescott (1989) have summarized the issues involved in the use of the MAC-R in settings with low prevalence; their work deserves careful reading by all clinicians.

The research on the MAC-R with polydrug patients clearly is less complete than with alcoholic patients (Greene & Garvin, 1988). Elevated scores on the MAC-R in polydrug patients indicate that the MAC-R is sensitive to the misuse of all types of substances, including alcohol. The MAC-R could more appropriately be called a "substance abuse" scale rather than an "alcoholism" scale. The "substances" that are misused do not have to be "street" drugs either, since legally prescribed medications also are prone to such misuse. There do not appear to be any ethnic differences between Black and White male polydrug patients in terms of their mean performance on the MAC-R. Yet the finding that Black male psychiatric patients score nearly in the same range as Black polydrug and alcoholic patients suggests that the MAC-R probably is less effective with members of other ethnic groups. Finally, data are needed on the performance of the MAC-R in other samples of polydrug patients such as women and adolescents. Until such information is available, the MAC-R should be used cautiously in these groups, too.

Since the AAS and APS are relatively new MMPI-2 scales, there is little information on them. They do appear to have utility in identifying individuals who have problems with alcohol or drugs. These scales, similar to the MAC-R, do not discriminate alcohol abuse from drug abuse but rather identify substance abuse in general. Clinicians should explore the issue of alcohol or drug abuse with any person who elevates AAS to a T score of 65 or higher, since the items relate directly to substance abuse. The APS does not appear to have significant gender effects like those seen on the MAC-R, so the APS may be more appropriate for screening women.

Finally, clinicians need to review item 489

on the MMPI-2 ("I have a drug or alcohol problem") with all persons, since a "true" response highlights a major treatment issue. Clinicians also may decide that the endorsement of any items on the AAS is worthy of further investigation.

FREQUENTLY OCCURRING CODETYPES

Several conclusions can be drawn from the performance of alcoholic patients on the standard MMPI-2 validity and clinical scales (Graham & Strenger, 1988; Greene & Garvin, 1988). First, it is clear that there is no unitary alcoholic personality. Instead, there seems to be a number of smaller, more discrete subgroups of alcoholics, although the composition of these subgroups depends on the method used to identify them. The codetype research would suggest several subgroups (2-4/4-2, 2-7/7-2, 4-9/9-4) in both men and women alcoholics and additional codetypes that are specific to men (1-2/2-1) and women (3-4/4-3, 4-6/6-4, and 4-8/8-4). Empirical methods such as cluster analysis also identify subgroups of alcoholic patients (2-7-8-4, 4-9, and 1-2-3-4), which have some degree of overlap with those identified by codetype research. These subgroups, however, account for only 25–35% of alcoholic patients. Second, there has been only limited work to examine whether these subgroups of alcoholics have different treatment outcomes/processes and/or drinking histories. It would be interesting to know whether specific subgroups of alcoholic patients are more successful in a particular type of treatment or that they have a particular history of substance use. Finally, groups other than the typical White male alcoholics are rarely examined, so it is difficult to be totally confident in applying these conclusions to other ethnic groups.

A number of conclusions also can be drawn from the MMPI-2 performance of polydrug patients. First, it is clear that there is no unitary polydrug personality, just as there is no unitary alcoholic personality. Instead, there seems to be a number of smaller, more discrete subgroups of polydrug patients, although the composition of these subgroups differs from those seen in alcoholic patients. The codetype research would suggest several subgroups (4-8/8-4 and 4-9/9-4) are seen frequently in both men and women, White polydrug patients, and additional codetypes that are specific to White men (6-8/8-6, 7-8/8-7, and 8-9/9-8). Second, Black male polydrug patients appear to be less emotionally disturbed than White men. Third, and again similar to the alcoholic patients, there has been virtually no work to examine whether these subgroups of polydrug patients have different treatment outcomes and/or histories of drug use. The influence of the multitude of moderator variables such as education, social class, and clinical setting on these subgroups of polydrug patients has been given little consideration.

Clinicians need to be familiar with two other MMPI-2 profiles that occur frequently in alcohol or drug abuse patients: Within-Normal-Limit (WNL) profiles (no T score equal to 65 or higher) and overreported, "fake-bad" profiles. WNL profiles reflect a lack of emotional distress in these patients even though they are in a treatment program. This lack of distress underlies the limited motivation to change that is encountered all too often in these patients. Patients who overreport their emotional distress are at high risk for leaving treatment despite the severe level of distress they seemingly are reporting on the MMPI-2. It is not clear whether their level of distress reflects a response style or the presence of comorbid psychopathology that interferes with their participating in treatment. Regardless of its causation, these patients are prone to terminate treatment prematurely.

PRESENCE OF A COMORBID DISORDER

In recent years, increased attention has been given to the existence of comorbid disorders—some form of psychopathology in conjunction with substance abuse. When the MMPI-2 is administered during the first few days of treatment, many patients may appear anxious, depressed, or psychotic, and it is difficult to deter-

mine whether those pathological patterns reflect the effects of toxicity or more enduring personality characteristics. Therefore, it often is difficult to use early assessment data to differentiate between those patients who have a comorbid disorder and those whose symptoms are residuals of substance abuse. This difficulty in making an accurate assessment is a significant roadblock because of the need to initiate specific treatments for patients with comorbid disorders.

Substance abuse patients frequently meet the *DSM-IV* criteria for an additional mental disorder, such as anxiety disorder, mood disorder, or schizophrenia. Antisocial personality disorder also is a common additional diagnosis for substance abuse patients, although such patients also have been found to have a variety of other personality disorders. The presence of a comorbid disorder in a substance abuse patient has important treatment implications because the additional problems can affect the patient's responses to substance abuse treatment, as well as the length and outcome of treatment, and can require that substance abuse treatment be supplemented with additional treatment components designed to respond to the individual needs of the patient.

SUMMARY

The MMPI-2 can provide valuable information to the clinician, from screening for alcohol or drug abuse to identifying personality characteristics and comorbid disorders that can affect the course of treatment. Clinicians should consider the routine administration of the MMPI-2 to all patients in alcohol or drug treatment so that these issues can be handled appropriately.

References & Readings

Galanter, M. (Ed.) (1996). *Recent developments in alcoholism: Vol. 12. Alcoholism and women.* New York: Plenum Press.

Gottesman, I. I., & Prescott, C. A. (1989). Abuses of the MacAndrew Alcoholism Scale: A critical review. *Clinical Psychology Review, 9,* 223–242.

Graham, J. R., & Strenger, V. E. (1988). MMPI characteristics of alcoholics: A review. *Journal of*

Consulting and Clinical Psychology, 56, 197–205.

Greene, R. L., & Banken, J. A. (1995). Assessing alcohol/drug abuse problems. In J. N. Butcher (Ed.), *Clinical personality assessment: Practical approaches* (pp. 460–474). New York: Oxford University Press.

Greene, R. L., & Garvin, R. D. (1988). Substance abuse/dependence. In R. L. Greene (Ed.), *The MMPI: Use in specific populations* (pp. 159–197). San Antonio, TX: Grune and Stratton.

Jacobson, G. R. (1989). A comprehensive approach to pretreatment evaluation: I. Detection, assessment, and diagnosis of alcoholism. In R. K. Hester & W. R. Miller (Eds.), *Handbook of alcoholism treatment approaches* (pp. 17–53). Elmsford, NY: Pergamon Press.

30   MILLON CLINICAL MULTIAXIAL INVENTORY (MCMI-III)

Theodore Millon & Roger D. Davis

Diagnostic instruments are most useful when developed on the basis of a comprehensive theory of psychopathology and coordinated with a recognized diagnostic system. Both the MCMI's Personality Disorder (Axis II) and Clinical Syndrome (Axis I) categories meet these criteria. In the MCMI-III, further parallelism has been achieved by rephrasing major criteria of the *DSM-IV* constructs and validating these items in the self-report mode. Accordingly, the diagnostic efficiency of the MCMI-III (Millon, Millon, & Davis, 1994) shows an incremental increase over that of the MCMI-II (Davis, Wenger, & Guzman, 1997). Few diagnostic instruments currently available are as fully consonant as the MCMI-III with the nosological format and conceptual terminology of the *DSM-IV*.

DESCRIPTION

The inventory itself consists of 24 clinical scales (presented as a profile in Table 1) and 3 "modifier" scales. The purpose of these first three indices, Disclosure, Desirability, and Debasement (X, Y, and Z), is to identify distorting tendencies in clients' responses. The next two sections constitute the basic personality disorder scales, reflecting Axis II of the *DSM*. The first section (1–8B) appraises the moderately severe personality pathologies, ranging from the Schizoid to the Self-Defeating (masochistic) scales; the second section (Scales S, C, and P) represents more severe personality pathologies: the Schizotypal, Borderline, and Paranoid. The following two sections cover several of the more prevalent Axis I disorders,

TABLE 1. Sample Profile Illustrating the Structure and Scales of the MCMI-III

Category		Raw	BR	Profile of BR Scores	Diagnostic Scales
		Score		0 60 75 85 115	
Modifying indices	X	135	79		Disclosure
	Y	18	84		Desirability
	Z	7	56		Debasement
Clinical personality patterns	1	7	63		Schizoid
	2A	6	69		Avoidant
	2B	3	55		Depressive
	3	7	60		Dependent
	4	22	68		Histrionic
	5	27	103		Narcissistic
	6A	20	88		Antisocial
	6B	21	85		Aggressive (Sadistic)
	7	10	34		Compulsive
	8A	17	80		Negativistic
	8B	1	15		Masochistic
Severe personality pathology	S	2	37		Schizotypal
	C	11	69		Borderline
	P	9	63		Paranoid
Clinical syndromes	A	3	57		Anxiety Disorder
	H	2	57		Somatoform Disorder
	N	6	59		Bipolar Manic Disorder
	D	3	57		Dysthymic Disorder
	B	17	99		Alcohol Dependence
	T	12	70		Drug Dependence
	R	2	27		Posttraumatic Stress
Severe syndromes	SS	2	27		Thought Disorder
	CC	1	17		Major Depression
	PP	3	60		Delusion Disorder

ranging from the moderate clinical syndromes (Scales A to T) to those of greater severity (Scales SS, CC, and PP). The division between personality and clinical disorder scales parallels the multiaxial model and has important interpretive implications.

Development of the Millon inventories has been informed by several post-MMPI psychometric developments. When the MCMI was initially constructed, all item selections were based on target diagnostic groups contrasted with representative, but undifferentiated, psychiatric patients (rather than normals), thus increasing differential diagnostic efficiency. Item selection and scale development for both older and more recent forms progressed through three sequential validation stages (Loevinger, 1957): theoretical-substantive, internal-structural, and external-criterion. Such an approach builds validity into the instrument

from the beginning, upholding standards of developers committed to diverse construction and validation methods (Hase & Goldberg, 1967). The resulting scales are theoretically, statistically, and empirically valid. Because each item must survive each stage of refinement, the chance that any item will prove "rationally surprising," "structurally unsound," or "empirically indiscriminant" is greatly diminished. The final MCMI-III items are weighted either 2 points or 1 point, depending on the extent to which they fulfill this tripartite logic: centrality to their respective constructs, relation to other items on the same scale, and external validity. As might be expected, the likelihood of instrument generalizability is greatly increased by such an approach to instrument construction.

Actuarial base rate transformations were used as the final measure of pathology. These not only provide a basis for selecting optimal differential diagnostic cutting lines but also help ensure that the frequencies of MCMI-generated diagnoses and profile patterns are comparable to representative clinical prevalence rates. Although the use of base rate scores has been one of the most widely misunderstood aspects of the MCMI, their utility is easily understood intuitively when contrasted with the more familiar T score. On the MMPI, for example, T scores of 65 and above indicate pathology, with roughly equal numbers of patients scoring above this threshold. Clinical experience, however, shows the number of depressed patients, for example, to be greater than the number of patients with a thought disorder. Base rate scores are constructed to reflect these clinical realities, to yield more depressives than delusional patients, more borderlines and antisocials than schizoids, and so on, rather than to assume their numbers to be equal. In the construction of the MCMI, target prevalence rates were set according to reviews of epidemiological data, estimates derived from clinicians who participated in the development project, and the senior author's own expert judgment. Thus, if it was deemed that 8% of patients are most likely to resemble the schizoid prototype, then the lookup table for this personality was constructed so schizoid was the highest personality elevation for 8% of the patients in the normative sample.

A discussion of base rate scores often leads to considerations of local versus global base rates, that is, the fact that the prevalence rates for different disorders vary somewhat by clinical setting. When this is raised in criticism of the concept, it is usually intended to support the continued use of T scores. However, as noted earlier, the base rate scores of the MCMI are intended to remedy the global base rate assumptions made in the use of T scores. Thus, while the prevalence rates of some disorders in particular clinical settings may differ from the base rates assumed by the MCMI and in the use of T scores, the MCMI's base rate scores at least do not implicitly assume the prevalence rates of all disorders to be equal. More frequently, the distinction between local and global prevalence rates is made in support of the base rate concept by clinicians who realize its importance in improving diagnostic efficiency, that is, positive and negative predictive power, sensitivity, and specificity. These clinicians, far from reverting back to T scores, often wish to optimize the base rate scores for their particular setting.

USES, SETTINGS, AND LIMITATIONS

The primary purpose of the MCMI is to provide information to clinicians—psychologists, counselors, psychiatrists, and social workers—who must make assessments and treatment decisions about persons with emotional and interpersonal difficulties. Because of the simplicity of administration and the availability of hand-scoring and rapid computer-scoring and interpretive procedures, the MCMI can be used on a routine basis in outpatient clinics, community agencies, mental health centers, college counseling programs, general and mental hospitals, correctional institutions, forensic settings, and courts, as well as in general independent practice offices. Individual scale-cutting lines can be used to make decisions concerning personality disorders or clinical syndrome diagnoses. Similarly, elevation levels among subsets of scales can furnish grounds for judgments about impairment, severity, and chronicity of pathology. More comprehensive and dynamic interpretations of relationships among symptomatology, coping behavior, interpersonal style, and personality structure may be derived from an examination of the configural pattern of the clinical scales.

The MCMI-III, however, is not a general personality instrument to be used for "normal" populations. To administer the MCMI to a wider range of problems or class of participants, such as those found in business and industry, or to use it to identify neurological lesions or for the assessment of general personality traits among college students is to apply the instrument to settings and samples for which it is neither intended nor appropriate.

The MCMI is frequently used in research. Upwards of 500 publications to date have included or focused primarily on the MCMI, with some 60 or so new references currently published annually (a list of these references can be obtained from National Computer Systems, attention: Ginny Smith). A series of special grants for conducting research using the MCMI-III is currently available from National Computer Systems. Those interested should also request *Doing Publishable Research With the MCMI* (Hsu & Maruish, 1993) for helpful suggestions.

ADMINISTRATION AND SCORING

A principal goal in constructing the MCMI was to keep the total number of items small enough to encourage use in diverse diagnostic and treatment settings yet large enough to permit the assessment of a wide range of clinically relevant behaviors. At 175 items, the final form is much shorter than comparable instruments. Potentially objectionable items have been screened out, with terminology geared to an eighth-grade reading level. Most clients can complete the MCMI in 20–30 minutes, thereby minimizing client resistance and fatigue.

Administration follows a procedure similar to that of most self-report inventories. Test directions, a patient information chart, an identification grid, and special coding sections for clinicians are printed on the front page. No special conditions or instructions are required to achieve reliable results beyond those printed on the test booklet itself. Answer choices (true and false) are printed next to each of the 175 item statements. This increases the accuracy of patient markings and allows the clinician to scan individual item responses.

INTERPRETATION

Clinicians interpreting the MCMI should bear in mind that the richness and accuracy of all self-report measures are enhanced when their findings are viewed in the context of other clinical sources and data, such as demographic background, biographical history, and other clinical features. The personality and clinical features characterizing each of the separate scales should be reviewed before analyzing profile configurations. Configural interpretation is a deductive synthesis achieved by refining, blending, and integrating the separate characteristics tapped by each scale. The accuracy of such interpretations depends on the meaning and significance of the individual scales composing the profile. Such an interpretive procedure seeks to break the pattern of labeling patients and fitting them into Procrustean categories. Information concerning sex, age, socioeconomic class, mental status observations, and interviews should all be used to provide a perspective for assessing the MCMI profile.

A basic separation should be made in the initial phase of interpretation between those scales pertaining to the basic clinical personality pattern (1–8B), those pointing to the presence of severe Axis II personality pathology (S, C, and P), those signifying moderate Axis I clinical syndromes (A–R), and those indicating a severe clinical state (SS, CC, and PP). Each section of the profile reflects different and important dimensions of the clinical picture. Therefore, the clinician should begin by dividing the profile into a series of subsections, focusing first on the significance of scale elevations and profile patterns within each section. Once this is completed, the clinician can proceed with the step of integrating each subsection.

The theoretical framework and clinical characterizations associated with each personality style are available in *Modern Psychopathology* (Millon, 1969/1983), *Toward a New Personology: An Evolutionary Model* (Millon, 1990), and *Disorders of Personality: DSM-IV and Beyond* (Millon & Davis, 1996). Several synopses of the various personality styles that serve as useful aids to interpretation are included in these works. In each of these, the characteristics of personality have been usefully organized in a manner similar to distinctions drawn in the biological realm, that is, by dividing them into *structural* and *functional* attributes. Functional characteristics represent dynamic processes that transpire within the intrapsychic world and between the individual's self and psychosocial environment. They repre-

TABLE 2. Domain Descriptors for the Narcissistic Personality

Behavioral Level

(F) Expressively Haughty (e.g., acts in an arrogant, supercilious, pompous, and disdainful manner, flouting conventional rules of shared social living, viewing them as naive or inapplicable to self; reveals a careless disregard for personal integrity and a self-important indifference to the rights of others)

(F) Interpersonally Exploitive (e.g., feels entitled, is unempathic, and expects special favors without assuming reciprocal responsibilities; shamelessly takes others for granted and uses them to enhance self and indulge desires)

Phenomenological Level

(F) Cognitively Expansive (e.g., has an undisciplined imagination and exhibits a preoccupation with immature and self-glorifying fantasies of success, beauty, or love; is minimally constrained by objective reality, takes liberties with facts, and often lies to redeem self-illusions)

(S) Admirable Self-Image (e.g., believes self to be meritorious, special, if not unique, deserving of great admiration, and acting in a grandiose or self-assured manner, often without commensurate achievements; has a sense of high self-worth, despite being seen by others as egotistic, inconsiderate, and arrogant)

(S) Contrived Objects (e.g., internalized representations are composed far more than usual of illusory and changing memories of past relationships; unacceptable drives and conflicts are readily refashioned as the need arises, as are others often stimulated and pretentious)

Intrapsychic Level

(F) Rationalization Mechanism (e.g., is self-deceptive and facile in devising plausible reasons to justify self-centered and socially inconsiderate behaviors; offers alibis to place oneself in the best possible light, despite evident shortcomings or failures)

(S) Spurious Organization (e.g., morphologic structures underlying coping and defensive strategies tend to be flimsy and transparent, appear more substantial and dynamically orchestrated than they are in fact, regulating impulses only marginally, channeling needs with minimal restraint, and creating an inner world in which conflicts are dismissed; failures are quickly redeemed and self-pride is effortlessly reasserted)

Biophysical Level

(S) Insouciant Mood (e.g., manifests a general air of nonchalance, imperturbability, and feigned tranquility; appears coolly unimpressionable or buoyantly optimistic, except when narcissistic confidence is shaken, at which time either rage, shame, or emptiness is briefly displayed)

sent "expressive modes of regulatory action." Structural attributes represent a deeply embedded and relatively enduring template of imprinted memories, attitudes, needs, fears, conflicts, and so on, which guide experience and transform the nature of perceived events. These domains are further differentiated according to their respective data level, either biophysical, intrapsychic, phenomenological, or behavioral, reflecting the four historical approaches that characterize the study of psychopathology, namely, the biological, the psychoanalytic, the cognitive, and the behavioral.

Table 2 presents domain descriptors for the Narcissistic personality. A more complete set of descriptors is available in the above sources and in the MCMI-III manual. In addition, *Disorders of Personality* presents new adult subtypes for each of the various personality disorders. These descriptions form more specific prototypes against which real patients can be compared.

In addition to undertaking interpretation's on one's own, the Microtest Q program (available from National Computer Systems, attention: Ginny Smith) is available for generating rapid and convenient MCMI narratives. These integrate both the personological and symptomatic features of the patient; the final report is arranged in a style similar to those prepared by clinical psychologists. As the report is generated, data are drawn from both scale score elevations and profile configurations and are based on both actuarial research findings and the MCMI's theoretical schema (Millon, 1969/1983, 1986a, 1986b, 1990; Millon et al., 1994; Millon & Davis, 1996), as well as the *DSM-IV*. Following current psychodiagnostic thinking, the Interpretive Report focuses on a multiaxial framework of assessment and summarizes findings along its several axes: clinical syndrome, personality disorder, psychosocial stressors, and therapeutic implications. The latter section has been greatly expanded specifically for the MCMI-III. These reports prove highly accurate in about 55–65% of cases; are appraised as both useful and generally valid, but with partial misjudgments, in about another 25–30% of cases; and seem off target or appreciably in error about 10–15% of the time. These positive figures are in the quantitative range of 5–6 times greater than are random diagnostic assignments or chance (Millon, 1987). Note, however, that the report is intended to serve as a rich source of clinical hypotheses. What is selected, rejected, emphasized, or de-emphasized in the final analysis depends on the individual case and the user's experience and judgment. As noted by Wetzler and Marlowe (1992), "The test is only as good as its user" (p. 428). A more basic Profile Report is also available.

The MCMI's diagnostic scale cutoffs and profile interpretations are oriented to the majority of patients who take the inventory, that is, to those displaying psychic disturbances in the midranges of severity rather than those whose difficulties are either close to "normal" (e.g., workers' compensation litigants, spouses of patients) or of marked clinical severity (e.g., acute psychotics, chronic schizophrenics). Accordingly, narrative analyses of patients experiencing ordinary life difficulties or minor adjustment disorders will tend to be construed as more troubled than they are; conversely, analyses of the most serious pathologies will often be construed as less severe than they are.

CONCLUSION

Within the limitations of the self-report mode and the inherent restrictions of psychometric technology, all steps were taken to maximize the MCMI-III's concordance with its generative theory and the official classification system. Pragmatic and philosophical compromises were made where valued objectives could not be simultaneously achieved—instrument brevity versus item independence, representative national patient norms versus local base rate specificity, theoretical criterion considerations versus empirical data. As was the case with its forebears, the MCMI-III is not cast in stone. It is and will remain an evolving assessment instrument, upgraded and refined to reflect substantive advances in knowledge, be it from theory, research, or clinical experience.

References & Readings

Butcher, J. N. (Ed.) (1972). *Objective personality assessment*. New York: Academic Press.

Choca, J. P., Shanley, L. A., & Van Denburg, E. (1992). *Interpretive guide to the Millon Clinical Multiaxial Inventory*. Washington, DC: American Psychological Association.

Davis, R. D., & Millon, T. (1993). Putting Humpty Dumpty back together again: The MCMI in personality assessment. In L. Beutler (Ed.), *Integrative personality assessment* (pp. 240–279). New York: Guilford Press.

Davis, R. D., Wenger, A., & Guzman, A. (1997). Diagnostic efficiency of the MCMI-III. In T. Millon (Ed.), *The Millon inventories*. New York: Guilford Press.

Hase, H. D., & Goldberg, L. R. (1967). Comparative validity of different strategies of constructing personality inventory scales. *Psychological Bulletin, 67*, 231–248.

Hsu, F., & Maruish, M. (1993). *Doing publishable research with the MCMI*. Minneapolis, MN: National Computer Systems.

Loevinger, J. (1957). Objective tests as instruments of psychological theory. *Psychological Reports, 3*, 635–694.

McCann, J. T., & Dyer, F. J. (1996). *Forensic assessment with the Millon inventories*. New York: Guilford Press.

Millon, T. (1983). *Modern psychopathology: A biosocial approach to maladaptive learning* and functioning. Prospect Heights, IL: Waveland Press. (Original work published 1969.)

Millon, T. (1986a). Personality prototypes and their diagnostic criteria. In T. Millon & G. Klerman (Eds.), *Contemporary directions in psychopathology: Toward the DSM-IV*. New York: Guilford Press.

Millon, T. (1986b). A theoretical derivation of pathological personalities. In T. Millon & G. Klerman (Eds.), *Contemporary directions in psychopathology: Toward the DSM-IV*. New York: Guilford Press.

Millon, T. (1987). *Millon Clinical Multiaxial Inventory-II manual*. Minneapolis, MN: National Computer Systems.

Millon, T. (1990). *Toward a new personology: An evolutionary model*. New York: Wiley-Interscience.

Millon, T. (Ed.) (1997). *The Millon inventories: Contemporary clinical and personality assessment*. New York: Guilford Press.

Millon, T., & Davis, R. D. (1996). *Disorders of personality: DSM-IV and beyond*. New York: Wiley-Interscience.

Millon, T., Millon, C., & Davis, R. D. (1994). *Millon Clinical Multiaxial Inventory-III manual*. Minneapolis, MN: National Computer Systems.

Rosen, A. (1962). Development of the MMPI scales based on a reference group of psychiatric patients. *Psychological Monographs*, 76(527).

Wetzler, S., & Marlowe, D. (1992). What they don't tell you in the test manual: A response to Millon. *Journal of Counseling and Development*, 70, 427–428.

Related Topics

31 THUMBNAIL GUIDE TO THE RORSCHACH INKBLOT METHOD

Barry A. Ritzler

MATERIALS

The Rorschach Inkblot Method stimulus materials consist of 10 inkblots designed by Hermann Rorschach when he developed the method in the early 1920s (Rorschach, 1921). All 10 inkblots should be administered in numerical order (I–X). A notepad is necessary for verbatim note taking, with two sections on the same page for First Viewing responses and Inquiry (see "Administration Procedures"). A scoring summary sheet and a location chart (a page with miniature copies of the 10 blots) also should be used.

FREQUENTLY USED SYSTEMS

Four somewhat different systems are used with noticeable frequency by psychologists in the United States:

• The *Rorschach Comprehensive System* (Exner, 1993): First published in 1974, this system was derived from empirical analysis of the Rorschach to establish acceptable levels of reliability and validity. The Comprehensive System incorporates coding variables from several other systems and has become the most frequently used Rorschach system in the United States (Piotrowski & Keller, 1992).

- The *Beck System* (Beck, Beck, Levitt, & Molish, 1961): Prior to the development of the Comprehensive System, this was one of the two most frequently used systems.
- The *Klopfer System* (Klopfer & Kelley, 1942): This was the other most frequently used system before the Comprehensive System.
- The *Rapaport System* (Rapaport, Gill, & Schafer, 1946): Though less frequently used than the Beck and Klopfer Systems, the Rapaport System tends to be favored by psychoanalytically oriented psychologists because of its conceptual ties to the theory.

The Rorschach is used throughout the world, and numerous systems exist in other countries but have not been introduced in the United States. The International Rorschach Society (Weiner, 1994) is an organization that brings together Rorschach psychologists from many different countries for the exchange of views on different approaches to the Rorschach Method.

ADMINISTRATION PROCEDURES

Although administration procedures differ somewhat between the frequently used systems, some basic principles apply to all systems. For instance, the key to administration is to minimize the influence of the examiner. The Method should be introduced with a minimum of explanation. It usually is sufficient to indicate that the Method is a common procedure used by psychologists to assess personality. No more specific information about the Method should be conveyed before administration.

The initial instructions are very simple. For example, the Comprehensive System (Exner, 1993) simply asks the initial question "What might this be?" as the subject is handed the first inkblot.

For most systems, all 10 blots are presented consecutively for a First Viewing, which affords the subject an opportunity to respond to each blot with little intervention by the examiner, who primarily is occupied taking verbatim notes. After the initial responses to all 10 blots are recorded, the blots are presented again for an Inquiry period in which the examiner attempts to gain more information about the responses by making concise, nonleading inquiries. The subject's responses to these inquiries also are recorded verbatim. The only exception to this procedure is the Rapaport System (Rapaport et al., 1946), which administers the Inquiry immediately after the First Viewing response is obtained for each blot and before the next blot is presented. It was Rapaport's intention to obtain Inquiry information while the process of the First Viewing response was fresh in the subject's mind. The other systems are concerned that immediate Inquiry will bias the subject's responses on subsequent blots.

The purpose of the Inquiry is to determine where each response is located on the blot and what stimulus qualities of the blot influenced (or determined) the subject's responses (e.g., shape, color, or shading). The Inquiry also is used to clarify ambiguities in the subject's communication of the response.

Detailed administration manuals exist for each system and should be consulted for more specific instruction in proper administration.

CODING (SCORING)

The Rorschach Inkblot Method should not be used without the application of one of the accepted coding systems. Without coding, the psychologist cannot take advantage of the substantial empirical validation and systematic methods of interpretation that exist for the Method. Rorschach interpretation without coding risks an overly subjective assessment biased by the psychologist's idiosyncratic associations to the form and content of the subject's responses. Most Rorschach experts consider interpretation without coding to be a misuse of the Method (Exner, 1993; Allison, Blatt, & Zimet, 1968).

INTERPRETATION

Interpretation of personality functioning using the Rorschach Inkblot Method is based on tallies and variables calculated from the coding of all responses and the content of the responses. For all frequently used systems, the calculated variables yield interpretive hypotheses supported by empirical research. Content analysis complements and broadens the understanding of the subject's personality, but it should not be done without integration with interpretive hypotheses obtained from the Method's quantitative variables.

Although the Rorschach Inkblot Method yields much useful information, it should seldom, if ever, be used by itself for personality assessment. Integration must be made with other valid personality information from testing, behavioral observations, facts of the subject's life history and current living situation, and objectively reported symptoms.

TRAINING

The Society for Personality Assessment's Standards for Training (Society for Personality Assessment, 1995) set the minimum standard for training in the Rorschach and other assessment methods at two semesters of graduate school coursework followed by practicum, internship, and postdoctoral training in the methods. Surveys indicate that most American Psychological Association (APA)–approved graduate programs in applied psychology teach the Rorschach Inkblot Method (e.g., Ritzler & Alter, 1986) but that the majority of such programs offer only one semester of instruction, so that the student must often seek supplementary training. However, since the Rorschach is a frequently used clinical method (Piotrowski & Keller, 1992), it is not difficult to find internships that offer training in the Method. Also, opportunities exist for postdoctoral training in the Method through postdoctoral fellowships and/or widely advertised workshops presented by qualified instructors. Such training beyond the graduate school level is essential for development of expertise in the Rorschach Inkblot Method.

APPLICATIONS

The Rorschach Inkblot Method has proved useful in the following settings and situations, among others:

- Treatment planning for inpatients and outpatients in public and private settings
- School assessments, particularly for classroom behavioral and learning problems
- Forensic applications such as the assessment of competence and criminal insanity, parole evaluations, custody determinations, assessment of psychological trauma and injury, and sentencing consultation
- Research methodology (see especially Exner, 1995)
- Assessment of the personality consequences of brain dysfunction (in conjunction with neuropsychological assessment)
- Vocational assessment for such purposes as employee selection and placement, evaluation of individual vocational problems, and consultation for workplace relationship problems

SOURCES OF INFORMATION REGARDING THE RORSCHACH INKBLOT METHOD

Psychologists can follow current developments in the Rorschach Inkblot Method by consulting the following publications:

- *Journal for Personality Assessment* (journal published by the Society for Personality Assessment)
- *Psychological Assessment* (journal published by the American Psychological Association)
- *Assessment* (journal published by Psychological Assessment Resources)
- *Rorschachiana* (yearbook published by the International Rorschach Society)

References & Readings

Allison, J., Blatt, S., & Zimet, C. (1968). *The interpretation of psychological tests.* New York: Harper and Row.
Beck, S., Beck, A., Levitt, E., & Molish, B. (1961).

Rorschach's test I: Basic processes (3rd ed.). New York: Grune and Stratton.

Exner, J. (1993). *The Rorschach: A comprehensive system*. New York: Wiley.

Exner, J. (Ed.) (1995). *Issues and methods in Rorschach research*. Mahwah, NJ: Erlbaum.

Klopfer, B., & Kelley, D. (1942). *The Rorschach Technique*. Yonkers, NY: World Book.

Piotrowski, C., & Keller, J. (1992). Psychological testing in applied settings: A literature review from 1982–1992. *Journal of Training and Practice in Professional Psychology, 6,* 74–82.

Rapaport, D., Gill, M., & Schafer, R. (1946). *Diagnostic psychological testing* (Vols. 1 & 2). Chicago: Yearbook Publishers.

Ritzler, B., & Alter, B. (1986). Rorschach teaching in APA approved clinical graduate programs: A ten-year update. *Journal of Personality Assessment, 50,* 44–49.

Rorschach, H. (1921). *Psychodiagnostik.* Bern: Bircher; trans., Bern: Hans Huber Verlag, 1942.

Society for Personality Assessment (1995). *Membership directory.* Mahwah, NJ: Erlbaum.

Weiner, I. (1994). Speaking Rorschach: Building bridges of understanding. *Rorschachiana, 19,* 1–6.

Related Topics

32   RORSCHACH DIFFERENTIATION OF SCHIZOPHRENIA AND AFFECTIVE DISORDER

Irving B. Weiner

RORSCHACH IDENTIFICATION OF SCHIZOPHRENIA

For purposes of personality assessment, schizophrenia can be conceptualized as a breakdown in certain cognitive, interpersonal, and integrative psychological functions that is characterized by disordered thinking, inaccurate perception, interpersonal ineptness, and inadequate control of ideation, affect, and behavior.

The Schizophrenia Index (SCZI) in the Rorschach Comprehensive System provides valid assessment of those aspects of schizophrenia that involve dissociated and illogical thinking, impaired perception of reality, and faulty comprehension and judgment in social situations.

SCZI comprises the following criterion variables:

X+% < .61 and S−% < .41; or X+% < .50

X−% > .29

FQ− => FQu; or FQ− > (FQo+FQ+)

Sum Level 2 Special Scores > 1 and FAB2 > 0

Sum 6 Special Scores > 6; or Weighted Sum 6 Special Scores > 17

M− > 1; or X−% > .40

A score of 0–3 on SCZI has no interpretive significance and cannot be considered to rule out schizophrenia. A SCZI of 4–6 suggests the presence of a schizophrenia spectrum disorder including, in addition to schizophrenia, schizophreniform and delusional disorder and paranoid and schizotypal personality disorder.

False-positive inferences of schizophrenia spectrum disorder based on a SCZI of 5 or 6 are highly unlikely to occur. False-positives of 4 on SCZI do occur on occasion, usually in persons who are not thought-disordered but who have pronounced difficulties in reality testing and social relatedness. These include people with psychotic conditions of whatever origin; with bipolar affective disorder, especially during phases of mania; and with severe personality disorder, especially with antisocial features.

RORSCHACH IDENTIFICATION OF DEPRESSION

For purposes of personality assessment, depression can be conceptualized as maladaptive change in affective life that is characterized by dysphoric mood, pessimistic and self-critical attitudes, depleted energy and enthusiasm, and marked somatic complaints or concerns.

The Depression Index (DEPI) in the Rorschach Comprehensive System provides valid assessment of those aspects of depression that involve dysfunctional emotionality, negative cognitions, and, to a lesser extent, limited involvement with the world.

DEPI comprises the following criterion variables:

FV+VF > 0; or FD > 2

Color-Shading Blends > 0; or S > 2

Egocentricity Ratio > .45 and Fr+rF = 0; or Egocentricity Ratio < .33

Affective Ratio < .46; or Blends < 4

Sum Shading > FM+m; or Sum C' > 2

MOR > 2; or Intellectualization Ratio > 3

COP < 2; or Isolation Index > .24

A score of 0–4 on DEPI has no interpretive significance and cannot be considered to rule out depressive disorder. A DEPI of 5 suggests depressive features in a subject's clinical condi-

tion, and a DEPI of 6 or 7 suggests the presence of an affective spectrum disorder, including major depressive disorder, dysthymia, bipolar disorder, cyclothymia, and borderline personality disorder.

False-positive inferences of depressive features from a DEPI of 5 and of affective spectrum disorder from a DEPI of 6 or 7 are highly unlikely to occur. On the other hand, there are two kinds of circumstances in which DEPI may frequently yield false-negative findings. Because the DEPI criterion variables are largely measures of trait rather than state characteristics, the index is not particularly sensitive to acute and reactive episodes of depression (which are more likely to elevate Rorschach indices of distress and deprivation than the DEPI). Because the DEPI variables measure primarily affective and cognitive aspects of depression, the index is not particularly sensitive to the type of helplessness depression that is characterized not so much by disturbing feelings and ideas as by apathy, passivity, dependency, and withdrawal (which is more likely to be detected by the Coping Deficit Index in the Comprehensive System than by DEPI).

RORSCHACH IDENTIFICATION OF BIPOLAR DISORDER

For purposes of personality assessment, bipolar disorder can be conceptualized as a form of affective disorder in which underlying depression is defended against or warded off by mechanisms of denial and reversal that displace dejection with elation, pessimism and self-criticism with optimism and self-glorification, lethargy and inactivity with vibrancy and enthusiastic pursuits, and bodily concerns with an exaggerated sense of physical and mental well-being.

There is as yet no formal Rorschach index for bipolar disorder. However, the origin of mania as a defensive maneuver for warding off depression typically results in records that contain ample evidence of both what is being denied (underlying depression) and how it is being denied (through forced gaiety, heightened activity, and an inflated sense of one's talents, capacities, and good health).

Because of their underlying depression, bipolar individuals tend to elevate on DEPI, even when manifesting manic behavior. Additionally, in bipolar disorder Rorschach evidence of depression exists concurrently and alternates with such indications of affective pleasure, positive cognitions, abundant energy, and a sense of well-being as the following:

Elevated Affective Ratio with prominence of CF and C responses; Color Projection; thematic imagery stressing happiness and gaiety

Reflection responses with high Egocentricity Ratio; thematic imagery stressing attractive figures effectively engaged in admirable activities

Elevated R and/or long, elaborate, and complex responses, with low Lambda, high Zf, and high DQ+; thematic imagery stressing activity and enthusiasm

Thematic imagery stressing the strength, attractiveness, and vigorous good health of human and animal figures seen

The intense emotionality, mood swings, and self-centeredness or self-glorification associated with bipolar disorder are also commonly observed in persons with borderline personality disorder. Accordingly, the Rorschach protocols produced by persons with these two conditions are often quite similar, and the differentiation between them is challenging. A useful clue in this circumstance derives from the central role of strained interpersonal relatedness in borderline personality disorder, which typically involves pronounced concerns about attachment and separation and manifestations of object splitting. Neither object splitting nor any basic incapacity to form comfortable interpersonal relationships is central to the nature of affective disorders. Accordingly, in a Rorschach protocol otherwise suggesting either bipolar or borderline personality disorder, the absence of clear indications of disturbed object

relations points toward the former rather than the latter.

DIFFERENTIATING SCHIZOPHRENIA
AND BIPOLAR DISORDER

SCZI and DEPI are reasonably independent. Schizophrenic subjects ordinarily do not elevate on DEPI (especially not with a 6 or 7), and bipolar subjects ordinarily do not elevate on SCZI (especially not with a 5 or 6). In those rare instances in which both SCZI and DEPI are elevated, the possibility of schizoaffective disorder should be considered.

Consistent with the fact that schizophrenia is primarily a disorder of thinking, most schizophrenics show an introversive Experience Balance. Consistent with the fact that bipolar disorder is primarily a disorder of mood, most bipolar persons show an extratensive Experience Balance.

Although disordered thinking may appear in bipolar as well as schizophrenic persons, especially during phases of mania, manic thought disorder differs from schizophrenic thought disorder by being less pervasive (lower Sum6); less severe (lower WSum6 and fewer Level 2 Special Scores); and less likely to consist of arbitrary reasoning (FABCOM) than to consist of loose and circumstantial associations (DR). Schizophrenic thought disorder, along with being more pervasive, severe, and illogical than manic thought disorder, also tends to be more persistent over time and more distressing to the subject.

The interpersonal withdrawal, restraint, and mistrust that frequently characterize schizophrenic disorder are typically absent in bipolar disorder, which especially in its manic phases is likely to be accompanied by an open, affable, extroverted social style and considerable interest in interpersonal interaction. Accordingly, elevations on the Hypervigilance Index (HVI) and the Isolation Index (ISOL), combined with the absence of T, COP, and Pure H, are much more likely to suggest schizophrenic than bipolar disorder; conversely, low scores on HVI and ISOL combined with abundant T, COP, and H are more likely to be associated with bipolar than schizophrenic disorder.

The alternating and intermingled indications of dysphoria and ebullience, of self-criticism and self-glorification, and of expansiveness and constriction that frequently characterize bipolar disorder are typically absent in schizophrenia, in which variability and fluctuations in affective tone, self-attitudes, and energy level have little to do with the basic nature of the condition. Accordingly, elevations in DEPI, Sum C, CF+C, and the Affective Ratio suggest bipolar rather than schizophrenic disorder, as do elevations in reflections, the Egocentricity Index, and MOR.

References & Readings

Exner, J. E., Jr., & Weiner, I. B. (1995). *The Rorschach: A comprehensive system: Vol. 3. Assessment of children and adolescents* (2nd ed.). New York: Wiley.

Weiner, I. B. (1966). *Psychodiagnosis in schizophrenia*. New York: Wiley.

Weiner, I. B. (1992). *Psychological disturbance in adolescence* (2nd ed.). New York: Wiley.

Related Topics

Chapter 31, "Thumbnail Guide to the Rorschach Inkblot Method"

33 MEASURES OF CHILDREN'S PSYCHOLOGICAL DEVELOPMENT

Karen Levine

This chapter contains an annotated listing of measures of children's intellectual ability and emotional development. For a detailed and cohesive discussion of most of the tests listed here, please consult *Children's Psychological Testing* (Woodrich, 1997) or *Assessment of Children* (Sattler, 1988).

MEASURES OF INFANT DEVELOPMENT

Several standardized tests can be administered to infants. Because assessment of infants is more of an art than a science since infant behavior and cooperation are extremely variable from minute to minute, results must be interpreted with great caution. Infant testing can be very useful to identify infants showing devel-opmental challenges and to determine eligibility for services such as early intervention. Infant assessment can also lead to early detection of some developmental disabilities such as autism that, in many cases, can be significantly ameliorated by intensive early help. However, infant tests for typically developing children do not correlate with later measures of intelligence until 1½–2 years of age (Bayley, 1969). Hence infant testing is extremely valuable as a route to intervention but not as a predictor of later IQ.

Bayley Scales of Infant Development II

- Normed for 0–2½ years
- Very well standardized

- Widely accepted as a clinical and research tool
- Has Mental, Motor, and Behavior Scales
- Requires substantial hands-on training to administer

Brazelton Neonatal Behavioral Assessment Scale (NBAS)

- Used primarily with premature infants or full-term newborns
- Requires substantial training and experience with infants to administer
- Improvements over time with repeated assessments correlate with later Bayley Scales (Lester, 1984).

Infant Screening Instruments

- Denver Developmental Screening Test
- Revised BRIGANCE® Diagnostic Inventory
- Battelle Developmental Inventory

PRESCHOOL INTELLIGENCE TESTS

Preschool-age children are typically referred for psychological testing for four primary reasons: kindergarten readiness, language delays, global delays, and/or attentional or behavioral difficulties. Preschool test instruments typically measure the child's abilities across several areas including the following: expressive and receptive language; visual-spatial processing; fine motor skills; visual-motor integration; memory; general knowledge; and preacademic skills (e.g., knowledge of letters and numbers). By preschool age, many children are able to attend and follow directions sufficiently to obtain reliable comprehensive test results across a broad set of learning areas, while other children, especially children with communication, attentional, and developmental problems, are not able to do so. Children's performance and skills at this age are also highly dependent on familial situation/experiences, as many children in this age range have had little or no exposure to school. However, careful and detailed psychological assessment of children at this age is very helpful in determining specific types of problems (e.g., language-processing problems),

as well as attentional difficulties. When language difficulties are suspected, a thorough speech and language evaluation is helpful.

Stanford-Binet Intelligence Scale-Fourth Edition

- Normed 2 years through adulthood, although scales vary substantially at different ages
- Widely used by psychologists
- Yields full-scale IQ
- Requires strong attention in young children
- Due to item range and scoring, the test is less useful for young children in mental retardation range.

Wechsler Preschool and Primary Scale of Intelligence-III

- Normed for children ages 3 years to 7 years 3 months
- Well normed
- Widely used by psychologists in educational systems and hospitals
- Highly correlated with WPPSI-R and to WISC-R
- Scores tend to be 8 points lower than on the WPPSI.

McCarthy Scales of Children's Abilities

- Normed for children ages 2½–8 years
- "Fun"; good for young children and children who are difficult to test
- Children with significant speech and language delays score erroneously lower than on WPPSI Performance Scales (Morgan, Dawson, & Kerby, 1992).

If children are easy to test with normal language and over age 6, the WPPSI-R is preferable due to more recent norms.

Kaufman Assessment Battery for Children

- Normed for children ages 2½–12 years
- "Fun"; good for young children and children who are difficult to test

- Well standardized
- The neuropsychological properties of the Simultaneous and Sequential Achievement factors have been controversial and broadly criticized (e.g., Sattler, 1988).
- Several subtests containing unique and appealing types of tasks can be useful for assessing abilities in difficult-to-test children (e.g., Face Recognition; Magic Window).

SCHOOL-AGE INTELLIGENCE TESTS

Wechsler Intelligence Scale for Children-III

- For children ages 6–16 years
- The most widely used IQ test for school-age children
- Very well normed
- Can detect substantial but not all subtle learning disabilities
- Involves a significant amount of cultural knowledge and experience
- Can assist in but should not be exclusive measure used in diagnosis of ADHD (Barkley, 1990)

Woodcock-Johnson Psycho-Educational Battery–Revised

- Well normed for ages 2 years and above
- Measures ability and achievement
- Yields up to 21 specific subtests
- Useful for identification of learning problems impacting school performance
- Most useful interpretations require thorough neuropsychological knowledge.

SCHOOL-AGE TESTS OF
SPECIFIC ABILITIES

Wide Range Assessment of Memory and Learning (WRAML)

- Normed for children ages 5–17 years
- Useful supplement to Wechsler scales
- Especially useful when memory or visual processing problems are suspected

Bender Visual-Motor Gestalt Test

- Brief shape-copying paper-and-pencil test
- Useful in about the 3–10 year range
- Assesses visual-spatial and visual-motor integration skills
- Good concurrent but poor predictive validity

Rey-Osterrieth Complex Figures Test

- Complex shape-copying task
- Useful in assessing visual-spatial, organizational, and learning style
- Often used as part of neuropsychological battery
- Multiple administration and scoring systems exist, with a great deal of research on each.

Peabody Picture Vocabulary Test-Revised

- Normed for children ages 2½ through adulthood
- Test of receptive vocabulary
- Requires ability to sustain attention
- Can be adapted to be used with eye gaze instead of pointing
- Correlates with verbal IQ
- Useful as a screening instrument
- Does not identify language-processing or language-formulation problems

TESTS FOR SPECIAL POPULATIONS

Individuals from cultures different from those of the norming sample should be tested only with great caution and reservation. Whenever possible, these individuals should be tested by a psychologist from the same culture as the child and, when possible, using instruments normed on other children from that culture. For example, many of the traditionally used language and intelligence tests in the United States have Spanish equivalents. Clearly these conditions will not always be possible. Often omitting testing and conducting interviews and observations is the best option. However, when it is deemed that some sort of testing will be in the child's best interest for a specific reason, such as access to a program, then test results should be interpreted very cautiously and combined with extensive observations, parent and teacher interviews, and evaluation of progress over time.

Many individuals with developmental disabilities cannot be validly assessed using standardized measures. For example, individuals who are nonverbal cannot be validly assessed using tests involving language. Individuals who have significant motor difficulties cannot be assessed using tasks involving motor skills. Individuals with motor and communication issues present an even greater challenge. Significant sensory difficulties and significant attentional difficulties also impact valid assessment.

Specific assessment measures have been designed for some populations. These measures contain items that do not rely on systems that are impacted by the specific disability, and they also generally are normed on groups of individuals with the same disability. However, these tests are generally normed on smaller groups and are less frequently revised and renormed than are the more traditional tests. Hence, when a more traditional test is felt to yield valid information, it is preferable. The following are some tests for special populations.

The Hiskey-Nebraska Test of Learning Aptitude

- Normed for children ages 3–16 years
- Separate norms for hearing impaired
- For children with hearing impairment
- Contains many traditional subtests in visual form (e.g. number recall with plastic numerals), easing interpretation

Pictorial Test of Intelligence

- Normed for children ages 3–8 years
- Useful for young children who have significant motor and/or language deficits, including many children with spastic quadriplegic cerebral palsy
- Children respond to questions by pointing or eye gaze
- Measures a variety of processing, memory, and achievement domains

The Merrill-Palmer Scale of Mental Tests

- Normed for children ages 2½–6 years
- Uses an array of interesting and appealing visual materials, most of which are self-explanatory
- Nonverbal items useful for children with little language and/or children who are difficult to test
- Most useful as a qualitative rather than a quantitative IQ instrument

Leiter International Performance Scale and Arthur Adaptation

- Normed for children ages 2–18 years
- Based on increasingly complex one-to-one matching (e.g., by shape, color, genus)
- Does not yield subtests/factors
- Useful for nonverbal children or children who speak language other than that of the examiner
- Can also be adapted for children with little motor ability through use of eye gaze

TESTS OF ADAPTIVE FUNCTIONING

It can often be very helpful to obtain information about a child's level of independent functioning in areas such as self-care and dressing in younger children, community functioning, and social functioning. While this information is helpful to obtain in assessing any child, it can be particularly valuable when assessing children for whom traditional tests are not valid.

Vineland Adaptive Behavior Scales

- A comprehensive and thorough interview measure of social, self-care, motor, and community functioning
- Parent and teacher versions, as well as Spanish parent and teacher versions

References & Readings

Barkley, R. A. (1990). *Attention deficit hyperactivity disorder: A handbook for diagnosis and treatment*. New York: Guilford Press.

Bayley, N. (1969). *Manual for the Bayley Scales of Infant Development*. New York: Psychological Corporation.

Lester, B. M. (1984). Data analysis and prediction. In T. B. Brazelton (Ed.), *Neonatal Behavioral Assessment Scale*. Philadelphia: Lippincott.

Morgan, R. L., Dawson, B., & Kerby, D. (1992). The performance of preschoolers with speech/language disorders on the McCarthy Scales of Children's Abilities. *Psychology in the Schools, 29*, 11–17.

Sattler, J. M. (1988). *Assessment of children*. San Diego, CA: Jerome M. Sattler.

Woodrich, D. L. (1997). *Children's psychological testing: A guide for nonpsychologists* (3rd ed.). Baltimore: Brooks.

Related Topics

34   CHILD BEHAVIOR OBSERVATIONS

Janice Ware

WHY USE DIRECT OBSERVATION?

Direct observation of child behavior is probably the most accurate means of assessing behavior, despite the many limitations of the available techniques. Direct observational data are multipurpose. In addition to their most frequent use for treatment planning, they also provide an important mechanism for evaluating treatment outcomes and are used as a base for developing theoretical understanding of childhood problems. Methods range from brief, informal single-session observations to highly structured techniques requiring extensive examiner training and considerable time input. Observations should serve not as a stand-alone tool but as an important component of a multimethod assessment. Direct observation is particularly effective when used as a complement to parent and/or self-report. Factors influencing the choice of an appropriate observational technique include (a) the stage of the evaluation process, (b) the nature of the behaviors of interest, (c) the setting in which the behavior occurs, and (d) the resources required to implement the observations.

WHAT METHODOLOGICAL CONCERNS EXIST?

The psychometric properties of specific observation strategies reflect a wide range of variability. Many of the most frequently used tools offer the least stable properties, including problems of objectivity, reliability, validity, reactivity, observer bias, and drift.

A vast number of semistructured and structured direct observation tools are available. The published tools that systematize observations range from broad-based observations of overall child functioning to quantification of specific child behaviors in specific patient populations. Currently, there is a strong movement to develop population-specific techniques that are sensitive to the developmental characteristics of children.

WHAT TECHNIQUES ARE AVAILABLE FOR DIRECT OBSERVATION?

Observation sites include naturalistic settings and simulated settings, such as role playing. Frequency/rate, duration, latency, intensity, topography, and locus are aspects of behavior that can be systematically measured regardless of the setting. Data are collected using either continuous or sampling techniques. Observation codes that measure various aspects of child noncompliance and adult response to the behaviors are used extensively.

The worth of these tools depends largely on the quality of the data documenting adult antecedent and consequent behavior to the child's oppositional patterns. O'Neill, Horner, Albin, Storey, and Sprague (1990) have expanded these observational strategies to include codes for documenting severely maladaptive behavioral patterns of individuals with developmental disabilities.

Home visit observations offer the unique opportunity to investigate the multiplicity of ecological influences contributing to a developmental problem. Typical observed influences include the family's living conditions, the level of parental attachment, the degree of structure present in the home, the presence of appropriate play materials, and the degree of family cohesion. Tools for assessing these factors range from highly structured coding tools to the taking of clinical notes. Regardless of the level of structure involved in the home observation, the actual writing and note taking are best deferred until after the visit in order not to detract from the spontaneity of the visit.

The most commonly used tool for home observation is the Home Observation for Measurement of the Environment Inventory (HOME; Caldwell & Bradley, 1978). HOME uses standardized norms and a simple dyadic coding system to identify at-risk family settings. HOME is frequently criticized because of its high correlation with family socioeconomic status and its reliance on maternal report to supplement direct observations. Despite its shortcomings, HOME has made important contributions by systematically focusing the attention of the observer on characteristics of the home environment that are known to be important influences on developmental outcome.

TECHNOLOGICAL ADVANCES

Innovative techniques ranging from the use of fiber-optic televideo network systems (known as *televideo* or *teleassessment*) to the more readily available use of audio/videotape equipment are increasingly incorporated as standard procedure in child assessment. The use of video and TV provides additional opportunities to collect developmental observations when it is not possible or desirable for an examiner to be present. Comparisons of coding from live and videotaped situations indicate that little information is lost. Observational studies that have been found to be effective in minimizing psychometric concerns use behavior sampling techniques such as intermittently activated tape recorders or time-lapse video procedures.

Teleassessment is now successfully incorporated into many developmental and psychiatric assessment centers and is especially useful for sites serving remote locations. Research reveals high levels of patient and provider satisfaction with the technique. This technique has been particularly successful in settings where multidisciplinary assessment is desirable but prohibitive because of the cost involved in transporting a team of professionals to a remote location. Typical uses of televideo include multidisciplinary neurodevelopmental evaluation of high-risk infants and provision of child and adolescent psychiatric interviews in areas underserved by specialty providers.

Review of audio/videotape segments provides an opportunity for the therapist to help the patient and the family reconcile differing perceptions of the problem behaviors. This can be a practical time- and cost-effective technique because of the wide availability of portable home video equipment. It also can minimize the need for costly home and school visits. Parental reluctance to use videotaped material as a part of the clinical assessment may be due to unfamiliarity with the potential benefits of the procedure.

Parents will want to know what confidentiality procedures have been put in place to safeguard their child. Parental concerns about confidentiality and potential misuse of the tapes can be markedly diminished by identifying the parents at the outset of the audio/videotaping discussion as the "keepers" of the tape. Informed consent procedures, including obtaining written permission for taping, must be closely followed prior to the first taping session. Increasingly, school systems require written parental permission from the parents of each child present in the classroom when the videotaping takes place, regardless of whether or not their child is targeted for observation.

FREQUENTLY USED OBSERVATION TOOLS FOR COMMONLY REFERRED CHILDHOOD PROBLEMS

Attachment Behavior

No standard, widely used clinical tool exists for assessing the attachment of the young child to his or her primary caregiver. Although the descriptive categories of disordered attachment generated through Main and Ainsworth's Strange Situation Procedure (SSP; Ainsworth, Blehar, Waters, & Wall, 1978) are frequently applied in clinical settings (e.g., the "secure," "avoidant," "resistant," or "disorganized" child), the SSP is a research rather than a clinical tool normed on children aged 12–18+ months. Caution should be used in attempting to apply SSP findings to situations where child behavior is observed under either clinical or naturalistic conditions. Nevertheless, the SSP procedure has served as a foundation for several clinical assessment tools, such as the work of Gaensbauer and Harmon (1981) that assesses infant social and emotional functioning in structured settings, including attachment behavior.

Many unstructured informal observational variations of the SSP have evolved to evaluate the young child's attachment to a primary caregiver. These paradigms focus on observing child proximity seeking to the attachment figure and reciprocal attachment figure–child emotional responsivity following a separation.

Clinical observations of attachment parameters can be further enhanced by use of the nosological categories of attachment disorder outlined by Lieberman and Pawl (1988). This system can be used to describe disorders diagnosed in children between the ages of 1 and 4–5 years.

Attention-Deficit Disorder

The cost of obtaining direct observations for children with attention problems most often precludes the inclusion of this valuable technique into standardized assessment batteries. Observations of children with attentional problems are used to confirm the diagnosis and treatment plan and to evaluate stimulant medication effects. The most widely published observation system for assessing attention-deficit disorder (ADD) is that developed by Routh and his colleagues (Routh & Schroeder, 1976). Many modifications to this system have been made by subsequent authors, including a clinic analogue system (Barkley, 1997).

Stimulant medications are well-known elicitors of different effects for different domains of development. For example, a symptom trade-off may occur, such as achieving optimal academic performance at the cost of increasing impulsivity. Thus, observational techniques documenting stimulant medication effects must be multidimensional.

Well-regarded tools for evaluating child behavior in the classroom include specifics of the target child's behavior, as well as critical information on classroom environmental factors unlikely to be available through parent or teacher report. These tools record behaviors such as being off task or out of seat, attentional shifts, and amount of motor activity. The same tool used for gathering baseline attentional data should be readministered to monitor medication effects, including the critical variable of dosage increments. Observer bias can be minimized through the use of crossover designs that alternate placebo with treatment over the course of several weeks such that the observer is unaware of the child's status at the time of the observation.

An interesting and alternative strategy for assessing attentional problems in preschoolers is the Goodman Lock Box, a play-based observational coding system for use in clinical settings (Goodman, 1981). In addition to attention, the Lock Box assesses other aspects of preschool children's mental organization, such as sequencing skills and perceptual-motor and visuospatial capacities.

Autism and Mental Retardation

Autism and mental retardation are two of the most frequently diagnosed developmental disorders. They are particularly complex to diagnose and treat because of the high degree of behavioral inconsistencies that interfere with the ability to use standardized assessment tools (Schopler, Reichler, & Renner, 1988). Consequently, differential diagnosis relies heavily on the adequacy of the behavioral observations, coupled with caregiver reports of typical behavior. Comorbidity between the two conditions also increases the importance of careful observations of specific behaviors so that the diagnoses can be discriminated and/or confirmed as coexisting. Similar observation strategies and tools are used for both disorders.

Parent-Child Interactions

Behavioral observations of parent-child interactions during infancy assess the parent's capacities across different situations to provide an emotional scaffolding for the child. The most widely used tools for assessing the parent-child dyad are the tests embedded within the Nursing Childhood Assessment Tool (NCAST; Barnard, 1979). The paradigm on which the NCAST scales are based assumes that parent-child interaction is reciprocal and, therefore, that distinct parent and child contributions to the interaction can be discriminated.

The NCAST Teaching Scale observes and rates parent and child responses to parental efforts to "teach" a common play task of childhood such as block building. The task is taught under semistructured circumstances. The NCAST Feeding Scale offers a variation of this task and is an observation of parent-child interactions during an actual child feeding situation.

Strengths of the NCAST system are its ability to capture the contingent and reciprocal nature of the interaction using both the infant and the parent's behavior as data. The NCAST system is difficult for some programs to incorporate because it requires specialized training by a certified instructor.

Play Assessments

Developmental aspects of childhood behavior such as interaction inhibition often make standardized assessments nearly impossible, rendering play observations an important medium for gathering critical information. The systematic observation of play can provide a useful, unobtrusive means to understand and interpret child behavior. Play observations are typically nonthreatening to parent and child alike, often offering an enjoyable means for parents to learn about their children.

The majority of structured, clinical play-based assessments address representational and cognitive capacities rather than the broader range of developmental tasks, including social and emotional development. However, inferences based on observed affective displays, ability to socially reference others during the play episode, general interest in social relatedness, joint attention capacities, and mastery motivation are often drawn from structured and unstructured play tasks.

For children with disabilities, play provides a wealth of otherwise unobtainable information. Populations that lend themselves to developmental play observations include children with general cognitive delay and children with sensory and language disabilities and behavior problems seen in autism, elective mutism, and conduct disorders.

There are a tremendous number of play observation tools (Schaefer, Gitlin, & Sandgrund, 1991). Advantages and disadvantages of the various play observation tools should be carefully considered (Cohen, Stern, & Balaban, 1983).

References & Readings

Ainsworth, M. S., Blehar, M. D., Waters, E., & Wall, S. (1978). *Patterns of attachment: A psychological study of the Strange Situation*. Hillsdale, NJ: Erlbaum.

Barkley, R. A. (1997). *Defiant children: A clinician's manual for assessment and parent training* (2nd ed.). New York: Guilford Press.

Barnard, K. E. (1979). *Instructor's learning resource manual.* Seattle: NCAST Publications, University of Washington.

Caldwell, B. M., & Bradley, R. H. (1978). *Manual for the home observation of the environment.* Little Rock: University of Arkansas Press.

Cohen, D., Stern, V., & Balaban, N. (1983). *Observing and recording the behavior of young children.* New York: Teachers College Press.

Gaensbauer, T. G., & Harmon, R. J. (1981). Clinical assessment in infancy utilizing structured playroom situations. *Journal of the American Academy of Child Psychiatry, 20,* 264–280.

Goodman, J. F. (1981). The Lock Box: A measure of psychomotor competence and organized behavior in retarded and normal preschoolers. *Journal of Consulting and Clinical Psychology, 49,* 369–378.

Lieberman, A. F., & Pawl, J. H. (1988). Clinical applications of attachment theory. In J. Belsky and T. Nezworski (Eds.), *Clinical implications of attachment* (pp. 88–93). Hillsdale, NJ: Erlbaum.

Linder, T. W. (1996). *Transdisciplinary play-based assessment: A functional approach to working with young children.* Baltimore: Paul H. Brooks.

Mash, E. J., & Terdal, L. G. (1988). *Behavioral assessment of childhood disorders* (2nd ed.). New York: Guilford Press.

O'Neill, R. E., Horner, R. H., Albin, R. W., Storey, K., & Sprague, J. R. (1990). *Functional analysis of problem behavior: A practical assessment guide.* Sycamore, IL: Sycamore.

Routh, D. K., & Schroeder, C. S. (1976). Standardized playroom measures as indices of hyperactivity. *Journal of Abnormal Child Psychology, 4,* 199–207.

Schaefer, C. E., Gitlin, K., & Sandgrund, A. (Eds.) (1991). *Play diagnosis and assessment.* New York: Wiley.

Schopler, E., Reichler, R. J., & Renner, B. R. (1988). *The childhood autism rating scale.* Los Angeles: Western Psychological Services.

Related Topics

Chapter 18, "Interviewing Parents"
Chapter 33, "Measures of Children's Psychological Development"

35   MILLON ADOLESCENT CLINICAL INVENTORY (MACI)

Theodore Millon & Roger D. Davis

The Millon Adolescent Clinical Inventory (MACI; Millon, Millon, & Davis, 1993) is an expansion of the earlier Millon Adolescent Personality Inventory (MAPI; Millon, Green, & Meagher, 1982). It is a 160-item, 31-scale, self-report inventory designed specifically for assessing clinically troubled adolescent personalities, their typical areas of concern, and Axis I clinical syndromes. Table 1 lists the MACI scales

and reports scale changes from the MAPI to the MACI. The MACI and its forerunners were developed in consultation with psychiatrists, psychologists, and other mental health professionals who work with adolescents, and they reflect issues most relevant to understanding adolescents' behavior and concerns. The MACI was developed primarily for use in clinical, residential, and correctional settings. The Expressed

TABLE 1. A Comparison of MACI and MAPI Scales

MACI	MAPI
Personality Scales	
1. Introversive (schizoid)	1. Introversive (schizoid)
2A. Inhibited (avoidant)	2. Inhibited (avoidant)
2B. Doleful (depressive)	
3. Cooperative (dependent)	3. Cooperative (dependent)
4. Sociable (histrionic)	4. Sociable (histrionic)
5. Confident (narcissistic)	5. Confident (narcissistic)
6A. Unruly (antisocial)	6. Unruly (antisocial)
6B. Forceful (sadistic)	
7. Respectful (compulsive)	7. Respectful (compulsive)
8A. Negative (negativistic)	
8B. Sensitive (self-defeating)	8. Sensitive (self-defeating)
9. Borderline tendency	
Expressed Concerns	
A. Identify diffusion	A. Self-concept
B. Self-devaluation	B. Personal esteem
C. Body disapproval	C. Body comfort
D. Sexual discomfort	D. Sexual acceptance
E. Peer insecurity	E. Peer security
F. Social insensitivity	F. Social tolerance
G. Family discord	G. Family rapport
H. Childhood abuse	
	H. Academic confidence
Clinical Indices and Behavioral Correlates	
AA. Eating dysfunctions	
BB. Substance abuse proneness	
CC. Delinquent predisposition	TT. Societal conformity
DD. Impulsive propensity	SS. Impulsive control
EE. Anxious feelings	
FF. Depressive affect	
GG. Suicidal tendency	
	UU. Scholastic achievement
	WW. Attendance consistency

Concerns scales of the MACI assess teenagers' attitudes regarding significant developmental problems, while the Personality Patterns and Clinical Syndromes scales reflect significant areas of pathological feelings, thoughts, and behavior that require professional attention.

HISTORICAL DEVELOPMENT

The original Millon Adolescent Inventory (MAI) was developed in 1974. The MAI served as the forerunner to the MAPI, first published and distributed by National Computer Systems (NCS) in 1982. The MAI and the MAPI were identical in item content but differed in their norms and intended purposes. The MAPI was subsequently divided into two forms. The MAPI-Clinical was designed to aid mental health workers in assessing adolescent difficulties among youngsters who were in a diagnostic or treatment setting at the time of testing; the MAPI-Guidance was designed for school settings, primarily to help counselors better understand adolescent personalities and to identify students who might benefit from further psychological evaluations.

The decision to develop a purely clinical reference group with appropriate, comparison norms served as the impetus for development of the MACI. The MAPI-C, useful as it was for diagnostic assessment, was not sufficiently broad-based to encompass the full range of clinical populations. There was also clearly a need to strengthen its psychometric features, make it more consonant with developments in its guiding theory, and fortify its coordination with the descriptive characteristics in the most recent *DSM* classifications. Like the other Millon inventories, the MACI's personality and clinical scales are grounded on a comprehensive theory (Millon, 1969, 1981, 1986a, 1986b, 1990, 1997), significantly increasing the instrument's clinical utility. Item selection and scale development progressed through three validation stages: theoretical-substantive, internal-structural, and external-criterion. This approach created an instrument that meets the standards of developers who are committed to diverse construction and validation methods (Hase & Goldberg, 1967). Each item had to pass satisfactorily through all three stages of development to be retained in the inventory.

ADMINISTRATION AND SCORING

The MACI was constructed specifically with an adolescent population in mind. Questions are presented in language teenagers use, with content that deals with their concerns and experiences. Both reading level and vocabulary were set to allow for ready comprehension by the vast majority of adolescents. The final 160-item inventory, geared to a sixth-grade reading level, can be completed by most adolescents in approximately 20 minutes. The brevity and clarity of the instrument facilitate quick administration with a minimum of youngster resistance. Norms were established employing samples of 13- to 19-year-olds in clinical settings (its use with other normative age-groups is inappropriate and may lead to erroneous diagnostic judgments). The presence of overwhelming anxiety, a confusional state, drug intoxication, or sedation may also significantly alter test results. If the instrument is adminis-

tered under such circumstances, the client should be retested at a later date.

The MACI is available in two paper-and-pencil formats, one for hand scoring and one for computer scoring. Hand-scoring materials include a reusable test booklet and a separate answer sheet. For computer scoring, there is a combination test booklet and answer sheet and an on-line format. Audiocassette recordings of the MACI are available for use with both English- and Spanish-speaking clients. While mail-in scoring is available through NCS, on-site computer scoring is the fastest and most convenient scoring option. Both options allow the user to select either a Profile Report or an Interpretive Report based on the examinee's scores.

Instructions for completing the MACI are printed on the test and are largely self-explanatory. No special conditions or instructions beyond those printed on the test are required. Accordingly, administration can be readily and routinely handled by properly trained assistants in clinic settings. The brevity of the test and the minimal facilities required make it convenient for use in settings where time, space, and privacy are limited. However, the MACI should not be mailed to clients or sent home with them for completion.

The MACI, like all the Millon inventories, employs actuarial base rate or prevalence data to establish scale cutting lines. These not only provide a basis for selecting optimal differential diagnostic cutting lines but also help ensure that the frequencies of MCMI-generated diagnoses and profile patterns are comparable to representative clinical prevalence rates. While the use of base rate scores has been one of the most widely misunderstood aspects of the MCMI, their utility is easily and intuitively understood when contrasted with the more familiar T score. On the MMPI, for example, T scores of 65 and above indicate pathology, with roughly equal numbers of patients scoring above this threshold. Clinical experience, however, shows the number of depressed patients, for example, to be greater than the number of patients with a thought disorder. Base rate scores are constructed to reflect these clinical realities, yielding more depressives than delusional patients, more borderlines and antisocials than schizoids, and so on, rather than assuming their numbers to be equal. In the construction of the MACI, target prevalence rates were set according to reviews of epidemiological data, estimates derived from clinicians who participated in the development project, and the senior author's own expert judgment. Thus, if it was deemed that 8% of patients are most likely to resemble the introversive prototype, then the lookup table for this personality was constructed so schizoid was the highest personality elevation for 8% of the patients in the normative sample.

A discussion of base rate scores often leads to considerations of local versus global base rates, that is, the fact that the prevalence rates for different disorders vary somewhat by clinical setting. When this is raised in criticism of the concept, it is usually intended to support the continued use of T scores. However, as noted earlier, the base rate scores of the MACI are intended to remedy the global base rate assumptions made in the use of T scores. Thus, while the prevalence rates of some disorders in particular clinical settings may differ from the base rates assumed by the MACI and in the use of T scores, the MACI's base rate scores at least do not implicitly assume the prevalence rates of all disorders to be equal. More frequently, the distinction between local and global prevalence rates is made in support of the base rate concept by clinicians who realize its importance in improving diagnostic efficiency: positive and negative predictive power, sensitivity, and specificity. These clinicians, far from reverting back to T scores, often wish to optimize the base rate scores for their particular setting.

SCALE DESCRIPTIONS

The major personality patterns, expressed psychosocial concerns, and clinical syndromes typical of adolescents have been organized into the following formal scales.

Personality Patterns

Twelve personality patterns are included, based on the senior author's theoretical schema (Millon, 1969, 1981, 1986a, 1986b, 1990, 1997) and similar material in the *DSM-IV*.

- *Introversive* (Scale 1): High scorers keep to themselves, appearing rather quiet, unemotional, apathetic, listless, distant, and asocial. Affectionate needs and feelings are minimal. Not only do they not get emotionally involved, they simply do not often feel strongly about things, lacking the capacity to experience both joy and sadness in any depth. They do not avoid others, but they are indifferent about the presence of others and the possibilities inherent in relationships.

- *Inhibited* (Scale 2A): High scorers are quite shy and ill at ease with others. Although they would like to be close to others, they have learned that it is better to keep their distance, and they do not readily trust friendship. Although they often feel lonely, they avoid close interpersonal contact, fearing rejection, and they closet feelings that are often very strong.

- *Doleful* (Scale 2B): High scorers characteristically exhibit a dejected and gloomy mood, perhaps since childhood. Their outlook on life is sad, brooding, and pessimistic. Most are prone to guilty and remorseful feelings, viewing themselves as inadequate or even worthless.

- *Submissive* (Scale 3): High scorers tend to be softhearted, sentimental, and kindly in relationships with others. They are extremely reluctant to assert themselves, however, and avoid taking initiative or assuming a leadership role. They are not only inclined to be quite dependent but also exhibit clinging behavior and a fear of separation. They typically play down their own achievements and underestimate their abilities.

- *Dramatizing* (Scale 4): High scorers tend to be talkative, charming, and frequently exhibitionistic or emotionally expressive. They tend to have intense but brief relationships with others. These adolescents look for interesting experiences and new forms of excitement. They often find themselves becoming bored with routine and long-standing relationships.

- *Egotistic* (Scale 5): High scorers tend to be quite confident of their abilities and are often seen by others as self-centered and narcissistic. They rarely doubt their own self-worth, and they act in a self-assured manner. These individuals tend to take others for granted, are often arrogant and exploitative, and do not share or concern themselves with the needs of others.

- *Unruly* (Scale 6A): High scorers tend to act out in an antisocial manner, often resisting efforts to make them adhere to socially acceptable standards of behavior. These adolescents may display a pervasively rebellious attitude that could bring them into conflict with parents and school or legal authorities.
- *Forceful* (Scale 6B): High scorers are strong-willed and tough-minded, tending to dominate and abuse others. They frequently question the rights of others and prefer to control most situations. They are often blunt and unkind, tending to be impatient with the problems or weaknesses of others.
- *Conforming* (Scale 7): High scorers are very serious-minded, efficient, respectful, and rule-conscious individuals who try to do the "right" and "proper" things. They tend to keep their emotions under check and to be overcontrolled and tense. They prefer to live their lives in a very orderly and well-planned fashion, avoiding unpredictable and unexpected situations.
- *Oppositional* (Scale 8A): High scorers tend to be discontented, sullen, passive-aggressive, and unpredictable. They may be outgoing and pleasant one moment but hostile and irritable the next. Often they are confused and contrite about their moodiness but are unable to control these swings for long.
- *Self-demeaning* (Scale 8B): High scorers tend to be their own worst enemies, acting in self-defeating ways, at times seeming content to suffer. Many undermine the efforts of others to help them. Often they deny themselves pleasure and sabotage their own efforts to achieve success.
- *Borderline tendency* (Scale 9): High scorers exhibit severe personality dysfunctions, displaying more pathological variants of the preceding personality traits and features. They may also exhibit marked affective instabilities, erratic interpersonal relationships, behavioral capriciousness, impulsive

hostility, fear of abandonment, and self-destructive actions.

Expressed Concerns

The following eight scales focus on areas of life that troubled adolescents often find problematic. The intensity of the problem is reflected in the elevation of the scale score.

- *Identity diffusion* (Scale A): High scorers are confused about who they are, what they want from life, and what they would like to become. Free-floating and unfocused about future goals and values, they are unclear and directionless about the course of their future development.
- *Self-devaluation* (Scale B): Although high scorers have a sense of who they are, they are very dissatisfied with that self-image. They speak openly about feelings of low self-esteem, find little to admire in themselves, and fear that they will fall far short of what they aspire to be.
- *Body disapproval* (Scale C): High scorers are discontent with what they perceive to be shortcomings or deviance in their physical maturation or morphology. They may also express dissatisfaction with their level of physical attractiveness and social appeal.
- *Sexual discomfort* (Scale D): High scorers find sexual thoughts and feelings confusing or disagreeable. They are troubled by their impulses and often fear the expression of their sexuality. They may be preoccupied with or in conflict over the roles their sexuality requires.
- *Peer insecurity* (Scale E): High scorers report dismay and sadness concerning perceived peer rejection. Wanting the approval of peers but unsuccessful in attaining it, many are likely to withdraw and become even more isolated.
- *Social insensitivity* (Scale F): High scorers are cool and indifferent to the welfare of others. Willing to override the rights of others to achieve personal ends, they lack empathy and show little interest in building warm personal ties.
- *Family discord* (Scale G): High scorers re-

port that their families are tense and full of conflict. They note few sources of support and possess a general feeling of estrangement from parents. Depending on the individual's personality, these difficulties may reflect either parental rejection or adolescent rebellion.

- *Childhood abuse* (Scale H): High scorers report shame or disgust about having been subjected to verbal, physical, or sexual abuse from parents, siblings, relatives, or family friends.

Clinical Syndromes

The final seven scales of the MACI involve areas of direct clinical significance that call for intervention on the part of a therapist. These diagnostic categories represent difficulties that are found in a significant proportion of adolescents who are seen by mental health professionals.

- *Eating dysfunctions* (Scale AA): High scorers exhibit distinct tendencies toward anorexia nervosa or bulimia nervosa. Though already below normal weight, they fear "getting fat." They may engage in uncontrolled eating, followed by self-induced vomiting or the misuse of laxatives or diuretics.
- *Substance-abuse proneness* (Scale BB): High scorers exhibit a pattern of alcohol or drug abuse that has led to significant impairment of performance and behavior. Some spend inordinate amounts of time obtaining their substances, behave in an unacceptable social manner, and continue substance use despite cognizance of its long-term harmful effect on their life.
- *Delinquent predisposition* (Scale CC): High scorers behave in ways or involve themselves in situations in which the rights of others are likely to be violated. In doing so, any number of societal norms or rules may be broken, including threats, use of weapons, deception and lying, stealing, and other antisocial behaviors.
- *Impulsive propensity* (Scale DD): High scorers have poor control over sexual and aggressive impulses and are likely to act out their feelings with minimal provocation. Easily

excited over minor matters, these adolescents may discharge their urges in sudden, impetuous, and often foolhardy ways.

- *Anxious feelings* (Scale EE): High scorers have a sense of foreboding, an apprehensiveness about all sorts of matters. Uneasy, disquieted, fretful, and nervous, they are often on pins and needles as they fearfully await the coming of unknown torments or calamitous events.
- *Depressive affect* (Scale FF): High scorers show a decreased level of activity, clearly distinct from that which has been characteristic of them in the past. They exhibit a notable decrease in effectiveness, feelings of guilt and fatigue, a tendency to be despairing about the future, social withdrawal, loss of confidence, and diminished feelings of adequacy and attractiveness.
- *Suicidal tendency* (Scale GG): High scorers admit to suicidal thoughts and plans. They express feelings of worthlessness and purposelessness and a sense that others would be better off without them. High scores call for professional attention and alertness on the part of family members.

CLINICAL INTERPRETATION AND COMPUTER-GENERATED REPORTS

Configural interpretation of the MACI is essentially similar to that of the MCMI-III (see chapter 30), proceeding from single-scale to configural syntheses, with appropriate integration of auxiliary data. Considerable interpretive material related to personality disorders, and on Millon's evolutionary theory, is presented in various writings, most notably *Modern Psychopathology* (Millon, 1969), *Toward a New Personology: An Evolutionary Model* (Millon, 1990), and *Disorders of Personality: The DSM-IV and Beyond* (Millon & Davis, 1996).

The MACI automated interpretive reports are substantially more detailed than those of the MAPI. They are based on clinically derived configurations and statistical clusters as synthesized by the underlying theory. MACI results can be furnished either in profile form or as an automated interpretive report. The profile provides limited information and assumes knowledge of the relevant clinical literature. The more comprehensive and detailed interpretive report is considered a professional-to-professional consultation. Its function is to serve as one component in the evaluation of the adolescent, and it should be viewed by the clinician as a series of probabilistic rather than definitive judgments. Although this information is appropriate for use in developing a therapeutic program, sharing the report with adolescents or their families is discouraged. Careful rephrasing of text interpretations may be undertaken with appropriate clients, using sound clinical judgment to assure a constructive outcome.

An actuarial system, particularly one that is supplemented by a systematic clinical theory, should yield reports as good as those prepared by human interpreters. Moreover, a computer database is far more substantial in scope and variety than are the disorders seen by the average clinician. Diagnosticians must resort to highly tenuous speculations when they encounter novel profile configurations. In contrast, a computer database is well supplied with comparable cases to be drawn upon for interpretive reference. In a few seconds, the computer can match a profile with comparable configurations and generate an appropriate narrative report. From a purely practical viewpoint, automated reports provide a significant savings of professional time and effort.

Computer-generated MACI interpretive reports include (a) a cover page, a summary page providing the raw and BR scores for each scale and a score profile, test validity information, and the personality code; (b) an initial paragraph noting the appropriate context, limitations, and restrictions of the use, a demographic summary, and a judgment as to the probable validity and reliability of test data given the adolescent's response tendencies and biases; (c) a series of paragraphs describing the major features of the teenager's personality patterns, the manner in which difficulties are manifested, and the probable course of relationships with therapists; (d) a series of descriptive statements characterizing the primary areas of concern as expressed by the youngster; (e) an interpretive summary of the nature and character of the highest Clinical Syndromes scales in order of their magnitude; (f) a section called "Noteworthy Responses," which indicates problem areas that call for closer inspection and further evaluation; (g) a summary section of "Diagnostic Hypotheses" related to the DSM-IV, arranged in a multiaxial format; and (h) a series of paragraphs pointing out the treatment implications of the preceding information.

References & Readings

Hase, H. D., & Goldberg, L. R. (1967). Comparative validity of different strategies of constructing personality inventory scales. *Psychological Bulletin, 67,* 231–248.

Millon, T. (1969). *Modern psychopathology*. Philadelphia: Saunders.

Millon, T. (1981). *Disorders of personality: DSM-III, Axis II*. New York: Wiley.

Millon, T. (1986a). Personality prototypes and their diagnostic criteria. In T. Millon & G. Klerman (Eds.), *Contemporary directions in psychopathology: Toward the DSM-IV*. New York: Guilford Press.

Millon, T. (1986b). A theoretical derivation of pathological personalities. In T. Millon & G. Klerman (Eds.), *Contemporary directions in psychopathology: Toward the DSM-IV*. New York: Guilford Press.

Millon, T. (1990). *Toward a new personology: An evolutionary model*. New York: Wiley-Interscience.

Millon, T. (Ed.) (1997). *The Millon inventories: Contemporary clinical and personality assessment*. New York: Guilford Press.

Millon, T., & Davis, R. D. (1996). *Disorders of personality: The DSM-IV and beyond*. New York: Wiley-Interscience.

Millon, T., Green, C. J., & Meagher, R. B., Jr. (1982). *Millon Adolescent Personality Inventory manual*. Minneapolis, MN: National Computer Systems.

Millon, T., Millon, C., and Davis, R. D. (1993). *Millon Adolescent Clinical Inventory manual*. Minneapolis, MN: National Computer Systems.

Related Topics

36 ASSESSING THE QUALITY OF A PSYCHOLOGICAL TESTING REPORT

Gerald P. Koocher

This chapter describes 10 key points that should be addressed in conducting *any* psychological assessment for which a report is prepared. The quality of the report can be evaluated by assessing the thoroughness and accuracy with which each of these 10 points is addressed.

REFERRAL QUESTIONS AND CONTEXT

- Does the report explain the reason the client was referred for testing and state the assessment questions to be addressed?
- Does the report note that the client was informed about the purpose of the assessment?
- Is the relevant psychological ecology of the client mentioned (e.g., recently divorced, facing criminal charges, candidate for employment)?
- If the evaluation is being undertaken at the request of a third party (e.g., a court, an employer, or a school), does the examiner note that the client was informed of the limits of confidentiality and whether a release was obtained?

CURRENT STATUS/BEHAVIORAL OBSERVATIONS

- What was the client's behavior like during the interview, especially with respect to any aspects that might relate to the referral questions or the validity of the testing (e.g., mood, ability to form rapport, concentration, mannerisms, medication side effects, language problems, cooperation, phenotype, or physical handicaps)?

- Were any deviations from standard testing administration or procedures necessary?

LISTING OF INSTRUMENTS USED

- Is a complete list (without jargon or abbreviations) of the tests administered presented, including the dates administered?
- Does the report explain the nature of any unusual instruments or test procedures used?
- If more than one set of norms or test forms exists for any given instrument, does the psychologist indicate which forms or norms were used?

RELIABILITY AND VALIDITY

- Does the psychologist comment specifically on whether or not the test results in the present circumstances are to be regarded as reasonably accurate (e.g., the test administration was valid and the client fully cooperative)?
- If there are mediating factors, are these discussed in terms of reliability and validity implications?
- Are the tests used valid for assessing the aspects of the client's abilities in question? (This should be a special focus of attention if the instrument used is nonstandard or is being used in a nonstandard manner.)

DATA PRESENTATION

- Are scores presented and explained for each of the tests used? (If an integrated narrative or description is presented, does this address all the aspects assessed, such as intellectual functioning, personality structure, etc.?)

- Are the meanings of the test results explained in terms of the referral questions asked?
- Are examples or illustrations included if relevant?
- Are technical terms and jargon avoided?
- Does the report note whether the pattern of scores (e.g., variability in measuring similar attributes across instruments) is a consistent or heterogeneous one?
- For IQ testing, are subtest scatter and discrepancy scores mentioned?
- For personality testing, does the psychologist discuss self-esteem, interpersonal relations, emotional reactivity, defensive style, and areas of focal concern?

SUMMARY

- If a summary is presented, does it err by surprising the reader with material not mentioned earlier in the report?
- Is it overly redundant?

RECOMMENDATIONS

- If recommendations are made, is it evident why or how these flow from the test results mentioned and discussed earlier?
- Do the recommendations mention all relevant points raised as initial referral questions?

DIAGNOSIS

- If a diagnosis is requested or if differential diagnosis was a referral question, does the report specifically address this point?

IS THE REPORT AUTHENTICATED?

- Is the report signed by the individual who conducted the evaluation?

- Are the credentials/title of the person noted (e.g., Mary Smith, Ph.D., Staff Psychologist, or John Doe, M.S., Psychology Intern)?
- If the examiner is unlicensed or a trainee, is the report co-signed by a qualified licensed supervisor?

FEEDBACK

- Is a copy of the report sent to the person who made the referral?
- Is some mechanism operational for providing feedback to the client, consistent with the context of testing and original agreement with the client?

References & Readings

American Psychological Association (1993). Record keeping guidelines. *American Psychologist, 48,* 308–310.

American Psychological Association, American Educational Research Association, & National Council on Measurement in Education (1985). *Standards for educational and psychological testing.* Washington, DC: American Psychological Association.

American Psychological Association, American Educational Research Association, & National Council on Measurement in Education (1998). *Standards for educational and psychological testing.* Washington, DC: American Psychological Association.

Bersoff, D. N., & Hofer, P. J. (1995). Legal issues in computerized psychological testing. In D. N. Bersoff (Ed.), *Ethical conflicts in psychology* (pp. 291–294). Washington, DC: American Psychological Association.

Conoley, J. C., & Impara, J. C. (Eds.) (1994). *Supplement to the 11th mental measurements yearbook.* Lincoln: University of Nebraska Press.

Eyde, L. D., Robertson, G. J., Krug, S. E., Moreland, K. L., Robertson, A. G., Shewan, C. M., Harrison, P. L., Proch, B. E., Hammer, A. L., & Primoff, E. S. (1993). *Responsible test use: Case studies for assessing human behavior.* Washington, DC: American Psychological Association.

Koocher, G. P., & Keith-Spiegel, P. C. (1998). *Ethics in psychology: Professional standards and cases* (2nd ed.). New York: Oxford University Press.

Matarazzo, J. D. (1990). Psychological assessment versus psychological testing: Validation from Bitnet to the school, clinic, and courtroom. *American Psychologist, 45*, 999–1016.

Moreland, K. L., Eyde, L. D., Robertson, G. J., Primoff, E. S., et al. (1995). Assessment of test user qualifications: A research-based measurement procedure. *American Psychologist, 50*, 14–23.

Tranel, D. (1994). The release of psychological data to nonexperts: Ethical and legal considerations. *Professional Psychology: Research and Practice, 25*, 33–38.

Wetter, M. W., & Corrigan, S. K. (1995). Providing information to clients about psychological tests: A survey of attorneys' and law students' attitudes. *Professional Psychology: Research and Practice, 26*, 474–477.

37 TYPES OF TEST SCORES AND THEIR PERCENTILE EQUIVALENTS

Thomas P. Hogan

This chapter defines the converted or normed scores commonly used with psychological and educational tests and presents their percentile equivalents. In addition, Figure 1 and Table 1 show the relationships among many of these normed scores. Figure 1 illustrates the equivalence of the various scores that are based on the normal curve. The figure has insufficient resolution for making conversions among the scores for practical or clinical purposes. However, Table 1 allows for such conversions. The table is constructed with percentile ranks as the reference columns on the left and right. The body of the table shows conversions to several types of scores, each of which is defined below. Slightly different values might be entered for any particular percentile depending on how one rounds the entries or reads up or down for points covering multiple scores. This is particularly true at the extremes of the distribution.

Figure 1 and Table 1 treat the equivalence of different score modes, not the equivalence of different standardization groups. Scores from tests standardized on different groups cannot be equated simply by using the equivalencies illustrated here. It should also be noted that some tests may have independently determined norms for two different score modes (e.g., in standard scores and in percentiles); if the norms are independently determined, they will not correspond exactly with the equivalencies given here.

STANDARD SCORES

Standard scores constitute one of the most frequently used types of norms. Standard scores convert raw scores into a system with an arbitrarily chosen mean and standard deviation.

TABLE 1. Percentile Equivalents of Several Standard Score Systems

Percentile	Stanine	NCE	IQ (15)	IQ (16)	W Sub	T Score	SAT	Z Score	Percentile
99	9	99	133	135	17	73	730	2.33	99
98	9	93	130	132	16	70	700	2.05	98
97	9	90	129	130		69	690	1.88	97
96	9	87	127	128		68	680	1.75	96
95	8	85	125	126	15	66	660	1.65	95
94	8	83	123	125				1.56	94
93	8	81	122	124		65	650	1.48	93
92	8	80	121	123		64	640	1.40	92
91	8	78	120	122				1.34	91
90	8	77	119	121	14	63	630	1.28	90
89	8	76		120				1.23	89
88	7	75	118	119		62	620	1.18	88
87	7	74	117	118				1.13	87
86	7	73	116	117		61	610	1.08	86
85	7	72						1.04	85
84	7	71	115	116	13	60	600	.99	84
83	7	70						.95	83
82	7	69	114			59	590	.92	82
81	7	68	113	114				.88	81
80	7	68						.84	80
79	7	67	112	113		58	580	.81	79
78	7	66						.77	78
77	7	66	111	112				.74	77
76	6	65				57	570	.71	76
75	6	64	110	111	12			.67	75
74	6	64						.64	74
73	6	63	109	110		56	560	.61	73
72	6	62						.58	72
71	6	62		109				.55	71
70	6	61	108					.52	70
69	6	60		108		55	550	.50	69
68	6	60	107					.47	68
67	6	59		107				.44	67
66	6	59	106			54	540	.41	66
65	6	58		106				.38	65
64	6	58						.36	64
63	6	57	105		11			.33	63
62	6	56		105		53	530	.31	62
61	6	56	104					.28	61
60	6	55		104				.25	60
59	5	55						.23	59
58	5	54	103			52	520	.20	58
57	5	54		103				.18	57
56	5	53						.15	56
55	5	53	102	102				.13	55
54	5	52				51	510	.10	54
53	5	52	101					.08	53
52	5	51		101				.05	52
51	5	50						.02	51
50	5	50	100	100	10	50	500	.00	50
49	5	50						−.02	49
48	5	49		99				−.05	48

TABLE 1. Percentile Equivalents of Several Standard Score Systems (*continued*)

Percentile	Stanine	NCE	IQ (15)	IQ (16)	W Sub	T Score	SAT	Z Score	Percentile
47	5	48	99					−.08	47
46	5	48				49	490	−.10	46
45	5	47	98	98				−.13	45
44	5	47						−.15	44
43	5	46		97				−.18	43
42	5	46	97			48	480	−.20	42
41	5	45						−.23	41
40	5	45		96				−.25	40
39	4	44	96					−.28	39
38	4	44		95		47	470	−.31	38
37	4	43	95		9			−.33	37
36	4	42						−.36	36
35	4	42		94				−.38	35
34	4	41	94			46	460	−.41	34
33	4	41		93				−.44	33
32	4	40	93					−.47	32
31	4	40		92		45	450	−.50	31
30	4	39	92					−.52	30
29	4	38		91				−.55	29
28	4	38						−.58	28
27	4	37	91	90		44	440	−.61	27
26	4	36						−.64	26
25	4	36	90	89	8			−.67	25
24	4	35				43	430	−.71	24
23	4	34	89	88				−.74	23
22	3	34						−.77	22
21	3	33	88	87		42	420	−.81	21
20	3	32						−.84	20
19	3	32	87	86				−.88	19
18	3	31	86			41	410	−.92	18
17	3	30		85				−.95	17
16	3	29	85	84	7	40	400	−.99	16
15	3	28						−1.04	15
14	3	27	84	83		39	390	−1.08	14
13	3	26	83	82				−1.13	13
12	3	25	82	81		38	380	−1.18	12
11	3	24		80				−1.23	11
10	2	23	81	79	6	37	370	−1.28	10
9	2	22	80	78				−1.34	9
8	2	20	79	77		36	360	−1.40	8
7	2	19	78	76		35	650	−1.48	7
6	2	17	77	75				−1.56	6
5	2	15	76	74	5	34	340	−1.65	5
4	2	13	74	72		32	320	−1.75	4
3	1	10	72	70		31	310	−1.88	3
2	1	7	70	68	4	29	290	−2.05	2
1	1	1	67	65	3	27	270	−2.33	1

Note: IQ (15) is for IQ tests with $M = 100$ and $SD = 15$, such as Wechsler Verbal, Performance, and Total Scores. IQ (16) is for IQ tests with $M = 100$ and $SD = 16$, such as Stanford-Binet and Otis-Lennon. W Sub is for Wechsler subtests, where $M = 10$ and $SD = 3$. SAT covers any of the several tests that use $M = 500$ and $SD = 100$; these scores are usually reported to two significant digits (i.e., with the farthest right digit always 0), and that is how they are presented here.

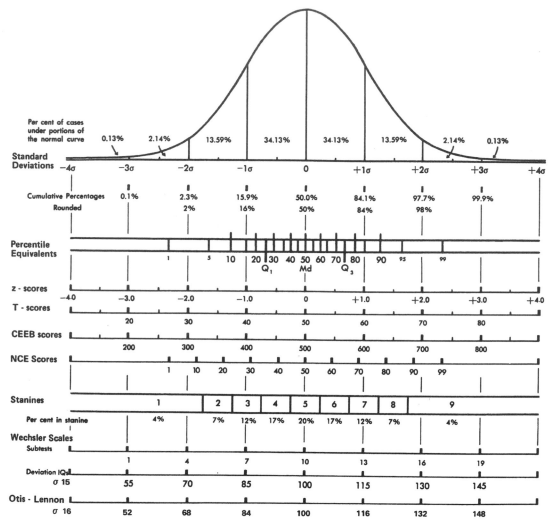

FIGURE 1. Equivalences of Several Standard Scores in the Normal Distribution (Reprinted by permission of the Psychological Corporation from Seashore, n.d.)

Although the standard score mean and standard deviation are "arbitrarily" chosen, they are selected to yield round numbers such as 50 and 10 or 500 and 100.

Standard scores may be either linear or nonlinear transformations of the raw scores. It will usually not be apparent from a table of standard score norms whether they are linear or nonlinear; the test manual (or publisher) must be consulted for this purpose. Nonlinear transformations are used either to yield normal distributions or to approximate an equal interval scale (as in Thurstone scaling). When used for this latter purpose, particularly in connection

with multilevel tests, the standard scores are sometimes called *scaled scores*, and they usually do not have a readily interpretable framework.

COMMON STANDARD
SCORE SYSTEMS

The following are commonly used standard score systems. In these descriptions, M = mean and SD = standard deviation.

IQs: The "IQ" scores on most contemporary intelligence tests are standard scores with M =

100 and *SD* = either 15 or 16, based on age groupings in the standardization sample.

T scores: T scores (sometimes called McCall's T scores) are standard scores with *M* = 50 and *SD* = 10. T scores are frequently used with personality tests, such as the MMPI-2 and NEO PI-R.

Wechsler subtests: Wechsler subtests use standard scores with *M* = 10 and *SD* = 3.

SAT, GRE scores: The Scholastic Assessment Test (SAT; formerly Scholastic Aptitude Test) Verbal and Mathematical Tests; the Graduate Record Examination (GRE) Verbal, Quantitative, and Analytical Tests; the GRE Subject Tests; and the Graduate Management Admissions Tests (GMAT) all use standard score systems with *M* = 500 and *SD* = 100. In determining total scores for these tests (e.g., SAT Total), means are additive but *SD*s are not. Hence, the mean for SAT Total (Verbal + Mathematical) is 1,000, but the *SD* is not 200; it is less than 200, since the two tests being added are not perfectly correlated.

Other tests: The ACT (American College Test) uses a score scale ranging from 1 to 36, with *M* = 16 for high school students and *M* = 19 for college-bound students and *SD* = 5. The LSAT (Law School Admission Test) has *M* = 150 and *SD* = 10.

Stanines: Stanines (a contraction of "standard-nine") are standard scores with *M* = 5 and *SD* = 2 (approximately), thus dividing the distribution into nine intervals (1–9), with stanines 2–8 spanning equal distances (each stanine covers ½ *SD*) on the base of the normal curve. Stanines are usually determined from their percentile equivalents, thus normalizing the resulting distribution. Stanines are frequently used with achievement tests and group-administered ability tests but are not used much outside these types of tests.

Stens: Stens (a contraction of "standard-ten") are standard scores that span the normal curve with 10 units and with *M* = 5.5 and *SD* = 2; each sten covers ½ *SD*.

Z scores: Z scores are standard scores with *M* = 0.0 and *SD* = 1.0. These scores are used frequently in statistical work but virtually never for practical reporting of test results.

Normal curve equivalents: Normal curve equivalents (NCEs) are a type of standard score designed to match the percentile scale at points 1, 50, and 99. Thus an NCE of 1 equals a percentile of 1, an NCE of 50 equals a percentile of 50, and an NCE of 99 equals a percentile of 99. The NCE scale divides the base of the normal curve into equal units between percentiles of 1 and 99. Using these criteria, NCEs work out to have *M* = 50 and *SD* = 21.06. NCEs were designed for use in federally funded programs in elementary and secondary schools and are used almost exclusively in that context.

PERCENTILES AND PERCENTILE RANKS

Percentiles and percentile ranks are among the most commonly used normed scores for all types of tests. A *percentile* is a point in the distribution at or below which the given percentage of cases falls. A *percentile rank* is the position of a particular score in the distribution expressed as a ranking in a group of 100. There is a fine, technical distinction between percentiles and percentile ranks, but the terms are often used interchangeably without harm.

Quartiles, quintiles, and deciles are offshoots of the percentile system, dividing the distribution of scores into quarters, fifths, and 10ths, respectively. Unfortunately, there is no uniformity in designating the top and bottom portions of each of these divisions. For example, the "second" quartile may be either the second from the bottom (25th–49th percentiles) or the second from the top (50th–74th percentiles). Hence, special care is needed on this point when communicating results in any of these systems.

AGE/GRADE EQUIVALENTS

Age and grade equivalents are normed scores, but they are very different in important respects from standard scores and percentiles. Hence, they cannot be represented conveniently in Figure 1 or in Table 1.

An *age equivalent* score converts a raw score into an age—usually years and months —corresponding to the typical (usually median) raw score attained by a specified group. The specified group is ordinarily defined within a fairly narrow age range (e.g., in 3-month intervals in the standardization group).

Age equivalents are used almost exclusively with tests of mental ability, in which case they are referred to as *mental ages*. However, they are also used with anthropometric measurements (e.g., height and weight) for infants and children.

Grade equivalents convert raw scores into a grade in school typical for the students at that grade level. "Typical" is usually defined as the median performance of students at a grade level. The grade equivalent (GE) is ordinarily given in school year and 10th of a year, in which the 10ths correspond roughly to the months specified below. Exact definitions of 10ths may vary by half months from one test series to another. Levels above grade 12.9 are sometimes given a nonnumerical descriptor such as PHS for "post–high school."

Sept.	Oct.	Nov.	Dec.	Jan.
.0	.1	.2	.3	.4
Feb.	Mar.	Apr.	May	June
.5	.6	.7	.8	.9

One of the peculiarities of age and grade equivalents is that their standard deviations are not equal across different age and grade levels. It is this feature that prevents them from being charted in Figure 1. Generally the standard deviations increase with successively higher age or grade levels.

References & Readings

Aiken, L. R. (1997). *Psychological testing and assessment* (9th ed.). Boston: Allyn and Bacon.

Anastasi, A., & Urbina, S. (1997). *Psychological testing* (7th ed.). Upper Saddle River, NJ: Prentice Hall.

Cohen, R. J., Swerdlik, M. E., & Phillips, S. M. (1996). *Psychological testing and assessment: An introduction to tests and measurement* (3rd ed.). Mountain View, CA: Mayfield.

Mitchell, B. C. (n.d.). *Test service notebook 13: A glossary of measurement terms*. San Antonio, TX: Psychological Corporation.

Seashore, H. G. (n.d.). *Test service notebook 148: Methods of expressing test scores*. San Antonio, TX: Psychological Corporation.

Related Topics

Chapter 38, "Popular Psychological Tests"
Chapter 39, "Sources of Information About Psychological Tests"

38   POPULAR PSYCHOLOGICAL TESTS

Pamela Brouillard

The American Psychological Association (APA) estimates that at least 20,000 new psychological tests are developed annually (American Psychological Association, 1993). Whereas clinical practice and training dictate that only a select number of tests will be used routinely, the popularity of a given test should not be considered synonymous with test quality. Prior to selecting any psychological test for use, the following issues should be considered.

- Psychological tests vary enormously in terms of their psychometric properties, ease of administration, and clinical utility.

- No single individual test will provide the user with sufficient information from which to make sound clinical decisions.
- Is the test well standardized, with clear instructions for administration and scoring?
- Is the normative sample representative of the general population and stratified for age, sex, education, and other variables?
- Does the reliability of the test meet current standards for use?
- Has the test been shown to be valid for the given area of interest?
- Is the test user qualified by training and education as well as specific licensing standards to use a given test?

Although the potential array of psychological tests from which one may select is enormous, most psychological tests can be categorized as falling within the two broad areas of use: tests of intellectual/cognitive functioning and achievement and tests of personality (objective and projective) and emotional functioning. The characteristics and uses of 10 popular psychological tests from these categories are described below. These descriptions should not be considered exhaustive in terms of either test selection or content. They are intended to highlight the salient characteristics of prominent psychological tests currently in use.

TESTS OF INTELLECTUAL/COGNITIVE
FUNCTIONING AND ACHIEVEMENT

Wechsler Intelligence Scale for Adults-Third Edition (WAIS-III; Wechsler, 1997a)

Revised in 1997, the WAIS-III retains the basic format of its predecessor, the WAIS-R, with several noteworthy modifications.

- Individual administration time of 60–90 minutes.
- Standardized on 2,450 adults aged 16–89 with an expanded upper age range of 15 years and stratified for age, sex, race/ethnicity, education, and geographic region according to census data. Co-normed with the Wechsler Memory Scale-Revised (1997b).

- Yields three general measures of intelligence: a Full Scale (FSIQ), Verbal (VIQ), and Performance IQ (PIQ) based on 11 subtests and expressed as standard scores (mean $[M]$ = 100, standard deviation $[SD]$ = 15; range of 45–155). Includes scaled scores on 11 core/3 supplemental subtests (M = 10, SD = 3); and 5 factor indices (M = 100, SD = 15).
- New subtests include Matrix Reasoning, replacing Object Assembly in the calculation of IQ, and supplemental subtests Symbol Search and Letter-Number Sequencing.
- Individual raw scores on the WAIS-III are converted to age-scaled scores for both global and subtest scores. On the WAIS-R, standard scores for all age ranges were derived by comparison to a single 20- to 34-year-old norm group.
- The reliability of the Wechsler tests is considered excellent. Interpretation of the WAIS-III will initially be guided by information obtained on the WAIS-R, with modifications expected as it continues to be evaluated.
- Provides both a technical and an administration manual with clear instructions for administration and scoring.
- Cost: basic kit $548.00; record forms 25/ $65.00; computer scoring program $125.00.

Wechsler Intelligence Scale for Children-Third Edition (WISC-III; Wechsler, 1991)

- Individual administration time of 50–70 minutes (85 with optional subtests).
- Standardized on 2,200 children aged 6 years to 16 years 11 months and stratified for age, gender, race/ethnicity, region, and parental education representative of census data.
- Yields three general measures of intelligence: a Full Scale (FSIQ), Verbal (VIQ), and Performance IQ (PIQ) expressed as standardized scores (M = 100, SD = 15; range 40–160); scaled scores on 10 core/3 supplemental subtests (M = 10, SD = 3); and 4 factor indices (M = 100, SD = 15).
- Cost: basic kit $577.50; record forms 25/ $65.00; computer scoring program $121.00.

Wechsler Preschool and Primary Scale of Intelligence-Revised (WPPSI-R; Wechsler, 1989)

- Individual administration time of 75 minutes (85 with optional subtests).
- Standardized on 1,700 children aged 3 years to 7 years 3 months and stratified for age, gender, race/ethnicity, geographic region according to census data.
- Yields three general measures of intelligence: a Full Scale (FSIQ), Verbal (VIQ), and Performance IQ (PIQ) based on 10 subtests and expressed as standard scores ($M = 100$, $SD = 15$) with a range of 41–160; scaled scores on 10 core/2 supplemental subtests ($M = 10$, $SD = 3$); and 4 factor indices ($M = 100$, $SD = 15$).
- Reliability with this young population is considered good for global scores in all age-groups except age 7.

Wide Range Achievement Test-3 (WRAT3; Wilkinson, 1993)

- Individually administered brief test of academic achievement (15–30 minutes, depending on age) with two alternate forms for ages 5–75.
- Standardized on 4,433 persons and stratified for age, region, gender, ethnicity, and socio-economic status according to U.S. census data.
- Yields standard scores ($M = 100$, $SD = 15$) on three subtests: Reading, Spelling, and Arithmetic, as well as percentile ranks and grade equivalents.
- Cost: basic kit $105.00; record forms 25/$26.00.

Woodcock-Johnson Pyscho-Educational Battery-Revised (WJ-R; Woodcock & Johnson, 1989)

- Individually administered comprehensive assessment of achievement (14 subtests; 50–60 minutes administration time) and cognitive abilities (40–80 minutes) for ages 2–79.
- Standardized on 6,359 subjects and stratified for region, community size, race, educational level, and occupation.

- Yields scores of broad cognitive ability (similar to IQ), aptitude (e.g., written language), and achievement (e.g., Reading Comprehension) based on cluster scores and individual subtest scores.
- Standard scores are expressed as age-equivalent, grade-equivalent, and W scores ($M = 100$, $SD = 15$).
- Hand and computerized scoring are available, with computer scoring recommended because hand scoring is difficult and time-consuming.
- Reliability and validity data are considered good for the achievement tests but are mixed for the cognitive abilities section.
- Cost: achievement test $254.00; cognitive test $460.00; protocols 25/$44.00; computer scoring software $220.00–$348.00 (with narrative).

Bender Visual-Motor Gestalt Test (Bender, 1946)

A test of visual-motor skill, the Bender-Gestalt consists of a series of figure drawings printed on cards, which the patient is asked to copy on a sheet of paper. While this test is sometimes used as a neuropsychological screening instrument, patients with brain damage may exhibit no impairment on this task and many newer, more comprehensive instruments are now available for this task.

- Individual administration time of 5–15 minutes for children and adults.
- Numerous scoring strategies exist; thus reliability can be variable.
- Sometimes interpreted as a projective test of personality, but its validity for this purpose is questionable.

PERSONALITY ASSESSMENT (OBJECTIVE)

Minnesota Multiphasic Personality Inventory-2 (MMPI-2; Butcher, Dahlstrom, Graham, Tellegen, & Kaemmer, 1989)

The MMPI-2 is an empirically developed paper-and-pencil test consisting of 567 true/false items that assess a wide range of psychopathology (e.g., hypochondriasis, depression). The validity of both the MMPI-2 and the MMPI-A rests largely on that of the original MMPI, one of the most widely used and researched of all psychological tests.

- Administration time of 60–90 minutes in individual, group, computer, and audiotaped formats. Requires a sixth- to eighth-grade reading level.
- Standardized on 2,600 adults aged 18–85 with a mean educational level of 13 years and stratified for gender, ethnicity, and socioeconomic level according to census data.
- Norms are reported separately for women and men.
- Yields normalized T scores ($M = 50$, $SD = 10$) on 10 clinical scales, 7 validity scales, as well as measures of test-taking attitude and numerous supplemental scores.
- Hand-scoring templates and mail-in computer scoring are available.
- Cost: test booklet $35.00; answer forms 25/$15.00; manual $42.00; user's guide $17.00; hand-scoring templates $65.00–$325.00.

Minnesota Multiphasic Personality Inventory-Adolescent (MMPI-A; Butcher et al., 1992)

The MMPI-A is an adolescent version of the MMPI specifically designed for use with 14- to 18-year-olds. While it is similar in structure and content to the original MMPI, several factors specifically related to its use with adolescents were considered in the development of this test.

- Contains 478 true/false items with a shorter administration than the MMPI, which may be an important consideration with adolescents; requires a seventh-grade reading level.
- Standardized on 1,620 adolescents from several geographic regions with ethnically diverse areas but does not conform to census data.
- Separate male and female norms are reported.

- Yields T scores ($M = 50$, $SD = 10$) on the same clinical and validity scales as the MMPI-2, as well as scores on additional scales designed to measure special problems associated with adolescence (i.e., school and family problems).
- Hand-scoring templates and mail-in computer scoring are available.
- The MMPI-A shares considerable interpretive overlap with MMPI-2 scales but requires additional investigation of the new scales.
- Cost: test booklet $35.00; answer forms 25/$15.00; manual $42.00; user's guide $18.00; hand-scoring templates $65.00–$195.00.

PERSONALITY TESTS (PROJECTIVE)

Rorschach

Originally developed by Swiss psychiatrist Hermann Rorschach, the Rorschach personality test requires an individual to verbally respond to 10 bilateral symmetrical inkblots. Interpretation of individual responses is based on the projective hypothesis that what patients see in the inkblots and how they see it are suggestive of their overall habitual problem-solving style and psychological needs. The test is used for diagnosis and treatment planning with a variety of psychological problems. (For additional information, please see chapter 31.)

- Individual administration time of 45–60 minutes (no time limit) for ages 5 to adult.
- Standardized administration, scoring, and interpretive procedures are available using the Exner Comprehensive System (Exner, 1993), which has greatly improved the reliability and validity of this test.
- Yields a structural summary with a variety of scores that organize responses across emotional and cognitive domains based on coding for content and organization of blots and many other features.
- Norms for adults, children, and adolescents as well as psychiatric reference samples are available.
- Both hand and computer scoring are available.

- Cost: stimulus plates $106.00; summary forms 100/$40.50; location forms 100/$29.00; computer scoring software $241.50–$566.50; requires additional texts for scoring.

Thematic Apperception Test (TAT)

Based on the needs press personality theory of Henry Murray (1943), the TAT provides a sample of oral storytelling behavior in response to standardized drawings that depict social situations and interpersonal relationships. Responses are believed to reflect the unconscious motivations and needs of the individual.

- For ages 7 and older; often used as an adjunct to the Rorschach.
- Administration time varies, depending on the number of drawings selected. Short forms typically require 30–45 minutes to administer.
- Stimulus materials are 39 picture drawings on cards, some of which are designated for specific age and sex groups.
- Several hand-scoring systems are available but are not well standardized, thus interscorer reliability tends to be poor. Interpretation focuses on recurrent themes across responses to drawings.
- Cost: basic kit $48.00; requires additional texts for scoring.

RESOURCES

Additional information about these and other tests can be found in the following sources.

- Professional guidelines for responsible test use such as the *Standards for Educational and Psychological Testing* (American Psychological Association, 1985).
- The test manual supplied by the publisher, which contains information on standardization, norms, reliability, and validity.
- Published reviews and descriptions of tests (e.g., *The Eleventh Mental Measurements Yearbook*; Kramer & Conoley, 1992).
- Published scoring and interpretive guide-

lines and supporting normative and comparative studies found in psychological books, journals, and other sources (e.g., Exner, 1993).
- Surveys of psychological test use (e.g., Piotrowski & Keller, 1992) in clinical settings.

References & Readings

American Psychological Association (1985). *Standards for educational and psychological testing*. Washington, DC: American Psychological Association.

American Psychological Association (1993, January). Call for book proposals for test instruments. *APA Monitor, 24,* 12.

Bender, L. (1946). *Bender Motor Gestalt Test: Cards and manual of instructions*. New York: American Orthopsychiatric Association.

Butcher, J. N., Dahlstrom, W. G., Graham, J. R., Tellegen, A., & Kaemmer, B. (1989). *Minnesota Multiphasic Personality Inventory-2 (MMPI-2): Manual for administration and scoring*. Minneapolis: University of Minnesota Press.

Butcher, J. N., Williams, C. L., Graham, J. R., Archer, R. P., Tellegen, A., Ben-Porath, Y. S., & Kaemmer, B. (1992). *MMPI-A (Minnesota Multiphasic Personality Inventory-Adolescent: Manual for administration, scoring, and interpretation*. Minneapolis: University of Minnesota Press.

Exner, J. E., Jr. (1993). *The Rorschach: A comprehensive system: Vol. 1. Basic foundations* (3rd ed.). New York: Wiley.

Kramer, J. J., & Conoley, J. C. (Eds.) (1992). *The eleventh mental measurements yearbook*. Lincoln: Buros Institute of Mental Measurements of the University of Nebraska.

Murray, H. A. (1943). *Thematic Apperception Test manual*. Cambridge, MA: Harvard University Press.

Piotrowski, C., & Keller, J. W. (1992). Psychological testing in applied settings: A literature review from 1982–1992. *Journal of Training and Practice in Professional Psychology, 6,* 74–82.

Wechsler, D. (1989). *WPPSI-R: Wechsler Preschool and Primary Scale of Intelligence-Revised*. San Antonio, TX: Psychological Corporation.

Wechsler, D. (1991). *WISC-III: Wechsler Intelligence Scale for Children-Third Edition*. San Antonio, TX: Psychological Corporation.

Wechsler, D. (1997a). *WAIS-III: Wechsler Intelli-*

gence Scale for Adults–Third Edition. San Antonio, TX: Psychological Corporation.

Wechsler, D. (1997b). *WMS-III: Wechsler Memory Scale-Third Edition*. San Antonio, TX: Psychological Corporation.

Wilkinson, G. S. (1993). *WRAT3: Wide Range Achievement Test-Third Edition*. Wilmington, DE: Jastak Associates.

Woodcock, R. W., & Johnson, M. B. (1989). *WJ-R: Woodcock-Johnson Psycho-Educational Battery-Revised*. Allen, TX: DLM Teaching.

Related Topics

39   SOURCES OF INFORMATION ABOUT PSYCHOLOGICAL TESTS

Thomas P. Hogan

Tests are an essential tool in the work of many psychologists. So many psychological tests are now available that it is impossible to be familiar with all of them or even a significant fraction of them. Hence, it is important to be familiar with sources of information about the many tests that one may evaluate, use, or encounter. This chapter presents an overview of six major sources of information about psychological and psychoeducational tests.

TEST LOCATOR SERVICE

Currently, the most exciting and revolutionary development regarding information about tests is the availability of the Test Locator on the World Wide Web. The Test Locator is a joint project of the ERIC Clearinghouse on Assessment and Evaluation at the Catholic University of America, the Library and Reference Services Division of the Educational Testing Service, the Buros Institute of Mental Measurements at the University of Nebraska, and Pro-Ed, a publisher of test reviews. Hard-copy materials available from each of these sources are listed below. The Test Locator allows accessing information from all these sources with the convenience of on-line searching. One can access the Test Locator through any of the following Web sites: http://ericae2.educ.cua.edu, http://www.unl.edu/buros, or http://www.ets.org.

Within the Test Locator, there is a Test Review Locator. One enters the name of a test, and the Test Locator lists references to reviews of the test appearing in the *Mental Measurements Yearbook (MMY)* or *Test Critiques* (see below for further descriptions of these sources). The service provides for fax or mail delivery of test reviews appearing in *MMY* (for a fee). There is also a Test Publisher Locator. One enters the name of a publisher, and the locator lists publisher contact information. Finally, the Test Locator provides access to the ETS Test

File (i.e., the ETS Test Collection database of over 10,000 tests; see below for further description of this resource).

SYSTEMATIC REVIEWS

Two published sources systematically provide reviews of tests: the *Mental Measurements Yearbooks* and *Test Critiques*. Both limit themselves to commercially available tests published in English. Both are updated every few years, providing reviews of new or revised tests. These two sources are the only ones that give thorough, professional reviews of a wide variety of tests.

The *Twelfth Mental Measurements Yearbook* (Conoley & Impara, 1995) is the most recent in the classic series of reviews sometimes referred to simply as *MMY* or "Buros," after Oscar K. Buros, who compiled and published the first volume in 1938. The *MMY* series is now prepared by the Buros Institute of Mental Measurements at the University of Nebraska and published by the University of Nebraska Press (P.O. Box 880484, 312 North 14th Street, Lincoln, NE 68588-0484; 402-472-3584 or 800-755-1105; Buros Institute, 402-472-6203). A new edition of *MMY* is published about every 3 or 4 years. The *Thirteenth Mental Measurements Yearbook* is scheduled for publication in 1998 (Impara & Plake, 1998). The 11th *MMY* was published in 1992, the 10th *MMY* in 1989. Each new yearbook contains references to reviews in earlier yearbooks. Beginning in 1989, the Buros Institute introduced a series of supplements to *MMY*. Supplements are published on an alternate schedule with full editions of *MMY*. Each supplement contains the same types of reviews as in the regular *MMY*; reviews in the supplements are incorporated into the next regular edition of *MMY*. The most recent issue in this series is the *Supplement to the Twelfth Mental Measurements Yearbook* (Impara & Conoley, 1996).

Subsets of reviews in *MMY* have been published as separate volumes from time to time. These publications, for tests in such categories as intelligence, personality, and reading, contain material available in the main *MMY* vol-

umes and in the *Tests in Print* series (see below) and hence are not separately referenced here. *MMY* reviews for the three most recent volumes are also available on CD-ROM from SilverPlatter (SilverPlatter Information, Inc., 100 River Ridge Drive, Norwood, MA 02062-5043; 781-769-2599).

The second source of systematic reviews is *Test Critiques* (*TC*; Keyser & Sweetland, 1994). This series is now available in 10 volumes, the first having been issued in 1984, the most recent in 1994. Individual reviews in *TC* are roughly comparable in scope to those in *MMY*. Each volume of *TC* covers about 100 tests. Like *MMY*, each new volume of *TC* contains a systematic listing of reviews contained in earlier volumes. *Test Critiques* is published by Pro-Ed (8700 Shoal Creek Boulevard, Austin, TX 78757-6897; 512-451-3246).

COMPREHENSIVE LISTINGS

Several sources give comprehensive listings of tests. Generally, these sources provide basic information about the tests (e.g., target age levels, publisher, types of scores) but refrain from giving any evaluative comments. These sources are most helpful for two purposes. First, if one needs to know what tests are available for a particular purpose, these listings will provide an initial pool of possibilities for more detailed review. Second, if one knows the name of a test but nothing else about it, information in these listings will provide a brief description of the test and its source.

The venerable series known as *Tests in Print* is now in its fourth edition: *Tests in Print IV* (Murphy, Conoley, & Impara, 1994). Usually referred to as *TIP-IV*, the current edition contains entries for 3,009 tests. Earlier editions appeared in 1961, 1974, and 1983. The *TIPs* are prepared by the Buros Institute of Mental Measurements (see above for contact information).

Tests: A Comprehensive Reference for Assessments in Psychology, Education, and Business (Maddox, 1997) is a continuing series by the company that publishes *Test Critiques*. Earlier editions in 1983 (with a supplement in

1984), 1986, and 1991 were edited by Sweetland and Keyser, editors of *Test Critiques*. The source presents, for the three areas identified in the title, lists of tests from over 400 publishers. Each entry includes the age/grade range for the test, purpose, timing, type of scoring, publisher, cost, and a brief description of the test structure and content. (See *Test Critiques* above for contact information.)

The ETS Test Collection is a library of approximately 10,000 tests and other measurement devices maintained by the Educational Testing Service in Princeton, New Jersey. Entries in the collection are accessible through the Test Locator service described above. The collection attempts to include tests available from any source: commercial publishers, individual authors, universities, journals, and so on. The collection has issued the following six volumes to provide information about tests in selected areas in hard-copy form: Volume 1, *Achievement Tests and Measurement Devices*, 2nd ed., 1993; Volume 2, *Vocational Tests and Measurement Devices*, 2nd ed., 1995; Volume 3, *Tests for Special Populations*, 1989; Volume 4, *Cognitive Aptitude and Intelligence Tests*, 1990; Volume 5, *Attitude Tests*, 1991; Volume 6, *Affective Measures and Personality Tests*, 1992. All are published by Oryx Press (4041 North Central at Indian School Road, Phoenix, AZ 85012-3397; 602-265-2651 or 800-279-6799).

The ETS Test Collection also provides *Tests in Microfiche*, a microfiche collection of unpublished instruments, and *Test Bibliographies* on selected topics. For further information on all these derivatives from the Test Collection, contact 609-734-5687 or 609-921-9000; e-mail: pstanley@ets.org; or use the ETS Web site address given above.

The *Directory of Unpublished Experimental Mental Measures* (Goldman & Mitchell, 1995) is a multivolume effort published by the American Psychological Association. As suggested by the title, the work concentrates exclusively on tests that are not available from regular publishers. The volumes include information (name, purpose, source, format, timing, etc.) for about 1,300 tests in a wide variety of areas.

SPECIAL-PURPOSE COLLECTIONS

A number of books provide collections of tests and/or test reviews within a relatively narrow band of interest. The following list is not intended to be exhaustive but is illustrative of the books in this category. Fischer and Corcoran (1994) provide a collection of simple, paper-and-pencil measures of clinically relevant constructs. There are two volumes, one concentrating on measures for families, children, and couples, the other on measures for adults. Robinson, Shaver, and Wrightsman (1991) provide an excellent collection of over 100 measures of attitudes, broadly conceived to include such areas as self-concept, locus of control, values, and life satisfaction. The work includes both published and unpublished measures; for unpublished measures, generally the entire test is included in the entry. Shaw and Wright (1967) is another excellent, although somewhat dated, collection of attitudinal measures, mostly unpublished, in such areas as social institutions, significant others, and social practices. All these references provide basic descriptive information about the measures included, plus at least some evaluative commentary on matters such as reliability and validity.

Health and Psychosocial Instruments (HaPI) is a database of instruments produced by Behavioral Measurement Database Services (P.O. Box 110287, Pittsburgh, PA 15232-0787; 412-687-6850). It is available on CD-ROM.

PUBLISHERS' CATALOGS

All the major test publishers have catalogs listing their products. The publisher's catalog is the best source of information about the most recent editions of a test, including variations such as large-print editions and foreign language versions; costs of materials and scoring; types of scoring services; and ancillary materials. Catalogs are usually issued on an annual or semiannual schedule.

Publishers' representatives, either in the field or in the home office, are also an important source of information, especially about new products and services. A call to a publisher's representative can often save hours of looking for information about a price or scoring service.

For contact information for major test publishers, see chapter 40. Contact information is also available in the Test Publisher Locator service described above.

OTHER USERS

Finally, a valuable but often overlooked source of information about tests is other users of tests. Experienced colleagues can be especially helpful in describing tests widely used in a particular field and the peculiarities of certain tests. In effect, colleagues can provide brief, informal versions of the lengthier reviews one would find in the formal sources cited above.

References & Readings

Conoley, J. C., & Impara, J. C. (Eds.) (1995). *The twelfth mental measurements yearbook.* Lincoln: University of Nebraska Press.

Fischer, J., & Corcoran, K. (1994). *Measures for clinical practice: A sourcebook* (2nd ed., Vols. 1 & 2). New York: Free Press.

Goldman, B. A., & Mitchell, D. F. (1995). *Directory of unpublished experimental mental measures* (Vol. 6). Washington, DC: American Psychological Association.

Impara, J. C., & Conoley, J. C. (Eds.) (1996). *Supplement to the twelfth mental measurements yearbook.* Lincoln: University of Nebraska Press.

Impara, J. C., & Plake, B. S. (Eds.) (1998). *The thirteenth mental measurements yearbook.* Lincoln: University of Nebraska Press.

Keyser, D. J., & Sweetland, R. C. (Eds.) (1994). *Test critiques* (Vol. 10). Austin, TX: Pro-Ed.

Maddox, T. (1997). *Tests: A comprehensive reference for assessments in psychology, education, and business* (4th ed.). Austin, TX: Pro-Ed.

Murphy, L. L., Conoley, J. C., & Impara, J. C. (Eds.) (1994). *Tests in print IV.* Lincoln: University of Nebraska Press.

Robinson, J. P., Shaver, P. R., & Wrightsman, L. S. (Eds.) (1991). *Measures of personality and social psychological attitudes.* San Diego, CA: Academic Press.

Shaw, M. E., & Wright, J. M. (1967). *Scales for the measurement of attitudes.* New York: McGraw-Hill.

Sweetland, R. C., & Keyser, D. J. (1991). *Tests: A comprehensive reference for assessments in psychology, education, and business* (3rd ed.). Austin, TX: Pro-Ed.

Related Topics

Chapter 38, "Popular Psychological Tests"

Chapter 40, "Publishers of Psychological and Psychoeducational Tests"

40   PUBLISHERS OF PSYCHOLOGICAL AND PSYCHOEDUCATIONAL TESTS

The following is a list of major publishers of psychological and psychoeducational tests in the United States and some of their most popular tests. Neither the list of publishers nor the list of their popular products is exhaustive. Rather, the lists are intended for quick reference and direction to the appropriate supplier.

American Association of State Psychology Boards
P.O. Box 4389
Montgomery, AL 36103
Phone: 334-832-4580
Publishes the Examination for Professional Practice
in Psychology

American College Testing Program (ACT)
P.O. Box 168
Iowa City, IA 52243
Phone: 319-337-1000
Publishes the ACT Career Planning and the ACT
Proficiency Examinations

American Guidance Service (AGS)
4201 Woodland Road
P.O. Box 99
Circle Pines, MN 55014-1796
Phone: 800-328-2560; 203-322-6135
Publishes the Kaufman Assessment Battery for
Children (K-ABC), the Peabody Picture Vo-
cabulary Test-Revised (PPVT-R), the Vineland
Adaptive Behavior Scales-Revised, and the Wood-
cock Reading Mastery Tests-Revised

The College Board
45 Columbus Avenue
New York, NY 10023-6992
Phone: 212-713-8000
Publishes the College Board Achievement Tests,
the Graduate Record Examinations, and the Test
of English as a Foreign Language (some tests are
sponsored jointly with the Educational Testing
Service)

Consulting Psychologists Press (CPP)
3803 East Bayshore Road
P.O. Box 10096
Palo Alto, CA 94303
Phone: 800-624-1765; 415-969-8901
Publishes the Adjective Check List, the California
Psychological Inventory (CPI), the Myers-Briggs
Type Indicator (MBTI), and the Strong Interest
Inventory (SII)

Educational and Industrial Testing Service (EdITS)
P.O. Box 7234
San Diego, CA 92167
Phone: 800-416-1666; 619-222-1666
Publishes the Personal Orientation Dimensions
(POD), the Comrey Personality Scales (CPS), the
Eysenck Personality Inventory (EPI), and the
Profile of Mood States (POMS)

Educational Testing Service (ETS)
Rosedale Road
Princeton, NJ 08541
Phone: 609-921-9000
Publishes the Advanced Placement Examinations,
the College Level Examination Program, the
Scholastic Assessment Test, the Secondary Level
English Proficiency Test (some tests are spon-
sored jointly with the College Board)

Harvard University Press
79 Garden Street
Cambridge, MA 02138
Phone: 800-448-2242; 617-495-2600
Publishes the Thematic Apperception Test

Institute of Personality and Ability Testing (IPAT)
P.O. Box 1188
Champaign, IL 61824-1188
Phone: 800-225-4728; 217-352-4739
Publishes the IPAT Anxiety Scale, the IPAT Depres-
sion Scale, and the 16 Personality Factor (16PF)

Jastak Associates
P.O. Box 3410
Wilmington, DE 19804
Phone: 800-221-WRAT
Publishes the Wide Range Achievement Test-3

Lafayette Instrument Company
P.O. Box 5729
Lafayette, IN 47903
Phone: 800-428-7545
Publishes the Purdue Pegboard

McBer
116 Huntington Avenue
Boston, MA 02116
Phone: 800-729-8074
Publishes the Learning Style Inventory (LSI)

Multi-Health Systems (MHS)
908 Niagara Falls Boulevard
North Tonawanda, NY 14120-2060
Phone: 800-456-3003
Publishes the Children's Depression Inventory
(CDI) and the Connors' Rating Scales; distrib-
utes the Wisconsin Card Sorting Test (WCST)

National Computer Systems (NCS)
Assessment Division
5605 Green Circle Drive
Minnetonka, MN 55343
Phone: 800-627-7271

Publishes the Millon Clinical Multiaxial Inventory-III (MCMI-III) and computer scoring services; distributes the Minnesota Multiphasic Personality Inventory-2 (MMPI-2)

PRO-ED
8700 Shoal Creek Boulevard
Austin, TX 78757-6897
Phone: 512-451-3246
Publishes the Detroit Tests of Learning Aptitude-2, the Draw A Person: Screening Procedure for Emotional Disturbance (DAP: SPED), Test of Visual Motor Integration (TVMI), and the Test of Nonverbal Intelligence-2

Psychological Assessment Resources (PAR)
P.O. Box 998
Odessa, FL 33556
Phone: 800-331-TEST
Publishes the Adaptive Behavior Scales, the Beery Developmental Test of Visual-Motor Integration, the NEO-Personality Inventory-Revised, the Eating Disorder Inventory-2, the Rogers Criminal Responsibility Assessment Scales, the Self-Directed Search, and the Wisconsin Card Sorting Test (only the manual, software, and record booklet)

Psychological Corporation/Harcourt Brace
555 Academic Court
San Antonio, TX 78204
Phone: 800-228-0752; 516-543-6914; 202-342-2205
Publishes the Bayley Scales of Infant Development, the Beck Depression Inventory (BDI), the McCarthy Scales of Children's Abilities, the Otis-Lennon School Ability Test, the Wechsler Adult Intelligence Scale-Revised (WAIS-R), the Rorschach Test (a distributor), the Wechsler Intelligence Scale for Children-III (WISC-III), the Wechsler Preschool and Primary Scale of Intelligence-Revised (WPPSI-R), the Wechsler Memory Scale-Revised, and the Western Aphasia Battery

Reitan Neuropsychology Laboratory
2920 South Fourth Avenue
Tucson, AZ 85713-4819
Phone: 520-882-2022
Publishes the Halstead-Reitan Neuropsychological Test Batteries

Riverside Publishing
425 Spring Lake Drive
Itasca, IL 60143
Phone: 800-323-9540
Publishes the AAMR Adaptive Behavior Scale, the Cognitive Abilities Test, the Stanford-Binet Intelligence Scale: Fourth Edition, the Stroop Color and Word Test, and the Woodcock-Johnson Psycho-Educational Battery-Revised

Sigma Assessment Systems
P.O. Box 610984
Port Huron, MI 48061-0984
Phone: 800-265-1285
Publishes the Personality Research Form (PRF) and the Jackson Personality Inventory

Slosson Educational Publishing
P.O. Box 280
East Aurora, NY 14052
Phone: 800-828-4800; 716-652-0930
Publishes the Leiter International Performance Scale, the Slosson Intelligence Test, and the Slosson Oral Reading Test

University of Minnesota Press
111 Third Avenue South, Suite 290
Minneapolis, MN 55455
Phone: 800-388-3863; 612-627-1970
Publishes the Minnesota Multiphasic Personality Inventory-2 (MMPI-2) and the Minnesota Multiphasic Personality Inventory-Adolescent (MMPI-A)

Western Psychological Services
12031 Wilshire Boulevard
Los Angeles, CA 90025
Phone: 800-222-2670
Publishes the Bender Visual-Motor Gestalt Test (children's version), the Hand Test, and the Luria-Nebraska Neuropsychological Battery; distributes the Bender Visual-Motor Gestalt Test (adult version)

Wonderlic Personnel Test, Inc.
1509 North Milwaukee Avenue
Libertyville, IL 60048-1380
Phone: 800-323-3742; 847-680-4900
Publishes the Wonderlic Personnel Test

Related Topics

Chapter 38, "Popular Psychological Tests"

PART III
Psychotherapy and Treatment

41 PATIENTS' RIGHTS IN PSYCHOTHERAPY

Dorothy W. Cantor

Patients who enter psychotherapy have rights that psychologists are responsible for honoring and rights for which third-party payers and other entities are responsible. It is the obligation of treating psychologists to respect the rights of patients and, to the limits of their ability, to assist patients to press third-party payers and other entities to do likewise.

1. *Confidentiality:* Confidentiality is the cornerstone of the psychotherapy process. Therefore, patients have the right to be guaranteed the protection of the confidentiality of their relationship with a psychologist, except when laws or ethics dictate otherwise.

- Patients should not be required to disclose confidential information, other than diagnosis, prognosis, type of treatment, time and length of treatment, and cost.
- Patients should make only time-limited disclosure with full written informed consent.
- Any entity receiving information about a patient should maintain clinical informa-

tion in confidence with the same rigor and subject to the same violation as the direct provider of care.

- Information technology should be used for transmission, storage, or data management *only* with methodologies that remove individual identifying information and assure the protection of the patients' privacy. Information should not be transferred, sold, or otherwise utilized.

2. *Respectful treatment:* Patients have the right to courtesy, respect, dignity, responsiveness, and timely attention to their needs.

3. *Respect for boundaries:* Patients have the right to expect their therapists to honor the boundaries between them and not to intrude in areas that go beyond the therapeutic relationship.

- Psychologists do not engage in sexual intimacies with current patients or with former patients for at least 2 years after treatment has ended.

- Psychologists do not accept as therapy patients persons with whom they have engaged in sexual intimacies.
- Psychologists do not exploit patients. They refrain from entering into or promising another relationship—personal, scientific, professional, financial, or otherwise—with a patient.

4. *Respect for individual differences:* Patients have the right to quality treatment, without regard to race, color, religion, national origin, gender, age, sexual orientation, or disabilities.

- Patients have the right to expect their therapists to have competency in dealing with their individual differences.
- Patients can expect their therapists to respect their values, attitudes, and opinions, even when they differ from their own.

5. *Knowledge of the psychologist's professional expertise:* Patients have the right to receive full information about the psychologist's knowledge, skills, preparation, experience, and credentials. They also have the right to be informed about their options for treatment interventions.

6. *Choice:* Patients have the right to choose their therapists, according to their own preferences and without pressure from third-party payers to select from a limited panel.

7. *Informed consent to therapy:* Patients have the right to informed consent. The language of that consent must be comprehensible. The patient should be informed of significant information concerning the treatment or assessment being entered into.

8. *Determination of treatment:* Patients have the right to have recommendations about their treatment made by the treating psychologist in conjunction with them or their family, as appropriate. Treatment decisions should not be made by third-party payers. The patient has the right to make final decisions regarding treatment.

- Patients have the right to continuity of care and to not be abandoned by their therapist.
- Patients can expect a psychologist to terminate a professional relationship when it becomes reasonably clear that the patient no longer needs the service, is not benefiting, or is being harmed by continued service.
- Patients can expect that prior to termination, whatever the reason, there will be a discussion of their needs and views and suggestions for alternative services and that reasonable steps will be taken to facilitate transfer to another therapist, if appropriate.

9. *Parity:* Patients have the right to receive benefits for mental health and substance abuse treatment on the same basis as for any other illnesses, with the same provisions, co-payments, lifetime benefits, and catastrophic coverage in both insurance and self-funded/self-insured health plans.

10. *Right to know:* Patients have the right to full disclosure regarding terms of their health insurance coverage.

- *Benefits:* Patients have the right to be provided information from the purchasing entity (such as employer, union, or public purchaser) and the insurance/third-party payer describing the nature and extent of their mental health and substance abuse treatment benefits. This information should include details on procedures to obtain access to services, on utilization management procedures, and on appeal rights. The information should be presented clearly in writing with language that the individual can understand.
- *Contractual limitations:* Patients have the right to be informed by the psychologist of any arrangements, restrictions, and/or covenants established between the third-party payer and the psychologist that could interfere with or influence treatment recommendations. Patients have the right to be informed of the nature of information that may be disclosed for the purposes of paying benefits.
- *Appeals and grievances:* Patients have the right to receive information about the methods they can use to submit complaints or grievances regarding provision of care by the psychologist to the licens-

ing board and to the professional association. Patients also have the right to be provided information about the procedures they can use to appeal benefit utilization decisions to the third-party payer system, to the employer or purchasing entity, and to external regulatory entities.

11. *Treatment review:* To assure that treatment review processes are fair and valid, patients have the right to be guaranteed that any review of their mental health and substance abuse treatment shall involve a professional having the training, credentials, and licensure required to provide the treatment in the jurisdiction in which it will be provided. The reviewer should have no financial interest in the decision and is subject to the section on confidentiality.

12. *Accountability:* Patients have the right to have both the psychologist treating them *and* the third-party payer be accountable to them.

- Psychologists may be held accountable and liable to individuals for any injury caused by gross incompetence or negligence on the part of the professional. The psychologist has the obligation to advocate for and document necessity of care and to advise the patient of options if payment authorization is denied.

- Payers and other third parties may be held accountable and liable to patients for any injury caused by gross incompetence or negligence or by their clinically unjustified decisions.

13. *Benefit usage:* Patients are entitled to the entire scope of the benefits within the benefit plan that will address their clinical needs.

14. *Nondiscrimination:* Patients who use their mental health and substance abuse benefits shall not be penalized when seeking other health insurance or disability, life, or any other insurance benefits.

References & Readings

American Psychological Association (1992). Ethical principles of psychologists and code of conduct. *American Psychologist, 47,* 1597–1611.

Mental Health Bill of Rights Project (1997). Principles for the provision of mental health and substance abuse treatment services. *Independent Practitioner, 17*(2), 57–58.

Related Topics

42 SAMPLE PSYCHOTHERAPIST-PATIENT CONTRACT

Eric A. Harris & Bruce E. Bennett

This draft psychotherapist-patient contract has been prepared for two reasons. First, it allows

one to comply with the requirement that practitioners have the informed consent of their patients (American Psychological Association, 1992, Standard 4.02). Second, it allows a therapist to establish a legally enforceable business relationship with the patient and avoids risks that such business issues will become the basis of a malpractice suit or an ethics or licensing board complaint. Most commentators suggest that full informed consent is both ethically necessary and a good risk management strategy.

This draft was designed for psychotherapy practices. It can and should be modified to include other practice areas such as psychological evaluations, testing, neuropsychological assessment, family therapy, and group psychotherapy if these are part of a practitioner's work.

There is a great variety of business practices among psychologists. You should redraft the contract to fit your business practices rather than adjusting your practices to fit the contract. Since regulations and laws governing certain institutions are somewhat different than those governing private practitioners, these forms may also need to be modified before they can be used in hospitals, clinics, or other institutional settings.

This document includes some basic, general language about the risks and benefits of psychotherapy; these should be supplemented, either in writing or orally, by the therapist on a case-by-case basis. This approach was selected because the risks and benefits of therapy can vary considerably from case to case. Therefore, it is hard to design a single draft that is appropriate for all situations. For example, it is probably important to have a much more thorough discussion of risks and benefits with those patients considered to be either most difficult or most risky. If one is a group or family therapist, additional issues may need to be included. The psychologist may orally provide whatever additional information is required and make a note in the record about what was said. Of course, this will not be as protective as a signed agreement, but in most cases it makes the most sense clinically.

Although this model contract was originally developed for Massachusetts psychologists, most of it can be used anywhere. There are two exceptions: (a) patients' access to their own records and (b) the laws and regulations governing therapeutic confidentiality and testimonial privilege, as well as exceptions to these protections of the psychotherapist-patient relationship. The model provides sufficient alternative sections to cover almost all variations regarding record access. However, there is much variation from state to state in laws governing privilege, confidentiality, and exceptions to both, so an adaptation should be made for each state in which a psychologist practices.

The reader is strongly advised to have his or her personal attorney review the informed consent document prior to implementation. The document should be in compliance with local and state statutes regulating the practice of psychology. It should also avoid language that could be interpreted as a guarantee or implied warranty regarding the services rendered.

This consent form is the property of the American Psychological Association Insurance Trust (APAIT), and copyright to the form is owned by the APAIT. ©1997 American Psychological Association Insurance Trust. This form is used with permission.

What follows is a specific draft text that you may adapt for your practice or agency. Sections of the draft where you should insert numbers are designated *XX*, and sections you may want to specially modify are bracketed [thus].

Outpatient Services Contract

Welcome to my practice. This document contains important information about my professional services and business policies. Please read it carefully and jot down any questions that you might have so that we can discuss them at our next meeting. Once you sign this, it will constitute a binding agreement between us.

Psychological Services

Psychotherapy is not easily described in general statements. It varies depending on the personality of both the therapist and the patient and the particular problems which the patient brings. There are a number of different approaches which can be utilized to address the problems you hope to address. It is not like visiting a medical doctor, in that psychotherapy requires a very active effort on your part. In order to be most successful, you will have to work on things we talk about both during our sessions and at home.

Psychotherapy has both benefits and risks. Risks sometimes include experiencing uncomfortable feelings such as sadness, guilt, anxiety, anger and frustration, loneliness, and helplessness. Psychotherapy often requires discussing unpleasant aspects of your life. Psychotherapy has also been shown to have benefits for people who undertake it. Therapy often leads to a significant reduction in feelings of distress, better relationships, and resolutions of specific problems. But there are no guarantees about what will happen.

Our first few sessions will involve an evaluation of your needs. By the end of the evaluation, I will be able to offer you some initial impressions of what our work will include and an initial treatment plan to follow, if you decide to continue. You should evaluate this information along with your own assessment about whether you feel comfortable working with me. Therapy involves a large commitment of time, money, and energy, so you should be very careful about the therapist you select. If you have questions about my procedures, we should discuss them whenever they arise. If your doubts persist, I will be happy to help you to secure an appropriate consultation with another mental health professional.

Meetings

My normal practice is to conduct an evaluation which will last from two to four sessions. During this time, we can both decide whether I am the best person to provide the services which you need in order to meet your treatment objectives. If psychotherapy is initiated, I will usually schedule one 50-minute session (one appointment hour of 50 minutes' duration) per week at a mutually agreed time, although sometimes sessions will be longer or more frequent. Once this appointment hour is scheduled, you will be expected to pay for it unless you provide *XXX* hours/days advance notice of cancellation [or unless we both agree that you were unable to attend due to circumstances which were beyond your control]. [If it is possible, I will try to find another time to reschedule the appointment.]

Professional Fees

My hourly fee is $*XXX*. In addition to weekly appointments, it is my practice to charge this amount on a prorated basis for other professional services you may require such as report writing, telephone conversations which last longer than *XX* minutes, attendance at meetings or consultations with other professionals which you have authorized, preparation of records or treatment summaries, or the time required to perform any other service which you may request of me. If you become involved in litigation which requires my participation, you will be expected to pay for the professional time required even if I am compelled to testify by another party. [Because of the complexity and difficulty of legal involvement, I charge $*XXX* per hour for preparation for and attendance at any legal proceeding.]

Billing and Payments

You will be expected to pay for each session at the time it is held, unless we agree otherwise or unless you have insurance coverage which requires another arrangement. Payment schedules for other professional services will be agreed to at the time these services are requested. [In circumstances of unusual financial hardship, I may be willing to negotiate a fee adjustment or installment payment plan.]

If your account is more than 60 days in arrears and suitable arrangements for payment have not been agreed to, I have the option of using legal means to secure payment, including collection agencies or small claims court. [If such legal action is necessary, the costs of bringing that proceeding will be included in the claim.] In most cases, the only information which I release about a client's treatment would be the client's name, the nature of the services provided, and the amount due.

Insurance Reimbursement

In order for us to set realistic treatment goals and priorities, it is important to evaluate what resources are available to pay for your treatment. If you have a health insurance policy, it will usually provide some coverage for mental health treatment. I will provide you with whatever assistance I can in facilitating your receipt of the benefits to which you are entitled including filling out forms as appropriate. However, you, and not your insurance company, are responsible for full payment of the fee which we have agreed to. Therefore, it is very important that you find out exactly what mental health services your insurance policy covers.

You should carefully read the section in your insurance coverage booklet which describes mental health services. If you have questions, you should call your plan administrator and inquire. Of course, I will provide you with whatever information I can based on my experience and will be happy to try to assist you in deciphering the information you receive from your carrier. If necessary to resolve confusion, I am willing to call the carrier on your behalf.

The escalation of the cost of health care has resulted in an increasing level of complexity about insurance benefits which sometimes makes it difficult to determine exactly how much mental health coverage is available. "Managed Health Care Plans" such as HMOs and PPOs often require advance authorization before they will provide reimbursement for mental health services. These plans are often oriented toward a short-term treatment approach designed to resolve specific problems that are interfering with one's usual level of functioning. It may be necessary to seek additional approval after a certain number of sessions. In my experience, while quite a lot can be accomplished in short-term therapy, many clients feel that more services are necessary after insurance benefits expire. [Some managed care plans will not allow me to provide services

to you once your benefits are no longer available. If this is the case, I will do my best to find you another provider who will help you continue your psychotherapy.]

You should also be aware that most insurance agreements require you to authorize me to provide a clinical diagnosis and sometimes additional clinical information such as a treatment plan or summary or in rare cases a copy of the entire record. This information will become part of the insurance company files, and, in all probability, some of it will be computerized. All insurance companies claim to keep such information confidential, but once it is in their hands, I have no control over what they do with it. In some cases they may share the information with a national medical information data bank. If you request it, I will provide you with a copy of any report which I submit.

Once we have all of the information about your insurance coverage, we will discuss what we can expect to accomplish with the benefits that are available and what will happen if the insurance benefits run out before you feel ready to end our sessions. It is important to remember that you always have the right to pay for my services yourself and avoid the complexities which are described above.

Contacting Me

I am often not immediately available by telephone. While I am usually in my office between 9 A.M. and 5 P.M., I usually will not answer the phone when I am with a client. I do have call-in hours at *XXXXX* on *XXXXX*. When I am unavailable, my telephone is answered by an automatic [answering machine] which I monitor frequently [is answered by my secretary, or answering service who usually knows where to reach me, or voice mail which I monitor frequently]. I will make every effort to return your call on the same day you make it with the exception of weekends and holidays. If you are difficult to reach, please leave some times when you will be available. [In emergencies, you can try me at my home number.] If you cannot reach me, and you feel that you cannot wait for me to return your call, you should call your family physician or the emergency room at the nearest hospital and ask for the [psychologist or psychiatrist] on call. If I am unavailable for an extended time, I will provide you with the name of a trusted colleague whom you can contact if necessary.

Professional Records

Both law and the standards of my profession require that I keep appropriate treatment records. You are entitled to receive a copy of the records, but if you wish, I can prepare an appropriate summary. Because these are professional records, they can be misinterpreted and/or can be upsetting to lay readers. If you wish to see your records, I recommend that you review them in my presence so that we can discuss the contents. [I am sometimes willing to conduct such a meeting without charge.] Clients will be charged an appropriate fee for any preparation time which is required to comply with an information request.

Professional Records

[This section is for psychologists who practice in states that do not require that psychologists provide clients with access to their records.]

As I am sure you are aware, I am required to keep appropriate records of [the professional services I provide] [your treatment] [our work together]. Because these records contain information which can be misinterpreted by someone who is not a mental health professional, it is my general policy that clients may not review them. However, if you request, I will provide you with a treatment summary unless I believe that to do so would be emotionally damaging. If that is the case, I will be happy to forward the summary to another appropriate mental health professional who is working with you. [This service will be provided without any additional charge.] [You should be aware that this will be treated in the same manner as any other professional (clinical) service and you will be billed accordingly.] [There will be an additional charge for this service.]

Professional Records

[This section is for psychologists who practice in states that require psychologists to provide clients with access to their records unless to do so would cause emotional damage, upset, etc.]

Both law and the standards of my profession require that I keep appropriate treatment records. You are entitled to receive a copy of the records, unless I believe that seeing them would be emotionally damaging, in which case, I will be happy to provide them to an appropriate mental health professional of your choice. Because these are professional records, they can be misinterpreted and/or can be upsetting, so I recommend that we review them together so that we can discuss what they contain. [I am sometimes willing to conduct such a meeting without charge.] Clients will be charged an appropriate fee for any preparation time which is required to comply with an information request.

Minors

If you are under 18 years of age, please be aware that the law may provide your parents with the right to examine your treatment records. It is my policy to request an agreement from parents that they consent to give up access to your records. If they agree, I will provide them only with general information about our work together unless I feel that there is a high risk that you will seriously harm yourself or another, in which case I will notify them of my concern. I will also provide them with a summary of your treatment when it is complete. Before giving them any information I will discuss the matter with you, if possible, and will do the best I can to resolve any objections you may have about what I am prepared to discuss.

Confidentiality

In general, the confidentiality of all communications between a client and a psychologist is protected by law, and I can only release information about our work to others with your written permission. However, there are a number of exceptions.

In most judicial proceedings, you have the right to prevent me from providing any information about your treatment. However, in some circumstances such as child custody proceedings and proceedings in which your emotional condition is an important element, a judge may require my testimony if he or she determines that resolution of the issues before him or her demands it.

There are some situations in which I am legally required to take action to protect others from harm, even though that requires revealing some information about a client's treatment. For example, if I believe that a child, an elderly person, or a disabled person is being abused, I must [may be required to] file a report with the appropriate state agency.

If I believe that a client is threatening serious bodily harm to another, I am [may be] required to take protective actions, which may include notifying the potential victim, notifying the police, or seeking appropriate hospitalization. If a client threatens to harm himself or herself, I may be required to seek hospitalization for the client or to contact family members or others who can help provide protection.

These situations have rarely arisen in my practice. Should such a situation occur, I will make every effort to fully discuss it with you before taking any action.

I may occasionally find it helpful to consult about a case with other professionals. In these consultations, I make every effort to avoid revealing the identity of my client. The consultant is, of course, also legally bound to keep the information confidential. Unless you object, I will not tell you about these consultations unless I feel that it is important to our work together.

While this written summary of exceptions to confidentiality should prove helpful in informing you about potential problems, it is important that we discuss any questions or concerns which you may have at our next meeting.

The laws governing these issues are quite complex, and I am not an attorney. While I am happy to discuss these issues with you, should you need specific advice, formal legal consultation may be desirable. If you request, I will provide you with relevant portions or summaries of the applicable state laws governing these issues.

Your signature below indicates that you have read the information in this document and agree to abide by its terms during our professional relationship.

References & Readings

American Psychological Association (1992). Ethical principles of psychologists and code of conduct. *American Psychologist, 47,* 1597–1611.

Bennett, B. E., Bryant, B. K., VandenBos, G. R., & Greenwood, A. (1990). *Professional liability and risk management.* Washington, DC: American Psychological Association.

Berglas, S., & Levendusky, P. G. (1985). The Therapeutic Contract Program: An individual-oriented psychological treatment community. *Psychotherapy, 22,* 36–45.

Greene, G. L. (1989). Using the written contract for evaluating and enhancing practice effectiveness. *Journal of Independent Social Work, 4,* 135–155.

Koocher, G. P., & Keith-Spiegel, P. C. (1998). *Ethics in psychology: Professional standards and cases* (2nd ed.). New York: Oxford University Press.

Miller, L. J. (1990). The formal treatment contract in the inpatient management of borderline personality disorder. *Hospital and Community Psychiatry, 41,* 985–987.

Selzer, M. A., Koenigsberg, H. W., & Kernberg, O. F. (1987). The initial contract in the treatment of borderline patients. *American Journal of Psychiatry, 144,* 927–930.

Yoemans, F. E., Selzer, M. A., & Clarkin, J. F. (1992). *Treating the borderline patient: A contract-based approach.* New York: Basic Books.

Related Topics

43 CLIENT-THERAPIST COMPATIBILITY

Sam S. Hill III

If there were a formula or book for selecting a therapist, it would reach the best-seller list in record time. The problems faced by the general population in selecting a mental health professional, whether a psychotherapist, a counselor, or a psychiatrist, are formidable. Most individuals seem to rely on word of mouth. A good report by a trusted friend may still be the best way to find a mental health professional. But what about the professional? What criteria do we use to "select" our clients?

IS GEOGRAPHY DESTINY?

- Urban centers allow practitioners to be more selective in choosing their clientele. The numbers of people searching for the right therapist and the numbers of professionals competing for them are greater in the populous areas, although this may be changing with the arrival of wider participation in managed care programs.
- Rural areas and smaller cities generally require that the few psychologists who practice be more generalists. There is simply not enough business to keep the doors open if you specialize in a particular population or modality of therapy.

As a result, there is a tendency for the latest methods and most current research to take place in urban areas and in tertiary medical centers, where both the populations and the funding are available for those dedicated to applied research and scholarship.

POPULATION CHARACTERISTICS

Does the patient meet the personal characteristics with which you are familiar and have adequate training and experience? If you were trained in a child clinical program and the presenting patient is an octogenarian you may want to ask yourself if this is a patient you should be taking on.

- *Age:* Is the patient of an age with which you have had training, familiarity, and supervision?
- *Gender:* Is the patient the sex with whom you work frequently and with whom you have adequate training and experience? If you have worked full-time for the last 20 years in a Veterans Administration Medical Center and the presenting patient is a woman with issues of childhood sexual abuse, are you the best person for her to see?
- *Race:* With less than 5% of all psychologists people of color, it is inevitable that we will treat people of other races. In and of itself this is not a problem if we are aware of the issues and differences among different races and the subtleties of their cultures.
- *Culture:* Time and experience have disabused us of the notion that the United States, United Kingdom, Australia, Russia, China,

or any large society contains a culturally homogeneous population. The notion that just living long enough in one country reduces everyone to a single culture has not proved true. Culture heavily influences values and the ethical framework of the individual. It is essential that the therapist understand the client's culture and value system and what constitutes health and normality within that culture.

- *Language/nationality:* It is important to be able to understand what your client is saying to you. If your client has an accent that you cannot understand and you do not speak his or her native language, you should refer the client elsewhere. The subtleties of language are important in the expression of feelings and thoughts in psychotherapy. Clients should feel that they have the full range of language to express themselves. Therapists who can participate in therapy in the client's first language have a distinct advantage.
- *Psychopathology:* Make sure that you have both the training and the experience in the disorders you are treating.

COMPATIBILITY WITH THEORETICAL ORIENTATION

- *Eclecticism:* Choose the treatment modality that best suits the client and his or her presenting problem.
- *Single orientation:* If you have a single theoretical orientation, ensure that your therapy will be the most effective for the client.

COMPETENCE

- *Experience:* If you have never dealt with a particular disorder, you may want to refer that person to another clinician. In some areas there may be little choice. You may be the only psychologist in your part of the state or community; the patient may be in serious distress, and you are his or her only option. It may still be better to decline the case. Call a colleague and seek supervision.

- *Training:* If you feel you are lacking the necessary expertise or that your training is now out of date, you must acquire additional training. The form that training takes can vary, but it should meet the "minimum standards of practice" criteria.
- *Supervision:* In most cases, a clinician is a generalist who treats a variety of patients with a variety of disorders. When you feel out of your depth, it is usually because you can't touch bottom. Seek formal supervision from someone who is known to be skilled in the area of practice in which you are working.

TRANSFERENCE/ COUNTERTRANSFERENCE

Be aware of your thoughts, feelings, and actions with your clients. Subject these to rigorous examination and engage in peer review of these issues. If you have strong feelings in either a positive or a negative direction, ask a colleague for help. We all too often become isolated and talk to no one about these problems. Without the help of another perspective, we can slip into problems without being aware of the risk to our psychological well-being and our professional status.

ECONOMICS

For whom do we work? This question was an easy one to answer just 10 years ago. Today the answer is not so simple. It is increasingly difficult for those who are on managed care panels, which use a capitation payment base to refuse patients for any reason, let alone those mentioned above. You can imagine the response of a large HMO when you say you cannot take a specific patient because you are unfamiliar with his or her subculture or native language or have never worked with a member of his or her race. It would be even worse if you should say that you prefer not to work with certain kinds of personality disorders because you seem to have a negative countertransference due to unresolved problems in your psychology.

AGENCIES

Agencies, both private and public, have a host of priorities, and client-therapist compatibility may not be at the top of the list.

- *Public:* These agencies are often exempt from licensing laws for professionals, but the professional codes of ethics still apply. In some settings, the client-therapist match is the subject of much thought and planning. In others it is more a matter of caseload sharing.
- *Private:* Private agencies are becoming more popular, especially in states where the privatization of state-run health care is more economical. Here, as in other areas of managed care, the rights and benefits of the client and therapist must be weighed against the profitability of the company. Special care should be taken in deciding who is the client.

References & Readings

Barnlund, D. C. (1990). Talking to strangers: Mediated therapeutic communication. In F. Gumpert & S. L. Fish (Eds.), *Communication and information science.* Norwood, NJ: Ablex.

Beutler, L. E., Clarkin, J. F., Crago, M., & Bergan, J. (1991). Client therapist matching. In C. R. Snyder, R. Donelson, & F. Forsyth (Eds.), *Handbook of social and clinical psychology: The health perspective* (Pergamon General Psychology Series, Vol. 162). Elmsford, NY: Pergamon Press.

Derlega, V. J., Hendrick, S. S., Winstead, B. A., & Berg, J. H. (1991). *Psychotherapy as a personal relationship.* New York: Guilford Press.

Related Topics

44   CHOICE OF TREATMENT FORMAT

John F. Clarkin

The final goal of psychological treatment is symptom relief, whether it be one or a constellation of symptoms or conflicts/difficulties in interpersonal relationships. However, for the mental health professional operating on a clinical (i.e., single case) basis, making the initial probes required to determine a treatment plan necessitates focusing on patient symptoms and diagnosis, the natural course of those symptoms, the personality of the patient in whom the symptoms reside, and process and mediating goals of the therapy. The key treatment planning factors include the patient's diagnosis and related problem areas; mediating and final goals of treatment; patient enabling factors; and treatment choice points (treatment setting, format, technique, somatic treatments, and duration and frequency; Clarkin, Frances, & Perry, 1992). The focus of this chapter is to articulate the principles guiding the choice of treatment format (i.e., individual, marital/family, group), given the information of patient di-

TABLE 1. Selection Criteria for Format: Individual, Marital/Family, and Group

Individual	Marital/Family	Group
1. Adolescent who is striving for autonomy 2. Patient symptoms based on internal conflict that is expressed in environmental situations	1. Family/marital problems are presented as such 2. Symptoms are predominantly within the family/marital situation 3. Family presents with current structured difficulties in its relationships 4. Adolescent acting-out behavior 5. Sexual dysfunction in the marital dyad	1. Patient's problems are interpersonal, both outside and inside family situations. 2. Patient presents with problems that fit the focus of specialized groups (e.g., alcohol or drug abuse)

agnosis and mediating and final goals of treatment. Table 1 summarizes several of these selection criteria.

Because the individual treatment format is familiar, private, relatively flexible, and built on the basic trust inherent in a dyadic relationship, it remains the most prevalent format of psychological treatment. Over the past 40 years, partly because the limitations of an individual format have become more widely appreciated and partly because the field has shifted toward theoretical models that emphasize interpersonal rather than intrapsychic dynamics, clinicians have increasingly used family/marital and group treatment formats.

There are clinical, cultural, and economic issues that guide the clinician to choose among individual, marital/family, and group treatment formats: (a) patient problem/diagnosis; (b) problem demonstration, that is, in marital, family, or group display; (c) model of treatment intervention; (d) patient preference; and (e) efficiency of treatment.

can be explored in the family therapy context to address a possible interaction between adolescent impulsivity and parental skills in setting limits.

The Axis V diagnosis or GAF rating may be of particular importance in choosing a treatment format. Independently of the particular Axis I (and Axis II) diagnosis, the relative level of the GAF score may relate to the nature and process of differential treatment planning. In several contexts it has been suggested that relatively healthy individuals (those with GAF scores roughly between 100 and 70) are most likely to respond to most formats of therapeutic intervention and may even be the most likely to be able to cope with difficulties without intervention. At the other end of the spectrum, those patients with severe and chronic difficulties (with GAF scores of roughly 30 to 0) may improve relatively little from most interventions without the assistance of significant others. This would suggest a family format of treatment.

PATIENT PROBLEM/DIAGNOSIS

Many patient problems and/or diagnoses lend themselves to specific treatment formats. For example, a sexual dysfunction with one's spouse in the context of marital disputes and with no physical reasons for the dysfunction may lend itself to treatment in the marital format, where the contributions of both parties to the dysfunction can be identified and explored. Alternately, an adolescent acting-out problem

PROBLEM DEMONSTRATION

Where is the problem presented by the individual patient demonstrated? For example, is it a hostility problem in a 43-year-old male who has this problem with his wife but not in social and work situations? Or, alternately, is he hostile in multiple environments in his life? Thus, the environment in which the problem arises is a clue to the selection of the treatment format.

MEDIATING GOALS OF TREATMENT

The alleviation or elimination of a particular diagnostic entity or symptom complex is the typical final goal of treatment. However, the mediating goals of treatment—those intermediate goals that must be reached in order to achieve the final goals—are not always so obvious. They are dictated by the model of the diagnosis/symptom picture/problem area or successive steps to health. These mediating goals will depend on the particular diagnosis/problem area, the theoretical orientation of the assessor, and current understanding of the particular diagnosis/problem area in question. The nature and extent of these mediating goals provide the indications for the various therapeutic settings, formats, strategies/techniques, somatic treatments, and treatment durations. Therefore, in the evaluation and treatment planning for any case, the clinician must be as precise as possible about the mediating goals of treatment.

These mediating goals of treatment go beyond the mere description of the symptoms/behaviors present and hypothesize causal relationships between the symptoms and other biological, intrapsychic, and environmental factors. There are many pathways to a common descriptive diagnosis of, for example, major depression. Thus, treatment will depend not only on the descriptive diagnosis but also on the variables that contribute to this symptom state.

The phrase "mediating goals of treatment" refers to those essential subgoals that must be achieved for the treatment or combination of treatments to achieve their final goal. There are two types of mediating goals: (a) the goals of the treatment process itself and (b) the successive approximations to health that are expected to occur sequentially in the patient's/family's behavior. The former goals are related to the enabling factors that the patient brings to therapy; the latter are related to the model of the illness that is being treated and to the particular school of therapy and its understanding of the covariance of certain patient behaviors.

One can articulate mediating goals of treatment that are consistent with each of the treatment formats. Individual treatment is consistent with mediating goals of treatment that include changes in the individual patient's cognitions and attitudes. Marital treatment is consistent with mediating goals that include changes in the interaction between two marital partners. Family treatment is congruent with goals that include the change in parenting behavior toward a child or adolescent. Group treatment is consistent with goals in the change of social behavior in the individual.

PATIENT PREFERENCE

Most patients, as thinking individuals and problem solvers in their own right, have hypotheses about what caused their problems and what changes are necessary to alleviate them. Couples who call a therapist for marital treatment have a different conceptualization of the problem than a married individual with marital conflict who calls for individual treatment. The family that sends the adolescent to individual treatment is different from the family that together seeks assistance in dealing with the teenage son's acting out. These patient preferences for a particular treatment format confront the clinician with a decision. The clinician should heed the ideas of the patient, at least initially, and whenever possible follow the treatment preferences of the patient and significant others.

TREATMENT EFFICIENCY

Psychologists increasingly function in a managed care world that emphasizes treatment efficiency. The most efficient treatment format is obviously group treatment, in which one (or two) professionals can treat some eight patients at one time. Therefore, a guiding issue is what treatment can be delivered as effectively in a group format as in other formats? In fact, there may be situations in which the group format is not only more efficient than the individual format but also more effective because of the mutual support and confrontation of fellow patients.

References & Readings

Beutler, L. E., & Clarkin, J. F. (1990). *Systematic treatment selection*. New York: Brunner/Mazel.

Clarkin, J. F., Frances, A., & Perry, S. (1992). Differential therapeutics: Macro and micro levels of treatment planning. In J. Norcross & M. Goldfried (Eds.), *Handbook of psychotherapy integration*. New York: Basic Books.

Feldman, L. B. (1992). *Integrating individual and family therapy*. New York: Brunner/Mazel.

Frances, A., Clarkin, J. F., & Perry, S. (1984). *Differential therapeutics: A guide to the art and science of treatment planning in psychiatry*. New York: Brunner/Mazel.

Perry, S., Frances, A., & Clarkin, J. F. (1990). *A DSM-III-R casebook of treatment selection*. New York: Brunner/Mazel.

Related Topics

45 COMPENDIUM OF CURRENT PSYCHOTHERAPY TREATMENT MANUALS

Michael J. Lambert, Jeremy A. Chiles,
Shelli R. Kesler, & David A. Vermeersch

The earliest treatment manuals were developed in the early 1960s. Manuals were originally created to provide specific definitions of treatment parameters for psychotherapy research (Strupp, 1992). By utilizing manuals in clinical trials, researchers can reduce variability among therapists by evaluating their adherence to the different treatment modalities under investigation (Luborsky & Barber, 1993; Crits-Christoph et al., 1991). Manuals have also been used to train and guide novice therapists (Moras, 1993) and have now become a means of delivering empirically validated treatments (Addis, 1997).

In clinical practice, the use of manuals has several advantages. Manuals provide a succinct theoretical framework for treatment, concrete descriptions of therapeutic techniques, and case examples of appropriate applications (Addis, 1997). The increased precision in detailing treatment techniques has generated much enthusiasm among professionals and third-party providers (Strupp & Anderson, 1997). However, others have expressed concerns over the use of treatment manuals in clinical practice. Among these concerns are questions regarding treatment efficacy and therapist adherence in clinical practice as opposed to controlled research settings (Addis, 1997), the engenderment of therapist rigidity and inflexibility (Strupp & Anderson, 1997; Lambert & Ogles, 1988), the neglect of nonspecific factors, and

Treatment Manuals

Author/Year	Title	Orientation	Patient Population	Modality	Strengths
Anxiety Disorders					
Barlow & Cerny (1988)	Psychological Treatment of Panic	Cognitive-behavioral	Panic disorder	Individual	1, 2, 3, 4
Beck, Emery, & Greenberg (1985)	Anxiety Disorders and Phobias: A Cognitive Perspective	Cognitive	Phobias	Individual	1, 2, 3
Bouman & Emmelkamp (1996)	Panic Disorder and Agoraphobia*	Cognitive-behavioral	Agoraphobia	Individual	1, 2, 3
Brown, O'Leary, & Barlow (1993)	Generalized Anxiety Disorder***	Cognitive-behavioral	GAD	Individual	1, 2, 3, 4
Calhoun & Resick (1993)	Posttraumatic Stress Disorder***	Cognitive-behavioral	Trauma	Individual/group	1, 2, 3, 4
Clark & Salkovskis (1996)	Treatment Manual for Focused Cognitive Therapy for Panic Disorder	Cognitive	Panic disorder	Individual	1, 2, 4
Craske & Barlow (1993)	Panic Disorder and Agoraphobia***	Cognitive-behavioral	Agoraphobia	Individual	1, 2, 3, 4
Crits-Christoph, Crits-Christoph, Wolf-Palacio, Fichter, & Rudick (1995)	Brief Supportive-Expressive Psychodynamic Therapy for Generalized Anxiety Disorder**	Dynamic	GAD	Individual	1, 2, 3, 4
Gaston (1995)	Dynamic Therapy for Posttraumatic Stress Disorder**	Dynamic	Trauma	Individual	1, 2, 3
Hope & Heimberg (1993)	Social Phobia and Social Anxiety***	Cognitive-behavioral	Social phobia/social anxiety	Group	1, 2, 3, 4
Kozak & Foa (1996)	Obsessive-Compulsive Disorder*	Behavioral-cognitive	Obsessive-compulsives	Individual	1, 2, 3
Riggs & Foa (1993)	Obsessive-Compulsive Disorder***	Cognitive-behavioral	Obsessive-compulsives	Individual	1, 2, 3
Scholing, Emmelkamp, & Oppen (1996)	Cognitive-Behavioral Treatment of Social Phobia*	Cognitive-behavioral	Social phobia	Individual	1, 2, 3, 4
Shear, Cloitre, & Heckelman (1995)	Emotion-Focused Treatment for Panic Disorder: A Brief, Dynamically Informed Therapy**	Dynamic	Panic disorder	Individual	1, 2, 3
Turner & Beidel (1988)	Treating Obsessive-Compulsive Disorder	Behavioral	Obsessive-compulsives	Individual	1, 2, 3, 4
Depressive Disorders					
Beck, Rush, Shaw, & Emery (1979)	Cognitive Therapy of Depression	Cognitive	Depression	Individual	1, 2, 3, 4, 5
Becker, Heimberg, & Bellack (1987)	Social Skills Training Treatment for Depression	Behavioral	Depression	Individual/group	1, 2, 3
Bellack, Hersen, & Himmelhoch (1996)	Social Skills Training for Depression*	Behavioral	Depression	Individual/group	1, 2, 3
Klerman, Weissman, Rounsaville, & Chevron (1984)	Interpersonal Psychotherapy of Depression	Interpersonal	Depression	Individual	1, 2, 3, 4, 5

(continued)

Treatment Manuals (*continued*)

Author/Year	Title	Orientation	Patient Population	Modality	Strengths
Lewinsohn (1984)	The Coping With Depression Course: A Psychoeducational Intervention for Unipolar Depression	Behavioral	Depression	Group	1, 2, 3, 4
Luborsky, Mark, Hole, Popp, Goldsmith, & Cacciola (1995)	Supportive-Expressive Dynamic Psychotherapy of Depression: A Time-Limited Version**	Dynamic	Depression	Individual	1, 2, 3
Rehm (1982)	Self-Control Manual: Treatment for Depression With Combined Behavioral and Cognitive Targets	Cognitive-behavioral	Depression	Group	1, 2, 4
Thase (1996)	Cognitive Behavior Therapy Manual for Treatment of Depressed Inpatients*	Cognitive-behavioral	Depression/inpatient	Individual	1, 2, 3, 4
Yost, Beutler, Corbishley, & Allender (1986)	Group Cognitive Therapy: A Treatment Approach for Depressed Older Adults	Cognitive	Depression	Group	1, 2, 3, 4
Young, Beck, & Weinberger (1993)	Depression***	Cognitive	Depression	Individual	1, 2, 3, 4
Dissociative Identity Disorders					
Kluft (1995)	Psychodynamic Psychotherapy of Multiple Personality Disorder and Allied Forms of Dissociative Disorder Not Otherwise Specified**	Dynamic	Dissociative disorder	Individual	1, 2, 3
Eating Disorders					
Sansone & Johnson (1995)	Treating the Eating Disorder Patient With Borderline Personality Disorder: Theory and Technique**	Dynamic	Eating/personality disorder	Individual	1, 2, 3
Wilson & Pike (1993)	Eating Disorders***	Cognitive-behavioral	Eating disorders	Individual	1, 2, 3, 4
Outpatient Treatments					
Daldrup, Beutler, Engle, & Greenberg (1988)	Focused Expressive Psychotherapy	Experiential	Outpatient	Individual	1, 2, 3, 4
Luborsky (1984)	Principles of Psychoanalytic Psychotherapy: A Manual for Supportive-Expressive Treatment	Dynamic	Outpatient	Individual	1, 2, 3, 4, 5
Rennie (1987)	Person-Centered Psychotherapy	Rogerian	Outpatient	Individual	
Sifneos (1987)	Short-Term Dynamic Psychotherapy	Dynamic	Outpatient	Individual	1, 2, 3, 4
Strupp & Binder (1984)	Psychotherapy in a New Key	Dynamic	Outpatient	Individual	1, 2, 3, 4
Toukmanian (1984)	Experiential-Cognitive Psychotherapy	Rogerian-cognitive	Outpatient	Individual	

Personality Disorders					
Beck & Freeman (1990)	Cognitive Therapy of Personality Disorders	Cognitive	Personality disorders	Individual	1, 2, 3
Benjamin (1996)	Interpersonal Diagnosis and Treatment of Personality Disorders	Dynamic	Personality disorders	Individual	1, 2, 3, 4
Linehan & Kehrer (1993)	Borderline Personality Disorder***	Behavioral	Personality disorders	Individual	1, 2, 3, 4
Piper, Rosie, Joyce, & Azim (1996)	Time-Limited Day Treatment for Personality Disorders: Integration of Research and Practice in a Group Program	Eclectic	Personality disorders	Group	1, 2, 3, 4
Relationship Problems					
Cordova & Jacobson (1993)	Couple Distress***	Behavioral	Couples difficulties	Couple	1, 2, 3
Greenberg & Johnson (1988)	Emotionally Focused Therapy for Couples	Experiential	Couples difficulties	Couple	1, 2, 3, 4
Weiss & Halford (1996)	Managing Marital Therapy: Helping Partners Change*	Behavioral	Marital discord	Couple	1, 2, 3
Schizophrenia					
Karon & Teixeira (1995)	Psychoanalytic Therapy of Schizophrenia**	Dynamic	Schizophrenia	Individual	1, 2, 3
Wong & Liberman (1996)	Biobehavioral Treatment and Rehabilitation for Persons with Schizophrenia*	Biobehavioral (medication & social skills)	Schizophrenia	Individual/group	1, 2, 3
Sex Offender Treatments					
Marshall & Eccles (1996)	Cognitive-Behavioral Treatment of Sex Offenders*	Cognitive-behavioral	Sex offenders	Group	1, 2, 3
Sexual Dysfunction Disorders					
Carey, Winzce, & Meisler (1993)	Sexual Dysfunction: Male Erectile Disorder***	Cognitive-behavioral	Sexual dysfunction	Individual/couple	1, 2, 3

(continued)

Treatment Manuals (*continued*)

Author/Year	Title	Orientation	Patient Population	Modality	Strengths
Jehu (1979)	Sexual Dysfunction: A Behavioural Approach to Causation, Assessment, and Treatment	Behavioral	Sexual dysfunction	Individual/couple	1, 2, 3
McConaghy (1996)	Treatment of Sexual Dysfunctions*	Cognitive-behavioral	Sexual dysfunction	Individual/couple	1, 2, 3
Sleep Disorders					
Van Brunt, Riedel, & Lichstein (1996)	Insomnia*	Behavioral/ pharmacotherapy	Sleep disturbance	Individual	1, 2, 3
Substance-Related Disorders					
Levin (1995)	Psychodynamic Treatment of Alcohol Abuse**	Dynamic	Alcohol abuse	Individual/group	1, 2, 3
Luborsky, Woody, Hole, & Velleco (1995)	Supportive-Expressive Dynamic Psychotherapy for Treatment of Opiate Drug Dependence**	Dynamic	Opiate dependence	Individual	1, 2, 3, 4
Mark & Faude (1995)	Supportive-Expressive Therapy of Cocaine Abuse**	Dynamic	Cocaine abuse	Individual/group	1, 2, 3, 4
McCrady (1993)	Alcoholism***	Behavioral	Alcohol abuse	Individual/couple/ group	1, 2, 3, 4
Paolantonio (1990)	Relapse Prevention Training Manual	Cognitive-behavioral	Drug and alcohol relapse	Group	1, 2, 4
Sobell & Sobell (1993)	Problem Drinkers: Guided Self-Change Treatment	Behavioral	Alcohol abuse	Individual	1, 2, 3, 4
Trichotillomania					
Stanley & Mouton (1996)	Trichotillomania Treatment Manual*	Behavioral	Hair pulling	Individual	1, 2, 3, 4
Weight Management Treatments					
Brownell & O'Neil (1993)	Obesity***	Cognitive-behavioral	Obesity	Individual/group	1, 2, 3
Friedman & Brownell (1996)	A Comprehensive Treatment Manual for the Management of Obesity*	Cognitive-behavioral	Obesity	Group	1, 2, 3
Williamson, Champagne, Jackman, & Varnado (1996)	Lifestyle Change: A Program for Long-Term Weight Management*	Behavioral	Weight management	Group	1, 2, 3, 4
Miscellaneous Cognitive-Behavioral Treatments					
Cash & Grant (1996)	Cognitive-Behavioral Treatment of Body-Image Disturbances*	Cognitive-behavioral	Body dissatisfaction	Individual/group	1, 2, 3, 4

Author (year)	Title	Approach	Population	Modality	Criteria
Ferguson & Mittenberg (1996)	Cognitive-Behavioral Treatment of Postconcussion Syndrome: A Therapist's Manual*	Cognitive-behavioral	Brain trauma	Individual	1, 2, 3, 4
Larkin & Zayfert (1996)	Anger Management Training With Essential Hypertensive Patients*	Cognitive-behavioral	Anger difficulties	Group	1, 2, 3, 4
Martin (1993)	Psychological Management of Chronic Headaches	Cognitive-behavioral	Headaches	Individual	1, 2, 3, 4

Miscellaneous Dynamic Treatments

DeRoche (1995)	Psychodynamic Psychotherapy With the HIV-Infected Client**	Dynamic	HIV	Individual	1, 2, 3
Eells (1995)	Relational Therapy for Grief Disorders**	Dynamic	Adjustment difficulties	Individual	1, 2, 3, 4

Miscellaneous Social Skills Training

Beidel, Bellack, Turner, Hersen, & Luber (1981)	Social Skills Training for Chronic Psychiatric Patients: A Treatment Manual	Behavioral	Chronic psychiatric	Group	1, 2, 3, 4

Miscellaneous Systems Treatment

Meyers, Dominguez, & Smith (1996)	Community Reinforcement Training With Concerned Others*	Systems	Families of patients	Family	1, 2, 3, 4

*Contained in *Sourcebook of Psychological Treatment Manuals for Adult Disorders.*
**Contained in *Dynamic Therapies for Psychiatric Disorders (Axis I).*
***Contained in *Clinical Handbook of Psychological Disorders: A Step-by-Step Treatment Manual.*

Note:
Strengths of Manual Criteria
1 A presentation of the main principles behind the techniques of the form of psychotherapy.
2 Concrete examples of each technical principle/treatment intervention.
3 Description of etiology and/or assessment approaches.
4 Specifically delineated description of treatment program (e.g., session-by-session, step-by-step phases)
5 Scales to guide independent judges in evaluating samples of sessions to determine the degree of conformity to the manual.

Publishers' Phone Numbers
Basic Books
  Phone: 800-225-5945
  Fax: 908-302-2300
Plenum Press
  Phone: 800-221-9369
  Fax: 212-463-0742

Wiley & Sons
  Phone: 800-225-5945
  Fax: 908-302-2300

the inadequacy of manuals for use in integrative approaches (Goldfried, 1993).

It is in light of the possible advantages afforded by treatment manuals and with consideration of expressed concerns regarding them that we present the following inventory of current treatment manuals. The manuals are listed in alphabetical order by author and are grouped into patient disorder and diagnostic categories, with miscellaneous categories listed at the end of the table. Orientation, patient population, and modality are given for each manual. The contents of each manual are also rated in the "Strengths" column according to five criteria. Three of these criteria were adapted from previous work by Luborsky and Barber (1993), who stated that a true manual must present the main principles behind techniques, provide concrete examples of each technique, and include means of evaluating therapist adherence. The other two criteria are a specific description of the treatment program and inclusion of scales to guide independent judges in evaluating conformity to the manual.

The interested clinician can obtain manuals by calling or writing the publishing companies that produce the manuals. A partial list of phone numbers is included to assist in this task. Unpublished manuals will need to be requested from the manual author. New manuals appear at a rapid rate, and it is likely that this list fails to include a number of important manual-based treatments. We invite interested readers to inform us of published manuals that have come to their attention.

References & Readings

Addis, M. E. (1997). Evaluating the treatment manual as a means of disseminating empirically validated psychotherapies. *Clinical Psychology: Science and Practice, 4,* 1–11.

Barber, J. P., & Crits-Christoph, P. (Eds.) (1995). *Dynamic therapies for psychiatric disorders (Axis I).* New York: Basic Books.

Barlow, D. H. (Ed.) (1993). *Clinical handbook of psychological disorders: A step-by-step treatment manual* (2nd ed.). New York: Guilford Press.

Barlow, D. H., & Cerny, J. A. (1988). *Psychological treatment of panic.* New York: Guilford Press.

Beck, A. T., Emery, G., & Greenberg, R. L. (1985). *Anxiety disorders and phobias: A cognitive perspective.* New York: Basic Books.

Beck, A. T., & Freeman, A. (1990). *Cognitive therapy of personality disorders.* New York: Guilford Press.

Beck, A. T., Rush, A. J., Shaw, B. F., & Emery, G. (1979). *Cognitive therapy of depression.* New York: Guilford Press.

Becker, R. E., Heimberg, R. G., & Bellack, A. S. (1987). *Social skills training treatment for depression.* New York: Pergamon Press.

Beidel, D. C., Bellack, A. S., & Turner, S. M. (1981). *Social skills training for chronic psychiatric patients: A treatment manual.* Unpublished manuscript, University of Pittsburgh.

Benjamin, L. S. (1996). *Interpersonal diagnosis and treatment of personality disorders.* New York: Guilford Press.

Clark, D. M., & Salkovskis, P. M. (1996). *Treatment manual of focused cognitive therapy.* Unpublished manuscript, Oxford University.

Crits-Christoph, P., Baranackie, K., Kurcias, J. S., Beck, A. T., Carroll, K., Perry, K., Luborsky, L., McLellan, A. T., Woody, G. E., Thompson, L., Gallagher, D., & Zitrin, C. (1991). Meta-analysis of therapist effects in psychotherapy outcome studies. *Psychotherapy Research, 1,* 81–91.

Daldrup, R. J., Beutler, L. E., Engle, D., & Greenberg, L. S. (1988). *Focused expressive psychotherapy: Freeing the overcontrolled patient.* New York: Guilford Press.

Garfield, S. L., & Bergin, A. E. (1994). Introduction and historical overview. In A. E. Bergin & S. L. Garfield (Eds.), *Handbook of psychotherapy and behavior change* (4th ed.). New York: Wiley.

Goldfried, M. R. (1993). Commentary on how the field of psychopathology can facilitate psychotherapy integration. Special issue: What can the field of psychotherapy offer to psychotherapy integration? *Journal of Psychotherapy Integration, 3,* 353–360.

Greenberg, L. S., & Johnson, S. M. (1988). *Emotionally focused therapy for couples.* New York: Guilford Press.

Jehu, D. (1979). *Sexual dysfunction: A behavioural approach to causation, assessment, and treatment.* New York: Wiley.

Klerman, G. L., Weissman, M. M., Rounsaville, B. J., & Chevron, E. S. (1984). *Interpersonal psychotherapy of depression.* New York: Basic Books.

Lambert, M. J., & Ogles, B. M. (1988). Treatment manuals: Problems and promise. *Journal of In-*

tegrative and Eclectic Psychotherapy, 7, 187–205.

Luborsky, L. (1984). *Principles of psychoanalytic psychotherapy: A manual for supportive-expressive treatment.* New York: Basic Books.

Luborsky, L., & Barber, J. P. (1993). Benefits of adherence to psychotherapy manuals and where to get them. In N. E. Miller, L. Luborsky, J. P. Barber, & J. P. Docherty (Eds.), *Psychodynamic treatment research.* New York: Basic Books.

Martin, P. R. (1993). *Psychological management of chronic headaches.* New York: Guilford Press.

Moras, K. (1993). The use of treatment manuals to train psychotherapists: Observations and recommendations. *Psychotherapy, 30,* 581–586.

Paolantonio, P. (1990). *Relapse prevention training manual.* Unpublished manuscript.

Piper, W. E., Rosie, J. S., Joyce, A. S., & Azim, H. F. A. (1996). *Time-limited day treatment for personality disorders: Integration of research and practice in a group program.* Washington, DC: American Psychological Association.

Rehm, L. P. (1982). *Treatment for depression with combined behavioral and cognitive targets.* Unpublished manuscript, University of Houston.

Sifneos, P. E. (1987). *Short-term dynamic psychotherapy: Evaluation and technique* (2nd ed.). New York: Plenum Press.

Sobell, M. B., & Sobell, L. C. (1993). *Problem drinkers: Guided self-change treatment.* New York: Guilford Press.

Strupp, H. H. (1992). The future of psychodynamic psychotherapy. *Psychotherapy, 29,* 21–27.

Strupp, H. H., & Anderson, T. (1997). On the limitations of therapy manuals. *Clinical Psychology: Science and Practice, 4,* 76–82.

Strupp, H. H., & Binder, J. L. (1984). *Psychotherapy in a new key: A guide to time-limited dynamic psychotherapy.* New York: Basic Books.

Turner, S. M., & Beidel, D. C. (1988). *Treating obsessive-compulsive disorder.* New York: Pergamon Press.

Van Hasselt, V. B., & Hersen, M. (1996). *Sourcebook of psychological treatment manuals for adult disorders.* New York: Plenum Press.

Yost, E. B., Beutler, L. E., Corbishley, M. A., & Allender, J. R. (1986). *Group cognitive therapy: A treatment approach for depressed older adults.* Elmsford, NY: Pergamon Press.

Related Topics

Chapter 46, "Empirically Validated Treatments"

46 EMPIRICALLY VALIDATED TREATMENTS

Dianne L. Chambless

Since 1993, the Division of Clinical Psychology of the American Psychological Association has sponsored an endeavor to identify empirically supported psychological interventions and to publicize the existence of these treatments to clinical psychologists and training programs. The goals are to serve the public and the profession by (a) helping psychologists and training programs to readily identify promising treatments on which their training efforts might, in part, be focused; and (b) aiding psychologists in practice to provide data supporting their choice of psychological interventions and the efficacy of their treatment procedures in order to make their services available and to obtain reimbursement for them. This effort is akin to movements within American psychiatry and British medicine to foster evidence-based practice by educating clinicians about the research base for practice. Within clinical psychology, this work may be seen as a logical extension of the Boulder model of scientist-practitioner training.

A succession of task forces appointed by presidents of the Division of Clinical Psychology have constructed and elaborated a list of empirically supported treatments. This work continues to evolve. The most recent (1997) list of treatments identified appears in Table 1. This list is necessarily incomplete: Not all treatments have yet been reviewed, and new evidence for treatments emerges monthly. Several factors need to be taken into account when using this list. First, the task forces have concentrated on specific treatments for specific psychological problems or issues, mainly in adult populations. That psychotherapy in general is beneficial for the average psychotherapy client is well known. The Empirically Validated Treatments (EVTs) list is an attempt to provide more focused information. Second, the task forces have followed a number of decision rules in determining what is sufficient evidence for listing a treatment. Decisions are largely based on randomized controlled studies that must have passed muster for methodological soundness, and the preponderance of the data across studies must have been positive (see Chambless & Hollon, in Chambless & Kendall, in press). At minimum, for a designation of *well established*, there must be two sound studies by independent investigators in which the EVT was demonstrated to be superior to another treatment or to a placebo condition or equivalent in efficacy to another treatment already designated well established. Under three conditions an EVT might be designated as *probably efficacious*: (a) when there is only one study meeting criteria for well established; (b) when all investigations have been conducted by one research team; or (c) when the only controlled comparisons have been to no-treatment control groups. In the last case, at least two studies by independent investigators must have attested to the efficacy of the EVT in comparison to no treatment.

The EVT project has been lauded and condemned. Those who favor it appear to be those who believe that training in specific psychological interventions is meaningful, that is, that there are important differences among approaches to psychotherapy and among approaches for different disorders. Those who believe that individual difference variables (e.g., characteristics of the client, the therapist, or the particular therapeutic relationship) are of the utmost importance in treatment outcome are less likely to find the EVT list useful, as are those who believe that psychologists are not yet able to define clients' problems or even their own interventions in terms meaningful enough to allow fruitful matching of treatments to target problems. Indeed, there is still debate about whether symptom relief (the primary, although not the sole, focus of EVT evidence) or less-well-specified growth is important and whether the most important changes clients make in experiential and psychodynamic therapies can be reliably and validly assessed.

Reactions to the EVT list also differ according to whether readers view the identification of evidence-based treatments as a support or a threat to clinical practice. A review of Table 1 will readily demonstrate that most, although not all, of the treatments identified to date are behavioral or cognitive-behavioral in nature, reflecting the greater research activity of psychotherapy treatment outcome researchers of that orientation. This in no way means that all treatments not appearing on the list are ineffective. In many cases their effectiveness simply has not been demonstrated to the satisfaction of the task force members—usually because of a dearth of evidence. Some practitioners of other orientations have expressed fear that their access to third-party payments will be cut off because they do not practice treatments on the list. Others have found that they can draw on the list to promote the efficacy and desirability of their treatment plans. To some degree, this particular controversy also centers around beliefs about the best ways to react to the demands for more efficient use of health care dollars. Those who believe it is possible to return to the era when psychologists were reimbursed for their services by third-party payers without reference to their efficacy appear to

TABLE 1. Examples of Empirically Validated Treatments

Well-Established Treatments	Citation for Efficacy Evidence
Anxiety and Stress	
Cognitive-behavior therapy for panic disorder with and without agoraphobia	Barlow et al. (1989)
	Clark et al. (1994)
Cognitive-behavior therapy for generalized anxiety disorder	Butler et al. (1991)
	Borkovec et al. (1987)
Exposure treatment for agoraphobia	Trull et al. (1988)
Exposure/guided mastery for specific phobia	Bandura et al. (1969)
	Öst et al. (1991)
Exposure and response prevention for obsessive-compulsive disorder	van Balkom et al. (1994)
Stress Inoculation Training for coping with stressors	Saunders et al. (1996)
Depression	
Behavior therapy for depression	Jacobson et al. (1996)
	McLean & Hakstian (1979)
Cognitive therapy for depression	Dobson (1989)
Interpersonal therapy for depression	DiMascio et al. (1979)
	Elkin et al. (1989)
Health Problems	
Behavior therapy for headache	Blanchard et al. (1980)
	Holroyd & Penzien (1990)
Cognitive-behavior therapy for bulimia	Agras et al. (1989)
	Thackwray et al. (1993)
Multicomponent cognitive-behavior therapy for pain associated with rheumatic disease	Keefe et al. (1990a,b)
	Parker et al. (1988)
Multicomponent cognitive-behavior therapy with relapse prevention for smoking cessation	Hill et al. (1993)
	Stevens & Hollis (1989)
Problems of Childhood	
Behavior modification for enuresis	Houts et al. (1994)
Parent training programs for children with oppositional behavior	Walter & Gilmore (1973)
	Wells & Egan (1988)
Marital Discord	
Behavioral marital therapy	Azrin et al. (1980a)
	Jacobson & Follette (1985)

Probably Efficacious Treatments	Citation for Efficacy Evidence
Anxiety	
Applied relaxation for panic disorder	Öst (1988)
Applied relaxation for generalized anxiety disorder	Barlow et al. (1992)
	Borkovec & Costello (1993)
Cognitive-behavior therapy for social phobia	Heimberg et al. (1990)
	Feske & Chambless (1995)
Cognitive therapy for obsessive-compulsive disorder	van Oppen et al. (1995)
Couples communication training adjunctive to exposure for agoraphobia	Arnow et al. (1985)
Eye Movement Desensitization/Reprocessing for civilian posttraumatic stress disorder (PTSD)	Rothbaum (in press)
	Wilson et al. (1995)

(continued)

TABLE 1. Examples of Empirically Validated Treatments (*continued*)

Probably Efficacious Treatments	Citation for Efficacy Evidence
Exposure treatment for PTSD	Foa et al. (1991)
	Keane et al. (1989)
Exposure treatment for social phobia	Feske & Chambless (1995)
Stress Inoculation Training for PTSD	Foa et al. (1991)
Relapse prevention program for obsessive-compulsive disorder	Hiss et al. (1994)
Systematic desensitization for animal phobia	Kirsch et al. (1983)
	Öst (1978)
Systematic desensitization for public speaking anxiety	Paul (1967)
	Woy & Efran (1972)
Systematic desensitization for social anxiety	Paul & Shannon (1966)

Chemical Abuse and Dependence

Behavior therapy for cocaine abuse	Higgins et al. (1993)
Brief dynamic therapy for opiate dependence	Woody et al. (1990)
Cognitive-behavior relapse prevention therapy for cocaine dependence	Carroll et al. (1994)
Cognitive therapy for opiate dependence	Woody et al. (1990)
Cognitive-behavior therapy for benzodiazepine withdrawal in panic disorder patients	Otto et al. (1993)
	Spiegel et al. (1994)
Community Reinforcement Approach for alcohol dependence	Azrin (1976)
	Hunt & Azrin (1973)
Cue exposure adjunctive to inpatient treatment for alcohol dependence	Drummond & Glautier (1994)
Project CALM for mixed alcohol abuse and dependence (behavioral marital therapy plus disulfiram)	O'Farrell et al. (1985)
	O'Farrell et al. (1992)
Social skills training adjunctive to inpatient treatment for alcohol dependence	Eriksen et al. (1986)

Depression

Brief dynamic therapy	Gallagher-Thompson & Steffen (1994)
Cognitive therapy for geriatric patients	Scogin & McElreath (1994)
Reminiscence therapy for geriatric patients	Arean et al. (1993)
	Scogin & McElreath (1994)
Self-control therapy	Fuchs & Rehm (1977)
	Rehm et al. (1979)
Social problem-solving therapy	Nezu (1986)
	Nezu & Perri (1989)

Health Problems

Behavior therapy for childhood obesity	Epstein et al. (1994)
	Wheeler & Hess (1976)
Cognitive-behavior therapy for binge-eating disorder	Telch et al. (1990)
	Wilfley et al. (1993)
Cognitive-behavior therapy adjunctive to physical therapy for chronic pain	Nicholas et al. (1991)
Cognitive-behavior therapy for chronic low back pain	Turner & Clancy (1988)
EMG biofeedback for chronic pain	Flor & Birbaumer (1993)
	Newton-John et al. (1995)
Hypnosis as an adjunct to cognitive-behavior therapy for obesity	Bolocofsky et al. (1985)
Interpersonal therapy for binge-eating disorder	Wilfley et al. (1993)
Interpersonal therapy for bulimia	Fairburn et al. (1993)
Multicomponent cognitive therapy for irritable bowel syndrome	Lynch & Zamble (1989)
	Payne & Blanchard (1995)
Multicomponent cognitive-behavior therapy for pain of sickle-cell disease	Gil et al. (1996)
Multicomponent operant-behavior therapy for chronic pain	Turner & Clancy (1988)
	Turner et al. (1990)

TABLE 1. Examples of Empirically Validated Treatments (*continued*)

Probably Efficacious Treatments	Citation for Efficacy Evidence
Scheduled, reduced smoking adjunctive to multicomponent behavior therapy for smoking cessation	Cinciripini et al. (1994)
	Cinciripini et al. (1995)
Thermal biofeedback for Raynaud's syndrome	Freedman et al. (1983)
Thermal biofeedback plus autogenic relaxation training for migraine	Blanchard et al. (1978)
	Sargent et al. (1986)
Marital Discord	
Emotionally focused couples therapy for moderately distressed couples	James (1991)
	Johnson & Greenberg (1985)
Insight-oriented marital therapy	Snyder & Wills (1989)
	Snyder et al. (1991)
Problems of Childhood	
Behavior modification of encopresis	O'Brien et al. (1986)
Cognitive-behavior therapy for anxiety (overanxious, separation anxiety, and avoidant disorders)	Kendall (1994)
	Kendall et al. (1997)
Exposure for simple phobia	Menzies & Clarke (1993)
Family anxiety management training for anxiety disorders	Barrett et al. (1996)
Sexual Dysfunction	
Hurlbert's combined treatment approach for female hypoactive sexual desire	Hurlbert et al. (1993)
Masters and Johnson's sex therapy for female orgasmic dysfunction	Everaerd & Dekker (1981)
Zimmer's combined sex and marital therapy for female hypoactive sexual desire	Zimmer (1987)
Other	
Behavior modification for sex offenders	Marshall et al. (1991)
Dialectical behavior therapy for borderline personality disorder	Linehan et al. (1991)
Family intervention for schizophrenia	Falloon et al. (1985)
	Randolph et al. (1994)
Habit reversal and control techniques	Azrin et al. (1980b)
	Azrin et al. (1980c)
Social skills training for improving social adjustment of schizophrenic patients	Marder et al. (1996)
Supported employment for severely mentally ill clients	Drake et al. (1996)

Note: Studies cited for efficacy evidence are linked to specific treatment manuals or to procedures well described in the study's report. The operational definition of the treatment is to be found in those manuals; the labels used here do not suffice to identify the particular treatment judged to be efficacious.

view the EVT movement as caving in to managed care. Others accept it as inevitable that, if psychologists are to be paid for their services, they will be called to account to demonstrate their benefit.

Finally, the EVT movement seems to displease psychologists to the degree that they see identifying efficacious treatments which are described in treatment manuals (a requirement for consideration by the task force) as threats to their autonomy and creativity. To the degree

that one believes psychotherapy is based on artistry rather than science, an emphasis on EVTs may be viewed as a restriction. The fear seems to be that psychologists will be reduced to automatons who use a Procrustean bed to fit the same treatment to all types of clients with a given diagnosis, regardless of their needs. Others see no reason that manual-based treatments cannot be combined and altered into the best configuration for a particular client.

However controversial, the EVT movement

has gained sufficient credence so that didactic instruction and clinical supervision in empirically supported treatments are now specified in the *Guidelines and Principles for Accreditation of Programs in Professional Psychology* for both internships and doctoral training programs. Thus, future generations of students should have exposure to one or more scientifically based treatments. Training for those in practice is likely to be more difficult, in that the various task forces working on the EVT effort have concluded that practitioners wishing to learn a new EVT sharply different from treatments in their current repertoire need supervised clinical work to acquire sufficient skill for ethical practice. Better vehicles for continuing education than the current 3-hour to 3-day workshop approach need to be developed.

References & Readings

Agras, W. S., Schneider, J. A., Arnow, B., Raeburn, S. D., & Telch, C. F. (1989). Cognitive-behavioral and response-prevention treatments for bulimia nervosa. *Journal of Consulting and Clinical Psychology, 57*, 215–221.

Arean, P. A., Perri, M. G., Nezu, A. M., Schein, R. L., Christopher, F., & Joseph, T. X. (1993). Comparative effectiveness of social problem-solving therapy and reminiscence therapy as treatments for depression in older adults. *Journal of Consulting and Clinical Psychology, 61*, 1003–1010.

Arnow, B. A., Taylor, C. B., Agras, W. S., & Telch, M. J. (1985). Enhancing agoraphobia treatment outcome by changing couple communication patterns. *Behavior Therapy, 16*, 452–467.

Azrin, N. H. (1976). Improvements in the CR approach to alcoholism. *Behaviour Research and Therapy, 14*, 339–348.

Azrin, N. H., Bersalel, A., Bechtel, R., Michalicek, A., Mancera, M., Carroll, D., Shuford, D., & Cox, J. (1980a). Comparison of reciprocity and discussion-type counseling for marital problems. *American Journal of Family Therapy, 8*, 21–28.

Azrin, N. H., Nunn, R. G., & Frantz, S. E. (1980b). Habit reversal vs. negative practice treatment of nailbiting. *Behaviour Research and Therapy, 18*, 281–285.

Azrin, N. H., Nunn, R. G., & Frantz-Renshaw, S. (1980c). Habit reversal treatment of thumbsucking. *Behaviour Research and Therapy, 18*, 395–399.

Bandura, A., Blanchard, E. B., & Ritter, B. (1969). Relative efficacy of desensitization and modeling approaches for inducing behavioral, affective, and attitudinal change. *Journal of Personality and Social Psychology, 13*, 173–199.

Barlow, D. H., Craske, M. G., Cerny, J. A., & Klosko, J. S. (1989). Behavioral treatment of panic disorder. *Behavior Therapy, 20*, 261–282.

Barlow, D. H., Rapee, R. M., & Brown, T. A. (1992). Behavioral treatment of generalized anxiety disorder. *Behavior Therapy, 23*, 551–570.

Barrett, P. M., Dadds, M. R., & Rapee, R. M. (1996). Family treatment of childhood anxiety: A controlled trial. *Journal of Consulting and Clinical Psychology, 64*, 333–342.

Blanchard, E. B., Andrasik, F., Ahles, T. A., Teders, S. J., & O'Keefe, D. (1980). Migraine and tension headache: A meta-analytic review. *Behavior Therapy, 11*, 613–631.

Blanchard, E. B., Theobold, D. E., Williamson, D. A., Silver, B. V., & Brown, D. A. (1978). Temperature biofeedback in the treatment of migraine headaches. *Archives of General Psychiatry, 35*, 581–588.

Bolocofsky, D. N., Spinler, D., & Coulthard-Morris, L. (1985). Effectiveness of hypnosis as an adjunct to behavioral weight management. *Journal of Clinical Psychology, 41*, 35–41.

Borkovec, T. D., & Costello, E. (1993). Efficacy of applied relaxation and cognitive-behavioral therapy in the treatment of generalized anxiety disorder. *Journal of Consulting and Clinical Psychology, 61*, 611–619.

Borkovec, T. D., Mathews, A. M., Chambers, A., Ebrahimi, S., Lytle, R., & Nelson, R. (1987). The effects of relaxation training with cognitive or nondirective therapy and the role of relaxation-induced anxiety in the treatment of generalized anxiety. *Journal of Consulting and Clinical Psychology, 55*, 883–888.

Butler, G., Fennell, M., Robson, P., & Gelder, M. (1991). Comparison of behavior therapy and cognitive behavior therapy in the treatment of generalized anxiety disorder. *Journal of Consulting and Clinical Psychology, 59*, 167–175.

Carroll, K. M., Rounsaville, B. J., Gordon, L. T., Nich, C., Jatlow, P., Bisighini, R. M., & Gawin, F. H. (1994). Psychotherapy and pharmacology for ambulatory cocaine abusers. *Archives of General Psychiatry, 51*, 177–187.

Chambless, D. L., Baker, M. J., Baucom, D. H., Beutler, L. E., Calhoun, K. S., Crits-Christoph, P., Daiuto, A., DeRubeis, R., Detweiler, J., Haaga, D. A. F., Bennett Johnson, S., McCurry, S.,

Mueser, K. T., Pope, K. S., Sanderson, W. C., Shoham, V., Stickle, T., Williams, D. A., & Woody, S. R. (in press). Update on empirically validated therapies, II. *Clinical Psychologist.*

Chambless, D. L., & Kendall, P. C. (Eds.) (in press). Special section on empirically supported therapies. *Journal of Consulting and Clinical Psychology.*

Chambless, D. L., Sanderson, W. C., Shoham, V., Bennett Johnson, S., Pope, K. S., Crits-Christoph, P., Baker, M., Johnson, B., Woody, S. R., Sue, S., Beutler, L., Williams, D. A., & McCurry, S. (1996). An update on empirically validated therapies. *Clinical Psychologist, 49,* 5–18.

Cinciripini, P. M., Lapitsky, L. G., Seay, S., Wallfisch, A., Kitchens, K., & van Vunakis, H. (1995). The effects of smoking schedules on cessation outcome: Can we improve on common methods of gradual and abrupt nicotine withdrawal? *Journal of Consulting and Clinical Psychology, 63,* 388–399.

Cinciripini, P. M., Lapitsky, L. G., Wallfisch, A., Mace, R., Nezami, E., & van Vunakis, H. (1994). An evaluation of a multicomponent treatment program involving scheduled smoking and relapse prevention procedures: Initial findings. *Addictive Behaviors, 19,* 13–22.

Clark, D. M., Salkovskis, P. M., Hackman, A., Middleton, H., Anastasiades, P., & Gelder, M. (1994). A comparison of cognitive therapy, applied relaxation, and imipramine in the treatment of panic disorder. *British Journal of Psychiatry, 164,* 759–769.

DiMascio, A., Weissman, M. M., Prusoff, B. A., Neu, C., Zwilling, M., & Klerman, G. L. (1979). Differential symptom reduction by drugs and psychotherapy in acute depression. *Archives of General Psychiatry, 36,* 1450–1456.

Dobson, K. S. (1989). A meta-analysis of the efficacy of cognitive therapy for depression. *Journal of Consulting and Clinical Psychology, 57,* 414–419.

Drake, R. E., McHugo, G. J., Becker, D. R., Anthony, W. A., & Clark, R. E. (1996). The New Hampshire supported employment study. *Journal of Consulting and Clinical Psychology, 64,* 391–399.

Drummond, D. C., & Glautier, S. (1994). A controlled trial of cue exposure treatment in alcohol dependence. *Journal of Consulting and Clinical Psychology, 62,* 809–817.

Elkin, I., Shea, M. T., Watkins, J. T., Imber, S. D., Sotsky, S. M., Collins, J. F., Glass, D. R., Pilkonis, P. A., Leber, W. R., Docherty, J. P., Fiester, S. J., & Parloff, M. B. (1989). National Institute of Mental Health Treatment of Depression Collaborative Research Program: General effectiveness of treatments. *Archives of General Psychiatry, 46,* 971–982.

Epstein, L. H., Valoski, A., Wing, R. R., & McCurley, J. (1994). Ten-year outcomes of behavioral family-based treatment for childhood obesity. *Health Psychology, 13,* 373–383.

Eriksen, L., Bjornstad, S., & Gotestam, K. G. (1986). Social skills training in groups for alcoholics: One-year treatment outcome for groups and individuals. *Addictive Behaviors, 11,* 309–329.

Everaerd, W., & Dekker, J. (1981). A comparison of sex therapy and communication therapy: Couples complaining of orgasmic dysfunction. *Journal of Sex and Marital Therapy, 7,* 278–289.

Fairburn, C. G., Jones, R., Peveler, R. C., Hope, R. A., & O'Conner, M. (1993). Psychotherapy and bulimia nervosa: Longer-term effects of interpersonal psychotherapy, behavior therapy, and cognitive behavior therapy. *Archives of General Psychiatry, 50,* 419–428.

Falloon, I. R. H., Boyd, J. L., McGill, C. W., Williamson, M., Razani, J., Moss, H. B., Gilderman, A. M., & Simpson, G. M. (1985). Family management in the prevention of morbidity of schizophrenia: Clinical outcome of a two year longitudinal study. *Archives of General Psychiatry, 42,* 887–896.

Feske, U., & Chambless, D. L. (1995). Cognitive behavioral versus exposure only treatment for social phobia: A meta-analysis. *Behavior Therapy, 26,* 695–720.

Flor, H., & Birbaumer, N. (1993). Comparison of the efficacy of electromyographic biofeedback, cognitive-behavioral therapy, and conservative medical interventions in the treatment of chronic musculoskeletal pain. *Journal of Consulting and Clinical Psychology, 61,* 653–658.

Foa, E. B., Rothbaum, B. O., Riggs, D. S., & Murdock, T. B. (1991). Treatment of posttraumatic stress disorder in rape victims: A comparison between cognitive-behavioral procedures and counseling. *Journal of Consulting and Clinical Psychology, 59,* 715–723.

Freedman, R. R., Ianni, P., & Wenig, P. (1983). Behavioral treatment of Raynaud's disease. *Journal of Consulting and Clinical Psychology, 51,* 539–549.

Fuchs, C. Z., & Rehm, L. P. (1977). A self-control behavior therapy program for depression. *Journal of Consulting and Clinical Psychology, 45,* 206–215.

Gallagher-Thompson, D., & Steffen, A. M. (1994). Comparative effects of cognitive-behavioral and brief dynamic therapy for depressed family caregivers. *Journal of Consulting and Clinical Psychology, 62,* 543–549.

Gil, K. M., Wilson, J. J., Edens, J. L., Webster, D. A., Abrams, M. A., Orringer, E., Grant, M., Clark, W. C., & Janal, M. N. (1996). The effects of cognitive coping skills training on coping strategies and experimental pain sensitivity in African American adults with sickle cell disease. *Health Psychology, 15,* 3–10.

Heimberg, R. G., Dodge, C. S., Hope, D. A., Kennedy, C. R., & Zollo, L. J. (1990). Cognitive behavioral group treatment for social phobia: Comparison with a credible placebo control. *Cognitive Therapy and Research, 14,* 1–23.

Higgins, S. T., Budney, A. J., Bickel, W. K., Hughes, J. R., Foeg, F., & Badger, G. (1993). Achieving cocaine abstinence with a behavioral approach. *American Journal of Psychiatry, 150,* 763–769.

Hill, R. D., Rigdon, M., & Johnson, S. (1993). Behavioral smoking cessation treatment for older chronic smokers. *Behavior Therapy, 24,* 321–329.

Hiss, H., Foa, E. B., & Kozak, M. J. (1994). Relapse prevention program for treatment of obsessive-compulsive disorder. *Journal of Consulting and Clinical Psychology, 62,* 801–808.

Holroyd, K. A., & Penzien, D. B. (1990). Pharmacological versus nonpharmacological prophylaxis of recurrent migraine headache: A meta-analytic review of clinical trials. *Pain, 42,* 1–13.

Houts, A. C., Berman, J. S., & Abramson, H. (1994). Effectiveness of psychological and pharmacological treatments for nocturnal enuresis. *Journal of Consulting and Clinical Psychology, 62,* 737–745.

Hunt, G. M., & Azrin, N. J. (1973). A community reinforcement approach to alcoholism. *Behaviour Research and Therapy, 11,* 91–104.

Hurlbert, D. F., White, C. L., & Powell, R. D. (1993). Orgasm consistency training in the treatment of women reporting hypoactive sexual desire: An outcome comparison of women-only groups and couple-only groups. *Journal of Behavior Therapy and Experimental Psychiatry, 24,* 3–13.

Jacobson, N. S., Dobson, K. S., Truax, P. A., Addis, M. E., Koerner, K., Gollan, J. K., Gortner, E., & Prince, S. E. (1996). A component analysis of cognitive-behavioral treatment for depression. *Journal of Consulting and Clinical Psychology, 62,* 295–304.

Jacobson, N. S., & Follette, W. C. (1985). Clinical significance of improvement resulting from two behavioral marital therapy components. *Behavior Therapy, 16,* 249–262.

James, P. S. (1991). Effects of a communication training component added to an emotionally focused couples therapy. *Journal of Marital and Family Therapy, 17,* 263–275.

Johnson, S. M., & Greenberg, L. S. (1985). Differential effects of experiential and problem-solving interventions in resolving marital conflict. *Journal of Consulting and Clinical Psychology, 53,* 175–184.

Kazdin, A. E. (Ed.) (1996). Special section on validated treatments. *Clinical Psychology: Science and Practice, 3,* 216–267.

Keane, T. M., Fairbank, J. A., Caddell, J. M., & Zimering, R. T. (1989). Implosive (flooding) therapy reduces symptoms of PTSD in Vietnam combat veterans. *Behavior Therapy, 20,* 245–260.

Keefe, F. J., Caldwell, D. S., Williams, D. A., Gil, K. M., Mitchell, D., Robertson, C., Martinez, S., Nunley, J., Beckham, J. C., & Helms, M. (1990a). Pain coping skills training in the management of osteoarthritic knee pain: A comparative study. *Behavior Therapy, 21,* 49–62.

Keefe, F. J., Caldwell, D. S., Williams, D. A., Gil, K. M., Mitchell, D., Robertson, C., Martinez, S., Nunley, J., Beckham, J. C., & Helms, M. (1990b). Pain coping skills training in the management of osteoarthritic knee pain: II. Follow-up results. *Behavior Therapy, 21,* 435–447.

Kendall, P. C. (1994). Treating anxiety disorders in children: Results of a randomized clinical trial. *Journal of Consulting and Clinical Psychology, 62,* 100–110.

Kendall, P. C., Flannery-Schroeder, E., Panichelli-Mindel, S. M., Southam-Gerow, M., Henin, A., & Warman, M. (1997). Therapy for youths with anxiety disorders: A second randomized clinical trial. *Journal of Consulting and Clinical Psychology, 65,* 366–380.

Kirsch, I., Tennen, H., Wickless, C., Saccone, A. J., & Cody, S. (1983). The role of expectancy in fear reduction. *Behavior Therapy, 14,* 520–533.

Law, M., & Tang, J. L. (1995). An analysis of the effectiveness of interventions intended to help people stop smoking. *Archives of Internal Medicine, 155,* 1933–1941.

Lichtenstein, E., & Glasgow, R. E. (1992). Smoking cessation: What have we learned over the past decade? *Journal of Consulting and Clinical Psychology, 50,* 509–524.

Linehan, M. M., Armstrong, H. E., Suarez, A., All-mon, D., & Heard, H. L. (1991). Cognitive-behavioral treatment of chronically parasuicidal borderline patients. *Archives of General Psychiatry, 48,* 1060–1064.

Lynch, P. M., & Zamble, E. (1989). A controlled behavioral treatment study of irritable bowel syndrome. *Behavior Therapy, 20,* 509–523.

Marder, S. R., Wirshing, W. C., Mintz, J., McKenzie, J., Johnston, K., Eckman, T. A., Lebell, M., Zimmerman, K., & Liberman, R. P. (1996). Two-year outcome of social skills training and group psychotherapy for outpatients with schizophrenia. *American Journal of Psychiatry, 153,* 1585–1592.

Marshall, W. L., Jones, R., Ward, T., Johnston, P., & Barbaree, H. E. (1991). Treatment outcome with sex offenders. *Clinical Psychology Review, 11,* 465–485.

McLean, P. D., & Hakstian, A. R. (1979). Clinical depression: Comparative efficacy of outpatient treatments. *Journal of Consulting and Clinical Psychology, 47,* 818–836.

Menzies, R. G., & Clarke, J. C. (1993). A comparison of in vivo and vicarious exposure in the treatment of childhood water phobia. *Behaviour Research and Therapy, 31,* 9–15.

Newton-John, T. R. O., Spence, S. H., & Schotte, D. (1995). Cognitive-behavioral therapy versus EMG biofeedback in the treatment of chronic low back pain. *Behaviour Research and Therapy, 33,* 691–697.

Nezu, A. M. (1986). Efficacy of a social problem-solving therapy approach for unipolar depression. *Journal of Consulting and Clinical Psychology, 54,* 196–202.

Nezu, A. M., & Perri, M. G. (1989). Social problem-solving therapy for unipolar depression: An initial dismantling investigation. *Journal of Consulting and Clinical Psychology, 57,* 408–413.

Nicholas, M. K., Wilson, P. H., & Goyen, J. (1991). Operant-behavioral and cognitive-behavioral treatment for chronic low back pain. *Behaviour Research and Therapy, 29,* 225–238.

O'Brien, S., Ross, L. V., & Christophersen, E. R. (1986). Primary encopresis: Evaluation and treatment. *Journal of Applied Behavior Analysis, 19,* 137–145.

O'Farrell, T. J., Cutter, H. S. G., Choquette, K. A., Floyd, F. J., & Bayog, R. D. (1992). Behavioral marital therapy for male alcoholics: Marital and drinking adjustment during the two years after treatment. *Behavior Therapy, 23,* 529–549.

O'Farrell, T. J., Cutter, H. S. G., & Floyd, F. J. (1985). Evaluating behavioral marital therapy for male alcoholics: Effects on marital adjustment and communication from before to after treatment. *Behavior Therapy, 16,* 147–167.

Öst, L.-G. (1978). Fading vs. systematic desensitization in the treatment of snake and spider phobia. *Behaviour Research and Therapy, 16,* 379–389.

Öst, L.-G. (1988). Applied relaxation vs. progressive relaxation in the treatment of panic disorder. *Behaviour Research and Therapy, 26,* 13–22.

Öst, L.-G., Salkovskis, P. M., & Hellstrom, K. (1991). One-session therapist-directed exposure vs. self-exposure in the treatment of spider phobia. *Behavior Therapy, 22,* 407–422.

Otto, M. W., Pollack, M. H., Sachs, G. S., Reiter, S. R., Meltzer-Brody, S., & Rosenbaum, J. F. (1993). Discontinuation of benzodiazepine treatment: Efficacy of cognitive behavioral therapy for patients with panic disorder. *American Journal of Psychiatry, 150,* 1485–1490.

Parker, J. C., Frank, R. G., Beck, N. C., Smarr, K. L., Buescher, K. L., Phillips, L. R., Smith, E. I., Anderson, S. K., & Walker, S. E. (1988). Pain management in rheumatoid arthritis patients: A cognitive-behavioral approach. *Arthritis and Rheumatism, 31,* 593–601.

Paul, G. L. (1967). Insight vs. desensitization in psychotherapy two years after termination. *Journal of Consulting Psychology, 31,* 333–348.

Paul, G. L., & Shannon, D. T. (1966). Treatment of anxiety through systematic desensitization in therapy groups. *Journal of Abnormal Psychology, 71,* 123–135.

Payne, A., & Blanchard, E. B. (1995). A controlled comparison of cognitive therapy and self-help support groups in the treatment of irritable bowel syndrome. *Journal of Consulting and Clinical Psychology, 63,* 779–786.

Rainer, J. P. (Ed.) (1996). Special issue on psychotherapy outcomes. *Psychotherapy, 33*(2).

Randolph, E. T., Eth, S., Glynn, S., Paz, G. B., Leong, G. B., Shaner, A. L., Strachan, A., Van Vort, W., Escobar, J., & Liberman, R. P. (1994). Behavioural family management in schizophrenia: Outcome from a clinic-based intervention. *British Journal of Psychiatry, 144,* 501–506.

Rehm, L. P., Fuchs, C. Z., Roth, D. M., Kornblith, S. J., & Romano, J. M. (1979). A comparison of self-control and assertion skills treatments of depression. *Behavior Therapy, 10,* 429–442.

Rothbaum, B. O. (in press). A controlled study of eye movement desensitization and reprocessing in the treatment of posttraumatic stress disordered sexual assault victims. *Bulletin of the Menninger Clinic.*

Sargent, J., Solbach, P., Coyne, L., Spohn, H., & Segerson, J. (1986). Results of a controlled experimental outcome study of non-drug treatment for the control of migraine headache. *Journal of Behavioral Medicine, 9,* 291–323.

Saunders, T., Driskell, J. E., Hall, J., & Salas, E. (1996). The effect of stress inoculation training on anxiety and performance. *Journal of Occupational Health Psychology, 1,* 170–186.

Scogin, F., & McElreath, L. (1994). Efficacy of psychosocial treatments for geriatric depression: A quantitative review. *Journal of Consulting and Clinical Psychology, 62,* 69–74.

Snyder, D. K., & Wills, R. M. (1989). Behavioral versus insight-oriented marital therapy: Effects on individual and interspousal functioning. *Journal of Consulting and Clinical Psychology, 57,* 39–46.

Snyder, D. K., Wills, R. M., & Grady-Fletcher, A. (1991). Long-term effectiveness of behavioral versus insight-oriented marital therapy: A 4-year follow-up study. *Journal of Consulting and Clinical Psychology, 59,* 138–141.

Spiegel, D. A., Bruce, T. J., Gregg, S. F., & Nuzzarello, A. (1994). Does cognitive behavior therapy assist slow-taper alprazolam discontinuation in panic disorder? *American Journal of Psychiatry, 151,* 876–881.

Stevens, V. J., & Hollis, J. F. (1989). Preventing smoking relapse, using an individually tailored skills-training technique. *Journal of Consulting and Clinical Psychology, 57,* 420–424.

Task Force on Promotion and Dissemination of Psychological Procedures (1995). Training in and dissemination of empirically-validated psychological treatments. *Clinical Psychologist, 48*(1), 3–23.

Telch, C. F., Agras, W. S., Rossiter, E. M., Wilfley, D., & Kenardy, J. (1990). Group cognitive-behavioral treatment for the nonpurging bulimic. *Journal of Consulting and Clinical Psychology, 58,* 629–635.

Thackwray, D. E., Smith, M. C., Bodfish, J. W., & Meyers, A. W. (1993). A comparison of behavioral and cognitive-behavioral interventions for bulimia nervosa. *Journal of Consulting and Clinical Psychology, 61,* 639–645.

Trull, T. J., Nietzel, M. T., & Main, A. (1988). The use of meta-analysis to assess the clinical significance of behavior therapy for agoraphobia. *Behavior Therapy, 19,* 527–538.

Turner, J. A., & Clancy, S. (1988). Comparison of operant behavioral and cognitive-behavioral group treatment for chronic low back pain. *Journal of Consulting and Clinical Psychology, 56,* 261–266.

Turner, J. A., Clancy, S., McQuade, K. J., & Cardenas, D. D. (1990). Effectiveness of behavioral therapy for chronic low back pain: A component analysis. *Journal of Consulting and Clinical Psychology, 58,* 573–579.

van Balkom, A. J. L. M., van Oppen, P., Vermeulen, A. W. A., Nauta, N. C. E., Vorst, H. C. M., & van Dyck, R. (1994). A meta-analysis on the treatment of obsessive compulsive disorder: A comparison of antidepressants, behaviour, and cognitive therapy. *Clinical Psychology Review, 14,* 359–381.

VandenBos, G. R. (Ed.) (1996). Special issue on outcome assessment of psychotherapy. *American Psychologist, 51*(10).

van Oppen, P., de Haan, E., van Balkom, A. J. L. M., Spinhoven, P., Hoogduin, K., & van Dyck, R. (1995). Cognitive therapy and exposure in vivo in the treatment of obsessive compulsive disorder. *Behaviour Research and Therapy, 33,* 379–390.

Walter, H. I., & Gilmore, S. K. (1973). Placebo versus social learning effects in parent training procedures designed to alter the behavior of aggressive boys. *Behavior Therapy, 4,* 361–377.

Wardle, J., Hayward, P., Higgitt, A., Stabl, M., Blizard, R., & Gray, J. (1994). Effects of concurrent diazepam treatment on the outcome of exposure therapy in agoraphobia. *Behaviour Research and Therapy, 32,* 203–215.

Wells, K. C., & Egan, J. (1988). Social learning and systems family therapy for childhood oppositional disorder: Comparative treatment outcome. *Comprehensive Psychiatry, 29,* 138–146.

Wheeler, M. E., & Hess, K. W. (1976). Treatment of juvenile obesity by successive approximation control of eating. *Journal of Behavior Therapy and Experimental Psychiatry, 7,* 235–241.

Wilfley, D. E., Agras, W. S., Telch, C. F., Rossiter, E. M., Schneider, J. A., Cole, A. G., Sifford, L., & Raeburn, S. D. (1993). Group cognitive-behavioral therapy and group interpersonal psychotherapy for the nonpurging bulimic individual: A controlled comparison. *Journal of Consulting and Clinical Psychology, 61,* 296–305.

Wilson, S. A., Becker, L. A., & Tinker, R. H. (1995). Eye movement desensitization and reprocessing (EMDR) treatment for psychologically traumatized individuals. *Journal of Consulting and Clinical Psychology, 63,* 928–937.

Woody, G. E., Luborsky, L., McLellan, A. T., & O'Brien, C. P. (1990). Corrections and revised analyses for psychotherapy in methadone maintenance patients. *Archives of General Psychiatry, 47,* 788–789.

Woy, R. J., & Efran, J. S. (1972). Systematic desensitization and expectancy in the treatment of speaking anxiety. *Behaviour Research and Therapy, 10,* 43–49.

Zimmer, D. (1987). Does marital therapy enhance the effectiveness of treatment for sexual dysfunction? *Journal of Sex and Marital Therapy, 13,* 193–209.

Related Topics

47 THUMBNAIL SYSTEMATIC ASSESSMENT AND TREATMENT MATCHING

Larry E. Beutler & Oliver B. Williams

This treatment selection synopsis has two major subdivisions: assessment items and therapy decisions. The assessment items section contains items targeted toward five areas of patient characteristics. Once these areas have been assigned specific values, treatment selection decisions can be addressed logically and algorithmically. The therapy decision section is divided into two parts: level of care and treatment approaches. Level of care covers basic patient functionality, safety, treatment setting, and the potential for medical consultation (mode). In the section on treatment approaches, a combination of the quantities derived from the assessment items is used to target and hone matched treatment selection.

ASSESSMENT

Five basic domains of patient characteristics can be rapidly assessed to capture an optimal range of variance for matched treatment effectiveness and differential psychotherapy. These domains are (a) severity and functionality; (b) patient and problem complexity; (c) distress; (d) the patient's overall level of reactance or resistance; and (e) the patient's general coping style. Findings from our research show that items used to capture these patient characteristic areas can be answered reliably by a clinician during the course of an intake session or by a clinician viewing a tape of the intake session. The items presented here are not comprehensive and exhaustive scales that approach psychometric nirvana. They are ideal representatives extracted from our research on clinician estimation of patient characteristics for matched treatment selection and should be seen as guides and suggestions to help the clinician, rather than as standardized psychological tests. Based on the relative levels of these characteristic dimensions, the clinician should be better able to select matched targeted therapeutic approaches tailored to specific patients.

These assessment and treatment dimensions, and the decisions that they portend, derive from a continuing study of differential treatment selection. A more complete process of relating patient characteristics to treatment decisions is embodied in Systematic Treatment Selection (STS), a software system (Beutler & Williams, 1995) designed to help clinicians develop empirically based treatment plans and track patient progress. (Information about standalone or network versions of the computer program Systematic Treatment Selection for Windows [3.1 or Win95] may be obtained from New Standards, Inc., 1080 Montreal Avenue, Suite 300, St. Paul, MN 55116, 800-755-6299.) This work is continually evolving, and the guidelines offered are in a state of flux as new information and research accumulate. The relationships proposed here are derived from those originally hypothesized by Beutler and Clarkin (1990).

Severity and Functionality

The safety of the patient and the safety of those around him or her are central to the issue of level of care. Additionally, the patient's ability to conduct primary tasks necessary to physical and social living determines functionality and is also central to level of care. The factors of severity and functionality prescribe the treatment setting and environment, as well as the amount of restriction necessary to maintain the patient's safety and/or the safety of others.

Answer the following questions:

S1. Is the patient actively suicidal, or has he or she attempted suicide within the past 6 months?

S2. Does the patient currently exhibit violent behavior, or has he or she previously been treated or incarcerated for violent or impulsive behavior?

S3. Has the patient lost control and cannot stop taking alcohol or another psychoactive substance?

S4. Is the patient so psychotic, vegetative, or disoriented that he or she cannot take care of himself or herself?

S5. Does the patient own a firearm?

Add Items 1–4. If the answer to Item 5 was "Yes," then add 2 to the sum of 1–4. Do not count a "Yes" response to Item 5. This score is Severity.

Patient and Problem Complexity

The depth, history, and thematic nature of the patient's profile provide important indicators to prognosis and length of treatment. Situational problems suggest a more acute symptom architecture where brief and targeted psychotherapeutic procedures are indicated. More complex profiles are reflected in longstanding and thematic complaints that recur in almost all facets of the patient's life. A "Yes" response to each of the following questions suggests greater complexity and chronicity. Call the total number of "Yes" responses Complexity.

C1. Does the patient have more than one Axis I diagnosis?

C2. Has the patient had the current or another diagnosable psychiatric condition continuously for more than 6 months?

C3. Does the patient have recurrent and distressful thoughts and feelings about his or her nuclear family (mother, father, close relatives)?

C4. Can the patient also be diagnosed with an Axis II disorder?

Distress

We conceptualize distress along three contributing factors: (a) comfort level as the patient would report it; (b) how the clinician perceives the patient's distress level; and (c) the patient's self-esteem, where low self-esteem is indicative of psychological distress. These distress factors are independent of diagnoses and are manifested as "psychic pain" no matter what the presenting problem.

Answer the following criteria to guide your estimate of patient distress. Based on your evaluation of these distress items, total the number of "Yes" responses. Call this sum Distress.

The patient . . .

D1. Would probably frequently report, "I often feel nervous, anxious, or restless even when things are going OK."
D2. Appears to be nervous, anxious, or restless.
D3. Feels guilt, unworthiness, or self-dislike most of the time.
D4. Is very uncertain about the future.
D5. Feels unhappy or sad.
D6. Has many symptoms of emotional distress.

Resistance Potential

The domain of resistance potential or reactance level connotes an individual's relative sluggishness or alacrity in accepting the therapist's direction. Reactance can be conceptualized as a kind of "psychological inertia." Analogously, the more inertia an object has, the more effort is required to move it or to change its course and direction. Consider the following comments about the patient. Add the number of "Yes" responses and call the total score Reactance.

R1. Is likely to accept and follow the directions of those in authority.
R2. Has strong and unbendable opinions about things.
R3. Is prone to criticize others.
R4. Is controlling in relationships.
R5. Is distrustful and suspicious of others' motives.
R6. Often breaks "the rules."
R7. Is passive-aggressive.

Coping Style

Coping style is the predominant manner in which an individual manages anxiety and stress. Anxiety can be exhibited through outward expression into one's physical and social environment, called externalization. It can also be focused inwardly by containment of feelings and thoughts, called internalization. Individuals are not uniformly characterized by one dimension or the other but rather by a composite of internalization and externalization. The degree and ratio of the two coping style factors facilitate an almost infinite variety of coping characterizations.

Respond to the following items with a "Yes" or "No" to indicate what you believe is true of the patient. Call the total number of "Yes" responses Externalization.

E1. Enjoys loud parties and festive occasions.
E2. Has used alcohol/drugs excessively at one time.
E3. Gets frustrated easily.
E4. Often gets into trouble because of his or her behavior.
E5. Gets bored easily.
E6. Blames others for his or her problems.

Respond to the following items with a "Yes" or "No" to indicate what you believe is true of the patient. Call the total number of "Yes" responses Internalization.

I1. More likely to feel hurt than angry.
I2. Worries or ruminates a lot.
I3. Feels more than passing guilt, remorse, or shame about minor things.
I4. Is more interested in ideas than in taking action.
I5. Is timid.
I6. Likes to be alone.

THERAPY DECISIONS

Treatment decisions are complex and, accordingly, are developed from weighting and integrating a number of separate patient and treatment dimensions. Weighting and balancing various factors in clinical practice are usually done through an idiosyncratic process that relies heavily on one's personal clinical experience. Even expert clinicians are limited in how effectively they can objectively integrate the many patient and environmental dimensions that have implications for treatment planning. This section contains a suggested method of weighting variables identified in the course of assessment and combining them in a systematic way to make general decisions about the level of care and an approach to treatment that might be effective. These are suggestions rather than guidelines, however. More specific recommendations than those presented here are possible, but they require more psychometrically sound assessment procedures and the use of more complex weightings of patient and treatment variables than those suggested for consideration. A computer-based version of this assessment process derives complex algorithms that include many dimensions and interactions in order to help clinicians select appropriate therapists, identify particular models of treatment that fit the patient, and select particular techniques that are likely to be effective. The abbreviated and psychometrically impure items presented here do not allow this level of specificity.

Level of Care

Severity = 0: Treatment in a restrictive setting does not appear warranted for this patient at this time. Optional treatment settings could include the site of difficulty, office treatment, the home, or any combination of these environments during the course of treatment. The clinician may want to consider how the present environment optimally affects and facilitates treatment outcome.

S1 is Yes or S2 is Yes or S3 is Yes and S5 is No: Treatment is indicated for this patient. The level of problem severity suggests that the patient will be manageable as an outpatient.

S1 and S5 are Yes: The patient may require protective controls against suicide potential. Acute hospitalization should be considered while the patient becomes stabilized on a treatment regimen.

Severity ≥ 3: Serious consideration must be given to providing a protective environment along with medical management and consultation.

Severity = 1 and Axis I Count < 4 and Complexity = 1: The patient presents problems of mild to moderate severity. Most of the symptomatic presentations probably can be expected to resolve within a period of 6 months of regular treatment. If the problems prove to be complicated by personality disorder or multiple problems, a reconsideration of this projection will be indicated.

Severity > 1 and C3 = Yes and Complexity ≥ 2: This patient presents with chronic and difficult problems. These difficulties are likely to resolve slowly. While one may expect some increased optimism and dissipation of some symptoms within a period of less than 6 months, substantial change may require both long-term care and periods in which the frequency of visits and varieties of care are increased.

S2 is Yes and S5 is Yes: The patient is prone to aggressive acts, which may involve risk to other people. Protections against these acts are indicated. At least short-term hospitalization or legal management may be indicated.

Treatment Approaches

(Complexity = 1 or 2) and Distress ≥ 3: Chronicity and acuteness are indicated, where acuteness has exacerbated long-standing problems. The first goal should be narrow focus and symptom removal; the second goal should be long-term behavioral management.

There are indications that this patient's problems reflect persistent and long-term conflicts. Thus, the long-term goals of treatment should not be constrained to symptom removal. This patient is likely to have conflicts and recurrent dysfunctional behaviors in interpersonal relationships that prevent the long-term resolution of symptoms. An understanding of the patient's intrapersonal dynamics and interpersonal problems is necessary in addressing these problems. It often helps to define (a) the dominant interpersonal needs or desires that motivate the initiation of interpersonal relationships; (b) the avoided and feared responses that are expected to come from others as the patient tries to meet these needs or achieve these wants; and (c) the acts of the patient to attempt a compromise between personal desires and feared consequences.

Distress ≥ 3 and Complexity = 0: Indicators suggest focus and outcome objectives should be on symptom removal. There is little indication of a persistent and continuing problem beyond situational disturbance.

Since this patient's presenting problems are relatively situational, this should not pose a major difficulty for the treatment. Good and even lasting outcomes have been noted with procedures that are designed to induce rapid symptom change. Indeed, insight-oriented treatments are often more time-consuming than warranted by the problems presented by patients such as this.

It may be possible to restrict the goals of treatment to symptom removal. If so, treatment can be expected to produce some diminution of the major symptoms of depression and anxiety within 20–30 sessions or weeks. If more focal symptoms are being presented, such as sleep, sexual, or impulse control problems, they may require a somewhat longer period. Treatment should be addressed to symptom removal, to the reduction of subjective distress, and to the increase in objective life adjustment. Cognitive control strategies, contingency programs for symptomatic control, and response prevention interventions should be considered.

Complexity ≥ 2 and Distress > 3: Complexity suggests chronic and long-standing symptoms. Treatment objectives and focus should be on long-term behavioral management. There are indications that this patient's problems reflect

persistent and long-term conflicts. Thus, the long-term goals of treatment should not be constrained to symptom removal.

This patient is likely to have conflicts and recurrent dysfunctional behaviors in interpersonal relationships that prevent the long-term resolution of symptoms. An understanding of the patient's intrapersonal dynamics and interpersonal problems is necessary in addressing these problems. It often helps to define (a) the dominant interpersonal needs or desires that motivate the initiation of interpersonal relationships; (b) the avoided and feared responses that are expected to come from others as the patient tries to meet these needs or achieve these wants; and (c) the acts of the patient to attempt a compromise between personal desires and feared consequences.

Distress < 3 and Complexity < 2: Given the low level of personal distress, this raises a question as to why this person is seeking treatment at this time. Careful consideration must be given to the need for and advisability of treatment, and especially the motivations that are determining a referral for treatment at the present time.

C3 = Yes and Complexity > 1: Family therapy appears to be indicated. This therapy should focus on conflicts in the patient's current family. The role of other symptoms and problems may be either ancillary or primary in the family problems, but the significance of family disruption nonetheless warrants direct attention.

Externalization > 3 and Reactance > 3 and S2 is Yes: The patient exhibits possible explosive outbursts. Thus, caution is advised, and treatment should include behavioral protections such as the initiation of nonviolence contracts, monitoring of impulsivity, and ongoing assessment of escalating emotional intensity. Training in emotional recognition, identification of risk environments, and cognitive management skills is indicated.

(Severity > 0 and Severity < 3) and Distress > 3 and Externalization > Internalization: The patient appears to be in sufficient distress to provide motivation for ongoing psychotherapy. Nonetheless, treatment progress is often slow with such individuals. They tend to work inconsistently in treatment, even withdrawing from treatment prematurely when their distress lessens. They have difficulty seeing their own contribution to their problems, tending to blame others and to attribute their difficulties to forces outside of their personal control. Treatment would do well to reinforce assumptions of personal responsibility. Sometimes, group therapies have been useful in providing a level of confrontation that encourages the assumption of personal responsibility for initiating change.

Externalization > 3 and Reactance > 3: Behaviorally focused and cognitive change therapies may be particularly helpful for this patient. However, because the patient tends to be more resistant to direction than usual, modifications of the treatments may be necessary. Such modifications may employ self-help manuals and efforts to make homework assignments more flexible than usual.

Severity = 1 and Distress > 2 and Internalization > Externalization: Treatment is indicated for this patient, and the level of problem severity suggests that the patient will be manageable as an outpatient. Moreover, the patient appears to be in sufficient distress to provide motivation for ongoing psychotherapy. Such individuals tend to work quite well in psychotherapy relationships, especially if they have a history of being able to form social attachments. Their motivation for treatment is typically to reduce stress, however, and rapid change of symptoms may reduce their motivation.

Severity = 0 and Distress ≥ 3 and Externalization > Internalization: While the patient has little impairment functionally, the level of internal distress indicates the desirability of treatment. This distress level is sufficient to provide motivation for treatment and indicates that engagement in outpatient treatment is possible. Engaging such patients in the process of therapy is difficult because they often have difficulty assessing their role in causing or maintaining their problems. A focus on problematic behaviors and cognitions with short-

term, measurable objectives is more likely to be effective than insight-oriented treatments.

Severity = 0 and Distress ≥ 3 and Internalization > Externalization: While the patient has little impairment functionally, the level of internal distress indicates the desirability of treatment. This distress level is sufficient to provide motivation for treatment and indicates that engagement in outpatient treatment is possible. The patient is self-reflective, suggesting that insight is possible and even desirable as a treatment goal. Insight into unwanted feelings may prove to be advantageous.

Severity = 0 and Distress < 3 and Externalization > Internalization: This patient apparently has minimal impairment of functioning. Coupled with the low level of personal distress, this raises a question as to why this person is seeking treatment at this time. Careful consideration must be given to the need for and advisability of treatment, and especially the motivations that are determining a referral for treatment at the present time.

Engaging such patients in the process of therapy is difficult because they often have difficulty assessing their role in causing or maintaining their problems. A focus on problematic behaviors and cognitions with short-term, measurable objectives is more likely to be effective than insight-oriented treatments.

Severity = 0 and Distress < 3 and Internalization > Externalization: This patient also apparently has minimal impairment of functioning. Coupled with the low level of personal distress, this raises a question as to why this person is seeking treatment at this time. Careful consideration must be given to the need for and advisability of treatment, and especially the motivations that are determining a referral for treatment at the present time.

However, the patient is self-reflective, suggesting that insight is possible and even desirable as a treatment goal. Insight into both hidden motives and unwanted feelings may prove to be advantageous.

Severity > 2: This patient may require a very structured and concrete approach to treatment, including pretreatment preparation, clearly established goals, and an outline of in-treatment and outside-of-treatment expectations.

References & Readings

Beutler, L. E. (1979). Toward specific psychological therapies for specific conditions. *Journal of Consulting and Clinical Psychology, 47,* 882–897.

Beutler, L. E., & Clarkin, J. (1990). *Systematic treatment selection: Toward targeted therapeutic interventions.* New York: Brunner/Mazel.

Beutler, L. E., & Williams, O. B. (1995). Computer applications for the selection of optimal psychosocial therapeutic interventions. *Behavioral Healthcare Tomorrow, 4,* 66–68.

Beutler, L. E., & Williams, O. B. (1996). Systematic treatment selection for Windows [Computer program]. St. Paul, MN: New Standards.

Gaw, K. E, & Beutler, L. E. (1995). Integrating treatment recommendations. In L. E. Beutler & M. Berren (Eds.), *Integrative assessment of adult personality* (pp. 280–319). New York: Guilford Press.

Related Topics

Chapter 45, "Compendium of Current Psychotherapy Treatment Manuals"

Chapter 46, "Empirically Validated Treatments"

Chapter 49, "Stages of Change: Prescriptive Guidelines for Behavioral Medicine and Psychotherapy"

48 PSYCHOTHERAPY TREATMENT PLAN WRITING

Arthur E. Jongsma, Jr.

HISTORICAL BACKGROUND

Over the past 30 years, formalized treatment planning has gradually become a vital aspect of the entire health care delivery system, whether it is treatment related to physical health, mental health, child welfare, or substance abuse. What started in the medical sector in the 1960s spread into the mental health sector in the 1970s as clinics, psychiatric hospitals, agencies, and others began to seek accreditation from bodies such as the Joint Commission on Accreditation of Healthcare Organizations (JCAHO) to qualify for third-party reimbursements. To achieve accreditation, most treatment providers had to develop or strengthen their documentation skills in the area of treatment planning. Previously, most mental health and substance abuse treatment providers had, at best, a rudimentary plan that looked similar for most of the individuals they treated. As a result, patients often were uncertain as to what they were trying to attain in psychiatric treatment. Goals were vague, objectives were nonexistent, and interventions were applied equally to all patients. Outcome criteria were not measurable, and neither the patient nor the treatment provider knew exactly when treatment was completed.

Treatment planning has gained even greater importance since the coming of managed care in the 1980s. Managed care systems insist that clinicians move rapidly from assessment of the problem to the formulation and implementation of the treatment plan. The purpose of managed care organizations' emphasis on early treatment planning is to move the patient to focus on progressing toward change as soon as possible. Treatment plans must be specific as to the problems and interventions, individualized to meet the patient's needs and goals, and measurable in terms of setting milestones that can be used to chart the patient's progress. Pressure from third-party payers, accrediting agencies, and other outside parties has therefore increased the need for clinicians to produce effective, high-quality treatment plans in a short time frame. However, the pressure on clinicians from these outside sources to produce individualized treatment plans has brought with it several concomitant rewards.

TREATMENT PLAN UTILITY

Detailed, written treatment plans can benefit not only the patient, therapist, treatment team, insurance community, and treatment agency but also the overall psychotherapy profession. The patient is served by a written plan because it stipulates the issues that are the focus of the treatment process. It is very easy for both provider and patient to lose sight of what the issues were that brought the patient into therapy. The treatment plan is a guide that structures what the therapeutic contract is meant to focus on. Although issues can change as therapy progresses, the treatment plan must be viewed as a dynamic document that can and must be updated to reflect any major change of problem, definition, goal, objective, or intervention.

Patients and therapists benefit as a result of the treatment plan forcing both to think about therapy outcomes. Behaviorally stated, measurable objectives clearly focus the treatment endeavor. Patients no longer have to wonder what therapy is trying to accomplish. Clear objectives also allow the patient to channel effort into specific changes that will lead to the long-term goal of problem resolution. Therapy is no longer a vague contract to just talk honestly and openly about emotions and thoughts until the patient feels better. Both patient and therapist are concentrating on specifically stated objectives using specific interventions.

Providers are aided by treatment plans because they force them to think analytically and critically about therapeutic interventions that are best suited for objective attainment for specific patients. Therapists were traditionally trained to "follow the patient," but now a formalized plan is the guide to the treatment process. The therapist must give advance attention to the technique, approach, assignment, or cathartic target that will form the basis for interventions.

Clinicians benefit from clear documentation of treatment that becomes a part of the permanent record because it provides added protection against a disgruntled patient's litigation. Malpractice suits are increasing in frequency, and insurance premiums are soaring. The first line of defense against allegations is a complete clinical record that includes detail regarding the treatment process. A written, individualized, formal treatment plan that is the guideline for the therapeutic process, has been reviewed and signed by the patient, and is coupled with problem-oriented progress notes is a powerful defense against exaggerated or false claims.

A well-crafted, problem-focused treatment plan that clearly stipulates intervention strategies facilitates and guides the treatment process that must be carried out by all team members in an inpatient, residential, or intensive outpatient setting. Good communication between team members is critical about what approach is being implemented and who is responsible for each intervention. Team meetings to discuss patient treatment used to be the only communication approach, and often therapeutic conclusions or assignments were not recorded. Now a thorough treatment plan stipulates in writing the details of objectives and the varied interventions (pharmacological, milieu, group therapy, didactic, recreational, individual therapy, etc.) and who will implement them.

Every treatment agency or institution is constantly looking for ways to increase the quality and uniformity of the documentation in the clinical record. A standardized, written treatment plan with problem definitions, goals, objectives, and interventions in every patient's file enhances that uniformity of documentation. This uniformity eases the task of record reviewers inside and outside the agency. Outside reviewers, such as the JCAHO, insist on documentation that clearly outlines assessment, treatment, progress, and discharge status.

The demand for accountability from third-party payers and HMOs is partly satisfied by a written treatment plan and complete progress notes. More and more managed care systems are demanding a structured therapeutic contract that has measurable objectives and explicit interventions. Clinicians cannot avoid this move toward being accountable to those outside the treatment process.

The psychotherapy profession stands to benefit from the use of more precise, measurable objectives to evaluate success in mental health treatment. Outcome data can be more easily collected regarding interventions that are effective in achieving specific objectives. Comparisons between different treatment strategies involving various objectives and interventions will be possible by clinicians and researchers. Treatment planning computer software has been published that assists in creating a treatment plan but also tracks patients' progress, analyzing and graphing outcome data (Jongsma, Peterson, & McInnis, 1997).

HOW TO DEVELOP A TREATMENT PLAN

The process of developing a treatment plan involves a logical series of steps that build on each other much as one would construct a house. The foundation of any effective treatment plan is the data gathered in a thorough biopsychosocial assessment. When the patient presents for treatment, the clinician must sensitively listen to and understand the patient's struggles in terms of family of origin issues, current stressors, emotional status, social network, physical health, coping skills, interpersonal conflicts, self-esteem, and so on. Assessment data may be gathered from a social history, physical exam, clinical interview, psychological testing, behavioral observations, or contact with a patient's significant others. The integration of all this information by the clinician or members of the multidisciplinary treatment team is a critical first step in arriving at an understanding of the patient and the focus of the patient's struggle. From this clinical formulation should evolve a list of problems that form the structure around which a treatment plan is created. An accurate and complete assessment of the nature of the patient's problems will provide focus in developing a specific treatment plan (Scholing, Emmelkamp, & Van Oppen, 1996). The development of the treatment plan from the integrated biopsychosocial assessment data is a six-step process.

Step One: Problem Selection

The problem list is like the structural beams that support the framework of a house under construction. Although the patient may discuss a variety of issues during the assessment, the clinician must ferret out the most significant problems on which to focus the treatment process. Usually a primary problem will surface, and additional secondary problems will also be evident. Some other problems may have to be set aside as not urgent enough to require treatment at this time. An effective treatment plan can deal with only a few selected problems or treatment will lose its direction.

As the problems to be selected become clear to the clinician or the treatment team, it is important to include opinions from the patient about his or her prioritization of issues for which he or she seeks help. A patient's motivation to participate in and cooperate with an eventual treatment process will depend somewhat on the degree to which treatment addresses his or her greatest needs.

Step Two: Problem Definition

The problem definition is similar to the specifications of what the structural beams are made of. Each individual patient presents with unique behavioral manifestations of the problem. Therefore, each problem that is selected for treatment focus requires a specific definition of how it is evidenced in this particular patient. The symptom pattern should be associated with diagnostic criteria and codes such as those found in *DSM-IV* or the *ICD-9*.

Step Three: Goal Development

The goals represent the rendering of what the finished house will look like. Setting broad goals for the resolution of the target problem is the next step in the treatment plan development process. These statements need not be crafted in measurable terms but can be global, long-term goals that indicate a desired positive outcome to the treatment procedures. One goal statement for each problem is all that is required in a treatment plan.

Step Four: Objective Construction

The objectives are like the building materials (the bricks, mortar, studs, and drywall) of the house under construction—the elements necessary to achieve the final product. In contrast to long-term goals, objectives must be stated in behaviorally measurable language. It must be clear when the patient has achieved the established objectives; therefore, vague, subjective objectives are not acceptable. Review agencies (e.g., JCAHO), HMOs, and managed care organizations insist that psychological treatment outcome be more measurable, so objectives must be crafted to meet this demand for accountability. The clinician must exercise professional judgment regarding which objectives are most appropriate for a given patient.

Each objective should be developed as a step toward attaining the broad treatment goal. In essence, objectives can be thought of as a series of steps that, when completed, will result in the achievement of the long-term goal. There should be at least two objectives for each problem, but the therapist should construct as many as necessary for goal achievement. New objectives should be added to the plan as the individual's

treatment progresses. When all the necessary objectives have been achieved, the patient should have resolved the target problem successfully and achieved the treatment goal. Additional accountability is required as reviewers demand that target attainment dates be assigned to each objective. This is an attempt to shorten and focus the counseling process because the emphasis is on brief symptom resolution rather than personality change or personal growth.

Step Five: Intervention Creation

Interventions represent the creative skills of the architect—the tools of the trade—that guide the building process. Interventions are the actions of the clinician to help the patient complete the objectives. The clinician may choose from cognitive, dynamic, behavioral, pharmacological, family treatment, or solution-focused brief therapeutic interventions. There should be at least one intervention for every objective. New interventions should be added as the original interventions have been implemented but the patient has not yet accomplished the objective. Addition of new interventions and objectives to promote treatment success is especially appropriate given the recent trend toward a patient's progression through various levels of a continuum of care in mental health and substance abuse programs. The clinical skills of the provider are tested as therapeutic intervention strategies must be created to assist the patient in achieving the objectives. Treatment planning books are available that provide a menu of concise suggestions for behavioral definitions of problems, long-term goals, short-term objectives, as well as therapeutic interventions (Jongsma & Peterson, 1995; Jongsma, Peterson, & McInnis, 1996). Treatment plan resources that are more general and theoretically based are also available (e.g., Gabbard, 1995). The therapeutic approach of the clinician will influence what type of intervention statements are written.

Assigning interventions to a specific provider is most relevant if the patient is being treated by a team in an inpatient, residential, or intensive outpatient setting. Within these settings, personnel other than the primary clinician may be responsible for implementing a specific intervention. Review agencies require that stipulation of the provider's name be attached to every intervention if the patient is being treated by a multidisciplinary team.

Step Six: Diagnosis Determination

The determination of an appropriate diagnosis is based on an evaluation of the patient's complete clinical presentation. The clinician must compare the behavioral, cognitive, emotional, and interpersonal symptoms that the patient presents to the criteria for diagnosis of a mental illness condition as described in the *DSM-IV*. The issue of differential diagnosis is admittedly a difficult one that research has shown to have rather low interrater reliability. Psychologists have also been trained to think more in terms of maladaptive behavior than in terms of disease labels. In spite of these factors, diagnosis is a reality that exists in the world of mental health care, and it is a necessity for third-party reimbursement. (However, recently, managed care agencies have become more interested in behavioral indices that are exhibited by the patient than in the actual diagnosis.) It is the clinician's thorough knowledge of *DSM-IV* criteria and a complete understanding of the patient assessment data that contribute to the most reliable, valid diagnosis. An accurate assessment of behavioral indicators will also contribute to more effective treatment planning.

One final but important aspect of an effective treatment plan is that it must be designed to deal with each individual patient specifically. Treatment plans, like quality homes, are not to be mass-produced with the same plan applied to all patients, even if they have similar problems. The individual's strengths and weaknesses, unique stressors, social network, family circumstances, and symptom pattern must be considered in developing a treatment strategy (Axelrod, Spreat, Berry, & Moyer, 1993). A treatment plan that takes into account the uniqueness of the patient's dynamics, traits, and circumstances will stand a greater chance of producing a satisfactory, measurable outcome in a shorter time frame.

Note

This chapter was adapted from Introduction, in A. E. Jongsma & L. M. Peterson, *The Complete Psychotherapy Treatment Planner* (New York: Wiley, 1995), pp. 1–7. Reprinted with permission.

References & Readings

Axelrod, S., Spreat, S., Berry, B., & Moyer, L. (1993). A decision-making model for selecting the optimal treatment procedure. In R. Van Houten and S. Axelrod (Eds.), *Behavior analysis and treatment: Applied clinical psychology* (pp. 183–202). New York: Plenum Press.

Gabbard, G. O. (1995). *Treatment of psychiatric disorders* (2nd ed., Vols. 1 & 2). Washington, DC: American Psychiatric Press.

Jongsma, A. E., Jr., & Peterson, L. M. (1995). *The complete psychotherapy treatment planner*. New York: Wiley.

Jongsma, A. E., Jr., Peterson, L. M., & McInnis, W. P. (1996). *The child and adolescent psychotherapy treatment planner*. New York: Wiley.

Jongsma, A. E., Jr., Peterson, L. M., & McInnis, W. P. (1997). TheraScribe 3.0: The computerized assistant to psychotherapy treatment planning (Version 3.0) [Computer software]. New York: Wiley.

Scholing, A., Emmelkamp, P. M., & Van Oppen, P. (1996). Cognitive-behavioral treatment of social phobia. In V. B. Van Hasselt & M. Hersen (Eds.), *Sourcebook of psychological treatment manuals for adult disorders* (pp. 123–177). New York: Plenum Press.

STAGES OF CHANGE

49

Prescriptive Guidelines for Behavioral Medicine and Psychotherapy

James O. Prochaska, Carlo C. DiClemente, & John C. Norcross

Over the past 20 years our research has focused on the structure of change that underlies both self-mediated and treatment-facilitated modification of problem behavior (for summaries, see Prochaska, DiClemente, & Norcross, 1992; Prochaska, Norcross, & DiClemente, 1995). From an integrative or transtheoretical perspective, this chapter summarizes prescriptive and proscriptive guidelines for psychosocial interventions based on the client's stage of change.

DEFINITIONS OF STAGES

The following are brief descriptions of each of the five stages. Each stage represents a period of time, as well as a set of tasks needed for movement to the next stage. Although the time an individual spends in each stage may vary, the tasks to be accomplished are assumed to be invariant.

Precontemplation is the stage at which there is no intention to change behavior in the foreseeable future. Most individuals in this stage are unaware or underaware of their problems. Families, friends, neighbors, or employees, however, are often well aware that the precontemplators have problems. When precontemplators present for psychotherapy, they often do so because of pressure from others. Usually they feel coerced into changing by a spouse who threatens to leave, an employer who threatens to dismiss them, parents who

threaten to disown them, or courts that threaten to punish them.

There are multiple ways to measure the stage of change. In our studies employing the discrete categorization measurement of stages of change, we ask if the individual is seriously intending to change the problem behavior in the near future, typically within the next 6 months. If not, he or she is classified as a precontemplator. Even precontemplators can *wish* to change, but this is quite different from intending or seriously considering change. Items that are used to identify precontemplation on the continuous stage of change measure include "As far as I'm concerned, I don't have any problems that need changing" and "I guess I have faults, but there's nothing that I really need to change." Resistance to recognizing or modifying a problem is the hallmark of precontemplation.

Contemplation is the stage in which people are aware that a problem exists and are seriously thinking about overcoming it but have not yet made a commitment to take action. People can remain stuck in the contemplation stage for long periods. In one study of self-changers we followed a group of 200 smokers who were in the contemplation stage for 2 years. The modal response of this group was to remain in the contemplation stage for the entire 2 years of the project without ever moving to significant action (Prochaska & DiClemente, 1983).

Contemplators struggle with their positive

evaluations of their dysfunctional behavior and the amount of effort, energy, and loss it will cost to overcome it. On discrete measures, individuals who state that they are seriously considering changing the addictive behavior in the next 6 months are classified as contemplators. On the continuous measure these individuals would be endorsing such items as "I have a problem and I really think I should work on it" and "I've been thinking that I might want to change something about myself." Serious consideration of problem resolution is the central element of contemplation.

Preparation is a stage that combines intention and behavioral criteria. Individuals in this stage are intending to take action in the next month and have unsuccessfully taken action in the past year. As a group, individuals who are prepared for action report some small behavioral changes, such as smoking five fewer cigarettes or delaying their first cigarette of the day for 30 minutes longer than precontemplators or contemplators (DiClemente et al., 1991). Although they have made some reductions in their problem behaviors, individuals in the preparation stage have not yet reached a criterion for effective action, such as abstinence from smoking, alcohol abuse, or heroin use. They are intending, however, to take such action in the very near future. On the continuous measure they score high on both the contemplation and action scales.

Action is the stage in which individuals modify their behavior, experiences, and/or environment in order to overcome their problems. Action involves the most overt behavioral changes and requires considerable commitment of time and energy. Modifications of the addictive behavior made in the action stage tend to be most visible and receive the greatest external recognition. Individuals are classified in the action stage if they have successfully altered the dysfunctional behavior for a period from 1 day to 6 months. On the continuous measure individuals in the action stage endorse statements like "I am really working hard to change" and "Anyone can talk about changing; I am actually doing something about it." They score high on the action scale and lower on the other scales. Modification of the target behavior to an accept-

able criterion and significant overt efforts to change are the hallmarks of action.

Maintenance is the stage in which people work to prevent relapse and consolidate the gains attained during action. For addictive behaviors this stage extends from 6 months to an indeterminate period past the initial action. For some behaviors, maintenance can be considered to last a lifetime. Being able to remain free of the addictive behavior and/or being able to consistently engage in a new incompatible behavior for more than 6 months are the criteria for considering someone to be in the maintenance stage. On the continuous measure, representative maintenance items are "I may need a boost right now to help me maintain the changes I've already made" and "I'm here to prevent myself from having a relapse of my problem." Stabilizing behavior change and avoiding relapse are the hallmarks of maintenance.

Spiral pattern: As is now well known, most people taking action to modify dysfunctional behavior do not successfully maintain their gains on their first attempt. With New Year's resolutions, for example, the successful self-changers typically report 3 to 5 years of consecutive pledges before maintaining the behavioral goal for at least 6 months (Norcross, Ratzin, & Payne, 1989). Relapse is the rule rather than the exception across virtually all behavioral disorders.

Accordingly, change is not a linear progression through the stages. Most clients actually move through the stages of change in a spiral pattern: People can progress from contemplation to preparation to action to maintenance, but most individuals will relapse. During relapse, individuals regress to an earlier stage. Some relapsers feel like failures—embarrassed, ashamed, and guilty. These individuals become demoralized and resist thinking about behavior change. As a result, they return to the precontemplation stage and can remain there for various periods of time. Approximately 15% of smokers who relapsed in our self-change research regressed to the precontemplation stage. Fortunately, most—85% of smokers, for example—move back to the contemplation stage and eventually back into preparation and action.

PRESCRIPTIVE GUIDELINES

1. *Assess the client's stage of change:* Probably the most obvious and direct implication is the need to assess the stage of a client's readiness for change and to tailor interventions accordingly.

Stages of change can be ascertained by multiple means, of which three self-report methods will be described here. The first and most efficient is to ask the patient a simple series of questions to identify his or her stage, for example, "Do you think behavior X is a problem for you now?" (if yes, then contemplation, preparation, or action stage; if no, then maintenance or precontemplation stage) and "When do you intend to change behavior X?" (if someday or not soon, then contemplation stage; if in the next month, then preparation; if now, then the action stage). A second method is to assess the stage from a series of mutually exclusive questions (DiClemente et al., 1991), and a third is a continuous measure that yields separate scales for precontemplation, contemplation, action, and maintenance (McConnaughy, Prochaska, & Velicer, 1983; McConnaughy, DiClemente, Prochaska, & Velicer, 1989).

2. *Beware of treating all patients as though they are in action:* Professionals frequently design excellent action-oriented treatment and self-help programs but then are disappointed when only a small percentage of addicted people register or when large numbers drop out of the program after registering. The vast majority of people are *not* in the action stage. Aggregating across studies and populations, we estimate that 10–15% are prepared for action, approximately 30–40% are in the contemplation stage, and 50–60% are in the precontemplation stage. Thus, those professionals who approach patients and work sites only with action-oriented programs are likely to underserve or misserve the majority of their target population.

3. *Assist clients in moving one stage at a time:* If clients progress from one stage to the next during the first month of treatment, they can double their chances of taking action in the next 6 months. Among smokers, for example, of the precontemplators who were still in precontemplation at 1-month follow-up, only 3%

took action by 6 months. For the precontemplators who progressed to contemplation at 1 month, 7% took action by 6 months. Similarly, of the contemplators who remained in contemplation at 1 month, only 20% took action by 6 months. At 1 month, 41% of the contemplators who progressed to the preparation stage attempted to quit by 6 months. These data indicate that treatment programs designed to help people progress just one stage in a month may be able to increase the chances of participants taking action on their own in the near future.

4. *Recognize that clients in the action stage are far more likely to achieve better and quicker outcomes:* The amount of progress clients make during treatment tends to be a function of their pretreatment stage of change. For example, in an intensive action- and maintenance-oriented smoking-cessation program for cardiac patients, 22% of precontemplators, 43% of contemplators, and 76% of those in action or prepared for action at the start of the study were not smoking 6 months later (Ockene, Ockene, & Kristellar, 1988). This repeated finding has direct implications for selecting and prioritizing treatment goals.

5. *Facilitate the insight-action crossover:* Patients in successful treatment evidence steady progression on the stages of change. Patients entering therapy are typically in the contemplation or preparation stage. In the midst of treatment, patients typically cross over from contemplation into action. Patients who remain in treatment progress from being prepared for action into taking action over time. That is, they shift from thinking about their problems to doing things to overcome them. Lowered precontemplation scores also indicated that, as engagement in therapy increases, patients reduce their defensiveness and resistance. The progression from contemplation to action is postulated to be essential for beneficial outcome regardless of whether the treatment is action-oriented or insight-oriented.

6. *Anticipate recycling:* Most self-changers and psychotherapy patients will recycle several times through the stages before achieving long-term maintenance. Accordingly, intervention programs and personnel expecting people to progress linearly through the stages are likely to gather disappointing and discouraging results. Be prepared to include relapse-prevention strategies in treatment, anticipate the probability of recycling patients, and try to minimize therapist guilt and patient shame over recycling.

7. *Conceptualize change mechanisms as processes, not as specific techniques:* Literally hundreds of specific psychotherapeutic techniques have been advanced; however, a small and finite set of change processes or strategies underlie these multitudinous techniques.

Change processes are covert and overt activities that individuals engage in when they attempt to modify problem behaviors. Each process is a broad category encompassing multiple techniques, methods, and interventions traditionally associated with disparate theoretical orientations. These change processes can be used within therapy sessions, between therapy sessions, or without therapy sessions.

The processes of change represent an intermediate level of abstraction between metatheoretical assumptions and specific techniques spawned by those theories. While there are 400-plus ostensibly different psychotherapies, we have been able to identify only 12 different processes of change based on principal components analysis.

Table 1 presents the eight processes receiving the most theoretical and empirical support in our work, along with their definitions and representative examples of specific interventions. A common and finite set of change processes has been repeatedly identified across diverse disorders.

8. *Do the right things (processes) at the right time (stages):* Twenty years of research in behavioral medicine, self-change, and psychotherapy converge in showing that different processes of change are differentially effective in certain stages of change. In general terms, change processes traditionally associated with the experiential, cognitive, and psychoanalytic persuasions are most useful during the earlier precontemplation and contemplation stages. Change processes traditionally associated with the existential and behavioral traditions, by contrast, are most useful during action and maintenance.

In the transtheoretical model, particular change processes will be optimally applied at each stage of change. During the precontemplation stage, individuals use the change processes significantly less than people in any of the other stages. Precontemplators process less information about their problems, devote less time and energy to reevaluating themselves, and experience fewer emotional reactions to the negative aspects of their problems. In therapy, these are the most resistant or the least active clients.

Individuals in the contemplation stage are most open to consciousness-raising techniques, such as observations, confrontations, and interpretations, and are much more likely to use bibliotherapy and other educational techniques. Contemplators are also open to emotional arousal, which raises emotions and leads to a lowering of negative affect if the person changes. As individuals become more conscious of themselves and the nature of their problems, they are more likely to reevaluate their values, problems, and themselves both affectively and cognitively.

Both movement from precontemplation to contemplation and movement through the contemplation stage entail increased use of cognitive, affective, and evaluative processes of change. Some of these changes continue during the preparation stage. In addition, individuals in preparation begin to take small steps toward action.

During the action stage, people use higher levels of self-liberation or willpower. They increasingly believe that they have the autonomy to change their lives in key ways. Successful action also entails effective use of behavioral processes, such as counterconditioning and stimulus control, in order to modify the conditional stimuli that frequently prompt relapse. Contingency management also comes into frequent use here.

Just as preparation for action was essential for success, so too is preparation for maintenance. Successful maintenance builds on each of the processes that came before. Specific preparation for maintenance entails an assessment of the conditions under which a person would be likely to relapse and development of

TABLE 1. Titles, Definitions, and Representative Interventions of Eight Processes of Change

Process	Definition: Interventions
1. Consciousness-raising	Increasing information about self and problem: observations; confrontations; interpretations; bibliotherapy
2. Self-reevaluation	Assessing how one feels and thinks about oneself with respect to a problem: value clarification; imagery; corrective emotional experience
3. Emotional arousal (or dramatic relief)	Experiencing and expressing feelings about one's problems and solutions: psychodrama; grieving losses; role playing
4. Social liberation	Increasing alternatives for nonproblem behaviors available in society: advocating for rights of repressed; empowering; policy interventions
5. Self-liberation	Choosing and commitment to act or belief in ability to change: decision-making therapy; New Year's resolutions; logotherapy techniques; commitment-enhancing techniques
6. Counterconditioning	Substituting alternatives for anxiety related behaviors: relaxation; desensitization; assertion; positive self-statements
7. Stimulus control	Avoiding or countering stimuli that elicit problem behaviors: restructuring one's environment (e.g., removing alcohol or fattening foods); avoiding high risk cues; fading techniques
8. Contingency management	Rewarding oneself or being rewarded by others for making changes: contingency contracts; overt and covert reinforcement; self-reward

Source: Adapted from Prochaska, DiClemente, & Norcross, 1992.

alternative responses for coping with such conditions without resorting to self-defeating defenses and pathological responses. Continuing to apply counterconditioning, stimulus control, and contingency management is most effective when based on the conviction that maintaining change supports a sense of self that is highly valued by oneself and significant others.

9. *Prescribe stage-matched "relationships of choice" as well as "treatments of choice":* Psychotherapists invariably customize their interpersonal stance to different patients. One way to conceptualize the matter, paralleling the notion of "treatments of choice" in terms of techniques, is how clinicians determine "therapeutic relationships of choice" in terms of interpersonal stances (Norcross, 1993; Norcross & Beutler, 1997).

The integration of stages of change and relationships of choice is an important practical guide for psychotherapists. Once you know a patient's stage of change, you will know which relationship stances to apply in order to help him or her progress to the next stage and eventually to maintenance. Rather than apply the relationship stances in a haphazard or trial-and-error manner, practitioners can use them in a more systematic and efficient style across the course of psychotherapy.

The research and clinical consensus on the therapist's stance at different stages can be characterized as follows. With precontemplators, often the role is like that of a *nurturing parent* joining with the resistant and defensive youngster who is both drawn to and repelled by the prospects of becoming more independent. With contemplators, the role is akin to that of a *Socratic teacher* who encourages clients to achieve their own insights into their condition. With clients who are in the preparation stage, the stance is more like that of an *experienced coach* who has been through many crucial matches and can provide a fine game plan or review the person's own plan. With clients who are progressing into action and maintenance, the psychotherapist becomes more of a *consultant* who is available to provide expert advice and support when action is not progressing as smoothly as expected.

10. *Avoid mismatching stages and processes:* A person's stage of change provides proscriptive as well as prescriptive information on treatments of choice. Action-oriented therapies may be quite effective with individuals who are in the preparation or action stage. These same programs may be ineffective or detrimental, however, with individuals in the precontemplation or contemplation stage.

We have observed two frequent mismatches. First, some therapists and self-changers appear to rely primarily on change processes that are most indicated for the contemplation stage —consciousness raising, self-reevaluation— while they are moving into the action stage. They try to modify behaviors by becoming more aware, a common criticism of classical psychoanalysis: Insight alone does not necessarily bring about behavior change. Second, other therapists and self-changers rely primarily on change processes that are most indicated for the action stage—contingency management, stimulus control, counterconditioning—without the requisite awareness of decision making and readiness provided in the contemplation and preparation stages. They try to modify behavior without awareness, a common criticism of radical behaviorism: Overt action without insight is likely to lead to temporary change.

11. *Think complementarily:* Competing systems of psychotherapy have promulgated apparently rival processes of change. However, ostensibly contradictory processes can become complementary when embedded in the stages of change. Although some psychotherapists insist that such theoretical integration is philosophically impossible, our research has consistently documented that ordinary people in the natural environment and psychotherapists in their consultation rooms can be remarkably effective in synthesizing powerful change processes across the stages of change.

References & Readings

DiClemente, C. C. (1991). Motivational interviewing and the stages of change. In W. R. Miller & S. Rollnick (Eds.), *Motivational interviewing: Preparing people for change.* New York: Guilford Press.

DiClemente, C. C., & Hughes, S. L. (1990). Stages of change profiles in alcoholism treatment. *Journal of Substance Abuse, 2,* 217–235.

DiClemente, C. C., Prochaska, J. O., Fairhurst, S. K., Velicer, W. F., Velasquez, M. M., & Rossi, J. S. (1991). The process of smoking cessation: An analysis of precontemplation, contemplation, and preparation stages of change. *Journal of Consulting and Clinical Psychology, 59,* 295–304.

McConnaughy, E. A., DiClemente, C. C., Prochaska, J. O., & Velicer, W. F. (1989). Stages of change in psychotherapy: A followup report. *Psychotherapy, 26,* 494–503.

McConnaughy, E. A., Prochaska, J. O., & Velicer, W. F. (1983). Stages of change in psychotherapy: Measurement and sample profiles. *Psychotherapy, 20,* 368–375.

Norcross, J. C. (1993). The relationship of choice: Matching the therapist's stance to individual clients. *Psychotherapy, 30,* 402–403.

Norcross, J. C., & Beutler, L. E. (1997). Determining the therapeutic relationship of choice in brief therapy. In J. N. Butcher (Ed.), *Objective psychological assessment in managed health care: A practitioner's guide.* New York: Oxford University Press.

Norcross, J. C., Prochaska, J. O., & DiClemente, C. C. (1995). The stages and processes of weight control: Two replications. In T. B. VanItallie & A. P. Simopoulos (Eds.), *Obesity: New directions in assessment and management.* Philadelphia: Charles Press.

Norcross, J. C., Ratzin, A. C., & Payne, D. (1989). Ringing in the New Year: The change processes and reported outcomes of resolutions. *Addictive Behaviors, 14,* 205–212.

Ockene, J., Ockene, I., & Kristellar, J. (1988). *The coronary artery smoking intervention study.* Worcester, MA: National Heart, Lung, and Blood Institute.

Prochaska, J. O. (1991). Prescribing to the stages and levels of change. *Psychotherapy, 28,* 463–468.

Prochaska, J. O., & DiClemente, C. C. (1983). Stages and processes of self-change in smoking: Toward an integrative model of change. *Journal of Consulting and Clinical Psychology, 5,* 390–395.

Prochaska, J. O., & DiClemente, C. C. (1984). *The transtheoretical approach: Crossing traditional boundaries of change.* Homewood, IL: Dow Jones/Irwin.

Prochaska, J. O., DiClemente, C. C., & Norcross, J. C. (1992). In search of how people change: Applications to addictive behaviors. *American Psychologist, 47,* 1102–1114.

Prochaska, J. O., & Norcross, J. C. (1998). *Systems of psychotherapy: A transtheoretical analysis* (4th ed.). Pacific Grove, CA: Brooks/Cole.

Prochaska, J. O., Norcross, J. C., & DiClemente, C. C. (1995). *Changing for good.* New York: Avon.

Prochaska, J. O., Norcross, J. C., Fowler, J., Follick, M., & Abrams, D. B. (1992). Attendance and outcome in a work-site weight control program: Processes and stages of change as process and predictor variables. *Addictive Behaviors, 17,* 35–45.

Related Topics

Chapter 47, "Thumbnail Systematic Assessment and Treatment Matching"

Chapter 48, "Psychotherapy Treatment Plan Writing"

50   ENHANCING ADHERENCE

Mireika Kobayashi, Thomas P. Smith, & John C. Norcross

Patient adherence is crucial for treatment success; conversely, failure to adhere is a frequent reason for therapeutic failure. The term *compliance* typically refers to the extent to which patients obediently and faithfully follow health care providers' instructions, assignments, and prescriptions. By contrast, the term *adherence* implies a more active, voluntary, and collaborative involvement of the patient in a mutually acceptable course of behavior that produces a desired preventive or therapeutic result (Meichenbaum & Turk, 1987). For this reason, we have chosen to use *adherence*, although the literature employs both terms.

The following guidelines are empirically supported and clinically tested methods for enhancing adherence. These are drawn from literature reviews, principally those of Meichenbaum and Turk (1987) and DiMatteo and DiNicola (1982).

- *Establish an open and honest partnership with the patient:* Research suggests that establishing a "partnering" relationship rather than an "authoritative" one can significantly enhance the accurate reporting of adherence difficulties by patients (e.g., Stone, 1979). Adherence has been found to be positively correlated with patients' perceptions of their physician's friendliness, caring, and interest (DiMatteo & DiNicola, 1982).

- *Listen to the patient:* Improve communication by involving patients in planning and implementing their treatment program, which involves listening to the patient's ideas and opinions. Pick up on any negative feedback. Nonadherence has been found to be correlated with difficulties in communication (DiMatteo & DiNicola, 1982).
- *Educate the patient:* Provide patients with information about their present condition, as well as treatment recommendations and adherence-enhancing strategies via, for instance, information booklets and videotapes. By gaining knowledge, patients are more likely to follow and understand the treatment regimen.
- *Cultivate positive expectations:* Orleans, George, Houpt, and Brodie (1985) discovered that the single biggest obstacle to getting physicians to help their patients with health behaviors is the physician's pessimism about people's ability to change. Numerous studies have shown that if physicians take a few minutes to counsel their patients about quitting smoking, they can double the number of their patients who are not smoking at the end of a year. Similarly, Leedham, Meyerowitz, Muirhead, and Frist (1995) found that positive expectations were associated with postoperative adherence behavior in transplant patients.
- *Give the patient a range of assignments from which to choose:* Research indicates that greater adherence is achieved if the patient is given a choice in making a decision. This may nurture the collaborative relationship and patient involvement in treatment planning.
- *Prescribe a self-care regimen that takes into account the patient's daily schedule:* Integrate the regimen into the patient's normal life. Cultural norms for behavior and cultural values are important factors that influence compliance. For example, a dietary regimen that does not fit easily into the dietary prescriptions of the patient's culture is certain to be ignored or, at best, followed inconsistently. Patients are both willing and able to make behavioral changes that conform to their social and cultural norms.

- *Keep the prescription as simple and concise as possible:* The more complex a prescription is, the more likely the nonadherence. Stone (1979), for example, found that the rate of nonadherence increases from 15% with only one drug prescribed, to 25% with two or three prescribed, to 35% when more than five drugs are prescribed.
- *Give clear instructions on the exact treatment regimen, preferably in writing:* Clear and explicit information is vital when prescribing a treatment regimen, so much so that its provision can, in some situations, completely solve the nonadherence problem. For example, patients must be told to take their psychotropic medication even after their symptoms disappear. This specific communication must be provided because "feeling better" is often mentioned by patients as the reason for discontinuing their medication (Meichenbaum & Turk, 1987).
- *Evaluate patient understanding:* The client must have an understanding of the treatment regimen in order to adhere to and maintain it. Ask the patient to repeat and/or demonstrate what is requested to be done. Clarify misunderstandings and reinforce the request.
- *Use behavioral contracting:* Behavioral contracts define the patient's mutual participation and responsibility, actively involve the patient in the therapeutic decision-making process, provide additional incentives (rewards) for achievement of treatment objectives, clarify mutually determined treatment goals, and minimize confusion (Meichenbaum & Turk, 1987). For all these reasons, contracts have been found to enhance adherence in both adult and child populations; however, they do not guarantee long-term maintenance.
- *Employ behavioral cues:* Multiple studies over the years have demonstrated that response priming increases outpatient use of prescribed medication. Similarly, cues such as calendars, linking treatment to other daily activities, and written reminders on the re-

frigerator or mirror have been shown to be successful for long-term adherence.

- *Teach and employ stimulus control:* Stimulus control—avoiding or countering stimuli that elicit problem behaviors—is one of the least frequently used but most powerful behavioral methods available to self-changers in their struggles with maintenance (Prochaska, Norcross, & DiClemente, 1994). Work with patients to identify stimulus control procedures that can restructure their home and work environments. Do not assume that patients will automatically employ obvious methods, such as removing alcohol or fattening foods from their homes or work sites.

- *Keep an active follow-up appointment:* Give a specific time and date for follow-up appointments. Call if an appointment is missed and discuss reasons for it. Research by DiMatteo, Sherbourne, Hays, and Ordway (1993) showed that adherence was higher among health care providers who made definite follow-up appointments.

- *Use appointment scheduling and reminder postcards:* Wolosin (1990) studied the effects of such techniques on women's likelihood of complying with recommendations for mammography screening. Women in one group were instructed to make appointments for themselves, whereas women in another group had appointments scheduled for them at the visit, which was followed up with a reminder postcard. The women who received scheduled appointments and reminder postcards had higher rates of adherence (73%) than did those who had to make their own appointments (54%).

- *Facilitate goal setting:* The health care professional must help patients set appropriate, explicitly defined, achievable goals. Studies show that subjects who use short-term or proximal rather than long-term or distal goals are most successful at maintenance (Meichenbaum & Turk, 1987).

- *Help clients set priorities:* One study with older adults examined obstacles to adherence and reported that some of the most common reasons for nonadherence included side effects, interference with vacation plans, unrelated illness, forgetting, and competing out-

side stressors (Atwood, Haase, Rees-McGee, & Blackwell, 1992). Health care professionals can help patients prioritize their competing demands.

- *Encourage self-monitoring and self-management:* These strategies help the client discover an appropriate focus for intervention, provide a baseline prior to treatment, identify antecedents and consequences of behavior problems, assist the patient in the actual adjustment to the treatment regimen, and lead to a better understanding of the disease (Meichenbaum & Turk, 1987). Self-monitoring and self-management are probably best used in conjunction with other behavioral measures.

- *Provide feedback on clients' progress and develop positive reinforcers for self-regulation:* The attainment of treatment goals is more likely if performance feedback is included. Such feedback should be accompanied by advice and encouragement from the clinician. The client is more likely to change if he or she notices present behavior and becomes aware of what is and is not being done.

- *Teach problem-solving skills:* Some researchers have increased adherence by having patients engage in a verbal and written evaluation of the anticipated benefits and costs of following a treatment regimen (e.g., Hoyt & Janis, 1975; Prochaska, DiClemente, & Norcross, 1992). Such decisional balance methods have been used successfully in fostering adherence in several clinical populations (e.g., chronic pain patients, cancer patients, alcoholics, obese patients).

- *Teach relapse prevention skills:* Relapse prevention is a self-control program designed to teach individuals who are trying to change their behavior how to anticipate and cope with relapse (see chapter 52). Repeated relapses can lower self-efficacy and the likelihood of sticking to future commitments. Distinguish between slips and falls (lapses and relapses), assist patients in creating "reminder cards" (what to do if they slip), and help them recognize that a slip need not necessarily lead to a fall.

- *Use graduated implementation, especially*

for complex regimens: Breaking the regimen down into a series of simple steps makes it manageable. For example, a patient who is ultimately trying to stop smoking may begin by cutting out a few cigarettes each day rather than going "cold turkey."

- *Acknowledge and reinforce efforts to adhere at each appointment:* The frequent use of rewarding communication strengthens reinforcement expectancies and patient adherence (Klingle & Burgoon, 1995).
- *Involve significant others, such as the patient's spouse, children, relatives, friends, and neighbors:* The treatment regimen should ideally be congruent with the patient's social, cultural, and environmental milieu. Those who are closest to the patient are influential in determining health beliefs and in maintaining health-related behavior.
- *Involve adjunctive services:* Take advantage of the multitude of community resources for education, support, and assistance. These include, to name a few, pharmacists, physical therapists, health educators, and self-help groups. Multimedia interventions, such as television programs, pamphlets, and community meetings, may also help to strengthen treatment adherence.
- *Repeat everything:* Information that is repeated is more likely to be retained and recalled than information that is not. Supplementing oral instructions with written communication is preferred. Written instructions can be referred to repeatedly by the patient.

No single intervention, by itself, is a self-sustaining panacea for long-term adherence. Multiple interventions must continue to be applied as long as adherence is required, especially in the instance of permanent lifestyle changes (see Cameron & Best, 1987; Prochaska et al., 1994).

References & Readings

Atwood, J. R., Haase, J., Rees-McGee, M. S., & Blackwell, G. (1992). Reasons related to adherence in community-based field studies. *Patient Education and Counseling, 19,* 251–259.

Azrin, N. H., & Powell, J. (1969). Behavioral engineering: The use of response priming to improve prescribed self-medication. *Journal of Applied Behavior Analysis, 2,* 39–42.

Cameron, R., & Best, J. A. (1987). Promoting adherence to health behavior change interventions: Recent findings from behavioral research. *Patient Education and Counseling, 10,* 139–154.

DiMatteo, M. R., & DiNicola, D. D. (1982). *Achieving patient compliance: The psychology of the medical practitioner's role.* Elmsford, NY: Pergamon Press.

DiMatteo, M. R., Sherbourne, C. D., Hays, R. D., Ordway, L., Kravitz, R. L., McGlynn, E. A., Kaplan, S., & Rogers, W. H. (1993). Physicians' characteristics influence patients' adherence to medical treatment: Results from the Medical Outcomes Study. *Health Psychology, 12,* 93–102.

Falvo, D. R. (1994). *Effective patient education: A guide to increased compliance.* Gaithersburg, MD: Aspen.

Haynes, R. B., Wang, E., & Da Mota Gomes, M. (1987). A critical review of interventions to improve compliance with prescribed medications. *Patient Education and Counseling, 10,* 155–166.

Hoyt, M. F., & Janis, I. L. (1975). Increasing adherence to a stressful decision via a motivational balance sheet procedure: A field experiment. *Journal of Personality and Social Psychology, 31,* 833–839.

Klingle, R. S., & Burgoon, M. (1995). Patient compliance and satisfaction with physician influence attempts: A Reinforcement Expectancy Approach to compliance-gaining over time. *Communication Research, 22,* 148–187.

Leedham, B., Meyerowitz, B. E., Muirhead, J., & Frist, W. H. (1995). Positive expectations predict health after heart transplantation. *Health Psychology, 14,* 74–79.

Meichenbaum, D., & Turk, D. C. (1987). *Facilitating treatment adherence: A practitioner's guidebook.* New York: Plenum Press.

Orleans, C. T., George, L. K., Houpt, J. L., & Brodie, K. H. (1985). Health promotion in primary care: A survey of U.S. family practitioners. *Preventive Medicine, 14,* 636–647.

Prochaska, J. O., DiClemente, C. C., & Norcross, J. C. (1992). In search of how people change. *American Psychologist, 47,* 1102–1114.

Prochaska, J. O., Norcross, J. C., & DiClemente, C. C. (1994). *Changing for good.* New York: Avon.

Stone, G. C. (1979). Patient compliance and the role

of the expert. *Journal of Social Issues, 35,* 34–59.

Wolosin, R. J. (1990). Effect of appointment scheduling and reminder postcards on adherence to mammography recommendations. *Journal of Family Practice, 30,* 542–547.

51 EARLY TERMINATION AND REFERRAL OF CLIENTS IN PSYCHOTHERAPY

Manferd D. Koch

Early identification of a nontherapeutic client-therapist relationship is important in designing strategies for effective treatment intervention. Responsibility is placed on the therapist to construct a therapeutic environment where healthy change can occur. When a therapeutic impasse develops, clinicians are encouraged to undergo self-evaluation and make every attempt to facilitate progress by considering alternative treatment approaches, consulting with colleagues, and seeking formal supervision. Certain problems and populations require specific skills for effective intervention, and client-therapist mismatches may become inefficient or even countertherapeutic. An individual therapist is not expected to have the specific expertise necessary to treat all clinical populations; therefore, referral of the client to another practitioner may be indicated. Koocher (1995) suggests that therapists learn to identify clients with whom they cannot or should not work and refer them immediately and appropriately to avoid causing the client personal discomfort or stress. One or more of the following issues may be a potential reason to refer a client to another psychotherapist:

- *Competence to treat:* A cornerstone of American Psychological Association (APA) ethical principles is to maintain high standards of competence by providing services for which one is qualified (American Psychological Association, 1992). Historically, therapists have demonstrated competence through education, training, experience, research, licensure, and recognition by colleagues. Technical competencies may be demonstrated by adherence to a training manual for specific therapies, such as experiential therapy (Greenberg, Rice, & Elliot, 1993). General abilities like sensitivity and insightfulness are harder to demonstrate. The boundaries of a therapist's competence may be questioned in malpractice actions when the therapist has been found to have used nontraditional therapies, to have limited experience with a unique cultural population, to have had little training in working with addiction or suicide, or to have not restricted practice. Limited self-study may not be sufficient to demonstrate competence. Formal continuing education provided by professional organizations is essential given the knowledge explosion in psychology, where the half-life of professional competence may be 10 years.

- *Dual relationships:* In psychotherapy, dual relationships occur when the therapist, the person in power, enters into a significantly different relationship with the client. Whether sequential or concurrent, such relationships may unintentionally produce inappropriate influence over the client and impair the therapist's judgment by blurring and distorting professional boundaries. When in doubt, the therapist should consult with the client and colleagues concerning possible adverse consequences prior to the development of potential dual relationships, such as therapist and social friend, therapist and business partner, and therapist and supervisor or teacher (Bennett, Bryant, VandenBos, & Greenwood, 1990). Sexual relationships with clients in therapy are always judged to be exploitative, forbidden, and in several states a felony crime. Nonerotic touching of clients in therapy is controversial and may be misinterpreted as sexual. Bartering for services and accepting gifts are questionable practices and should be avoided except in unusual circumstances and with the consultation of colleagues. Referral may be necessary when dual relationships are unavoidable and are deemed to be harmful or exploitative.

- *Countertherapeutic transference:* A client may develop unconscious feelings and behaviors toward a therapist based on significant relationships and conflicts originating early in the client's life. Such transference may eventually result in the client's having a positive infatuation toward the therapist or acting as if the therapist were infallible. Reliving previously repressed positive feelings in the form of a transference neurosis may have therapeutic value. However, the outcome of the therapy is dependent on the therapist's helping the client analyze and deal with maladaptive transference styles. In some cases, clients are so fearful of change that they refuse to abandon positive transference; consequently, the therapy should terminate, since continuation is not likely to produce significant change. In other instances, the client may quickly devalue the therapist and develop negative transference when the therapist cannot fulfill all of the client's needs. In other cases, transference is negative initially, and the client acts out feelings of mistrust, ambivalence, hostility, or aggression almost from the inception. The client who develops strong negative transference may be unconsciously motivated to act out hostile feelings in an escalating fashion and to passive-aggressively sabotage the therapy, even becoming suicidal and in rare instances homicidal. A client's verbal abuse and threats of physical harm can produce extreme anxiety and concerns about self-preservation for the therapist (Maier, 1993). Such actions on the part of the client and reactions from the therapist are countertherapeutic and potentially dangerous. These actions indicate that consultation with colleagues, referral to another therapist with different skills, or placement in a controlled facility is appropriate.

- *Unresolvable countertransference:* Subjective reactions of the therapist toward the client are termed *countertransference*. As with transference, these feelings may be positive, such as being overly attracted and solicitous toward a client, or negative, as in disliking and acting in a rejecting fashion toward the client. Therapist reactions may be the consequence of the manner in which the client treats the therapist, unresolved issues on the part of the therapist, or a combination of both. Positive and negative reactions of the therapist are real and need to be recognized but not acted out toward the client. In some instances, countertransference feelings may contain important information that could exert a therapeutic effect when shared with the client. Therapists can use their reactions to help the client understand the impact the client has on relationships with significant others. It is a therapeutic skill to recognize one's personal attitudes, feelings, and biases and not act them out in the therapy. Eventually therapists will encounter people who make them feel angry or frustrated or whom they simply dislike. Every attempt should be made by the therapist to deal with countertransference issues, including consultation, supervision, and personal therapy. However, if these actions are not productive, referral is indicated, since strong unresolved positive or negative feelings and actions toward the client will inevitably result in dissolution of the therapeutic relationship (Kleinke, 1993).

- *Failure to form a therapeutic alliance:* To make progress in therapy, a client and therapist must form a working alliance with agreed-upon goals, rules, and responsibilities. A productive alliance involves bonding together and collaborating to accomplish the tasks of the therapy. Misalliance can be the consequence of the actions or failure to act on the part of either the client or the therapist. The therapist may contribute to the misalliance through poorly designed, planned, and executed interventions; inappropriate attitudes; and lack of self/other understanding and by allowing disruptive outside influences to enter the therapy. Clients may believe that benefit should be derived solely from efforts on the part of the therapist, without active client participation. Others resist entering into a closely bonded relationship, while the fear of change may keep some clients from forming an alliance. Therapist tolerance for maladaptive acts during therapy inadvertently encourages the continuation of problematic behaviors outside of therapy. Strupp (1980) found little evidence that therapists confronted clients' hostility and negativity. Often a poor therapy outcome was the consequence of a negative cycle of client hostility and therapist counterhostility, ultimately destroying the therapeutic alliance. If it becomes clear after observation and consultation that elements of the client-therapist interaction block productive work, transferring the client should be considered.

- *Resistance and therapeutic impasse:* Analysis of resistance has been a central element of analytic therapy. Because therapy can be painful and threatens current psychic structures, clients maintain their defenses, which control anxiety. Typically, resistance on the part of the client results from the fear that change will force one to give up a desired object, feeling, or behavior. The therapist should accept the existence of this process while at the same time helping the client identify what is threatening. Resistance may take the form of withholding information, attempts to manipulate the therapist, violating rules of the therapy, and even open hostility. Transference resistance is the consequence of dynamic issues between therapist and client, which typically are a repetition of earlier modes of interacting with significant others. Another form of resistance is the result of the client's belief that talk therapy will not be useful in problem solving, while others may experience therapist intervention as a loss of personal freedom. When resistance hinders the process of change, therapists should encourage the client to work through the dysfunctional resistance. Nevertheless, resistance may become so strong that it curtails effective treatment and results in a therapeutic impasse. Therapists may also impede the therapeutic process by engaging in counterresistance, which serves to preserve the therapist's psychological status quo. This results in therapist and client collusion to preserve and defend dysfunctional role interactions (Stearn, 1993). When these conditions occur, referral to another therapist with different skills is indicated.

- *Compassion fatigue:* It is essential that therapists maintain their own mental health when working with others. Therapists should be aware of signs of fatigue, distress, burnout, or other impairment within themselves (Bennett et al., 1990). *Compassion stress* and *compassion fatigue* are terms applied to the effects felt by mental health professionals who work repeatedly with highly traumatized people. Therapists are encouraged to recognize their shortcomings and special vulnerabilities to stress and fatigue and to develop strategies for prevention of compassion fatigue (Figley, 1995). Some categories of clients are more demanding, difficult to treat, and problematic than others. Clients with borderline personality disorder, severe depression, terminal illness, psychosis, or suicidal or homicidal tendencies or those who have recently lost a child may be emotionally taxing for the therapist. Professionals are wise to restrict their caseload to only a few of these difficult clients at any one time. After working extensively with emotionally draining clients, the mental health professional may experience signs of burnout, which result in increased mental and physical fatigue, irritability, distancing from clients, and impairment of competence to treat. Because it is essential that therapists maintain emotional integrity until their own mental well-being is restored, they should refer rather than treat additional demanding clients.

References & Readings

American Psychological Association (1992). Ethical principles of psychologists and code of conduct. *American Psychologist, 47,* 1597–1611.

Bennett, B. E., Bryant, B. K., VandenBos, G. R., & Greenwood, A. (1990). *Professional liability and risk management.* Washington, DC: American Psychological Association.

Figley, C. R. (1995). Compassion fatigue: Toward a new understanding of the cost of caring. In B. H. Stamm (Ed.), *Secondary traumatic stress: self-care issues for clinicians, researchers, and educators* (pp. 3–25). Lutherville, MD: Sidran.

Greenberg, L. S., Rice, L. N., & Elliott, R. (1993). *Facilitating emotional change: The moment-by-moment process.* New York: Guilford Press.

Kleinke, C. L. (1993). *Common principles of psychotherapy.* Pacific Grove, CA: Brooks/Cole.

Koocher, G. P. (1995). Ethics in psychotherapy. In B. Bongar & L. E. Beutler (Eds.), *Comprehensive textbook of psychotherapy: Theory and practice* (pp. 456–473). New York: Oxford University Press.

Maier, G. J. (1993). Management approaches for the repetitively aggressive patient. In W. H. Sledge & A. Tasman (Eds.), *Clinical challenges in psychiatry* (pp. 181–213). Washington, DC: American Psychiatric Association.

Stearn, H. S. (1993). *Resolving counter-resistance in psychotherapy.* New York: Brunner/Mazel.

Strupp, H. H. (1980). Success and failure in time-limited psychotherapy: Further evidence. *Archives of General Psychiatry, 37,* 947–954.

Related Topics

52 GUIDELINES FOR RELAPSE PREVENTION

Lisa J. Roberts & G. Alan Marlatt

Relapse is the most common outcome for alcohol and substance abuse treatment programs with abstinence as the goal. In a classic review of outcome literature on alcoholics, heroin addicts, and habitual smokers, relapse curves across these different substances showed a strikingly similar pattern. Within 3 months of treatment completion, nearly two thirds of all the research participants had relapsed, with a majority of these relapses occurring within the first month following treatment termination (Hunt, Barnett, & Branch, 1971).

Early treatment approaches focused on changing behavior (e.g., quitting substance use) but not necessarily on maintaining those changes over time. This resulted in a "revolving door" phenomenon in which treatment completors returned to treatment following each relapse. As a result of the problem of relapse, increasing emphasis has been placed on the maintenance stage of the behavior change process. Relapse prevention (RP) offers an alternative to the "revolving door" relapse problem through an integration of behavioral skills training, cognitive interventions, and lifestyle change procedures (Dimeff & Marlatt, 1995; Marlatt & Gordon, 1985). Although initially developed for alcoholics and drug addicts, the principles and concepts of RP have been adapted to other addictive disorders and problems of impulse control, including smoking (Rustin, 1990; Shiffman, 1982), overeating (Brownell & Rodin, 1990; Sternberg, 1985), sexual offenses (Laws, 1989; Pithers et al., 1989; Ward & Hudson, 1996), and violence (Gondolf, 1988). In addition, RP techniques have been developed for individuals with co-occurring substance abuse and other serious psychiatric disorders such as schizophrenia (Daley, 1994; Roberts, Shaner, Eckman, Tucker, & Vaccaro, 1992) and borderline personality disorder (Linehan & Dimeff, 1995).

CLINICAL PRACTICE OF RP

Relapse prevention is a cognitive-behavioral self-management training program designed to enhance the maintenance stage of the habit-change process. With skills training as the cornerstone, RP teaches clients how to (a) understand relapse as a process; (b) identify high-risk situations; (c) learn how to cope with craving and urges to engage in the addictive behavior; (d) reduce the harm of relapse by minimizing the negative consequences and learning from

the experience; and (e) achieve a balanced lifestyle, centered on the fulcrum of moderation. The following are brief descriptions of these key themes, along with suggestions on how to implement them in clinical practice.

Reframe Relapse as a Process

Begin by exploring the client's subjective associations with the term *relapse*. There are two common definitions of relapse, one in which the term refers to an outcome and implies a dichotomous outcome of a person either being ill and having symptoms or being well and without symptoms. A second definition views relapse as a process and implies stages of relapse over time. Many clients view relapse in dichotomous terms ("I was either able to attain my goal or not"). We use the term *lapse* as the first episode of the behavior after the commitment to abstinence. It is used to describe a single event, a reemergence of a previous habit, which may or may not lead to a state of relapse. When a slip is defined as a lapse, it implies that corrective action can be taken. Such setbacks can be viewed as opportunities for new learning rather than indications of personal failure or lack of motivation (Marlatt, 1996).

Identify High-Risk Situations

Next, teach the client to recognize the high-risk situations that may precipitate or trigger a relapse. A high-risk situation is one in which the individual's sense of perceived control is threatened. High-risk situations can include an environmental occurrence, an interpersonal interaction, or an internal factor, including affect, cognitions, or physiological state. The procedures available to identify high-risk situations differ based on whether or not the client is still engaged in the target behavior at the time of assessment.

1. *Self-monitoring:* Ask the client to keep a continuous (usually daily) record of the target behavior (what time the behavior began and ended, amount consumed, amount of money spent, etc.), along with a brief description of such additional factors as set-

ting (where, who was present, doing what); events that may have occurred prior to the target behavior (what was happening, how you were feeling); amount consumed (be specific); and consequences (what happened, how you felt, what you were thinking). Self-monitoring can also be used to monitor urges to use, along with records of coping responses and whether or not the urge was followed by an addictive act. Self-monitoring can serve as both an assessment procedure and an intervention strategy, since the client's awareness of the target behavior increases as the assessment continues.

2. *Autobiographies:* Have clients provide a descriptive narrative of the history and development of their problem. Ask the client how and why he or she initiated or first became involved with the addictive behavior; how the patterns of engaging in the addictive behavior may have changed over time; what people, places, events, and so forth he or she associates with the addictive behavior.

3. *Other methods:* Numerous clinical aids have been developed by researchers and clinicians to help clients identify and prioritize their individual high-risk situations. These include the Inventory of Drinking Situations (Annis, 1982), the Inventory of Drug-Taking Situations (Annis, 1985), and the Identifying High-Risk Situations Inventory (Daley, 1986).

4. *Assess self-efficacy:* Once the high-risk situations have been identified, it is helpful to assess the client's degree of self-confidence in being able to resist urges to engage in the addictive behavior in those situations. One useful assessment tool is the Situational Confidence Questionnaire (Annis & Graham, 1988).

Learn How to Cope With Urges to Use in High-Risk Situations

1. *Assess coping skills:* Assessment of the client's coping skills is crucial since any situation can be considered high-risk to the extent that the person is incapable of responding to that situation with an appropriate coping response.

2. *Teach effective coping behaviors:* Next, teach the client to respond to cues (that either occur before or coexist with a high-risk situation) by engaging in an effective coping behavior. Coping skills can be behavioral (escape or avoidance), cognitive (advance planning, reminder of negative consequences, "urge surfing"), or a combination of the two. The goal is to teach clients how to plan ahead and respond to early warning signs of relapse. Discuss the role of cognitive setups, such as seemingly unimportant decisions, that may be warning signs of relapse.

The importance of skills training cannot be overemphasized. Relapse prevention combines practice in both general problem-solving skills and specific coping responses. Skills-training methods incorporate components of direct instruction, modeling and behavioral rehearsal and coaching, and feedback from the therapist. In those cases in which it is not practical to use new coping skills in real-life settings, the therapist can utilize imagery to represent high-risk situations.

Teach specific cognitive strategies, including "urge surfing" and reminding oneself of the potential negative consequences. Urge surfing is a metaphor for the conditioned response to stimuli associated with the addictive behavior. It is based on the analogy that urges are like ocean waves, in that they have a specific course of action, with a given latency of onset, intensity, and duration. Remind clients that these urges and craving responses will arise, subside, and then pass away on their own. Encourage the client to wait out the waxing and waning of the craving without engaging in the problem behavior. Eventually the internal pressure to respond will fade out through extinction.

Clients who are on the verge of using may only selectively attend to the positive expectancies of use. Help clients develop a decisional matrix that summarizes both immediate and delayed negative consequences of engaging in the behavior. A reminder card (also referred to as an *emergency card*) is one way of listing both cognitive and behavioral techniques that can be used in the event a client has an urge to use.

Train clients to be on the lookout for warning signs of impending high-risk situations and to take preventive action at the earliest possible point. Depending on the situation and the client's self-efficacy, the recommended action might be to avoid the high-risk situation. However, not all high-risk situations can be identified in advance. Many situations arise suddenly without warning, for example, being on a date with a supposed nonuser who offers drugs. In this type of situation, the individual must rely on previously acquired coping responses. Emphasize that the earlier one intervenes in the chain of events leading up to a high-risk situation, the easier it will be to prevent relapse.

Minimize the Negative Consequences of Relapse by Learning From the Experience

1. *Explain the AVE:* The client's attributional response to a slip can further increase the probability of a full-blown relapse. Clients who view relapse in dichotomous terms may believe that there is no going back once the line has been crossed. The *abstinence violation effect* (AVE) describes this transgression. The AVE results from two key cognitive-affective elements: cognitive dissonance (conflict and guilt) and a personal attribution effect (blaming oneself as the cause of the relapse). Teach the client that a slip does not have to turn into a full-blown relapse. In addition, the eventual outcome of a lapse may not always be negative. It is possible that a lapse may turn out to be a valuable learning experience that raises consciousness and teaches the client information about sources of life stress that need attending to.

2. *Conduct relapse debriefings:* One way to learn from lapses and relapses is through the use of relapse debriefings. Explore all aspects of the chain of events leading up to the relapse (or a particular temptation or lapse), including details concerning the high-risk situation, alternative coping responses, and inappropriate and appropriate cognitions. This process may be conducted in an individual or group format.

Achieve Lifestyle Balance That Is Centered on the Fulcrum of Moderation

Intervene in the client's overall lifestyle to increase capacity to deal with perceived hassles (shoulds) and perceived pleasures or self-fulfillment (wants). A key goal for lifestyle intervention is to provide alternative sources of reward and to replace the addictive behavior with other positive activities or positive addictions. A positive addiction is a behavior that may be experienced negatively at first but is highly beneficial in terms of the long-range effects. Examples include aerobic exercise and relaxation training.

EFFECTIVENESS OF RP

Carroll (1996) reviewed the literature on controlled clinical trials that have evaluated RP in the treatment of smokers, alcoholics, and drug users. Across substances, RP was found to be generally effective compared with no-treatment controls, whereas evidence regarding the superiority of RP relative to other active treatments is less consistent. Another interesting finding was that some RP treatment outcome studies showed delayed emergence of effects. In her study comparing RP and pharmacotherapy in the treatment of cocaine abuse, Carroll found that only those subjects who received RP showed significant continuing improvement at the 1-year follow-up. This delayed emergent effect is consistent with the skills acquisition basis of this approach. As with learning any new skill, clients become more experienced in acquiring and performing the skills, and their overall performance should improve over time.

References & Readings

Annis, H. M. (1982). *Inventory of drinking situations.* Toronto: Addiction Research Foundation.

Annis, H. M. (1985). *Inventory of drug-taking situations.* Toronto: Addiction Research Foundation.

Annis, H. M., & Davis, C. S. (1989). Relapse prevention. In R. K. Hester & W. R. Miller (Eds.), *Handbook of alcoholism treatment approaches:*

Effective alternatives (pp. 170–182). Elmsford, NY: Pergamon Press.

Annis, H. M., & Graham, J. M. (1988). *Situational confidence questionnaire (SCQ-39) user's guide.* Toronto: Addiction Research Foundation.

Brownell, K. D., Marlatt, G. A., Lichtenstein, E., & Wilson, G. T. (1986). Understanding and preventing relapse. *American Psychologist, 41,* 765–782.

Brownell, K. D., & Rodin, J. (1990). *The weight maintenance survival guide.* Dallas: LEARN Education Center.

Carroll, K. M. (1996). Relapse prevention as a psychological treatment: A review of controlled clinical trials. *Experimental and Clinical Psychopharmacology, 4,* 29–36.

Chiauzzi, E. J. (1991). *Preventing relapse in the addictions: A biosocial approach.* Elmsford, NY: Pergamon Press.

Daley, D. (1986). *Relapse prevention workbook for recovering alcoholics and drug dependent persons.* Holmes Beach, FL: Learning Publications.

Daley, D. (1994). *Preventing relapse: Dual diagnosis workbook series.* Center City, MN: Hazelden.

Dimeff, L. A., & Marlatt, G. A. (1995). Relapse prevention. In R. Hester & W. Miller (Eds.), *Handbook of alcoholism treatment approaches* (2nd ed., pp. 176–194). Boston: Allyn and Bacon.

Gondolph, F. (1988). *Staying stopped: A gender-based approach to preventing violence.* Unpublished manuscript.

Gorski, T. T. (1990). The Cenaps model of relapse prevention: Basic principles and procedures. *Journal of Psychoactive Drugs, 22,* 125–133.

Hunt, W. A., Barnett, L. W., & Branch, L. G. (1971). Relapse rates in addiction programs. *Journal of Clinical Psychology, 27,* 455–456.

Laws, D. R. (Ed.) (1989). *Relapse prevention with sex offenders.* New York: Guilford Press.

Linehan, M. M., & Dimeff, L. A. (1995). *Dialectical behavior therapy manual of treatment interventions for drug abusers with borderline personality disorder.* Unpublished manuscript, University of Washington, Seattle.

Marlatt, G. A. (1996). Models of relapse and relapse prevention: A commentary. *Experimental and Clinical Psychopharmacology, 4,* 55–60.

Marlatt, G. A., & Gordon, J. R. (1985). *Relapse prevention: Maintenance strategies in the treatment of addictive behaviors.* New York: Guilford Press.

Monti, P. M., Abrams, D. B., Kadden, R. M., & Cooney, N. L. (1989). *Treating alcohol dependence: A coping skills training guide.* New York: Guilford Press.

Pithers, W. D., Martin, G. R., & Cumming, G. F. (1989). Vermont treatment programme for sexual aggressors. In D. R. Laws (Ed.), *Relapse prevention with sex offenders* (pp. 292–310). New York: Guilford Press.

Roberts, L. J., Shaner, A., Eckman, T. A., Tucker, D. E., & Vaccaro, J. V. (1992). Effectively treating stimulant-abusing schizophrenics: Mission impossible? *New Directions for Mental Health Services, 53,* 55–65.

Rustin, T. A. (1990). *Quit and stay quit: Medical treatment program for smokers.* Houston: Discovery Publishing.

Shiffman, S. (1982). Relapse following smoking cessation: A situational analysis. *Journal of Consulting and Clinical Psychology, 50,* 71–86.

Sternberg, B. (1985). Relapse in weight control: Definitions, processes, and prevention strategies. In G. A. Marlatt & J. Gordon (Eds.), *Relapse prevention: A self-control strategy for the maintenance of behavior change* (pp. 521–545). New York: Guilford Press.

Ward, T., & Hudson, S. M. (1996). Relapse prevention: A critical analysis. *Sexual Abuse: A Journal of Research and Treatment, 8,* 177–200.

Wilson, P. H. (1992). *Principles and practices of relapse prevention.* New York: Guilford Press.

Related Topics

53 PLAY THERAPY

Charles E. Schaefer

In 1997, the International Association of Play Therapy adopted the following definition of play therapy: "Play Therapy is the systematic use of a theoretical model to establish an interpersonal process wherein trained play therapists use the therapeutic powers of play to help clients prevent or resolve psychosocial difficulties and achieve optimal growth and development."

HISTORY AND MAJOR THEORIES

Play was first used directly in the therapy of children in 1919 by Hug-Hellmuth, who felt it was an essential part of child analysis. However, Anna Freud and Melanie Klein wrote extensively on how they adapted traditional psychoanalytic techniques for use with children by incorporating play into their sessions. The primary goal of their approach was to help children work through difficulties or trauma by helping them gain insight. Although both women relied on play as part of treatment, they used it in very different ways.

In 1928, Anna Freud began to use play as a way of luring children into therapy. The rationale behind this technique involved the concept of a therapeutic alliance. Traditional psychoanalysis held that the majority of the work of analysis was accomplished once the healthy aspects of the patient's personality joined forces with the analyst to work against the patient's unhealthy self.

This joining of forces was termed the *therapeutic alliance*. Anna Freud was aware that most children do not come to therapy voluntarily; they are brought by their parents, and it is the parents, not the child, who have a complaint. In addition, she realized that the therapeutic techniques of free association and dream analysis were foreign to most children's means of relating. Therefore, to maximize the ability of the child to form an alliance with the therapist, Freud used play, the child's natural medium, to build a relationship with her child patients. She used games and toys to interest the child in therapy and the therapist. As the child developed a satisfactory relationship, the emphasis of the sessions slowly shifted from a focus on play to a focus on more verbal interactions. Since most children were unable to make use of the technique of free association, Freud concentrated on the analysis of dreams and daydreams. She found that children were often as able and interested in the work of dream analysis as their adult counterparts. She used the analysis of daydreams to encourage free association with children. She found they were often able to create mental images and, while visualizing their fantasies, were able to verbalize them.

Whereas Anna Freud advocated using play mainly to build a strong, positive relationship between a child patient and the therapist, Melanie Klein (1932) proposed using it as a direct substitute for verbalizations. Klein considered play to be the child's natural medium of expression. She felt that children's verbal skills were insufficiently developed to express satisfactorily the complete thoughts and affects they were capable of experiencing. In Kleinian play therapy there is no introductory phase; the therapist simply starts out making direct interpretations of the child's play behavior. And whereas Freud thought that analysis was most appropriate for neurotic children whose disorders were primarily anxiety based, Klein thought that any child, from the most normal to the most disturbed, could benefit from her style of "play analysis."

In the late 1930s a technique of play therapy, now known as *structured therapy*, was developed using psychoanalytic theory as a basis for a more goal-oriented approach. All of the therapies in this category share (a) a psychoanalytic framework, (b) at least a partial belief in the cathartic value of play, and (c) the active role of the therapist in determining the course and focus of the therapy. Levy (1938) developed a technique called *release therapy* to deal with children who had experienced a specific traumatic event. Levy provided the child with materials and toys aimed at helping the child recreate the traumatic event through play. The child was not forced into a set play pattern, but very few toys were made available other than those the therapist thought might be used to cathect the emotionally loaded event. The concept of this type of therapy was derived from Sigmund Freud's notion of the repetition compulsion. The idea here is that given security, support, and the right materials, a child could replay a traumatic event over and over until he or she was able to assimilate its associated negative thoughts and feelings.

Also in 1938, Solomon developed a technique called *active play therapy*, which was to be used with impulsive/acting-out children. Solomon thought that helping a child to express rage and fear through the medium of play would have an abreactive effect because the child could act out without experiencing the negative consequences he or she feared. Through interaction with the therapist, the child learns to redirect the energy previously used in acting out toward more socially appropriate play-oriented behaviors. Solomon also placed a heavy emphasis on building children's concept of time by helping them to separate out anxiety over past traumas and future consequences from the reality of their present life situations.

Hambridge (1955) set up play sessions in much the same way as Levy, but he was even more directive in setting up the specifics of the play situation. Whereas Levy made available materials that would facilitate reenactment of

a traumatic event, Hambridge directly re-created the event or anxiety-producing life situation in play in order to aid the child's abreaction. This technique was not used in isolation but rather was introduced as a middle phase in an already established therapeutic relationship with a child—that is, when he was sure that the child had sufficient ego resources to be able to manage such a direct and intrusive procedure. After the situation was played out, Hambridge allowed the child to play freely for a time to recoup before leaving the safety of the playroom.

Also in the 1930s there emerged a number of play techniques generally grouped together under the heading of *relationship therapies*. The original philosophical basis for such therapy comes from the work of Otto Rank (1936), who stressed the importance of the birth trauma in development. He believed that the stress of birth causes persons to fear individuation and thus leads them to cling to their past. He de-emphasized the importance of transference and the examination of past events in therapy and instead focused on the realities of the patient-therapist relationship and the patient's life in the here and now.

Taft (1933), Allen (1942), and Moustakas (1959) adapted Rank's line of thinking to work with children in play therapy. All three emphasized the negative effect of the birth trauma on the ability of the child to form deep positive relationships. Because of this trauma, susceptible children may have difficulty separating from their primary caretaker, becoming either clingy and dependent or isolated and unable to relate sufficiently to others. Through therapy the child is given a chance to establish a deep, concerned relationship with a therapist in a setting that, simply because of the basic therapeutic agreement, is safer than any he or she will ever experience again. Taft adopted an existential approach and focused on the interaction between the child and the therapist and the ability of the child to learn to use that relationship effectively. Moustakas focused on helping the child to individuate, to explore interpersonal situations, while using the secure relationship with the therapist as a safe base. Despite the tendency to emphasize the child-therapist relationship and to de-emphasize the significance of past events, the relationship therapists still maintain a strong tie to psychoanalytic theory. Rather than completely abandoning this theoretical framework, they seem to have rejected the "rules" of analysis while retaining the essential element, the therapeutic relationship.

In 1959, Carl Rogers developed the client-centered approach to therapy with adults, which was modified by Virginia Axline (1947) into a play-therapy technique. This approach is based on the philosophy that children naturally strive for growth and that this natural striving has been subverted in the emotionally disturbed child. Client-centered play therapy aims to restore the balance between the child and his or her environment so as to facilitate natural, self-improving growth. The basic rules of Axline's play technique (Axline, 1947, pp. 73–74) are reproduced here because they have become well known as the credo of the approach.

1. The therapist must develop a warm, friendly relationship with the child. Good rapport should be established as soon as possible.
2. The therapist accepts the child exactly as he or she is.
3. The therapist establishes a feeling of permissiveness in the relationship so that the child feels free to express his or her feelings completely.
4. The therapist is alert to recognize the feelings the child is expressing and reflects those feelings back in such a manner that the child gains insight into his or her own behavior.
5. The therapist maintains a deep respect for the child's ability to solve his or her own problems if given an opportunity to do so. The responsibility to make choices and to institute change is the child's.
6. The therapist does not attempt to direct the child's actions or conversation in any manner. The child leads the way; the therapist follows.
7. The therapist does not attempt to hurry the therapy along. It is a gradual process and must be recognized as such by the therapist.

8. The therapist establishes only those limitations necessary to anchor the therapy to the world of reality and to make the child aware of his or her responsibility in the relationship.

In 1949, Bixler wrote an article entitled "Limits Are Therapy" and, in a sense, ushered in a movement in which the development and enforcement of limits were considered the primary vehicle of change in therapy sessions. Bixler (1949, p. 2) suggested that the therapist set limits with which he or she is comfortable, including the following:

1. The child should not be allowed to destroy any property or facilities in the room other than play equipment.
2. The child should not be allowed to physically attack the therapist.
3. The child should not be allowed to stay beyond the time limit of the interview.
4. The child should not be allowed to remove toys from the playroom.
5. The child should not be allowed to throw toys or other material out of the window.

Ginott (1959, 1961) felt that the therapist, by properly enforcing limits, can reestablish the child's view of himself or herself as protected by adults. To say that this technique stresses limits is not to say that other techniques do not use limits. Many other therapists and therapy techniques use limits explicitly, but they are not seen as the major effective element of the therapy. The rationale in limit-setting therapy is that children who manifest specific acting-out behavior can no longer trust adults to react in consistent ways and therefore must constantly test their relation to adults. Limits allow the child to express negative feelings without hurting others and subsequently fearing retaliation. Further, limits allow the therapist to maintain a positive attitude toward the child because he or she does not feel compelled to tolerate the child's aggressive acting out.

In the past decade, play therapy has further diversified with the introduction of cognitive-behavioral and family play-therapy approaches (Kaduson & Schaefer, 1997; Schaefer, 1993).

TRAINING

In the past 20 years, numerous play-therapy training sites have been established across the country. The International Association of Play Therapy, headquartered in Fresno, California, offers a wide variety of symposia and workshops at its annual conventions. This association has also developed criteria for professionals to become registered play therapists. In addition, the Play Therapy Training Institute, located in New Jersey, has trained thousands of play therapists through its certificate program. Information in the United States is available by contacting the author at Fairleigh Dickinson University, 139 Temple Avenue, Hackensack, NJ 07601.

PLAY TOYS AND MATERIALS

Play therapists differ in the type of toys and play materials they have in their playrooms. Typically, however, play therapists present their clients with the following play materials:

- *Family toys:* Dolls, doll house, people puppets, soldiers
- *Representational toys:* Cars, boats, planes, trucks
- *Expressive toys:* Paper, paints, crayons, marking pencils
- *Sensory toys:* Clay, Play-Doh, plasticine
- *Structural materials:* Building blocks, puzzles
- *Motor toys:* Balls, ring-toss, Nok-Out Bench
- *Dependency toys (furry toys):* Animals, puppet animals
- *Aggression toys:* Aggressive animals, Bobo the Clown, guns
- *Board games:* Range of therapeutic games

suitable for different developmental levels, ages 5 to adulthood.

References & Readings

Allen, F. (1942). *Psychotherapy with children.* New York: Norton.

Axline, V. (1947). *Play therapy.* Boston: Houghton-Mifflin.

Bixler, R. (1949). Limits are therapy. *Journal of Consulting Psychology, 13,* 1–11.

Freud, A. (1928). *Introduction to the technique of child analysis* (L. P. Clark, Trans.). New York: Nervous and Mental Disease Publishing.

Ginott, H. (1959). The theory and practice of therapeutic intervention in child treatment. *Journal of Consulting Psychology, 12,* 160–166.

Ginott, H. (1961). *Group psychotherapy with children.* New York: McGraw-Hill.

Hambridge, G. (1955). Structured play therapy. *American Journal of Orthopsychiatry, 25,* 601–617.

Hug-Hellmuth, H. (1921). On the technique of child-analysis. *International Journal of Psycho-Analysis, 2,* 287–305.

Kaduson, H., & Schaefer, C. E. (1997). *The playing cure.* Northvale, NJ: Jason Aronson.

Klein, M. (1932). *The psychoanalysis of childen.* London: Hogarth.

Levy, D. (1938). Release therapy in young children. *Psychiatry, 1,* 387–389.

Moustakas, C. (1959). *Psychotherapy with children.* New York: Harper and Row.

Rank, O. (1936). *Will therapy.* New York: Knopf.

Rogers, C. (1959). A theory of therapy, personality, and interpersonal relationships as developed in the client-centered framework. In S. Koch (Ed.), *Psychology: A study of science* (Vol. 3). New York: McGraw-Hill.

Schaefer, C. E. (1993). *Therapeutic powers of play.* Northvale, NJ: Jason Aronson.

Solomon, J. (1938). Active play therapy. *American Journal of Orthopsychiatry, 8,* 479–498.

Taft, J. (1933). *The dynamics of therapy in a controlled relationship.* New York: Macmillan.

Related Topics

54 CHILD SEXUAL ABUSE
Treatment Issues

Kathryn Kuehnle

1. Sexually abused children are a heterogeneous group.

- Child sexual abuse is not a discrete clinical syndrome; rather, it is a life event or a series of life events, wherein not all sexually abused children are traumatized by these experiences.
- There is no symptom that is characteristic of the majority of sexually abused children, nor is there a child sexual abuse syndrome. Sexually abused children exhibit a wide range of symptoms and symptom intensity, as well as an absence of symptomatology.
- As discussed by Friedrich (1990), sexual abuse events interact with a complex matrix of factors, including the abuse characteristics, family dynamics, caretaker response to the abuse allegation, involvement in the legal system, and the premorbid personality of the victim.
- Sexually abused children's diversity must be considered when planning treatment strategies. This diversity suggests that one type of therapy will not be appropriate or effective for all children.

2. Not all sexually abused children will require professional treatment.

- Substantial numbers of asymptomatic child victims have been found in almost every study of the impact of sexual abuse.

  - A number of research studies have found one quarter to one third of child victims to be without symptoms on the studies' measures.
  - In a review of research on the effects of child sexual abuse, Browne and Finkelhor (1986) found asymptomatic children had been abused for shorter periods of time, without force, violence, or penetration, by someone who was not a father figure, and were living in a supportive and relatively well-functioning family.
  - Because of their cognitive immaturity, toddler and preschool-age children may be at decreased risk for development of symptoms in response to sexual victimization when physical violence is absent.

- There may be two diverse groups of asymptomatic children: those who are resilient and dealing successfully with their abuse and those who suppress conflicts related to the abuse but remain distressed at another psychological level.

3. Mediating factors found to be important in the child victims' psychological recovery involve the cognitive processing of the event and family support.

- Research by Runyan, Everson, Edelsohn, Hunter, & Coulter (1988) has shown that levels of distress in sexually abused children, psychological symptomatology, and speed of recovery are related to parental support.

  - Family supportiveness may be a possible alternative explanation to apparent treatment effects for sexually abused children.

- Differences in cognitions (e.g., attributions, optimism, and positive reframing) that are developed by victims may mediate the consequences of the sexual abuse experience.

  - Parental support may influence the child victims' cognitions.

4. A review of 45 studies by Kendall-Tackett, Williams, and Finkelhor (1993) found that sexually abused children had more symptoms than nonsexually abused children, with abuse accounting for 15–45% of the variance.

- No one symptom characterized a majority of sexually abused children.

  - Posttraumatic stress symptoms, fears, behavior problems, sexualized behaviors, and poor self-esteem were the most frequently identified symptoms.
  - Some symptoms were more common to certain ages (e.g., running away and substance abuse for adolescents).

- Friedrich et al. (1992) found that children who demonstrated unusually high levels of sexualized behaviors had experienced more severe sexual abuse, force, or threat of death and a greater number of abusers.

5. Relevant to treatment is the question of whether the problems exhibited by the sexually abused children actually have been caused by the sexual abuse experience.

- Based on his review of methodological issues in the study of sexual abuse effects, Briere (1992) concluded that researchers have yet to determine (a) the premorbid functioning of sexually abused children and the degree to which the effects of sexual abuse represent preexisting risk factors or psychological disturbance; (b) the exact role of a coexisting pathogenic family environment and other forms of child maltreatment; or (c) the differential impact of social or demographic factors.

  - Incestuous families are often characterized by conflict between parents.
  - Deblinger (1994) postulated that aggression in some sexually abused children may be a modeled behavior rather than a symptom of sexual abuse due to the high rate of family violence that is found in families where intrafamilial sexual abuse occurs.

6. Before treatment goals can be developed, typical problem behaviors must be discriminated from symptoms of trauma.

- According to a review of developmental research by Kuehnle (1996, chapter 2), high percentages of nonsexually abused preschool and elementary school–age children in the general population exhibit various problems such as nightmares, sudden changes in mood, poor concentration, fearfulness, disobedience, and temper tantrums.

- Nonsexually abused children also are sexually active in a number of different ways throughout their development.

  - A discussion of sexual development by Kelley and Byrne (1992, chapter 7) identifies early sexual climaxes typically to be the result of masturbation, which may begin by 8 months of age.
  - Children ages 2 through 12 exhibit a wide variety of sexual behaviors (e.g., self-stimulation and exhibitionism) at relatively high frequencies, whereas children of this age exhibit adult sexual behaviors (e.g., oral sex and anal or vaginal penetration) at very low frequencies.
  - Friedrich, Grambsch, Broughton, Kuiper, and Beilke (1991) found that higher frequencies of sexual behavior were exhibited by sexually abused and nonsexually abused children with children's exposure to parental nudity, witnessing parental sexual behavior, and exposure to sexual behavior in the media.

7. Longitudinal studies show that symptomatology of some sexually abused children diminishes without therapy.

- Research studies indicate that the majority of children show signs of improvement over a 12- to 24-month period, especially in the areas of posttraumatic stress symptoms and fearfulness.
- Research findings on the spontaneous improvement of other factors such as withdrawal, acting out, and depression are variable.

8. A number of post–sexual abuse events may negatively affect recovery.

- Lack of support from the nonoffending parent.
- The experience of a stressful medical examination.
- Involvement in a criminal case that continues for a lengthy time period.
- Parents' belief that the event of sexual abuse has permanently psychologically damaged their child may negatively influence the child's attributions and self-perception.
- Therapy, in some cases, may be iatrogenic.

9. There is widespread belief that child sexual abuse frequently results in serious symptoms that may not surface for years (i.e., sleeper effects).

- The existence of sleeper effects has not been empirically established. Pathogenic family environments are a confounding factor.
- Some of the delayed sleeper effects (e.g., sexual aggression, substance abuse, proneness to revictimization) are thought to be triggered by later developmental changes that may not be accessible to therapy implemented during an earlier developmental stage.

10. Reviews by Finkelhor and Berliner (1995) and O'Donohue and Elliott (1992) of treatment outcome studies using single subject, pretest and posttest, experimental, and quasi-experimental designs show scientific research has not been extensive enough to prove the effectiveness of any type of sexual abuse treatment.

- Preliminary results are consistent with the findings from the general literature on child psychotherapy that no reliable significant differences for treatment outcome have been found between group, individual, or play therapies.
- Several important conclusions are derived from research regarding treatment of specific symptoms and behavior problems.
  - Some children do not improve as much as other children in the same treatment group.
  - The variables that distinguish sexually abused children who make significant improvement in treatment from children who make no improvement have not been identified.
  - Sexual problems and externalizing behaviors (e.g., aggression, acting out) are more resistant to treatment.
  - Preschool children's externalizing symptoms may be less resistant to change when the treatment intervention includes helping parents to manage the acting-out behaviors.
  - Internalizing behaviors (e.g., depression, fearfulness) appear to be less entrenched and less resistant to treatment.

11. Within the mental health field, "abuse-specific" therapy, which is primarily supportive and psychoeducational in nature, currently is a preferred approach for treating sexually abused children.

- "Abuse-specific" therapy is effectively used with victims who will benefit from supportive and educational interventions, including the following:
  - The processing of their sexual abuse memories.
  - Exposure to other victims (e.g., group therapy) to decrease feelings of stigmatization and isolation.
  - Encouragement of expression of abuse-related feelings (e.g., confusion, anger).
  - Clarification of pathological beliefs that might lead to negative self-attributions.
  - Development of skills to prevent future abuse.
- James (1989) suggests that abuse therapy may need to be developmentally sequenced based on cognitive reassessment that occurs as a result of developmental maturation.
  - Certain concepts may not be processed until the child reaches a specific developmental level.
  - Children may need to return to therapy as they mature and reprocess the abuse at a more sophisticated conceptual level (e.g., fear of becoming a perpetrator).

12. It is debatable whether all children who have experienced sexual abuse must process their abuse experience(s) in therapy.

- It is unknown whether expression of abuse memories is beneficial for all children or if repression of abuse memories is beneficial for some children.
- Gil (1996) cautions that premature or overzealous pursuit of traumatic memories prior to the development of coping strategies and reinforcement of internal resources may be iatrogenic.
- "Abuse-specific" therapy or elements of this therapy may be inappropriate with specific subgroups of victims.
  - Elements of "abuse-specific" therapy (e.g., encouragement of expression of abuse-related feelings) are inappropriate when sexual abuse remains a question and cannot be substantiated.
  - Elements of "abuse-specific" therapy (e.g., exposure to other victims' abuse histories) may be inappropriate for preschool children and children who are mentally retarded, are diagnosed

with pervasive developmental disorder, or show psychotic symptoms or significant mental illness in which perceptions are distorted and thinking processes are disturbed.

- "Abuse-specific" therapy, because it is primarily supportive and educational, may be less effective with certain behavioral problems, including sexual behavior problems and externalized problem behaviors that require more targeted and intensive interventions.

13. The approach of viewing the sequelae of sexual abuse as being treatable by modifications of standard treatments appears promising.

- Sexually abused children typically enter therapy because they have experienced a potentially traumatizing event. Based on multiple premorbid factors, they are a psychologically heterogeneous group.

  - Many other nonsexually abused children enter therapy because they are exhibiting an emotional, social, or behavior disorder and are part of a homogeneous group based on the disorder.

- Individual evaluations of sexually abused children can target behavioral symptoms and pathological cognitions in order to create homogeneous groups for specific treatment interventions.

  - Research by Deblinger, Lippmann, and Steer (1996) indicates that parent treatment only and parent-child treatment combined are most effective in decreasing externalizing behaviors, whereas child treatment only and parent-child treatment combined are most effective in decreasing overall PTSD symptomatology.
  - Research indicates that sexually inappropriate behaviors, regardless of the reasons for these behaviors, respond more readily to behavioral interventions than to play therapy or psychodynamic treatment.

- Treatment goals must attempt to specify the therapeutic interventions and which aspects of these interventions (e.g., content of treatment) are expected to impact which behavioral symptoms and/or pathological cognitions.
- The prophylactic benefit of therapy in preventing later deterioration has not been adequately tested.

14. The treatment outcome literature seems to best support the efficiency of behavioral and cognitive-behavioral interventions (Cohen & Mannarino, 1996; Deblinger, Lippmann, & Steer, 1996; Stauffer & Deblinger, 1996), but because of the paucity of treatment outcome research, the effectiveness of other treatment models cannot be ruled out.

- Many of the treatment studies using behavioral and cognitive-behavioral interventions with sexually abused children have relied on skills training—particularly coping skills, problem-solving skills, and communication skills.
- A clear relationship between treatment duration and effectiveness has not been found.

15. Conjoint or combined (i.e., separate parent and separate child) treatment of the nonoffending parent is emerging as a critical element in the treatment of sexually abused children.

- The nonoffending parent's emotional support has been found to be related positively to the child's postabuse functioning.
- Parents may experience adverse emotional responses to the sexual abuse of their children that may impede their ability to provide support.
- Conjoint treatment may decrease premature termination of treatment and facilitate generalization of treatment gains.

16. Prevention training may be an important component of treatment.

- Prevention training has been used in the treatment of sexually abused children in order to reduce the danger of revictimization, for which abused children are at high risk.
- Prevention training views self-protection as involving specific skills and techniques.

  - The most important technique is disclosure. Disclosure may not stop the occurrence of the initial abuse incident but may result in intervention.
  - Secondary benefits from the development of self-protection skills may include decreasing fear and increasing self-esteem.

17. Because of the potential conflict of interest between the roles of therapist and forensic evaluator, a number of professional organizations have advised their members not to engage in these dual roles.

- The therapist should delineate the parameters of his or her role to the child's parent(s). The therapist should make clear to the parent(s) that the therapist's role is to provide treatment.
- Children should not be provided therapy for sexual abuse if there is a question of whether the child is or is not a victim of sexual abuse.
- Even in cases where child sexual abuse cannot be substantiated, the child can be provided therapy with other problem- or symptom-focused goals.

References & Readings

Briere, J. (1992). Methodological issues in the study of sexual abuse effects. *Journal of Consulting and Clinical Psychology, 60*(2), 196–203.

Browne, A., & Finkelhor, D. (1986). The impact of sexual abuse: A review of the research. *Psychological Bulletin, 99*, 66–77.

Cohen, J. A., & Mannarino, A. P. (1996). A treatment outcome study for sexually abused preschool children: Initial findings. *Journal of the American Academy of Child and Adolescent Psychiatry, 35*, 42–50.

Deblinger, E. (1994, August). *Update on treatment outcome studies.* Paper presented at the American Psychological Association Convention, Los Angeles, CA.

Deblinger, E., Lippmann, J., & Steer, R. (1996). Sexually abused children suffering posttraumatic stress symptoms: Initial treatment outcome findings. *Child Maltreatment, 1*(4), 310–321.

Finkelhor, D., & Berliner, L. (1995). Research on the treatment of sexually abused children: A review and recommendations. *Journal of American Academy of Child and Adolescent Psychiatry, 34*, 1408–1423.

Friedrich, W. N. (1990). *Psychotherapy of sexually abused children and their families.* New York: Norton.

Friedrich, W. N., Grambsch, P., Broughton, D., Kuiper, J., & Beilke, R. (1991). Normative sexual behavior in children. *Pediatrics, 88*, 456–464.

Friedrich, W. N., Grambsch, P., Damon, L., Hewitt, S. K., Koverola, C., Lang, R. A., Wolfe, V., & Broughton, D. (1992). Child sexual behavior inventory: Normative and clinical contrasts. *Psychological Assessment, 4*, 303–311.

Gil, E. (1996). *Treating abused adolescents.* New York: Guilford Press.

James, B. (1989). *Treating traumatized children: New insights and creative interventions.* Lexington, MA: Lexington Books.

Kelley, L., & Byrne, D. (1992). *Exploring human sexuality.* Englewood Cliffs, NJ: Prentice-Hall.

Kendall-Tackett, K. A., Williams, L. M., & Finkelhor, D. (1993). Impact of sexual abuse on children: A review and synthesis of recent empirical studies. *Psychological Bulletin, 113*, 164–180.

Kuehnle, K. (1996). *Assessing allegations of child sexual abuse.* Sarasota, FL: Professional Resource Press.

O'Donohue, W. T., & Elliott, A. N. (1992). Treatment of the sexually abused child: A review. *Journal of Clinical Child Psychology, 21*, 218–228.

Runyan, D. K., Everson, M. D., Edelsohn, G. A., Hunter, W. M., & Coulter, M. L. (1988). Impact of legal intervention on sexually abused children. *Journal of Pediatrics, 113*, 647–653.

Stauffer, L., & Deblinger, E. (1996). Cognitive behavior groups for nonoffending mothers and their young sexually abused children: A preliminary treatment outcome study. *Child Maltreatment, 1*(1), 65–76.

Related Topics

55

PRINCIPLES OF TREATMENT WITH THE BEHAVIORALLY DISORDERED CHILD

Esther Calzada, Arwa Aamiry, & Sheila M. Eyberg

We provide a set of principles for effective psychosocial treatment of children and adolescents with conduct-disordered behavior to which psychologists may refer in preparation for treating these youngsters. The scope of this chapter is limited to children and adolescents between the ages of 2 and 16 years whose problems are related to disruptive behavior disorders, including attention-deficit/hyperactivity disorder, oppositional defiant disorder, and conduct disorder. The challenges to treatment presented by these children and their families are considerable. The following eight principles are designed to maximize treatment effectiveness.

ESTABLISHING AND MAINTAINING RAPPORT

To conduct effective psychotherapy with a disruptive child or adolescent, the psychologist must first establish a safe and comfortable atmosphere for the child in the therapeutic situation. Disruptive children may express their initial apprehensions through behaviors that reflect oppositionality or defiance of the unfamiliar situation in which they may not be voluntarily involved. Providing a structure for the child in the initial stages of therapy will reduce the child's anxiety and help to motivate him or her to participate. This can be accomplished, for example, by reading together *A Child's First Book About Play Therapy* (Nemiroff & Annunziata, 1990) for the 4- to 7-year-old child, which provides age-appropriate information about therapy. Older children also require age-appropriate information about the purpose and process of therapy, presented in a positive but noncoercive atmosphere of understanding and acceptance. To establish a therapeutic alliance, it is always necessary to convey respect for the child and to avoid judging (e.g., belittling, siding with third persons) or laughing at/minimizing problems.

Certain communication techniques help establish and maintain rapport. The use of paraphrasing, for example, through either reflective or summary statements, conveys genuine interest and concern for the child. Paraphrasing also increases the child's willingness to provide information and to consider it and enables the psychologist to verify understanding of that information. Phrasing questions in ways that avoid leading (e.g., closed-ended questions) or blaming (e.g., "why" questions) helps the child feel at ease and consequently increases his or her willingness to participate as well. With disruptive children, key strategies for managing behavior must also be used to keep therapy progressing productively that include, for example, not reinforcing an adolescent for unacceptable verbalizations that are part of the target problem constellation (such as lying, sassing) but conveying respect for both self and client in a matter-of-fact response.

CONSIDERING AGE AND DEVELOPMENTAL LEVEL OF CHILD

Children are constantly undergoing biological, cognitive, social, and affective changes. The span of childhood and adolescence is a disjointed period during which there are rapid shifts in what is deemed appropriate in children's thinking, feeling, and behaving. Thus many expressions of children in therapy are ones that would characterize maladjustment in older or younger children but have no clinical significance for their age-group. Psychologists who work with children must have strong academic grounding in child development but also must keep current with fads and trends by observing normal children at different ages with their peers and by examining children's media and other sources for developmental information.

It is important to keep in mind that a child's rate of development is often not consistent across developmental domains. Knowledge of the child's level of cognitive development is a critical domain in psychotherapy, for many potential therapeutic approaches are cognitive. Even psychologists are prey to assumptions about intellectual functioning based on a child's verbosity and attractiveness. In general, cognitive therapy components of treatment should be reserved for school-age children, although certain preschoolers with exceptional cognitive capacities will benefit from such approaches, just as certain school-age children will require a more concrete therapeutic approach. Cognitive tasks that involve long-term planning are generally reserved for adolescents at or above a 14-year level of cognitive functioning.

DETERMINING DEGREE OF PARENT INVOLVEMENT AND MOTIVATION

To a large extent, the motivation of the parents will determine whether the child remains in therapy. Parents who are not motivated to seek treatment for their child may skip appointments, arrive late, convey to the child that taking him or her to therapy is an inconvenience, or even sabotage therapy, for example, by criticizing the therapy or the therapist to the child. Through parent counseling that addresses the nature and causes of their child's disorder and the notion of a "no-fault disorder," the importance of their child's therapy, and the expected benefits for both the child and themselves, psychologists may increase a parent's motivation.

Among parents who are motivated to bring their child to therapy, there may be significant life stressors that make it difficult for them to do so. For example, it is not uncommon for a single working mother with several young children to feel overwhelmed by the practical issues of her child's therapy such as the financial responsibility, care of her other children, and transportation issues. Psychologists must address these issues before beginning treatment. By anticipating practical solutions to these common problems, psychologists prepare parents for possible obstacles and provide ways to overcome them.

The decision to involve parents in the child's treatment depends in large part on the degree to which the parents are involved in the child's life and the role their behavior plays in the maintenance of the child's symptoms. For most children and adolescents, it is important to involve their parents in treatment (McNeil, Hembree-Kigin, and Eyberg, 1996).

CONSIDERING PARENT PSYCHOPATHOLOGY

A child's psychological functioning is related to the psychological functioning of his or her own parents. Psychological dysfunction in a primary caregiver may contribute powerfully to maintenance of behavior problems in his or her children; conversely, children with disruptive behavior problems create stressful situations that may exacerbate the parent's dysfunction. Thus assessment of the parent and of the parent-child interaction must precede child treatment. To treat a child successfully, it may be necessary to provide or obtain treatment for the parent as well.

Parent psychopathology must also be considered as it relates to the assessment of the child. Parent interview and parent report measures are the most typical and easiest methods of assessing the child's problems for treatment. Yet parents with significant psychopathology are likely to provide a distorted description and to exaggerate in either direction. Thus, additional sources of information are critical for determining and guiding the course of treatment. These may include teacher rating scales, simple behavior coding of targeted problem behaviors in the session, or use of other informants or methods relevant to the treatment goals.

USING ASSESSMENT TO GUIDE TREATMENT

A thorough understanding of the affective, behavioral, and cognitive functioning of the child is necessary for choosing and implementing a successful treatment. To evaluate the affective and behavioral domains of the child's problems, multiple assessment measures with established validity and reliability—including self-report inventories, ratings by others, and direct observation measures—should be used. Multiple measures provide a fuller understanding of the presenting problem(s) and allow the psychologist to draw on more than a single source of information.

Measures of intellectual functioning and academic achievement are necessary to determine the mode of treatment (e.g., parent training, individual treatment), the type of treatment (e.g., behavioral, insight-oriented), the communication strategies that may be beneficial (e.g., interpretation, instruction), as well as the multiple considerations in the preparation of the individual treatment activities and homework (e.g., What can the child read? How far apart can tangible incentives be used effectively? To what degree can the child understand metaphors?).

The initial assessment must also incorporate a description of the family's strengths and weaknesses in terms of the affective, behavioral, and cognitive factors to provide an understanding of the context in which the child's problems exist. For example, factors such as strong parent-child bonding or the borderline intellectual functioning of parents would have implications for the child's treatment plan. Exploring the physical, social, and cultural environment of the family is also important for determining the resources available to the child and the limitations imposed by them. All these individual child and family factors must be considered in selecting the most effective treatment.

MAINTAINING TREATMENT INTEGRITY

Integrity of treatment refers to the degree of achievement of application of intended treatment. This would include adherence to the techniques that constitute theoretically driven therapies; to specific, session-by-session content and process elements of manualized treatment protocols; and to individual session outlines based on assessment information from the child and family in treatment. Treatment integrity is difficult to maintain with highly complex interventions or with children whose families have multiple social adversities and psychopathologies. Such problems are more common in the treatment of conduct-disordered children than in children with some other disorders, and psychologists must guard against unproductive sidetracking while still helping children and families cope with life events that impinge on the progress of therapy. The integrity of a treatment is protected by preparation of detailed session plans that include specific guidelines for others involved even minimally in the child's treatment, as well as circumspect implementation of the plans. Yeaton and Sechrest (1995) suggest that treatment integrity is best ensured by constant monitoring of the child's change.

PLANNING FOR GENERALIZATION OF TREATMENT

Generalization occurs when the outcome of treatment results in changes extraneous to the original targeted change. These effects should be sought across all settings important to the child's life and across all behaviors relevant to treatment goals. To obtain generalization, it is essential to identify target behaviors that occur in many situations and settings. For example, teaching a young noncompliant child to comply to adult requests will have greater consequence than teaching the child to feed the bird when reminded. Psychologists need to include generalization explicitly within the treatment plan by targeting behaviors most apt to be reinforced in dissimilar natural settings. Psychologists, too, must reinforce occurrences of prosocial behavior within the treatment session with defiant children. Another technique to intensify generalization is through the use of diverse stimulus and response exemplars that broaden the context in which the child learns new and adaptive behaviors; the more diversity, the greater the generalization (Stokes & Osnes, 1989).

EVALUATING TREATMENT PROGRESS AND OUTCOME

Although the most comprehensive assessment takes place at the beginning of treatment, ongoing assessment is necessary to guide the course of treatment. Throughout the treatment process, frequent and regular assessment allows the psychologist to time strategic changes and to change strategies when progress is not maintained. Ongoing assessment also provides an objective basis on which to determine treatment termination. Monitoring measures must be ones that can be completed quickly and easily and typically are brief rating scales or behavioral frequency counts of target behaviors collected from parents and teachers or by the psychologist during the session.

At the time of termination, treatment outcome assessment allows the psychologist to evaluate the progress of the child and family in a comprehensive and quantified way by read-ministering measures used at the initial assessment. One criterion by which outcome can be measured is the restoration of the child to a level of functioning attained before the problem(s) developed. Another criterion might be the functioning of the child at a level present in a normative, or peer-relevant, population. In some cases, the criterion might be the return of a child to school or to the home. In addition to the target goals of treatment, the psychologist should document the associated or generalized areas of change, as well as the areas in which problems remain.

Follow-up assessments serve to evaluate the long-term impact of treatment and provide important information to document the degree to which treatment effects last. For chronic conditions such as the disruptive behavior disorders, it is important to implement multiple strategies for maintenance (see Eyberg, Edwards, Boggs, & Foote, in press, for a review). The knowledge that the psychologist will be checking in on the child or family after treatment ends often serves to enhance treatment maintenance. A follow-up assessment can also catch early relapse and occasion a booster session to reverse a turnaround. Psychologists should program specific strategies for maintenance into each treatment plan; discussion and planning for maintenance and follow-up with the child and family are always an important part of the treatment termination process.

SUMMARY

The principles of psychosocial treatment of children with disruptive behavior disorders outlined here address the treatment process from the initial assessment through follow-up and maintenance. The principles are applicable to psychosocial treatments broadly, regardless of theoretical orientation. They highlight the uniqueness of the individual child and family, as well as characteristics shared by disruptive children in the therapeutic process. By following these principles, therapists who treat the consequential problems of children with behavior disorders will have maximal efficacy and the highest likelihood of success.

References & Readings

Adams, P. (1982). *A primer of child psychopathology* (2nd ed.). Boston: Little, Brown.

Eyberg, S. (1992). Assessing therapy outcome with preschool children: Progress and problems. *Journal of Clinical Child Psychology, 21*, 306–311.

Eyberg, S., Edwards, D., Boggs, S., & Foote, R. (in press). Maintaining the treatment effects of parent training: The role of "booster sessions" and other maintenance strategies. *Clinical Psychology: Science and Practice.*

Foote, R., Eyberg, S., & Schuhmann, E. (in press). Parent-child interaction approaches to the treatment of child conduct problems. In T. Ollendick & R. Prinz (Eds.), *Advances in clinical child psychology.* New York: Plenum Press.

Foster, S., Bell-Dolan, D., & Burge, D. (1988). Behavioral observation. In A. Bellack & M. Hersen (Eds.), *Behavioral assessment: A practical handbook* (pp. 119–160). Elmsford, NY: Pergamon Press.

Jacobson, N., & Truax, P. (1992). Clinical significance: A statistical approach to defining meaningful change in psychotherapy research. In A. Kazdin (Ed.), *Methodological issues and strategies in clinical research* (4th ed., pp. 631–648). Washington, DC: American Psychological Association.

Jensen, P., Hibbs, E., & Pilkonis, P. (1996). From ivory tower to clinical practice: Future directions for child and adolescent psychotherapy research. In E. Hibbs & P. Jensen (Eds.), *Psychosocial treatments for child and adolescent disorders: Empirically based strategies for clinical practice* (pp. 701–711). Washington, DC: American Psychological Association.

Kanfer, R., Eyberg, S., & Krahn, G. (1992). Interviewing strategies in the child assessment. In C. E. Walker & M. C. Roberts (Eds.), *Handbook of clinical child psychology* (2nd ed., pp. 49–62). New York: Wiley.

Kazdin, A. (1988). *Child psychotherapy: Developing and identifying effective treatments.* Elmsford, NY: Pergamon Press.

McNeil, C. B., Hembree-Kigin, T., & Eyberg, S. M. (1996). *Short-term play therapy for disruptive children.* King of Prussia, AL: Center for Applied Psychology.

Nemiroff, M. A., & Annunziata, J. (1990). *A child's first book about play therapy.* Washington, DC: American Psychological Association.

Reisman, J., & Ribordy, S. (1993). *Principles of psychotherapy with children* (2nd ed.). New York: Lexington Books.

Steiner, H. (1996). *Treating adolescents.* San Francisco: Jossey-Bass.

Stokes, T., & Osnes, P. (1989). An operant pursuit of generalization. *Behavior Therapy, 20,* 337–355.

Yeaton, W. H., & Sechrest, L. (1995). Critical dimensions in the choice and maintenance of successful treatments: Strength, integrity, and effectiveness. In A. Kazdin (Ed.), *Methodological issues and strategies in clinical research* (4th ed., pp. 137–156). Washington, DC: American Psychological Association.

Related Topics

Chapter 19, "Medical Evaluation of Children With Behavioral or Developmental Disorders"
Chapter 53, "Play Therapy"

56 PSYCHOLOGICAL INTERVENTIONS IN CHILDHOOD CHRONIC ILLNESS

Robert J. Thompson, Jr. & Kathryn E. Gustafson

Although specific childhood illnesses are rare, approximately 1 million children (i.e., 2%) have a severe chronic illness that may impair their daily functioning, and an additional 10 million have a less serious chronic illness. Because of advances in health care, children and their families are, in increasing numbers, coping with chronic illness over substantial periods of their lives, which has caused concern about quality of life in general and psychological adjustment in particular (Thompson & Gustafson, 1996).

PART III • PSYCHOTHERAPY AND TREATMENT

It is estimated that children with chronic illness have a risk for psychological adjustment problems that is 1½–3 times as high as that of their healthy peers (Pless, 1984). These children seem to be particularly at risk for anxiety-based internalizing difficulties or a combination of internalizing difficulties and milder forms of externalizing problems such as oppositional disorders (Thompson & Gustafson, 1996). Parents and siblings are also at increased risk for adjustment problems. However, good adjustment is not only possible but the norm. Therefore, attention has been focused on delineating processes that account for this variability in adjustment and that may serve as salient intervention targets (Wallander & Thompson, 1995).

Systems-theory perspectives on human development focus on the progressive accommodations that occur throughout the life span between the developing organism and his or her changing environment. Chronic illness can disrupt normal processes of child development and family functioning, and it can be viewed as a potential stressor to which the individual and family systems endeavor to adapt. The goals of care are to diminish the impact of the illness and to prevent dysfunction (Perrin & MacLean, 1988). A major hypothesized mechanism of effect for the impact of chronic illness on children and their families is through disrupting normal processes of child development and family functioning (Perrin & MacLean, 1988).

Models of adaptation that incorporate biomedical, psychosocial, and developmental dimensions, such as the risk and resistance and transactional stress and coping models (Wallander & Thompson, 1995), suggest that the impact of chronic illness can be lessened and adaptation promoted through stress reduction, enhancement of support-eliciting social problem-solving skills, and effective parenting (Thompson & Gustafson, 1996). Additional intervention targets include enhancing adherence to medical regimens and pain management.

ENHANCING ADAPTATION

The focus of intervention efforts is on fostering positive adaptation by children and their families to the stresses associated with a chronic illness. One intervention target is stress reduction through multicomponent cognitive and behavioral treatment programs that address cognitive processes of appraisal of stress and methods of coping with stress. More specifically, a combination of emotion-focused and problem-focused coping skills is necessary to deal with the controllable and noncontrollable aspects of chronic illness and their treatments.

Enhancing social skills is another intervention target. In particular, perceived social support, especially classmate support, appears to serve as a protective factor in adaptation to chronic childhood illness. Social skills are necessary to elicit and maintain peer support. Intervention programs focus on developing social-cognitive problem-solving skills. Frequently these skills are developed in the context of school reentry programs designed to reintegrate the child into the school setting after the diagnosis of the chronic illness or a prolonged absence because of the illness and/or treatment regimen. This typically involves a three-pronged approach of enhancing the child's academic and social skills, modifying the school environment, and helping parents be effective advocates for the needs of their child (Thompson & Gustafson, 1996). To improve children's social skills and peer relationships, school reentry programs incorporate social skills training and social-cognitive problem-solving training. For example, one well-developed program has three modules (Varni, Katz, Colegrove, & Dolgin, 1993). The social-cognitive problem-solving module teaches children to identify the problems, explore possible solutions, and evaluate the outcome. The assertiveness-training module teaches children to express their thoughts, wishes, and concerns. The teasing module teaches children how to cope with verbal and physical teasing associated with changes in their physical appearance. The success of these multicomponent programs has been documented in children with cancer (Varni et al., 1993).

Intervention programs are beginning to target improved parenting as a method of fostering adaptation to chronic childhood illness. More specifically, systems theory perspectives suggest that adaptation can be enhanced by reducing parental stress and distress and developing parenting skills conducive to child cognitive and social development.The mental health and child development literature contains examples of parenting intervention programs that have proved effective in improving children's behavior problems (Forehand, 1993) and cognitive and social development (Gross, 1990). Parenting intervention programs to foster developmentally conducive parent-child interactions are beginning to be designed to meet the illness-related tasks of specific chronic illnesses. The multifamily group intervention for children with diabetes (Satin, La Greca, Zigo, & Skyler, 1989) is an example. The family component consisted of three to five families meeting together for six weekly sessions during which discussion facilitators promoted independent problem-solving skills for managing diabetes. The intervention also included a 1-week simulation component in which parents followed a meal and exercise plan; accomplished blood testing, twice-daily injections of normal saline, and measurement four times daily of urinary glucose and ketones using simulated urine; and recorded results in a diabetes-monitoring diary. Improvements in metabolic functioning relative to controls at both the 3- and 6-month assessment periods occurred for the participants in this multifamily group, with and without the simulated experience component.

ADHERENCE

The estimated adherence rate for medical regimens for the pediatric population is 50% (Dunbar-Jacob, Dunning, & Dwyer, 1993). Given the less than one-to-one correspondence between treatment and outcome and the movement to a family-centered, parent-professional, collaborative model of care, noncompliance is no longer viewed as an indicator of irresponsibility. Noncompliance can be a well-reasoned, adaptive choice (Deaton, 1985). Correspondingly, adherence intervention efforts are now directed to providing knowledge, developing specific procedural skills, and tailoring a management plan to the specific needs and realities of the family situation (Epstein & Cluss, 1982).

Educational and behavioral strategies have been developed for improving adherence to therapeutic regimens. It is clear that knowledge of the therapeutic regimen is necessary but not sufficient for improving adherence. There are three types of behavioral strategies: *stimulus control techniques* include flavoring pills and tailoring the drug regimen to specific daily events; *self-control techniques* include self-regulation of dosage and self-monitoring of both symptoms and medications; *reinforcement techniques* include reinforcing symptom reduction, medication use, and health contacts and feedback on whether drug levels are in the therapeutic range. In general, self-monitoring approaches are less effective than reinforcement or feedback approaches (Epstein & Cluss, 1982). Across a number of studies, the reported success rates for improving adherence were 64% for educational strategies, 85% for behavioral strategies, and 88% for combined educational and behavioral strategies (Haynes, 1976).

PAIN MANAGEMENT

Pain is a normative experience of everyday life and is also associated with illness and treatments. Pain involves a sensation component and a response component, which includes the psychological, emotional, and behavioral responses to the sensation. Pain management is one of the tasks associated with chronic illness (Thompson & Gustafson, 1996). Approaches to pain management can involve analgesics, cognitive-behavioral therapy, or a combination of both.

Children with illnesses typically confront two types of pain: pain associated with invasive medical procedures and recurrent pain. To address pain related to medical procedures, intervention efforts seek to develop children's and parents' cognitive-behavioral coping skills through multicomponent programs involving deep breathing, attention distraction, muscle relaxation, relaxing imagery, emotive imagery, and behavioral rehearsal (Dahlquist, 1992).

Recurrent pain is a frequent symptom of a number of illnesses such as sickle-cell disease, hemophilia, juvenile rheumatoid arthritis, and recurrent abdominal pain. Cognitive-behavioral treatment approaches to managing chronic and recurrent pediatric pain have been characterized by techniques to regulate pain perception and techniques to modify pain behavior. The self-regulatory techniques for pain perception include muscle relaxation, deep breathing, and guided imagery and active coping strategies, including diverting attention and reinterpreting pain sensations (Varni, Walco, & Katz, 1989). Pain behavior regulation techniques focus on identifying and modifying socioenvironmental factors that influence pain expression. Cognitive-behavioral family interventions call attention to the role of caregivers in providing discriminative cues and in selectively reinforcing behavioral expressions of pain and self-management skills through attention (Sanders, Shepherd, Cleghorn, & Woolford, 1994). Coping behaviors rather than distress behaviors are reinforced. The focus is on helping children maintain the pleasures afforded by their normal daily activities.

SUMMARY

Interventions based on social-learning theory are effective in relation to primary intervention targets. More specifically, cognitive-behavioral interventions improve stress management, enhance support-eliciting social problem-solving skills, enhance parental fostering of their children's cognitive and social development and management of children's behavior problems, and improve adherence and pain management skills. These cognitive-behavioral interventions have multiple components; are beginning to be incorporated within family systems approaches; and are being modified to fit the particular tasks and situations associated with specific chronic illnesses.

References & Readings

Dahlquist, L. M. (1992). Coping with aversive medical treatments. In A. M. La Greca, L. J. Siegel, J. L. Wallander, & C. E. Walker (Eds.), *Stress and coping in child health* (pp. 345–376). New York: Guilford Press.

Deaton, A. V. (1985). Adaptive noncompliance in pediatric asthma: The parent as expert. *Journal of Pediatric Psychology, 10,* 1–14.

Dunbar-Jacob, J., Dunning, E. J., & Dwyer, K. (1993). Compliance research in pediatric and adolescent populations: Two decades of research. In N. P. Krasnegor, L. Epstein, S. B. Johnson, & S. J. Yaffe (Eds.), *Developmental aspects of health compliance behavior* (pp. 29–51). Hillsdale, NJ: Erlbaum.

Epstein, L. H., & Cluss, P. A. (1982). A behavioral medicine perspective on adherence to long-term medical regimens. *Journal of Consulting and Clinical Psychology, 50,* 950–971.

Forehand, R. (1993). Twenty years of research on parenting: Does it have practical implications for clinicians working with parents and children? *Clinical Psychologist, 46,* 169–176.

Gross, R. T. (1990). Enhancing the outcomes of low birth weight, premature infants: A multisite, randomized trial. *Journal of the American Medical Association, 263,* 3035–3042.

Haynes, R. B. (1976). Strategies for improving compliance: A methodologic analysis and review. In D. L. Sackett & R. B. Haynes (Eds.), *Compliance with therapeutic regimens* (pp. 69–82). Baltimore: Johns Hopkins University Press.

Perrin, J. M., & MacLean, W. E., Jr. (1988). Children with chronic illness: The prevention of dysfunction. *Pediatric Clinics of North America, 35,* 1325–1337.

Pless, I. B. (1984). Clinical assessment: Physical and psychological functioning. *Pediatric Clinics of North America, 31,* 33–45.

Sanders, M. R., Shepherd, R. W., Cleghorn, G., & Woolford, H. (1994). The treatment of recurrent abdominal pain in children: A controlled comparison of cognitive-behavioral family intervention and standard pediatric care. *Journal of Consulting and Clinical Psychology, 62,* 306–314.

Satin, W., La Greca, A. M., Zigo, M. A., & Skyler, J. S. (1989). Diabetes in adolescence: Effects of multifamily group interventions and parent simulation of diabetes. *Journal of Pediatric Psychology, 14,* 259–275.

Thompson, R. J., Jr., & Gustafson, K. E. (1996). *Adaptation to chronic childhood illness.* Washington, DC: American Psychological Association.

Varni, J. W., Katz, E. R., Colegrove, R., Jr., & Dolgin, M. (1993). The impact of social skills training on the adjustment of children with newly diagnosed cancer. *Journal of Pediatric Psychology, 18,* 751–767.

Varni, J. W., Walco, G. A., & Katz, E. R. (1989). A

cognitive-behavioral approach to pain associated with pediatric chronic disease. *Journal of Pain and Symptom Management, 4*, 238–241.

Wallander, J. L., & Thompson, R. J., Jr. (1995). Psychosocial adjustment of children with chronic physical conditions. In M. C. Roberts (Ed.), *Handbook of pediatric psychology* (2nd ed., pp. 124–141). New York: Guilford Press.

Related Topics

Chapter 19, "Medical Evaluation of Children With Behavioral or Developmental Disorders"

Chapter 70, "Psychological Interventions in Adult Disease Management"

Chapter 71, "Thumbnail Guide to Medical Crisis Counseling^SM"

57 GUIDELINES FOR CONDUCTING ADOLESCENT PSYCHOTHERAPY

Alice K. Rubenstein

1. *Adopt an integrative framework:* The majority of difficulties facing adolescents today are systemic, requiring an integrative approach in regard to both diagnosis and treatment. Although effective psychotherapeutic interventions draw from the more traditional therapies, the focus is on system interventions and problem solving. It is critical to have an understanding of the ecological factors, including the social, economic, and cultural context in which an adolescent lives.

2. *Avoid traditional models:* Traditional models, developed for working with children and adults, are not appropriate. Adolescents are beyond the playroom, and most do not have the patience for the traditional "talk" therapies. Insight can come later. Focus on *their* concerns in the present.

3. *Begin with the first contact:* The first phone contact provides the opportunity to begin assessing the presenting problem(s) and ascertaining the adolescent's appropriateness for the therapist's skills and setting. Most often, initial contact is made by a parent and pro-

vides the opportunity to present the overall boundaries of treatment. Specific points to be covered include when, how, and what kind of feedback will be given to the parents; the likely need for collateral contacts with the systems and other professionals who interact with the adolescent; the confidential nature of your sessions with the adolescent; who will be responsible for getting the adolescent to his or her appointments; relevant payment and insurance coverage procedures; and the expectation of parental support and involvement in the adolescent's treatment. In those cases where the first contact is made by the adolescent, it is most often both legally and financially necessary to gain parental permission for treatment.

4. *Schedule an initial meeting with parents:* Most often, parents are an important, if not critical, resource for gathering diagnostic data. The decision to have an initial meeting with the parent(s) is based on a number of factors, including the age of the adolescent; the therapist's initial feel for the presenting problem(s); the parents' anxiety; and the therapist's style. The adolescent's confidentiality is best ensured by having such a meeting prior to, or soon after, the first few sessions with the adolescent. In addition to gathering diagnostic information, meeting with the parent(s) provides insight into such factors as parenting style and family dysfunction. It is helpful to have both parents attend this meeting, even in cases of separation or divorce. If a joint meeting is not possible, meet separately with each parent.

5. *Discuss insurance coverage early:* Insurance coverage for adolescents is often inadequate and does not address their specific treatment needs. Be sure to check on coverage for sessions with parents and collateral contacts. When possible, contact the insurance company case manager or peer reviewer. Educate them about the special needs of adolescents. Negotiate and clarify what will and will not be covered. Be prepared to justify your treatment plan in terms of goals and outcomes. Depending on the coverage provided, a separate financial agreement with the parents may be needed to cover collateral contacts and/or other interventions.

6. *Make contact with the adolescent:* In most cases, the parent(s) arrange the initial appointment for the adolescent. However, telephone confirmation directly with the adolescent is recommended. This not only communicates respect for the adolescent as a separate person but also provides data regarding the adolescent's interest in or resistance to treatment. The majority of adolescents have been bribed, forced, prodded, and/or coerced into entering treatment. Others come with little sense of how psychotherapy can help them. Most have difficulty owning and verbalizing their difficulties. Many will deny and blame others (e.g., parents, teachers) for their difficulties.

7. *Conduct individual and systems assessments:* When working with adolescents, two diagnostic assessments are being made simultaneously: the more traditional individual assessment of the adolescent as "patient" and, equally or more important, an assessment of the systems in which the adolescent lives. Assessment is interwoven with the ongoing process of listening, supporting, confronting, and reframing. Systems assessment is accomplished by exploring the adolescent's experience of all the systems in which they interact (e.g., family, school, community), as well as accessing as much direct information as possible from and about these systems. This includes an assessment of relevant stressors, such as parent-adolescent conflicts; peer group relationships; school achievement, including possible learning disabilities; daily stressors, including home and work responsibilities; and stressful life events, including geographic relocation, divorce, and/or death. Substance abuse, physical and/or sexual abuse, and involvement with the legal system are also essential.

8. *Make diagnoses in the context of adolescent development:* A developmental perspective, which takes into account the normative fluctuations of affect and behavior of adolescents, is critical in making an accurate diagnosis. Presenting symptomatology must be considered in the context of normal adolescent development. It is important to pay attention to comorbidity of clinical dysfunction in adolescents. Disorders of adolescence often require dual or multiple diagnoses. Adolescent depression often occurs with anxiety, eating disorders, learning disabilities, and/or substance abuse. It usually takes at least three sessions to establish the rapport necessary to identify the major contributors to the adolescent's dysfunctional affect and behavior.

9. *Refer for psychological testing:* Standardized assessment techniques may be useful, particularly if the therapist suspects intellectual, learning, and/or neurological problems. If this is the case, careful consideration should be given to who will conduct the testing. In light of the complexity of forming a therapeutic alliance with an adolescent, many clinicians refer any diagnostic testing to an outside resource.

10. *Consider the common clinical dysfunctions in adolescents:* Although the *DSM-IV* identifies a number of disorders with onset prior to adulthood, many disorders are more likely to first appear and/or have a significantly greater impact during adolescence. These include attention-deficit/hyperactivity disorder; conduct disorder; oppositional disorder; depression; biploar disorder; dysthymic disorder; substance abuse mood disorder; anxiety disorders;

eating disorders; substance abuse disorders; and learning disorders.

11. *Assure confidentiality:* In order to establish and maintain the integrity of a viable working relationship with both the adolescent and his or her parents, it is critical to have a clear and concrete understanding of the importance of confidentiality in the treatment process. The guidelines for confidentiality should be established at the time of initial contact with the parents and presented to the adolescent at the very beginning of treatment. Assuring confidentiality is the first step in empowering the adolescent. Explaining to parents the therapeutic value of confidentiality not only helps them to support the treatment process but also provides for developmentally appropriate separation between the adolescent and the parents.

12. *Clarify the boundaries of confidentiality:* Confidentiality requires that the therapist not repeat anything the adolescent tells him or her to anyone. In addition, adolescents need assurance that the therapist will not withhold from them any contact they have with the adolescents' parents and/or others involved with them. Parents, however, need assurance that the therapist is taking clinical responsibility for determining the boundaries of confidentiality. Both the adolescent and the parents should be informed that confidentiality will be waived if the therapist judges that the adolescent is in danger of harming himself or herself or another person or if certain statutory obligations present themselves. If this becomes necessary, it is best to tell the adolescent first. In keeping with the goal of empowerment, the adolescent should be encouraged to talk directly with his or her parents, possibly in the format of a family session. In cases where there is suspected physical and/or sexual abuse, the adolescent must be informed that you are required by law to notify the appropriate agency immediately.

13. *Involve parents:* In most cases, particularly with younger adolescents, therapeutic change necessitates parental involvement in the treatment process. Balancing confidentiality with parental involvement requires careful attention to boundaries, as well as a clear assessment of the parents' role in the adolescent's dysfunctional behavior. Whenever possible, sessions with parents should take place when the adolescent is present. Developmentally appropriate empowerment is enhanced by having the adolescent directly involved in negotiations with the family system. However, when clinical judgment suggests otherwise, separate meetings can be held with the parents. When this is the case, the adolescent should be provided with a summary of the parental contact. In some cases, particularly with older adolescents, clinical judgment may suggest extremely limited parental contact. In all cases, it is best to involve the adolescent in decisions regarding contact with his or her parents and teachers. A signed release should be secured from the parents *and* the adolescent before any collateral contacts are made. This is particularly important in regard to medical and/or legal issues. In terms of the parents, this is a legal necessity; with the adolescent, it is a therapeutic one. If treatment is court ordered, the waiver of privilege should be clearly spelled out to both the parents and the adolescent.

14. *Emphasize the first session:* Adolescents usually determine who they can trust in their first few minutes of contact. If there is a parent in the waiting room, greet the adolescent first. Cover the limits and boundaries of confidentiality as soon as possible. Ask the adolescent why he or she came and/or explain what has been communicated to you as the presenting problem(s). Find out what he or she wants. Be honest, and don't be afraid to use humor.

15. *Fit the therapist and office to the adolescent:* If the adolescent is coming straight from school or work, offer a snack. The therapist's attire should be casual, avoiding any image of power and/or authority. Consider your office environment. Adolescents do not wish to be confronted with how learned therapists are. Shelves stacked with books and/or journals can be distancing. The physical environment should be comfortable and inviting.

16. *Consider multiple treatment modalities:* Group or family therapy may be utilized as primary or supplementary treatment modalities for adolescents. Group therapy is often the treatment of choice for adolescents with dual or multiple diagnoses, particularly in cases of substance abuse, depression, and oppositional disorders. Group psychotherapy makes use of peer confrontation and support, while providing for connection and belonging. As increased autonomy emerges as a primary struggle during adolescence, family therapy can help to mediate parent-adolescent conflicts, as well as foster effective communication through the process of separation and individuation. As with individual psychotherapy, confidentiality, collateral contacts, and parental involvement must be clearly defined.

17. *Cultivate empowerment:* Psychotherapy with adolescents requires a very special kind of advocacy. It is a delicate balance between helping adolescents empower themselves while providing support, confrontation, and direct intervention when needed. Focus on what they need, not on why they were sent, and do not ruminate about their helplessness. It is important to begin to set operational goals early on. Consider tangible things they want to be different. Help them to identify exchanges or trade-offs they can make with those in power—for example, a C average in exchange for being able to get a driving permit. It is often helpful to make a list. Their goals might include such things as a later curfew, increased spending money, having more friends, getting a job, doing better in school, eliminating substance abuse, reducing delinquent behaviors, or surviving in one or more dysfunctional systems. Identify ways they can try to reach their goals by brainstorming with them. The process involves teaching and modeling how they can take control of their own lives. Be careful not to take responsibility for their reaching their goals. It is their job, so the success is theirs.

18. *Avoid splitting with the systems:* Many adolescents who enter treatment are angry with one or more of the systems with which they interact. While it is important for the therapist to be supportive of the adolescent's feelings, it is equally important not to pair with the adolescent against all of these systems and to engage in institutional splitting. In most cases, adolescents want and need the support and approval of these systems, even if they are dysfunctional. Whenever possible, the adolescent should be encouraged and helped to figure out ways to meet his or her own needs while at the same time finding ways to work with the systems with which he or she must interact. In the long run, an overly dependent relationship with an adolescent will not prove helpful.

19. *Monitor countertransference carefully:* It is critical for therapists to maintain a therapeutic boundary between themselves and the adolescents they work with. Overidentification with the adolescent can damage the therapeutic relationship and interfere with productive change. Adolescents must learn how to navigate their own systems, regardless of the degree of dysfunction. Empowerment necessitates appropriate boundaries.

20. *Intervene outside the office:* Since the world of adolescents is often significantly impacted by the systems in which they interact, it is important to be willing to leave the office setting. This may include meetings with teachers, youth leaders, probation officers, and so forth. Always inform the adolescent that such a meeting has been requested and/or that you would like to have such a meeting. Empower the adolescent to take an active role in effecting change by encouraging him or her to attend. Review with the adolescent what you will say at any meeting. Do whatever is necessary to ensure and keep his or her trust and connection.

21. *Be flexible and available:* Unlike most adults, adolescents require a great deal more flexibility and availability in the course of treatment. They often require far more phone contact, especially in a crisis. The therapist must establish a balance between keeping appropriate boundaries and becoming too rigid. It is helpful to let adolescents know if and how they can reach you between sessions. In addition, the course of treatment with an adolescent may well be more variable than it is with an adult. The frequency of sessions may vary from weekly to biweekly to monthly, depending on the issues at hand.

22. *Handle parental contact with care:* Phone calls from parents regarding their adolescent should be taken by the therapist. Listen but offer no information that might compromise confidentiality without first checking with the adolescent. The therapist is free to share with the adolescent all communications with his or her parent(s). Following the third or fourth session, with the adolescent's permission, arrange for a meeting with the parents. Encourage, but do not force, the adolescent to attend this session. If the adolescent chooses not to attend, provide him or her with a summary of the session.

23. *Model an appropriate termination:* The psychotherapeutic relationship is critical in adolescents' lives. Therefore, the process of termination has special ramifications and opportunities. Stress an open-ended arrangement and the ability to reinitiate contact. Emphasize the ongoing process of solving life problems. Reinforce their successes and the skills they have acquired. Discuss your position on future post-therapy contacts (e.g., writing, phone contact, graduations, birthdays, holiday cards, weddings). Encourage adolescents to discuss their feelings about termination. Within a therapeutic context, share your own feelings about the termination. Model a healthy and mature farewell.

References & Readings

Bratter, B., Bratter, C., & Bratter, T. (1995). Beyond reality: The need to (re)gain self-respect. *Psychotherapy, 32,* 59–69.

Bratter, T. (1977). The psychotherapist as advocate: extending the therapeutic alliance with adolescents. *Journal of Contemporary Psychotherapy, 8,* 119–126.

Bratter, T. (1989). Group psychotherapy with alcohol and drug addicted adolescents: Special clinical concerns and challenges. In F. J. Cramer Azima & L. H. Richmond (Eds.), *Adolescent group psychotherapy* (pp. 163-188). Madison, CT: International Universities Press.

Glasser, W. (1975). *Reality therapy: A new approach to psychiatry* (2nd ed.). New York: Harper Collins.

Haley, J. (1987). *Problem solving therapy* (2nd ed.). San Francisco: Jossey-Bass.

Holmbeck, G., & Updegrove, A. (1995). Clinical-developmental interface: Implications of developmental research for adolescent psychotherapy. *Psychotherapy, 32,* 16–33.

Kazdin, A. E. (1993). Adolescent mental health: Prevention and treatment programs. *American Psychologist, 48,* 127–141.

Petersen, A., Compas, B., Brooks-Gunn, J., Stemmler, M., Ey, S., & Grant, K. (1993). Depression in adolescence. *American Psychologist, 48,* 155–168.

Rubenstein, A. (1996a). Interventions for a scattered generation: Treating adolescents in the nineties. *Psychotherapy, 33,* 353–360.

Rubenstein, A. (1996b). *Practical psychotherapy with adolescents* (APA Psychotherapy Video Tape Series II). Washington, DC: American Psychological Association.

Rubenstein, A., & Zager, K. (1995). Training in adolescent treatment: Where is psychology? *Psychotherapy, 32,* 2–6.

Young, I., Anderson, C., & Steinbrecher, A. (1995). Unmasking the phantom: Creative assessment of the adolescent. *Psychotherapy, 32,* 34–38.

Related Topics

58 GUIDELINES FOR CONDUCTING COUPLE AND FAMILY THERAPY

Jay L. Lebow

The following guidelines stem from a review of the couple and family therapy literature; from research assessing couples, families, and couple and family therapy; and from clinical experience. The goal of this chapter is to suggest widely accepted generic guidelines for practice that transcend the numerous schools of couple and family therapy.

1. *Develop a systemic perspective:* A system consists of interacting components; in a family, these include such subsystems as couple, sibling, and individual. Individuals do not function in a vacuum but continually influence one another through feedback.

2. *Always consider context in attempting to understand couples and families:* Behavior that appears to make little sense often emerges as far more understandable when the surrounding conditions are understood. For example, a child's school phobia or a spouse's depression frequently becomes more intelligible when its meaning in the life of the family system is recognized.

3. *Understand multiple perspectives:* The therapist should attempt to grasp and communicate understanding of the respective viewpoints of various family members, which may vary considerably.

4. *Examine potential circular pathways of causality that may maintain problems:* The therapist should attempt to understand ways in which family members are influenced within circular pathways in which the behavior, thoughts, and feelings of one person promote those of another, which in turn promote those of the first person. Although not all causal pathways are circular, and even among circular causal chains the participation of family members may not be coequal, such cycles frequently block problem resolution. For example, parents' angry and punitive behavior may both lead to and flow from the acting-out behavior of a child. Regardless of where the cycle begins, the punitive behavior by the parents leads to more acting out by the child, which, in turn, leads to more parental punitive behavior.

5. *Respect the diversity of family forms:* Families assume many forms, including single-parent, remarried, and gay and lesbian. The therapist should become knowledgeable about typical life across this range of forms and, along with the families, should develop therapeutic goals that honor the family's form and culture.

6. *Understand the special ethical considerations of couple and family therapy, particularly concerning confidentiality:* Couple and family therapists face special ethical dilemmas, such as deciding who is the patient and who is entitled to confidentiality of communication. All clients who attend conjoint sessions become patients and should retain the same rights. In couple and family therapy, confidentiality should be broken only with agreement of all participants, except in those circumstances in which legal duty to report or warn takes precedence. The therapist should articulate a clear position about confidentiality for confidences made outside of sessions, as well as when participants vary across sessions. Therapists should understand state law about these and similar matters, as well as ethical guidelines.

7. *Begin assessment and intervention with the first phone call:* Couple and family therapies require more effort before the first session on the part of the therapist than do other therapies. Active efforts before the first session to include members who are clearly important to the problem or its solution substantially increase participation in therapy and thereby impact on treatment outcome.

8. *Determine and clarify who will be included in treatment:* There are a variety of methods in family therapy, ranging from some that include multiple generations to others that include only a few or even one member of the family. Who is and who is not part of the therapy always needs to be clearly designated and understood. In general, it is easier to include additional members of the family earlier in treatment rather than later, when alliances are well set. Involving fathers as well as mothers in the treatment of children promotes better outcome.

9. *Begin with an emphasis on engagement and alliance building:* The therapist must

build an alliance with each member of the family, with each subsystem, and with the family as a whole. Techniques such as eliciting input from each family member, joining with each around some aspect of the problem, and assimilating and adapting to the culture of the family help build such alliances. Pay particular attention to the alliance with those member(s) of the family who have most say in whether the therapy will continue. Alliance with the therapist appears to predict outcome regardless of the form of couple or family therapy.

10. *Assess through history gathering and observing interaction:* Assessment should have multiple foci, including the family system, its subsystems, and individuals. Assessment typically is intermixed with treatment, rather than a distinct phase. Assessment leads to a formulation of how to intervene.

11. *Understand that certain difficulties in family life are grossly underreported:* Family violence, sexual abuse, infidelity, alcoholism, and drug abuse, among other problems, are typically reported at much lower frequencies than they occur. Inquire about them in a standard noninvasive way.

12. *Understand each client's expectations and how well they are satisfied:* Family members bring a range of expectations about such issues as money, sex, and intimacy that are manifested at many levels, ranging from the behavioral to the psychodynamic. Relationship satisfaction is often more the product of unmet expectations than of particular problematic patterns. Help family members articulate and negotiate their expectations.

13. *Compile a genogram to understand how family of origin factors affect the system:* Elaborating on who is in the extended family, what the key experiences have been in the life of the family, and repetitive issues across the generations increases mutual understanding, promotes the working through of experiences, and potentially sets the stage for exploring individual and interactive patterns.

14. *Remember that couple and family therapy is usually brief:* Families typically are only willing to engage in therapies of under 10 sessions. Keep therapy accordingly focused.

15. *Promote better family relationships:* Relationships have a variety of positive effects beyond their intrinsic value in promoting better individual mental health, individual health, and child functioning.

16. *Promote solutions, a focus on coping, and a view of family health:* Families respond far better to a focus on creating solutions. Reframe behavior in a form that can be more positively understood. Stress the normal developmental aspects of what the couple or family is experiencing.

17. *Negotiate clear goals for treatment:* Family life presents endless possible goals, and participants often begin with varying agendas. Negotiating an agreed set of goals for therapy is an essential task early in treatment. Goals may be added or modified as therapy progresses.

18. *Establish control:* Therapists in couple and family therapy must intervene actively to move clients from habitual patterns. For example, the therapist must be able to interrupt habitual patterns of destructive arguing in couples.

19. *Develop a clear plan:* Couple and family therapy is innately complex and typically has multiple foci. A clear road map mitigates the dangers of losing focus. This road map may require revision as treatment progresses.

20. *Employ individual, biological, and macrosystemic interventions in the context of the treatment:* Empirical support is strongest for approaches that combine family therapy with other intervention strategies. Treatment of severe mental illness should include the use of medication; treatment of adolescent disorders should include a focus on school and peer systems; and treatment of depression should include "individual" therapy for the depression.

21. *Teach empathy, communication, how to deliver reinforcement, and other skills when such skills are inadequately developed:* Many couples and family members lack

the requisite skills to perform essential conjoint tasks. Instruction, modeling, in-session practice, and homework can help family members master these skills. Such instruction and practice can help premarital couples significantly reduce their risk of divorce and parents reduce the likelihood of child behavior problems.

22. *Suggest tasks that have a high likelihood of being carried out successfully:* Suggestions that are not followed are likely to increase client reactivity and resistance. For example, repeatedly proposing communication exercises to a family that is not ready to utilize them is likely to retard progress.

23. *Develop contracts between family members that are mutually satisfying:* Couples and families who are dissatisfied with their relationships typically have much lower rates of positive exchange and higher rates of coercion. Negotiating positive quid pro quo exchanges leads to more satisfying relationships.

24. *Promote clear family structure:* Flexible yet clear boundaries, shifting yet not chaotic patterns of alliance, and an age-appropriate distribution of power promote family health.

25. *Understand personal narratives and promote the development of a positive understanding of the narratives of other family members:* The stories created by family members often carry with them the seeds of difficulties. Reexamining these stories and helping create new ones that include positive connotation of motives and behaviors can lead to more harmonious family life and problem resolution.

26. *Coach individuals to take responsibility for their own behavior:* Blame leads to endless cycles of misunderstanding and alienation. Helping clients assume an "I" stance about their own behavior helps break such cycles.

27. *Promote the expression of underlying softer affect that lies behind anger and criticism:* Individuals often express defensive reactions rather than feelings such as sadness or fear. Exploring such underlying

feelings in a safe environment promotes understanding and empathic connection. For example, uncovering the sad affect that lies behind anger expressed toward a spouse in couple therapy can alter typical dysfunctional patterns of conflict.

28. *See couples with relationship distress conjointly:* Conjoint couples therapy is the only demonstrated effective form of treatment for couple adjustment problems. Although spouses who are unhappy with their relationships frequently seek individual therapy, there is no evidence that this helps the couple relationship and some evidence that it has a deleterious effect.

29. *Focus a major part of treatment on conjoint couple therapy when there is coexisting relationship difficulty along with depression:* Individual treatment of depression does not appear to impact on the relationship problems, and the presence of relationship difficulties predicts poor prognosis over time for depression. Depressed individuals who do not have comorbid couple difficulties do not require couple therapy, but they do benefit from some psychoeducational involvement of their partners.

30. *Recognize and target Gottman's four signs of imminent divorce—criticism, contempt, defensiveness, and stonewalling:* Clients presenting such patterns should be warned of their risk of divorce, and initial work should center directly on developing alternative patterns of relating. Couples are unlikely to benefit from treatment unless these signs change.

31. *In divorcing and remarried systems, promote good-enough communication to allow for coparenting:* Help families understand the typical stresses and coping strategies. Refer for mediation if substantial conflicts arise between coparents.

32. *Utilize psychoeducational interventions when dealing with severe mental illness:* Families in which there is severe individual dysfunction often fail to understand the origins of disorders and feel blamed when encountering therapists. An educative stance that teaches about the disorder and about typical family processes is enor-

mously helpful in gaining cooperation and reducing symptoms and recidivism. Reducing expressed emotion (i.e., highly emotional critical affect) appears to have particularly great value in the context of severe mental illness. Treatment that increases emotional arousal and conflict in these families is contraindicated.

33. *In disorganized families, promote the creation of stabilizing rituals:* In particular, families with alcoholic members fare much better when they maintain such rituals as a regular dinner hour.

34. *In family violence and abuse, protect safety first:* At times, couples and families present in situations where contact is dangerous. The ethical obligation must be first to safety and then to family therapy.

35. *In child behavior problems, train parents to engage in predictable schedules of reinforcement to reward and extinguish behavior:* Reinforcement may focus on a single behavior or may utilize a point system to focus on a constellation of targets.

36. *In oppositional children and in adolescent conduct disorder and substance abuse, utilize family therapy as part of a multisystemic approach that also addresses other relevant systems, such as school, peer, and legal systems, as well as the individual:* The relevant social system in these cases does not stop at the boundary of the family but extends into these various other domains. Research suggests treatment is more effective when these parts of the social system are considered.

37. *Attend to tasks of termination, such as planning for the future, throughout the treatment:* Families often end treatment abruptly, despite the best efforts of therapists for planned termination. Addressing termination issues as the treatment unfolds lessens the negative effect of unplanned termination.

38. *Assess the impact of treatment on each individual, each subsystem, and the system as a whole, as well as on the presenting problem:* Outcome in family systems is complex, including many stakeholders and numerous foci, such as the presenting problem, individual functioning, and family functioning.

39. *Promote the maintenance of change:* All treatment effects appear to wane over time. Promote maintenance of change through follow-up sessions, continuing homework, and self-monitoring of the family's processes.

40. *Be aware of the meaning of gender and culture:* The therapist joins with the family with a gender and as a member of a cultural group. The therapist's work should be informed by an understanding of the impact of gender and culture. Therapist gender and culture also affect treatment process, regardless of therapist behavior.

41. *Coordinate with other therapists, health providers, and agencies involved with a case:* Coordinating goals and efforts often is a major factor in treatment success; inconsistent goals and methods frequently create obstacles to success.

42. *Utilize couple and family therapies to engage difficult-to-engage cases:* There is considerable evidence that many difficult-to-engage clients, such as alcoholics, substance abusers, and oppositional and delinquent adolescents, more easily engage in couple and family therapy.

43. *Consider the effects on the family system of any therapy you conduct:* Potent effects of psychotherapy extend beyond the individual. When seeing a couple, consider the effects on children and extended family. When seeing an individual, consider the effects on spouse, parents, children, and other members of the family.

44. *Expect treatment to have an impact:* Couple and family therapies have been demonstrated to be effective in 75% of cases and have been shown to have effect sizes much like those of individual therapy. Specifically, couple and family therapy has been demonstrated efficacious in helping alleviate couple relationship problems, depression in unhappily married women, schizophrenia, agoraphobia, panic disorder, adolescent substance abuse, adolescent delinquent behavior, childhood oppositional behavior, alcoholism, eating disor-

ders, and the psychological consequences of physical illness.

References & Readings

Alexander, J. F., Holtzworth-Munroe, A., & Jameson, P. (1994). The process and outcome of marital and family therapy: Research review and evaluation. In A. E. Bergen & S. L. Garfield (Eds.), *Handbook of psychotherapy and behavior change* (4th ed.). New York: Wiley.

Goldner, V. (1985). Feminism in family therapy. *Family Process, 24*, 31–48.

Gottman, J. M., & Levenson, R. W. (1992). Marital processes predictive of later dissolution: Behavior, physiology, and health. *Journal of Personality and Social Psychology, 63*, 221–233.

Gurman, A. S., & Kniskern, D. P. (Eds.) (1981). *Handbook of family therapy*. New York: Brunner/Mazel.

Gurman, A. S., & Kniskern, D. P. (Eds.) (1991). *Handbook of family therapy* (Vol. 2). New York: Brunner/Mazel.

Gurman, A. S., Kniskern, D. P., & Pinsof, W. M. (1986). Research on marital and family therapies. In S. L. Garfield & A. E. Bergin (Eds.), *Handbook of psychotherapy and behavior change* (3rd ed., pp. 565–624). New York: Wiley.

Jacobson, N. S., & Gurman, A. S. (Eds.) (1995). *Clinical handbook of couple therapy*. New York: Guilford Press.

Lebow, J., & Gurman, A. S. (1995). Research assessing couple and family therapy. *Annual Review of Psychology, 46*, 27–57.

Mikesell, R. H., Lusterman, D. D., & McDaniel, S. H. (Eds.) (1995). *Family psychology and systems therapy: A handbook*. Washington, DC: American Psychological Association.

Pinsof, W. M., & Wynne, L. (Eds.) (1995). Special issue: The effectiveness of marital and family therapy. *Journal of Marital and Family Therapy, 21*.

Walsh, F. (Ed.) (1995). *Normal family processes* (2nd ed.). New York: Guilford Press.

Related Topics

59   TREATING HIGH-CONFLICT COUPLES

Susan Heitler

1. *Define conflict levels:* Conflict may be expressed in anxious tension, depression, disengagement (for fear of fights), and passive-aggressive or addictive behavior, as well as in overt anger, deprecating or demanding words and tone of voice, or, in the extreme, physical violence. *High conflict* refers to the frequency with which a couple locks into oppositional stances and also to the intensity of anger expressed in disagreements.

2. *Obtain requisite therapist skills:* In addition to traditional therapy skills, a high-conflict couple psychotherapist, like a professional mediator, needs referee skills for ensuring that the couple's dialogue stays safe, plus expert knowledge of the steps of conflict resolution.

3. *Arrange the therapy room for symmetry and interaction:* Place the three chairs in an equilateral triangle. Rollers on the therapist's chair are preferable so that the therapist can roll closer to the couple or to one or the other partner for interventions and then roll back when the couple's dialogue flows cooperatively. Do not seat the couple side by side on a sofa because this arrangement encourages the couple to talk to the therapist rather than to each other.

4. *Obtain a threefold diagnostic picture:*

- A history of each individual's symptoms and any personality disorder. Accelerate this assessment by having each partner fill out a symptom checklist before beginning treatment. If the symptom checklist or your interview questions suggest anger outbursts, obtain detailed individual reports of exactly what has happened, bearing in mind the tendency to minimize and deny rages, emotional abuse, and physical violence (Holtzworth-Munroe, Beatty, & Anglin, 1995).
- A laundry list of conflicts about which the couple fights.
- An initial assessment of communication and conflict resolution skills and deficits.

This threefold diagnostic workup organizes diagnostic information to correspond to the three main strands of treatment: Eliminate symptoms (excessive anger, depression, etc.); resolve each conflict on the laundry list and, in the process of resolving the conflicts, gain understanding of the central problematic relationships of childhood and their reenactments in the marriage (Lewis, 1997); and build skills so the partners learn to resolve conflicts without angry fighting.

5. *Note contraindications for couple therapy:*

- Unwillingness to agree that verbal and physical violence are out of bounds, at home and in the therapy session.
- Poor impulse control or other signs that therapy may be unsafe.
- Reprisals for talking openly about concerns in the sessions.
- A paranoid-like blaming stance with a rigidly held set of beliefs about the other

(a fixed ideational system), ego-syntonic controlling behavior, and projection.

If these symptoms can be addressed with individual treatment and/or medication, subsequent couple treatment may be productive. Also, individual therapy for the healthier partner often can help him or her to cope more effectively with the spouse.

6. *Audiotape the treatment sessions:* Listening to the tape can be assigned as homework to accelerate and consolidate learning. Taping is contraindicated, however, if potential court involvement could result in the tapes being used as evidence detrimental to either participant.

7. *Ensure safety:* Early in treatment teach disengagement/reengagement routines to prevent hurtful fights (see Table 1). Practice these routines in the session. Inquire intermittently about the couple's experiences with their exit routines to ensure their plan is fully effective.

8. *Intervene immediately if anger escalates in a session:* Redirect the outburst to you, away from the spouse, by engaging the angry person in dialogue. If the angry partner continues to escalate, stand between the two spouses and/or ask the receiving spouse to step out for a few moments. Simplifying the situation by having one partner leave enables tempers to de-escalate and calm to return. If an angry spouse threatens to leave the session, agree, inviting him or her to return when he or she feels calmer. Thank him or her for demonstrating self-awareness and self-control.

After an angry outburst, reiterate the angry person's underlying concerns in a quiet voice so that dialogue resumes in a calm mode and the angry person knows he or she is being heard. Detoxify the incident by reframing the contents of the outburst in nonblaming language and by discussing any hurt feelings that may have resulted from the outburst.

9. *Initiate a collaborative set:* Create a shared perspective on the part of each spouse that they are mutually responsible for the problems in the relationship and that they both need to change themselves if the relationship is going to improve (Christensen et al., 1995). To help make a transition from conflict to coopera-

TABLE 1. Time-Out Routines for Emotional Safety at Home

Initiate time outs when either of you
- Feels too upset or negative to talk constructively.
- Senses that the other is getting too emotional to dialogue constructively.

To initiate a time out
- Use a nonverbal signal, such as sports signals.
- Go to separate spaces immediately, without any further discussion.
- Self-soothe by doing something pleasant.
- Write in a journal if it feels helpful, but write primarily about yourself, not your partner.

To reengage
- Wait until you both have regained normal humor.
- Reengage first in normal activity before you attempt to talk again about a difficult subject.
- If a difficult subject again provokes unconstructive discussion, save it for therapy.

Exit rules
- No door slamming or parting comments.
- *Never* block the other from leaving or pursue the other when he or she needs to disengage.
- As soon as the going gets even a little bit hot, keep cool and exit. Prevention is preferable to destruction.

tion, develop face-saving explanations for the conflicts:

- Define the last comfortable phase of marriage and then identify external or developmental stresses that may subsequently have overloaded the system (e.g., arrival of children, illness, financial setbacks).
- Explain the role of insufficient communication and conflict resolution skills.
- Identify conflict resolution models in each spouse's family of origin. Explain that you speak French if your parents spoke French, and that you are likely to argue if you grew up in a household where adults fought about differences. Alleviate blaming of parents by looking compassionately at parents' family of origin histories.

10. *Begin by setting agendas:* In the initial session, ask what each spouse wants to accomplish overall from therapy. Begin each subsequent session by asking what each spouse wants to focus on in that session (e.g., skills, a difficult feeling or issue, an argument from the prior week).

Close sessions by summarizing progress on each agenda item. Connect side issues to the focal concerns. In general, in a 45- to 50-minute session, one main conflict can be brought to resolution and one main skill improved.

11. *Address symptoms immediately:* Symptoms that disrupt personal or couple functioning need to be addressed early in treatment, particularly if they pose safety concerns and/or interfere with treatment. If violence is involved, immediate steps must be taken to remove guns from the home, to assure escape options, to address impacts of alcohol and drugs on safety, to teach ways of controlling anger, to ensure that both partners understand the high danger of even "minor" violence (e.g., a small push can cause a serious head injury), and to implement a temporary separation if violence risk is high. Firmly adopt the stance that no violent acts are acceptable (Holtzworth-Munroe et al., 1995).

12. *Explain that a symptom is a solution, or a by-product of a solution, to a conflict* (Heitler, 1993): Anger may serve as a means of coercion in couples that settle their differences by means of dominant-submissive, winner-loser strategies. Anger expresses frustration when stances have polarized and defensiveness has replaced listening. Anger energizes increased voice volume in order to be heard or to have one's viewpoint prevail. It also may serve to prevent discussion of hidden behavior (e.g., gambling, an affair, drugs).

Other symptoms commonly occur in high-conflict couples. Anxiety arises when conflicts hover unaddressed. Depression is the by-product of dominant-submissive conflict resolution, that is, of submitting to the preferences or will of the other. Addictive and obsessive-compulsive disorders (including eating disorders and hypochondria) indicate attempts to escape from conflicts by means of distraction.

Symptoms generally can be removed by re-addressing conflicts with healthier dialogue patterns. Augmenting the couple treatment format with individual therapy sessions and/or additional symptom removal treatment strategies (e.g., medications) may be necessary. Wherever possible, one therapist for the full system is preferable to having different therapists for the individual and the couple work (two therapists will tend to pull the couple apart). On the other hand, it is vital to utilize referrals for additional specialized treatments such as medication or treatment for substance abuse.

13. *Teach about anger:* Explain that when we are angry, we may feel like we are "seeing red." Rather than attacking when we see red, as if we were bulls, we can interpret the red as a stop sign. Anger tells us to stop, look to identify the difficulty, listen to our and to our partner's concerns, and then choose a safe route for continuing. Angry feelings enable us to identify problems; angry actions, however, seldom effectively ameliorate problems.

14. *Resolve current disputes:* Once flagrant symptoms have been sufficiently calmed, guide conflicts through the three stages of conflict resolution:

- Express initial positions. Be sure that both spouses speak up *and* listen to each other.
- Explore underlying concerns. Be sure both spouses talk about their own thoughts and feelings, not about their partner's, and that both listen to absorb, not to criticize.
- Design a mutually satisfying plan of action, a solution set responsive to all the concerns of both spouses (Heitler, 1992).

15. *Utilize the four Ss* that are essential in conflict resolution (Heitler, 1997):

- Specifics lead to resolution; generalities breed misunderstandings.
- Short segments mean that for conflicts to move toward resolution, participants need to speak a paragraph at a time, not multiple pages. Lengthy monologues lose data and drain energy from dialogue. For spouses who ramble, suggest a three-sentence rule.
- Symmetry of air time gives a sense of fairness and equal power.
- Summaries consolidate understanding and propel conflict resolution forward.

16. *Have spouses talk with each other, not through you:* High-conflict couples need to learn to talk with each other when they have differences. To redirect comments when the partners are speaking to you instead of with each other, look at the listener rather than the speaker or use a hand or head gesture to indicate that the partners are to talk to each other. On the other hand, however, funneling the dialogue through you can be a way to de-escalate tensions when anger is escalating. Similarly, when a couple's dialogue skills are poor or when you are running out of time in a session, having the spouses speak to you may speed up the conflict resolution process.

17. *Identify core concerns:* Hot spots in a dialogue indicate strongly felt concerns. As you discuss conflicts, certain underlying concerns will surface repeatedly, raising strong feelings each time. Luborsky, Crits-Christoph, and Mellon (1986) call these transference issues—such as "I don't want to be controlled" or "People disappoint me by not doing what they should" —*core conflictual themes*. I call them *core concerns*.

Note where spouses' core concerns dovetail, repeatedly reengaging the other's central concerns in what Wachtel (1993) calls vicious cycles. For instance, her thought "I can't seem to please him" and resultant depressive withdrawal may interact with his "I never get the affection I want" and angry complaining stance. Her depressive withdrawal triggers his anger; his

TABLE 2. Protocol for Depth Dive Technique for Exploring and Loosening Transference Reactions

Point of entry
- When one partner shows a strong emotion or excessive response suggestive of a transference reaction or core concern.
- Instruct him or her to close eyes and focus on the feeling.

The dive
- Say, "As you focus on that feeling, allow a similar scene from your past to emerge, a scene in which you felt a similar feeling. Notice who you see, what they are doing, and how you responded then."
- Ask, "What elements feel to you the same as in the present situation?"
- Ask, "And what in the present situation is different?" And then, "Seeing these differences, what new options exist for you now?"

Debriefing
- Have patient open his or her eyes and then digest the experience aloud.
- Clarify that the emotional response made sense in its originating circumstance. Since the present has elements in common with the original circumstance, it is understandable that the response was similar.
- Begin to experiment with the new response options available now that the patient understands the ways in which the present situation differs from the past.

angry complaints trigger her withdrawal. Establish new solutions for these concerns, replacing negative cycles with positive ones (e.g., she greets him warmly when he comes home from work; he expresses appreciation for her dinner).

18. *Depth dive to access family of origin roots of core concerns:* As Norcross (1986) explains, deeper concerns are less accessible to conscious thought and generally arise from historically earlier life experiences. See Table 2 for the steps involved in a depth dive visualization (Heitler, 1995). During a depth dive, the nondiving spouse listens, holding his or her comments for the discussion after the depth dive.

19. *Allow only healthy communication:*

- Prevent poor skills by prompting spouses before they speak. For example, to prompt effective listening, suggest, "What makes sense to you in what your spouse just said?"
- If you did not succeed with prevention, rectify skill errors by inviting a redo.
- Alternatively, serve as translator, converting provocative comments into better form. For instance, after an accusatory "You don't do your part in keeping up the house," pull your chair next to the speaker and reiterate for him or her, "I feel like I'm doing more than my share."
- Repeat frequently simple iterations of basic communication rules, such as "You can talk about yourself or ask about the other; it's out of bounds to talk about the other." "What's right, what makes sense, what's useful in what your partner is saying?"

20. *Coach communication skills:* Design practice exercises to consolidate the essential skills:

- *Insightful self-expression:* Good spousal communication involves expressing one's own concerns and feelings instead of criticizing the other. Explain the difference between self-expression and "crossovers" (my term for crossing the boundary between self and other by talking about what you think the other is thinking or feeling or telling them what to do). Practice self-expressive when-you's ("When you left early, I felt rejected"). Emphasize that the subject of a when-you is the pronoun *I.*
- *Digestive listening:* Instead of listening like an adversary for what's wrong with what the other is saying, cooperative partners listen to learn, to sponge in what makes sense in what their partner says. "But . . ." indicates that the prior comments are being deleted, not digested.
- *Bilateral listening:* Two-sided listening to both self and other enables both partners' viewpoints to count. Bilateral listening

contrasts with either-or thinking and the belief that if one person is right the other is wrong.

21. *Convert blame after upsets to apologies and learning:* Teach the couple to piece together the puzzle of what happened, with each spouse describing his or her own feelings, thoughts, actions, and mistakes. Attribute the problem to a "mis-" (e.g., a misunderstanding, mistake, miscommunication). Guide apologies, with each spouse owning his or her part in the difficulties. Conclude with each having learned something that will help to prevent future similar upsets.

22. *Terminate therapy* when the symptoms have been ameliorated, the conflicts resolved, and dialogue is consistently cooperative.

References & Readings

Christensen, A., Jacobson, N. S., & Babcock, J. (1995). Integrative behavioral couple therapy. In N. S. Jacobson & A. S . Gurman (Eds.), *Clinical handbook of couple therapy* (pp. 31–64). New York: Guilford Press.

Heitler, S. (1992). *Working with couples in conflict* [audiotape]. New York: Norton.

Heitler, S. (1993). *From conflict to resolution.* New York: Norton.

Heitler, S. (1995). *The angry couple: Conflict-focused treatment.* In L. Schein (Ed.), *Assessment and treatment of psychological disorders* [Video series]. New York: Newbridge.

Heitler, S. (1997). *The power of two.* Oakland, CA: New Harbinger.

Holtzworth-Munroe, A., Beatty, S. B., & Anglin, K. (1995). The assessment and treatment of marital violence: An introduction for the marital therapist. In N. S. Jacobson & A. S. Gurman (Eds.), *Clinical handbook of couple therapy* (pp. 317–339). New York: Guilford Press.

Lewis, J. M. (1997). *Marriage as a search for healing.* New York: Brunner/Mazel.

Luborsky, L., Crits-Christoph, P., & Mellon, J. (1986). Advent of objective measures of the transference concept. *Journal of Consulting and Clinical Psychology, 54,* 39–47.

Norcross, J. (1986). In J. O. Prochaska (Ed.), Integrative dimensions for psychotherapy. *International Journal of Eclectic Psychotherapy, 5,* 256–274.

Wachtel, P. (1993). *Therapeutic communication.* New York: Guilford Press.

Related Topics

60   TREATMENT OF MARITAL INFIDELITY

Don-David Lusterman

Estimates of extramarital sex (EMS) vary widely. Glass and Wright (1992) found that 44% of husbands and 25% of wives had at least one extramarital experience. They found a correlation between extramarital involvement (EMI) and low marital satisfaction. A full-probability study ($N = 1,200$) conducted annually over a 5-year period (Smith, 1993) reports a roughly 15% incidence, including 21% of men and 12% of women. All studies find that married men are more frequently involved than are married women. The discovery of EMI is traumatic for spouses and the couple's children, families, and friends. The following observations and guidelines are based on clinical experience and the research literature.

1. *Definition:* Infidelity is the breaking of trust. While often thought of as sexual misconduct, it may also include nonsexual but secret relationships. The most distinguishing characteristic of all types of infidelity is secrecy. Most discoverers report that deceit is the most traumatic element of discovery. Thus, if a couple agrees that extramarital sex is acceptable, no infidelity has occurred. A negative answer to the therapist's question "Could you discuss your actions comfortably with your mate?" helps the patient to understand the relationship between deceit and infidelity. A wife's discovery that her husband has been involved in a "computer romance" might be as shocking to her as the discovery that he had been involved in a sexual adventure. If a partner in a foursome becomes secretly involved with another member of the foursome, it becomes an infidelity. The violation of intimacy boundaries may be much more crucial than that of sexual boundaries; an intense and secretive platonic relationship may be more threatening than a sexual relationship.

2. *Types of marital infidelity:* Humphrey (1987) categorizes EMI by the following criteria:

- Time
- Degree of emotional involvement
- Sexual intercourse or abstinence
- Single or bilateral EMS
- Heterosexual or homosexual

Lusterman (1995) suggests an additional criterion: number of EMI partners. He also differentiates one-night stands and philandering from protracted marital infidelity (affairs). Glass and Wright (1992) use three categories: *primarily sexual*, *primarily emotional*, and *combined-type*. Careful questioning of the involved partner using these sets of criteria helps the therapist to develop an understanding of the type and degree of involvement. Such questioning may reveal philandering. Philanderers are compulsively driven to have frequent and brief EMS. They avoid intimacy and are primarily interested in power over the other person (Pittman, 1989). They are best seen as suffering a personality disorder NOS, with narcis-

sistic features, and they require individual treatment parallel with conjoint therapy.

3. *Discovery:* EMI is a systemic phenomenon, involving the discoverer and the discovered and, if it takes the form of an affair, the third party as well. Children, families of origin, and friends are also often affected. Partners in "good" marriages rate as most important "trust in each other that includes fidelity, integrity and feeling 'safe'" and "permanent commitment to the marriage" (Kaslow & Hammerschmidt, 1992). The discovery of infidelity shatters these assumptions, producing great trauma (Janoff-Bulman, 1992). The discoverer feels betrayed, and the discovered person is often ashamed and fearful of the discoverer's responses.

4. *The initial session:* The discoverer often exhibits a rapid succession of conflicting emotions and behaviors. At one moment he or she may be sobbing, at another, ready to strike at the offending mate. The discovered partner may be by turns apologetic, defensive, and angry. The discovered person may deny the infidelity despite copious proof. Admission is often accompanied by the demand that there be no further discussion about it. The therapist's first responsibility is to indicate that avoiding the topic, while it may provide some momentary relief for the discovered party, will in the end cause more problems. The therapeutic approach, while sensitive to the affective issues, must also include a psychoeducational aspect. Couples and individuals alike find that clearly defined information brings a degree of relief and often helps to restore marital communication.

5. *Therapeutic ground rules:* The couple should be told that the purpose of the therapy is to help them change their relationship. With work, they will be moving toward a better marriage or a better divorce. In a better divorce, both accept mature responsibility for the failure of the marriage. This lays the groundwork for an amicable settlement that is in the best interests of their children, and it also permits them to leave the marriage with new insights about future relationships. A better marriage is characterized by open and honest communication about both positive and negative issues.

6. *Confidentiality:* Although it is crucial to establish a relationship with the couple, it is equally important that the therapist schedule a session to meet each member of the couple alone. (Not all authorities view confidentiality the same way; for other views, see Brown, 1991; Glass & Wright, 1995; and Pittman, 1989.) I believe that individual sessions enable the therapist to see whether there are issues that one or the other is not yet ready to reveal in conjoint sessions. Individual sessions also enable the therapist to know whether the affair or other extramarital and secret sexual activity is still going on. The therapist prepares the couple for individual sessions by assuring each partner that anything discussed in such meetings is confidential. While nothing will be divulged to the other partner, the information obtained will enable the therapist to organize a treatment plan. Making this contract with the couple provides the therapist with the freedom to decide whether subsequent sessions should be held with each individual, with the couple, or as some mix of individual and couples work. In some instances only one mate undertakes therapy when marital infidelity is involved. It may be the person who is suspicious of or has just discovered a mate's EMI or the person who is extramaritally involved and conflicted about it. A systemically oriented therapist will inform the person that it is probable that the mate will be included in the therapy at some point. It is very important to inform the involved person that at no time will conjoint therapy include the third party. The involved person who decides to confess the infidelity to the mate should be strongly cautioned not to do so in the therapist's office. This person may require coaching in order to develop an appropriate strategy for revealing the infidelity. Only after the person has acted on this responsibility should conjoint therapy be undertaken.

7. *Moratorium:* It is crucial that the therapist press the involved partner to declare a moratorium on the affair. Failing that, the involved person should be helped to disclose the affair to his or her partner. Until such time, the other partner should also be seen individually, so that both partners' perceptions of the marriage can be examined. Seeing the couple indi-

vidually greatly increases their anxiety. This tension helps to break the impasse of denial and brings them back to therapy to work more directly on the marital or divorce issues.

8. *Trust-building:* Many discoverers consider themselves "victims." In such a case, it is wise for the therapist to begin by accepting this perceptual frame. Only when the discoverer feels fully supported is it possible to examine the predisposing factors that often play a role in infidelity.

9. *Sequelae of victimhood:* When the discoverer experiences himself or herself as the victim, the therapist must validate these feelings and provide the couple with information about the nature of trauma. Many discoverers report or evidence the following symptoms:

- Difficulty staying or falling asleep
- Irritability or outbursts of anger
- Difficulty concentrating
- Hypervigilance
- Exaggerated startle response
- Physiological reactivity upon exposure to events that symbolize or resemble an aspect of the traumatic event (e.g., being unable to watch a TV show or movie about infidelity)

The discoverer's responses are best reframed as a *normal*, nonpathological response to the shock of discovery (Glass & Wright, 1995; Lusterman, 1995). The therapist should make clear to both husband and wife that these intrusive recollections and obsessive searching for more details or for evidence that the infidelity continues (when the mate has denied it) are all part of a posttraumatic stress reaction as described in *DSM-IV* (American Psychiatric Association, 1994). Working together, the couple can alleviate and even overcome this trauma. The therapist should explain to the discovered mate that he or she can play a crucial role in helping the discoverer, who needs to express grief, shock, and anger directly to the mate and requires honest answers to his or her questions. This process is crucial to the restoration of trust. If the offending party blocks this process, recovery is slowed. Dealing with trauma is the first order of business. Several sessions may pass during which the therapist has the illusion that the couple is beyond the posttraumatic phase, only to discover that a fight has broken out between sessions because the discoverer, once again, *feels* that the mate is lying, withholding, and/or unable to empathize with the discoverer's pain. The mate's ability both to admit the deception and to express remorse is a necessary step in the restoration of communication. In its absence, the prognosis for good recovery from the trauma is poor.

10. *Jealousy:* It is an error to label normal reactive jealousy following the affair as if it were a personality problem. Treating it as such is a frequent cause of premature termination of therapy. In rare instances, the discoverer *is* obsessively jealous, despite honest reassurance. If careful examination reveals a history of pathological jealousy predating the marriage, this problem may require separate treatment for the pathologically jealous mate, in conjunction with the marital therapy. Pathological jealousy is best seen as an aspect of a paranoid personality disorder.

11. *Predisposing factors:* Once the couple has negotiated the hurdle of discovery, it is then possible to begin a review of the prediscovery phase of the marriage. During this process, the therapist helps the couple to move beyond the issue of perceived victimhood and on to an examination of factors within the marriage that may have contributed to the affair. Such factors generally include low self-disclosure and consequent poor problem solving (Lusterman, 1989). During this phase, the therapist must be alert to the recurrence of posttraumatic signs. These can be precipitated, for example, by the discovery of old evidence, hang-up telephone calls, or stalking by the third party. Each time there is such a recurrence, it is important to address the posttraumatic issues before returning to the review process. Once the predisposing factors have been examined, the couple is ready for traditional marital therapy, with a focus on honest communication.

12. *Termination:* Couples are ready for termination when they have examined the context and meaning of the infidelity and have resolved that they can either proceed to a healthier relationship or move toward divorce. A better marriage includes an improvement in mutual empathy and joint responsibility (Glass & Wright, 1995).

Because the discoverer remains vulnerable to a possible recurrence, it is important to discuss with both mates the importance of a detection mechanism. The offending mate is reminded that, should the discoverer need reassurance, it must be patiently given. The discoverer is asked to agree with the offending mate that if there is a recurrence, the next stage will be divorce.

13. *Bibliotherapy:* As part of a psychoeducational approach, suggested readings can be helpful. Janoff-Bulman (1992), Lusterman (1989), Pittman (1989), and Vaughan (1989) have been found to be of value. A number of Web sites also provide an opportunity to receive information and participate in a bulletin board. Among these are the following:

- America On Line: *Extramarital Affairs Forum:* keyword: online psych; *Divorce and Separation Community:* keyword: better health; then, under "Community Connection," go to "Divorce and Separation"
- Internet Web site: *Vaughan & Vaughan Homepage:* http://www.vaughan-vaughan.com

References & Readings

American Psychiatric Association (1994). *Diagnostic and statistical manual of mental disorders* (4th ed.). Washington, DC: American Psychiatric Association.

Brown, E. (1991). *Patterns of infidelity and their treatment.* New York: Brunner/Mazel.

Glass, S., & Wright, T. (1992). Justifications for extramarital relationships: The association between attitudes, behavior, and gender. *Journal of Sex Research, 29,* 361–387.

Glass, S., & Wright, T. (1995). Reconstructing marriages after the trauma of infidelity. In K. Halford & H. Markman (Eds.), *Clinical handbook of marriage and couple interventions.* New York: Wiley.

Humphrey, F. (1987). Treating extramarital sexual relationships in sex and couples therapy. In G. Weeks & L. Hof (Eds.), *Integrating sex and marital therapy: A clinical guide.* New York: Brunner/Mazel.

Janoff-Bulman, R. (1992). *Shattered assumptions: Towards a new psychology of trauma*. New York: Free Press.

Kaslow, F., & Hammerschmidt, H. (1992). Long-term "good marriages": The seemingly essential ingredients. *Journal of Couples Therapy, 3(2/3)*, 15–38.

Lusterman, D.-D. (1989, May/June). Marriage at the turning point. *Family Networker, 13*, 44–51.

Lusterman, D.-D. (1995). Treating marital infidelity. In R. Mikesell, D.-D. Lusterman, & S. McDaniel (Eds.), *Integrating family therapy: Handbook of family psychology and systems theory*. Washington, DC: American Psychological Association.

Pittman, D. J. (1989). *Private lies: Infidelity and the betrayal of intimacy*. New York: Norton.

Smith, T. (1993). *American sexual behavior: Trends, socio-demographic differences, and risk behavior* (Version 1.2). Chicago: National Opinion Research Center, University of Chicago.

Vaughan, P. (1989). *The monogamy myth*. New York: Newmarket Press.

Related Topics

Chapter 58, "Guidelines for Conducting Couple and Family Therapy"

Chapter 59, "Treating High-Conflict Couples"

61 PRINCIPLES OF BRIEF AND TIME-EFFECTIVE THERAPIES

Brett N. Steenbarger & Simon H. Budman

The idea of change is fundamental to psychotherapy. People enter into therapeutic relationships to make changes in their lives: their relationships, behavior patterns, feelings, and thoughts. A matter of ongoing debate is the amount of time needed for such changes to occur. At one end of the spectrum of positions are the relatively nondirective therapies, such as Rogerian, client-centered approaches and classical psychoanalytic models, which rely heavily on the client to establish the pace of change and, hence, are *time-unlimited*. At the other end of the spectrum are *time-limited* models of treatment, which specify a fixed number of sessions as a formal part of treatment planning. Between these poles are a variety of treatment approaches that are brief but not necessarily time-limited (see Wells & Giannetti, 1990, for an overview). *Time-effectiveness*, rather than classical brevity, has thus become a prominent feature of the professional landscape (Budman & Gurman, 1992).

Brief therapy is time-effective by design rather than by default (Budman & Gurman, 1988). The use of strategies that facilitate efficient and effective change is consciously built into treatment plans. For this reason, short-term work is more than time-unlimited treatment packed into fewer sessions. An analogy would be lightning chess, in which players are allotted a fixed amount of time in which to play an entire game. Each move is rapid and must draw on the player's ability to quickly appraise and act on situations. If traditional chess players attempted to play the lightning version of the game without altering their approach, they would rarely see an endgame. The introduction of time demands creates a new game, requiring different skills (Budman & Steenbarger, 1997).

The brevity of short-term treatment is meaningfully related to several variables, including the proposed focus of change, the directivity of the change methods, and the aggressiveness with which between-session contexts for change are maximized. The briefest modalities tend to establish a highly specific focus for change and actively maintain this focus from session to session. Short-term models that are less brief, such as cognitive restructuring and dynamic work, seek change across broader cognitive and relationship patterns. Similarly, approaches that are prescriptive in their assignment of homework and directed tasks are briefer than models that are exploratory and dominantly focused on within-session change contexts.

Despite the considerable popularity and relevance of brief therapy, surprisingly few studies have been conducted to directly compare short-term versus long-term interventions. Indeed most psychotherapy outcome studies have been conducted with treatments of 20 sessions and fewer, so that much of the outcome literature can be construed as pertaining to brief work. Reviewers of process and outcome findings (Lambert & Bergin, 1994; Koss & Shiang, 1994; Steenbarger, 1992, 1994), however, emphasize the following findings of particular relevance to time-effective treatment.

- *Most therapy is brief in duration:* Studies conducted across multiple delivery systems find that clients average five sessions in treatment, with over 80% of clients finishing their therapy by the 10th visit (Phillips, 1992).
- *Change occurs most rapidly early in psychotherapy:* Gains are extended with additional sessions but with somewhat diminishing returns, especially among clients with low-severity concerns (Howard, Kopta, Krause, & Orlinsky, 1986).
- *Brief therapy is effective:* Meta-analytic studies suggest that therapies overall aver-

age one standard deviation of change, significantly exceeding changes associated with no-treatment controls and, to a somewhat lesser degree, inert placebos (Lambert & Bergin, 1994).
- *Nonspecific factors account for much of brief therapy's effectiveness:* Gains in brief therapy are not reliably different from one approach to another, nor do they necessarily exceed the gains produced by generic treatments offering support, reassurance, and expectations of change (Elkin, 1994).
- *Severity of the presenting problem is an important mediator of brief therapy outcome:* Evidence suggests that the trajectory of change (Howard et al., 1986) and the effectiveness of treatment (Lambert & Bergin, 1994) are attenuated when presenting problems are severe rather than mild.

There is general recognition that brief therapy is not appropriate for all clients and that the indiscriminate application of highly abbreviated treatments will yield significantly higher relapse rates (Steenbarger, 1992). Accordingly, the initial phase of treatment generally begins with an assessment to determine the degree to which brevity can be incorporated into treatment planning. The acronym DISC can be especially helpful in conceptualizing the following key indications for short-term work.

- *Duration:* Presenting problems that are chronic and long-standing are more apt to require ongoing treatment than are problems that are situational and developmental.
- *Interpersonal history:* A history of trauma and/or a history in which there is an absence of long-term, positive relationships often contraindicates brevity. Clients with stable, highly positive interpersonal histories are most likely to be able to form the rapid bonds with therapists that are needed for brief work.
- *Severity:* Problems that greatly interfere with a client's functioning in work, social, and emotional spheres are less likely to be resolved briefly than are problems that do not leave clients highly impaired.

- *Complexity:* Highly complex problems, with multiple emotional, behavioral, somatic, and cognitive components, tend to require more concerted and ongoing intervention than do highly focal presenting concerns.

Such criteria can form the backbone of data-driven triage and practice guidelines, creating a meaningful integration of research and practice in the clinical setting and enhancing both the quality and cost-effectiveness of care (Budman & Steenbarger, 1997).

A significant body of work suggests that elements common to the psychotherapies, not their unique and differentiating features, may be most responsible for their salutary impact (Garfield, 1994). This finding has led to a search for integrative models of therapy that maximize the effective ingredients of change across all modalities (Norcross & Goldfried, 1992). Similarly, a number of authors have proposed that the brief therapies share features that account for their ability to catalyze change (Budman & Gurman, 1988; Koss & Shiang, 1994; Steenbarger, 1992). These common principles include the following:

- *Focus:* The brief therapies do not attempt to reconstruct personality but instead limit changes to specific targets relevant to the client's presenting concerns.
- *Activity:* Brief therapists assume an active stance as a change agent, maintaining the focus and introducing change methods rather than allowing clients to establish the pace of treatment.
- *Therapist values:* Brief therapists tend to adopt a developmental approach to change, in which clients are viewed as engaged in ongoing adaptive efforts rather than as stuck at a level of pathology.
- *Client involvement:* Brief therapies make explicit efforts to actively engage clients in change efforts, both within and between sessions.
- *Novelty:* Brief therapies introduce novel skills, experiences, and understandings into treatment as ways of speeding up change processes.

To the extent that *any* therapy embodies these elements, it might be said to be time-effective, though not necessarily brief or time-limited (Budman & Gurman, 1992). Integrative accounts (Budman & Gurman, 1988; Steenbarger, 1992) help to delineate how change processes occur in such time-effective work. Clients enter treatment with established patterns that yield unwanted consequences in terms of mood, behavior, and relationships. By actively setting treatment foci and explicitly addressing time in treatment planning, therapists establish favorable expectations for change early in the helping process. The introduction of novel skills, understandings, and experiences—particularly under conditions of maximum client experiencing and involvement—appears to dislodge old problem patterns and facilitate the building of constructive alternatives. Rapid feedback and the use of between-session change contexts, as in homework exercises, help to cement initial changes, preventing relapse. The practice of time-effective work might thus be described as tripartite, with techniques devoted to the following:

- *Engagement:* Building trust and rapport, and helping clients identify focal goals for which they are prepared to take action
- *Discrepancy:* Creating situations in which clients are encouraged to think, feel, and act in ways that are discrepant from their accustomed problem patterns
- *Implementation and maintenance:* Using in- and out-of-session contexts to rehearse and elaborate changes, provide feedback, and facilitate the internalization of new patterns

At the level of technique, especially striking is the manner in which each of the various time-effective approaches incorporates strategies to move clients beyond traditional discourse to a level of greater experiencing. The skillful use of imagery, metaphor, in- and between-session exercises, confrontation, paradox, and rehearsal takes clients out of an accustomed mode of consciousness, allowing them to experience themselves and others in new ways. Sometimes the strategies are quieting, as in relaxation methods, guided imagery techniques, and other introspective devices. At other times, the modes are galvanizing, as in confrontation and the prescription of unusual tasks. It is very common for time-effective therapists to facilitate change in a "one-two punch," with shifts in consciousness preceding efforts at introducing novel action and thought patterns. An analogy would be to chaotic systems in physical science, in which small deviations in initial conditions undergo multiple iterations, leading to profound changes in outcome. The brief therapist, in a sense, treats clients as deviation-amplifying systems that can take the seemingly small novelties introduced in treatment and spread these across a life span. From this vantage point, it is the power of treatment to dislodge old patterns—not necessarily the duration of therapy per se—that accounts for its efficacy.

Several authors (Budman & Gurman, 1992; Prochaska, Norcross, & DiClemente, 1994; Steenbarger, 1994) have suggested that a stages-of-change framework may be helpful in understanding the processes common to the time-effective therapies. Clients at a relatively low level of readiness for change, as evidenced by the inability to articulate a treatment focus and unwillingness to take action, may benefit from exploratory approaches that facilitate an understanding of problems and the building of a treatment alliance. Those who enter therapy already committed to making specific changes, conversely, might best benefit from action-oriented methods that rapidly introduce novel cognitive, interpersonal, and behavioral patterns. It would thus make sense that highly abbreviated treatment would be most appropriate among clients who begin their treatment with clear, focused goals and a readiness to begin action. Those requiring self-exploration to understand problem patterns and commit to change will necessarily engage in therapy of longer duration.

References & Readings

Budman, S. H., & Gurman, A. S. (1988). *Theory and practice of brief therapy*. New York: Guilford Press.

Budman, S. H., & Gurman, A. S. (1992). A time sensitive model of brief therapy: The I-D-E approach. In S. H. Budman, M. F. Hoyt, & S. Friedman (Eds.), *The first session in brief therapy* (pp. 111–134). New York: Guilford Press.

Budman, S. H., & Steenbarger, B. N. (1997). *The essential guide to group practice in mental health: Clinical, legal, and financial fundamentals*. New York: Guilford Press.

Elkin, I. (1994). The NIMH Treatment of Depression Collaborative Research Program: Where we began, where we are. In A. E. Bergin & S. L. Garfield (Eds.), *Handbook of psychotherapy and behavior change* (4th ed., pp. 114–142). New York: Wiley.

Garfield, S. L. (1994). Research on client variables in psychotherapy. In A. E. Bergin & S. L. Garfield (Eds.), *Handbook of psychotherapy and behavior change* (4th ed., pp. 190–228). New York: Wiley.

Howard, K. I., Kopta, S. M., Krause, M. J., & Orlinsky, D. E. (1986). The dose-effect relationship in psychotherapy. *American Psychologist, 41,* 159–164.

Koss, M. P., & Shiang, J. (1994). Research on brief psychotherapy. In A. E. Bergin & S. L. Garfield (Eds.), *Handbook of psychotherapy and behavior change* (4th ed., pp. 664–700). New York: Wiley.

Lambert, M. J., & Bergin, A. E. (1994). The effectiveness of psychotherapy. In A. E. Bergin & S. L. Garfield (Eds.), *Handbook of psychotherapy and behavior change* (4th ed., pp. 143–189). New York: Wiley.

Norcross, J. C., & Goldfried, M. R. (Eds.) (1992). *Handbook of psychotherapy integration*. New York: Basic Books.

Phillips, E. L. (1992). George Washington University's international data on psychotherapy delivery systems: Modeling new approaches to the study of therapy. In L. E. Beutler & M. Crago (Eds.), *Psychotherapy research: An international review of programmatic studies* (pp. 263–273). Washington, DC: American Psychological Association.

Prochaska, J. O., Norcross, J. C., & DiClemente, C. C. (1994). *Changing for good*. New York: Avon.

Steenbarger, B. N. (1992). Toward science-practice integration in brief counseling and therapy. *Counseling Psychologist, 20,* 403–450.

Steenbarger, B. N. (1994). Duration and outcome in

psychotherapy: An integrative review. *Professional Psychology: Research and Practice, 25,* 111–119.

Wells, R. A., & Giannetti, V. J. (Eds.) (1990). *Handbook of the brief psychotherapies.* New York: Plenum Press.

62   TREATMENT AND MANAGEMENT OF THE SUICIDAL PATIENT

Bruce Bongar

Suicide has been found to be the most frequently encountered emergency situation for mental health professionals (Schein, 1976), with clinicians consistently ranking work with suicidal patients as the most stressful of all clinical endeavors (Deutsch, 1984). Recent empirical findings have shown that the average professional psychologist who is involved in direct patient care has almost a 1 in 3 chance of losing a patient to suicide at some time during his or her professional career (Greaney, 1995). In addition, one study found that a psychologist in training has a 1 in 7 chance of losing a patient to suicide (Brown, 1987).

A telling national survey found that psychologists responded to the loss of a patient to suicide in a manner akin to the death of a family member (Chemtob, Hamada, Bauer, Torigoe, & Kinney, 1988). Because the possibility of a patient's suicide is not a rare event in psychological practice, it must be considered a real occupational hazard for those clinicians involved in direct patient care (Chemtob, Hamada, Bauer, Torigoe, & Kinney, 1988). This hazard not only encompasses the threat of malpractice action but also entails the intense emotional toll that a patient's suicide can wreak on the survivors (including the patient's psychologist).

At the present time, malpractice actions against clinicians for the death of a patient are relatively rare, although increasing in frequency. The American Psychological Association's Insurance Trust (APAIT) has provided summary data that indicate that malpractice related to suicide of a patient was the sixth most frequent claim brought against psychologists, but it ranked second in the percentage of total costs (5.4% of the claims and 10% of the costs; APAIT Claims Frequency, 1990). However, as nonmedical clinicians seek expanded professional privileges such as hospital staff membership and admission and discharge privileges, they will find themselves exposed to many of the same malpractice liabilities as their colleagues in psychiatry (Gutheil & Appelbaum, 1982).

GENERAL PRINCIPLES

The mental health professional's assessment and treatment efforts represent an opportunity to translate knowledge (albeit incomplete) of elevated risk factors into a plan of action (Bongar, 1991). The management plan for patients who are at an elevated risk for suicide should ameliorate those risk factors that are most foreseeably likely to result in suicide or self-harm (Brent, Kupfer, Bromet, & Dew, 1988). Several general principles should guide the treatment of patients at elevated risk for suicide and apply across broad diagnostic categories:

- The most basic principle is that, because most suicide victims take their own lives or harm themselves in the midst of a psychiatric episode, it is critical to understand that a proper diagnosis and careful management/treatment plan of the acute psychiatric disorder could dramatically alter the risk of suicide (Brent et al., 1988). The data on adult suicides indicate that more than 90% of these suicide victims were mentally ill before their death.
- For acute management, special precautions must be taken when assessing and treating patients who present with chronic suicidal ideation and behavior (e.g., where the clinician takes repeated calculated risks in not hospitalizing). Gutheil (1990) noted that here the mental health clinician will feel the tension between short-term solutions (e.g., a protected environment) and long-term solutions (e.g., actual treatment of the chronicity).
- Family involvement for support and improved compliance.
- Diagnosis and treatment of any comorbid medical and psychiatric condition.
- The provision of hope, particularly to new-onset patients.
- The restriction of the availability of lethal agents; and indications for psychiatric hospitalization (Brent et al., 1988).
- To this list, a risk management perspective would add the critical necessity of assessing personal and professional competences in order to treat at-risk patients.

- Meticulous documentation and the routine involvement of a "second opinion," through consultation (Bongar, 1991; Bongar, Peterson, Harris, & Aissis, 1989).

All our assessment and management activities also should include a specific evaluation of the patient's competence to participate in management and treatment decisions, especially the patient's ability to form a therapeutic alliance (Bongar, 1991; Gutheil, 1984, 1990; Kahn, 1982; Luborsky, 1990). An essential element in strengthening this alliance is the use of informed consent; that is, patients have the right to participate actively in making decisions about their psychological/psychiatric care (Bongar, 1991). Clinicians need to directly and continuously evaluate the quality of this special relationship—to understand that the quality of this collaborative alliance is inextricably part of any successful treatment/management plan (Bongar et al., 1989, 1991; Gutheil, 1984, 1990; Kahn, 1982; Luborsky, 1990; Motto, 1979; Shneidman, 1981, 1984; Simon, 1987, 1988).

RISK ASSESSMENT AND MANAGEMENT

Suicide results from the complex interplay of a number of diagnostic (psychiatric and medical), constitutional, environmental, occupational, sociocultural, existential, and chance causal elements. It is not simply the result of misdiagnosis or inadequate treatment. Courts sometimes have trouble understanding that psychotherapists are "ordinary mortals struggling with" this conundrum (Simon, 1987, p. 264) and that mental health professionals are not able to guarantee control over the behavior of their patients, particularly patients in outpatient treatment. Additionally, Maltsberger and Goldblatt (1996) noted:

Suicide risk assessment, a clinical activity, refers to the establishment of a clinical judgement of risk in the very near future, based on the weighing of a very large mass of available clinical detail. From time to time confused clinicians conclude that because suicide cannot be predicted, clinical risk assessment is a chimerical pursuit, and that one might as well toss a coin. Risk assessment carried out in a systematic, disciplined way (Maltsberger, 1992) is more than a guess or an intuition (Motto, 1989, 1992). The best clinical risk assessment is a reasoned, inductive process, and it is a responsibility that we cannot escape. (Maltsberger & Goldblatt, 1996, p. 481)

As a first step in risk management, clinicians need to determine their own technical and personal competence to work with such high-risk patients. Although the law does not record a case to date of negligent psychotherapy where the basis was a failure to cure or to relieve a psychiatric symptom, verbal psychotherapies are not without their own risks (Simon, 1987). Patients who are improperly diagnosed or given an inappropriate type of psychotherapy may indeed regress and present with suicidal ideation or behavior (Simon, 1987; Stone, 1989a, 1989b). Unusual or extreme therapies, innovative or regressive therapies, as well as sexual seduction by therapists and malignant countertransferences can be taken as evidence of treatment gone awry. The presence of such factors may increase the risk of suicide significantly (Simon, 1987). Stone (1989b) has cautioned about the risks of forcing a patient to see that his or her reality situation is empty of possible gratification; he has also emphasized the need to be cautious when the context of this malignant insight is such that the patient feels even more hopeless and helpless. At times, therapy is less than adequate because of ideological, theoretical, or technical prejudices (Lesse, 1989). "Not all psychiatrists and other psychotherapists are equipped emotionally or technically to manage suicidal patients" (Lesse, 1989, p. 215).

In coming to terms with their own limitations, therapists must remember that all mental health providers are limited to varying degrees in their specific professional competences. As Welch noted: "One might further argue that the greatest threat to 'quality of care' comes not from those with limited training but from those with a limited recognition of the limitations of their own training" (1989, p. 28).

One of the initial tasks of the mental health professional who is called upon to treat the suicidal patient is the need to have evaluated a priori the strengths and limitations of his or her own training, education, and experience in the treatment of specific patient populations in specific clinical settings (e.g., an understanding of the therapist's own technical proficiencies, as well as emotional tolerance levels for the intense demands required in treating suicidal patients).

Honest errors of judgment are inevitable in clinical practice, and the courts have recognized that "the accurate prediction of dangerous behavior, and particularly suicide and homicide, are almost never possible. Thus, an error of prediction, or even of judgment does not necessarily establish negligence" (Stromberg et al., 1988, p. 468).

Based on my clinical and forensic experience, there are common themes in complaints lodged against outpatient therapists, reflecting possible breaches in the duty of care and the practitioner's failure to act in a reasonable and prudent manner. Attention to these "failures" may therefore represent an opportunity to develop appropriate treatment and risk management strategies. Table 1 details the most common failure scenarios in outpatient care.

Previously, I have operationalized a consultation model that seeks to maximize clinical, legal, and ethical standards of care for suicidal patients. The model suggested first emphasizes the importance of developing a strong therapeutic alliance, facilitated via informed consent procedures at treatment initiation. The informed consent procedure should begin an "ongoing process of information-giving and collaboration" with the client (Bongar, 1991, p. 177). By involving patients and their families, when appropriate, as "collaborative risk management partners" (Bongar, 1991, p. 177), cooperation with treatment is improved, the protective net is widened, responses to treatment are more closely monitored, and the quality and quantity of available data are improved.

Second, the model emphasizes the importance of retaining appropriate consultants. These consultants should be senior or expert in the field or should have forensic experience, or both. They should be retained on a regular basis for formal (as opposed to informal) con-

TABLE 1. Outpatient Suicide: Common Failure Scenarios

1. Failure to properly evaluate the need for psychopharmacological intervention, or unsuitable pharmacotherapy.
2. Failure to specify criteria for and to implement hospitalization.
3. Failure to maintain appropriate clinician-patient relationships (e.g., dual relationships, sexual improprieties and dual relationships with patients)
4. Failures in supervision and consultation.
5. Failure to evaluate for suicide risk: at intake.
6. Failure to evaluate for suicide risk: at management transitions.
7. Failure to secure records of prior treatment/inadequate history taking.
8. Failure to conduct a mental status exam.
9. Failure to diagnose.
10. Failure to establish a formal treatment plan.
11. Failure to safeguard the outpatient environment.
12. Failure to adequately document clinical judgments, rationales, and observations.

Source: Bongar, Berman, Litman, & Maris, 1992.

sultation. That is, "In order for the consultation to be more forensically effective it must be a formal one, one where the psychologist and the consultant provide notes for the written record and where both consultant and psychologist of record formally acknowledge that a consultant relationship is in effect" (Bongar, 1991, p. 185). This written record is necessary in order for the consultation to be legally recognized and unquestioned (Bongar, 1991). Finally, consultants should be given sufficient information to provide reasonable advice.

What follows is a detailed list of issues the consultant should be asked to address when the clinical situation is one of risk, uncertainty, or danger. These include reviewing

1. The overall management of the case, specific treatment issues, and uncertainties in the assessment of elevated risk or in diagnosis. This can include a review of the mental status examination, history, information from significant others, the results of any psychological tests and data from risk estimators, suicide lethality scales, and so forth. The psychologist's formulation of the patient's (*DSM-IV*) diagnosis, together with any other specific psychotherapeutic formulations, clinical assessments, and evaluation of any special treatment and management issues (e.g., co-morbidity of alcohol/substance abuse, physical illness), should also be reviewed.

2. Issues of managing the patient with chronically suicidal behavior, violent behavior, patient dependency, patient hostility and manipulation, toxic interpersonal matrices, lack of psychosocial supports, and the patient's competence to participate in treatment decisions. An assessment of the quality of the therapeutic alliance and the patient's particular response to the psychologist and to the course of treatment (e.g., intense negative or positive transference) should also be discussed.

3. The psychologist's own feelings about the progress of treatment and feelings toward the patient (e.g., the psychologist's feelings of fear, incompetence, anxiety, helplessness, or even anger) and any negative therapeutic reactions such as countertransference and therapist burnout.

4. The advisability of using medication or the need for additional medical evaluation (e.g., any uncertainties regarding organicity or neurological complications) or both. Reevaluation of any current medications that the patient is taking (e.g., effectiveness, compliance in taking medication, side effects, polypharmacy) should be included in this review of medication options.

5. The indications and contraindications for hospitalization. Considerations should include what community crisis intervention resources are available for the patient with

few psychosocial supports, day treatment options, emergency and backup arrangements and resources, and planning for the psychologist's absences.

6. Indications and contraindications for family and group treatment. This discussion should include the possible use of other types of psychotherapy and somatic interventions and questions on the status of and progress in the integration of multiple therapeutic techniques.

7. The psychologist's assessment criteria for evaluating dangerousness and imminence (e.g., whether the consultant agrees with the clinician's assessment of the level of perturbation and lethality). The specifics of the patient's feelings of despair, depression, hopelessness, impulsivity, and cognitive constriction and his or her impulses toward cessation should also be discussed.

8. The issues of informed consent and confidentiality and the adequacy of all current documentation on the case (e.g., intake notes, progress notes, utilization reviews, family meetings, supervisor notes, telephone contacts).

9. Whether the consultant agrees with the psychologist's current risk-benefit analysis and management plan. Does the consultant agree that the dual issues of foreseeability and the need to take affirmative precautions have been adequately addressed? (Bongar, 1991, pp. 183–184)

SUMMARY GUIDELINES

In *The Suicidal Patient: Clinical and Legal Standards of Care*, Bongar (1991, pp. 202–204) made the following eight points for the most optimal care:

1. For each patient seen as part of a clinician's professional practice activities, there must be an initial evaluation and assessment, regular ongoing clinical evaluations and case reviews, consultation reports and supervision reports (where indicated), and a formal treatment plan. All these activities need to demonstrate specifically a solid understanding of the significant factors used to assess elevated risk of suicide and how to manage such risk—with a documented understanding of the prognosis for the success (or possible paths to failure) of subsequent outpatient (or inpatient) treatment or case disposition.

2. Clinicians must be aware of the vital importance of documentation. In cases of malpractice, courts and juries often have been observed to operate on the simplistic principle that "if it isn't written down, it didn't happen" (no matter what the subsequent testimony or elaboration of the defendant maintains). Defensive clinical notes, written after the fact, may help somewhat in damage control, but there is no substitute for a timely, thoughtful, and complete chart record that demonstrates (through clear and well-written assessment, review, and treatment notes) a knowledge of the epidemiology, risk factors, and treatment literature for the suicidal patient. Such a case record should also include (where possible) a formal informed consent for treatment, formal assessment of competence, and documentation of confidentiality considerations (e.g., that limits were explained at the start of any treatment).

3. Clinicians must obtain, whenever possible, all previous treatment records and must consult with previous psychotherapists. When appropriate, mental health practitioners should involve the family and significant others in the management or disposition plan. The family and significant others are good sources of information (both current and background) and can serve as an integral and effective part of the support system.

4. Clinicians should routinely obtain consultation and/or supervision (or make referrals) on any case where suicide risk is determined to be elevated, as well as after a patient suicide or serious suicide attempt. They also should obtain consultation and/or supervision on (or refer) cases that are outside their documented training, education, or experience, as well as when they are unsure of the best avenue for initiating or continuing treatment. A guiding principle in moments

of clinical uncertainty is that two perspectives are better than one.

5. Clinicians should be knowledgeable about the effects of psychotropic medication and make appropriate referrals for a medication evaluation. If the clinician decides that medication is not indicated in the present instance, he or she should thoroughly document the reasoning for this decision in the written case record. Where appropriate, the patient (and, when indicated, the patient's family or significant others) should be included in this decision-making process. Clinicians need to know the possible organic etiologies for suicidality and seek immediate appropriate medical consultation for the patient when they detect any signs of an organic condition.

6. Clinicians who see suicidal patients at elevated risk levels should have access to the full armamentarium of resources for voluntary and involuntary hospital admissions, day treatment, 24-hour emergency backup, and crisis centers. This access can be direct or indirect (through an ongoing collaborative relationship with a psychologist or psychiatrist colleague).

7. If a patient succeeds in committing suicide (or makes a serious suicide attempt), the clinician should be aware not only of his or her legal responsibilities (e.g., the clinician must notify his or her insurance carrier in a timely fashion) but also, and more important, of the immediate clinical necessity of attending both to the postvention needs of the bereaved survivors and to the clinician's own emotional needs. (The clinician must acknowledge that it is both normal and difficult to work through feelings about a patient's death or near death, and that he or she, having lost a patient to suicide, is also a suicide survivor.) The concern should be for the living. After consultation with a knowledgeable colleague and an attorney, not only is immediate clinical outreach to the survivors sensitive and concerned clinical care, but also in helping the survivors to deal with the catastrophic aftermath via an effective clinical postvention effort, the clinician is practicing effective risk management.

8. Most important, clinicians must be cognizant of all the above standards and take affirmative steps to ensure that they have the requisite knowledge, training, experience, and clinical resources prior to accepting high-risk patients into their professional care. This requires that all these mechanisms be in place before the onset of any suicidal crisis.

Note

Portions of this chapter are adapted from Bruce Bongar, *The Suicidal Patient: Clinical and Legal Standards of Care* (Washington, DC: American Psychological Association, 1991), and Bruce Bongar, N. Peruzzi, and S. Greaney, "Risk Management and the Suicidal Patient," in P. Kleespies (Ed.), *Handbook of Psychological Emergencies* (in press). Reprinted with permission.

References & Readings

Bongar, B. (1991). *The suicidal patient: Clinical and legal standards of care.* Washington, DC: American Psychological Association.

Bongar, B., Berman, A. L., Litman, R. E., & Maris, R. (1992). Outpatient standards of care in the assessment, management, and treatment of suicidal persons. *Suicide and Life-Threatening Behavior, 22,* 453–478.

Bongar, B., Peruzzi, N., & Greaney, S. (in press). Risk management and the suicidal patient. In P. Kleespies (Ed.), *Handbook of psychological emergencies.*

Bongar, B., Peterson, L. G., Harris, E. A., & Aissis, J. (1989). Clinical and legal considerations in the management of suicidal patients: An integrative overview. *Journal of Integrative and Eclectic Psychotherapy, 8*(1), 53–67.

Brent, D. A., Kupfer, D. J., Bromet, E. J., & Dew, M. A. (1988). The assessment and treatment of patients at risk for suicide. In A. J. Frances & R. E. Hales (Eds.), *American Psychiatric Press review of psychiatry* (Vol. 7, pp. 353–385). Washington, DC: American Psychiatric Press.

Brown, H. N. (1987). The impact of suicides on therapists in training. *Comprehensive Psychiatry, 28*(2), 101–112.

Chemtob, C. M., Hamada, R. S., Bauer, G. B., Torigoe, R. Y., & Kinney, B. (1988). Patient suicide: Frequency and impact on psychologists. *Professional Psychology: Research and Practice, 19,* 416–420.

Deutsch, C. J. (1984). Self-report sources of stress among psychotherapists. *Professional Psychology: Research and Practice, 15,* 833–845.

Greaney, S. (1995). *Psychologists' behavior and attitudes when working with the non-hospitalized suicidal patient.* Unpublished doctoral dissertation, Pacific Graduate School of Psychology, Palo Alto, California.

Gutheil, T. G. (1984). Malpractice liability in suicide. *Legal Aspects of Psychiatric Practice, 1,* 1–4.

Gutheil, T. G. (1990). Argument for the defendant—Expert opinion: Death in hindsight. In R. I. Simon (Ed.), *Review of clinical psychiatry and the law* (pp. 335–339). Washington, DC: American Psychiatric Association.

Gutheil, T. G., & Appelbaum, P. S. (1982). *Clinical handbook of psychiatry and the law.* New York: McGraw-Hill.

Kahn, A. (1982). The stress of therapy. In E. L. Bassuk, S. C. Schoonover, & A. D. Gill (Eds.), *Lifelines: Clinical perspectives on suicide* (pp. 93–100). New York: Plenum.

Lesse, S. (1989). The range of therapies with severely depressed suicidal patients. In S. Lesse (Ed.), *What we know about suicidal behavior and how to treat it* (pp. 193–217). Northvale, NJ: Jason Aronson.

Litman, R. E. (1988, May). Treating high-risk chronically suicidal patients. In D. G. Jacobs & J. Fawcett (Chairs), *Suicide and the psychiatrist: Clinical challenges.* Paper presented at a symposium conducted by the Suicide Education Institute of Boston, in collaboration with the Center of Suicide Research and Prevention, at the American Psychiatric Association Annual Meeting, Montreal, Quebec, Canada.

Luborsky, L. (1990). Who is helped by psychotherapy? *Harvard Medical School Mental Health Letter, 7*(2), 4–5.

Maltsberger, J. T., & Goldblatt, M. J. (Eds.) (1996). *Essential papers on suicide.* New York: New York University Press.

Motto, J. A. (1979). Guidelines for the management of the suicidal patient (Weekly Psychiatry Update Series, Lesson 20, Vol. 3, pp. 3–7). [Available from Biomedia, Inc., 20 Nassau Street, Princeton, NJ 08540.]

Motto, J. A. (1989). Problems in suicide risk assessment. In D. G. Jacobs & H. N. Brown (Eds.), *Suicide: Understanding and responding* (pp. 129–142). Harvard Medical School perspectives on suicide. Madison, CT: International Universities Press.

Schein, H. M. (1976). Obstacles in the education of psychiatric residents. *Omega, 7,* 75–82.

Shneidman, E. S. (1981). Psychotherapy with suicidal patients. *Suicide and Life-Threatening Behavior, 11,* 341–348.

Shneidman, E. S. (1984). Aphorisms of suicide and some implications for psychotherapy. *American Journal of Psychotherapy, 38,* 319–328.

Simon, R. I. (1987). *Clinical psychiatry and the law.* Washington, DC: American Psychiatric Press.

Simon, R. I. (1988). *Concise guide to clinical psychiatry and the law.* Washington, DC: American Psychiatric Press.

Stone, A. A. (1989a). A response to Dr. Klerman. *Harvard Medical School Mental Health Letter, 6*(1), 3–4.

Stone, A. A. (1989b). Suicide precipitated by psychotherapy. In S. Lesse (Ed.), *What we know about suicidal behavior and how to treat it* (pp. 307–319). Northvale, NJ: Jason Aronson.

Stromberg, C. D., Haggarty, D. J., Leibenluft, R. F., McMillan, M. H., Mishkin, B., Rubin, B. L., & Trilling, H. R. (1988). *The psychologist's legal handbook.* Washington, DC: Council for the National Register of Health Service Providers in Psychology.

Welch, B. (1989). A collaborative model proposed. *American Psychological Association Monitor, 20*(10), 28.

Related Topics

63 CRISIS INTERVENTION

Kenneth France

1. *Clients who need crisis intervention:* A crisis exists when a person's usual coping methods fail to successfully handle current pressures and the individual feels overwhelmed by seemingly unresolvable difficulties. Finding oneself in crisis usually results in new coping efforts (Folkman, Lazarus, Dunkel-Schetter, DeLongis, & Gruen, 1986), which may include actions such as contacting a psychologist. A person reaching out in this way is desperate for an end to the stress and is likely to welcome the professional's crisis intervention assistance (Halpern, 1973, 1975). Together they work in a problem-solving alliance that draws on the client's knowledge and experience to forge the beginnings of an adaptive resolution. Empirical research has demonstrated that crisis intervention can result in client benefits such as decreased anxiety, confusion, anger, and helplessness, as well as improved performance in career and family roles (Bunn & Clarke, 1979; Capone, Westie, Chitwood, Feigenbaum, & Good, 1979; Viney, Clarke, Bunn, & Benjamin, 1985).

2. *Clients who need emergency mental health intervention:* An emergency is a life-threatening or other potentially catastrophic situation in which immediate action is necessary in order to rescue those at risk. Sometimes the situation involves a person who has struggled in crisis for so long that he or she is now withdrawing from the world either voluntarily (through contemplated suicide) or involuntarily (through personality disorganization). For psychologists, however, it is more common to encounter a patient who has a long history of emotional difficulties and who is again showing behaviors that have been problematic in the past. In either of these cases, the goal of an emergency mental health intervention is to arrange an appropriate disposition, which may involve the imposition of a solution (such as involuntary hospitalization and treatment).

3. *Choosing between crisis intervention and emergency mental health intervention:* Crisis intervention is appropriate if the person is in crisis and is able to participate in logical problem solving. Emergency mental health intervention is necessary when active guidance and assertive decision making by the psychologist are required to decrease imminent danger. Making the right choice between these two options is crucial. Individuals in crisis who are simply told what to do often fail to implement the suggestion. Consequently, emergency mental health intervention is inappropriate for most persons in crisis. Likewise, problem solving does not work with someone who is incapable of rational decision making. Thus, crisis intervention is doomed to failure with such individuals.

4. *Making the most of the time you have:* In a 50-minute session, you must make an early decision as to whether you should employ crisis intervention or emergency mental health intervention. If emergency mental health intervention is your choice, then the session's activities may involve the following: determining appropriate diagnoses; surveying previous treatment; exploring issues related to suicidal/homicidal danger, availability of support, and level of cooperation; and securing necessary authorizations from service gatekeepers. When you choose crisis intervention, there may be some exploration relating to danger and suicide lethality, but the majority of the time will be spent in collaborative problem solving.

5. *Characteristics of crises:* A crisis is precipitated by an identifiable event that overwhelms the person's ability to cope. We all encounter such distressing episodes, so crises are a normal part of being human. Because each of us has our own personal values and perspectives, what causes a crisis for one person may not bother another individual. There also can be pronounced differences among those who are in crisis. Some may fall into coping characterized by repression, denial, distortion, cognitive restriction, drug and alcohol abuse, or physical difficulties. Others may strive for accurate understanding, acceptance, gradual progress, and optimism. But one way or another, most crises are resolved within a matter of weeks. In the minority of instances in which that is not the case, the person eventually may be at risk for suicide or personality disorganization.

6. *The philosophy of crisis intervention:* The minimum goal in crisis intervention is restoration of the previous level of functioning. The optimal goal is for the crisis to become a learning experience that leaves the person better able to cope with future pressures. Positive outcomes are more likely when intervention is immediately available. Although the response from the psychologist is an active one, all efforts recognize and use the client's abilities. As a secondary prevention activity, crisis intervention catches the difficulties in their early stages, thereby decreasing the episode's duration and severity. Such progress is brought about by engaging the individual in a problem-solving process.

7. *Problem solving:* The central endeavor in crisis intervention is problem solving. Although there are many approaches to this activity, one strategy is to think of it as involving three phases: exploring thoughts and feelings, considering alternatives, and developing a plan (France, 1996). And while a variety of communication styles can be effective, the use of reflec-

tion, along with a judicious number of open-ended questions, tends to be beneficial. (Open questions usually begin with the word *what* or *how*. Reflection involves using new words to summarize central ideas and emotions communicated by the other person.)

8. *Exploring thoughts and feelings:* During this phase of problem solving, the task is for the client and the psychologist to develop a joint understanding of the issues confronting the person and the emotions associated with those topics. Specific events should be discussed in conjunction with the related feelings, so that a shared view develops as to how the crisis came about and what has been happening. As long as new material continues to emerge, the exploration phase should continue. It ends with agreement on three areas: the nature of the distressing circumstances, how the person is feeling about them, and what changes the individual desires.

9. *Considering alternatives:* Once there is an understanding of the issues, the interaction moves to deciding what to do about them. The goal of this phase is to identify and consider two or three solid options. One tactic for generating these possibilities is to explore three questions: What has the client already tried? What has the client thought about doing? And, right now as you are talking, what other ideas can the client generate? (Only after strongly pulling for options from the client would it be appropriate for the crisis intervener to make a suggestion.) When exploring in detail a promising possibility, have the client consider the likely positive and negative consequences associated with that option. This phase ends with agreement on an approach, or a combination of approaches, that can become the person's plan.

10. *Developing a plan:* The one absolute requirement of an initial crisis intervention contact is the development of a plan that has four characteristics. The plan is collaboratively created rather than dictated by the psychologist (Deci & Ryan, 1987); it focuses on current issues, and there are aspects of it that the client can begin working on the same day or the next day; it involves specific tasks that have been thought through; and it is likely, not just possible, that the individual will carry out those tasks. Once a negotiated, present-focused, concrete, and realistic plan has been developed, the client should review its major components. Clarify any misunderstandings or ambiguities that become apparent, and arrange a subsequent contact.

11. *Subsequent contact:* The initial activity of a subsequent contact is to review the client's efforts in implementing the plan. Successes should be highlighted, and difficulties should be identified. Negotiate necessary modifications in existing components of the plan, and engage in problem solving with regard to important issues that still need to be addressed.

12. *Suicide lethality assessment:* Both in crisis intervention and in emergency mental health intervention, it is appropriate to ask if the client has been thinking about suicide. An affirmative response to this question necessitates further exploration. If you believe there is an ongoing risk of suicide, you may want to examine the following five factors that have been shown to increase the probability of suicide: the existence of a plan for suicide that is specific, available, and deadly (or the person believes is deadly; Michel, 1987); feelings of hopelessness or depression (initial improvement during a clinical depression is an especially dangerous time); past suicide attempts by the client (although most people who die by suicide kill themselves on the first attempt) and past attempts or completed suicide by close relatives or friends; a recent upsurge in difficulties experienced by the client (Earle, Forquer, Volo, & McDonnell, 1994); and significant object loss associated with the current crisis (Heikkinen, Aro, & Lonnqvist, 1993).

13. *Intervening with a suicidal person:* If the client has attempted suicide or is currently at risk, keep in mind the following five endeavors. Arrange an immediate medical evaluation for an individual who has just engaged in self-harm. Determine the appropriate intervention or combination of interventions: crisis intervention for a person in crisis who wants help, ongoing treatment for an individual with long-

standing problems, and hospitalization for a client who is either ambivalent about wanting to be alive or certain about wanting to be dead. Decrease the availability of lethal means; for example, develop a plan for removing firearms from the person's residence. Engage the individual in problem solving that begins to move him or her toward adaptive ways of relieving the pain. For a client who remains suicidal, recognize the potential for homicide. (A study by Asnis, Kaplan, van Pragg, and Sanderson, 1994, focused on 403 psychiatric outpatients and found that of the 127 who had made a suicide attempt, 35% also had contemplated or attempted homicide.)

14. *Deciding whether to support outpatient therapy or hospitalization:* Bengelsdorf, Levy, Emerson, and Barile (1984) developed the Crisis Triage Rating Scale to assist clinicians in deciding whether a person needs outpatient or inpatient services. The evaluator assigns scores for dangerousness, support, and cooperation, then adds the numbers together. Bengelsdorf and his colleagues believe that a total score of 9 or lower suggests a need for hospitalization, whereas a score of 10 or higher tends to indicate outpatient services as being appropriate. The scale's scoring criteria are described below.

DANGEROUSNESS

1. Threats of suicidal or homicidal behavior, a recent dangerous attempt, or unpredictable violence
2. Threats of suicidal or homicidal behavior or a recent dangerous attempt, but sometimes views such ideas and actions as unacceptable, or past violence but no current problems
3. Ambivalence associated with life-threatening thoughts, a "suicide attempt" not intended to end in death, or impulse control that is inconsistent
4. Some ongoing or past life-threatening behavior or ideas but clearly wants to control such behavior and is able to do so
5. No life-threatening ideas or actions and no history of problems with impulse control

SUPPORT

1. Inadequate support from family members, friends, and community resources
2. Possible support but effect is likely to be small
3. Appropriate support possibly developed but with difficulty
4. Appropriate support possibly developed, but some components may not be reliable
5. Access to appropriate support

COOPERATION

1. Unwilling or unable to cooperate
2. Little appreciation or understanding of ongoing intervention efforts
3. Passively accepts intervention efforts
4. Ambivalence or limited motivation regarding intervention efforts
5. Actively requests outpatient services and wants to productively participate in therapy

References & Readings

Asnis, G. M., Kaplan, M. L., van Praag, H. M., & Sanderson, W. C. (1994). Homicidal behaviors among psychiatric outpatients. *Hospital and Community Psychiatry, 45,* 127–132.

Bengelsdorf, H., Levy, L. E., Emerson, R. L., & Barile, F. A. (1984). A Crisis Triage Rating Scale: Brief dispositional assessment of patients at risk for hospitalization. *Journal of Nervous and Mental Disease, 172,* 424–430.

Bunn, T. A., & Clarke, A. M. (1979). Crisis intervention: An experimental study of the effects of a brief period of counselling on the anxiety of relatives of seriously injured or ill hospital patients. *British Journal of Medical Psychology, 52,* 191–195.

Capone, M. A., Westie, K. S., Chitwood, J. S., Feigenbaum, D., & Good, R. S. (1979). Crisis intervention: A functional model for hospitalized cancer patients. *American Journal of Orthopsychiatry, 49,* 598–607.

Deci, E. L., & Ryan, R. M. (1987). The support of autonomy and the control of behavior. *Journal of Personality and Social Psychology, 53,* 1024–1037.

Earle, K. A., Forquer, S. L., Volo, A. M., & McDonnell, P. M. (1994). Characteristics of outpatient suicides. *Hospital and Community Psychiatry, 45,* 123–126.

Folkman, S., Lazarus, R. S., Dunkel-Schetter, C., DeLongis, A., & Gruen, R. J. (1986). Dynamics of a stressful encounter: Cognitive appraisal, coping, and encounter outcomes. *Journal of Personality and Social Psychology, 50,* 992–1003.

France, K. (1996). *Crisis intervention: A handbook of immediate person-to-person help* (3rd ed.). Springfield, IL: Charles C. Thomas.

Halpern, H. A. (1973). Crisis theory: A definitional study. *Community Mental Health Journal, 9,* 342–349.

Halpern, H. A. (1975). The Crisis Scale: A factor analysis and revision. *Community Mental Health Journal, 11,* 295–300.

Heikkinen, M., Aro, H., & Lonnqvist, J. (1993). Life events and social support in suicide. *Suicide and Life Threatening Behavior, 23,* 343–358.

Michel, K. (1987). Suicide risk factors: A comparison of suicide attempters with suicide completers. *British Journal of Psychiatry, 150,* 78–82.

Viney, L. L., Clarke, A. M., Bunn, T. A., & Benjamin, Y. N. (1985). Crisis-intervention counseling: An evaluation of long- and short-term effects. *Journal of Counseling Psychology, 32,* 29–39.

Related Topics

Chapter 62, "Treatment and Management of the Suicidal Patient"
Chapter 64, "Impact of Disasters"
Chapter 108, "Model for Clinical Decision Making With Dangerous Patients"

64 IMPACT OF DISASTERS

Eric M. Vernberg & R. Enrrique Varela

This chapter describes important concepts and issues in evaluating the impact of disasters on individuals. Items are arranged chronologically in relation to the disaster events: predisaster planning, impact and short-term adaptation phases, and long-term adaptation phase.

PREDISASTER PLANNING

Almost every community in the United States has a local emergency management network in place, yet the emphasis on mental health aspects of disasters varies greatly. More widespread disasters require involvement of a state, regional, or national emergency management network. Participation in planning activities at one or more of these levels is a necessity for psychologists who want to be involved in the crisis management aspects of disaster mental health. Disasters, especially those receiving intense media coverage, often draw a tremendous number of offers of help from a broad range of mental health service providers. Understandably, emergency management personnel have difficulty processing such offers in the aftermath of a disaster and prefer to rely instead on relationships developed earlier.

Disaster Response Network

The American Psychological Association Disaster Response Network (DRN) was established in 1991 to organize psychologists within each state into a disaster response network with formal ties to the American Red Cross (ARC) and local emergency management services. The DRN offers short-term crisis inter-vention at disaster sites at the request of the ARC and is a useful resource for clinicians working with disaster survivors. To obtain information about the DRN in your state, contact the APA Practice Directorate at 202-336-5898.

The ARC offers a 2-day training program for psychologists who wish to provide emergency mental health services as part of a Red Cross disaster team. Contact your local ARC chapter or the DRN for a schedule of training opportunities.

IMPACT AND SHORT-TERM ADAPTATION PHASES

The *disaster impact phase* refers to the period when a disaster is occurring. Exposure to traumatic events of an overwhelming nature is a central characteristic of this phase, and mental health roles often involve acute crisis management. The *short-term adaptation phase* includes the period after the overwhelming disaster events end and the tasks of inventorying losses and developing a plan for recovery are accomplished. This phase generally requires 3–9 months to complete. Emergency services and intense media activity are generally withdrawn within this period.

Elements of Traumatic Exposure

The nature of exposure to trauma is an important indicator of risk for acute or chronic mental health sequelae of disasters. Indeed, most research finds a dose-response relationship between traumatic exposure and subsequent symptomatology. A useful typology distinguishes the following elements of traumatic exposure (Green, 1990; selected structured questions are included from the DIS/DS, Robins & Smith, 1993).

- *Threat to one's life or bodily integrity:* "At any time did you think you might die?"
- *Physical harm or injury to self:* "Did you have any illness or injuries as a result of the disaster?"
- *Receipt of intentional injury or harm:* "Do you think the disaster was just an act of God or nature, or do you think the people who were involved were in part to blame?"
- *Exposure to the grotesque:* "Sometimes people in disasters have to see or do things they find disgusting. Did this happen to you?"
- *Violent/sudden loss of a loved one:* "Were any of your family, friends, or companions injured or killed as a result of the disaster?"
- *Witnessing or learning of violence to a loved one:* "Did you see anyone get injured or killed?"
- *Exposure to toxins with long-term effects:* "Do you know of any health problems that could be caused by what happened to you in the disaster?"

Not all elements of traumatic exposure are equally likely to produce symptomatology. Additional important distinctions include the duration of exposure, the cause of the disaster (e.g., natural vs. human-made; accidental vs. deliberate or negligent), the proportion of the community affected, the degree of geographic dislocation, and the potential impact on the survivor's life (e.g., permanent disability, catastrophic economic loss, multiple deaths in family).

Context of Evaluation and Intervention

Hearing detailed descriptions of traumatic experiences may be troubling for family members or others who were not directly exposed. Detailed descriptions in group contexts should be solicited only among individuals who shared similar levels of traumatic exposure. Mixed groups of survivors and rescue workers (other than mental health personnel acting as facilitators) are not appropriate. Initial evaluation and intervention in community settings rather than clinical settings are preferable to minimize stigmatization and resistance to mental health services.

Psychological First Aid

Common initial reactions to overwhelming traumatic exposure include confusion, disorganization, and emotional numbness. Basic mental health roles during and shortly after the impact phase may be categorized as *psychological first aid* to connote the clear distinction from more traditional mental health interventions. Psychological first aid *does not* deal with chronic, long-term, or intrapsychic problems. Instead, the focus is on the here and now, enhancing current functioning, and providing sufficient environmental support to prevent further injury. Appropriate activities include the following:

- Providing direct, instrumental assistance with problem solving and practical needs; this may include active advocacy on behalf of survivors
- Providing factual information about the disaster, typical reactions, and resources for support and assistance
- Offering assistance in evaluating information and formulating responses
- Activating social support systems, including family and community networks and access to other survivors

Specific forms of psychological first aid include the following. *Debriefing and defusing* refer to sessions in which individuals or groups of survivors are encouraged to review the major elements of a traumatic experience soon after exposure. The goals of these interventions include emotional release, enhancing social support, reducing social isolation, translating iconic memories into language (to facilitate cognitive processing of the traumatic events), and providing education, information, and stress-management strategies. Debriefing and defusing sessions also offer opportunities to screen for severe impairment that may require additional evaluation and treatment (American Red Cross, 1991).

Although formal debriefing and defusing are widely practiced and strongly embraced by many disaster mental health workers, evidence for their efficacy in general or the superiority of one protocol over another remains sparse (Gist & Lubin, 1998).

Crisis reduction counseling is conducted with an individual or family and focuses on assessing psychological states, validating and normalizing thoughts and feelings, identifying and prioritizing current problems, and identifying sources of support (American Red Cross, 1991). Discussion is limited to issues related to the disaster recovery process.

Crisis intervention is carried out with an individual or family to mitigate extreme emotional distress in the immediate aftermath of a disaster or traumatic event. The goals are to assess the extent of current mental health impairment in relation to pretrauma functioning, to provide pragmatic emotional support, and to give information and advice to help regain emotional equilibrium. Depending on the psychological state, this may include information on the process of recovery from trauma, maladaptive versus adaptive coping strategies, resources and supports, and indicators of the need for further mental health assistance (American Red Cross, 1991).

Guidelines for Providing More Intensive Services

In the course of receiving psychological first aid, individuals should be provided with more extensive evaluations or treatments under the following conditions (American Red Cross, 1991):

- Preexisting serious mental disorder that is exacerbated by the disaster
- Extremely impaired functioning, including thought disturbances, dissociative episodes, extreme overarousal or mood lability, or inability to care for personal needs
- Acute risk of harm to self or others, including suicidality, homicidal ideation, extreme

substance abuse, or inappropriate anger or abuse of others
- Evidence of a life-threatening health condition (e.g., heart problems, diabetes, high blood pressure) that is not currently being treated and appears to be causing problems

LONG-TERM ADAPTATION PHASE

Mental health issues related to long-term adaptation following disasters begin to fit more traditional approaches to clinical assessment and treatment. Still, several issues deserve special attention in assessing and treating disaster survivors in the months and years after traumatic exposure.

Common Mental Health Problems After Disasters

Anxiety, depression, and somatic complaints: The most consistent mental health problems found in studies of disaster survivors are symptoms of anxiety (including posttraumatic stress disorder), depression, and somatic symptoms.

Substance abuse: Although widely believed to be affected by disasters, increases in substance abuse problems among disaster survivors have been reported less consistently than the anxiety/depression/somatic complaint symptoms described above. The topic needs further study, as some studies have found increases in alcohol use (and other substances, such as tranquilizers) among disaster-exposed populations in the United States and others have not.

Aggression and anger: Problems with anger and aggression appear to be linked to disasters, although there is less evidence for this than for anxiety, depression, and somatic complaints. A number of studies have found anger and irritability to be higher in disaster-exposed populations than in nonexposed comparison groups, and there is some suggestion that these problems may be quite persistent over time. There is surprisingly little research documenting increases in actual aggression after disasters.

Factors Influencing Recovery

Social support: Social support is swiftly mobilized by most disasters but often is depleted and diminished long before recovery is accomplished (Kaniasty & Norris, 1997). This sense of declining support may contribute to distress. Assessment of access to needed support is essential in designing interventions for disaster survivors. Improving access to needed forms of social support is a major goal for mental health providers. Risk of poor access to social supports following disasters is especially high for marginalized members of communities (e.g., poorer, less educated individuals; geographically isolated individuals).

Ongoing disruptions: Many disasters cause serious disruptions for individuals long after the identified disaster event has ended. It is extremely important to inquire about ongoing stressful circumstances that follow many severe disasters. These include economic struggles, dislocation, rebuilding, employment disruption, changes in household composition, and increases in "daily hassles." When ongoing disruption is high, it is appropriate to continue the functions characteristic of psychological first aid long after the primary disaster event has ended.

Psychological resources: Several psychological resources have been linked to resilience following traumatic events of varying types. Religious faith and philosophical perspectives that in some way enable individuals to make sense of disaster experiences appear to be important resources following disasters. A second set of psychological resources includes at least average intelligence, good communication skills, and strong beliefs of self-efficacy.

Socioeconomic status: Education and financial status may influence recovery from disasters and even levels of exposure to traumatic experiences during disasters. Education may influence an individual's ability to cope with the demands for documentation and careful completion of applications for disaster assistance. Education is also linked to skills in seeking information regarding resources. Financial status exerts multiple possible influences on postdisaster functioning. In terms of increased exposure to traumatic experiences during disasters, housing built of less durable materials (e.g., mobile homes) or in less desirable locations (e.g., flood-prone land) is more likely to be damaged by disasters in the first place. This places poorer individuals, on average, at greater risk for loss of personal possessions and exposure to life-threatening circumstances. Following disasters, individuals with few financial resources (including personal property insurance) may find it virtually impossible to repair or replace lost belongings. Even for poorer families with some insurance, months of waiting may be required before claims are settled, placing extreme financial pressures on those with few financial reserves. Many lower-paying, lower-occupational-status jobs offer little in the way of paid personal leave or scheduling flexibility. This may further complicate postdisaster recovery by making it difficult for individuals to find the time to pursue aid or repairs.

Age-Related Issues

Age is related to disaster response in numerous ways, and children and the elderly are typically viewed as "special populations" in the disaster literature. Children and some of the elderly are similar in their greater dependence on others to meet basic needs for food, clothing, and shelter. Impairment in individuals or systems that meet these dependency demands places both groups at risk for mental health disturbance, and possibly for physical danger.

Children and adolescents: Children of different ages have different types of difficulties related to disasters. *Infants and toddlers* are often very sensitive to disruptions in caretaking and may show increases in feeding problems, irritability, and sleep problems. These behavioral problems in turn place increased demands on caretakers, who may themselves be highly distressed by a disaster.

Preschool children are beginning to use language in relatively sophisticated ways but are very limited in their understanding of disaster-related events. This limited understanding often leads to fears that may seem unwarranted to older children and adults (e.g., extreme fears during thunderstorms that occur after a flood or tornado). These fears may lead to dramatic reactions to relatively harmless postdisaster events.

School-age children understand the physical environment much better than preschoolers but may be very preoccupied by the loss of possessions or pets or by memories of traumatic events. Elementary school–age children also are often able to recognize distress in their caretakers and may be quite worried about the safety and security of their families. Children of this age can do relatively little to help actively in the recovery process, which may increase feelings of isolation and helplessness. Children over 8 years old generally are competent reporters of psychiatric symptoms (especially internalizing symptoms) when given appropriate measures. Children typically report more postdisaster symptoms than others (e.g., parents, teachers) report for them (Vogel & Vernberg, 1993). Relying solely on parent or teacher reports to identify postdisaster mental health problems in school-age children is almost certain to underestimate these problems.

Adolescents are more competent to help with recovery and are less dependent than younger children. At the same time, adolescents may engage in greater risk-taking behaviors after disasters. Adolescents also may have intense feelings of being cheated out of expected experiences (e.g., athletic and social events that are canceled or postponed) after disasters.

Young and middle-aged adults: There is some evidence of differences in disaster-related distress between young adults (18–40) and middle-aged adults (40–65), with the latter group typically faring worse. Middle-aged adults are more likely than other age cohorts to have responsibility for children and elderly parents during and after disasters, and this increased responsibility may contribute to psychological distress.

Older adults: Health status (including mental health) and competence to perform tasks of daily living are also important aspects in determining postdisaster needs of the elderly. Sensory changes accompanying aging are important to consider. Hearing and vision problems may make it more difficult for the elderly to obtain information regarding disaster relief efforts or to provide information to others. Noisy, crowded settings (such as disaster shelters or Disaster Assistance Centers) may be particularly problematic because it becomes increasingly difficult with age to filter out competing noises during conversations. Decreased sense of smell and taste tend to make the elderly prefer foods with more flavor, and elders may respond to bland food provided through disaster relief teams by adding salt (which aggravates hypertension) or reducing food intake (which may result in malnutrition). The relationship between cognitive functioning and physical health becomes increasingly strong during late adulthood, and declines in physical health due to poor nutrition or disruptions in medications may contribute to significant mental health problems, including confusion, disorientation, and depression. Similarly, loss of social support and disruptions in routines following disasters may produce poor health behaviors, leading to increased dysfunction. Sudden changes in living arrangements are difficult for older adults, especially those with cognitive, physical, or sensory impairments. Many elderly also attach a strong stigma to the use of mental health services, and substantial efforts may be required to make such service acceptable. Some older adults who are aware of their diminished capabilities may fear that they will be placed in nursing homes or other restrictive settings if their difficulties become known to relief workers. It is important to communicate that mental health workers are attempting to help the elderly live as independently as possible and that they may help garner the resources and support needed for this to occur.

References & Readings

American Red Cross (1991). *Disaster services regulations and procedures* (ARC Document 3050M). Washington, DC: American Red Cross.

Gist, R., & Lubin, B. (Eds.) (1998). *Response to disaster: Psychosocial, community, and ecological approaches.* Bristol, PA: Taylor and Francis.

Green, B. L. (1990). Defining trauma: Terminology and generic stressor dimensions. *Journal of Applied Social Psychology, 20,* 1632–1642.

Hobfoll, S. E., & de Vries, M. W. (Eds.) (1995). *Extreme stress and communities: Impact and intervention.* Dordrecht, the Netherlands: Kluwer Academic Publishers.

Kaniasty, K., & Norris, F. H. (1997). Social support dynamics in adjustment to disasters. In S. Durk (Ed.), *Handbook of personal relationships* (pp. 595–622). New York: Wiley.

Robins, L. N., & Smith, E. M. (1993). *Diagnostic interview schedule: Disaster supplement.* St. Louis, MO: Washington University School of Medicine, Department of Psychiatry.

Saylor, C. F. (Ed.) (1993). *Children and disasters.* New York: Plenum Press.

Ursano, R. J., McCaughey, B. G., & Fullerton, C. S.

(Eds.) (1994). *Individual and community responses to trauma and disaster: The structure of human chaos.* Cambridge, England: Cambridge University Press.

Vernberg, E. M., & Vogel, J. M. (1993). Interventions with children following disasters. *Journal of Clinical Child Psychology, 22,* 485–498.

Vogel, J. M., & Vernberg, E. M. (1993). Children's psychological reactions to disasters. *Journal of Clinical Child Psychology, 22,* 464–484.

Related Topics

Chapter 63, "Crisis Intervention"

65 KEY PRINCIPLES IN THE TREATMENT OF BORDERLINE PERSONALITY DISORDER

John F. Clarkin & Pamela A. Foelsch

Patients with borderline personality disorder (BPD) are characterized by identity diffusion, affective dyscontrol, impulsivity, and chaotic interpersonal relations. Often they exhibit repetitive self-mutilating or frank suicidal behaviors. These patients rarely present with BPD alone but manifest comorbid *DSM-IV* Axis II conditions, most frequently histrionic, narcissistic, and antisocial features or disorders, and common *DSM-IV* Axis I conditions of major depression, eating disorders, and substance abuse. This is a group of patients who have serious pathology, which is frightening to therapists because of the safety and legal implications, and they elicit intense countertransference feelings.

Based on the growing body of research and our own extensive experience, we present 10 important areas for consideration in the assessment and treatment of these patients.

1. Determine the specific criteria for BPD met by the individual patient. Since Axis II is polythetic in nature, patients may receive the diagnosis of BPD by meeting any 5, 6, 7, 8, or 9 *DSM-IV* criteria. This means that mathematically there are 256 ways of obtaining the diagnosis. Just on the BPD criteria themselves, the patients are quite heterogeneous. A factor analysis of the BPD criteria (Clarkin, Hull, & Hurt, 1993) suggests three factors: an identity diffu-

sion factor, an affect disregulation factor including suicidal behavior, and an impulsive factor. Thus, BPD patients can be identity diffused patients primarily, or identity and impulsive, or affective with suicidal behavior. The prominence of the three factors is most important in setting and prioritizing treatment goals.

2. Carefully assess for comorbid Axis I and Axis II conditions. Only rarely does a patient meet criteria for BPD alone. The common comorbid Axis I conditions include affective disorder, eating disorders, and substance use and abuse. Common Axis II conditions include histrionic, narcissistic, and antisocial personality disorders/traits.

3. In the assessment, carefully explore two areas of pathology: (a) the manner in which the patient has used or abused prior treatments and (b) the interpersonal behaviors between patient, therapist, and significant others, particularly surrounding prior self-mutilating and suicidal behaviors. These prior behaviors must be considered in structuring the next treatment. For example, if the patient has destroyed a prior treatment by not talking during the regular session then telephoning the therapist on the weekend and insisting on crisis help, the likelihood of this happening in the new therapy will be discussed, along with how the therapist will structure the therapy.

4. Structure the treatment from the beginning with a clear verbal contract delineating the patient's treatment role and responsibilities and the therapist's role and responsibilities. This need for a structured treatment contract is recognized in both psychodynamic and cognitive-behavioral orientations (Yeomans, Selzer, & Clarkin, 1992; Linehan, 1993). It is especially around destruction of the patient (i.e., suicidal behavior) and destruction of the therapy (e.g., coming to sessions intoxicated, refusing to talk during sessions) that the roles and responsibilities of patient and therapist must be delineated. This verbal agreement provides both a structure within which the therapy can proceed and a treatment frame that the therapist can refer to later should difficulties arise.

5. Focus the treatment around goals identified early in the assessment and treatment phases. These goals should be determined by the nature of the patient's pathology and the therapist's orientation to treatment. Two prominent treatment orientations are the cognitive-behavioral orientation (Linehan, 1993), which strives for reduction of therapy-interfering behaviors and for an increase in social skills, and the psychodynamic orientation (Clarkin, Yeomans, & Kernberg, in press; Kernberg, Selzer, Koenigsberg, Carr, & Appelbaum, 1989), which focuses on the here-and-now transference with the goal of increasing identity as opposed to identity diffusion. One can also use a supportive orientation, which may be of assistance in achieving some equilibrium and maintenance of that status (Rockland, 1992). Still others (Horwitz et al., 1996) suggest tailoring the treatment with a balance of expressive and supportive techniques.

6. At times of crisis, especially those involving serious suicidal ideation and/or threats, hospitalization to control this behavior must be considered. The advantage of hospitalization in protecting the patient briefly from suicidal potential must be weighed against the possibility of rewarding suicidal threats with the comfort of around-the-clock attention, which may reinforce future suicidal ideation.

7. While individual treatment is often recommended for these patients, other treatment formats could be considered. One cognitive-behavioral approach uses a combination of individual treatment and group treatment for skills enhancement (Linehan, 1993). Others (Munroe-Blum, 1992) have used group treatment alone with these patients. Because there is insufficient research on the question of treatment format, the clinician must consider the specific goals and practicality in deciding on the individual case. Group treatment is more economical, but this advantage must be weighed against the high dropout rate

of these patients, who strongly prefer individual treatment if given a choice.

8. Medication can be considered as an adjunct to a consistent therapeutic relationship (Koenigsberg, 1997). Medications can be of assistance with depressive symptoms and possibly with impulsive behaviors. Attention must be paid to the patient's tendency to seek medications as a "quick fix" and/or to undermine therapy. A strong working relationship between therapist and psychopharmacologist is essential.

9. The therapist should be alert to the clinical and legal standards of care when dealing with these patients, who are often suicidal. This includes information about legal perspectives, assessment of suicide risk, and risk management, such as documentation of clinical decisions and consultation with other professionals when appropriate. It is strongly recommended that the clinician consult the excellent book by Bongar (1991) on this topic.

10. Borderline patients, especially those who are suicidal with comorbid narcissistic and antisocial traits/disorders, are extremely difficult to treat. Their behavior in sessions is complicated by identity diffusion and intense affect, often of a hostile and aggressive nature. All these factors suggest that clinicians, even experienced ones, should be comfortable seeking consultation with colleagues about certain situations. Some therapists who treat borderline patients form a peer group with other professionals treating these patients.

References & Readings

Bongar, B. (1991). *The suicidal patient: Clinical and legal standards of care*. Washington, DC: American Psychological Association.

Clarkin, J. F., Hull, J. W., & Hurt, S. W. (1993). Factor structure of borderline personality disorder criteria. *Journal of Personality Disorders, 7*, 137–143.

Clarkin, J. F., & Lenzenweger, M. F. (1996). *Major theories of personality disorder*. New York: Guilford Press.

Clarkin, J. F., Marziali, E., & Munroe-Blum, H. (1992). *Borderline personality disorder: Clinical and empirical perspectives*. New York: Guilford Press.

Clarkin, J. F., Yeomans, F. E., & Kernberg, O. F. (in press). *Psychodynamic treatment of borderline personality organization*. New York: Wiley.

Horwitz, L., Gabbard, G. O., Allen, J., Frieswyk, S. H., Colson, D. B., Newsom, G. E., & Coyne, L. (1996). *Borderline personality disorder: Tailoring the psychotherapy to the patient*. Washington, DC: American Psychiatric Press.

Kernberg, O. F. (1984). *Severe personality disorders: Psychotherapeutic strategies*. New Haven, CT: Yale University Press.

Kernberg, O. F. (1992). *Aggression in personality disorders and perversions*. New Haven, CT: Yale University Press.

Kernberg, O. F., Selzer, M. A., Koenigsberg, H. W., Carr, A. C., & Appelbaum, A. H. (1989). *Psychodynamic psychotherapy of borderline patients*. New York: Basic Books.

Koenigsberg, H. W. (1997). Integrating psychotherapy and pharmacotherapy in the treatment of borderline personality disorder. *In Session: Psychotherapy in Practice, 3*, 39–56.

Linehan, M. M. (1993). *Cognitive-behavioral treatment of borderline personality disorder*. New York: Guilford Press.

Meissner, W. W. (1984). *The borderline spectrum: Differential diagnosis and developmental issues*. New York: Jason Aronson.

Munroe-Blum, H. (1992). Group treatment of borderline personality disorder. In J. F. Clarkin, E. Marziali, & H. Munroe-Blum (Eds.), *Borderline personality disorder: Clinical and empirical perspectives* (pp. 288–299). New York: Guilford Press.

Rockland, L. H. (1992). *Supportive therapy for borderline patients: A psychodynamic approach*. New York: Guilford Press.

Stone, M. H. (1990). *The fate of borderline patients: Successful outcome and psychiatric practice*. New York: Guilford Press.

Yeomans, F. E., Selzer, M. A., & Clarkin, J. F. (1992). *Treating the borderline patient: A contract-based approach*. New York: Basic Books.

Related Topics

66 PSYCHOTHERAPY WITH RELUCTANT AND INVOLUNTARY CLIENTS

Stanley L. Brodsky

When therapists offer counseling from the same frame of reference for reluctant and involuntary clients as they do for eager, voluntary clients, they set up themselves and their clients for considerable frustration. Some reluctant clients will never fully participate in counseling; for them, quick termination of the treatment may be the decision of choice. For other clients, the reluctance becomes transformed into active participation and the treatment itself becomes a productive venture. The beginning points in approaching treatment of reluctant clients are awareness of therapist assumptions and of client roles and rights.

REACTIONS TO RELUCTANT CLIENTS

Therapists have a need to present themselves as expert and trustworthy in their therapeutic roles (Beutler, Machado, & Neufeldt, 1994). If therapists are frustrated by clients, these needs may rise to prominence, occasionally in exaggerated form. The resultant events are often confrontational demands by the therapists for clients to give up their reluctance or a facade by clients of conformity to the patient role.

Therapists enter their professions in part altruistically, to feel good about helping others (Guy, 1987). Reluctant clients are unappreciative and do not provide the customary positive feedback therapists want as part of their work. Many therapists take this lack of appreciation personally and feel threatened, incapable, and frustrated. In order to avoid becoming impaired in working with the client, they need to

be able to address the threat and frustration as foreground personal issues.

THE MENTAL HEALTH–CRIME FALSE SYLLOGISM

Law violators are the most frequent category of reluctant client, often explicitly coerced to enter psychotherapy as a condition of probation or parole or as proof of progress toward being a desirable candidate for parole or privileges within prison. It is incorrectly concluded by many clinicians that being a serious offender is prima facie evidence of need for psychotherapy. This conclusion takes the form of the following implicit false syllogism (Davis & Brodsky, 1992):

> Most people are not offenders.
> Most people are not mentally ill.
> Therefore most offenders are mentally ill.

A fundamental rule emerges from this principle: Do not attempt to cure antisocial behavior per se through psychotherapy. Instead, treatment services should be offered without institutional pressures to offenders who request such services (Monahan, 1980).

THE RIGHT TO REFUSE TREATMENT

Every client's right to decline treatment as well as to choose treatment knowledgeably should be respected. The choice to refuse treatment, as fully as to participate in therapy, should be an informed one, particularly when there are institutional, occupational, or family consequences of not entering therapy. Clients should know precisely what choices they are declining. The therapist's responsibility is to ensure that the client understands the alternatives of what treatment is available, how long it lasts and how well it works, the nature of the therapeutic procedures, and the assumption of client self-determination in continuing therapy. Contracts with clients and outlines of information to be given to clients have been gathered in Bersoff (1995, pp. 305–334).

REFERRAL CLARIFICATION: WHY IS A CLIENT HERE?

Often agencies do not know exactly why they have referred a client. They know something is wrong and that the client needs help or an intervention but little more. Thus, the therapist should find out why a coercive referral has been made. The specific information needed includes the treatment aims, the referrer's anticipation of success, the time constraints, the legal or familial frames of reference, and the influences of the client's transient situation. These actions consist of clarifying and redefining the referral. Otherwise therapists become engaged in a vague plan of "just doing therapy."

LOW TRUST–HIGH CONTROL DILEMMAS

With voluntary clients, the customary therapeutic relationship is characterized by high trust and little effort to control the other's behaviors. With confined populations and clients pressured to enter therapy, mutual distrust of motives is often accompanied by the therapist having considerable control over client living conditions, privileges, and release (Harris & Watkins, 1987). The subsequent therapist fear of manipulation produces a role conflict between helping and "supervising." The normal trust and rapport between therapist and client become dis-

placed by a concern over being used and by excessive control measures, which themselves are antagonistic to good treatment. The resolution of these dilemmas lies in explicit delineation of limits, as well as absolute separation of therapeutic roles from evaluative and organizational roles (Brodsky, 1973; Davis & Brodsky, 1992).

WHO IS THE CLIENT?

Therapists may be classified as falling on a continuum from system professional to system challenger, depending on the extent to which they accept the existing aims of the agency. Therapists need to define their stances and consider client versus agency responsibilities, coercion effects, and other values implicit in treatment activities. All psychotherapy has implicit values. The therapist needs to be especially sensitive to social values and imposing normative behaviors. This dilemma is best resolved by making explicit on an a priori basis the social values with which one is practicing.

Confidentiality is often the playing field on which these conflicts become tested. Confidentiality is not absolute. Explicit agreement from the beginning on confidentiality is important, with all parties being informed in writing and in advance about the level of confidentiality (Report of the Task Force on the Role of Psychology in the Criminal Justice System, 1980).

TREATING THE ABRASIVE CLIENT

Abrasive clients are individuals who have a special knack for irritating others. They know how to get under others' skin to annoy. They become adept at jabbing at the vulnerabilities of their therapists. Sometimes it is done with subtlety; therapists become aware of this process when they find themselves getting annoyed without apparent good reason. According to Wepman and Donovan (1984), abrasive individuals have both a high need for human intimacy and a fear of closeness. The need for intimacy brings them toward therapists emotionally, whereas their fear leads them to push therapists away. Clients who have criticized a therapist's clothing, family, office decor, facial expression, tone of voice, ethnicity, or personal appearance succeed when they are rejected. The treatment is to try to respond to the hurt and the desire for closeness: "The alliance must be made with the wounded, vulnerable aspects of the personality" (Wepman & Donovan, 1984, p. 17).

THERAPY AS AN AVERSIVE CONTINGENCY FOR INAPPROPRIATE BEHAVIOR

If the treatment itself is a negative experience for clients, it can be used as an aversive stimulus following undesirable behavior. In a discussion of behavioral treatment of delinquents, Levinson, Ingram, and Azcarate (1973) described just such an effective program with confined, severely antisocial youthful offenders. The youths were able to earn the right to discontinue mandatory group therapy by going 3 successive months without being sent to segregation. Once this program was introduced, misconduct reports among group members dropped 43% in a 6-month period after therapy. In other settings, such as family therapy, anecdotal reports have indicated that children's problem behaviors have diminished or disappeared with the promise that attendance in therapy would no longer be required.

ERRORS IN TECHNIQUE

When the criterion for success is reduced recidivism, nondirective and traditional psychodynamic therapies, as well as any approach with low-risk offenders, have little payoff (Gendreau, 1996). Therapy that is vaguely targeted and not intensive in nature seems to fail. With diagnosed psychopaths, these failures become even more compelling. Insight-oriented therapies and group therapies, in particular, are associated with higher rates of future crime (Hare, 1996). Therapy is best offered for specific behaviors that disrupt criminogenic social networks and to provide relapse prevention training.

Therapy also fails when therapists (a) passively accept problematic aspects of the client's behavior and attitudes, such as evasiveness and negativism; (b) fail to address deficiencies in the therapeutic relationship; or (c) present destructive or poorly timed interventions (Sachs, 1983). Effective therapists do not sit back and wait in the therapy office but instead are active. Timing, specificity of focus, and intense involvement in therapeutic work are crucial.

UTILIZING RESISTANCE

When clients actively resist involvement and change, therapists should not be in direct opposition. Instead, they should consider aiming at second-order change so that clients accept in an oppositional way the view therapists would originally have wanted. Thus, one can ask resistant clients, "Why should you change?" or instruct clients to "go slow." In the same spirit, one might tell a distrustful client to never trust the therapy fully. These procedures may be conceptualized as co-opting clients' cognitive space. Teyber's (1988) interpersonal process in psychotherapy addresses this approach by explicitly using what he calls "honoring the client's resistance."

LITIGIOUS CLIENTS

Therapists and clients alike can become influenced by fears of lawsuits. Clients who think about suing are poor candidates for therapeutic progress. Therapists fearful of lawsuits become legalistic, distant, overly cautious, and less effective. The therapist's role will be addressed here rather than that of the client. Most therapists' fears of litigation are excessive and irrational (Brodsky, 1988). The litigaphobic therapist becomes what he or she fears—a surrogate lawyer, second-guessing every action. The alternative is to assess realistically the base rate for such suits—statistically low—and to get consultation as necessary to manage such fears. A scale is available for assessing the extent of fear of litigation (Breslin, Taylor, & Brodsky, 1976).

OBJECTIVE SELF-AWARENESS

This phenomenon, described by Duval and Wicklund (1972), has powerful implications for reluctant clients. When clients are encouraged to listen in at staff meetings about their cases and discussions of their therapeutic progress, as well as to read documents written about them, they become, in effect, outside observers of themselves. As a result, they become motivated and fascinated. This principle can be used by sharing with clients the videotapes and audiotapes of sessions, ongoing therapy records, and especially the opportunity to hear discussions of their dynamics and progress (Brodsky & Myers, 1986).

LIFE SKILLS ENHANCEMENT

In enhancement of life skills, therapeutic efforts are offered as short courses that are closed ended and based on a published curriculum. Each unit of instruction attends to narrowly defined areas of functioning. The short courses have scheduled beginnings and endings, the use of pass or fail criteria, and the advance identification of specific treatment content. In this alternative to conventional open-ended therapies, topics that are addressed include conflict management, human sexuality, assertiveness training, and fairness awareness (Scapinello, 1992).

FOUR MORE PRACTICAL APPROACHES

1. *Keep the client for three sessions:* One third of therapy clients never return for a second appointment even after a definite time has been set. An additional 40% stop before the sixth session. In their research using the Vanderbilt Psychotherapy Process Scale, O'Malley, Suh, and Strupp (1983) found no relationship whatever between first-session events and eventual outcome. A strong relationship was found between third-session events and outcome. By that time, patients became involved, and that involvement made a difference. Thus, the therapist should set up contracts or trial therapy agreements for three or four sessions.

2. *Common foundations for therapy:* When conventional approaches to building rapport do not work, the therapist should consider adapting the "group conversation method" developed by DuBois and Li (1971). In this method, clients are asked to take turns describing sensory memories (such as smells and tastes from childhood), activities at school or home, or particular holidays. The questions include: How did you use to spend Halloween? What are your memories of worst teachers? Best teachers? Christmas smells? Where you grew up? Earliest religious memories? Otto (1973), who has called this network of positive formative experiences the Minerva experience, suggests the joint recollection of such experiences is a positive bonding.

3. *Time and therapy:* Our experiences are captured by conventions of time. Therapists become entrained by 50-minute hours and appointment books, and they believe that "good" clients should comply as well. As a beginning point with difficult clients, experiment with very short or long sessions. More broadly, however, try to understand the meaning of time in clients' lives. Responsibility and personal development are concepts seated in part in elements of time, such as continuity and comprehension of consequences (McGrath, 1988). How do the clients experience time passing? Five years from now, will they look back at the present with envy? With feelings of wasted living? Regret? One book compellingly develops this theme: Grudin's *Time and the Art of Living* (1982), which asserts that when time becomes a foreground issue, it can serve to help with problems in living and in therapy.

4. *Concrete changes:* Giving clients immediate and concrete self-coping methods yields good motivation to continue with therapy. For example, in the case of anxiety problems and panic attacks, cognitive therapies and teaching of diaphragmatic breathing and relaxation techniques lead to rapid improvement. Help with sleep problems has an especially strong impact, given that about 40% of the general population and 80% of institutionalized persons have sleeping difficulties. Clients welcome assistance in managing insomnia, difficulties falling asleep, and waking easily during the night.

SUMMARY

Therapists should not automatically assume that traditional therapies with voluntary and cooperative clients apply to reluctant and involuntary clients. Instead, referral questions, definitions of client, and confidentiality should be examined carefully. Milieu demands for control of client behavior can compromise therapeutic relationships, as can abrasive and resistant client behaviors. Therapists should consider utilizing client resistances, ensuring that therapy continues through at least three sessions, and adapting the length of therapy sessions to individual clients. With these clients, concrete and immediate changes are important, along with promoting objective self-awareness and using closed-ended short-term treatments.

References & Readings

Bersoff, D. N. (Ed.) (1995). *Ethical conflicts in psychology*. Washington, DC: American Psychological Association.

Beutler, L. E., Machado, P. P. P., & Neufeldt, S. A. (1994). Therapist variables. In A. E. Bergin & S. L. Garfield (Eds.), *Handbook of psychotherapy and behavior change* (4th ed., pp. 229–269). New York: Wiley.

Breslin, F. A., Taylor, K. R., & Brodsky, S. L. (1986). Development of a litigaphobia scale: Measurement of excessive fear of litigation. *Psychological Reports, 58,* 547–550.

Brodsky, S. L. (1973). *Psychologists in the criminal justice system*. Urbana: University of Illinois Press.

Brodsky, S. L. (1988). Fear of litigation in mental health professionals. *Criminal Justice and Behavior, 15,* 492–500.

Brodsky, S. L., & Myers, H. H. (1986). In vivo rotation: An alternative method of psychotherapy supervision. In F. W. Kaslow (Ed.), *Supervision and training: Models, dilemmas, and challenges* (pp. 95–104). New York: Haworth.

Davis, D. L., & Brodsky, S. L. (1992). Psychotherapy with the unwilling client. *Residential Treatment for Children and Youth, 9*(3), 15–27.

DuBois, R. D., & Li, M.-S. (1971). *Reducing social tension and conflict through the group conversation method*. New York: Association Press.

Duval, S., & Wicklund, R. A. (1972). *A theory of objective self-awareness*. New York: Academic Press.

Gendreau, P. (1996). Offender rehabilitation: What we know and what needs to be done. *Criminal Justice and Behavior, 23,* 144–161.

Grudin, R. (1982). *Time and the art of living*. New York: Ticknor and Fields.

Guy, J. D. (1987). *The personal life of the psychotherapist*. New York: Wiley.

Hare, R. D. (1996). Psychopathy: A clinical construct whose time has come. *Criminal Justice and Behavior, 23,* 25–54.

Harris, G. A., & Watkins, D. (1987). *Counseling the involuntary and reluctant client*. College Park, MD: American Correctional Association.

Levinson, R. B., Ingram, G. L., & Azcarate, E. (1973). Aversive group therapy: Sometimes good medicine tastes bad. In J. S. Stumphauzer (Ed.), *Behavior therapy with delinquents* (pp. 159–163). Springfield, IL: Thomas.

McGrath, J. E. (Ed.) (1988). *The social psychology of time*. Newbury Park, CA: Sage.

Monahan, J. (Ed.) (1980). *Who is the client? The ethics of psychological intervention in the criminal justice system*. Washington, DC: American Psychological Association.

O'Malley, S. S., Suh, C. S., & Strupp, H. H. (1983). The Vanderbilt Psychotherapy Process Scale: A report on the scale development and a process-outcome study. *Journal of Consulting and Clinical Psychology, 51,* 581–586.

Otto, H. A. (1973). *Ways of growth: Approaches to expanding awareness*. New York: Penguin.

Sachs, J. S. (1983). Negative factors in brief psychotherapy: An empirical assessment. *Journal of Consulting and Clinical Psychology, 51,* 557–564.

Scapinello, K. F. (1992). *Specialized services offered by the Psychology Department* (Programme Report No. PR92-2). Brampton: Ontario Correctional Institute.

Teyber, E. (1988). *Interpersonal process in psychotherapy: A guide to clinical training*. Boston: Dorsey.

Wepman, B. J., & Donovan, M. W. (1984). Abrasiveness: Descriptive and dynamic issues. *Psychotherapy Patient, 1,* 11–20.

Related Topics

67 TREATMENT MATCHING IN SUBSTANCE ABUSE

Carlo C. DiClemente

"Different strokes for different folks" certainly characterizes the treatment of substance abuse. Consider what substances of abuse encompass: (a) multiple classes of drugs (sedatives, stimulants, opiates); (b) different sources of drug availability (cocaine and crack; beer, wine, and hard liquor; cigarettes and smokeless tobacco); (c) varied routes of administration (oral, nasal, intravenous); and (d) a broad range of abusing individuals representing every social class, ethnicity, educational level, and profession.

The past few decades have witnessed a substantial increase in methods for treating substance abusers and a more differentiated view of the critical differences and similarities across the various substances of abuse. Although interventions for alcohol, nicotine, and illegal drugs have been developed in parallel and not with a common or collaborative treatment development strategy, there is today an increasing level of communication and cross-fertilization among researchers and clinicians working in substance abuse. There is also a growing realization that substance abuse is a biobehavioral problem and that both pharmacological and psychosocial interventions are needed to adequately address the problem and promote effective change. Psychosocial treatments and treatment matching are the focus of this chapter.

TREATMENT APPROACHES

A variety of psychosocial treatments and treatment modalities have been applied to substance abuse problems (Onken & Blaine, 1990; Hester & Miller, 1995). Among the most popular are the following:

- *Group therapy*, whether dynamically oriented (Brown, 1995) or a skills-based/relapse-prevention approach (Marlatt & Gordon, 1985), has been the treatment of choice for drug abuse in most treatment settings, usually along with some case management or individual counseling and a referral to Alcoholics Anonymous, Narcotics Anonymous, Cocaine Anonymous, Rational Recovery, or some other self-help support group.
- *Cognitive-behavioral treatment* includes a combination of treatment strategies to change habitual patterns of thoughts and behaviors that make up the substance abuse problem. Counterconditioning techniques, including relaxation training and cue extinction; thought-stopping and countering techniques; skills training for affect management, assertiveness, and interpersonal interactions; efficacy-enhancing exercises; and relapse-prevention training, including recognizing cues and triggers, teaching drink and drug refusal skills, encouraging changes in the social environment, and coping with expectancies and triggers that promote relapse, are all standard components in the cognitive-behavioral treatment of substance abuse (Rotgers, Keller, & Morgenstern, 1996).
- *Cognitive therapy* for substance abusers is a recent adaptation of various cognitive therapy approaches (Beck, Wright, Newman, & Liese, 1993) specifically to treat alcohol and

drug abuse clients. These approaches typically focus on changing the beliefs, thoughts, and expectations that appear to underlie both the use of the substances and the difficulties in changing or quitting the substance abuse, including enduring withdrawal symptoms and craving.

- *Couples, family, and social network therapies:* Since the spouse and significant others play a role in the pattern of use and abuse as either collaborators or critics, this approach focuses on the mutual interactions and how to change these interactions in order to facilitate change or, at minimum, not interfere with the change process (McCrady & Epstein, 1996). These approaches have brought into the treatment spouses, friends, family members, colleagues, ministers, and so forth in order to influence and support the substance abuser in the process of change.

- *Behavior-focused treatments* entail changing the reinforcements and contingencies associated with the substance use. They have been incorporated into what has been called a *community reinforcement approach*, which attempts to increase the positive reinforcers associated with work, social networks, and personal functioning in order to change the environment of the drug abuser (Rotgers, Keller, & Morgenstern, 1996). Token economies and offering rewards or punishments contingent on *not engaging* in the drug abuse have often been used quite effectively to achieve short-term change but have had difficulty maintaining that change after the contingencies are removed.

- *Motivational interventions:* Motivational interviewing strategies developed by Miller and Rollnick (1991) use motivation and decision-making theory to deal with the ambivalence and resistance that are often associated with changing an addictive behavior. However, confrontation, which has often been the hallmark of many approaches dealing with drug addicts, is notably absent in this motivational approach. Instead, personal responsibility for the behavior change is emphasized, and the treatment provider's role is one of feedback and advice in the context of an empathic, listening, and reflective style.

- *12-step approaches,* which are based on the principles of Alcoholics Anonymous and usually include attendance at AA or other similar meetings, are very common in most community-based treatment programs. They have been incorporated into numerous more comprehensive, medically oriented treatment approaches, including detox and inpatient programs.

- *Residential treatment* settings offer psychosocial rehabilitation based on either a 12-step or a more confrontive therapeutic community model. Often they employ psychological principles, including counterconditioning, reinforcement management, and relapse prevention.

- *Stage-based methods:* Since, at any point in time, most substance abusers are not ready to change their behavior, action-oriented interventions could be expected to have low levels of success. Viewing treatment as involving movement through a series of sequential steps and attempting to increase motivation prior to offering action-oriented interventions like skills training and relapse prevention is becoming a common approach among treatment providers (Prochaska, DiClemente, & Norcross, 1992; Shaffer, 1992).

- *Court-mandated treatment:* Many judges and probation officials are generating large numbers of clients referred by the courts as a condition of their probation for offenses that involve substance abuse. Mandated treatment increases the numbers of individuals who come to treatment but does not necessarily produce internal motivation for change. The first challenge for the treatment provider with the more difficult, less motivated substance abuser is to promote internal motivation for change in order to enable the client to move toward seriously considering change and ultimately to develop a plan of action and follow through with that plan.

- *Relapse prevention and recycling treatments:* Relapse, or a return to the problematic behavior, is frequent with addictive behaviors. In fact, most clients experience multiple relapses and quitting attempts as they recycle through the process of change before achieving sustained change. Most programs have a specific component devoted to relapse prevention that usually employs the strategies outlined in the cognitive-behavioral treatments described above (Marlatt & Gordon, 1985).

TREATMENT MATCHING

Over the past 30 years, psychologists have assumed that the extensive heterogeneity in substance abusers necessitated differentiation in treatment. Instead of focusing on the differences in the drugs of abuse, many hypothesized that clients with certain characteristics (e.g., antisocial personality, cognitive impairment, levels of cognitive complexity, severity of dependence) would respond differently to different types of treatments either to increase or to decrease the efficacy of that treatment approach. This so-called matching hypothesis, which assumes a client attribute by treatment interaction (ATI), has been explored both in educational settings and in the treatment of mental health and substance abuse problems. Although a number of individual studies have supported the matching hypothesis, they are typically small-N studies that often found matching post hoc.

In the largest single trial of psychosocial treatments of its kind, the National Institute on Alcohol Abuse and Alcoholism and a large group of senior alcoholism and addiction investigators examined the question of treatment matching in its more traditional form through Project MATCH (Project MATCH Research Group, 1993, 1997). Do certain patient characteristics interact with certain types of treatments to produce differential outcomes? This randomized, clinical trial yielded several interesting and important findings:

1. Compliance of these alcohol-dependent clients with all three of the individual treatments (cognitive-behavioral, 12-step facilitation, and motivational enhancement) was substantial, with patients receiving on average two thirds of the prescribed treatment dose over a 12-week period.

2. There were dramatic changes in drinking from pre- to posttreatment, with few differences in outcomes among the treatments. Although there was no treatment control comparison to definitively test for treatment effects, the changes in drinking were significant and were well sustained throughout the 12 months posttreatment and even extending out to 39 months posttreatment. Three years after treatment there continued to be significant and dramatic differences from the pretreatment level of drinking for the MATCH participants.

3. There was only minimal support for the primary treatment matching hypotheses tested in this study, so that individuals with very different characteristics could be assigned to any of these treatments with little difference in outcome.

4. Despite intensive efforts at control, there were site differences, indicating that replication of findings is critical.

Project MATCH studied a more static conceptualization of treatment matching, relying on the assumption that a single characteristic at a single point in time would interact with one type of treatment to produce better outcomes. If the process of change is a dynamic one represented by stages of change, a static model as a basis for matching would not be the most appropriate model, since the individual engaged in changing a behavior represents a moving target and not a static entity (DiClemente, Carbonari, & Velasquez, 1992). Some data indicate that, when treatments are targeted at the stages and processes of change in a more dynamic type of matching, these interventions can be more effective. However, this requires complex individualization of the treatment process. Newer technologies, including computer-generated feedback, make it possible to create more individualized interventions that can target shifting client decisional considerations, current coping activities, levels of self-efficacy to abstain or refrain from the substance, and psychosocial risk factors. Early indications suggest that this more dynamic, process-oriented type of matching can aid the delivery and outcome of efforts to promote successful, sustained behavior change among substance abusers (Prochaska, DiClemente, Velicer, & Rossi, 1993).

PRACTICAL SUGGESTIONS
FOR TREATMENT

Although there are no compelling data for specific treatment matching to client characteristics, current research does yield the following specific suggestions for treatment:

1. There is significant co-occurrence of alcohol and drug problems with many psychiatric syndromes. Some screening for alcohol or drug abuse and dependence should be included in clinical intake procedures.
2. Individuals currently experiencing serious withdrawal symptoms or those who have had indications of delirium tremens (alcohol) or another drug-related organic brain syndrome need supervised detoxification from alcohol or drugs prior to psychosocial treatment.
3. Individuals with intact marriages and a spouse willing to attend treatment do better with some behavioral marital therapy.
4. Individuals with multiple psychosocial problems, including financial, social, housing, and occupational, do better when given access to multiple services or treatments addressing these problems in addition to the psychosocial treatment of the drinking or drug problems. Concurrent interventions, as in the community reinforcement approach or social network therapy, are recommended.
5. Brief interventions consisting of 30–60 minutes of discussion and advice appear to produce significant change in drinking and possibly drug use. At minimum, practitioners should offer some brief intervention of feedback and advice to everyone who screens positive for alcohol or drug abuse and dependence.
6. Intensity of treatment (outpatient, inpatient) appears to have little relation to treatment outcome for a broad range of individuals with alcohol problems. Engagement and retention of individuals in treatment appear to be the most important dimension. Offering

choice and engaging the client in the treatment are important strategies with substance abusers.
7. Motivation to change the substance use is an important dimension to consider in designing treatments. Clients with low motivation need interventions that acknowledge the client's perspective and are proactive in keeping the client in treatment. Confrontation appears to increase defensiveness and denial.
8. There is a crucial role for behavioral and psychosocial interventions to be given in conjunction with pharmacological treatments such as nicotine replacement, naltrexone or other drugs used to reduce craving for opiates and alcohol, and disulfiram and other drugs used as antagonists for alcohol and other drugs.

Results of ongoing and new research currently being conducted in the area of substance abuse treatment will be available in the next 5 years and should offer the practitioner direction for greater specification of treatment options.

References & Readings

Beck, A. T., Wright, F. D., Newman, C. F., & Liese, B. S. (1993). *Cognitive therapy of substance abuse*. New York: Guilford Press.

Brown, T. (Ed.) (1995). *Treating alcoholism*. San Francisco: Jossey-Bass.

DiClemente, C. C., Carbonari, J. P., & Velasquez, M. M. (1992). Alcoholism treatment mismatching from a process of change perspective. In R. R. Watson (Ed.), *Treatment of drug and alcohol abuse* (pp. 115–142). Totowa, NJ: Humana Press.

Hester, R. K., & Miller, W. R. (1995). *Handbook of alcoholism treatment approaches: Effective alternatives* (2nd ed.). Needham Heights, MA: Allyn and Bacon.

Marlatt, G. A., & Gordon, J. R. (Eds.) (1985). *Relapse prevention: Maintenance strategies in the treatment of addictive behaviors*. New York: Guilford Press.

McCrady, B. S., & Epstein, E. E. (1996). Theoretical bases of family approaches to substance abuse treatment. In F Rotgers, D. S. Keller, & J. Morgenstern (Eds.), *Treating substance abuse: Theory and technique* (pp. 117–142). New York: Guilford Press.

Miller, W. R., & Rollnick, S. (1991). *Motivational interviewing: Preparing people to change addictive behavior.* New York: Guilford Press.

Onken, L. S., & Blaine, J. D. (Eds.) (1990). *Psychotherapy and counseling in the treatment of drug abuse* (NIDA Research Monograph 104, DHHS Publication No. ADM 90-1172). Washington, DC: Superintendent of Documents.

Prochaska, J. O., DiClemente, C. C., & Norcross, J. C. (1992). In search of how people change: Applications to addictive behaviors. *American Psychologist, 47,* 1102–1114.

Prochaska, J. O., DiClemente, C. C., Velicer, W. F., & Rossi, J. S. (1993). Standardized, individualized, interactive, and personalized self-help programs for smoking cessation. *Health Psychology, 12,* 399–405.

Project MATCH Research Group (1993). Project MATCH: Rationale and methods for a multisite clinical trial matching alcoholism patients to treatment. *Alcoholism: Clinical and Experimental Research, 17,* 1130–1145.

Project MATCH Research Group (1997). Matching alcoholism treatments to client heterogeneity: Project MATCH posttreatment drinking outcomes. *Journal of Studies on Alcohol, 58,* 7–29.

Rotgers, F., Keller, D. S., & Morgenstern, J. (Eds.) (1996). *Treating substance abuse: Theory and technique* (pp. 174–201). New York: Guilford Press.

Shaffer, H. J. (1992). The psychology of stage change: The transition from addiction to recovery. In J. H. Lowinson, P. Ruiz, & R. B. Millman (Eds.), *Substance abuse: A comprehensive textbook* (2nd ed., pp. 100–105). Baltimore: Williams and Wilkins.

Related Topics

68 MOTIVATIONAL INTERVIEWING

Theresa B. Moyers

Clients attempting to give up entrenched and self-destructive behaviors, such as pathological use of substances, are frequently uncertain or ambivalent about their desire for change. Such ambivalence is often labeled as poor motivation, and the therapist may then increase the level of confrontation in an effort to elicit more willingness to change. Clients typically respond to confrontation with increased resistance, leaving both parties unsatisfied with the outcome of the session.

Motivational interviewing (Miller & Rollnick, 1991) is an alternative approach that enables therapists to reconceptualize ambivalence and utilize specific skills to help clients resolve it and move toward positive behavior change. It is typically most useful in initial sessions with substance-abusing clients, but it forms an important "safety net" when ambivalence recurs throughout the therapy process.

Within the motivational interviewing paradigm, ambivalence is viewed as a normal part of the process of change (Prochaska, DiClemente, & Norcross, 1992). Clients who are uncertain about changing their pathological substance use are *not* viewed as having a peculiarly high level of denial or as being unmotivated for treatment. Instead, the therapist interprets such ambivalence as a normal road block experienced by all individuals who successfully change destructive behaviors.

GUIDING PRINCIPLES

- *Expressing empathy:* Therapist empathy is conveyed through the use of active listening skills and an attitude of acceptance. The therapist works hard to understand matters from the client's perspective and to convey this understanding in the use of both careful body language and accurate reflections of content. Reflective listening is viewed as the most important initial intervention and one that is the foundation for all further motivational interviewing strategies. It is a fallback position, which the therapist may always choose to use and remain consistent with a motivational interviewing approach.

- *Developing discrepancy:* The therapist will help clients to recognize the discrepancy between their current substance abuse and the goals and values they hold most deeply. This may be accomplished by an open-minded exploration of the costs and benefits of the substance use. Another strategy to develop discrepancy might be a values clarification exercise in which the client discusses the things most important to himself or herself and any barriers that prevent consistency with those values. Finally, therapists can question clients about hopes and plans for the future, as well as concerns they have about how their substance abuse may interfere. Therapists should not fall into the trap of trying to convince clients of the need for change. Ideally, *clients* will present the arguments for change, essentially talking themselves into making the desired move.

- *Avoiding argumentation:* The therapist recognizes that resistance will increase if client choices are threatened and will avoid arguing while using motivational interviewing. Specifically, the therapist refrains from direct confrontation of self-destructive attitudes and behaviors. This may mean that clients will persist in refusing to label themselves as alcoholic, will continue to minimize

the impact of their drinking on others, or will reject the need for professional help. The therapist does not challenge such views with a logical argument, recognizing that doing so may cause clients to become more firmly entrenched by causing them to argue against change. Therapists avoid arguments by reminding themselves that clients bear the ultimate responsibility for change and that their interaction with the client may be one of only many that will tip the balance in favor of change. If the therapist is tempted to argue with clients, a safe fallback is to express empathy by using active listening skills.

- *Rolling with resistance:* The therapist works to "invite" the client to examine new choices by (a) reframing concerns, (b) offering collaborative treatment plans, (c) using mutual metaphors and language, and (d) paying explicit attention to the fact that not changing is always an option.

- *Supporting self-efficacy:* The therapist actively conveys the message that the client is capable of change. The client is viewed as the expert in solving the problem and is encouraged to personalize a recovery plan by utilizing his or her particular strengths and ideas. Therapists place themselves in a consultative role, offering options that clients may not have considered from a broad menu of change strategies.

AVOIDING TRAPS

In attempting to use motivational interviewing, the following "traps" may be encountered that snare both client and therapist:

- *The blaming trap:* When therapists or family members attempt to assign blame for substance abuse, usually to the client, and the client disagrees, resistance to change increases. This is the antithesis of motivational interviewing. This trap can be avoided by adopting a "no-fault" policy for the problem at hand and making this explicit to the client.

- *The question-answer trap:* When therapists ask closed-ended questions, the patient falls into the passive role of answering only yes or no. Such a trap discourages the exploration of the patient's deepest concerns, which is the goal of motivational interviewing. This can be avoided by using open-ended queries and reserving questions asking for specific information until the end of the session.

- *The confrontation-denial trap:* When therapists feel they must impress upon clients the seriousness of their substance abuse, a predictable *decrease* in client concern is likely to result. Therapists may avoid this trap by reflecting a client's lack of concern rather than confronting it or diagnosing it as denial.

- *The labeling trap:* Clients often refuse to accept labels that are important to therapists. They may not be willing to call themselves an "alcoholic" or a "heroin addict," even when they are quite motivated to change destructive substance use. Accepting a label has not been shown to produce better treatment outcomes (Orford, 1973), and a therapist using a motivational interviewing approach need not insist that clients adopt diagnostic labels but instead will search for a common language to discuss the problem.

- *The premature focus trap:* Ambivalent clients will typically enter the therapist's office with a variety of concerns, only some of which will relate to substance abuse. The therapist refrains from focusing on the client's substance use too early without careful exploration of the broader spectrum of the client's distress.

COGNITIVE TRAPS

In addition to these behavioral traps, cognitive barriers may stymie clinicians who are attempting to use motivational interviewing for the first time.

- Therapists may feel as if this technique places them in a passive role. This cognitive trap may be overcome by an appreciation for the effortfulness and skill necessary for active listening when it is done well.

- The therapist may fear that motivational interviewing reinforces a client's denial. The therapist may overcome this barrier by an examination of the literature indicating that direct confrontation of denial often produces resistance, the opposite of the desired outcome (Miller & Sovereign, 1989).

- The therapist may be concerned that motivational interviewing implies that the client can decide not to change. Clinicians can assist themselves with this discomfort by examining their clients' ultimate freedom to choose whether they wish to give up destructive behaviors. Also, as Rogers (1957) points out, clients may paradoxically be most able to change when they are least compelled to do so.

SKILL AND RESEARCH

In general, a therapist who is skillfully using motivational interviewing is active, warm, and highly selective in what he or she chooses to reflect and elaborate upon in the session. His or her clients should experience a sense of increased personal power regarding their ability to change their pattern of substance abuse. Resistance behaviors, such as arguing and disagreeing, should decrease over the therapy hour.

Evidence for the effectiveness of motivational interviewing is substantial. Eleven clinical trials have evaluated motivational interviewing in inpatient, outpatient, and primary care settings (Noonan & Moyers, 1997). Problem drinkers from all points of the abuse continuum, as well as drug abusers, have been included in these studies. Motivational interviewing has consistently produced superior results when compared with confrontation of denial (Miller, Benefield, & Tonigan, 1993) and when used as an enhancement to traditional treatment (Bien, Miller, & Boroughs, 1993; Brown & Miller, 1993).

Note

The author wishes to thank William R. Miller, Ph.D., for reviewing this article.

References & Readings

Bien, T., Miller, W. R., & Boroughs, J. M. (1993). Motivational interviewing with alcohol outpatients. *Behavioral and Cognitive Psychotherapy, 21,* 347–356.

Brown, J., & Miller, W. R. (1993). Impact of motivational interviewing on participation and outcome in residential alcoholism treatment. *Psychology of Addictive Behaviors, 7,* 211–218.

Miller, W. R., Benefield, R. G., & Tonigan, J. S. (1993). Enhancing motivation for change in problem drinking: A controlled comparison of two therapist styles. *Journal of Consulting and Clinical Psychology, 61,* 455–461.

Miller, W. R., & Rollnick, S. (1991). *Motivational interviewing: Preparing people for change.* New York: Guilford Press.

Miller, W. R., & Sovereign, R. G. (1989). The checkup: A model for early intervention in addictive behaviors. In T. Loberg, W. R. Miller, P. E. Nathan, & G. A. Marlatt (Eds.), *Addictive behaviors: Prevention and early intervention* (pp. 219–231). Amsterdam: Swets and Zeitlinger.

Noonan, W. C., & Moyers, T. B. (1997). Motivational interviewing. *Journal of Substance Misuse, 2,* 8–16.

Orford, J. (1973). A comparison of alcoholics whose drinking is totally controlled and those whose drinking is mainly controlled. *Behaviour Research and Therapy, 11,* 565–576.

Prochaska, J. O., & DiClemente, C. C. (1986). Toward a comprehensive model of change. In W. R. Miller & N. Heather (Eds.), *Treating addictive behaviors: Process of change* (pp. 3–27). New York: Plenum Press.

Prochaska, J. O., DiClemente, C. C., & Norcross, J. C. (1992). In search of how people change: Applications to addictive behaviors. *American Psychologist, 47,* 1102–1114.

Rogers, C. (1957). The necessary and sufficient conditions for therapeutic personality change. *Journal of Consulting Psychology, 21,* 95–103.

Related Topics

69   ANXIETY/ANGER MANAGEMENT TRAINING

Richard M. Suinn

Anxiety and stress present major concerns for the general population. Primary care practitioners report that anxiety ranks next highest as the major reason patients see their physicians. Anxiety can be at the core of various disorders:

- Generalized anxiety disorder or phobic disorders
- The blocking of coping behaviors, healthy lifestyles, educational attainment, or successful performance
- Biomedical consequences

Anger is now being recognized as another crucial problem area. Severe angry episodes are experienced by as high as 20 percent of the population. Anger is the source of varied social and personal problems:

- Child or family abuse
- Physical or verbal assault
- Community property damage
- Disruption of work performance
- Interference with health and the immune system

Developed in the 1970s, Anxiety Management Training (AMT) was designed as a brief intervention for anxiety (Suinn, 1990, 1995). Since then, empirical results have proved its application for anger. It is a six- to eight-session structured procedure that trains patients in using relaxation to deactivate anxiety or angry emotional states.

APPLICATIONS: EMPIRICAL VALIDATION

Empirical results confirm the value of AMT for the following:

- Generalized anxiety disorder (Shoemaker, 1976)
- Mathematics anxiety (Suinn & Richardson, 1971)
- Essential hypertension (Jorgensen, Houston, & Zurawski, 1981)
- Diabetes (Rose, Firestone, Heick, & Faught, 1983)
- Dysmenorrhea (Quillen & Denney, 1982)
- Depression (Jannoun, Oppenheimer, & Gelder, 1982; Cragan & Deffenbacher, 1984)
- Type A characteristics (Hart, 1984; Nakano, 1990)

- Anger (Deffenbacher, in press; Suinn & Deffenbacher, 1988)
- Removing anxiety blocking patient's ability to respond to traditional psychotherapy (Van Hassel, Bloom, & Gonzales, 1982)

ADVANTAGES OF AMT

A major advantage of AMT is the fact that it is a brief therapy using a self-control approach that permits generalization. Moreover, because the procedure is structured, it is possible to determine progress at each session and to determine the need for additional or fewer sessions. The step-by-step characteristics of AMT also allow monitoring of gains from session to session. Such concrete information can be most useful for the practitioner who wishes to carefully monitor progress or for the researcher who wishes to study variables involved in change from each session.

HOW TO CONDUCT SESSIONS

Among the basic or core characteristics of the AMT method are the following:

- Guided imagery for anxiety or anger arousal
- Relaxation for deactivating the arousal
- Practice for self-control
- Homework for generalization

The guided imagery involves use of anxiety or anger imagery from the patient's experience to precipitate arousal. Anxiety or anger arousal is precipitated during the sessions in order to aid the client in the use of relaxation to reduce an actual experience of anxiety or anger. Thus, the client can first practice controlling his or her anxiety in the safe setting of the treatment environment, prior to being assigned homework in real-life applications. AMT covers six to eight sessions.

Session 1 involves relaxation training using the standard Jacobsen tension/relaxation method (1938) or biofeedback.

Session 2 involves identification of an anxiety (or anger scene for anger treatment), relaxation, and anxiety (or anger arousal) followed by relaxation. The anxiety (anger) scene involves a real experience that has been associated with a moderately high level of anxiety (anger). After the client is relaxed, anxiety (anger) arousal is initiated through the therapist's instruction to switch on this scene and use it to reexperience anxiety (anger). Instructions include description of both scene-setting and anxiety (anger)–arousal details to aid in arousal. After about 10–15 seconds of exposure, the scene is terminated and the therapist reintroduces the relaxation.

Session 3 follows the steps used in session 2, with the addition of self-initiated relaxation and attention to the client's personal signs associated with anxiety (anger). This might involve symptoms such as heightened respiration, clenched fists, catastrophic thoughts, and so on. After the client obtains arousal, the therapist instructs the client to pay attention to the anxiety (anger) symptoms. The following instructions are given: "Pay attention to how you experience anxiety [anger]; perhaps it is in body signs such as your hands or neck tensing, or your heart rate, or in some of your thoughts." Then relaxation is again retrieved, with the therapist taking responsibility for guiding the relaxation. This cycle of arousal, attention to anxiety (anger) signs, and retrieval of relaxation is continued to the end of the hour—a cycle of about three to five repetitions.

Session 4 adds two new major components. First, a high-intensity anxiety (or anger) scene is identified. During this session, this scene will be alternated with the moderate-level scene used in sessions 2 and 3. Second, the session requires the client to assume more responsibility for regaining self-control after anxiety (anger) arousal. Instead of the therapist terminating the anxiety (anger) scene and reinitiating the relaxation, the client decides when to end the anxiety (anger) scene and takes responsibility for relaxation retrieval.

Session 5 completes the fading out of therapist control and the completion of client self-control. At the start of the session, the client self-initiates relaxation, signaling its achievement. Although the therapist switches on the

anxiety (anger) scene, all activities from this point are client controlled.

Sessions 6–8 repeat the session 5 format until self-control appears complete. New anxiety (anger) scenes may be employed as needed to increase generalization.

References & Readings

Cragan, M. K., & Deffenbacher, J. L. (1984). Anxiety management training and relaxation as self-control in the treatment of generalized anxiety in medical outpatients. *Journal of Counseling Psychology, 1,* 123–131.

Deffenbacher, J. (1994). Anger reduction: Issues, assessment, and intervention strategies. In A. Siegman & T. Smith (Eds.), *Anger, hostility, and the heart* (pp. 239–269). Hillsdale, NJ: Lawrence Erlbaum.

Hart, K. (1984). Stress management training for Type A individuals. *Journal of Behavioral Medicine, 12,* 133–140.

Jacobsen, E. (1938). *Progressive relaxation.* Chicago: University of Chicago Press.

Jannoun, L., Oppenheimer, C., & Gelder, M. (1982). A self-help treatment program for anxiety state patients. *Behavior Therapy, 13,* 103–111.

Jorgensen, R., Houston, B., & Zurawski, R. (1981). Anxiety management training in the treatment of essential hypertension. *Behavior Research and Therapy, 19,* 467–474.

Nakano, K. (1990). Effects of two self-control procedures on modifying Type A behavior. *Journal of Clinical Psychology, 46,* 652–657.

Quillen, M. A., & Denney, D. R. (1982). Self-control of dysmenorrheic symptoms through pain management training. *Journal of Behavior Therapy and Experimental Psychiatry, 13,* 123–130.

Rose, M., Firestone, P., Heick, H., & Faught, A. (1983). The effects of anxiety management training on the control of juvenile diabetes mellitus. *Journal of Behavioral Medicine, 27,* 381–395.

Shoemaker, J. (1976). *Treatment for anxiety neurosis.* Unpublished doctoral dissertation, Colorado State University, Ft. Collins.

Suinn, R. (1990). *Anxiety management training: A behavior therapy.* New York: Plenum Press.

Suinn, R. (1995). Anxiety management training. In K. Craig & K. Dobson (Eds.), *Anxiety and depression in adults and children* (pp. 159–179). Thousand Oaks, CA: Sage.

Suinn, R., & Deffenbacher, J. (1988). Anxiety management training. *Counseling Psychologist, 16,* 31–49.

Suinn, R., & Richardson, F. (1971). Anxiety management training: A non-specific behavior therapy program for anxiety control. *Behavior Therapy, 2,* 498–512.

Van Hassel, J., Bloom, L. J., & Gonzales, A. C. (1982). Anxiety management training with schizophrenic outpatients. *Journal of Clinical Psychology, 38,* 280–285.

70 PSYCHOLOGICAL INTERVENTIONS IN ADULT DISEASE MANAGEMENT

Carol D. Goodheart

Chronic illnesses are now the primary cause of disability and death in the United States, a change from the acute conditions of the past. Over a 25-year span, the number of people with chronic conditions will increase by 35 million, from 99 million in 1995 to 134 million in 2020 (Institute for Health and Aging, 1996). The chronic illnesses form a spectrum of diseases; they may be life-threatening, progressive, manageable, unpredictable, or of known or unknown etiology. Such illnesses include cancer, cardiovascular disease, diabetes, asthma, arthritis, HIV disease, Alzheimer's disease, postviral syndromes, and gastrointestinal disorders, among many others.

Behavior, genetics, and the environment interact to produce or prevent disease. The Human Capital Initiative (1995) reports the state of the psychological research agenda on health and behavior, which fosters the understanding of basic processes necessary for the prevention and treatment of chronic illness.

Once disease is present, symptomatology may be affected by behavior, cognition, emotion, and interpersonal dynamics. Overall, the application of psychological interventions to disease management results in improvements in mental health functioning and reductions in medical service use (Lechnyr, 1992; Pallak, Cummings, Dorken, & Henke, 1994; Schlesinger, Mumford, Glass, Patrick, & Sharfstein, 1983). The following summary highlights the key elements in the psychological treatment of adults with chronic illnesses.

There are many models of psychological intervention during illness, with variations according to theoretical orientation, population, setting, and emphasis. Among the diverse approaches, however, there are common themes for the clinician (Goodheart & Lansing, 1997).

1. *Obtain medical information:* Clinicians need not become medical experts, but they must obtain sufficient background to understand the choices, treatments, and experiences of the adult with a chronic condition. Collaboration with the patient's physician can provide information on the outcome, process, etiology, and management needs of a particular disease (the acronym OPEN makes the list easy to remember). Other important medical resources are available through the Internet, medical reference libraries, federal and state government health agencies (on-line, mail, and facsimile transmissions), and specific disease organizations such as the American Cancer Society, the American Diabetes Association, and the American Heart Association. *The Merck Manual of Diagnosis and Therapy* (Berkow & Fletcher, 1992) provides a medical overview of most conditions a clinician will encounter.

2. *Assess response to illness and psychological status:* The adult's capacity to cope with illness is affected by premorbid personality organization, life stage roles and tasks, maturational development, internal resources such as temperament and intelligence, and external resources such as socioeconomic status, family support, and level of access to health care. These factors are evaluated through clinical interview and, in some situations, through specific standardized assessment measures/scales for depression, anxiety, somatization, hostility, or other relevant indices.

3. *Integrate theoretical orientation and illness:* Cross-fertilization between and among differing schools of psychological theory often occurs when clinicians work with chronically ill adults. Dynamic clinicians add behavioral and educational components; cognitive clinicians add inferred self- and relational components; family systems, feminist theory, humanistic, and eclectic clinicians add to the diversity. In general, clinicians tend to borrow from other clinicians' attitudes and techniques. Regardless of orientation, the focus on coping with illness is enhanced when clinicians understand the patient's global mastery-competence level and how the patient manages reality, affect, and anxiety, interpersonal relationships, and cognitive functions. Examples of three treatment approaches with theoretically different underpinnings are *Medical Family Therapy* (McDaniel, Hepworth, & Doherty, 1992), a family systems orientation; *Managing Chronic Illness: A Biopsychosocial Perspective* (Nicassio & Smith, 1995), a cognitive-behavioral orientation; and *Treating People With Chronic Disease: A Psychological Guide* (Goodheart & Lansing, 1997), a psychoanalytic-psychodynamic orientation. All three texts are based on a biopsychosocial model of understanding and intervention. All recommend an interdisciplinary collaborative approach to health care and are appropriate for community practice and medical settings. Another key reference guide is *Clinical Health Psychology in Medical Settings: A Practitioner's Guidebook* (Belar & Deardorff, 1995).

4. *Offer a menu of interventions:* The selection of interventions is based on the changing needs and capacities of the chronically ill adult and the knowledge and skills of the clinician. Interventions may be directed toward prevention of further illness (e.g., smoking cessation, weight control); toward screening for disease (e.g., decreasing the avoidance of warranted HIV testing or mammograms); or toward management of disease. Disease management interventions include the following:

- *Focused psychotherapy:* a time-limited approach to problem solving, based on biopsychosocial stressors and resources.
- *Decision making:* helping adults arrive at the best decisions for their personal circumstances from among the medical choices they are given.
- *Medical symptom reduction:* helping adults decrease pain, lessen side effects of treatments (e.g., anticipatory nausea associated with chemotherapy), or decrease frequency or intensity of acute episodes (e.g., incidents of asthma exacerbation).
- *Coping enhancement:* helping adults to plan actively, elicit support, seek information, develop new habits, reduce anxiety, and facilitate mourning while preventing depression.
- *Treatment adherence:* helping adults develop motivation and overcome obstacles to maintaining adherence to prescribed medical treatment regimens.

- *Stress and pain reduction:* helping adults learn techniques of progressive relaxation, hypnosis, biofeedback, visualization, meditation, or focused breathing.
- *Interpersonal techniques:* helping adults learn new or improved skills for communication, assertion, and conflict resolution with medical personnel, family, partners, employers, coworkers, friends.
- *Adaptation:* helping adults make quality-of-life adjustments to an altered reality due to the losses of illness, effects of medications, aftereffects of medical treatments, or disability.
- *Crisis management:* helping adults mobilize internal and external supportive resources to regain control, for use when the patient is flooded with affect and overwhelmed by anxiety and when the patient's ability to cope on his or her own is compromised.
- *Anger management:* helping adults control anger through the use of shame reduction, guided imagery, anger arousal, and relaxation (an adaptation of anxiety management training; Deffenbacher, Demm, & Brandon, 1986; Suinn, 1996) and through improved self-efficacy in communication and problem solving.
- *Nonverbal psychotherapeutic techniques:* helping adults express affect and experience through art therapy, sand play, or movement therapy. Rarely used alone, these visual, tactile, motile techniques are particularly useful in adults with learning disabilities, posttraumatic stress disorder, or a blocked, regressed, dissociated, or concrete state of functioning.
- *Family involvement:* helping the caregivers, partners, and family members of adults with chronic illness by conjoint treatments and the development of coping and support structures within the home care system.
- *Support for self disease management:* helping adults contribute to their own well-being through self-selected adjunctive activities (e.g., personal illness diaries, exercise and nutrition programs [within limits of medical recommendations], religious and spiritual participation, humorous tapes and books).
- *Referral:* helping adults decrease their isolation and increase the support network available to them through disease support groups and community services.
- *Handling uncertainty and fear of death:* helping adults with the anxiety and depression that often accompany disease progression. The primary technique for death anxiety is to listen fully, which may be difficult under severe and threatening circumstances. To listen fully means to listen without judgment, without withdrawal, without denial, and without interference to the patient's hopes. To listen fully is to be present, with the patient, in facing death.

It is not possible within the limits of this entry to detail the implementation of each intervention given. Even experienced clinicians may not be skilled in every type of intervention listed above. For example, most clinicians are trained in graduate school to offer crisis management, but few are trained to offer hypnosis for pain management. For further training in specific modalities, clinicians may turn to appropriate postdoctoral continuing education programs (e.g., the American Society for Clinical Hypnosis offers hypnosis training throughout the United States).

5. *Match the focus of intervention to the need:* No single intervention is sufficient if used exclusively. Individuals with chronic illness vary in their willingness or ability to make use of the strategies. Nevertheless, important overlapping areas of need that represent common impediments to functioning have been identified in chronically ill adults:

- Isolation, losses and dependency, fear of death, confines of illness, lack of familiarity with medical culture (Shapiro & Koocher, 1996).
- Separation, loss of key roles and autonomy and control, disruption of plans, assault on self-image and self-esteem, uncertain and unpredictable futures, distressing emotions (Turk & Salovey, 1995).

• Decreased self-esteem associated with body image changes, mourning associated with losses, negative affects associated with physical, psychological, and social discomfort (Goodheart & Lansing, 1997).

6. *Face the personal impact of working with chronically ill adults:* Clinicians have their own idiosyncratic responses to the presence of disease and to patients' characterological reactions to disease. Entering into a therapeutic relationship with a chronically ill adult carries special challenges. Like everyone else, clinicians have deeply held personal attitudes toward bodily needs, functions, disfigurements, and pains and toward caretaking and dependency. They have personal fears about debilitation, decline, and death. Working with ill patients often induces countertransference reactions in clinicians, which may be expressed as

• Anxiety (e.g., exposure to death, failure, vulnerability, or loss may stimulate anxiety).
• Affect (e.g., anger may be a marker of frustration with the toll of disease or with patients who complain more than the clinician thinks is necessary; disgust or distaste may be evoked by the graphic details of illness).
• Defensive reactions (e.g., withdrawal, denial, moralizing, minimizing, or rescuing may occur if clinicians' anxieties or negative affects are aroused sufficiently).

It is not always possible to resolve these issues in ideal ways, but it is realistic to identify and manage clinicians' personal responses that interfere with clinical care. Potential signs of difficulty include the following:

• Preoccupation with thoughts of the patient out of session.
• Persistent intense feelings about the patient.
• Depressive constellation of discouragement, fatigue, and pessimism.
• Treatment impasse.
• Feedback from patient, supervisor, colleagues, family, or friends regarding affects, anxieties, or reactions to the work.

SUMMARY

Psychological interventions in adult chronic illness are becoming increasingly important as the number of people with chronic conditions grows. The research literature on interactions among behavior, biology, and disease provides the basis for increasingly targeted psychological intervention strategies. The overview framework for these strategies includes obtaining sufficient medical information, assessing response to illness and psychological status, integrating psychological theory and the illness, offering a varied selection of interventions, matching the focus of intervention to the need, and facing the personal impact of working with chronically ill adults.

References & Readings

Belar, C. D., & Deardorff, W. W. (1995). *Clinical health psychology in medical settings: A practitioner's guidebook.* Washington, DC: American Psychological Association.

Berkow, R., & Fletcher, A. (Eds.) (1992). *The Merck manual of diagnosis and therapy.* Rahway, NJ: Merck.

Deffenbacher, J., Demm, P., & Brandon, A. (1986). High general anger: Correlates and treatment. *Behavior Research and Therapy, 24,* 481–489.

Goodheart, C., & Lansing, M. (1997). *Treating people with chronic disease: A psychological guide.* Washington, DC: American Psychological Association.

Human Capital Initiative (1995). *Do the right thing: A research plan for healthy living.* Washington, DC: American Psychological Association.

Institute for Health and Aging, University of California, San Francisco (1996). *Chronic care in America: A 21st century challenge.* Princeton, NJ: Robert Wood Johnson Foundation.

Lechnyr, R. (1992). Cost savings and effectiveness of mental health services. *Journal of the Oregon Psychological Association, 38,* 8–12.

McDaniel, S. H., Hepworth, J., & Doherty, W. J. (1992). *Medical family therapy.* New York: Basic Books.

Nicassio, P. M., & Smith, T. W. (Eds.) (1995). *Managing chronic illness: A biopsychosocial perspective.* Washington, DC: American Psychological Association.

Pallak, M. S., Cummings, N., Dorken, H., & Henke, C. J. (1994). Effects of mental health treatment on medical cost. *Mind/Body Medicine, 1,* 7–16.

Schlesinger, H. J., Mumford, E., Glass, G. V., Patrick, C., & Sharfstein, S. (1983). Mental health treatment and medical care utilization in a fee for service system: Outpatient mental health treatment following the onset of a chronic disease. *American Journal of Mental Health, 73,* 422–429.

Shapiro, D. E., & Koocher, G. P. (1996). Goals and practical considerations in outpatient medical crises intervention. *Professional Psychology: Research and Practice, 27,* 109–120.

Suinn, R. (1996, January 9). Anger: A disorder of the future, here today: Part 2. Treatment. *Alaska Psychologist, 11.*

Turk, D. C., & Salovey, P. (1995). Cognitive-behavioral treatment of illness behavior. In P. M. Nicassio & T. W. Smith (Eds.), *Managing chronic illness: A biopsychosocial perspective.* Washington, DC: American Psychological Association.

Related Topics

Chapter 56, "Psychological Interventions in Childhood Chronic Illness"
Chapter 71, "Thumbnail Guide to Medical Crisis Counseling^SM"

71 THUMBNAIL GUIDE TO MEDICAL CRISIS COUNSELING^SM

Irene S. Pollin & Gerald P. Koocher

Medical Crisis Counseling^SM (Pollin, 1994, 1995) is a systematic mode for meeting the psychological needs of patients with lifelong illness using a brief treatment program of 10 sessions or less. It is based on an integrative theoretical approach that focuses on the manner in which chronic illness disrupts normal developmental tasks and trajectories. The intervention involves the use of cognitive coping strategies, enhancement of social support, and basic concepts of several therapeutic systems, including therapeutic techniques of self-psychology, along with client-centered and rational-emotive elements.

The intervention model can be effectively illustrated and summarized by considering the issues or fears that commonly affect patients confronting chronic illness and their families. These fears include fear of loss of control, fear of loss of self-image, fear of dependency, fear of stigma, fear of abandonment, fear of anger, fear of isolation, and fear of death.

- *Unit of treatment:* Those treated are chiefly individual adult or adolescent medical patients because mobilization of personal coping resources is central to the intervention. However, there are times when spouses, parents, or other sources of social support (or tensions) may be brought into the session with the patient's permission. In the case of child patients, parents or other caretakers will invariably be drawn into the intervention at appropriate times in order to advance and maintain the patient's progress.

- *Therapist's role:* The therapist serves as facilitator, problem solver, health educator, and coach to the patient with a solution-focused orientation. Empathic listening and helping the patient to frame his or her concerns is the central role, although the therapist must also be prepared to assume an active problem-focused orientation to help patients progress when they are feeling "stuck." The therapist also serves as a validator of the patient's experiences to the extent that emotional reactions are placed in the context of normal responses to abnormal circumstances.

- *Patient's role:* Patients are encouraged to take an active coping stance. The ideal role exists when the patient becomes consumer-oriented and functions in partnership with the physician and the psychotherapist.

SETTING THE STAGE FOR ASSESSMENT AND INTERVENTION: THE FIRST SESSION

The therapist's initial orientation should be focused on the patient's strengths. The emphasis should be placed on framing any distress being experienced as a normal reaction to serious illness, as opposed to reflecting psychopathology. The patient needs to hear the message "You may feel out of control, but that doesn't mean you're going crazy; it means you're experiencing the normal reaction of people in similar circumstances." Within this frame of reference, it is important for the therapist to evidence both empathy and a sense of confidence that the interventions to follow can make a difference. Therapists should also convey their role as supportive consultants who will assist patients in gaining a renewed sense of personal control in coping with their illness.

Therapist Activities

1. After orienting the patient to the nature of the intervention, the therapist asks the patient to review the onset of the medical illness or the particular crisis leading to the referral for counseling (if other than diagnosis). During this conversation, the therapist should be listening carefully for elements related to specific fears, as well as other concerns linked to the illness. Exercises include the following:

- Invite the patient to recount the nature of the experiences that accompanied or triggered the diagnosis or current crisis. If more than one family member is present, each should be encouraged to describe events from his or her own perspective. Typical inquiries might include "Tell me about what happened when you first became ill. What happened when you realized something was wrong? How did the change in your condition affect you psychologically? What steps did you take or avoid taking when you first sensed that something was wrong?"

- Inquire about what the patient knows or has been told about the illness or crisis and who provided the information. Inquire about how the patient rates communication with the primary medical caregiver(s). Ask whether patients are comfortable asking questions of the physician(s) treating them. Ask whether the patient is confused about any of the advice given to him or her and whether the patient needs or wants additional information. Assess the accuracy of information reported by the patient, if possible, but generally accept what the patient says as valid because that is how he or she experiences the illness. However, also be prepared to offer or refer the patient for new educative information as needed.

- Explore any attributions of meaning or beliefs about the illness or crisis event. Typical inquiries might include "Why do you think this happened? How have you tried to make sense of what was happening? What are your thoughts about how these events came to pass?"

- Ask how things have changed since the diagnosis as a result of the illness or medical crisis event. Encourage the patient to talk about changes from the perspective of his or her own beliefs, feelings, and fears, as well as any changes he or she has sensed or experienced in relationships with other important people in his or her life.

- Ask about other difficult or stressful challenges the patient has faced in life and what (if anything) was helpful in coping with those events. This can be initiated in the context of the current illness being one of these most difficult or stressful circumstances the patient has had to face, although some patients may cite other life events as more stressful. Answers to this question can provide hints to "what works" or what does not help for some patients. Note what sort of thoughts and activities were helpful in prior coping efforts.

2. Based on the information collected in the earlier portion of the interview, engage the patient in formulating a series of steps that form a basis for exerting some control over what is happening to the patient. This might initially include helping the patient to do the following:

   • Begin a problem list that identifies symptoms or aspects of the physical illness that are problematic or disruptive. Make a list of the patient's goals in his or her own words. Retain this list for use in summing up at the final session.
   • Identify emotional or interpersonal challenges that have been brought on or become exacerbated by the medical crisis.
   • Recognize aspects of the medical care system that are presenting adjustment problems, including any gaps in information or education about the illness and treatment course. Help the patient to focus on the most important goals of communication (e.g., "What is most important for you to communicate to your family or your physician?") and then strategize about different ways to get the point across.

3. At the conclusion of the first session, after reviewing the initial goals that have been established, it is important to assess the patient's sense of optimism or hopefulness and begin to mobilize it. Ask, "How effective do you think this program will be in addressing your needs?" Listen carefully to the response and note any expressed reservations. These may form a good basis for beginning the next session.

TECHNIQUES AND STRATEGIES FOR THE MAIN INTERVENTION (MIDDLE SESSIONS)

During the intermediate sessions (between number 2 and number 9), it is important to assist the patient in addressing the eight primary sources of potential anxiety and depression related to his or her medical condition described earlier. The patient can be helped to recognize each as it emerges, identify or label it as an issue that can be dealt with, and actively strategize about how to address and overcome the coping challenges presented.

Therapist Activities

1. Using examples or descriptions provided by the patient, label the particular source of distress and help to put it in context. For example, it is normal to feel out of control when one has been diagnosed with a chronic illness, the course of which is unpredictable or unknown at the time. It is normal to feel that one is different, less capable, or less attractive as the sense of self-image shifts in response to changes related to the medical crisis or subsequent treatment regimen.

   • The patient may find it useful to take stock of his or her current status. Use of a personal journal or a therapeutic homework assignment might be helpful here. The patient can be asked to summarize the nature of the disease, stage or status, and prognosis; inventory his or her emotional status; document disruptions in his or her normal life that are attributable to the illness; and list any other stressors in the environment.
   • The patient can also be asked to inventory his or her normal responses to stresses and coping capacities by asking questions such as "How do you usually respond when you are feeling tense or sad at home? How could someone who knows you tell when you are feeling stressed? What is your response to pressure at work? What helps you to cope with these problems?" The answers can then be dis-

cussed as they apply to illness-related stresses. It is important for patients to understand the point in time at which their life changed because of the illness. This theme should be reiterated during the course of the intervention, focusing on how things have changed or not. In this way, patients can see the changes as they occur and place responsibility on the illness, not on spouses or other family members.

- If the patient is at a loss to describe coping strategies, illustrations can be given. For example, ask, "Some people tell jokes; some keep worries all to themselves; some turn to family, friends, or faith; some tell everyone who will listen; and others raid the refrigerator. What do you usually do?" Explore how the preferred coping methods of the past are affected by the illness.

2. To the extent that a patient avoids talking about any of the key issues, the therapist should initiate a discussion of that content area at an appropriate time in a middle session.

- Invite the patient to recount the nature of the experiences that accompanied or triggered the diagnosis or current crisis. If more than one family member is present, each should be encouraged to describe events from his or her own perspective. The key issues may actually present themselves in the context of these discussions, providing the therapist an opportunity to explore them further.
- If the patient seems to have unanswered questions or concerns about inadequate communication with the primary medical caregiver, consider ways to help address the problem. For example, assist the patient in writing down questions to ask the physician, ask permission to relay these concerns to the physician for the patient, or consider whether the patient might benefit from educational materials or programs. Explore the patient's level of confidence in the physician and beliefs about

whether the doctor truly cares about him or her.
- To the extent that a breakdown in communications with one or more family members has occurred, consider these strategies. Help the patient to think about how his or her coping style differs from those of the other people in question. Plan strategies for opening new channels of communication. Use role playing to prepare the patient. Consider inviting the other party or parties to join a future session with the patient.

3. Make certain the patient has the opportunity to address all of the eight common fears cited earlier, as well as other issues that may be unique to him or her or characteristic of this particular illness.

- To the extent that a patient has omitted reference to some particular stress area, the therapist should inquire directly (e.g., the cancer patient who is obviously experiencing hair loss as the result of chemotherapy but who makes no reference to it or to changes in self-image should be asked directly: "How do you feel about losing your hair? What has that been like for you?").

4. Attend to solving real problems, including difficulties communicating or getting one's needs met by physicians, nurses, other health care providers, and family members.

- Ask the patient to take an inventory of the relationships that are most important in coping with the illness. Ask questions such as "How easy or difficult is it for you to know and trust people? Who are you close to?" For each relationship or individual named, encourage the patient to list both positive and negative aspects. Help the patient consider how to strengthen the positive factors and overcome the negative factors. For example, a patient who has been drawing on a single source of social support can be helped to identify and draw on support from multiple sources.

How Many Sessions Are Needed?

Some patients may show significant benefit and progress in fewer than 10 sessions. In such cases it is perfectly appropriate to conclude the intervention with a summary session and advise the patient that he or she is welcome to return should any new issues emerge or an exacerbation follow. It is not unusual for some patients to require brief intermittent "tune-up" sessions, especially when the illness is prolonged or has a highly variable course.

The key factor in determining whether to terminate would be the degree to which the goals stated in the initial consultation session have been achieved. With some patients it may soon become clear that more extended treatment is needed (e.g., patients who acknowledge significant histories of depression or anxiety disorders or who display signs of suicide risk). Consider referral for medication consults as warranted. Consider referrals for more intensive or extensive treatment as dictated by the patient's condition. At the point of termination it may be appropriate to refer some patients for other services (e.g., rehabilitation counseling, vocational guidance).

SUMMING UP: THE FINAL SESSION

Session 10 (or the final session, if fewer than 10 sessions are needed) should provide a forum to review the progress of the previous sessions. This is the final session because integration and consolidation will have taken place on an ongoing basis. Review the goals set out in the first session and written down in the patient's own words. Go back to those words and review them with the patient.

Therapist Activities

1. This is a time to review the concerns or problems that brought the patient to counseling and to examine what progress has been made. It is especially helpful to focus on steps that the patient has taken to address any problems that were noted during the earlier sessions.

   • Help the patient to consider long-term planning, anticipate future events that may be stressful, and consider what strategies to apply in the context of what has worked for him or her previously.
   • Goals set out in the first session were written down in the patient's own words. Go back to those words and review them with the patient. Acknowledge the patient's successes and accomplishments.

References & Readings

Koocher, G. P., & Pollin, I. (1995). Medical Crisis Counseling: A new service delivery model. *Journal of Clinical Psychology in Medical Settings, 1,* 291–299.

Meyer, E. C., DeMaso, D. R., & Koocher, G. P. (1996). Mental health consultation in the pediatric intensive care unit. *Professional Psychology: Research and Practice, 27,* 130–136.

Pollin, I. (1994). *Taking charge: Overcoming the challenges of long-term illness.* New York: Times Books.

Pollin, I. (1995). *Medical Crisis Counseling: Short-term treatment for long term illness.* Evanston, IL: Norton.

Shapiro, D. E., & Koocher, G. P. (1996). Goals and time considerations in outpatient medical crises intervention. *Professional Psychology: Research and Practice, 27,* 109–120.

Related Topics

72 ASSESSING AND TREATING NORMATIVE MALE ALEXITHYMIA

Ronald F. Levant

Alexithymia literally means the inability to put emotions into words. The term is composed of a series of Greek roots: *a* ("without"), *lexus* ("words"), and *thymos* ("emotions")—"without words for emotions." This condition was originally described by Sifneos (1967) and Krystal (1982) to characterize the severe emotional constriction they encountered in their (primarily male) patients who were psychosomatic, drug-dependent, or affected by posttraumatic stress disorder (PTSD) (see also Sifneos, 1988). They were dealing with cases of severe alexithymia, which is at the far end of the continuum of this disorder. Through my work on this topic at the Boston University Fatherhood Project (Levant & Kelly, 1989) and in my subsequent research and clinical practice (Levant & Kopecky, 1995), I have found that alexithymia also occurs in "garden-variety" or mild to moderate forms and in these forms is very widespread among men. I have come to call this "normative male alexithymia."

Simply put, as a result of the male role socialization ordeal, boys grow up to be men who are genuinely unaware of their emotions and sometimes even their bodily sensations. When men are required to give an account of their emotions and are unable to identify them directly, they tend to rely on their cognition to logically deduce what they should feel under the circumstances. They cannot do what is so easy, and almost automatic, for most women— to simply sense inward feelings and let the verbal description come to mind.

This widespread inability among men to identify emotions and put them into words has enormous consequences. It blocks men who

suffer from it from utilizing the most effective means known for dealing with life's stresses and traumas—namely, identifying, thinking about, and discussing one's emotional responses to a stressor or trauma with a friend, family member, or therapist. Consequently, it predisposes such men to deal with stress in ways that make certain forms of pathology more likely, such as substance abuse, violent behavior, sexual compulsions, stress-related illnesses, and early death. It also makes it less likely that such men will be able to benefit from psychotherapy as traditionally practiced.

I hasten to point out that by characterizing men's traditional inability to put emotions into words as a mild form of alexithymia I do not mean to pathologize men. Rather, I hope to engage the reader in a consideration of the idea that this aspect of traditional masculinity does not serve men well in today's world and is therefore dysfunctional, although it did serve a purpose in earlier historical eras.

As I have discussed in detail elsewhere, normative alexithymia, like the more severe forms, is a result of trauma—in this case, the trauma of the male role socialization process that is so normative that we do not think of it as trauma at all (Levant, 1995; Levant & Kopecky, 1995). In brief, the male role socialization ordeal, through the combined influences of mothers, fathers, and peer groups, suppresses and channels natural male emotionality to such an extent that boys grow up to be men who develop an action-oriented variant of empathy, cannot readily sense their feelings and put them into words, and tend to channel or transform their vulnerable feelings into anger and their caring feelings into sexuality.

My approach to helping men identify and process their emotions integrates cognitive-behavioral, psychoeducational, skills-training, and family systems components. The program I have developed is an active, problem-solving approach that relies on the use of homework assignments. I have found that many men find such an approach very congenial because it is congruent with aspects of the male code. In addition, men who are demoralized for one reason or another may find that it restores their sense of agency.

Helping men overcome normative alexithymia is useful at the beginning stages of therapy for many men because it enables them to develop the skills of emotional self-awareness and emotional expressivity that will empower them to wrestle with deeper issues.

ASSESSMENT

During the first interview, in addition to taking a standard history, I also assess the man's ability to become aware of his emotions and put them into words. I typically use the following format.

1. To what extent is the patient aware of discrete emotions, as contrasted with either the neuroendocrinological and musculoskeletal components of emotions (i.e., tension in the forehead, tightness in the gut) or signs of stress (i.e., feeling "overloaded" or "zapped")? Some specific questions are, Do you have feelings that you can't quite identify? Is it easy for you to find the right words for your feelings? Are you often confused by what emotion you are feeling? Do you find yourself puzzled by sensations in your body? (Questions reproduced or adapted from the Taylor Alexithymia Scale or TAS-20; Bagby, Taylor, & Parker, 1994.)

2. What emotions does the patient become aware of? Is he aware of his emotions in the vulnerable part of the spectrum—that is, emotions that make him feel vulnerable,

such as worry, fear, anxiety, sadness, hurt, dejection, disappointment, rejection, or abandonment? A typical question is, When you are upset, do you know if you are sad, frightened, or angry? (Question adapted from the TAS-20; Bagby et al., 1994.) If he is not aware of his vulnerable emotions, are these emotions transformed into anger and expressed as anger, rage, or violence?

3. Is the patient aware of his emotions in the caring/connection part of the spectrum, such as caring, concern, warmth, affection, appreciation, love, neediness/dependency, closeness, or attachment? Is he limited in his ability to express caring/connection emotions? Does he express them primarily through the channel of sexuality?

4. Is the patient aware of his emotions in the anger part of the spectrum? Does he become aware of an emotion—such as anger—only where it is very intense?

5. At what intensities does the patient experience his emotions? Some specific questions are, Would "cool, calm, and collected" describe you? When you are angry, is it easy for you to still be rational and not overreact? Does your heart race at the anticipation of an exciting event? Do sad movies deeply touch you? When you do something wrong, do you have strong feelings of shame and guilt? (Questions reproduced or adapted from the Affect Intensity Measure or AIM; Larsen & Diener, 1987.)

TREATMENT

The program I have developed for the treatment of alexithymia consists of five steps.

Step 1: Psychoeducation About Normative Alexithymia

In order for the patient to be able to make sense of his experience and utilize the treatment techniques, he needs to know the limitations of his ability to know and express his emotions and how these limitations came about. An important part of this step is helping the patient develop his ability to tolerate certain emotions (such as fear or sadness) that he may regard as unmanly and therefore shameful (Krugman, 1995). I tailor this step to the individual patient (see also Krystal, 1979).

Step 2: Develop a Vocabulary for Emotions

Since men tend not to be aware of emotions, they usually do not have a very good vocabulary for emotions. This also follows from the research literature on the gender-differentiated development of language for emotions. The next step, then, is to help the man develop a vocabulary for the full spectrum of emotions, particularly the vulnerable and caring/connection emotions. I ask patients to record as many words for emotions as they can during the course of a week.

Step 3: Learn to Read the Emotions of Others

The third step involves learning to apply emotional words to feeling states. Since it is often less threatening to do this with other people than with oneself, and since men can readily build on their action-empathy skills to learn emotional empathy, I recommend focusing on other people at this stage. I teach patients to read facial gestures, tone of voice, and other types of "body language" in other people. I encourage them to learn to identify the emotions of other people, in conversations, while observing other people or while watching movies. I instruct them to ask themselves questions during this process, such as, What is that person feeling? What does this feel like from that person's perspective?

Step 4: Keep an Emotional Response Log

The next step involves teaching the patient to apply emotional words to his own experience. To do this, I ask him to keep an emotional response log, noting when he experienced a feeling that he could identify or a bodily sensation or sign of stress that he became aware of and

what circumstances led up to it. The instructions for keeping an emotional response log are as follows:

- Record the bodily sensation or sign of stress (or feelings, if you notice them) that you become aware of and when you first started to experience it.
- Describe the social or relational context within which the emotion was aroused: Who was doing what to whom? How did that affect you?
- Go through your emotional vocabulary list and pick out the words that seem to best describe the emotion that you were experiencing.

Step 5: Practice

The fifth and final step involves practice. Emotional self-awareness is a skill, and like any other skill, it requires practice to become an automatic part of one's functioning. In structured groups, I use role plays, videotaped for immediate feedback, to practice the skill. Men are taught to tune in to their feelings through watching and discussing immediate playbacks of role plays in which feelings were engendered. By pointing out the nonverbal cues and asking such questions as, What were your feelings when you grimaced in that last segment?, men learn how to access the ongoing flow of emotions within.

Although working on these matters in a group context with video feedback is obviously advantageous, one can also practice this skill without such arrangements. By systematically keeping an emotional response log and discussing the results in therapy, one can gradually improve the ability to recognize feelings and to put them into words.

References & Readings

Bagby, R. M., Taylor, G. J., & Parker, J. D. A. (1994). The twenty-item Toronto Alexithymia Scale: II. Convergent, discriminant, and concurrent validity. *Journal of Psychosomatic Research, 38*, 33–40.

Krugman, S. (1995). Male development and the

transformation of shame. In R. F. Levant & W. S. Pollack (Eds.), *A new psychology of men* (pp. 91–126). New York: Basic Books.

Krystal, H. (1979). Alexithymia and psychotherapy. *American Journal of Psychotherapy, 33,* 17–30.

Krystal, H. (1982). Alexithymia and the effectiveness of psychoanalytic treatment. *International Journal of Psychoanalytic Psychotherapy, 9,* 353–378.

Larsen, R. J., & Diener, E. (1987). Affect intensity as an individual difference characteristic: A review. *Journal of Research in Personality, 21,* 1–39.

Levant, R. F. (1995). Toward the reconstruction of masculinity. In R. F. Levant & W. S. Pollack (Eds.), *A new psychology of men* (pp. 229–251). New York: Basic Books.

Levant, R. F. (1996). The new psychology of men. *Professional Psychology, 27,* 259–265.

Levant, R. F. (in press). Desperately seeking language: Understanding, assessing, and treating normative male alexithymia. In W. S. Pollack & R. F. Levant (Eds.), *New psychotherapy for men: A case approach.* New York: Wiley.

Levant, R. F., & Kelly, J. (1989). *Between father and child.* New York: Viking.

Levant, R. F., & Kopecky, G. (1995). *Masculinity reconstructed.* New York: Dutton.

Pleck, J. H. (1995). The gender role strain paradigm: An update. In R. F. Levant & W. S. Pollack (Eds.), *A new psychology of men* (pp. 11–32). New York: Basic Books.

Sifneos, P. E. (1967). Clinical observations on some patients suffering from a variety of psychosomatic diseases. *Proceedings of the Seventh European Conference on Psychosomatic Research.* Basel, Switzerland: Kargel.

Sifneos, P. E. (1988). Alexithymia and its relationship to hemispheric specialization, affect, and creativity. *Psychiatric Clinics of North America, 11,* 287–292.

Taylor, G. J. (1994). The alexithymia construct: Conceptualization, validation, and relationship with basic dimensions of personality. *New Trends in Experimental and Clinical Psychiatry, 10,* 61–74.

Related Topics

73 ASSESSING AND TREATING MALE SEXUAL DYSFUNCTION

Joseph LoPiccolo & Lynn M. Van Male

Assessing and treating sexual dysfunction in men is a challenging and multifaceted undertaking. In this overview we will present a brief summary of the theoretical concepts and principles underlying postmodern sex therapy for men, as well as summarize the major technologies available for treating erectile failure, premature ejaculation, and male orgasmic disorder.

POSTMODERN SEX THERAPY:
A SUMMARY OF THEORETICAL
CONCEPTS AND PRINCIPLES

Postmodern sex therapy is conceptualized as a blend of cognitive therapy, systems theory, and behavioral psychotherapy (LoPiccolo, in press). This approach identifies five basic categories of causes of sexual dysfunction, which are applicable to both men and women:

- *Family of origin learning history*, including parental prohibitions against childhood masturbation and sex play, parental negativism about adolescent dating and premarital sexual experience, and unpleasant or traumatic sexual experiences in childhood and adolescence
- *Systemic issues in the couple's relationship*, including lack of attraction to partner, poor sexual skills of the partner, general marital unhappiness, fear of closeness or intimacy, lack of basic trust, differences between the couple in degree of "personal space" desired in the relationship, passive-aggressive solutions to a power imbalance, poor conflict resolution skills, and inability to blend feelings of love and sexual desire
- *Intrapsychic or cognitive issues*, including "performance anxiety," religious orthodoxy, gender identity conflicts, homosexual orientation or conflict, anhedonic or obsessive-compulsive personality, sexual phobias or aversions, fear of loss of control over sexual urges, masked sexual deviation, fears of having children, unresolved feelings about death or loss of a previous partner or spouse, underlying depression, aging concerns, and attempting sex in a context or situation that is not psychologically comfortable for the patient
- *Operant issues in the couple's day-to-day environment* or the reinforcing consequences of the dysfunction that come not from the relationship with the partner or from the patient's own psyche but from the external world
- *Physiological or medical issues*, including any of a number of illnesses and/or diseases that cause pain, chronic fatigue, restriction of movement, reduction of blood flow to the pelvis, or impairment in the neurological system that controls arousal and orgasm (e.g., diabetes, heart disease, spinal-cord injury, multiple sclerosis, pituitary/hypothalamic tumors, and end-state renal disorder); commonly prescribed medications (e.g., antihypertensive, antianxiety, antidepressant,

and antipsychotic medications); chronic substance use/abuse (e.g., alcohol, marijuana, heroin, cocaine, and barbiturates); and hormonal imbalances (e.g., too much or too little prolactin, testosterone, estrogen)

Although different practitioners may emphasize one of these five elements more than another, an examination of all factors is necessary to gain a complete understanding of the original causes and current maintainers of a sexual dysfunction. Failure to attend to the individual or couple dynamic relationship needs that are being served by the sexual dysfunction often creates a situation in which symptom removal can be disruptive, thus leading to "resistance" to therapeutic progress. We cannot overemphasize the importance of examining contextual factors prior to utilizing the specific sex therapy technologies enumerated later in this overview. (For further reading on postmodern sex therapy, see LoPiccolo, in press.)

MECHANISMS OF CHANGE

Currently, sex therapy consists of a complex, multifaceted package of procedures. However, given that the postmodern view espouses considering the sexual problem in its full systemic context, treatment often focuses not only on the individual but also on the couple. We conceptualize couple sex therapy as involving nine major general principles:

- *Mutual responsibility:* Sexual dysfunctions are most often shared disorders. Thus, even if the nondysfunctional partner is not directly involved in causing or maintaining the dysfunction, both partners will need to change for therapy to help them in the solution of their problems.
- *Information and education:* In the present age of increased patient access to self-help books, magazine articles, and videos on sexuality, only rarely are people who enter sex therapy completely ignorant of the basic anatomy and physiology of the human sexual response. Nonetheless, even in cases where there are other complex causes and

maintainers of the sexual dysfunction, it is always useful to include a specific informational and educational component to get maximally effective results. Zilbergeld (1992) provides an excellent source of such material.

- *Attitude changes:* For the specific technologies of sex therapy to be effective, positive attitude change and acceptance of sexuality as a normal, healthy part of being human often need to be addressed in treatment.

- *Elimination of performance anxiety:* Quite often patients in sex therapy experience anxiety as a result of "keeping score" and being goal-oriented or orgasm-focused. Since it is precisely this goal-directedness that interferes with arousal, the effect of focusing on pleasure and enjoying the sexual *process* automatically has the side effect of facilitating the goal of normal sexual functioning.

- *Increase of effective communication:* Sexually dysfunctional couples tend to be unable to tell each other what they like and dislike about sex. Postmodern sex therapy encourages open, clear, and effective communication about sexual techniques, preferences, responses, and the initiation and refusal of sexual activity.

- *Change of destructive sex roles and lifestyles:* Patients may need to be encouraged to examine issues such as rigidly adhering to a societally determined stereotypes about what men and women "should" want in sexual relationships, disengaging from in-laws who are a destructive influence on their relationship, withdrawing from their adult children's problems, or quitting a job that requires one of them to commute too far to and from work.

- *Change of disruptive marital systems and enhancement of the marital relationship:* Often it is not possible to directly intervene in the sexual problem without also directly intervening in the marital relationship. When the couple is having significant difficulties over finances, child rearing, or other issues, it is unrealistic to expect them to leave these issues outside the bedroom door when they begin to have a sexual session assigned by the therapist.

- *Physical and medical interventions:* As mentioned earlier, several major classes of medical diseases and chemical agents may interfere with sexual functioning. Thus, concurrent medical care is often necessary in the treatment of sexual dysfunction. In the event physiological antecedents to sexual dysfunction are not addressable, the patient's focus of treatment may not be on regaining full sexual functioning but rather on the appropriate adaptation to alternative erotic and intimate activities.

- *Prescription of direct changes in sexual behavior and teaching of effective sexual technique:* Although the eight types of procedures listed above are key elements in postmodern sex therapy, the truly distinctive element of sex therapy, as opposed to other psychotherapeutic approaches, is the prescription by the therapist of a series of specific sexual behaviors for the patients to perform in their own home. The particular behavioral prescriptions vary with the dysfunction and are summarized below.

Erectile Failure

Treatment of erectile failure consists of reducing performance anxiety and increasing stimulation (LoPiccolo, 1992). The following list summarizes the main steps in treating erectile failure.

- *Sensate focus:* Initially, attempts to have intercourse—and even to have an erection—are proscribed. Instead, during sensate focus, the couple learns the "tease technique," in which, if he gets an erection in response to her caressing, they stop until he loses it. This exercise teaches them that erections occur naturally in response to stimulation, as long as the couple does not focus on performance. More recently, increasing direct stimulation of the penis has been focused on in addition to reducing performance anxiety. Many men with erectile failure have either mild organic impairment or normal aging changes in erectile responsiveness, which make direct stimulation of the penis necessary for erection to occur. While this may seem obvious, many cases seen in current clinical practice involve unwillingness of the female partner—or sometimes the male himself—to engage in direct stimulation of the penis. In such cases, negative attitudes are explored, and the couple is helped to engage in normal "foreplay" stimulation of the penis.

- *"Stuffing" technique:* When the couple is ready to resume penile-vaginal intercourse, the man lies on his back and the woman kneels above him and uses her fingers to push his nonerect penis into her vagina. This procedure, known as the "stuffing technique," frees him from having to have a rigid penis to accomplish entry. The couple is instructed to achieve the woman's orgasms through manual or oral sex, again reducing pressure on the male to perform.
- *Intercourse:* When the couple has mastered sensate focus and "stuffing," they are ready to resume intercourse in their preferred position (e.g., female superior, male superior, side-by-side).

This set of procedures seems to work well in cases in which there is no major organic impairment of erection. Physical intervention is often indicated, however, for men with significant physical problems underlying or complicating their difficulty with erection. For these men, the following approaches may be suggested.

- *Penile prostheses:* One type of penile prosthesis consists of a semirigid rod made of rubber and wire, which, when surgically implanted, produces an artificial erection. It can be bent down so that the man can wear normal clothing but bent up to an erect position when the man wants to have intercourse. Another type of prosthesis consists of inflatable hollow cylinders inserted into the penis, a reservoir of fluid placed under the abdominal wall, and tubing connecting the penile cylinders and the reservoir to a pump inserted in the scrotum. When the man wants to have sex, he squeezes the pump, forcing fluid from the reservoir to the penile cylinders, which expand and produce an erection.

These prostheses are expensive (between $5,000 and $15,000, depending on the type), but over 25,000 were installed in 1988 in the United States. In recent years, prostheses have become less commonly used as nonsurgical medical interventions (i.e., the vacuum erection device and penile injections) have become available.

- *Vacuum erection device (VED):* A hollow cylinder is placed over the penis and pushed against the body to create an airtight seal. The cylinder is connected to a hand pump, which pumps the air out of the cylinder and leaves the penis in a partial vacuum. The resultant pressure differential draws blood into the penis and produces an erection. The cylinder is removed, and a rubber constriction ring is placed around the base of the penis to maintain the erection. The VED is less expensive ($300–$600), but it interferes with the spontaneity of sex, since the man must take time to use it during lovemaking. The vacuum device is most often used for men whose erectile failure is caused by diabetes or neurological problems, and it seems to work well for these men (LoPiccolo, 1992).
- *Chemical vasodilators:* Another nonsurgical treatment for men with medically based erectile failure is injection of drugs that dilate the penile arteries. Drugs that were formerly used for this purpose tended to cause scarring in the penis over long periods of use and so were used more as a short-term "confidence booster" for men with situational erectile failure. However, the drugs that are now used do not seem to have this effect, and injection therapy has become common for long-term treatment of organically based erectile failure (Wagner & Kaplan, 1993).

Premature Ejaculation

Premature ejaculation is treated with almost a 100% success rate by direct behavioral retraining procedures (Masters & Johnson, 1970). The following summarizes the steps in this typically effective treatment.

- *"Stop-start" or "pause" procedure:* In this technique, the penis is manually stimulated until the man is fairly highly aroused. The couple then pauses until the man's arousal subsides, then the stimulation is resumed. This sequence is repeated several times before stimulation is carried through to ejaculation, so the man ultimately experiences much more total time of stimulation than he has ever experienced before and learns to have a higher threshold for ejaculation.
- *"Squeeze" procedure:* This technique is much like the "stop-start" procedure, except that when stimulation stops, the woman firmly squeezes the penis between her thumb and forefinger, at the place where the head of the penis joins the shaft. This squeeze seems to reduce arousal further.
- *Vaginal containment:* After a few weeks of training involving "stop-start" and "squeeze" procedures, the necessity of pausing diminishes. Then the couple may progress to putting the penis in the vagina, but without any thrusting movements. Again, if the man rapidly becomes highly aroused, the penis is withdrawn and the couple waits for arousal to drop off.
- *Active thrusting:* When good tolerance for inactive containment of the penis is achieved, the training procedure is repeated during active thrusting. Generally, 2 to 3 months of practice are sufficient to enable a man to enjoy prolonged intercourse without any need for pauses or squeezes.

Male Orgasmic Disorder

Male orgasmic disorder is treated by reducing performance anxiety and ensuring adequate stimulation. The couple is instructed that during sex the penis is to be caressed manually (and, if acceptable to them, orally) until the man is aroused, but that stimulation is to stop whenever he feels he might be close to having an orgasm. This paradoxical instruction reduces goal-focused anxiety about performance

and allows the man to enjoy the sexual pleasure provided by the caressing. An electric vibrator may be used to increase the intensity of stimulation. For men with neurological damage, therapy is likely to include some physiological treatment, possibly a drug that increases arousal of the sympathetic nervous system or stimulation of the anus with a vibrator to trigger the ejaculation reflex (LoPiccolo, 1996).

References & Readings

LoPiccolo, J. (1992). Post-modern sex therapy for erectile failure. In R. C. Rosen & S. R. Leiblum (Eds.), *Erectile failure: Diagnosis and treatment* (pp. 171–197). New York: Guilford Press.

LoPiccolo, J. (1996). Premature ejaculation and male orgasmic disorder. In G. O. Gabbard & S. D. Atkinson (Eds.), *Synopsis of treatments of psychiatric disorders* (pp. 797–804). Washington, DC: American Psychiatric Press.

LoPiccolo, J. (in press). Sex therapy: A post modern model. In J. Lynn & J. P. Garske (Eds.), *Contemporary psychotherapies*. Monterey, CA: Brooks-Cole.

Masters, W. H., & Johnson, V. E. (1970). *Human sexual inadequacy*. Boston: Little, Brown.

O'Donohue, W., & Geer, J. H. (Eds.) (1993). *Handbook of sexual dysfunctions: Assessment and treatment*. Boston: Allyn and Bacon.

Wagner, G., & Kaplan, H. S. (1993). *The new injection treatment for impotence*. New York: Brunner/Mazel.

Wincze, J. P., & Carey, M. P. (1991). *Sexual dysfunction: A guide for assessment and treatment*. New York: Guilford Press.

Zilbergeld, B. (1992). *The new male sexuality*. New York: Bantam Books.

74 ASSESSING AND TREATING FEMALE SEXUAL DYSFUNCTION

Joseph LoPiccolo & Lynn M. Van Male

The assessment and treatment of sexual dysfunction in women are no less challenging and multifaceted than the assessment and treatment of sexual dysfunction in men. In addition to presenting a brief summary of the theoretical concepts and principles underlying postmodern sex therapy, this chapter reviews the major technologies available for treating female arousal and orgasm dysfunctions, vaginismus, dyspareunia, and low sexual desire and aversion to sex. (A detailed discussion of theoretical concepts and mechanisms of change is given in the overview of male sexual dysfunction in chapter 73.)

POSTMODERN SEX THERAPY: A SUMMARY OF THEORETICAL CONCEPTS AND PRINCIPLES

Postmodern sex therapy is an amalgamation of cognitive therapy, systems theory, and behavioral psychotherapy. The following five categories are theorized to account for the causes and maintainers of sexual dysfunction:

- Family of origin learning history
- Systemic issues in the couple's relationship
- Intrapsychic or cognitive issues
- Operant issues in the couple's day-to-day environment
- Physiological or medical issues

The degree to which each of these factors contributes to the development or maintenance of a sexual dysfunction varies case by case. However, a thorough examination of all five types of factors is necessary to gain a complete understanding of a sexual dysfunction. The sexual dysfunction often serves an important role in the individual or couple dynamic; thus attempts to remove it without attending to the need(s) it fulfills can meet with great resistance on the part of the individual or the couple. We cannot overemphasize the importance of examining contextual factors prior to utilizing the specific sex therapy technologies enumerated later in this overview. (For further reading on postmodern sex therapy, see LoPiccolo, in press.)

MECHANISMS OF CHANGE

Currently, sex therapy consists of a complex, multifaceted package of procedures. However, given that the postmodern view espouses considering the sexual problem in its full systemic context, treatment often focuses not only on the individual but also on the couple. It is possible to conceptualize couple sex therapy as involving nine general principles:

- Mutual responsibility
- Information and education
- Attitude changes
- Elimination of performance anxiety
- Increase of effective communication
- Change of destructive sex roles and lifestyles
- Change of disruptive marital systems and enhancement of the marital relationship
- Physical and medical interventions
- Prescription of direct changes in sexual behavior and teaching of effective sexual technique

A Note on Sexual Victimization

Although sexual victimization is by no means the only route into the manifestation of sexual dysfunction, it is not uncommon for patients who have sexual dysfunction(s) to have a history of sexual trauma or childhood molestation. For such cases, it is vital to stress that the therapist's first objective is to address sexual victimization issues prior to treating any sexual dysfunction(s). For example, for an inorgasmic survivor of sexual trauma, some of the orgasm triggers mentioned below may serve as triggers for flashback rather than assisting in achieving orgasm. Thus, for patients with both a sexual dysfunction and a history of sexual trauma or childhood molestation, additional therapeutic procedures are indicated. These procedures are described in other works, such as Courtois (1988).

Female Arousal and Orgasm Dysfunctions

Global, Lifelong Inorgasmia Specific treatment techniques for female arousal and orgasm dysfunctions include self-exploration, body awareness, and directed masturbation training (Heiman & LoPiccolo, 1988). Masters and Johnson (1970) stressed the use of couple sensate-focus procedures for such cases, but later experience showed that it is more effective for the woman to learn to have orgasm by herself first and then share this knowledge with her partner. The directed masturbation program that has been most successful in our work has nine steps and a "pre-step":

- *Exploration of beliefs about sexuality:* Before the woman even begins the program steps, it is important for her to explore her beliefs and possible fears about becoming a fully sexual woman. What does she risk losing by becoming orgasmic?
- *Education:* In step 1 the woman uses diagrams and reading materials simply to learn about her body, her genitals, and the female sexual response.
- *Full-body exploration:* In step 2 she explores her whole body visually (with the aid of a mirror) and by touch.
- *Finding pleasure zones:* Step 3 consists of locating erotically sensitive areas on her entire body (lips, thighs, the curve of her waist, etc.), with a focus on her breasts and genitals, especially her clitoris.
- *Erotic self-pleasuring:* Actual stimulation (masturbation) of the areas identified in step 3 is the focus of step 4.
- *Enhanced erotic self-pleasuring:* Step 5 is erotic masturbation accompanied by sexual pictures, stories, and the woman's own fantasies. Women are encouraged to write their own erotic stories, as well as reading commercially published collections of women's sexual fantasies.
- *Masturbation aids, enactment, and "orgasm triggers":* Step 6 has three elements. First, if the woman has not yet experienced an orgasm, it is suggested that she begin to use an electric vibrator to increase the intensity of stimulation. Second, she will be instructed to act out or role-play a very exaggerated orgasm to overcome any fears about losing control or looking silly when she has a real orgasm. Finally, she will use "orgasm triggers," such as tilting her head back, holding her breath with diaphragm tensed as if trying to exhale, arching her feet and pointing her toes, contracting her pelvic muscles, tensing her leg muscles, and thrusting her pelvis.
- *Sensate focus and mutual masturbation:* Step 7 integrates the Masters and Johnson's sensate focus procedure with the woman's individual progress. This training in communication and sexual skill teaches her to demonstrate for her partner how she prefers to be stimulated and how she can have an orgasm. Because most women find it easier to demonstrate how they like to be touched if they have the opportunity to observe how their partner prefers to be erotically stimulated, we suggest partners be the first to demonstrate self-stimulation to orgasm in order to help disinhibit clients.
- *Partner-assisted orgasm:* In step 8 her partner rests his hand on hers as she masturbates to orgasm. Once she is comfortable

with this, she may guide his hand to teach him how she likes to be touched, and then the couple may move on until he is able to bring her to orgasm with manual, oral, or vibrator stimulation.

- *Intercourse:* In the last step, the woman and her partner practice intercourse in positions that permit one or the other of them to continue to stimulate her clitoris while the penis is in the vagina.

This training program has been found to be very effective: over 90% of women learn to have an orgasm during masturbation, about 80% during caressing by their partner, and about 30% during intercourse. Because it is a structured program, it works equally well in group therapy and even as a self-treatment, since the woman can go through the program without a therapist, using a self-help book (Heiman & LoPiccolo, 1988) and instructional videotape (LoPiccolo, 1980).

Situational Orgasmic Dysfunction In contrast to women with global, lifelong lack of orgasm, some women are able to have an orgasm in some way but not in a way that is satisfactory to them. Such types of situational orgasmic dysfunction include being able to reach orgasm only in solitary masturbation or only in some particular sexual activity, such as oral stimulation. Treatment for situational lack of orgasm includes a process of *gradual stimulus generalization.* This procedure is designed to help the woman expand the ways in which she reaches orgasm by the identification of numerous intermediate steps that will help her expand the situations in which she is able to achieve an orgasm.

For example, consider the case of a woman who can reach orgasm only when she is alone, through masturbating by pressing her thighs together, and cannot have orgasm in any way when her partner is present. The intermediate steps she and her therapist identify may include using thigh pressure but also putting her fingers on her clitoris, direct stimulation of her clitoris with her thighs spread apart, thigh pressure with her partner present, thigh pressure with her partner's fingers on her clitoris,

her partner's direct stimulation of her clitoris without thigh pressure, and direct clitoral stimulation during intercourse (Zeiss, Rosen, & Zeiss, 1977). This approach is quite effective in helping women learn to have orgasm with a partner.

Sex therapists do not consider lack of orgasm during intercourse to be a problem, provided the woman enjoys intercourse and can have orgasm when her partner caresses her. For this reason, reassurance about their normality, not treatment, is indicated for women whose only concern is situational lack of orgasm during intercourse. Although sex therapists agree that lack of orgasm during intercourse is not a problem, popular books and magazines continue to suggest ways for women to achieve orgasm during intercourse. One such suggestion is the "high ride" position, in which the man positions his body upward on his partner until the top of her head is even with his shoulder area. This position bends the man's penis back until it is sliding along the woman's clitoris during intercourse. Although the "high ride" is supposed to lead to orgasm during intercourse, it does not seem to be effective and is also uncomfortable for many couples.

Vaginismus

Vaginismus refers to spastic contractions of the muscles around the vagina, which make it impossible for the penis to enter. The treatment for this dysfunction is shown in a video (LoPiccolo, 1981) and includes the following elements.

- *Deep muscle relaxation and breathing:* Vaginismic women are first taught how to relax the muscles of their bodies to promote somatic awareness prior to the focus of treatment being directed toward their presenting complaint. It is critical that the patient be allowed to progress at her own pace because "working hard" to make quick progress in the treatment of vaginismus is almost always countertherapeutic.
- *Voluntary control of the pubococcygeal muscle:* Vaginismic patients practice contracting and relaxing the pubococcygeal muscle, which

is part of the pelvic floor and surrounds the vagina, until they have acquired voluntary control over their vaginal muscles.

- *Graduated dilator containment:* To assist in overcoming their fear of penetration, vaginismic women are taught to use a set of gradually larger dilators, which they insert in their own vagina at home and at their own pace, so that they are not frightened or traumatized. It is critical to emphasize that dilator insertion is done gently, *not* with a vigorous thrusting motion. Additionally, the woman should not progress to the next larger dilator until she is able to comfortably contain the previous, smaller one.

- *Partner participation in dilator insertion:* Later, when the woman can comfortably insert the largest dilator, she begins to guide her partner as he slowly and gently inserts the dilators. Again, it is important to stress that dilator insertion is *not* done forcefully or with repetitive thrusting motions.

- *Vaginal containment of the penis:* As her partner lies passively on his back, the woman kneels above him and gradually inserts his penis at a pace that is comfortable to her.

- *Intercourse:* Once the woman is able to comfortably contain her partner's penis, the couple may begin to add thrusting motions and to explore various intercourse positions that are enjoyable to both of them.

The therapist stresses the need for effective stimulation, so that the patient learns to associate penetration with vaginal lubrication, pleasure, and arousal instead of with fear or pain. Some therapists use muscle-relaxing drugs or hypnosis during dilation, but this does not seem to be a necessary part of the treatment. Therapy for vaginismus is highly successful: over 90% of the women treated become able to have pain-free intercourse.

Dyspareunia

Dyspareunia refers to pain that a woman experiences during intercourse. Most cases of dyspareunia involve some physiological abnormality, such as unrepaired damage following childbirth. However, some cases are exclusively psychogenic in origin. There are no specific treatment procedures for psychogenic dyspareunia. Since psychogenic dyspareunia is actually caused by lack of arousal, the general sex therapy procedures and the specific techniques for enhancing female arousal and orgasm are used (O'Donohue & Geer, 1993). When the pain is caused by scars or lesions, the couple can be taught positions for intercourse that do not put pressure on the traumatized sites. Since most cases of dyspareunia are caused by undiagnosed physical problems, an examination by a gynecologist who is expert in this area is essential (O'Donohue & Geer, 1993).

Low Sexual Desire and Aversion to Sex

Low sexual desire refers to a condition in which the patient is markedly lacking in sexual drive and interest. Although the judgment of just how low sexual desire must be to be dysfunctional is somewhat subjective and frequently societally determined, most patients who experience this dysfunction have virtually no sexual interest. Sexual aversion is not just a lack of interest in sex but an actual negative emotional reaction such as revulsion, fear, or disgust that occurs when sexual activity is attempted. Although the steps for addressing hyposexual desire are addressed in this overview, which focuses on female sexual dysfunctions, the same procedures have been applied with equal success to male patients.

Because of the many difficult psychological issues that are likely to underlie hypoactive sexual desire and sexual aversion, these dysfunctions typically require a longer and more complex program of treatment than others. LoPiccolo and Friedman (1988) have described a widely used four-element sequential treatment model for hypoactive drive and aversion.

- *Affectual awareness:* The first stage of therapy focuses on helping the client become aware of her negative emotions regarding sex. Therapy sessions during which the patient visualizes sexual scenes help uncover feelings of anxiety, fear, resentment, vulnerability, and so forth. Many patients claim that they have overcome negative ideas about sex, but such changes are likely to be superficial, leaving a negative affectual (emotional or gut-level) residue hidden under a bland umbrella feeling of lack of interest in sex. The purpose of the affectual awareness stage of therapy is to get under this umbrella and make the patient aware that she is not just naturally uninterested in sex but that something is blocking the normal biological sex drive.

- *Insight:* The second phase of therapy helps patients understand why they have the negative emotions identified in the affectual awareness phase. Negative messages from their religion, culture, family, and current and past relationships are explored. In a sense, this and the previous step are preparatory. The more active treatment follows.

- *Cognitive and emotional change:* In this phase, cognitive techniques are applied to the irrational thoughts and emotions that inhibit sexual desire. Patients generate "coping statements" that help them change their negative emotions and thoughts. Typical statements might be "If I allow myself to enjoy sex, it doesn't mean I'll lose control," and "When I was younger I learned to feel guilty about sex, but I'm a grown-up now, and I don't have to feel that way anymore."

- *Behavioral interventions:* It is at this stage that sensate focus, skill training, and other general sex therapy procedures are introduced. Sex drive is heightened in a number of ways: having patients keep a "desire diary" in which they record sexual thoughts and feelings, having them read books and view films with good erotic content, and encouraging them to develop their own sexual fantasies. All of these activities make sexual thoughts and cues more readily available to the patient. Nonsexual affection, consisting of simple hugs, squeezes, and pats, and pleasurable shared activities such as dancing and walking together are also encouraged to help strengthen feelings of sensual enjoyment and sexual attraction.

This type of program seems to be fairly successful. In one study of the approach, frequency of sex increased from once a month to once a week for men who had experienced hypoactive sexual desire and from once every two weeks to more than once a week for female patients. Women who had experienced sexual aversion increased sexual intercourse from less than once every two weeks to more than once a week (Schover & LoPiccolo, 1982).

References & Readings

Courtois, C. A. (1988). *Healing the incest wound.* New York: Norton.

Heiman, J. R., & LoPiccolo, J. (1988). *Becoming orgasmic: A sexual and personal growth program for women.* New York: Simon and Schuster.

LoPiccolo, J. (1980). *Becoming orgasmic* [Videotape]. (Available from Focus International, 14 Oregon Drive, Huntington Station, NY 11746.)

LoPiccolo, J. (1981). *Treating vaginismus* [Videotape]. (Available from Focus International, 14 Oregon Drive, Huntington Station, NY 11746.)

LoPiccolo, J. (in press). Sex therapy: A post modern model. In S. Lynn & J. P. Garske (Eds.), *Contemporary psychotherapies.* Pacific Grove, CA: Brooks-Cole.

LoPiccolo, J., & Friedman, J. R. (1988). Broad spectrum treatment of low sexual desire: Integration of cognitive, behavioral, and systemic treatment. In S. Leiblum & R. Rosen (Eds.), *Sexual desire disorders* (pp. 107–144). New York: Guilford Press.

Masters, W. H., & Johnson, V. E. (1970). *Human sexual inadequacy.* Boston: Little, Brown.

O'Donohue, W., & Geer, J. H. (Eds.) (1993). *Handbook of sexual dysfunctions: Assessment and treatment.* Boston: Allyn and Bacon.

Schover, L., & LoPiccolo, J. (1982). Treatment effectiveness for dysfunctions of sexual desire. *Journal of Sex and Marital Therapy, 8,* 179–197.

Zeiss, A. M., Rosen, G. M., & Zeiss, R. A. (1977). Orgasm during intercourse: A treatment strategy for women. *Journal of Consulting and Clinical Psychology, 45,* 891–895.

Related Topics

PSYCHOTHERAPY WITH CLIENTS RECOVERING MEMORIES OF CHILDHOOD TRAUMA

Laura S. Brown

Research suggests that most therapists will likely see at least one client with "recovered memories" in their professional careers (Pope & Tabachnick, 1995). Such clients may enter therapy in the throes of intrusive recalls, flashbacks, or terrifying nightmares; alternatively, a person already in treatment for some other complaint may begin to report the onset of this type of frightening imagery of sexual abuse. Clients who present with this picture may be a source of potential challenges for the therapist, as a result of controversies that have emerged since 1992 about the issue of recovered memories of childhood abuse.

This article seeks to provide a brief synopsis of information and guidance to help clinicians when recovered memories are at issue. A basic assumption is that it is possible for people to recall in a delayed fashion reasonably accurate memories of traumatic events from childhood, as well as to present material that is not accurate about such events, and that the clinician's task is to respond in a compassionate and informed manner that empowers clients to become authors of their own narratives and the ultimate experts on their personal histories and realities. Readers seeking an expanded discussion of this issue are referred to Pope and Brown (1996), from which the following material is derived.

EFFECTS OF CHILDHOOD SEXUAL ABUSE

Evidence suggests that sexual abuse may be harmful to most, if not all, of those subjected to

it. Studies reviewing literature on both sexually abused children and adult survivors of sexual abuse find that abuse tends to be associated with a wide range of psychological, psychosomatic, and interpersonal difficulties, although there is also immense individual variability, representing differences in the experience of abuse and the resources of the abuse victim at the time of the abuse and afterward.

Beitchman, Zucker, Hood, daCosta, and Ackman (1991), while considering other possible sources of distress, including more general "family dysfunction," note that sexual abuse may be a risk factor, if not a direct cause, of adult emotional distress. Polusny and Follette (1995) reviewed research from 1987 onward on the long-term correlates of childhood sexual abuse; they found that persons with this experience were overrepresented in a variety of diagnostic categories and also had excess reports of abusive and sexually assaultive adult life experiences. The overrepresentation of sexual abuse survivors in both medical and psychiatric patient groups is a frequent finding, suggesting that child sexual abuse may be generally harmful (Bryer, Nelson, Miller, & Krol, 1987).

BASIC PREMISES OF WORKING WITH THE REMEMBERING CLIENT

A major premise underlying clinical work with a client who reports delayed recall of childhood trauma is that the issues in this area are poorly addressed by attempts to make a forced choice between the artificially created categories of "true" and "false" memories of trauma. It is difficult to find convincing evidence that a forced-choice dichotomy is accurate or that it necessarily leads to more valid and useful conclusions.

Another major premise of practice in this area is that science and practice must not proceed in ignorance of each other but must adequately inform one another if either is to claim intellectual integrity. Neither can be considered absent the other or as more important than the other.

Another major premise is that mental health professionals must always question their assumptions regarding what is "true" about delayed recall of childhood trauma. While various assertions made by authors on the topic of recovered memories may seem intuitively or clinically appealing or may resonate with one's prior beliefs or biases, they may also be erroneous to a degree that could lead to harm to clients. Many absolute statements on the topic of childhood sexual abuse may rely on strongly held beliefs, clinical experience, a collection of anecdotes, an appeal to authority, or countless other justifications. But accompanying the assertion with evidence of empirical validity allows a more scientific approach; therapists who are developing strategies for assessment and treatment of clients who have alleged memory recovery must pay careful attention to developing a scientific foundation for their work.

Yet another fundamental premise of working with such clients is that, in light of the current state of scientific data and knowledge, each report of recovered memory of abuse must be carefully and fairly evaluated on an individual basis. No claim can be reflexively assumed to be true, false, or somewhere in between prior to an informed and unbiased review of the data surrounding that assertion. The most plausible, coherent, and compelling report of abuse, even when it does not involve a period of forgetting, may describe something that never occurred in the life of the narrator. The most implausible, internally contradictory, and unpersuasive story, based on memory recovered after a long delay, may reflect abuse that actually was perpetrated on this person. Those who assert that

recovered memories of abuse are all completely false or all completely true or that there are characteristics of the reported memories that will prima facie reveal with absolute and total certainty whether the memories are valid or invalid have—perhaps with the best of motives—raced away from what is currently known.

RESEARCH ON MEMORY: WHAT DOES IT TELL US?

At first glance, the field of memory may baffle, overwhelm, and discourage practitioners, particularly the many who have long ago forgotten their introductory coursework in cognitive psychology. This complex, evolving field frustrates the search for quick concepts that would safely generalize to virtually all cases. It is little wonder that the very difficult question of delayed recall of trauma is one for which answers appear complex and often conflicting. It is helpful for mental health professionals who are searching for a useful scientific explanatory model for what is being observed clinically to be aware of this complexity, of the diversity of viewpoints within the science of memory, and of the continuing evolution of these viewpoints.

The current state of research appears to indicate several things:

1. Memory is reconstructive; it is not a camera or a video recorder. Not everything that occurs will be retained in normal memory; not everything that is retained will always be available for retrieval. Therefore, the absence of recollection for an event is not evidence of repression, dissociation, or other defensive forgetting; it may simply indicate that the event was never stored in memory.
2. Memory is affected by experience; how we remember what we remember is colored by mood, social context, and the demands of the interpersonal environment. Some things are more easily remembered in one set of circumstances than in another.
3. It is possible, via suggestion, to create false beliefs regarding events that have probably

not occurred in a person's life but may come to be experienced by that person as a "memory" of his or her life experience (Loftus, 1993). However, there is no evidence available to date that employing usual psychotherapeutic techniques can produce false beliefs that one was sexually abused. There is a fair amount of anecdotal evidence that therapists using coercion and social pressure (in other words, not practicing psychotherapy) can induce such false beliefs in clients. Studies that have purported to demonstrate that psychotherapy can easily implant false memories of childhood sexual abuse appear, on close examination, to lack generalizability to the therapy setting (Pope, 1995).

4. It is possible for a person to temporarily lose access to the memory of a trauma and then recall it at a later date. This is true for every variety of trauma (Elliott & Briere, 1995), not only childhood trauma. This phenomenon of posttraumatic amnesia has been observed and documented cross-situationally for over a century; it is not a recent invention or fad.

5. Not everything that a person recalls will be accurate, whether the memory is continuous or delayed. Memory is not history.

IS THERE A "FALSE MEMORY SYNDROME"?

Although various individuals and organizations have attempted to assert that false memory syndrome (FMS) exists, the evidence is weak. FMS has been defined as

a condition in which a person's identity and interpersonal relationships are centered around a memory of traumatic experience which is objectively false but in which the person strongly believes. Note that the syndrome is not characterized by false memories as such. We all have memories that are inaccurate. Rather, the syndrome may be diagnosed when the memory is so deeply engrained that it orients the individual's entire personality and lifestyle, in turn disrupting all sorts of other adaptive behaviors. The analogy to personality disorder is intentional. False Memory Syndrome is especially destructive be-

cause the person assiduously avoids confrontation with any evidence that might challenge the memory. Thus it takes on a life of its own, encapsulated, and resistant to correction. The person may become so focused on the memory that he or she may be effectively distracted from coping with the real problems in his or her life. (Kihlstrom, 1996)

However, there is a complete absence of empirical evidence to support this definition (Pope, 1996). Almost all of the reported cases of alleged FMS have been described by third parties with an interest in declaring the memories to be false—those accused of abuse and the people close to them. A number of those who have been described as having FMS have concrete proof of the reality of what they have recalled or have successfully subjected their allegations to a legal contest. As far as can be determined, so-called FMS is a name that was created by and for an advocacy organization; it is not appropriately utilized as a diagnosis at this time (Pope, 1996).

IMPORTANT TREATMENT CONSIDERATIONS

Primary to treatment of this group—indeed, of any client group—is obtaining careful and thorough informed consent to treatment. I have described the concept of "empowered consent" (Brown, 1994), which emphasizes the importance of making the consent process one in which the ongoing education of the client to become an active, collaborative, and authoritative partner in the treatment process is initiated. With clients who are experiencing delayed recall of childhood trauma, such empowerment is essential because it lays the groundwork for a therapy relationship in which the client takes ownership of what is real and of the authorship of his or her personal narrative.

Errors in treatment of clients who experience delayed recall are most likely to arise from various cognitive distortions by the clinician: overgeneralization, denial, or premature cognitive commitment. Statements such as "All sexual abuse survivors have symptom X" or "All reports of recovered memories are confabulations" represent this sort of cognitive distortion that could lead to both ineffective assessment and harmful treatment. One very common source of cognitive distortions regarding childhood sexual abuse is the lack of training and experience that most clinicians bring to this work. This is true as regards both formal training and experiential exposure to the topic. A national survey of clinicians concluded that from "any standpoint, these participants found that graduate training related to childhood and adult abuse was woefully lacking" (Feldman-Summers & Pope, 1994, p. 357) and rated their graduate training in every area of abuse but one (the exception: nonsexual violence against adults) as "very poor."

Therapists who work with the remembering client must thus pursue both intellectual and emotional competencies for working with this population. Intellectual competencies are developed when therapists become knowledgeable about working with the client population. They must become familiar with the professional literature on the treatment of adult survivors (e.g., Briere, 1996; Courtois, 1988; Herman, 1992; Pearlman & Saakvitne, 1995; Salter, 1995; or a recent scholarly article on the topic, Enns, McNeilly, Corkery, & Gilbert, 1995). They must obtain formal training and, where possible, ongoing consultation or supervision. Therapists working with this population must at a minimum become familiar with the range of literature on the following topics: developmental theory, trauma and trauma response, memory, suggestibility, and dissociation.

Trends that have emerged over the past decade regarding the treatment of adult survivors of childhood sexual abuse have emphasized containment and client empowerment as the goals for treatment. A focus on memory recall per se is rarely advised; rather, the integration of memory into a coherent personal narrative is emphasized. These emerging standards call for the clinician to respect the client's need for safety, as well as the client's timing and pacing of treatment. The use of techniques that supposedly assist in accessing unavailable memories is commonly seen as inadvisable in this standard; instead, there is a focus on assisting the client in the management of intrusive

recall if it occurs spontaneously. Additionally, this literature stresses the importance of tolerance for ambiguity. Many events that occur in a person's life will never be recalled; traumatic events may be recalled only in a fragmentary or incomplete fashion. Assisting clients to come to terms with these realities and moving with them toward enhanced functioning is an important component of trauma treatment with the remembering adult.

Particular stress should be placed on careful assessment, both clinically and when advisable psychometrically by the clinician working with the remembering adult. Careful differential diagnosis may assist a therapist and client in the development of a mutually satisfactory treatment plan. This sort of careful assessment is distinct from the notion, advanced by some authors (e.g., Yapko, 1994), that it is the task of the therapist to undertake to corroborate or disprove any materials presented by a client as delayed recalls of trauma. Rather, therapists must support clients in their own determinations regarding whether and how to search for corroboration.

Sophisticated models of distress, pathology, assessment, and diagnosis—and the degree to which they are informed by or isolated from current empirical research and scientific scholarship—are another fundamental resource when delayed memories of abuse are at issue. Unfortunately, some popular press and self-help books seem unaware of this resource. They may, for example, state or imply that childhood sexual abuse is the paramount or sole cause of many symptoms and syndromes. The current state of knowledge regarding sexual abuse in childhood is that it can be *a* (not *the*) risk factor for a range of possible disorders, such as posttraumatic stress disorder, dissociative identity disorder, borderline personality disorder, and various depressive disorders. However, and most important, *there is no one symptom, syndrome, or diagnosis that inevitably results from sexual abuse in childhood. No psychological symptom is pathognomic of a history of child sexual abuse.* For instance, flashbacks or flashback-like episodes, intrusive thoughts of sexual abuse experiences, or nightmares containing images of sexual abuse are not in and of themselves indicative of sexual abuse having taken place. This variability in presentation underscores the importance of a basic knowledge of the domain of psychopathology, so that careful differential diagnosis informs any treatment.

Another kind of competence, one that is less frequently addressed in the training of therapists, is emotional competence. This term refers to psychotherapists' emotional capacities to work effectively with people who may be despairing, terrified, sexually aroused, enraged, violent, frantic, or experiencing other intense feelings or impulses. It refers to the therapist's ability to carry on this work without responding to the emotional intensity through sealing themselves off, allowing their own personal issues or biases to distort the therapy, or feeling empty and resentful. Not all therapists can work with all clients or all kinds of problems. To acknowledge limitations and constantly monitor how close one is to them is not a sign of weakness; it is an essential part of clinical work.

This population is one that especially demands emotional competence from therapists. As Pearlman and Saakvitne (1995) note in their essential text on therapists' emotional responses to working with trauma survivors, the adult survivor of childhood sexual abuse is frequently the client most likely to evoke complex and painful affects in the therapist and most likely to challenge the therapist's cherished notions about families, the safety of children, and, at times, the nature of reality. Because it is not uncommon to encounter severe dissociative symptoms among adults having delayed recall of childhood sexual abuse (Kluft, 1990), therapists must also cope with their feelings about interacting with the challenging phemonenology of dissociative identity disorder. This is also a group that is at very high risk for revictimization by sexually exploitative therapists, given their early training to comply with and submit to sexual victimization (Pope, 1994).

FORENSIC CONSIDERATIONS

Clients with a history of childhood sexual victimization are more likely than the average therapy client to have experiences that might lead them to become the plaintiff in a litigation (Brown, 1996). These include a history of victimization by prior therapists or health care providers, sexual harassment, domestic violence (Walker, 1994), or the desire to sue a perpetrator under laws, now extant in more than half of the states (Pope & Brown, 1996), that toll the statute of limitations from the time at which recall of the abuse commences. Therapists treating this group are well advised to become familiar with differences between the roles of treatment provider and forensic expert and to seek legal consultation if and when the potential for involvement in litigation arises.

References & Readings

Beitchman, J., Zucker, K., Hood, J., daCosta, G., & Ackman, D. (1991). A review of the short-term effects of childhood sexual abuse. *Child Abuse and Neglect, 16*, 101–118.

Briere, J. N. (1996). *Therapy for adults molested as children* (Rev. 2nd ed.). New York: Springer.

Brown, L. S. (1994). *Subversive dialogues: Theory in feminist therapy*. New York: Basic Books.

Brown, L. S. (1996). Your therapy client as plaintiff: Clinical and legal issues for the treating therapist. In J. L. Alpert (Ed.), *Sexual abuse recalled: Perspectives for clinicians* (pp. 337–362). New York: Jason Aronson.

Bryer, J. B., Nelson, B. A., Miller, J. B., & Krol, P. A. (1987). Childhood sexual and physical abuse as factors in adult psychiatric illness. *American Journal of Psychiatry, 144*, 1426–1430.

Courtois, C. (1988). *Healing the incest wound: Adult survivors in therapy*. New York: Norton.

Elliot, D. M., & Briere, J. (1995). Posttraumatic stress associated with delayed recall of sexual abuse: A general population study. *Journal of Traumatic Stress, 8*, 629–647.

Enns, C. Z., McNeilly, C., Corkery, J., & Gilbert, M. (1995). The debate about delayed memories of child sexual abuse: A feminist perspective. *Counseling Psychologist, 23*, 181–279.

Feldman-Summers, S., & Pope, K. S. (1994). The experience of "forgetting" childhood abuse: A national survey of psychologists. *Journal of Consulting and Clinical Psychology, 62*, 636–639.

Herman, J. L. (1992). *Trauma and recovery*. New York: Basic Books.

Kihlstrom, J. (1996). False memory syndrome. *FMS Foundation brochure* [E-mail version]. Philadelphia: False Memory Syndrome Foundation.

Kluft, R. P. (Ed.) (1990). *Incest-related syndromes of adult psychopathology.* Washington, DC: American Psychiatric Press.

Loftus, E. F. (1993). The reality of repressed memories. *American Psychologist, 48,* 518–537.

Pearlman, L. A., & Saakvitne, K. (1995). *Trauma and the therapist.* New York: Norton.

Polusny, M. A., & Follette, V. M. (1995). Long-term correlates of child sexual abuse: Theory and review of the empirical literature. *Applied and Preventive Psychology, 4,* 143–166.

Pope, K. S. (1994). *Sexual involvement with therapists: Patient assessment, subsequent therapy, forensics.* Washington, DC: American Psychological Association.

Pope, K. S. (1995). What psychologists better know about recovered memories, research, lawsuits, and the pivotal experiment. *Clinical Psychology: Science and Practice, 2,* 304–315.

Pope, K. S. (1996). Memory, abuse, and science: Questioning claims about the false memory syndrome epidemic. *American Psychologist, 51,* 957–974.

Pope, K. S., & Brown, L. S. (1996). *Recovered memories of abuse: Therapy, assessment, forensics.* Washington, DC: American Psychological Association.

Pope, K. S., & Tabachnick, B. (1995). Recovered memories of abuse among therapy patients: A national survey. *Ethics and Behavior, 5,* 237–248.

Salter, A. (1995). *Transforming trauma: A guide to understanding and treating adult survivors of child sexual abuse.* Thousand Oaks, CA: Sage.

Walker, L. E. A. (1994). *The abused woman and survivor therapy.* Washington, DC: American Psychological Association.

Yapko, M. (1994). *Suggestions of abuse: True and false memories of childhood sexual trauma.* New York: Simon and Schuster.

Related Topics

76   HYPNOSIS, IMAGERY, AND SUGGESTION

Do's and Do Not's

Ray William London

The do's and do not's of hypnosis apply to the clinical and forensic process, no matter what it may be called. Hypnotic processes have been called altered states of consciousness, autogenic training, biofeedback, directed fantasy, dream analysis, fantasy-imaging processes, guided fantasy, guided imagery, imagery, meditation, relaxation, suggestion, and visualization. The differences between hypnosis and its progeny are more pecuniary and semantic than real. Here, the term *hypnosis* will be used to cover the range of treatment terms.

PREPARATION

DO

- Obtain adequate, appropriate, and accredited training, supervision, and consultation prior to using hypnotic treatment.
- Use the knowledge, skill, and care ordinarily possessed and employed by members of the profession in good standing.
- Use ordinary and reasonable care and diligence and your best judgment in the application of your skill to the case.
- Know and follow the hypnosis-related statutory and case law of your state of practice. Read and study the applicable law and decisions yourself.
- Obtain appropriate professional hypnosis consultation whenever necessary. Especially seek adequate consultations in new, complex, experimental, or unusual utilizations. Human subject standards of care must be followed.
- Seek consultation when using indirect messages like paradoxical, confusion, and deception techniques.
- Make the consultation formal. Both parties should provide documentation that the consultation occurred. Payment for the consultation clearly establishes a duty.
- Remember that when you are functioning as a consultant, your conduct can and often does extend your own potential liability.

DO NOT

- Do not use hypnosis as a therapeutic parlor game or a chance to use a new trick or technique.
- Do not practice outside of your licensure, education, training, experience, or the state of the art. If you would not work with a particular patient or situation without hypnosis, do not let hypnosis make you into something else.

INTAKE

DO

- Explain to the patient (and significant others) the diagnosis, treatment plan, and prognosis.

Make sure that the explanation is based on peer-reviewed and replicated research findings.
- Ask the patient if he or she has any questions or concerns.
- Recognize that many hypnosis patients may be confused and feel overwhelmed by their situation or condition. Remember that selective attention and cognitive filtering are realities with which we must all deal.
- Discuss with the patient when you, the agency, or the patient's insurance company requires that you balance treatment cost control against reasonable and necessary diagnostic tests and treatment.

DO NOT

- Do not rush into using hypnosis when there is a history of, or clinical indications of, intrapersonal and interpersonal concerns. Intrapersonal concerns include (a) suicidal ideation, gestures, attempts, or risk, (b) substance abuse, (c) sexual abuse, (d) impulse and anger control, and (e) active psychotic processes. Interpersonal dynamics include (a) spouse abuse, (b) blackmail or extortion, (c) dangerousness, and (d) significant Axis II disorders.
- Do not inappropriately use hypnosis with victims or witnesses to crimes. Carefully use hypnosis with patients who present with legal and prior treatment concerns. Legal history issues include (a) illegal behavior or (b) being a victim or witness to a crime. The patient's prior treatment history should be assessed for (a) dual relationships, (b) dissatisfaction with another professional's treatment, and (c) prior litigation or professional complaints.
- Do not readily hypnotize a patient with a history of doctor shopping, therapist switching, or professional litigation. Beware of patients who are highly manipulative.
- Do not present yourself as being "rude," "too busy," or "arrogant" or fail to give "adequate attention" to the patient's problem.
- Do not make office visits too brief, fail to promptly return telephone calls, fail to talk to the patient or his or her family, or have long waiting delays.

TREATMENT SELECTION

DO

- Base the treatment plan on acceptable assessment procedures and data, the presenting problems, a sound philosophical basis, and a research-verified treatment strategy.
- Obtain a full psychological and psychosocial history.
- Conduct a comprehensive diagnostic workup. The psychological assessment data must include objective data on hypnotic susceptibility.
- Attend to the full range of the patient's clinical needs.
- Attend to the patient's age, career pattern, marital status, relationships with the opposite sex, and children. Note what strengths were observed. Focus on his or her goals for the future.
- Follow published, peer-reviewed, scientifically validated research and guidelines to assist you in treating patients with a range of problems.
- Realize that even the best technique can backfire.
- Provide scientifically based therapeutic intervention, do no harm, and help the patient improve the quality of his or her life.
- Vigilantly assess secondary gain, resistance, and the impact of the therapeutic relationship.

DO NOT

- Do not ignore established research and sound clinical data.
- Do not believe that hypnosis is a one-technique-fits-all procedure.
- Do not use your hypnotic knowledge to confirm your expectations, see how many personalities can be found, or voyeuristically experience stories of deviant sexual accounts.
- Do not use your therapeutic role to be an advocate for political, sex role, or social causes.
- Do not use your hypnosis training to make you a clinical detective, police officer, judge, jury member, executioner, or lawyer's marketing agent.
- Do not believe everything that the patient says, in or out of hypnosis. Do not make an assumption-of-belief error.

- Do not rush to base your work on pop psychology books, press releases, lay presentations, or idiosyncratic workshop data.
- Do not fail to follow a reasonable and prudent strategy and established professional guidelines.

HIGH-RISK PATIENTS/CLIENTS

DO

- Follow the specific forensic safeguards with victims and witnesses. The guidelines have been established to protect the welfare of the subject, the public, and you.
- Limit the use of hypnotically enhanced recall to the investigative, not the testifying, process.
- Remember that the subject may not later testify based on the hypnotically refreshed memories.
- Explore and document the subject's expectations, fantasies, and misconceptions regarding hypnosis.
- Obtain an informed consent.
- Make a psychological assessment of the subject's state of mind prior to the induction of hypnosis.
- Use test suggestions of known difficulties to determine the subject's ability to respond to the approach.
- Obtain and document from the subject a detailed description of the facts as he or she remembers them.
- Carefully avoid adding any new elements to the witness's description of the events before, during, or after the formal induction of hypnosis.
- Remember that, traditionally, there must be at least one free and unpressured narrative recall of the material with no questions about specifics.
- Use nonleading questions throughout the process.
- Maintain an empathetic, nonjudgmental, and neutral stance.
- Avoid prejudging the cause of the patient's difficulties or the veracity of the patient's reports. Prejudging can interfere with appropriate assessment and treatment.

- Document the session at least by audiotape but preferably videotape, especially when the focus of the work involves any actual or potential victim or witness of a "crime."
- Tape the entire session—from first to last contact.
- Remember that a failure to follow established guidelines can contaminate the hypnotized patient's memory and can lead to disqualification to testify in subsequent proceedings.
- Be independent of, not regularly employed by, and not responsible to the prosecutor or investigators.
- Limit the session to the "hypnotists" and the subject. There may be an exception in unusual situations (such as FBI work).
- Maintain clinical distance and objectivity.
- Deal with the dysfunction, disease, feelings, beliefs, and delusions, not esoteric explanations.
- Caution against making major life decisions during the acute phase of treatment.
- Debrief the patient and explore the subject's response to the termination of the sessions or the approach.

DO NOT

- Do not tell or imply to patients that their memories of past events are always completely and historically accurate.
- Do not tell patients that they should divorce their spouses, believe that they know who a perpetrator was, or recommend litigation.
- Do not conduct hypnosis sessions unless you are a licensed psychologist or psychiatrist skilled and trained in the clinical and investigative uses of hypnosis.
- Do not get involved in the drama and wonder of the patient's presentation. Your being spellbound does not help the patient.
- Do not jump to believe, express disbelief, or exert pressure to believe in events that may not have occurred.
- Do not make public statements about the veracity or other features of individual reports. Do not confuse your personal biases and prejudices with your public statements.
- Do not identify or personally indicate a named perpetrator.

- Do not rush to judgment with patients or peers. Avoid finger-pointing.
- Do not ignore your own biases, countertransference, or interpretation. Make sure that you have all the facts before making an assessment.
- Do not further "victimize" the patient or place yourself, the hypnosis professional, at risk.

PREINDUCTION

DO

- Explore and attempt to correct the patient's unrealistic expectations or irrational misconceptions regarding hypnosis and the treatment.
- Obtain a full informed consent prior to the use of the procedure. Present the patient or guardian with sufficient scientifically based, theoretically sound, and valid information to appreciate the alternatives and the reality of potential risks.
- Periodically update and renew the consent, based on new knowledge and court decisions.
- Have the consent form that you select reviewed by your own attorney. Your attorney should be experienced in malpractice cases within your major professional identification in your state of practice.
- Make and maintain a complete recording of the work, especially with memory refreshment work, victims, and witnesses to crimes.
- Document preprocedure discussions concerning the nature of the proposed treatment, the alternatives presented, potential and realistic risks, and complications. Note if a patient declines to accept the hypnosis professional's offer.
- Explain and document the potential consequences of a refusal of treatment.
- Explore the patient's beliefs, expectations, and prior hypnotic experiences.

DO NOT

- Do not forget to document.
- Do not blindly accept a canned informed consent. Such consents cannot always reflect your professional practices or the law of your state of practice.

INDUCTION

DO

- Recognize that the hypnotic process begins before the formal induction and ends after reorientation.
- Select an induction process based on the patient's abilities and needs.
- Individualize the induction.
- Separate the beliefs, facts, and dogma in the field.
- Carefully monitor your use of hypnosis, behavior, screening, observations, suggestions, timing, word choice, images, and debriefing.

DO NOT

- Do not play with age regression and uncovering techniques without adequate training and consultation.
- Do not tell patients or believe yourself that hypnosis can ever be a truth-detection device.

POSTINDUCTION

DO

- Attend to the patient's entire system.
- Attend to expressions of anger, discomfort, dissatisfaction, or unhappiness by a patient or family member.
- Make sure that the patient is reoriented and prepared to return to regular activities.

DO NOT

- Do not believe that once the session is over, your responsibilities end.
- Do not ignore possible posttreatment complications.
- Do not believe that hypnosis is an all-powerful, controlling, evil process or a quick fix.

FOLLOW-UP

DO

- Pay special attention to a failure to return for a scheduled treatment or complaints regarding or failure to pay the bill.
- Document details regarding the hypnosis, techniques, responses, and validity.

- Recognize that when a record is incomplete or inaccurate, you may have to provide more information.
- When making chart corrections, clearly note the date of late entry, with a preface explaining the reason for the new information.
- Make sure that everyone who sees the correction will easily recognize it as a late entry.

DO NOT

- Do not recklessly alter a record after a bad result or the occurrence of a "red flag." Such a correction or addendum must not be placed on the original record page. The correction should be placed on a separate piece of paper, properly dated, and held in a safe place for potential use.
- Do not delude yourself into thinking that just because you say something is a myth, you are able to destroy some of the irrational beliefs held by the patient, his or her family, your colleagues, or attorneys.
- Do not recommend premature disruption of important relationships or making other important decisions based on clinical speculations.
- Do not recommend litigation based solely on hypnotic memories or without a full informed consent.
- Do not fail to document potential limitations of the hypnotic experience.

References & Readings

American Medical Association (1985). Council report: Scientific status of refreshing recollection by the use of hypnosis. *Journal of the American Medical Association, 253,* 1918–1923.

American Medical Association (1994). *Council report: Memories of childhood abuse* (C.S.A. Report 5-A-94). Chicago: American Medical Association.

Forensic uses of hypnosis (1979). Special issue, *International Journal of Clinical and Experimental Hypnosis, 27*(4).

Forensic uses of hypnosis, II (1990). Special issue, *International Journal of Clinical and Experimental Hypnosis, 38*(4).

London, R. W. (1997). Forensic implications in clinical practice [Invited master class]. *International*

Journal of Clinical and Experimental Hypnosis, 45(1), 6–17.

MacHovec, F. J. (1986). *Hypnosis complications: Prevention and risk management.* Springfield, IL: Charles C. Thomas.

Measures of hypnotizability (1979). Special issue, *American Journal of Clinical Hypnosis, 21* (2 & 3).

People v. Shirley, 31 Cal. 3d 18, 641 P.2d 775, 181 Cal. Rept. 243 (1982).

Perry, C., Orne, M. T., London, R. W., & Orne, E. C. (1996a). Rethinking per se exclusions of hypnotically elicited recall as legal testimony. *International Journal of Clinical and Experimental Hypnosis, 44,* 66–81.

Rock v. Arkansas, 483 U.S. 44, 61 (1987).

State v. Fertig, A-19-95 (1996).

State v. Hurd, 86 N.J. 525, 432 A.2d 86 (1981).

Related Topics

77 GROUP PSYCHOTHERAPY
An Interpersonal Approach

Victor J. Yalom

Group psychotherapy is an extremely effective modality and potentially a more efficient use of professional resources than individual psychotherapy. Its efficacy has been demonstrated in treating a wide range of disorders, yet it continues to be underutilized or misused by clinicians who are not sufficiently trained in group techniques. The current pressures toward providing briefer, more cost-effective treatment provide a renewed opportunity for a broader utilization of group methods of treatment.

APPLICATIONS

Psychotherapy groups generally consist of between 6 and 10 clients and one or two therapists. Some formats, such as multifamily groups, may be much larger. Groups are run in almost every setting, from private practice to hospitals, and are applicable for almost every conceivable clinical population. For some populations, such as substance abusers or domestic violence offenders, groups are generally considered the preferred method of treatment.

THEORY

The interactional or interpersonal approach described here assumes that patients' presenting symptoms and underlying difficulties are to a large extent the result of maladaptive patterns of interpersonal relationships. A major therapeutic factor in group psychotherapy occurs in the form of interpersonal learning—that is, group members become more aware of and modify their maladaptive interpersonal behaviors and beliefs. Through the course of a successful group therapy, patients obtain direct and repeated feedback about the effects of their behavior on others—honest feedback, which they are unlikely to receive in a constructive and supportive manner anywhere else in their lives. Other important therapeutic factors in groups include the feeling of support and belonging, catharsis, the instillation of hope, and the experience of altruism in helping other members.

With the therapist's active promptings, members will increase their awareness and understanding of how their behaviors impact other group members: which behaviors elicit positive reactions, such as compassion, empathy, attraction, and a desire for increased emotional closeness, and which provoke negative reactions, such as anger, hurt, fear, and a general desire to withdraw. They then have the opportunity to "try out" new behaviors in the relative safety of the group, learning how to develop social relationships that are more fulfilling. Success begets success, and patients begin to internalize these experiences, altering some of their negative self-images. Finally, they apply these new social skills and internalized identities in their relationships outside the group.

A basic assumption underlying this process of change is that the group is a "social microcosm"—that is, that the types of relationships patients tend to form in their daily lives will eventually be re-created within the group itself. Thus the concept of transference from individual psychotherapy is broadened to include the "parataxic distortions," as coined by Harry Stack Sullivan, which occur in all relationships. Because of the variety and number of group members, the opportunity to work through the multiple transferences or distortions that develop is much richer than in individual therapy.

Because of this phenomenon, the most powerful and efficacious way to learn from these recapitulated relationships is to focus on them as they continuously recur during the course of therapy. This is referred to as the "here-and-now," because the focus is here (in the group) and now (interactions that occur during the therapy session). Accordingly, past events or relationships outside the group are used primarily as jumping-off points, which then

guide the here-and-now work in the group rather than remaining the central focus.

For example, if a group member complains of repeated conflicts with his or her boss, it is usually of limited benefit to hear a lengthy recounting of these conflicts, since the patient's report is undoubtedly a skewed one, biased by the member's needs and distorted perceptions. Attempts to interpret or make suggestions about the work situation are often unproductive because the patient always has the upper hand, being privy to infinitely more information about the situation than the other group members or leader. Instead, the therapist draws attention to the manner in which the group member engages in, or avoids, conflict with other group members—with the assumption that in some way his or her troublesome relationship with the boss will be reenacted here. Because all the group members can witness his or her exchanges in the group, they are able to give feedback that is more accurate and compelling.

TASKS OF THE GROUP THERAPIST

Given the premise that interpersonal learning is maximized in a group that operates largely in the here-and-now, what must the therapist do for this to occur? First and foremost, the therapist must actively assist patients in translating their presenting complaints into interpersonal issues. For example, a patient who initially requests therapy because of a feeling of depression would be urged to explore the interpersonal context of his or her depression—for example, the depression might be triggered by feelings of rejection by a lover, with subsequent loneliness or humiliation. This initial reformulation of the problem must then be broadened so that it can be addressed in the group. With additional effort the therapist might help the patient restate the complaint as "I feel depressed when others don't give me the attention I want, and yet I am unable to state my needs directly." In this manner the complaint has been transformed into one that can be addressed in the here-and-now of the therapy group: the patient can explore how he or she experiences similar feelings of rejection by other group members and yet has difficulty in letting them know what he or she wants from them.

The other main task of the therapist is to help the group continuously attend to the interpersonal dynamics that occur within the group. This can be broken down into two subtasks. The first is to help plunge the group into the here-and-now, allowing the members to interact with each other as much as possible. The second is to help them reflect back on these interactions and learn from them.

The therapist must, in a very active manner, help the group members to interact directly with each other and to share their observations and feelings about one another. During the initial session, it is common for the members to take turns talking about themselves, including their reasons for seeking therapy and the areas in which they would like to change. From this very first meeting, the astute therapist will look for every opportunity to direct the interactions toward the here-and-now. For example, if a patient states that he or she is feeling quite anxious, a few probing questions may reveal that the patient invariably compares himself or herself with others and usually concludes that they will look down on him or her because of lack of education and sophistication. The therapist can bring this general concern into the here-and-now by asking, "Of the people in this group, which ones have you imagined are having critical thoughts of you?"

Although the group members may initially resist the leap into the here-and-now, with time and reinforcement they will begin to engage with each other more spontaneously. This is not to suggest that the therapist can relax and expect the group to internalize these norms enough to be a self-correcting mechanism; members are far too preoccupied attending to the issues that brought them to the group. The leader must continuously attend to the group process and seize upon or create opportunities to steer the group into productive here-and-now exchanges. But, over time, productive working groups should require less guidance into the here and now if the therapist consistently reinforces this norm.

The experiential element of these interactions is crucial but by itself is insufficient. Experience, like catharsis, rarely by itself leads to personal change. It is necessary for the here-and-now experience to be linked with some mechanism that helps patients understand and learn from these interactions. In other words, the patients need to be able to look back and reflect upon the encounters they experience in the group.

To facilitate this, therapists must first have a clear understanding of group process. Process can be most easily defined in contradistinction to content: Whereas content consists of the actual words or topics discussed, process refers to the meaning that these conversations have in terms of the relationships between the group members. Thus, from a process orientation, the same utterance by a patient will have vastly different connotations depending on the manner in which it was delivered, the timing, and the context of the group discussion.

Therapists thus must find ways to help the group reflect back on its own process. Again this is an area where therapists must be very active, since group members themselves are unlikely to initiate this type of activity. Process comments can range from simple observations by the therapist of specific incidents (e.g., "I noticed that when you said that your fists were clenched") to more generalized interpretations (e.g., "You seem to instinctively challenge whatever the other men say in the group; I wonder if you feel the need to be competitive with them?"). Over the course of therapy, process comments serve to heighten patients' awareness of how their behavior appears to others in the group. Ultimately patients become aware of how they determine the quality of the interpersonal world they live in, and with this awareness comes the possibility for true behavior change, leading to more satisfying relationships.

COMMON ERRORS

One of the most common errors of novice group psychotherapists is to practice some form of individual psychotherapy in the group.

In this scenario the therapist typically spends an inordinate amount of time focusing on some issue or problem that a group member is experiencing, attempting to solve or analyze that problem. This approach has several obvious drawbacks. The first is that it reinforces the therapist as the expert, disempowering other group members. The experience group members gain in being able to give and receive help from each other is in itself extremely therapeutic and should be cultivated as much as possible. The second drawback is that a prolonged exchange between the therapist and a group member leaves the other members on the sideline, uninvolved, and likely to become disinterested. Group therapists need to be alert to ensure that the unique ingredients of the psychotherapy group—that is, a number of individuals who are motivated to come together to help each other grow and gain relief from suffering under the direction of a skilled leader—are fully utilized. This is accomplished by keeping the group interactive, with members participating fully, taking risks, and giving each other feedback and support.

The other most vexing misuse, or underutilization, of the group format is a failure to work in the here-and-now. This is usually caused by therapists leading groups without proper training or supervision. Once therapists have observed and understood the power and energy that here-and-now interactions generate, they will be more likely to develop the skills necessary to use this approach. Another reason for avoiding the here-and-now is the fear that this will lead to excessive conflict. A successful course of group psychotherapy, as with individual psychotherapy, involves the experience and expression of a wide range of feelings: anger, disappointment, and hurt, as well as caring, support, and even joy. The skilled therapist facilitates the direct expression of conflict rather than going underground but also ensures that difficult feelings are aired in a safe, nonabusive manner. Only rarely does conflict dominate the interactions and threaten group cohesion; in fact, in most settings the therapist needs to be more active in facilitating the expression of conflict rather than in containing it.

OBSTACLES TO FORMING AND STARTING GROUPS

Getting groups up and running can be the most challenging aspect of conducting group psychotherapy. The solo private practitioner needs a large base of clients to put together an appropriate mix in a timely fashion; if the process of group formation is stretched out too long, some individuals may drop out before the group begins. On the other hand, starting a group with fewer than five members is likely to be problematic. With anticipated absences and unanticipated dropouts, some meetings will have as few as two or three clients. These meetings lack the richness of exchanges and overall dynamism experienced in larger group sessions. Furthermore, they are likely to engender in the members (and the leader) fears about group survival, which are unproductive and distract from the therapeutic goals.

Thus therapists need a steady referral base or an ability to effectively market their groups. Often it is easier to publicize groups targeted to specific populations, such as incest survivors, teens with eating disorders, or recovering alcoholics. Another possibility is for therapists to team up as coleaders, which allows them to draw patients from their combined practices, making it easier to fill groups and keep them filled as openings occur. This also has other advantages for the therapists, including complementing each other's clinical skills and combating the isolation of private practice.

Group practices, clinics, and managed care organizations offer their own set of hurdles to developing successful group psychotherapy programs. Although they have the advantage of having large numbers of patients necessary for conducting multiple groups, they pose challenges in appropriately and tactfully funneling these patients to the therapists leading these groups. It is quite common to encounter a great deal of resistance (conscious and unconscious) at every level of an organization—from intake workers to front-line therapists to administrators—to implementing a group program. Many clinicians still have limited knowledge and training regarding groups and view group psychotherapy suspiciously as a second-class form of treatment. Unfortunately, some large institutions that are successful in running large numbers of groups unwittingly encourage these beliefs by emphasizing to their staffs the necessity to accommodate large patient populations rather than the particular treatment benefits of groups.

To overcome this, each level of the organization must in essence be retrained to think "group" as one of the treatment options for each patient. Telephone intake workers should think in interpersonal terms as they ask about presenting symptoms and should inform callers of available group treatments. If a client appears to be a good candidate for a group, he or she should be referred directly to the group leader, who can do a more in-depth assessment. If the client is a good fit, then it is essential that the therapist spend some time preparing the client for the group to increase acceptance of the referral and decrease the likelihood of early dropout. Both intake workers and therapists need to fully understand how groups work so they can intelligently discuss how the group will address the particular concerns of each client. For example, a chronically shy individual may at first be quite reluctant to accept a referral for a social skills training group but might become more enthusiastic when it is explained how the therapist will assist in working directly on his or her shyness via interactions with other group members.

Needless to say, top administrators must fully support any attempt to increase group psychotherapy utilization, taking significant concrete steps to ensure the success of these efforts. Group psychotherapists should be given adequate training and supervision. Also, it is important that reimbursement or other institutional rewards encourage the use of group psychotherapy. For example, if therapists are required to provide a specified amount of direct services per week, a 90-minute group should be counted as more than 1½ hours because of the extra paperwork, phone calls, and effort involved in starting the group. Without institutional support, therapists are likely to be discouraged from leading groups.

ISSUE-FOCUSED GROUPS

Most groups being led today are formed for clients who possess shared symptoms, such as panic attacks, depression, or posttraumatic stress disorder, or have common life experiences, such as incest survivors or single parents. These homogeneous groups offer several advantages. They are often easier to form, and from a community mental health perspective, they help to destigmatize the symptoms, thus making group treatment more accessible to many who otherwise might not seek out psychiatric or psychological services. Once the group has been formed, the commonality, either of symptoms or of life experiences among the members, can increase the group's cohesion. Because these groups are often time-limited, a sense of cohesion is especially important, since it accelerates the development of safety and, hence, of risk taking.

However, the therapist should be aware of and strive to avoid potential pitfalls with homogeneous groups. There is a tendency among patients to focus on the commonalties of their symptoms and conditions rather than on their unique individual experiences. Thus they avoid taking responsibility for their current dilemmas and the areas they would like to change. The therapist must steer the group away from theoretical discourses about the nature of their symptoms, excessive advice giving, and personal historical accounts and instead address the ways in which their symptoms manifest in their day-to-day relationships. This is not to say that a psychoeducational approach is not useful but to suggest that ultimately the group leader should highlight the interpersonal components of the issues or symptoms under discussion and utilize the group format to work directly on those issues in the here-and-now.

References & Readings

Leszcz, M. (1992). The interpersonal approach to group psychotherapy. *International Journal of Group Psychotherapy, 42,* 37–62.

Roller, B. (1997). *The promise of group psychotherapy*. San Francisco: Jossey-Bass.

Rutan, J. S., & Stone, W. N. (1993). *Psychodynamic group psychotherapy* (2nd ed.). New York: Guilford.

Sadock, H., & Kaplan, B. (Eds.) (1993). *Comprehensive group psychotherapy* (3rd ed.). Baltimore: Williams and Wilkins.

Vinogradov, S., & Yalom, I. D. (1989). *Concise guide to group psychotherapy*. Washington DC: American Psychiatric Press.

Yalom, I. D. (1983). *Inpatient group psychotherapy*. New York: Basic Books.

Yalom, I. D. (1995). *The theory and practice of group psychotherapy* (4th ed.). New York: Basic Books.

Related Topics

78   ASSESSING AND REDUCING RISK OF INFECTION WITH THE HUMAN IMMUNODEFICIENCY VIRUS

Michael P. Carey

Epidemiologic data from the Centers for Disease Control and Prevention confirm that the acquired immunodeficiency syndrome (AIDS) can affect anyone who comes into contact with the human immunodeficiency virus (HIV). Although AIDS was originally thought to be a disease that affected only gay Caucasian men, recent data refute this notion. Rates of new infections among gay men have declined, whereas rates among heterosexual men and women have either remained stable or increased. It has been estimated that 71% of HIV-infected cases worldwide involve heterosexual transmission (Ehrhardt, 1992). HIV does not discriminate among persons on the basis of sexual orientation, gender, or race. In the United States, 650,000–900,000 persons are infected with HIV (Karon et al., 1996), and there have been more than 500,000 documented cases of AIDS; of the persons with AIDS, more than 300,000

have already died. AIDS is now the leading cause of death among young adults in the United States; more deaths result from AIDS than from accidents, murders, suicides, cancer, or heart disease in this age-group.

Neither cure nor vaccine exists for HIV and AIDS; thus, behavioral avoidance of the virus provides the only protection against infection. Every psychologist is obliged to know the basics of HIV transmission and prevention, to evaluate clients for their risk of infection, and to provide risk reduction counseling when indicated. Because few psychologists have the time to become experts in infectious disease or sexual behavior, in this chapter I overview three areas necessary for ethical practice. First, I summarize the key information regarding HIV transmission. Second, I provide guidelines for the screening of HIV risk in a time-efficient manner; by asking a few simple questions, a psychologist will communicate concern for his or her clients' safety and, in some cases, help them to identify their risk of contracting a life-threatening disease. Third, I provide basic guidelines for counseling clients regarding risk reduction. Finally, I identify resources for further study and consultation.

HIV TRANSMISSION

The good news about HIV transmission is that HIV is a fluid-borne agent. What this means is that, unlike tuberculosis or other airborne infectious agents, HIV is not spread through sneezing, coughing, sharing eating utensils, or other forms of casual contact. For HIV transmission to occur, an infected person's blood, semen, vaginal secretions, or breast milk must enter the bloodstream of another person. The three most common routes of transmission are (a) *unprotected sexual intercourse* (anal, vaginal, or oral) with an infected partner; (b) *sharing unsterilized needles* (most commonly in the context of recreational drugs but also in tattooing, steroid use, and other needle uses) with an infected person; and (c) *maternal-child transmission* (e.g., infection through the placenta before birth and perhaps through breast-feeding after birth) when the mother is infected. Transmission can also occur through blood transfusions (when receiving but not when giving blood) and through a variety of accidental exposures (e.g., trauma situations, occupational needle-sticks), but these routes are relatively rare.

ASSESSMENT OF RISK

Careful listening serves as the cornerstone of the assessment process. Some clients may freely offer their concerns about HIV-related risk as a reason for therapy. Despite the importance of sexual health, not all health professionals know how to listen when it comes to the sexual sphere. It is not uncommon for clients to report that they had tried previously to discuss sexual concerns with a health care professional but were met with avoidance, embarrassment,

or apparent lack of interest; as a result, the clients did not pursue their concerns. Thus, the first guideline is to be open to clients' self-disclosures regarding sexual, drug-use, and other risk behaviors and to be aware of subtle messages you might convey to discourage the disclosure of such material.

Even when a therapist is open to self-disclosure on such topics, many clients will be reluctant to independently raise their concerns regarding sexual or other risk behaviors. In these cases, the therapist will need to actively assess the client's risk in a sensitive and efficient manner. Assessment of risk should take place after a client and therapist have established a basic rapport and the therapist has assured the client of confidentiality. Specific risk assessment should always begin with an appropriate introduction for the client(s). During this time the reasons for asking questions about sexual and other socially sensitive behaviors should be provided. For example, one might say that a standard practice is to inquire about risk for HIV just as one routinely inquires about suicidal ideation, personal safety, and other important matters; thus, all clients get asked, and no client will feel singled out as being at unique risk. Although sensitivity is advised, it is also important to ask questions in a direct fashion, without apology or hesitancy (Kinsey, Pomeroy, & Martin, 1948). If the clinician appears embarrassed about or unsure of the appropriateness of the questions, a client may detect this and provide incomplete or ambiguous responses. After the introductory remarks, the client should be invited to ask any questions he or she might have.

When assessing sexual behavior, we have found it helpful to adopt certain assumptions in order to gather the most accurate information without wasting time and effort (Wincze & Carey, 1991). These assumptions reflect the preferred direction of error. Thus, for example, it is better to assume a low level of understanding on the part of the client so that information is conveyed in a clear, concrete manner. Other examples of useful assumptions include the notions that (a) clients will be embarrassed about and have difficulty discussing sexual matters; (b) clients will not understand medical terminology; and (c) clients will be misinformed about HIV and AIDS. As the clinician learns more about the client, these assumptions are adjusted.

Depending on the client and the context, it may be useful to sequence the inquiry from the least to the most threatening questions. Thus, questions about receipt of blood transfusions might precede questions regarding needle sharing or sexual behavior. Experience in the assessment of sexual behavior also suggests that it can be helpful to place the "burden of denial" on the client (Kinsey et al., 1948). That is, rather than ask whether a client has engaged in a particular activity, the clinician might ask the patient how many times he or she has engaged in it. Use of this strategy will depend on the nature of the relationship that has been established with the client.

Given these process considerations, the content of the risk screening follows the transmission categories identified earlier. We advise inquiring about each of the following domains and pursuing follow-up questions as appropriate.

1. "When were you last tested to determine if you are infected with HIV (the virus that causes AIDS)? What were the results of that test?" Knowledge of the date of the test is important for the determination of subsequent risk activity. Because of the "window period" (i.e., the amount of time between exposure to and infection with the virus and the development of antibodies detectable with serological tests), one should assess risk behavior going back at least 6 months prior to the most recent antibody test. If a client discloses that he or she is infected with HIV (i.e., is HIV-positive or HIV+), you will need to address the many health, relationship, and social issues associated with HIV disease. This is a complex set of clinical challenges that is beyond the scope of this chapter. Kalichman (1995) provides an excellent guide to mental health care for infected persons.

2. "Since your last HIV antibody test, have you received a blood transfusion (or treatment for a blood clotting problem)? If so, was it between 1977 and 1985?" Since 1985, donated blood has been tested for antibod-

ies to HIV; thus, the risk of receiving HIV-infected blood during a transfusion in the United States is extremely low (1 in 60,000).

3. "Since your last HIV antibody test, with how many *men* have you had sex (oral, anal, or vaginal)? Did you always use condoms when having sex? If yes, did you use condoms during *every* penetrative contact, including oral sex? Did you always use *latex* condoms? Have any of your male partners had sex with other men?" Most experts agree that anal sex is more risky than vaginal sex, which is more risky than oral sex. Experts disagree regarding the probability of HIV transmission through oral sex, although this vector of transmission has been demonstrated in analogue laboratory studies with animals (Baba et al., 1996). Experts agree that condoms protect against HIV only when used consistently and correctly with all partners. Because HIV is smaller than sperm cells, natural or lambskin condoms allow the virus to pass through and should not be used. Gay and bisexual men still account for the largest number of infected persons in the United States.

4. "Since your last HIV antibody test, with how many *women* have you had sex (oral, anal, or vaginal)? Did you always use condoms or other barrier protection (e.g., dental dam) when having sex?" Transmission of HIV from an infected woman is less likely than from an infected male, but some risk is still involved.

5. "How many times have you shared or borrowed a needle, or used another person's works (cotton, corker, cooker), to prepare or inject drugs? Did you disinfect the needle prior to reusing it? If so, how did you do this?" Contaminated needles are responsible for the second-largest number of infections in the United States. Although needles can be properly disinfected (e.g., by flushing with a bleach solution two or more times), they are typically shared without cleaning or after improper cleaning.

6. "Have you ever had sex with a person who used injection drugs?" All else being equal, injection drug users (IDUs) are more

likely to be infected with HIV than are non-IDUs.

7. "Have you ever had a sexual partner whom you knew or suspected was HIV infected or had AIDS? If so, did you always use condoms when you had sex?" Having a partner known to be infected with HIV introduces the greatest risk of infection.

8. "Are you at all concerned that you might have been infected with the virus?" This leaves the door open for people who may not have felt comfortable responding to the earlier questions.

RISK REDUCTION COUNSELING

Three levels of counseling may be appropriate. First, if a client reports that he or she has engaged in any high-risk activity (e.g., unprotected intercourse), it may be appropriate to encourage the client to seek testing for HIV. Early detection of infection can help clients to obtain preventive medical care, as well as psychosocial services. Knowledge of serostatus may enhance motivation for risk reduction practices in order to avoid infecting others. The recommendation to seek antibody testing is complex, involving legal, ethical, and political issues (e.g., confidentiality, possible discrimination, and duty to warn).

Clients who express concern despite apparent low risk may also be advised to consider testing. Clients who have been abstinent or those who strongly believe themselves to have been in a mutually monogamous sexual relationship with a HIV-negative partner and have never shared an injection drug needle can be reassured and counseled to maintain low risk.

Information about HIV-antibody testing is available from numerous sources, including American Red Cross chapters and local health departments. Two types of testing are available: with *confidential* testing, the results are recorded in the client's medical files and may be disclosed to those with legal access to records; with *anonymous* testing, a code number is given when blood is drawn, and this number must be presented by the client to receive the results. The client's name is not associated with test results. Many states offer anonymous and/or confidential tests, without charge. Although sites that offer HIV testing are required to provide pretest and posttest counseling, therapists should be prepared to supplement such counseling, regardless of the outcome.

A second level of counseling involves simple education. If a client is misinformed about the basics of HIV and AIDS or has questions about transmission and prevention of HIV infection, most psychologists should be able to help immediately. If a client has been involved in risky sexual or drug-use practices, he or she should be advised promptly and specifically which behaviors enhance risk and what preventive action can be taken to reduce risk for infection. An at-risk client may require more than simple education, however.

The third level of intervention involves the provision of intensive risk reduction counseling. Intervention programs have been developed that are well grounded in psychological theory and have been evaluated in clinical trials with many populations (Kalichman, Carey, & Johnson, 1996). An excellent example of such a program is Kelly's (1995); his readable manual provides a step-by-step guide for implementing an empirically validated risk reduction program. Psychologists can also refer to the sources cited herein and can call local, state, and national hot lines to learn of additional resources (e.g., National AIDS Hotline at 800-342-7514; National AIDS Hotline TTY/TDD service at 800-243-7889; and National AIDS Information Clearinghouse at 800-458-5231).

References & Readings

Baba, T. W., Trichel, A. M., An, L., Liska, V., Martin, L. N., Murphey-Corb, M., & Ruprect, R. M. (1996). Infection and AIDS in adult macaques after nontraumatic oral exposure to cell-free SIV. *Science, 272,* 1486–1489.

Ehrhardt, A. A. (1992). Trends in sexual behavior and the HIV pandemic. *American Journal of Public Health, 82,* 1459–1461.

Kalichman, S. C. (1995). *Understanding AIDS: A guide for mental health professionals.* Washington, DC: American Psychological Association.

Kalichman, S. C., Carey, M. P., & Johnson, B. T.

(1996). Prevention of sexually transmitted HIV infection: A meta-analytic review of the behavioral outcome literature. *Annals of Behavioral Medicine, 18*, 6–15.

Karon, J. M., Rosenberg, P. S., McQuillan, G., Khare, M., Gwinn, M., & Petersen, L. R. (1996). Prevalence of HIV infection in the United States, 1984 to 1992. *Journal of the American Medical Association, 276*, 126–131.

Kelly, J. A. (1995). *Changing HIV risk behavior: Practical strategies.* New York: Guilford Press.

Kinsey, A. C., Pomeroy, W. B., & Martin, C. E.

(1948). *Sexual behavior in the human male.* Philadelphia: Saunders.

Wincze, J. P., & Carey, M. P. (1991). *Sexual dysfunction: A guide for assessment and treatment.* New York: Guilford Press.

Related Topics

Chapter 67, "Treatment Matching in Substance Abuse"
Chapter 68, "Motivational Interviewing"
Chapter 80, "Assessment and Treatment of Lesbians, Gay Men, and Bisexuals"

79 GUIDELINES FOR TREATING WOMEN IN PSYCHOTHERAPY

Susan L. Williams-Quinlan

Traditional psychotherapeutic approaches with women have been roundly criticized on many grounds. A short list would include an androcentric perspective, focusing on intrapsychic conflicts as the cause of women's concerns while negating the influence of societal and cultural factors, using diagnostic categories in a sexist manner, and reinforcing sex role stereotypical behaviors that limit the goals of treatment and the empowerment of women (Worell & Remer, 1992).

This chapter addresses the psychological treatment of women in psychotherapy by means of four abbreviated guidelines: the American Psychological Association (APA) "Guidelines for Therapy With Women" (American Psychological Association, 1978); principles of nonsexist therapy (adapted from Matlin, 1996; Rawlings & Carter, 1977; Worell & Remer, 1992); principles of feminist therapy (adapted from

Matlin, 1996; Rawlings & Carter, 1977; Worell & Remer, 1992); and salient questions to ask female clients (adapted from Kaschak, 1992).

APA GUIDELINES FOR THERAPY WITH WOMEN

- The conduct of therapy should be free of constrictions based on gender-defined roles, and the options explored between client and practitioner should be free of sex role stereotypes.
- The psychologist should recognize the reality, variety, and implications of sex-discriminatory practices in society and should facilitate client examination of options in dealing with such practices.
- The psychologist should be knowledgeable about current empirical findings on sex

roles, sexism, and individual differences resulting from the client's gender-defined identity.

- The theoretical concepts employed by the therapist should be free of sex bias and sex role stereotypes.
- The psychologist should demonstrate acceptance of women as equal to men by using language free of derogatory labels.
- The psychologist should avoid establishing the source of personal problems within the client when they are more properly attributable to situational or cultural factors.
- The psychologist and a fully informed client should agree upon aspects of the therapy relationship such as treatment modality, time factors, and fee arrangements.
- The psychologist should recognize the importance of the availability of accurate information to a client's family but acknowledge that the privilege of communication about diagnosis, prognosis, and progress ultimately resides with the client, not the therapist.
- The psychologist whose female client is subjected to violence in the form of physical abuse or rape should recognize and acknowledge that the client is the victim of a crime.
- The psychologist should recognize and encourage exploration of a woman client's sexuality and should recognize her right to define her own sexual preferences.
- The psychologist should not have sexual relations with a client or treat her as a sex object.

PRINCIPLES OF NONSEXIST THERAPY

- Because of the pervasiveness of sexism in our society and the value-laden nature of therapy, therapists should be aware of their own values, especially with regard to sexism.
- Therapists should not use their power in the therapeutic relationship to encourage women, however subtly, toward more stereotypically "feminine" behavior.
- Therapists should avoid using any language that degrades women (such as referring to

all persons as "he" or using infantilizing terms like "chick" or "babe").

- Clients should make decisions regarding their life choices based on their individual needs and talents rather than limiting themselves to options based on restrictive gender roles.
- Gender-role reversals and variations (e.g., fathers who stay home full-time with their children, women who choose not to have children, or mothers who work outside the home in high-paying, powerful positions) should not be seen as pathological.
- Marriage is not viewed as any better an outcome of therapy for a woman than for a man.
- Women and men should not be expected to differ in characteristics such as nurturance, assertiveness, autonomy, and expressiveness.
- Theories based on biological determinism (e.g., Freud and Erickson) should be rejected due to their androcentric bias and general devaluation of women.

PRINCIPLES OF FEMINIST THERAPY

- Women have been assigned an inferior status because they have less political and economic power than men.
- The primary source of women's problems is social rather than personal. Women have individual problems due to living in a society that devalues, limits, and discriminates against them.
- Society should be changed to be less sexist; women should not be encouraged to adjust to sexist social conditions.
- The focus on society as a primary source of pathology should not be used as an excuse to avoid individual responsibility; women must take charge of their own lives.
- Clients learn that they have been taught "socially appropriate" behaviors but that these behaviors may be far from ideal.
- Society may have encouraged the client not to value herself, but the client can be empowered to value herself in therapy. In so doing, the client can identify her areas of

strengths, which can then be used to help her recognize and solve problems.

- Women must work toward economic and psychological independence, and their relationship with other women and men should be marked by equality in personal power.
- Many clients experience long-term psychological consequences of violence and sexual abuse.
- Other women should not be seen as the enemy; they can often provide valuable emotional support. However, men are not necessarily the enemy either; viewing all men as villains simply reverses the discrimination.
- Relationships of friendship, love, and marriage should be equal in personal power.
- The therapist-client relationship is viewed as egalitarian. If women clients are placed in subordinate roles in therapy, the situation may echo women's inferior status in society.
- Therapists' self-disclosure of relevant information about their own life experiences helps in reducing the power differential.
- Throughout therapy, clients are encouraged to become more self-confident and independent and to develop skills to help themselves.
- Group therapy can often be used to emphasize the client's power and to minimize the therapist's power.
- Inequalities with respect to ethnicity, age, sexual orientation, economics, and disabilities should all be addressed; gender is not the only inequality.

AREAS TO ASSESS

Kaschak (1992) recommends that the following areas are important to assess with female clients through the therapy process in order to begin to understand more fully the source of their successes and difficulties.

- Quality and centrality of relationships with other women, men, and children: How much and in what ways do these relationships determine the sense of self and of self-esteem? In what ways are these relationships helpful and/or hurtful to others and to the client herself?

- History and current experience of limitations imposed by parents, peers, teachers, the media, and other significant sources
- Previous experiences with violations of the self, including the more obvious ones of violence, incest, and rape
- Own evaluation of appearance and the importance it plays in the client's life
- Physical presentation of self, including habitual aspects of posture, carriage, gait, expression, musculature, and movement, and the manner in which this changes when dealing with specific issues in therapy
- Degree of fragmentation experienced physically and psychologically
- Sense of invisibility and hypervisibility in general and in specific situations
- Importance and meaning of food, eating, and dieting experiences
- Losses and disappointments, especially loss of other possibilities and of the sense of self
- From an antigonal psychology framework, anger at and loss of the mother (Jocasta) and enmeshment with an individual father or cultural (Oedipal) fathers
- Extent to which the client has a tendency to watch and evaluate herself through the male perspective
- Extent of sense of responsibility for events and behaviors of people whom the client cannot control
- Experiences of shame
- Sense of self and of self-esteem

Of utmost importance in feminist psychotherapy with women is the valuing of their personal experiences; viewing their concerns in the broader social, political, and cultural context of the society they live in; acknowledging how this environment can serve to undermine their goals; and helping them to recognize their unique abilities and voices as they strive toward positive change rather than adjustment to sexist societal norms.

Source: American Psychological Association, "Guidelines for Therapy With Women: Task Force on Sex Bias and Sex Role Stereotyping in Psychotherapeutic Practice," *American Psychologist, 33,* 1122–1123, copyright © 1978 American Psychological Association. Adapted with permission.

References & Readings

American Psychological Association (1975). Report on the task force on sex bias and sex-role stereotyping in psychotherapeutic practice. *American Psychologist, 30,* 1169–1175.

American Psychological Association (1978). Guidelines for therapy with women: Task force on sex bias and sex role stereotyping in psychotherapeutic practice. *American Psychologist, 33,* 1122–1123.

Brodsky, A. M., & Hare-Mustin, R. T. (Eds.) (1980). *Women and psychotherapy: An assessment of research and practice.* New York: Guilford Press.

Brook, E. P. (Eds.) (1993). *Women, relationships, and power: Implications for counseling.* Alexandria, VA: American Counseling Association.

Brown, L. S., & Root, M. P. P. (Eds.) (1990). *Diversity and complexity in feminist therapy.* New York: Haworth.

Cantor, D. W. (Ed.) (1990). *Women as therapists: A multitheoretical casebook* (pp. 78–95). New York: Springer.

Dutton-Douglas, M. A., & Walker, L. E. (Eds.) (1988). *Feminist psychotherapies: Integration of therapeutic and feminist systems.* Norwood, NJ: Ablex.

Gilligan, C., Rogers, A. G., & Tolman, D. L. (Eds.) (1991). *Women, girls, and psychotherapy: Reframing resistance.* New York: Harrington.

Jordan, J. V., Kaplan, A. G., Baker Miller, J., Stiver, I. P., & Surrey, J. L. (1991). *Women's growth in connection.* New York: Guilford Press.

Kaschak, E. (1992). *Engendered lives: A new psychology of women's experience.* New York: Basic Books.

Matlin, M. W. (1996). *The psychology of women* (3rd ed.). Fort Worth, TX: Harcourt Brace.

Mirkin, M. P. (Ed.) (1994). *Women in context: Toward a feminist reconstruction of psychotherapy.* New York: Guilford Press.

Mowbray, C. T., Lanir, S., & Hulce, M. (Eds.) (1985). *Women and mental health: New directions for change.* New York: Harrington.

Rave, E. J., & Larsen, C. C. (1995). *Ethical decision making in therapy: Feminist perspectives.* New York: Guilford Press.

Rawlings, E. I., & Carter, D. K. (1977). *Psychotherapy for women: Treatment toward equality.* Springfield, IL: Charles C. Thomas.

Unger, R., & Crawford, M. (1996). *Women and gender: A feminist psychology* (2nd ed.). New York: McGraw-Hill.

Worell, J., & Remer, P. (1992). *Feminist perspectives in therapy: An empowerment model for women.* New York: Wiley.

Related Topics

80 ASSESSMENT AND TREATMENT OF LESBIANS, GAY MEN, AND BISEXUALS

Robin A. Buhrke & Douglas C. Haldeman

Nearly 25 years have passed since psychology and psychiatry, in consideration of the scientific evidence, removed homosexuality from the list of mental disorders (Bayer, 1981). Since that time, the database supporting this decision has grown exponentially. We know that lesbian, gay, and bisexual individuals exist everywhere, do not always self-identify, and, because of socially instituted stigma, are more likely to be consumers of psychological services than heterosexuals (Garnets, Hancock, Cochran, Peplau, & Goodchilds, 1991). A study commissioned by the American Psychological Association's (APA's) Committee on Lesbian and Gay Concerns (Garnets et al., 1991) found that 90% of psychologists surveyed had treated a lesbian or gay individual, yet many reported a wide range of prejudicial and unfounded assumptions about lesbians and gay men. Given the lack of attention to this issue in most training programs, guidance for practitioners and trainers is necessary.

In this brief overview, guidelines on the assessment and treatment of lesbian, gay, and bisexual individuals are addressed. Assessment focuses on the construct of sexual orientation and how best to assist those struggling with sexual orientation–related concerns. Our discussion of treatment will focus on concerns that are common among lesbian, gay, and bisexual individuals.

ASSESSMENT GUIDELINES

The assessment of sexual orientation is made challenging by the fluid nature of the construct itself. Early work (e.g., Kinsey, Pomeroy, & Martin, 1948) defined sexual orientation as a continuum, as opposed to dichotomous. Subsequent models (e.g., Coleman, 1987) have included gender-based, social, and affectional variables in the construction of sexual orientation. Regardless of the model, sexual orientation is a complex phenomenon; for some, the behavioral aspects thereof may not be the most significant. That is, one can *identify* as lesbian, gay, or bisexual without ever having engaged in same-sex sexual behavior. Similarly, one can engage in same-sex sexual behavior and not identify as lesbian, gay, or bisexual. Sense of identity, internalized sociocultural expectations, importance of social/political affiliations, and fantasies are some of the variables that need to be examined in order to assist the patient in arriving at a cogent self-perception of sexual ori-

entation. This makes the process of identifying as lesbian, gay, or bisexual laden with both practical and existential considerations.

Competence in serving lesbian, gay, and bisexual patients is measured by the ability to recognize and neutralize antigay bias and to refrain from assuming that normalcy implies heterosexuality. This may be accomplished by familiarizing oneself with the extant literature, as well as by developing a sense of "cultural literacy"—that is, an understanding of what the normative life experiences of lesbians, gay men, and bisexuals may entail. Ultimately, this implies a familiarity with normative developmental, familial, social, and vocational concerns faced by many lesbians, gay men, and bisexuals throughout the life span (D'Augelli & Patterson, 1994). Further, an appreciation for the added burdens of social stigma and the potential for discrimination and violence faced by many lesbians, gay men, and bisexuals is necessary to adequately understand the experiences of these groups. Finally, the clinician may benefit from an examination of personal values around same-gender sexual orientation.

Psychological research has firmly established that same-gender sexual orientation is not, in itself, a sign of poor psychological adjustment, psychopathology, or emotional disturbance (e.g., Gonsiorek, 1991; Reiss, 1980). Lesbians and gay men do not differ from heterosexual women and men on measures of psychological adjustment and self-esteem or in the capacity for decision making, vocational adjustment, or competence in family roles (as parent or spouse). Further, the development of a positive lesbian or gay identity is correlated with better psychological adjustment for lesbians and gay men. Self-identifying as lesbian or gay, accepting this as an aspect of identity, self-disclosing, and feeling accepted by others have been found to be strongly related to psychological adjustment (Bell & Weinberg, 1978; Murphy, 1989). Similarly, a more positive lesbian or gay male identity has been found to be correlated with significantly fewer symptoms of neurotic or social anxiety, higher ego strength, less depression, and higher self-esteem (Hammersmith & Weinberg, 1973; Savin-Williams, 1989). Generally, psychological adjustment appears to be highest among gay men and lesbian women who are committed to their lesbian, gay, or bisexual identity, reject the notion that homosexuality is an illness, are uninterested in changing their homosexuality, and have close and supportive associations with other gay people (Bell & Weinberg, 1978).

This is not meant to encourage clinicians to impose a "pro-gay" agenda, or any agenda at all, upon the confused or questioning patient. Rather, it is the clinician's responsibility to provide a safe, value-neutral environment for exploration, as well as accurate, scientific information about same-gender sexual orientation. The therapeutic task with many lesbian, gay, and bisexual patients is the neutralization of the toxic effects of internalized social opprobrium. This cannot be accomplished if the clinician is unaware of the scientific data regarding sexual orientation, is unacquainted with the lives of well-adjusted, high-functioning lesbians, gay men, and bisexuals, or attempts to work while harboring unexamined antigay prejudices.

Thus, a clinician who bases treatment on antiquated and scientifically unproven theories about the nature of same-gender sexual orientation can do little more than reinforce the societal stigma that causes many lesbian, gay, and bisexual individuals to seek help in the first place. This is particularly true with patients who seek to change their sexual orientation. Davison (1991) views "reparative" or "conversion" therapy as part of the inhospitable social context that causes many distressed lesbians and gay men to seek sexual orientation change. Conversion therapy programs are founded on unproven and biased theories and yield no support to the notion that sexual orientation can be changed, even if it were desirable to do so (Haldeman, 1994). No clinician should attempt to change an individual's sexual orientation, or instruct a homosexually oriented individual in heteroerotic activities, without carefully assessing the history and motives behind such a request and making certain that the patient is well aware of the damaging effects of internalized antigay prejudice and is acquainted with the normative life experiences of lesbians, gay men, and bisexuals.

What, then, should the clinician who is interested in conducting competent assessments with lesbians, gay men, and bisexuals take into consideration? Garnets et al. (1991) identify several themes that reflect exemplary practice:

1. Clinicians recognize that same-gender sexual orientation is not pathological.
2. Clinicians do not automatically attribute a patient's concerns to his or her sexual orientation and are able to recognize that negative attitudes about homosexuality, as well as experiences of rejection, harassment, and discrimination, can cause emotional distress.
3. Clinicians affirm that lesbians and gay men can and do lead productive and fulfilling lives and participate in healthy, long-term relationships, despite the lack of institutional support for them.

These themes, together with the literature on which they are based, form the foundation from which a competent clinical assessment of lesbian, gay, and bisexual individuals can be made. We now turn our attention to treatment.

TREATMENT CONSIDERATIONS

Most often, when lesbians, gay men, and bisexuals come to treatment, they do so to address the same types of issues that their heterosexual counterparts address: depression, anxiety, self-esteem, career concerns, relationship problems, and so on. There are a great deal more similarities between heterosexual patients and lesbian, gay, and bisexual patients than there are differences. However, there are important experiences that are unique for lesbians, gay men, and bisexuals, and these issues may arise in treatment.

Perhaps the major issue facing lesbians, gay men, and bisexuals is that of "coming out." Coming out is the developmental process in which lesbians, gay men, and bisexuals become aware of their sexual orientation (Gonsiorek & Rudolph, 1991). This process occurs over a period of time, ranging anywhere from a few days to years, and may be extended for many bisexuals (Matteson, 1996). Many times, because of being raised in environments that are antigay or stigmatizing, early awareness of same-sex attractions may result in anxiety, shame, fear, and guilt. Patients who are questioning their sexual orientation may present to clinicians with confusion and sometimes even requests for help in ridding themselves of these unpleasant feelings. It is important for clinicians to help patients work through these feelings, identify environmental pressures that contribute to these feelings, and find resolution and affirmation, regardless of the outcome of their explorations.

Coming out also refers to disclosing one's sexual orientation to others. If clinicians are heterosexually biased—that is, if they assume that all patients are heterosexual—they may never know otherwise. If a clinician responds to a male patient's statements about his "partner" with questions about "her," a gay or bisexual man will be less likely to disclose that his partner is male. Keeping his sexual orientation hidden not only reinforces homophobic bias but also establishes a barrier between the patient and the clinician, which undermines the therapeutic process.

Because most lesbians, gay men, and bisexuals are invisible to the heterosexual majority, a number of consequences occur: There is a considerable underestimation of the numbers of lesbians, gay men, and bisexuals; we tend to stereotype based on those who are out and visible or those who come to treatment; and few role models exist for newly coming out lesbians, gay men, and bisexuals. This invisibility often creates marginalization and isolation, which clinicians can avoid perpetuating by educating themselves about normative lesbian, gay, or bisexual life experience and refraining from making heterosexist assumptions about patients' lives.

Marginalization and isolation are often magnified for lesbians, gay men, and bisexuals of color because of their multiple-minority status. An African American lesbian is often forced to choose between her sexual orientation and her ethnicity by overt or covert questions such as "Are you Black or are you gay?" It is important for the clinician to not perpetuate this splitting of patients' identities and to recognize each pa-

tient as an integrated whole. It is also important to recognize that these same patients may not feel at home in the lesbian, gay, and bisexual community because of being Black, while at the same time, because of being gay, they are not accepted in the Black community.

Family issues may raise particular problems for lesbians, gay men, and bisexuals. In many jurisdictions, lesbians, gay men, and bisexuals can lose custody of their children simply because of their sexual orientations. This places an incredible stress on parents in choosing between acknowledging their sexual orientations and risking their families. Without knowing clear boundaries of confidentiality, patients may be reluctant to disclose their sexual orientations to their clinicians for fear that that information may later be used against them in court cases. For lesbians, gay men, and bisexuals who have children, blending families can pose some unique problems —what and how to tell the children, how to deal with schools, and so on. For those who want children but don't have them, creating a family is more difficult, whether by natural or adoptive means.

Additionally, it is important to be sensitive to the potential for internalized reactions to prejudice, discrimination, and violence in lesbian, gay, and bisexual clients. In most jurisdictions, it is legal to deny housing, employment, and custody of children solely on the basis of sexual orientation. This reality places a high level of stress on many lesbians, gay men, and bisexuals. Falco (1996) presents eight stressors and strengths that are common among lesbian and bisexual women, which may be generalized to gay men as well. Clinicians should be mindful of the level of stress this lack of protection may place on many lesbians, gay men, and bisexuals.

• *Disclosure choices are continual:* Coming out or disclosing one's sexual orientation is not a onetime occurrence. It is a lifelong process, with decisions to be made about how much to tell and to whom with each new person met. And each decision to disclose has the potential to be met with antipathy and rejection.

- *Nondisclosure generalizes to other areas:* Most lesbians, gay men, and bisexuals do not disclose to everyone they meet. The process of hiding one aspect of oneself may generalize to other areas, and self-esteem may suffer as a result of interpreting "hidden" aspects as "bad."
- *Lack of support:* The absence of social support for and negative cultural attitudes about lesbians, gay men, and bisexuals can effect one's sense of self, as well as the stability of relationships. Bisexuals may be particularly prone to marginalization, since they are not often accepted in either the heterosexual or the lesbian and gay communities.
- *Absence of role models and cultural history:* Although lesbians, gay men, and bisexuals have a rich culture and history, most of it is invisible. As a result, many mistakenly believe that they are "the only one."
- *Internalized homophobia:* Some lesbians, gay men, and bisexuals have internalized the negative messages about homosexuality from their culture, and they, too, believe that heterosexuality is preferred. This can create a great deal of conflict and anguish for the patient.
- *Identity development:* The process of establishing a lesbian, gay, or bisexual identity is complex and complicated. Although few individuals march through the stages of development in a lockstep manner, the models can be useful for clinicians in understanding their patients and in formulating appropriate interventions.
- *Androgyny and ego strength:* In order to recognize and accept their same-sex attractions, lesbians, gay men, and bisexuals must deviate from social norms. This calls for a certain amount of ego strength. Further, lesbians and gay men tend to have a greater capacity for both feminine and masculine traits, which is generally associated with better psychological health (Falco, 1991).
- *Gender socialization and its impact on relationships:* Same-sex relationships are, by their very nature, composed of two people with similar gender socialization histories. While this may serve as a source of commonality and connection, it can also create

some difficulties. For example, as a result of their female socialization, both women in a lesbian or bisexual relationship may be sexually unaggressive and reluctant to initiate intimate contact.

The life experiences of lesbian, gay, and bisexual individuals presenting for psychotherapy are tremendously varied. Competent clinical practice with these groups does not require one to be lesbian, gay, or bisexual. Rather, it is based on the ability to understand the lesbian, gay, or bisexual individual in his or her own frame of reference. This means approaching treatment with a nonstigmatizing view of sexual orientation and avoiding a heterocentric model for intervening. These basic principles enable the lesbian, gay, or bisexual individual to grow in a therapeutic environment free of the stigma that is so widespread in the sociocultural environment.

References & Readings

Bayer, R. (1981). *Homosexuality and American psychiatry: The politics of diagnosis.* Princeton, NJ: Princeton University Press.

Bell, A. P., & Weinberg, M. S. (1978). *Homosexualities: A study of diversity among men and women.* Bloomington: Indiana University Press.

Cabaj, R. P., & Stein, T. S. (Eds.) (1996). *Textbook of homosexuality and mental health.* Washington, DC: American Psychiatric Association.

Coleman, E. (1987). The assessment of sexual orientation. *Journal of Homosexuality, 14,* 9–24.

D'Augelli, A. R., & Patterson, C. J. (1995). *Lesbian, gay, and bisexual identities over the lifespan.* New York: Oxford University Press.

Davison, G. (1991). Constructionism and morality in therapy for homosexuality. In J. Gonsiorek & J. Weinrich (Eds.), *Homosexuality: Research implications for public policy* (pp. 137–148). Newbury Park, CA: Sage.

Falco, K. L. (1991). *Psychotherapy with lesbian clients.* New York: Brunner/Mazel.

Falco, K. L. (1996). Psychotherapy with women who love women. In R. P. Cabaj & T. Stein (Eds.), *Textbook of homosexuality and mental health* (pp. 397–412). Washington, DC: American Psychiatric Association.

Garnets, L., Hancock, K., Cochran, S., Peplau, L., & Goodchilds, J. (1991). Issues in psychotherapy with lesbians and gay men: A survey of psychologists. *American Psychologist, 46,* 964–972.

Garnets, L. D., & Kimmel, D. C. (Eds.) (1993). *Psychological perspectives on lesbian and gay male experiences.* New York: Columbia University Press.

Gonsiorek, J. D. (1982). *Homosexuality and psychotherapy: A practitioner's handbook of affirmative models.* New York: Haworth.

Gonsiorek, J. (1991). The empirical basis for the demise of the illness model of homosexuality. In J. Gonsiorek & J. Weinrich (Eds.), *Homosexuality: Research issues for public policy* (pp. 115–136). Newbury Park, CA: Sage.

Gonsiorek, J. D., & Rudolph, J. R. (1991). Homosexual identity: Coming out and other developmental events. In J. D. Gonsiorek & J. D. Weinrich (Eds.), *Homosexuality: Research implications for public policy* (pp. 161–176). Newbury Park, CA: Sage.

Gonsiorek, J. D., & Weinrich, J. D. (Eds.) (1991). *Homosexuality: Research implications for public policy.* Newbury Park, CA: Sage.

Haldeman, D. C. (1994). The practice and ethics of sexual orientation conversion therapy. *Journal of Consulting and Clinical Psychology, 62,* 221–227.

Hammersmith, S. K., & Weinberg, M. S. (1973). Homosexual identity: Commitment, adjustments, and significant others. *Sociometry, 36,* 56–78.

Kinsey, A. C., Pomeroy, W. B., & Martin, C. E. (1948). *Sexual behavior in the human male.* Philadelphia: Saunders.

Matteson, D. R. (1996). Psychotherapy with bisexual individuals. In R. P. Cabaj & T. Stein (Eds.), *Textbook of homosexuality and mental health* (pp. 433–450). Washington, DC: American Psychiatric Association.

Murphy, B. (1989). Lesbian couples and their parents: The effects of perceived parental attitudes on the couple. *Journal of Counseling and Development, 68,* 46–51.

Reiss, B. F. (1980). Psychological tests in homosexuality. In J. Marmor (Ed.), *Homosexual behavior: A modern reappraisal* (pp. 296–311). New York: Basic Books.

Savin-Williams, R. C. (1989). Coming out to parents and self-esteem among gay and lesbian youth. *Journal of Homosexuality, 13,* 101–109.

Weinberg, M. S., & Williams, C. J. (1974). *Male homosexuals: Their problems and adaptations.* New York: Oxford University Press.

Related Topics

Chapter 72, "Assessing and Treating Normative Male Alexithymia"
Chapter 79, "Guidelines for Treating Women in Psychotherapy"

81 PSYCHOTHERAPY WITH OLDER ADULTS

Margaret Gatz & Bob G. Knight

1. *Case formulation:* When a therapist is seeing an older adult for treatment, an initial task is to create a picture of the older adult, including the individual's strengths and ways of functioning in the world, as well as the nature of the problem that has brought the person to treatment. This picture can be conceptualized in any of several ways: as building a model of the person, as describing the individual's characteristic defense mechanisms, or as identifying preferred coping styles.

2. *Cohort and culture:* In understanding an older adult client, it may be helpful to apply concepts from the study of cultural differences. The identity of an older adult will inevitably reflect the historical time during which he or she has matured. Working with a person who matured in a different time is similar in many ways to working with a client who matured in a different cultural context; the therapist must be careful about cohort- or culture-bound assumptions, word use, and values. Cohorts and cultures can also interact in the sense that earlier-born older adults may have a specific and strong sense of ethnic identity with regard to ethnicities that are no longer identified as separate or disadvantaged (e.g., Irish or Italian).

3. *Epidemiology of disorder:* Other than the dementias, prevalence of psychological disorders is lower in older adults than in adults of other ages. This statement flies in the face of stereotypes of old age as inevitably depressing or anxiety provoking. In fact, most older adults seem to have developed sufficient psychological resilience that they do not develop new disorders in response to the transitions and life stressors that accompany aging. At the same time, depression and other disorders may be quite high in older adults with comorbid medical disorders, in both inpatient and outpatient medical care settings, and among those who are living in nursing homes. (Review chapters concerning various diagnostic entities and the influence of physical disease and medication can be found in Carstensen, Edelstein, & Dornbrand, 1996.)

4. *Differential diagnosis:* In older adults who are seen by a mental health professional, multiple problems typically coexist; these may include emotional distress, cognitive impairment, chronic physical conditions, and changes in social network or environmental context. The classical differential diagnostic distinction is between depression and dementia (LaRue, 1992); indeed, one frequent assessment question concerns the explanation for perceived changes in memory. A more encompassing way to consider differential diagnosis is through a decision tree: first, whether the pattern of functioning reflects normal aging versus some pathological process; second, what combination of emotional distress versus neuropathological changes (e.g., Alzheimer's disease, Parkinson's disease) is suggested; and third, what aspects of the problem are reversible. Sometimes following a case over time is the most certain way of distinguishing among assessment hypotheses.

5. *Assessment:* Psychological assessment is often complex in older adults and often requires a working knowledge of neuropsychological assessment, as well as the use of personality and emotional assessment techniques with appropriate age norms. Simple screening devices, such as mental status examinations and brief scales to measure depression and anxiety, can be helpful in day-to-day practice, if their limitations are understood. (Review chapters about assessing dementia and depression, as well as a directory of instruments and norms, can be found in Storandt & VandenBos, 1994. See also Lawton & Teresi, 1994, for a compendium of chapters about assessment issues.)

6. *Age of onset:* Early in the assessment, a key question to evaluate is whether the current problem is a new situation altogether or a continuation, recurrence, or exacerbation of a previous problem. This consideration influences both etiologic inferences and choices about treatment (Gatz, Kasl-Godley, & Karel, 1996).

7. *Emergencies:* Older adults often seemingly wait to see a mental health professional until there is some emergency, whether financial, psychiatric, or physical. In such instances, the therapist must first resolve the emergency and then deal with the psychological circumstances (Sherman, 1981).

8. *Suicide:* Older adults, especially older white males, are the age-group at highest risk for suicide (Conwell, 1994). This is due, in part, to the fact that the ratio of suicide attempts to suicide completions is much lower among older adults. Older adults with depression or substance abuse and those with dementing illnesses who are aware of their cognitive impairment and depressed about it should be assessed for suicide risk. Older clients can, and do, make distinctions among not wanting to live, wanting to die, and wanting to kill themselves. While society debates the legality of rational suicide and assisted suicide, psychologists must be alert to those whose suicidal impulses are motivated by psychological distress.

9. *Access:* The majority of older adults who meet diagnostic criteria for a mental disorder are not seen by any mental health professional. For this reason, the role of the psychologist includes home visits, medical hospital and nursing home consultation, outreach to senior centers, and cooperation with primary care physicians (Smyer, 1993).

10. *Family:* The family constitutes the primary social context of older adults. If an older adult is declining physically or cognitively, his or her health-related dependencies and needs for assistance have radiating effects on the family. Consequently, the family must be considered in the treatment plan, while at the same time respecting the confidentiality of the patient.

11. *Spectrum of interventions:* As different theoretical approaches to psychotherapy have emerged, each has been applied to older adults (e.g., psychoanalysis, behavior modification, community mental health consultation, and cognitive therapy). In addition, efforts have been made to use the knowledge base from research about developmental processes in later life in order to inform intervention. Research has shown that older adults respond well to a variety of forms of psychotherapy. Cognitive-behavioral, brief psychodynamic, and interpersonal therapies have shown utility in the treatment of depression, anxiety, and sleep disturbance, as have 12-step programs with older alcohol abusers. Cognitive training techniques, behavior modification strategies, and environmental modifications have relevance for improving functional abilities in cognitively impaired older adults. Finally, use of reminiscence or life review is common with older adults, both as an element of other therapies and as a separate, special technique. (The empirical evidence is summarized in Gatz et al., in press. Overview chapters about implementing this array of treatments may be found in Zarit & Knight, 1996, whereas Niederehe, 1994, focuses on depression.)

12. *Relationship issues:* From the begin-

ning of psychotherapeutic work with older adults, therapists have noted the potential for differences in the therapeutic relationship when the client is older than the therapist. Older clients confront the therapist with aging issues in an "off time" way; that is, the therapist confronts reactions to aging, illness, disability, and death before these issues have arisen in the therapist's own life. Older clients may remind the therapist of older relatives and elicit countertransferential reactions related to parents, grandparents, or others (Knight, 1996). Therapists may share social stereotypes about the elderly and expect their older clients to be boring, unattractive, or asexual. Biases may also influence diagnosis; therapists are inclined to interpret the same symptoms as reflecting brain disorder in an older person but depression in a younger client.

13. *Interface with medical care system:* Older adults with significant mental health problems are most often seen by various nonspecialists, such as primary care physicians. Psychologists who see older adults must be prepared to work in interdisciplinary settings and to cooperate with other professionals. Moreover, they must inform themselves about the reimbursement system and become advocates for making the system responsive to their clients (Koenig, George, & Schneider, 1994).

14. *When to refer to a specialist or to seek more training in clinical geropsychology:* When older clients have problems similar to younger clients and there is no reason to suspect a dementing illness, psychotherapy with older adults is very similar to that with younger adults. As assessment issues become more complex and more subtle, such as needing to disentangle multiple possible causes of symptoms, more specialized knowledge is needed. Practitioners working in an age-segregated environment (e.g., nursing homes) or becoming more specialized in treating older adults need more training in clinical geropsychology. Continuing education in clinical geropsychology can often be found through the American Psychological Association, sponsored by Section II (clinical geropsychology) of Division 12 (clinical psychology) or by Division 20 (adult development and aging); through state and local psychologi-

cal associations; and through some universities and medical centers, especially those with Alzheimer's disease research centers.

References & Readings

Carstensen, L. L., Edelstein, B. A., & Dornbrand, L. (Eds.) (1996). *The practical handbook of clinical gerontology*. Thousand Oaks, CA: Sage.

Conwell, Y. (1994). Suicide in elderly patients. In L. S. Schneider, C. F. Reynolds III, B. D. Lebowitz, & A. J. Friedhoff (Eds.), *Diagnosis and treatment of depression in late life: Results of the NIH Consensus Development Conference* (pp. 397–418). Washington, DC: American Psychiatric Press.

Gatz, M., Fiske, A., Fox, L. S., Kaskie, B., Kasl-Godley, J. E., McCallum, T. J., & Wetherell, J. L. (in press). Empirically-validated psychological treatments for older adults. *Journal of Mental Health and Aging*.

Gatz, M., Kasl-Godley, J. E., & Karel, M. J. (1996). Aging and mental disorders. In J. E. Birren & K. W. Schaie (Eds.), *Handbook of the psychology of aging* (4th ed., pp. 367–382). San Diego, CA: Academic Press.

Knight, B. G. (1996). *Psychotherapy with older adults* (2nd ed.). Thousand Oaks, CA: Sage.

Koenig, H. G., George, L. K., & Schneider, R. (1994). Mental health care for older adults in the year 2020: A dangerous and avoided topic. *Gerontologist, 34*, 674–679.

LaRue, A. (1992). *Aging and neuropsychological assessment*. New York: Plenum Press.

Lawton, M. P., & Teresi, J. A. (Eds.) (1994). *Annual review of gerontology and geriatrics: Focus on assessment techniques*. New York: Springer.

Niederehe, G. T. (1994). Psychosocial therapies with depressed older adults. In L. S. Schneider, C. F. Reynolds III, B. D. Lebowitz, & A. J. Friedhoff (Eds.), *Diagnosis and treatment of depression in late life: Results of the NIH Consensus Development Conference* (pp. 293–315). Washington, DC: American Psychiatric Press.

Sherman, E. (1981). *Counseling the aging*. New York: Free Press.

Smyer, M. A. (Ed.) (1993). *Mental health and aging*. New York: Springer.

Storandt, M. A., & VandenBos, G. R. (Eds.) (1994). *Neuropsychological assessment of dementia and depression in older adults: A clinician's guide*. Washington, DC: American Psychological Association.

Zarit, S. H., & Knight, B. G. (Eds.) (1996). *A guide to psychotherapy and aging: Effective clinical interventions in a life-stage context*. Washington, DC: American Psychological Association.

Related Topics

82   REFUSAL SKILLS TRAINING

Robert Henley Woody & Jennifer Kate Henley Woody

Nancy Reagan's assertion to "just say no!" became a clarion call, particularly against substance abuse, in the 1980s. While an overly simple idea, it served as an impetus for the development of professional psychological programs that have gained marked acceptance in the 1990s.

Refusal Skills Training (RST) aims to counteract the occurrence and maintenance of highly damaging behavior, such as tobacco smoking, substance abuse, and risky sexual activity. Predicated primarily on learning theory, RST seeks to educate the client about maladaptive approach behaviors and provide a set of personally implemented resistance skills. Commonly, the intervention is tailored to the client's personal weakness or behavior problems. An RST program can be provided on an individual or group basis (the latter seems to be the most popular format and allows peer reinforcers). While especially useful as proaction (i.e., prevention), RST can be used as reaction (i.e., remediation).

FORMS AND EXAMPLES OF
RST PROGRAMS

RST emphasizes two forms of influence: informational influence and normative influence. *Informational influence* is directed at the pressures or reinforcers experienced by the client in everyday life, such as advertisements of products and mass media depictions of behaviors that could reinforce unhealthy outcomes. This is clearly an educational approach, and it requires astute teaching methods and highly relevant informational materials. *Normative influence* is directed at the pressures or reinforcers that the client encounters, especially those emitted by other persons such as peers.

The modality for RST deserves consideration. Generally, the training programs seem to rely on informational influence disseminated by a pamphlet or other material, perhaps supplemented with brief individual or group counseling. The normative influence is offered through behavioral rehearsal or modeling techniques (either in vivo or by videotape). A variety of studies indicate that electronic media, especially those involving video stimuli, can enhance learning (Herrmann & McWhirter, 1997). While there are innumerable variables that would have to be considered in the unique program, it would appear that normative influence may be the most effective

for behavior change (Poler, Warzak, & Woody, 1997).

RST employs multiple interventions that may vary in the psychological processes that are emphasized. Goldstein, Reagles, and Amann (1990) suggest six types of interventions: cognitive, environmental, affective/interpersonal, therapeutic, school alternative, and social learning. While all of these approaches could be implemented proactively (i.e., before the development of a problem), the therapeutic and school alternative approaches are most often reactive (i.e., after the problem has occurred).

Cognitive interventions promote informational influence but can also involve normative influence. Using a variety of techniques and formats, the cognitive approach provides information that will presumably enable the client/student to make informed decisions (e.g., not to use drugs). Similarly, some strategies have sought cognitive change through aversive information, say, about detrimental substances or behaviors. Fear-arousing and punishment tactics have proved ineffective in altering high-risk behavior; moreover, Hansen et al. (1988) found that informational programs, such as explaining how a drug or alcoholic substance works or what it looks like, might actually arouse curiosity or promote experimentation. The latter result might occur especially if the information is presented in, say, a peer context and the positive message is subverted by adverse normative influence.

Environmental interventions are those that target the context in which the high-risk behavior takes place. For example, since the school is a critical site in a young person's life and has legal authority to restrict behavior, schools have implemented drug intervention strategies, such as strict policies, detection methods, and prevention/intervention organizations (Goldstein et al., 1990). This approach combines the possibility of informative and normative influence.

Affective/interpersonal interventions, which emphasize information and instruction, target the student's self-concept, self-acceptance, and decision-making processes. Again, research on these strategies, such as values clarification, has shown little assured effect on behavioral change (Goodstat & Sheppard, 1983). Although informative influence dominates, a group program or the descriptions in the information can draw upon normative influence.

Therapeutic interventions involve the student entering into individual or group counseling. The therapeutic focus is on the high-risk behavior or maladaptive behavior. Beyond any change that might occur from insight (e.g., improved definition of personal needs or development of coping abilities), the interpersonal relationships (e.g., with the therapist or other group members) introduce normative influence. Certainly, counseling provided in a group context creates the possibility of powerful normative influence.

School alternative interventions, like the therapeutic approach, tend to be employed when a behavioral problem already exists. With the former, the student enters into individual or group counseling, with a focus on the high-risk behavior or maladaptive behavior. With the latter, the student with an incorrigible behavior pattern (including, e.g., substance abuse and/or criminal conduct) is placed in an environment that includes treatment (e.g., an alternative school or group residence). The alternative approach, if managed properly, makes normative influence possible; if managed poorly, adverse modeling can occur.

Social learning interventions most closely parallel the normative influence approach, although informative influence occurs as well. This strategy commonly incorporates observational learning, behavioral rehearsal, and reinforcement contingencies. The majority of social skill and refusal skill curricula fall under this rubric. Most often, these programs rely on providing information, developing social and self-regulatory skills, skill enhancement through guided practice (e.g., modeling appropriate skills, student role playing/behavioral rehearsal), and social support for behavioral change (e.g., providing peer/adult feedback, discussion, and real-world practice/reinforcement). A social learning approach can function in a preventive as well as a corrective manner. Further, behavioral rehearsal allows students to practice these skills in a socially valid context (e.g., with their peers, in a school setting).

EMPIRICAL RESEARCH ON RST PROGRAMS

Increasingly, research has demonstrated the effectiveness of RST that employs social learning/normative approaches (Goldstein, 1981, 1988; Katz, Robisch, & Telch, 1989; Reardon, Sussman, & Flay, 1989; Schinke & Blythe, 1982; Schinke & Gilchrist, 1984). The efficacy of a given RST program will depend, in part, on the age and gender of the clients (e.g., McQuillen, Higginbotham, & Cummings, 1984; Hops et al., 1986). Clearly, additional research is needed to evaluate the effectiveness of RST with lower-income and minority populations and with consideration for age and gender.

One of the primary attractions of RST is that its programs can be clearly defined and structured. When considering the status of any therapeutic intervention, including RST, efficacy and effectiveness should be distinguished; a differentiation should be made between "the efficacy study, in which patients are randomly assigned to different conditions and in which considerable control is often exerted over the nature and duration of the treatment provided," and "the effectiveness study, in which observations are made, but patients are free to pursue whatever type of treatment they prefer (subject to market forces), and the nature of the treatment is left uncontrolled" (Hollon, 1996, p. 1025).

The research results for RST are, for the most part, efficacy studies. Despite an effort to carefully structure the intervention and the use of a particular educationally oriented program that can be defined, the research seldom, if ever, controls and measures the presence or absence (or degree of influence from) the interpersonal conditions that could facilitate learning and behavioral change for the client. Consequently, the effects of the interpersonal conditions remain unmeasured and likely contaminate the efficacy attributed to RST. In addition, the various RST programs contain unique contents, and "making comparison across programs is inherently difficult" (Herrmann & McWhirter, 1997, p. 177).

Since RST programs are finding ready reception in schools, the use of peers as models or leaders, either in vivo or by video recordings, is common. As would be expected, the results have been positive, such as enhancing the efforts of teachers or counselors (Perry, 1989).

From their review of the research, Herrmann and McWhirter (1997) conclude that RST (which they refer to as Refusal and Resistance Skills, or RRS) programs defy generalization: "In other words, neither general endorsements nor general criticisms of RRS programs are appropriate because a number of different mediating factors (including target behaviors and process variables) interact to determine the efficacy of different programs. Moreover, the quality of program delivery plays an important role in determining overall program effectiveness" (p. 184). They also believe that the research supports early intervention (e.g., perhaps as young as the first grade and certainly by the fourth grade); caution that it remains unproved that refusal and resistance skills will actually be implemented behaviorally; and endorse a comprehensive prevention curriculum and use of peer facilitation.

Certainly, it is known that most therapeutic interventions, especially those based on promoting insight, do not modify maladaptive behavioral problems, such as tobacco smoking, substance abuse, and risky sexual activity. Therefore, there is nothing to lose and potentially much to gain from capitalizing on the proven informational and normative influences that can be included in behaviorally based RST programs. If supplemented with nurturance, empathy, and other facilitative conditions, RST programs, particularly in a peer-group context, most likely will lead to cognitive restructuring and behavioral shaping and become the intervention of choice for smoking, alcohol and substance abuse, delinquency, gang behavior, and risky sexual activity.

Anticipating Resistance

Different RST groups may create specific challenges. In regard to high-risk behavior, there is a tendency for youth to find nonrefusal conduct to be highly rewarding, both intrinsically (especially if a mental identification with a role model occurs) and extrinsically (especially if peer reinforcement occurs). Goldstein et al. (1990) found one critical obstacle to RST effectiveness in relation to drug refusal: "Resistance to participate . . . or to learn and use the refusal skills may occur when the youths' involvement in drug use is highly rewarding relative to its financial, interpersonal, or physiological costs" (p. 93). This concern is applicable to any high-risk behavior, such as sexual or criminal activity. To counteract the problem of resistance, Goldstein et al. (1990) suggest the systematic use of intrinsic/extrinsic rewards and the use of a curriculum that maximizes the relevance of the training in the real world.

Promoting Maintenance

Possibly the most important criterion for the success of RST programs is maintenance. The question becomes: How can professionals ensure that a student who masters a skill within the therapeutic context will, in fact, use the skill in real-world experiences? Skill generalization should be addressed in any RST program. Transfer-enhancing procedures may include such strategies as overlearning, stimulus variability, and mediated generalization (e.g., self-recording, self-reinforcement). Maintenance-enhancing strategies incorporate the use of prompt fading, reinforcement fading/withdrawal, booster sessions, and natural reinforcers (Goldstein et al., 1990).

Clarifying the Intervention

Each RST program has an indiosyncratic theoretical basis, which means that even if the intervention strategies appear to be the same or comparable, the underlying nuances may be quite different and, thus, the effects are like the proverbial "apples and oranges." For example, it would seem that the majority of RST programs rely, to varying degrees, on learning theory, yet there is also use of interpersonal relationships (which may or may not actually adhere to a reinforcement paradigm). Analysis of the RST programs reveals both behavioral modification and cognitive restructuring techniques, as evidenced by "(1) an emphasis on the present and near future; (2) a problem-solving orientation that focuses on changing cognitions and/or overt behavior; and (3) attention to conscious rather than to unconscious determinants of behavior" (Robertson & Woody, 1997, p. 178). Thus, the practitioner should carefully delineate the change mechanisms for the purposes of practice improvement and clinical research.

GUIDELINES FOR PRACTICE

There is a solid behavioral science rationale for implementing RST programs, especially for prevention; other behavioral modification approaches may be as good as or better than RST for changing existing maladaptive behaviors. Before offering an RST program, the practitioner should, of course, be mindful of previous statements regarding anticipating resistance, promoting maintenance, and clarifying the interventions. The following 10 guidelines provide a step-by-step approach.

1. Determine the characteristics of the clients/students. While it is feasible to establish a given RST program and then select clients/students who are seemingly compatible, it is preferable to first evaluate generally the pool of potential clients/students. Knowing the characteristics of possible recipients of RST services allows one to tailor the program to their needs.
2. Delineate and define the behavior that is to be targeted (e.g., tobacco smoking, substance abuse, or risky sexual activity), and establish reinforcement contingencies that rely on information and/or normative influence. These decisions should be stated in writing and critiqued by at least one other professional source.
3. Determine whether the format will be individual or group. Given the importance of peer interactions, generally a group format should be considered before deciding on an individual format. In keeping with research on group dynamics, five to eight students is appropriate to facilitate peer interactions.
4. If using a group format, structure for heterogeneity of skill proficiency. Clients/students with more proficient refusal skills provide supportive modeling and reinforcement for the group members with less proficient refusal skills.
5. Communication of information should be tailored to the developmental, emotional, and cognitive levels of the clients/students. Consideration should be given to how maturation, existing emotional and/or behavioral problems, and intellectual limits restrict or impact on general curriculum content and the specific information that is delivered. Stated simply, the content and delivery style should be understandable to the clients/students.
6. Determine and adhere strictly to a behavior management plan. In accord with the behaviors that were delineated and defined, introduce, monitor, and maintain rules. A behavior/rule contract signed by each client/student is advisable (e.g., required attendance, completing homework assignments). Relying on the behavior management plan allows individual and group behaviors to be reinforced systematically. At least initially, natural/tangible reinforcers are needed. The plan should state the number of sessions that will be provided.
7. From the initial session and throughout the first phase particularly, emphasis should be placed on establishing client/student rapport with the professional and motivation to benefit from the RST program. Empathic understanding and other facilitative conditions should preface any information that might be perceived as confrontive by the clients/students; these qualities should continue throughout the RST program. Generally, each client/student should be comfortable with the professional and the other clients/students before being challenged by an RST task. The client/student who is insecure, shy, or eas-

ily threatened or who lacks expressive skills may merit special attention, within or outside the group.

8. Group dynamics should be monitored and managed. If a group format is used, special attention should be given to promoting cohesion. Care should be taken to avoid interpersonal conflicts that cannot be used therapeutically, as well as unnecessary dissonance and cleavage. Gamelike strategies may be useful for reinforcing critical dynamics in the group.

9. Techniques for maintaining the effects of the RST program outside the sessions should be applied. It is often helpful to use homework assignments, self-monitoring, journal writing, or booster sessions (in person or by telephone with, say, a designated "buddy" from the same program or with the professional). Family and social contacts should be enlisted to help the clients/students progress in real-life situations. The results of these external efforts or events should be discussed in the sessions.

10. When an RST program is completed, make a thoughtful evaluation of the successes and failures, individually and at the group level. By understanding the effects of an RST program, professionals will potentially design more effective future offerings.

References & Readings

Goldstein, A. P. (1981). *Psychological skill training.* Elmsford, NY: Pergamon Press.

Goldstein, A. P. (1988). *The Prepare Curriculum: Teaching prosocial skill competencies.* Champaign, IL: Research Press.

Goldstein, A. P., Reagles, K. W., & Amann, L. L. (1990). *Refusal skills: Preventing drug use in adolescents.* Champaign, IL: Research Press.

Goodstat, M., & Sheppard, M. (1983). Three approaches to alcohol education. *Journal of Studies on Alcohol, 44,* 362–380.

Hansen, W. B., Graham, J. W., Wolkenstein, B. H., Lundy, B. Z., Pearson, J., Flay, B. R., & Johnson, C. A. (1988). Differential impact of three alcohol prevention curricula on hypothesized mediating variables. *Journal of Drug Education, 18,* 143–153.

Herrmann, D. S., & McWhirter, J. J. (1997). Refusal and resistance skills for children and adolescents: A selected review. *Journal of Counseling and Development, 75,* 177-187.

Hollon, S. D. (1996). The efficacy and effectiveness of psychotherapy relative to medications. *American Psychologist, 51,* 1025–1030.

Hops, H., Weissman, W., Biglan, A., Thompson, R., Faller, C., & Severson, H. H. (1986). A taped situation test of cigarette refusal skill among adolescents. *Behavioral Assessment, 8,* 145–154.

Katz, R. C., Robisch, C. M., & Telch, M. J. (1989). Acquisition of smoking refusal skills in junior high school students. *Addictive Behaviors, 14,* 201–204.

McQuillen, J. S., Higginbotham, D. C., & Cummings, M. C. (1984). Compliance-resisting behaviors: The effects of age, agent, and types of requests. In R. N. Bostrom (Ed.), *Communication yearbook 9* (pp. 747–762). Beverly Hills, CA: Sage.

Perry, C. L. (1989). Prevention of alcohol use and abuse in adolescence: Teacher- vs. peer-led intervention. *Crisis, 10,* 52–61.

Poler, M., Warzak, W. J., & Woody, R. H. (1997). *Acceptability of refusal skills training modalities: A comparison of adolescents' and professionals' preferences.* Unpublished manuscript, University of Nebraska Medical Center.

Reardon, K. K., Sussman, S., & Flay, B. R. (1989). Are we marketing the right message: Can kids "just say no" to smoking? *Communication Monographs, 56,* 307–324.

Robertson, M. H., & Woody, R. H. (1997). *Theories and methods for practice of clinical psychology.* Madison, CT: International Universities Press.

Schinke, S. P., & Blythe, B. (1982). Cognitive-behavioral prevention of children's smoking. *Child Behavior Therapy, 3,* 25–42.

Schinke, S. P., & Gilchrist, L. D. (1984). *Life skills counseling with adolescents.* Baltimore: University Park Press.

Related Topics

Chapter 68, "Motivational Interviewing"

Chapter 95, "Sexual Feelings, Actions, and Dilemmas in Psychotherapy"

83 APSAC STUDY GUIDES

Jeannie Baker & Sam S. Hill III

The American Professional Society on the Abuse of Children (APSAC) is the nation's largest interdisciplinary professional society for those working in the field of child abuse and neglect. The APSAC's mission is to improve society's response to the abuse and neglect of its children by promoting effective interdisciplinary approaches to the identification, intervention, treatment, and prevention of child maltreatment. The APSAC currently has three study guides available: Volume 1, *Assessment of Sexual Offenders Against Children* (Quinsey & Lalumiere, 1996); Volume 2, *Evaluating Children Suspected of Having Been Sexually Abused* (Faller, 1996); and Volume 3, *Medical Evaluation of Physically and Sexually Abused Children* (Jenny, 1996). These study guides are intended to provide an outline of information in specific aspects of child maltreatment and to direct the professional to available research material. The content of these study guides is summarized in the following pages.

ASSESSMENT OF SEXUAL
OFFENDERS AGAINST CHILDREN

The APSAC Study Guide, Volume 1, *Assessment of Sexual Offenders Against Children* (Quinsey & Laluminere, 1996), is written for health care professionals involved in the assessment of child molesters. It is not intended to be a "how-to" manual but rather an outline of the key elements that constitute assessment of child molesters. This guide also provides direction to available research in this area.

- *Defining the sexual offender:* Child molestation is defined as a common, transcultural, historical occurrence. There are key differences between forensic assessment and nonforensic clinical assessment. An explanation for offender behavior must be theorized.
- *Characteristics of sexual offenders against children:* Certain characteristics are peculiar to child molesters. Level of social competence and social skills is one variable. Studies have been made of sexual offenders' cognitive beliefs and patterns. Sexual preferences of child molesters are a function of sexual response patterns and sexual history. There is a relationship between personality test results and psychopathology. Differences in hormone and brain dysfunction in child molesters are suggested. Taxonomic research has been conducted. Situational determinants can be predictors.
- *Implications for practice:* Assessment utilizing the clinical interview, psychological testing, phallometric assessment, and polygraph tests is necessary.
- *Appraising risk:* Recidivism risk appraisal is necessary.
- *Treatment planning:* Treatability and treatment needs should be determined.
- *Ethical issues:* The referral source and client should be determined and confidentiality amid reporting mandates should be maintained according to professional and legal guidelines.
- *The report:* Conflicts of interest are possible in making a report. Reports should provide the necessary information.

- *Recommended assessment instruments:* The standard assessment battery assesses the risk of recidivism, treatment needs, and supervision needs. The battery also includes (when relevant) measures of personality, psychopathology, social skills, and brain and hormonal dysfunction.

EVALUATING CHILDREN SUSPECTED OF HAVING BEEN SEXUALLY ABUSED

The APSAC Study Guide, Volume 2, *Evaluating Children Suspected of Having Been Sexually Abused* (Faller, 1996), is written to familiarize the health care professional with the basics of (alleged) child sexual abuse assessment. The study guide also provides the reader with information necessary to evaluate current research, conduct a comprehensive evaluation, and defend his or her findings.

- *Models for evaluating child sexual abuse:* The most widely used and accepted model for determining an allegation of sexual abuse is the Child Interview model. Less widely used for evaluating sexual abuse allegations is the Parent-Child Interaction Model. The Comprehensive Evaluation Model is best suited for assessment of allegations of intrafamilial sexual abuse, where complexity and multiple victims/offenders may be present.
- *Interviewer objectivity and allegations of sexual abuse:* Gender, profession, and age differences, as well as other factors, affect evaluation objectivity. Research on false allegations by children is discussed.
- *Number of child interviews:* Repetition of allegations to multiple professionals increases the risk of contamination of disclosure and trauma to the child. There are advantages and disadvantages of both too few and too many interviews by a single professional. Children have individual differences in disclosing sexual victimization. Situational and logistical factors affect the interview.
- *Documentation:* Videotaping has both advantages and disadvantages. The specifics of

videotaping procedure should be determined. It is necessary to obtain informed consent of the child, including familiarization with the equipment and professionals involved. The child's overall functioning over and above the sexual abuse can be assessed through audio/visual documentation.
- *Standardized tests:* Psychological testing can be used in differentiating the sexually abused child. Behavior checklists can be utilized for symptomology in the victim by third-party report. Projective tests can elicit information related to the victim's sexual experience.
- *Questioning techniques:* Avoid the use of leading questions (i.e., yes or no questions or multiple choice), as well as coercive techniques. Use open-ended questions instead, primarily, or in combination with free narrative.
- *Media for interviewing children:* Anatomical dolls can be used to elicit sexualized doll play. Sexually abused children are more likely to engage in sexual behavior with anatomical dolls than are nonabused children. In general, there is no significant difference between the use of anatomical versus nonanatomical dolls as "props" to elicit responses from sexually abused children. It is preferable that experienced professionals use anatomical dolls. Opinions vary as to how to use anatomical dolls. In general, take cues from the child and vary techniques circumstantially. Anatomical drawings can be used as a substitute for, or prelude to, anatomical dolls. Anatomical drawings are not as controversial as anatomical dolls and can become a permanent part of case record.
- *Special considerations for cases involving very young children:* Chronological age can differ from developmental age. It is necessary to rely on caregiver report. Observation of alleged abuser-child interaction is an alternative. Multiple interviews are necessary. Play themes should be assessed.
- *Children as witnesses:* An abundance of analogue studies are needed to assess the accuracy of sexual abuse experiences. Ecological validity of child participation and ecological validity of questioning procedures must be

determined. Children's memory of events varies by age and context of experience. Children are fairly resistant to suggestive questioning, with children under 4 years of age being less resistant than their older peers. Children are more likely to make errors of omission than commission. Use of positive reinforcement appears to affect the responses of younger children more than older children. Children take what adults communicate to them seriously; that is, if an adult communicates certain facts about a situation of which a child has no direct knowledge, the child assumes the adult is telling the truth. Young children can be programmed to believe they have had experiences which they have not.

- *False allegations:* It is necessary to determine the difference between a false allegation and an unsubstantiated allegation. Consensually arrived at criteria are the most valid measures to identify false allegations. False allegations generated by adults are more common than false allegations generated by children. False accusations of sexual abuse by children are quite uncommon but are more likely to be made by older children, usually adolescents. Very young children may make fictitious allegations, primarily to please the evaluator or in response to leading questions. Custody and/or visitation battles between parents occasionally result in false allegations. Children also occasionally identify the wrong abuser—someone less feared or less loved.
- *Criteria for deciding whether an allegation is valid:* Various professionals suggest guidelines for determining sexual abuse. The child interview is central to any sexual abuse evaluation, especially documentation of affect consistent in the abuse description, details of the sexual abuse, and advanced sexual knowledge.
- *Forming conclusions:* Conclusions regarding the truthfulness of the child and about whether the child has been sexually abused utilize supporting evidence. Evaluations can be inconclusive or require an extended evaluation. The child may need to be protected when the evaluation is inconclusive.

MEDICAL EVALUATION OF PHYSICALLY AND SEXUALLY ABUSED CHILDREN

The APSAC Study Guide, Volume 3, *Medical Evaluation of Physically and Sexually Abused Children* (Jenny, 1996), has been designed to familiarize the health care professional with the broad range of information contained in the medical literature about the physical and sexual abuse of children. It is not intended to be a textbook on child abuse but rather to serve as a guide to the best information available and to help the professional locate that information. Also included in the study guide is a glossary of medical terms in "layperson's" terms.

- *Child physical abuse—epidemiology, risk factors, and evaluation:* It is necessary to obtain a complete medical and psychosocial history of circumstances leading to the injury in question, including a report by the child, where appropriate. Make an environmental assessment of the abuse site, including interviews with neighbors and others present at the time of the alleged incident. An examination should be performed as soon as the child is stable and should include growth chart measurements and a detailed comprehensive head-to-toe physical, including genitalia and anus. Siblings should also be interviewed and examined. Skeletal X rays, bone scans, computerized tomography (CT) scans, and magnetic resonance imaging (MRI) are recommended, as well as blood work. Findings should be thoroughly documented in the child's chart.
- *Abdominal trauma:* Small bowel injuries are uncommon. Diagnosis can be difficult and symptoms nonspecific. Stomach injuries are also less common, frequently presenting as peritonitis from gastric rupture. Liver injuries can be very difficult to diagnose, especially in the absence of a history of trauma. Urinalysis and blood tests are useful. Pancreatic injuries, especially pancreatitis, can be diagnosed by CT, ultrasound, or blood work. Urinary tract injuries are not commonly reported but can be life-threatening. Adrenal gland and cardiac injuries are un-

common but do occur. Suspected chest and abdominal trauma can be confirmed through CT, ultrasound, or upper gastrointestinal (GI) tract series.

- *Burns:* Burns, a common form of child abuse, are categorized by burn depth as it relates to the layer of skin affected. First-degree or epidermal burns affect the outermost skin layer, causing only redness. Second-degree, or partial thickness, burns involve both the epidermal and dermal layers. They can be superficial or deep. Third-degree, or full thickness, burns completely destroy the dermis. Depth of hot-liquid burn depends on the temperature of the water and the length of time in the water. Hot-liquid burns are often accidental, the result of a child pulling a pan of water or grease from a stove. These burns are especially damaging. Cigarettes, electric irons, hair dryers, and cigarette lighters cause pattern (contact) burns. Like other burns, their severity depends on the temperature of the object and the length of exposure. Open flames, such as a gas stove, or flammable liquids cause flame burns, often accompanied by smoke inhalation. Heat stroke frequently occurs when neglectful caregivers leave children in parked cars. Heat stroke results in cerebral edema and bleeding, liver and kidney failure, and circulatory collapse. Predictive factors associated with child abuse by burning include delay in seeking medical assistance and an injury not consistent with the reported cause of injury. Psychological factors in children with abusive burn injuries include depression, language deficits, inappropriate affect, withdrawal, attention deficits, and tactile defensiveness. Social factors associated with abused burn victims include low socioeconomic status, adolescent parents, premature birth, postnatal illness, and physical or mental handicap.
- *Chest injuries:* Chest injuries, other than rib fractures from squeezing or shaking an infant's thorax, are seldom noted as a consequence of child abuse. The most frequently noted chest area injuries associated with abuse include injuries to the lungs, heart, and mediastinal (esophageal) areas.

- *Injuries to the face, ears, mouth, throat, and nose:* Orofacial trauma is routinely encountered in physically abused children. According to recent studies, facial contusions are the most common. Injuries to the lips, tongue, and teeth are frequent. Facial fractures are less common, but when present they involve the nose, jawbone, temporal bone, and eye socket. Other frequent orofacial injuries occur to the palate, pharynx, larynx, nose, and ears.
- *Fractures:* Certain fractures occur more frequently as a result of abuse than as a result of accident. Periosteal elevation is not often seen in nonabused children. Long bone fractures reflect the type of force applied to the bone, either spiral fractures from rotational force, transverse fractures from translational forces, or compression fractures from axial loading. Metaphysical fractures are rarely seen as the result of an accidental injury. These fractures usually occur in children under the age of 2 as the result of child abuse. Nine other types of fractures that are moderately to highly indicative of abuse include fractures of the posterior rib, scapular fractures, spinous process fractures, fractures of the sternum, multiple fractures in any location, epiphyseal plate (growth plate) fractures, vertebral fractures, fractures of the small bones of the hands and feet, and complex skull fractures. Differential diagnosis is important in distinguishing between abuse and nonabuse fractures. Specific guidelines are available for imaging of suspected child abuse victims. Healing of fractures varies by injury site and between individual children.
- *Head injuries:* The most lethal form of child abuse is head trauma. When such injuries are not fatal, children often are left with permanent neurological illnesses such as seizures, cerebral palsy, blindness, or deafness. Infants are more vulnerable to head trauma because of a softer brain with immature neurons and unmyelinated nerves, as well as the presence of more cerebrospinal fluid and proportionately larger heads. Types of abusive head injuries include injuries to the scalp, hair loss, bleeding under the scalp, bleeding under the external periosteum of

the skull, skull fractures, epidural and subdural hematomas, dural tears, brain tissue injury, and spinal cord injuries.

- *Retinal hemorrhages and other eye injuries:* Retinal hemorrhages are unusual in accidental head injuries. The chief sign of abusive head traumas, especially "shake baby syndrome," is retinal hemorrhage. Other eye injuries include traumatic retinoschisis, retinal detachment, retinal folds around the macula, bleeding into the optic nerve sheath, and traumatic avulsion of the nerve from the back of the eye. Retinal hemorrhage differential diagnosis is extensive. Retinal hemorrhage from causes other than trauma are rare.
- *Injuries to the skin:* Injuries to the skin are uncommon in children 9 months old and younger. Common skin trauma includes bruises, abrasions, and lacerations. Other skin lesions found on abused children include bite marks, ecchymotic mask, stun gun injuries, tattoos or other symbolic lacerations, and lesions caused by folk medicine practices or constriction devices.
- *Child sexual abuse—epidemiology, risk factors, and evaluation:* Recent research indicates sexual abuse to be a common experience of children. Studies indicate that 7 out of every 10,000 children are victims of sexual abuse. However, this figure is lower than the actual number of children being abused because many cases go unreported. Reports by adults of sexual abuse during childhood vary from 6% to 62% in women and from 3% to 30% in men. Girls are more likely to be abused than boys and are more likely to report abuse. The greatest risk is among children 8–10 years old, as well as among those from socially isolated families, those with an absent parent or unavailable parents, or those growing up in homes with a nonbiologically related father or father figure. Availability of evidence in sexual assault depends on type of assault, age of child, orifices assaulted, and postassault activities of the victim. Immediate physical exam—within 72 hours of contact—is crucial. Behavioral reactions in sexually abused children are similar to posttraumatic stress disorder (PTSD). Sexual "acting out" behavior is frequently seen in sexually abused children. A coordinated, comprehensive medical and psychosocial history is essential. When possible, a single interview with all professionals present (i.e., physician, law enforcement officer, social worker, and prosecutor) can minimize further trauma to the child. Children's responses to interviews vary by their level of cognitive development, emotional development, behavioral development, circumstances of the sexual abuse, and response of individuals in the child's immediate sphere of contact. Physical examination documentation is important. Equally important is enlisting the child's cooperation and participation. Allowing the child to have control of certain elements of the exam, as well as advance knowledge of procedures, can reduce fearfulness. Photographs and/or drawings of injury sites are essential. Retraumatizing a child during genital exam should be avoided. Numerous techniques can be utilized to reduce discomfort and embarrassment to the child. Examining physician should be familiar with the differences between abnormal and normal anatomy, including nonsexual abuse trauma that can be easily mistaken for sexual abuse trauma. Sexual abuse trauma can be documented as acute, subacute, or chronic. Photoculposcope usage has both advantages and disadvantages. It is widely used to evaluate child sexual abuse, allowing for confirmation of findings and consistency of diagnosis. Colposcopy results can be easily evaluated for second opinions and effectively presented in court. The major disadvantage is cost. Detailed, comprehensive documentation, including observations of the victim's affect and language skills, as well as remarks made by the child, will go a long way in assisting the medical professional in being an effective witness.
- *Forensic examination of the sexually assaulted child:* Forensic examinations should be conducted according to specific protocols. Protocols are provided by law enforcement agencies or particular medical facilities. Proper collection, handling, and storage of forensic specimens are crucial to court pre-

sentation. Medical records can be used as evidence in court. Accurate, legible, and complete documentation will greatly assist the presentation. Direct quotes from the child should be used whenever possible. Photographs and/or drawings are also a key element in documentation.

• *Sexually transmitted diseases in children:* Common nonvenereal pathogens not caused by sexually transmitted diseases (STDs) include vaginitis, vulvitis, and anal infections. Pinworms and foreign bodies also account for genital and anal discomfort. STDs in children may differ from those in adults. Most often STDs in children indicate sexual abuse. Common STDs include syphilis, gonorrhea, chlamydia, human papillomavirus (HPV), herpes, and *Trichomonas vaginalis.* Guidelines for STD diagnostic tests are recommended by the Centers for Disease Control.

• *Glossary of medical terms in physical abuse:* Medical terms frequently used in evaluating physical abuse are defined in easy-to-understand language.

• *APSAC guidelines on descriptive terminology in child sexual abuse medical evaluations:* Descriptive terminology used in medical evaluations of sexually abused children is given.

References & Readings

Briere, J., Berliner, L., Bulkley, J. A., Jenny, C., & Reid, T. (Eds.) (1996). *The APSAC handbook on child maltreatment.* Thousand Oaks, CA: Sage.

Faller, K. C. (1996). *Evaluating children suspected of having been sexually abused.* Thousand Oaks, CA: Sage.

Jenny, C. (1996). *Medical evaluation of physically and sexually abused children.* Thousand Oaks, CA: Sage.

Kuehnle, K. (1996). *Assessing allegations of child sexual abuse.* Sarasota, FL: Professional Resource Press.

Quinsey, V. L., & Laluminere, L. L. (1996). *Assessment of sexual offenders against children.* Thousand Oaks, CA: Sage.

Related Topics

Chapter 54, "Child Sexual Abuse: Treatment Issues"

Chapter 75, "Psychotherapy With Clients Recovering Memories of Childhood Trauma"

Chapter 110, "Interviewing Children When Sexual Abuse Is Suspected"

84 PRACTICE GUIDELINES FOR MAJOR DISORDERS

Sam S. Hill III

Practice guidelines are found in a variety of sources, but few have the authority of those published by the American Psychiatric Association. These guidelines were first printed in the *American Journal of Psychiatry* in February 1993. Although published by the American Psychiatric Association, the guidelines are reviewed by individuals and organizations throughout the world who work in the field of mental health. These reviewers are as diverse as one can imagine, from the National Institute of Mental Health and the American Psychological Association to the National Alliance for the Mentally Ill. With this broad range of comment and input, they have developed what many believe to be the state of the art when treating certain disorders.

ORGANIZATION OF THE PRACTICE GUIDELINES

The guidelines are organized into one hardcover volume containing the oldest guidelines and three softcover booklets with the most recent. The hardcover volume contains the guidelines on psychiatric evaluation of adults, eating disorders, major depressive disorder in adults, treatment of patients with bipolar disorder, treatment of patients with substance use disorders, and a short entry on the practice guideline development process. The softcover individual-practice guidelines have been released in 1996 and 1997 and address the treatment of patients with nicotine dependence, treatment of patients with Alzheimer's disease and other dementias of late life, and treatment of patients with schizophrenia. These guidelines are all slightly different in organization, but they follow the same principles, which are as follows:

- The disorders are both prevalent and serious.
- The disorders are relevant to practice.
- The disorders are researchable.
- There is an established body of knowledge about the subject.
- The area is one in which more attention and involvement are needed.

Contributors are typically members of a working group that is put together based on the members' knowledge and experience in the topic area. Although all of the contributors and the overwhelming majority of reviewers are physicians, other disciplines are involved in the commentary process. This is mentioned so that there is no doubt about the theoretical orientation of the guidelines. They are based on the medical model and are within the empirical tradition. This will give comfort to some, but not all, clinicians.

The format of the practice guidelines is essentially the same:

- Executive summary of recommendations
- Disease definition, epidemiology, natural history
- Review of available treatments: goals, efficacy, side effects, implementation
- Development of a treatment plan for the individual patient
- Clinical features influencing treatment
- Research directions
- Reviewers and consultants
- Organizations submitting comments

The section on executive summary of recommendations contains recommendations based on the empirical proof of efficacy, including those with substantial clinical confidence, those with moderate clinical confidence, and those offered on the basis of individual circumstances.

The section on disease definition, epidemiology, and natural history gives the diagnostic criteria using the fourth edition of the American Psychiatric Association's *Diagnostic and Statistical Manual of Mental Disorders (DSM-IV)*.

The next section reviews the available treatments, which are organized into three categories: psychiatric management, psychosocial interventions, and somatic interventions. Each subsection is organized by

- Goals of treatment
- Efficacy data
- Side effects and safety
- Implementation issues

The other sections are explained by their titles. The American Psychiatric Association intends to update these guidelines every 3–5 years.

EXAMPLES OF TREATMENT GUIDELINES

All of the treatment strategies incorporate general principles of a comprehensive multidisciplinary assessment and a coordinated treatment strategy. Rather than reiterate all of the treatment guidelines, only the guidelines on eating disorders and depression are reviewed as examples of the very valuable information available in these volumes.

Anorexia Nervosa

- Outpatient treatment is recommended initially, with partial hospitalization and hospitalization to follow if the early setting was unproductive.
- The aims of treatment are survival based: (a) to regain a healthy weight; (b) to restore healthy eating habits; (c) to treat physical complications; (d) to address dysfunctional beliefs; (e) to approach those dysfunctional thoughts, feelings, and beliefs; (f) to deal with affective and behavioral issues; (g) to deal with associated or contributory psychological difficulties; (h) to include family therapy when appropriate and possible; and (i) to teach relapse prevention.
- Dietary consultation is recommended to educate patients on the health qualitative and quantitative aspects of eating.
- Pharmacological therapy consultation is recommended. Although medications are not recommended routinely, it is a good idea to consult a psychiatrist or the patient's primary care physician following weight gain when the psychological effects of the disorder are resolving.
- Discharge criteria is based on the patient's weight and on whether anorexia behaviors are under control.
- Long-term goals include improving mood, resolving personality disturbances, and improving interpersonal relationships and social functioning.
- Family therapy is seen as very important for children with anorexia; couples therapy is important for adults who have anorexia and are married or in relationships. It is less important in the treatment of single adults who live independently.
- Individual therapy should be tailored to the patient. This therapy will likely be long-term, depending on any comorbid conditions.
- The chronicity of eating disorders is considered in the concluding recommendation.

Bulimia Nervosa

- Outpatient, partial hospitalization and inpatient treatment are again recommended.
- Antidepressant medications are recommended next. These are not seen as or recommended to be the only course of treatment.
- Psychotherapy is recommended next in order of importance due to the high rates of comorbid conditions.
- Family therapy is recommended, especially in children and adolescents.
- Malnutrition and/or concurrent substance abuse, if they exist, should be treated before the bulimia.

Major Depression

The guideline begins with the diagnostic criteria for depressive episode, which follows the *DSM-IV*. The qualitative factors or specific features of the diagnosis are also considered in this introductory section. Next, the reader is given the natural history and course of the disorder, and finally the first section ends with the epidemiology of depression.

In the section on treatment principles and alternatives, the authors introduce treatment in the order designated by the editors. The advantages of inpatient and outpatient treatment are designated by the phase of the depression: *acute, continuation,* or *maintenance.*

- Psychotherapeutic interventions: Each therapy is rated for phase and efficacy if there is sufficient empirical data to endorse it. If there is insufficient research, then the guideline says so.

  1. Supportive therapies
  2. Psychodynamic psychotherapy and psychoanalysis
  3. Brief therapy
  4. Interpersonal therapy
  5. Behavior therapy
  6. Cognitive behavioral therapy
  7. Marital therapy and family therapy
  8. Group therapy (the efficacy is based on clinical experience rather than on controlled studies)

- Somatic interventions
- Antidepressant medications
- Electroconvulsive therapy
- Light therapy

A discussion of medication-resistant depression is undertaken, with proposed solutions for these patients. The guideline ends with clinical features influencing treatment and a summary. These guidelines provide a good working list of references and an impressive, if not one-dimensional, listing of consultants and reviewers.

References & Readings

American Psychiatric Association (1994). *Diagnostic and statistical manual of mental disorders* (4th ed.). Washington, DC: American Psychiatric Press.

American Psychiatric Association (1996). *Practice guidelines.* Washington, DC: American Psychiatric Press.

Related Topics

Chapter 46, "Empirically Validated Treatments"
Chapter 47, "Thumbnail Systematic Assessment and Treatment Matching"

85 THERAPIST SELF-CARE CHECKLIST

James D. Guy, Jr. & John C. Norcross

Although an escalating number of empirical studies have examined the sources of practitioner distress and burnout, far fewer attempts have addressed how psychotherapists understand and ameliorate this distress in a constructive manner. As in their clinical activities, psychologists in their personal lives are frequently more adept at cataloging their psychopathology than at identifying their self-care and self-change strengths.

Our overarching aims in this brief chapter are threefold: first, to remind busy practitioners of the personal and professional need to tend to their own psychological health; second, to provide a field-tested diversity of methods to prevent burnout and to nourish themselves; and third, to generate a positive message of self-renewal and growth.

The following list summarizes frequently used and commonly recommended methods of alleviating the distress of conducting psychotherapy or, more optimistically, of nourishing and replenishing the practitioner. Unfortunately, the extant literature on the "person of the therapist" and "burnout" has not progressed to the point where definitive self-care recommendations can be offered (Norcross & Aboyoun, 1994; Schaufeli, Maslach, & Marek, 1993); thus, it is not an exhaustive or empirically driven compilation. Nonetheless, the list is a practical synthesis of clinical wisdom, research literature, and therapist experience on a multitude of self-care methods from disparate theoretical traditions. The list is adapted from a more extensive catalog of self-care activities published in our book, *Leaving It at the Office* (in press), and is divided into 10 broad categories of self-care strategies.

RECOGNIZE THE HAZARDS OF THE "IMPOSSIBLE PROFESSION"

- All accounts indicate that clinical practice exacts a negative toll on the practitioner, particularly in the form of problematic anxiety, moderate depression, and emotional under-involvement with family members (Norcross & Aboyoun, 1994). Have you identified how clinical practice has impacted you and your loved ones?
- Reading about and reflecting on the stresses of psychotherapy lead to the realization that similar strains are experienced by virtually all mental health professionals. Can you affirm the universality of these stresses and disconfirm your feelings of unique limitation?
- Consider the amount of physical isolation that you experience each day. What steps can you take to create more opportunities for contact with other clinicians?
- Try to include phone calls, special lunches, and coffee breaks in your workday at least once or twice each week to provide contact with family and friends.
- Consider taking steps to create variety in your day, such as intermingling psychotherapy sessions with supervision, consultations, study breaks, a trip to the gym, and so on.
- Invite family and friends to point out when you become too interpretive and "objective" when it is more appropriate to be spontaneous and genuine.
- Take Coach John Wooden's advice and refuse to believe either your most idealizing or your most demeaning client—you are neither God nor the devil.
- How much confidential client material do you share with your spouse or significant other? Have you thought out all the implications of what you do share?
- Reflect on the number of clients you've said good-bye to over the years. What has been the accumulated impact of these terminations?
- Therapists tend to minimize their own limi-

tations and needs, particularly when talking with colleagues. With which colleague can you be truly honest?
- Consider why you became a psychotherapist and why you continue to practice. Look for ways to work through those motivations to practice that are unhealthy.
- Fortunately, burnout and impairment among therapists are relatively rare phenomena. What steps are you taking to reduce their likelihood?

REFOCUS ON THE REWARDS OF PRACTICING PSYCHOTHERAPY

- Focus on the rewards associated with clinical work that bring life and vitality. For example, recall the life-transforming psychotherapies in which you were privileged to participate.
- Your emotional growth is one of your most important therapeutic tools. Is your tool being properly and regularly sharpened?
- Satisfaction from helping others is essential. Be sure to include at least some clinical activities that demonstrate you're actually helping someone!
- Enjoy maintaining relationships with clients that span years, or even decades, that include intermittent courses of treatment.
- Ideally, your work will capitalize on both your natural and your acquired abilities. Do what you do well.
- Be careful when applying your expertise to your family of origin ("Fools rush in where angels fear to tread").
- How has clinical practice improved the quality of your friendships?
- Remember that you are self-employed, regardless of who you work for. Adopting this perspective begets freedom of choice.
- Clinical practice may not make you rich, but if it is your calling, it is a wonderful way to make a living.
- There are many more benefits than hazards associated with the practice of psychotherapy. If you've forgotten this, find some methods to help you remember.

NURTURE RELATIONSHIPS INSIDE AND OUTSIDE THE OFFICE

- In one study of "well-functioning" psychologists (Coster & Schwebel, 1997), peer support emerged as the highest priority. How does your peer support fare?
- Are you getting enough "alone" time? Do you know what to do with it when it's available?
- Name the three most nurturing people in your life. What can you do to increase the amount of support that you receive from them?
- Ongoing peer supervision or consultation is highly valued by experienced clinicians throughout their careers. Do you have such arrangements in your own life? Under what circumstances are you willing to seek supervision or consultation?
- During a typical workday, who "recharges your batteries" best and brightens your day?
- Identify the client who provides you with the greatest amount of nurturance. How does this make you feel? How are you handling this?
- What have you learned about yourself as a result of experiencing a sense of loss following completion of treatment with a "favorite" client?
- Identify your most significant "mentor" during your career. What made this relationship so important? How are your needs for mentoring being met today?
- A spouse or significant other is an important source of nurturance for many clinicians. How important is this in your life? Why or why not?
- Utilize your family-of-origin relationships to help you reality test and to confront your grandiosity. These folks will in all likelihood be honest with you if invited!
- Have your friendships become fewer in number and diminished in significance over the years of professional practice? Why or why not?
- Who is your personal "guru"? Who helps you derive meaning?
- Something is seriously wrong if you are giving out more nurturance than you are receiving. Take corrective action!

SET BOUNDARIES, CLARIFY RELATIONSHIPS

- Setting boundaries emerges in our research as the most frequent self-care strategy of mental health professionals (Norcross & Guy, in press). Be clear with your clients about personal needs, expectations, and boundaries.
- Clearly delineate your policies regarding extra sessions, late appointments, telephone contacts, payment for services rendered, and the like.
- Your work expresses a combination of personal style, theoretical orientation, and individual preference. You will bend to suit your clients' needs, but not much.
- Clarify your expectations of your clients early in your work. What are the ground rules for treatment?
- Saying good-bye to clients well requires clear statements concerning how, when, and why treatment may resume in the future.
- Understand what your client needs most, and don't allow that goal to be compromised by conflicting roles and agendas.
- Your clients are not there to meet your needs; treatment relationships are not reciprocal.
- Define your relationships with colleagues and staff with care. Transference influences these relationships, too.
- Establishing an identity apart from your role as a clinician will enrich your private life with variety and meaning. Don't get stale!
- Let your hair down with family and friends. They want you to be genuine, spontaneous, and "unprofessional."

EMPLOY COGNITIVE RESTRUCTURING

- Self-monitor your internal dialogue, either implicitly or explicitly, particularly in regard to countertransference feelings.

- Monitor what Ellis calls "stinking thinking" through introspection, reflection, using triple column logs, or sharing concerns with others.
- Think through your reactions to transferential feelings directed to you. To whom are they aimed, and to whom do they belong?
- Beware of absolutistic thinking: "musturbation" and the "tyranny of the shoulds." They can affect you as much as your patients.
- Dispute the common fallacy that "good psychotherapy is equivalent to having patients who like us." It is not!
- Yes, you are an expert on human behavior—but you're still nutty at times!
- Recall that the other side of caring consists of confrontation. At times, caring about others includes being tough.
- Reassure yourself that the conditions in psychotherapy, as well as in life, are not always easy. This is unfortunate but not the end of the world.
- To fail is human. To consider yourself a failure is not divine.
- Remind yourself that you cannot cure every patient.
- Dwell on your successes as well as your failures.
- Assertively lessen unrealistic demands made on you: don't take on more work than necessary or wrongly believe you're expected to do more.
- Catch yourself when you assume personal causality. Self-deprecation is self-defeating!
- Consider alternate explanations that may cause events. Psychotherapy is not the only causal event in clients' lives.
- Calculate real probabilities. The worst does not always happen—to you or to your patients.
- Evaluate events on a continuum to avoid dichotomous thinking; psychotherapy outcomes are rarely on either extreme of a continuum.

SUSTAIN HEALTHY ESCAPES

- We occasionally become so intent and focused on sophisticated self-care methods that we overlook the basics. What is the quality of your sleep, your nutrition, your body? Do you obtain sufficient exercise and healthy food during the day, or, as one of us discovered himself doing a few years ago, are you subsisting throughout the day without exercise and with only diet soda and hard pretzels?
- Increase your sensory awareness: Beholding your surroundings using vision, hearing, touch, gustation, and olfaction can be a powerful elixir and can counterbalance the primarily cognitive and affective work of psychotherapy.
- A sense of humor is one of your most important stress relievers. Practice!
- Take your own advice: Exercise and relax regularly.
- Take a minibreak between sessions to self-massage your face and neck muscles; perhaps schedule regular massages to nourish yourself and relieve muscle tension.
- Mahoney (1997) reports that over 80% of therapists routinely engage in reading or a hobby, take pleasure trips or vacations, and attend artistic events and movies as part of their self-care patterns. Is your life balanced?
- Monitor your vacation and down time. Is it less than you as a psychotherapist would recommend to patients in similarly stressful occupations?
- Pace your day, space appointments, and take a break or two.
- How much adventure and other diversions do you have away from the office? Is play a steady staple of your emotional diet?
- Support groups and peer supervision groups offer multiple advantages. Please consider joining one.
- Involvement in other professional activities balances your workload and expresses a full array of your skills. Psychotherapy, teaching, supervision, consultation, assessment, and writing are all part of the mental health professional landscape.
- Variety and intellectual stimulation are important. Mix up your therapy days: individual, marital, and family formats; younger and older patients; talk therapy and action

therapy. What else can you do to increase variety and novelty in your schedule?

UNDERGO PERSONAL THERAPY

- Freud (1964) recommended that every therapist should periodically—at intervals of 5 years or so—reenter or initiate psychotherapy *without shame* as a form of continued education. Do you heed his sage advice? Do you struggle with the shame?
- Between 52% and 65% of psychotherapists enter personal treatment following completion of formal training (Norcross & Guy, in press). Do you subscribe to the illusion —or perhaps the delusion—that mental health professionals do not experience a need for personal therapy once they are in practice?
- Can you give yourself 50 minutes of time every week or two in a holding environment? Are you practicing what you preach regarding the value of psychotherapy?
- If you do not participate in formal psychotherapy, consider an annual satisfaction checkup with a valued mentor, trusted colleague, or former therapist.

CREATE A FLOURISHING ENVIRONMENT

- In our research on the frequency of self-care methods (Brady, Norcross, & Guy, 1995), psychotherapists rate "making organizational changes at the practice" the least common method. We believe they do so at considerable risk. Do you fall prey to American individualism and neglect systemic forces inside and outside your office?
- Are your clinical talents and interpersonal interests poorly invested in paperwork? If so, consider a computer, a clerical assistant, or other alternatives.
- Look for ways to create a greater sense of freedom and independence in your work.
- Enhance your work environment: comfort in your furniture, aesthetics in your decor, replenishment in your refrigerator, and nourishment in your peers.

CULTIVATE SPIRITUALITY AND MISSION

- We emphasize the personal experience of spirituality, or what Maslow called "mission." Can you identify and resonate to an abiding mission or spirituality?
- What is your sense of "calling" to be a clinician? What are the spiritual antecedents to your career choice?
- Your work grows out of a legacy of "healers" that extends back for many centuries. Try to feel connected to that heritage and to the privilege of practicing psychotherapy.
- What are the spiritual sources of your hope and optimism regarding human nature?
- A sense of personal mission can fruitfully incorporate larger societal concerns, such as enhancing women's rights, promoting social justice, teaching conflict resolution, eradicating poverty, and abolishing sexual abuse. Where are your sympathies?
- If you've lost your enduring sense of care and concern for others, get help!
- Optimism and belief in the potential for personality change are prerequisites for good clinical practice. Assess yourself and then ask a friend to assess you.
- How does your belief in a mission, God, or a transcendent force serve as a resource for you? Are you squarely confronting your own yearnings for a sense of transcendence and meaning?
- Who serves as a "spiritual mentor" for you? Is this adequate?
- Since the practice of psychotherapy is not meant to provide ultimate meaning for your life, what does? What should?

FOSTER CREATIVITY AND GROWTH

- Opportunities for dedicated reflection and discernment are a professional obligation, not a luxury. How often do you engage in spiritual exercises, journaling, meditation, or other forms of renewal?

- Are you finding ways of nurturing your creativity? Are staleness and repetition starting to get you down?
- Attending clinical conferences, reading literature, and continuing your education are the lifesprings of a committed professional. Do you feel you are just "getting CE hours" or truly refining and building your skills?
- Kottler (1991, p. 238) declares, "Everything comes together for a therapist in the creative process." How are you coming together, nourishing yourself, and growing as a psychotherapist?

References & Readings

Brady, J. L., Norcross, J. C., & Guy, J. D. (1995). Managing your own distress: Lessons from psychotherapists healing themselves. In L. VandeCreek, S. Knapp, & T. L. Jackson (Eds.), *Innovations in clinical practice* (pp. 293–306). Sarasota, FL: Professional Resource Press.

Coster, J. S., & Schwebel, M. (1997). Well-functioning in professional psychologists. *Professional Psychology: Research and Practice, 28,* 5–13.

Dryden, W. (Ed.) (1995). *The stresses of counselling in action.* Thousand Oaks, CA: Sage.

Freud, S. (1964). Analysis terminable and interminable. In J. Strachey (Ed.), *Complete psychological works of Sigmund Freud.* London: Hogarth Press. (Original work published 1937.)

Freudenberger, H. J. (1980). *Burn-out.* New York: Bantam Books.

Guy, J. D. (1987). *The personal life of the therapist.* New York: Wiley.

Kilburg, R. R., Nathan, P. E., & Thoreson, R. W. (Eds.) (1986). *Professionals in distress: Issues, syndromes, and solutions in psychology.* Washington, DC: American Psychological Association.

Kottler, J. A. (1991). *The compleat therapist.* San Francisco: Jossey-Bass.

Mahoney, M. J. (1997). Psychotherapists' personal problems and self-care patterns. *Professional Psychology: Research and Practice, 28,* 14–16.

Norcross, J. C., & Aboyoun, D. C. (1994). Self-change experiences of psychotherapists. In T. M. Brinthaupt & R. P. Lipka (Eds.), *Changing the self* (pp. 253–278). Albany: State University of New York Press.

Norcross, J. C., & Guy, J. D. (in press). *Leaving it at the office: Understanding and alleviating the distress of conducting psychotherapy.* New York: Guilford Press.

Rippere, V., & Williams, R. (Eds.) (1985). *Wounded healers.* New York: Wiley.

Schaufeli, W. B., Maslach, C., & Marek, T. (Eds.) (1993). *Professional burnout: Recent developments in theory and research.* Washington, DC: Taylor and Francis.

Scott, C. D., & Hawk, J. (1986). *Heal thyself: The health of health care professionals.* New York: Brunner/Mazel.

Related Topics

PART IV
Pharmacotherapy

ADULT PSYCHOPHARMACOLOGY 1
Common Usage

Joseph K. Belanoff, Charles DeBattista,
& Alan F. Schatzberg

Make the appropriate diagnosis, but especially identify the target symptoms (see Table 1). Ideally, one would like to see the patient in a drug-free state for 1–2 weeks, although this is not always possible. Target symptoms are critical. Past history of medication response is quite predictive of current response. Family history of drug response is often helpful in making a medication choice.

MAJOR DEPRESSION

Major depression is a common debilitating illness (lifetime prevalence of approximately 16%). Success rates for psychopharmacological interventions are approximately 60–70%.

- *Monoamine oxidase inhibitors (MAOIs):* MAOIs are probably underutilized because of concern about tyramine-induced hypertensive crisis (extreme high blood pressure brought on by eating certain foods, including aged cheese, aged meat, and red wine, while using an MAOI).
- *Tricyclic antidepressants (TCAs):* TCAs have demonstrated proven efficacy in major depression but can produce side effects, ranging from the annoying (dry mouth) to the dangerous (arrhythmia). Least likely to produce sedation, postural hypotension, and anticholinergic side effects are desipramine and nortriptyline.
- *Selective serotonin reuptake inhibitors (SSRIs):* The release of fluoxetine in 1988 greatly expanded the number of patients with major depression treated pharmacologically. The SSRIs (fluoxetine, sertraline, paroxetine, and fluvoxamine) are virtually never lethal in overdose, and their side-effect profiles are relatively benign.
- *Trazodone and nefazodone:* Trazodone is an inhibitor of serotonin reuptake, an agonist at some serotonin receptors, and an antago-

TABLE 1. Adult Psychopharmacology

Indication	Class	Drug Name	Dosage	Blood Level
Major depression	MAOI	Phenelzine (Nardil)	45–70 mg	
	MAOI	Tranylcypromine (Parnate)	30–50 mg	
	TCA	Imipramine (Tofranil)	150–300 mg	150–300 μg/ml imipramine & desipramine
	TCA	Desipramine (Norpramin)	150–300 mg	150–300 μg/ml
	TCA	Amitriptyline (Elavil)	150–300 mg	100–250 μg/ml amiltriptyline & nortrip-tyline
	TCA	Nortriptyline (Pamelor)	50–150 mg	50–150 μg/ml
	SSRI	Fluoxetine (Prozac)	20–60 mg	
	SSRI	Sertraline (Zoloft)	50–200 mg	
	SSRI	Paroxetine (Paxil)	20–50 mg	
	SSRI	Fluvoxamine (Luvox)	50–300 mg	
		Trazodone (Desyrel)	300–600 mg	
		Nefazodone (Serzone)	300–600 mg (divided)	
		Venlafaxine (Effexor)	75–375 mg (divided)	
		Bupropion (Wellbutrin)	300–450 mg	
Antidepressant augmentation		Lithium	600–1,800 mg	0.5–0.8 mEq/L
		L-triodothyramine	25–50 mcg	
Bipolar disorder		Lithium	900–2,000 mg	0.8–1.2 mEq/L*
	Anticonvulsant	Carbamazepine (Tegretol)	400–1,600 mg	6–10 μg/ml
	Anticonvulsant	Divalproex sodium (Depakote)	750–2,250 mg (divided)	50–100 μg/ml
Schizophrenia	Low-potency antipsychotic	Chlorpromazine (Thorazine)	300–800 mg	
	High-potency antipsychotic	Haloperidol (Haldol)	6–20 mg	
	Atypical antipsychotic	Risperidone (Risperdal)	2–8 mg	
	Atypical antipsychotic	Clozapine (Clozaril)	300–900 mg	
	Atypical antipsychotic	Olanzapine (Zyprexa)	5–20 mg	
Panic disorder	Benzodiazepine	Alprazolam (Xanax)	1–6 mg	
Generalized anxiety disorder		Buspirone (BuSpar)	15–30 mg (divided)	
Obsessive-compulsive disorder	TCA	Clomipramine (Anafranil)	150–250 mg	
	SSRI	Fluvoxamine (Luvox)	100–350 mg	
Insomnia		Trazodone (Desyrel)	50–100 mg (at bedtime)	
	Antihistamine	Diphenhydramine (Benadryl)	25–50 mg (at bedtime)	
Narcolepsy	Psychostimulant	Dextroamphetamine (Dexedrine)	10–40 mg	
	TCA	Protriptyline (Vivactil)	10–40 mg	
Schizotypal personality disorder	Antipsychotic	Haloperidol (Haldol)	3 mg	
Borderline personality disorder	Antipsychotic	Loxapine (Loxitane)	5–25 mg	
	SSRI	Fluoxetine (Prozac)	10–40 mg	
Avoidant personality disorder	MAOI	Phenelzine (Nardil)	60 mg	
Alcohol withdrawal	Benzodiazepine	Chlordiazepoxide (Librium)	25–100 mg Q 6 h	
	Benzodiazepine	Lorazepam (Ativan)	1 mg Q 1 hr PRN pulse > 110, BP > 150/100	

TABLE 1. Adult Psychopharmacology (*continued*)

Indication	Class	Drug Name	Dosage	Blood Level
	Vitamin	Thiamine	100 mg 1–3 × Q D	
	Vitamin	Folic acid	1 mg Q D	
	Vitamin	Multivitamin	1 tablet Q D	
Heroin withdrawal	Opioid	Methadone	5 mg Q 4 h as needed on first day then decrease by 5 mg Q D until 0	
Relapse prevention		Disulfiram (Antabuse)	500 mg Q D for 2 weeks then 250 Q D (1st dose at least 12 h after last E to H use)	
	Opioid agonist	Naltrexone (ReVia)	25 mg Q D for 1–2 days then 50 mg (1st dose at least 7–10 days after last opioid use)	
Bulimia nervosa	SSRI	Fluoxetine (Prozac)	40–60 mg	
Alzheimer's dementia	Anticholinesterase	Tacrine (Cognex)	Start at 40 mg and raise by 40 mg every 6 weeks up to 110 mg	
	Anticholinesterase	Donezepil (Aricept)	5 mg	

*Levels ≥ 1.5 mEq/L may be toxic, and levels ≥ 2.5 mEq/L may be fatal.

nist at others. It is also an alpha-adrenergic blocker and an antihistamine, so common side effects include orthostatic hypotension and sedation. Although the primary indication for trazodone is major depression, it is quite effective in low doses (50–100 mg) as a hypnotic.

Nefazodone, a newer antidepressant, has complicated effects on the serotonin system. It, too, is a 5-HT2 antagonist, as well as an inhibitor of serotonin reuptake (this combination may lead to sensitization of 5-HT1A receptors).

- *Venlafaxine:* Like the TCAs, venlafaxine is a nonspecific reuptake inhibitor. Unlike the TCAs, venlafaxine does not block cholinergic, histaminergic, or adrenergic receptors, so its side-effect profile is much more benign.
- *Bupropion:* Bupropion was to be introduced in the United States in 1985 but was delayed after the occurrence of seizures in patients with bulimia. It was introduced in 1989 and has proved to be an effective, safe (and underutilized) antidepressant.
- *Electroconvulsive therapy (ECT):* When de-

pression is very severe or accompanied by delusions, ECT is the treatment of choice.

- *Adjunct therapy:* If a patient's depression has been nonresponsive to a 6-week course of antidepressants at appropriate dosages, adjunct therapy with either lithium or thyroid hormone is an alternative.
- *Atypical depression (hyperphagia, hypersomnia, leaden paralysis, rejection sensitivity, mood reactivity):* MAOIs have demonstrated superior efficacy compared with TCAs in treating this variation of major depression.
- *Psychotic (delusional) depression:* Antidepressant medication alone is usually ineffective. The combination of an antidepressant and an antipsychotic is effective in many patients. ECT is probably the most effective treatment.
- *Dysthymia:* For many years the prognosis for individuals with dysthymia was poor. There is now increasing evidence that long-term use of antidepressants, particularly SSRIs, is quite effective in improving dysthymia and perhaps in preventing declines into major depression.

BIPOLAR DISORDER

The most effective acute treatment for manic psychotic agitation (virtually always administered in the emergency room) is an antipsychotic medication (i.e., haloperidol) combined with a benzodiazepine (i.e., lorazepam). Shortly thereafter, sometimes following a negative toxicology screen, a mood-stabilizing agent must be started.

- *Lithium:* Lithium remains the gold standard for the treatment of bipolar disorder. Seventy to eighty percent of acutely manic patients respond to lithium, but it often takes 1–3 weeks for a full response.
- *Carbamazepine:* Primarily used as an anticonvulsant, carbamazepine also has been shown to be quite effective in treating bipolar disorder.
- *Valproic acid:* Valproic acid (primarily used now in divalproex sodium form) has been granted FDA approval for the treatment of bipolar disorder. It appears that valproate may be especially effective in the treatment of rapid-cycling bipolar disorder and mixed manic-depressive states. Because there are many drug-drug interactions with valproic acid, the prescribing physician must be made aware of all medication changes (including over-the-counter drugs).

SCHIZOPHRENIA

Antipsychotic medication is often divided into two groups, "typical" and "atypical." All "typical" antipsychotics are dopamine-2 receptor blockers. "Atypical" antipsychotics are less prominent dopamine-2 receptor blockers, and they tend to block many other receptors, particularly serotonin-2 receptors.

- *Dopamine receptor antagonists (D2 receptors):* All traditional antipsychotic medication works essentially the same way and has the same side-effect profile. Medications with a relatively low affinity for D2 receptors ("low potency") require a higher dose, and medications with a relatively high affin-

ity for D2 receptors ("high potency") require a lower dose.
- *Risperidone:* Risperidone is both a serotonin and a dopamine antagonist. At lower doses (under 6 mg), it is not a potent dopamine-2 receptor blocker, so its motor side effects are minimal.
- *Clozapine and olanzapine:* Clozapine and olanzapine are potent antipsychotic medications. Clozapine has been remarkably effective in improving previously treatment-resistant schizophrenia.

ANXIETY DISORDERS

Biological theories of anxiety disorders have pointed to problems in the norepinephrine, serotonin, and gamma-aminobutyric acid neurotransmitter systems. As a consequence, a wide variety of medications has been tried with varying success.

- *Panic disorder:* Antidepressants should be considered the first line of pharmacotherapy for patients with panic disorder. Benzodiazepines have also been shown to be effective in treating panic disorder but have a number of disadvantages over antidepressants. They often produce sedation, increase the effects of alcohol, produce dyscoordination, and are associated with dependence and withdrawal. Patients can have *severe* panic attacks while withdrawing from benzodiazapines.
- *Generalized anxiety disorder (GAD):* Benzodiazepines have been frequently used to treat patients with GAD. They are effective in the short run for symptom relief. However, for all of the reasons listed above, their longer-term use is problematic. Buspirone, a serotonin partial agonist, has been shown to be as effective as benzodiazepines in patients with GAD.
- *Social phobia:* Unfortunately, the pharmacological treatment of social phobia has lagged behind the treatment of other anxiety disorders. Alprazolam and phenelzine have been reported to produce improvement in symptoms of social phobia. Beta-blockers have

helped with performance anxiety (in events like public speaking) but not particularly with social phobia.

- *Obsessive-compulsive disorder (OCD):* OCD is both relatively common and quite responsive to pharmacotherapy. Clomipramine, a nonspecific (but very serotonergically potent) reuptake inhibitor, has been best studied and is often effective. All of the SSRIs have been shown to be effective in reducing the symptoms of OCD.

SLEEP DISORDERS

- *Insomnia:* Insomnia is a common symptom in many psychiatric illnesses, particularly major depression. Insomnia often resolves as the depressive episode resolves. However, when insomnia is particularly distressing to the patient, low doses of trazodone or diphenhydramine are often effective in improving sleep.
- *Narcolepsy:* Psychostimulants (i.e., amphetamines) have long been accepted as valuable treatment for the daytime sleepiness seen in narcolepsy. Stimulants do not prevent the cataplexy that some narcoleptic patients experience, but either TCAs or SSRIs in combination with stimulants may be helpful.

PERSONALITY DISORDERS

Despite the fact that pharmacotherapy has increasingly gained acceptance as a treatment option for severe personality disorders, there are few well-controlled studies that document pharmacological efficacy. In addition, many specific personality disorders have not been studied pharmacologically at all. Those that have include the following:

- *Schizotypal personality disorder:* It appears that schizotypal personality disorder has a genetic association with schizophrenia, so it is not surprising that there is some evidence for improvement with low-dose antipsychotic medication.
- *Borderline personality disorder (BPD):*

SSRIs seem to help in BPD, particularly with impulsive aggression and affective instability. Low-dose antipsychotic medication is often effective in improving hostility and cognitive perceptual disturbances. Anticonvulsants, particularly valproic acid, seem to improve behavioral dyscontrol; benzodiazepines often make behavioral dyscontrol worse.

- *Avoidant personality disorder:* There are no double-blind placebo-controlled studies, but there is evidence that MAOIs, SSRIs, beta-adrenergic receptor antagonists, and benzodiazepines may be useful in combination with psychotherapy.

PSYCHOACTIVE SUBSTANCE ABUSE AND WITHDRAWAL

- *Intoxication:* Most treatment for serious intoxication is focused on physiological support (controlling blood pressure, heart rate, respiration, etc.). The psychosis seen in amphetamine and cocaine intoxication may be treated with standard antipsychotics, often in combination with benzodiazepines (which help with agitation).
- *Withdrawal:* Withdrawal from alcohol, benzodiazepines, and barbiturates is similar and is potentially life-threatening. All of these withdrawals are best pharmacologically treated with benzodiazepines. Lorazepam (Ativan) is recommended for patients with significant liver disease because its metabolism is less impaired in advanced liver disease. Methadone and clonidine are used in opiate withdrawal.
- *Relapse prevention:* The prevalence of substance abuse disorders, particularly alcohol abuse and dependence, has sparked interest in pharmacological methods to help prevent relapse. Disulfiram (Antabuse) has been tried for many years, although its popularity has certainly declined. Naltrexone, a synthetic opioid antagonist, is used in the treatment of alcoholism and narcotic dependence. Naltrexone aids abstinence by blocking the "high" caused by narcotics.

SOMATOFORM DISORDERS

Most of the somatoform disorders are ineffectively treated with current medication, and unfortunately psychoactive medication therapies are probably overused significantly. The one exception is body dysmorphic disorder, where the effective use of serotonergic agents (particularly SSRIs) has dramatically improved the prognosis for affected patients.

EATING DISORDERS

- *Anorexia nervosa:* Unfortunately, there is no shining star of pharmacological treatment for this life-threatening illness. Antipsychotic medication has not worked, and cyproheptadine, amitriptyline, and fluoxetine have had limited success.
- *Bulimia nervosa:* Antidepressants work very well in the treatment of bulimia apart from their ability to elevate mood.

IMPULSE-CONTROL DISORDERS

Among the impulse-control disorders, intermittent explosive disorder and trichotillomania are most often treated pharmacologically.

- *Intermittent explosive disorder:* Anticonvulsants are used most often, although the results are mixed. Benzodiazepines often make matters worse, with more behavioral dyscontrol. There is increasing case evidence that buspirone (often in higher doses than used in generalized anxiety disorder) may be effective.
- *Trichotillomania:* New pharmacological studies are taking place with both serotonergic antidepressants and the anticonvulsant valproic acid.

References & Readings

Albani, F., Riva, R., & Baruzzi, A. (1995). Carbamazepine clinical pharmacology: A review. *Pharmacopsychiatry, 28*(6), 235–244.

Andrews, J. M., & Nemeroff, C. B. (1994). Contemporary management of depression. *American Journal of Medicine, 97,* 245–325.

Callahan, A. M., Fava, M., & Rosenbaum, J. F. (1993). Drug interactions in psychopharmacology. *Psychiatric Clinics of North America, 16,* 647–671.

Kunovac, J. L., & Stahl, S. M. (1995). Future direction in anxiolytic pharmacotherapy. *Psychiatric Clinics of North America, 18,* 895–909.

Naranjo, C. A., Herrmann, N., Mittmann, N., & Bremner, K. E. (1995). Recent advances in geriatric psychopharmacology. *Drugs and Aging, 7*(3), 184–202.

Related Topics

Chapter 87, "Adult Psychopharmacology 2: Side Effects and Warnings"
Chapter 88, "Pediatric Psychopharmacology"

87 ADULT PSYCHOPHARMACOLOGY 2
Side Effects and Warnings

Elaine Orabona

Psychopharmacology is a dynamic field that requires the practitioner to keep up to date on the regularly changing information regarding the pharmacodynamics and pharmacokinetics of psychoactive medications. Given this caveat, several variables do remain constant in the safe and effective practice of pharmacotherapy. The following is not meant to be exhaustive, but rather it highlights information from the average clinical assessment that can affect the interaction between drug and patient.

- *Age:* The elderly metabolize drugs at a slower rate, which is one reason for the axiom "Start low and go slow." The axiom also holds true for children.
- *Sex:* Psychotropic medications can have physical and behavioral teratogenic effects on the developing fetus and newborn (e.g., lithium has been associated with Ebstein's anomaly, a serious malformation in cardiac development, when taken during the first trimester). Therefore, the rule of thumb is to counsel all women of childbearing age about these risks and to avoid all but essential medications during pregnancy, especially the first trimester. When unavoidable, serotonin-specific reuptake inhibitors (SSRIs) have typically been the first-choice medications, although this is still controversial because tricyclic antidepressants (TCAs) have a longer track record of use in pregnancy and can be measured through blood serum levels. Women also metabolize drugs differently during menstrual cycle phases, pregnancy/lactation, and menopause. For example, Wisner, Perel, and Wheeler (1993) found that by the third trimester women on average required 1.6 times the nonpregnant dose of TCA.
- *Ethnicity:* Populations differ in their expression of genes that allow them to metabolize various drugs. The cytochrome P450 enzymes responsible for the metabolism of most psychotropic medications are IAD, IID6, and IIIA3/4. IID6, which is the enzyme responsible for the hydroxylation of many psychiatric medications, has been found to be deficient in 5–8% of Caucasians. Knowledge of genetic differences can help guide pharmacotherapy when individuals who are "fast" or "slow" metabolizers show either subtherapeutic response or excessive side effects.
- *Symptoms:* An assessment of symptoms will assist with establishing the target symp-

toms to be treated and monitored. The assessment must include pertinent negatives such as the *absence* of a history of mania because antidepressants can precipitate a switch into mania for those with a predisposition.
- *Past psychiatric history:* Look for previous psychotropic medication use, including family psychiatric history and use of psychotropic medications (if a drug worked or did not work for the patient's family members before, it is likely to repeat its performance in the future). Suicide history and current profile will suggest whether it is safe to utilize medications with narrow versus broad therapeutic windows.
- *Past medical history:* Medical illness and concomitant drug use—even over-the-counter medication, homeopathic remedies, or folk remedies—can affect the pharmacokinetics and pharmacodynamics of any psychotropic medication. Some combinations can be monitored with relative safety, while others are absolutely contraindicated, such as a monoamine oxidase inhibitor and meperidine or dextromethorphan.
- *Habits:* Regular alcohol use can either speed up or slow down the metabolism of psychotropic medications, depending on the stage of damage to the liver. Also, chronic alcohol withdrawal can lower the seizure threshold, which means drugs that lower the seizure threshold (e.g., bupropion, high doses of tricyclics, and low-potency antipsychotics) should be avoided in individuals with seizure history. Tobacco and caffeine can also induce (speed up) the metabolism of various drugs and should be considered when monitoring for possible subtherapeutic or interaction effects. Illicit drugs can cause a patient to appear depressed, psychotic, and/or anxious. These must always be considered because of their influence on diagnostic and treatment decisions (e.g., whether to withhold, use, or delay the timing of certain psychotropic medications).
- *Laboratory studies:* The most common laboratory studies for psychiatric patients include complete blood count (CBC) with differential; blood chemistries (typically include electrolytes, blood urea nitrogen [BUN], creatinine clearance, liver function

tests [LFTs]); thyroid function tests (TFTs); testing for sexually transmitted disease such as syphilis via RPR or VDRL; urinalysis with toxicology screen; blood alcohol level; drug serum levels (for those measurable); and HIV as appropriate. For women of child-bearing age, a pregnancy test such as blood or urine HCG should also be included. Some of these studies will assist with differential diagnoses, but they can also provide baselines for the introduction of new medications that can affect various systems. For example, carbamazepine, an anticonvulsant and mood stabilizer, can cause blood dyscrasia and liver disease, and therefore requires periodic monitoring for changes from baseline in CBCs and LFTs. Similarly, lithium is known to cause endocrine effects such as hypothyroidism and renal insufficiency; therefore, BUN, creatinine, and thyroid-stimulating hormone (TSH) should be monitored regularly after baseline levels are obtained.

- *TCAs:* All the TCAs cause varying degrees of anticholinergic effects (e.g., dry mouth, urinary retention, constipation, blurred vision); antihistaminic effects such as sedation and weight gain; orthostatic hypotension from alpha-1 blockade; sexual dysfunction; and the potential for cardiotoxicity because of the quinidinelike effects on the heart. In fact, cardiac conduction problems are a significant *contraindication* to treatment with TCAs.

- *MAOIs:* MAOIs are not used as first-line drugs because of their lethal interaction and overdose effects. A lethal hypertensive crisis can occur when these drugs are mixed with sympathomimetics or foods containing tyramine (a natural by-product of the fermentation process), such as cheeses, wines, beers, chopped liver, fava beans, and chocolate. Besides these agents, L-dopa and TCAs can also cause an excessive elevation in blood pressure, which can result in myocardial infarction and stroke. Other signs and symptoms of hypertensive crisis include severe headache, excessive sweating, dilated pupils, and cardiac conduction problems. MAOIs are also contraindicated with SSRIs, serotonin precursors, and some narcotic analgesics be-

cause they can cause central serotonin syndrome, characterized by rapid heart rate, hypertension, neuromuscular irritability, fever, and even coma, convulsions, and death. This is especially important when switching from an SSRI such as fluoxetine, which has a relatively long half-life, to an MAOI because this switch requires a longer waiting period (approximately 4 weeks). All these drugs can cause postural hypotension, sexual dysfunction, weight gain, and symptoms similar to those produced by muscarinic blockage (i.e., anticholinergic side effects). Insomnia and restlessness/activation are more commonly seen with tranylcypromine and not phenelzine.

- *SSRIs:* These drugs tend to show a milder side-effect profile than the older antidepressants. Common side effects include activation (sometimes experienced as anxiety), headache, gastrointestinal distress (e.g., nausea, vomiting, and diarrhea), sexual dysfunction (mainly delayed ejaculation/orgasm), and occasional asthenia. An interesting phenomenon is associated with SSRI side effects. SSRIs may cause either insomnia or sedation with no apparent predictability. Therefore, patients who are given a morning dosing schedule based on the common side effect of activation and insomnia will need to be educated about the freedom to switch to nighttime dosing should they experience sedation.

- *Trazodone and nefazodone:* Both of these drugs can cause sedation, postural hypotension, nausea, and vomiting. Trazodone has a greater potential for sedation, cardiac arrhythmias, and priapism (a sustained, painful engorgement of the penis or clitoris). Nefazodone appears to have a more benign side-effect profile, including headache, dry mouth, and asthenia.

- *Venlafaxine:* Venlafaxine's side effects are similar to the SSRI side-effect profile plus sweating, constipation, sedation, and dizziness. This drug is associated with a mild to moderate increase in diastolic blood pressure at higher doses; therefore, patients with hypertension should be monitored closely before dose increases.

- *Bupropion:* Bupropion shows various advantages over the SSRIs in that it does not have anticholinergic, postural hypotension, conduction arrhythmias, sexual dysfunction, or significant drug interaction effects. Side effects include activation and anorexia. In rare cases, bupropion has been associated with psychotic symptoms and seizure in doses over 450 mg per day.

- *Lithium:* Because of its low therapeutic index, lithium can easily result in toxicity. Toxic effects can be expected at serum levels above 1.5 mmol/L, with severe adverse effects occurring as low as 2.0 mmol/L and above. Signs of toxicity include sluggishness, impaired gait, slurred speech, tinnitus, abdominal distress, tremor, ECG abnormalities, low blood pressure, seizures, shock, delirium, and coma. Aside from toxic effects, lithium's side-effect profile includes nausea, vomiting, diarrhea, abdominal pain, sedation, tremor, muscular weakness, increased thirst and urination, swelling due to excessive fluid in body tissues, weight gain, dry mouth, and dermatological reactions. Chronic use can result in leukocytosis, hypothyroidism/goiter, acne, and ECG changes.

- *Carbamazepine:* Carbamazepine is associated with a number of rarely occurring toxicities, which include hepatitis, blood dyscrasias such as agranulocytosis and aplastic anemia, and exfoliative dermatitis (Stevens-Johnson syndrome). Incidents of leukopenia, thrombocytopenia, elevated liver enzymes, and dermatological reactions are typically reversible. Initial signs of toxicity include dizziness, blurred and double vision, sedation, and ataxia. Since carbamazepine is a potent inducer of hepatic enzymes, it speeds up metabolism and therefore can reduce the levels of several other drugs, including antipsychotics, valproate, TCAs, benzodiazepines, and hormonal contraceptives. Therapeutic drug monitoring is recommended.

- *Valproic acid:* Initial common side effects include gastrointestinal effects, sedation, tremor, and incoordination of involuntary muscle movements. With chronic use, there can be mild impairment of cognitive function, alopecia, and weight gain. Hematologi-cal effects include those seen commonly (e.g., thrombocytopenia, platelet dysfunction) and uncommonly (bleeding tendency). Hepatic effects include those seen commonly (benign increase of liver enzymes) and uncommonly (hepatitis/hepatic failure).

- *Benzodiazepines:* Predictably, the common side effects are sedation and fatigue. In addition, ataxia, slurred speech, and memory (usually anterograde amnesia) and cognitive function impairment may occur. Behavioral disinhibition can occur in the form of rage, aggression, impulse dyscontrol, and euphoria. All benzodiazepines can cause depression. Although these drugs tend to be safe in overdose, this is not the case when mixed with other CNS depressants, which, in combination, can result in respiratory depression. Patients should be counseled about this risk, particularly those who drink alcohol.

- *Buspirone:* This drug does not tend to produce sedation but can be initially activating. Side effects can include headache and gastrointestinal distress (e.g., nausea, diarrhea, heartburn). It is preferable to benzodiazepines in its side-effect profile since it shows virtually no sedation, cognitive and motor impairment, disinhibition, interaction with alcohol, or potential for dependence.

- *Traditional neuroleptics:* Three primary side effects include sedation, extrapyramidal symptoms, and anticholinergic effects. Extrapyramidal symptoms include parkinsonian symptoms such as rigidity, bradykinesia, and resting tremor; akathisia (internal restlessness); acute dystonias such as muscle contractions or spasms (e.g., ocular gyric crisis); and tardive dyskinesia. Some antipsychotics can also lower the seizure threshold, usually in a dose-dependent fashion.

- *Risperidone:* Although risperidone has a lower incidence of extrapyramidal symptoms, at higher doses it approximates the traditional neuroleptics. Other side effects include postural hypotension, sedation, cognitive impairment, asthenia, constipation, nausea, dyspepsia, tachycardia, headache, fatigue, sexual dysfunction, dizziness, galactorrhea, and weight gain.

- *Clozapine:* This is the only antipsychotic

that does not tend to produce tardive dyskinesia or extrapyramidal symptoms. Side effects include agranulocytosis, seizures, orthostatic hypotension, sedation, hypersalivation, tachycardia, constipation, hyperthermia, and eosinophilia.

- *Olanzapine:* Major side effects include somnolence, agitation, insomnia, nervousness, hostility, constipation, dry mouth, and weight gain.
- *Disulfiram:* Side effects include sluggishness, sedation, tremor, headache, impotence, dizziness, and complaints of malodor and bad breath.

Note

The opinions and assertions contained herein are the private views of the author and are not to be construed as the official policy or position of the U.S. government, the Department of Defense, or the Department of the Air Force.

References & Readings

Bezchilibenyk-Butler, K. Z., & Jefferies, J. J. (Eds.) (1997). *Clinical handbook of psychotropic drugs.* Toronto: Hogrefe and Huber.

Hahn, R. K., Albers, L. J., & Reist, C. (1997). *Current clinical strategies: Psychiatry.* Irvine, CA: Current Clinical Strategies Publishing.

Hyman, S. E., Arana, G. W., & Rosenbaum, J. F. (1995). *Handbook of psychiatric drug therapy.* Boston: Little, Brown.

Janicak, P. G., Davis, J. M., Preskorn, S. H., & Ayd, F. J. (1997). *Principles and practice of psychopharmacotherapy.* Baltimore: Williams & Wilkins.

Jensvold, M. F., Halbreich, U., & Hamilton, J. A. (Eds.) (1996). *Psychopharmacology and women.* Washington, DC: American Psychiatric Press.

Maxmen, J. S., & Ward, N. G. (1995). *Psychotropic drugs fast facts.* New York: Norton.

Preston, J., & Johnson, J. (1995). *Clinical psychopharmacology made ridiculously simple.* Miami, FL: MedMaster.

Schatzberg, A. F., & Nemeroff, D. B. (1995). *Textbook of psychopharmacology.* Washington, DC: American Psychiatric Press.

Wisner, K. L., Perel, J. M., & Wheeler, S. M. (1993). Tricyclic dose requirements across pregnancy. *American Journal of Psychiatry, 150,* 1541–1542.

Related Topics

88   PEDIATRIC PSYCHOPHARMACOLOGY

Timothy E. Wilens, Thomas J. Spencer, & Joseph Biederman

There is a growing awareness of psychiatric disorders in children and adolescents. Many of the children who suffer from psychopathology may benefit from psychopharmacological treatment. This chapter reviews the major psychopathology in childhood, potential risks, and treatment guidelines for using psychotropics in children and adolescents.

ATTENTION-DEFICIT/ HYPERACTIVITY DISORDER

Attention-deficit/hyperactivity disorder (ADHD) may affect from 5% to 9% of school-age children and persists into adulthood in approximately 50% of cases (Barkley, 1990). A child with ADHD is characterized by a degree of inattentiveness, impulsivity, and often hyperactivity that is inappropriate for the developmental stage of the affected child (Barkley, 1990). ADHD symptoms vary among children and may adversely influence all areas of function, including academic performance, overall behavior, and social/interpersonal relationships with adults and peers. More recent studies indicate that ADHD commonly co-occurs with oppositional-defiant, conduct, depressive, and anxiety disorders (Biederman, Newcorn, & Sprich, 1991). ADHD has a male preponderance and appears to run in families. The pharmacological management of ADHD relies on agents that affect dopaminergic and noradrenergic neurotransmission, namely, stimulants, antidepressants, and antihypertensives (Spencer et al., 1996).

Stimulants

The most commonly used stimulants are methylphenidate (Ritalin®), dextroamphetamine (Dexedrine), magnesium pemoline (Cylert), and amphetamine compounds (Adderall, Desoxyn). Stimulants have been shown to be effective in approximately 70% of patients and appear to operate in a dose-dependent manner in improving cognition and behavior (Wilens & Biederman, 1992). The beneficial effects of stimulants are of a similar quality and magnitude in patients of both sexes and across different ages, from preschool years to adulthood. Whereas methylphenidate and dextroamphetamine are both short-acting compounds, with slow-release preparations available, pemoline is given as a single dose in the morning. Dosing starts at 5 mg daily for the short-acting stimulants and increases up to 1–2 mg/kg/day of medication. The typical starting dose of pemoline is 37.5 up to 75–150 mg/day. There appears to be a dose-response relationship for both behavioral and cognitive effects of the stimulants in ADHD individuals (Wilens & Biederman, 1992). The most commonly reported short-term side effects associated with the stimulants are appetite suppression, sleep disturbances, dysphoria, irritability, and rebound phenomena. Pemoline has also been associated with abnormal motor movements and hepatotoxicity. Long-term side effects remain controversial and include tic development and height/weight decrement. Although the negative effects on growth velocity may be offset by drug holidays, the continuous use of stimulants on weekends and holidays should be determined individually.

Antihypertensives

The antihypertensive agent clonidine has been used increasingly for the treatment of ADHD, particularly in younger children and those with hyperactivity and aggressivity. Clonidine is a short-acting agent with daily dosing ranging from 0.05 mg to 0.6 mg given in divided doses up to four times daily. Clonidine is used adjunctly with the stimulants and antidepressants. Short-term adverse effects include sedation (which tends to subside with continued treatment), dry mouth, depression, confusion, ECG changes, and hypertension with abrupt withdrawal (Hunt, Minderaa, & Cohen, 1985). Abrupt withdrawal of clonidine has been associated with rebound; thus, slow tapering is advised. Guanfacine (Tenex) has also been used for ADHD. Guanfacine appears to be longer acting, less sedating, and more effective for attentional problems than clonidine (Spencer et al., 1996). Dosing in school-age children generally starts at 0.5 mg/day and gradually increases as necessary to a maximum of 4 mg/day in two or three divided doses.

Antidepressants

Second to the stimulants, the antidepressants have been the most studied pharmacological treatment for ADHD (Spencer et al., 1996). The tricyclic antidepressants (TCAs) have generally been considered second-line drugs of choice because of a long duration of action and minimal risk of abuse or dependence. The novel dopaminergic antidepressant bupropion has been reported to be effective and well tolerated in the treatment of ADHD children.

DEPRESSION

Juvenile depression may occur in up to 5% of adolescents. Symptoms of childhood depression include irritability, sad facial expression, low energy, isolation, withdrawal, negativism and aggression, and suicidality (Kashani & Schmid, 1992). Children with subsyndromal chronic depressive disorders may have dysthymic disorder. Childhood depression commonly co-occurs with anxiety, ADHD, conduct disorders, and substance use disorders. Juvenile mood disorders are chronic and highly recurrent. The antidepressants are the mainstay of treatment (Bostic, Wilens, Biederman, & Spencer, 1997).

Serotonin Reuptake Inhibitors

Serotonin reuptake inhibitors (SRIs), including fluoxetine (Prozac), paroxetine (Paxil), sertraline (Zoloft), and fluvoxamine (Luvox), are generally considered the first-line drugs of choice for juvenile depression (Emslie et al., 1997). These agents vary in how long they last and their adverse effects. Whereas fluoxetine has a long half-life of 7–9 days, paroxetine and sertraline have half-lives of approximately 24 hours (Baldessarini, 1996). Because of its long half-life, missed doses of fluoxetine have less effect on overall clinical stabilization than the other SRIs. In contrast, in children prone to develop mania, the selection of a shorter-acting SRI may be preferable.

Although not well established, the suggested daily doses in pediatric subjects approximate those in adults and vary among SRIs. Treatment generally begins with 5–10 mg of fluoxetine or paroxetine or 25 mg of sertraline or fluvoxamine and may be titrated upward to full adult doses in some cases (i.e., 20–30 mg of fluoxetine or paroxetine; 150–200 mg of sertraline or fluvoxamine). Common adverse effects of SRIs include agitation, gastrointestinal symptoms, irritability, insomnia, and headaches. Fluvoxamine may cause sedation and is useful in children with comorbid sleep difficulties. All the SRIs have been found to inhibit various hepatic (liver) enzymes and thereby increase blood levels of other medications.

Tricyclic Antidepressants

Tricyclic antidepressants (TCAs) include desipramine, nortriptyline, amitriptyline, and imipramine. Although these agents have not been demonstrated to be effective in controlled trials, they are often used in comorbid states. Treatment with a TCA should be initiated with a 10-mg or 25-mg dose and increased slowly every 4–5 days by 20–30%. Typical dose ranges for the TCAs are 2.0–5.0 mg/kg (1.0–3.0 mg/kg for nortriptyline). Common adverse effects of the TCAs include dry mouth, blurred vision, and constipation, as well as rashes, nightmares, and stomachaches. Overdose on TCAs can be fatal. Reports of sudden death in four children on TCAs (1990) have led to increased caution in the use of these compounds, including ECG monitoring by some physicians.

Other Antidepressants

Venlafaxine (Effexor) possesses both serotonergic and noradrenergic properties and may prove to be useful in the treatment of juvenile mood disorders with ADHD at typical doses of 50–150 mg/day. Adverse effects of venlafaxine are similar to those of the SRIs with the addition of nausea, which generally improves within the first week of use, and increased blood pressure.

Bupropion (Wellbutrin®) may be helpful in children with prominent mood lability, dysthymia, or comorbid ADHD. Similar to the management of ADHD, bupropion should be started at 37.5 mg/day and titrated upward as necessary to 150–399 mg/day. The major side effects include irritability, insomnia, tic exacerbation, and seizures.

BIPOLAR DISORDER

In children, mania is commonly manifested by an extremely irritable or explosive mood, unmodulated high energy such as overtalkativeness, racing thoughts, poor quality of sleep, or increased goal-directedness with associated poor functioning (Geller et al., 1995). The clinical course of juvenile mania is frequently chronic and mixed, with manic and depressive features co-occurring. For juvenile bipolar disorders, the mood stabilizers remain the treatment of choice.

Mood Stabilizers

Lithium is a salt that is considered one of the initial agents for labile mood disorders (Alessi, Naylor, Ghaziuddin, & Zubieta, 1994). The usual lithium starting dosage ranges from 150 to 300 mg in divided doses once or twice a day and increased based on response, side effects, and serum levels. Suggested serum levels are 0.6–1.5 mEq/L for acute episodes and levels of 0.4–0.8 mEq/L for maintenance therapy. Common short-term side effects include gastrointestinal symptoms, frequent urination and drinking, tremor, and somnolence. The chronic administration of lithium may be associated with weight gain, thyroid dysfunction, and renal impairment, necessitating renal and thyroid monitoring.

Alternative mood-stabilizing agents used in children include the anticonvulsants valproic acid (Depakote, valproate) and carbamazepine (Tegretol) (McElroy, Keck, Pope, & Hudson, 1992). Carbamazepine is dosed from 200 to 1,000 mg, leading to therapeutic blood levels of between 4 and 12 µg/ml. Common side effects include dizziness, drowsiness, nausea, blurred vision, white blood cell suppression, and serious rashes. Valproic acid is sometimes used as a first-line treatment and is dosed from 250 to 1,500 mg/day, leading to therapeutic blood levels of 50–100 µg/ml. Common short-term side effects in children include sedation, nausea, and thinning of hair. For both anticonvulsants, monitoring of blood counts and liver function is warranted during treatment (Baldessarini, 1996). Gabapentin (Neurontin), lamotroqine (Lamietal), and topiramate (Topimax) are also anticonvulsants that are recently being used in youth with prominent mood lability, although their efficacy and safety profiles in children remain unstudied.

ANXIETY DISORDERS

The anxiety disorders encompass a wide range of clinical conditions in which anxiety is the predominant feature (Reiter, Kutcher, & Gardner, 1992). These include childhood disorders such as separation anxiety, generalized anxiety, and social phobia. Also within the umbrella of anxiety disorders of childhood is posttraumatic stress disorder, in which there is an objective stressor outside the usual human experience along with the recurrent experiencing of the event and accompanying hypervigilance or dissociation. Children may also present with panic disorder and agoraphobia, a fear of places with limited escape. Children with anxiety disorders often have other coexisting emotional factors such as depression, as well as behavioral problems such as ADHD. The benzodiazepines and antidepressants are the mainstay of pharmacotherapy for children and adolescents with anxiety disorders.

Benzodiazepines

The benzodiazepines remain one of the most important agents for anxiety (Graae, Milner, Rozzotto, & Klein, 1994). Benzodiazepines are chosen based on how long they last and their strength. The more potent agents clonazepam (Klonopin) and lorazepam (Ativan) are often used in children with severe anxiety or panic, whereas the lower-potency agents like diazepam (Valium) can be helpful in generalized anxiety. Dosing varies between agents, which are usually given in divided daily doses. Short-term adverse effects are disinhibition and sedation. Although the benzodiazepines have a measurable abuse liability, there is little evidence that therapeutic use predisposes children to later abuse.

Antidepressants

Other pharmacological treatments that may be helpful for either uncomplicated or comorbid anxiety disorders include the use of the TCAs (nortriptyline and others), serotonin reuptake inhibitors (fluoxetine and others), or nefazodone (Serzone) as single agents or in combination with benzodiazepines (Birmaher et al., 1994).

OBSESSIVE-COMPULSIVE DISORDER

Obsessive-compulsive disorder (OCD) affects 1–2% of the population and is characterized by persistent ideas or impulses (obsessions) that are intrusive and senseless such as thoughts of becoming contaminated or self-doubting, repetitive, and purposeful behaviors (compulsions) such as hand washing, counting, or touching in order to neutralize the obsessive worries (Swedo, Leonard, & Rapoport, 1992). Trichotillomania, the compulsive pulling out of one's hair, may be related to OCD. The serotonergic antidepressants are the most effective medications for OCD.

Clomipramine

Clomipramine has been shown to be efficacious in youths with OCD (Swedo et al., 1992). Clomipramine is dosed from 50 to 200 mg daily and has side effects and monitoring requirements similar to those of the other TCAs.

Serotonin Reuptake Inhibitors

There is also an emerging literature on the efficacy of SRIs for juvenile OCD. Preliminary indications suggest relatively higher doses of SRIs may be necessary for adequate treatment of the condition (i.e., fluoxetine doses of 40–80 mg/day). Currently, sertraline (Zoloft) and fluvoxamine (Luvox) are FDA approved for OCD in youth.

TICS AND TOURETTE'S DISORDER

Tourette's disorder is a childhood-onset neuropsychiatric disorder that consists of multiple motor and phonic tics and other behavioral and psychological symptoms (Cohen, Bruun, & Leckman, 1988). Affected patients commonly have spontaneous waxing, waning, and symptomatic fluctuation. Tourette's disorder is commonly associated with OCD, ADHD, and anxiety disorders (Coffey, Frazier, & Chen, 1992). The pharmacotherapy of tic disorders has changed in recent years and is influenced by the presence of comorbid conditions.

Clonidine

Clonidine has been increasingly utilized as a first-line drug of choice for tics and Tourette's syndrome. The mechanism of action of clonidine's effectiveness remains unknown. Dosing for tics or Tourette's disorder appears similar to that employed for ADHD.

Antidepressants

More recently, the TCAs have been used in youth with this disorder. TCAs may be particularly helpful in reducing tic and ADHD symptoms in children with this comorbidity disorder (Singer et al., 1994). Patients with commonly comorbid OCD may need additional pharmacotherapy with serotonergic blocking drugs such as clomipramine or SRIs.

Antipsychotics

The antipsychotics remain the most efficacious agents for tics in children who fail to respond to other treatments (Cohen et al., 1988). The high-potency antipsychotics pimozide (Orap) and haloperidol (Haldol) are generally used in doses of 0.5–15 mg/day. However, antipsychotics have limited effects on the frequently associated comorbid disorders (ADHD and OCD) and carry a risk for the development of tardive dyskinesia.

PSYCHOSIS

Psychosis is used to describe abnormal behaviors of children with impaired reality testing such as the presence of delusions, hallucinations, or thought disorders. Psychosis is present in schizophrenia and related disorders and in some forms of unipolar or bipolar mood disorders. The antipsychotics (neuroleptics) are the major treatment for psychosis.

Traditional Antipsychotics

An extensive array of traditional agents are commonly classified based on their potency (strength). The low-potency agents requiring higher dosages include chlorpromazine (Thorazine) and thioridazine (Mellaril). The intermediate-potency agents include trifluoperazine (Stelazine), thiothixene (Navane), and perphenazine (Trilafon). The high-potency agents requiring lower doses include haloperidol (Haldol) and fluphenazine (Prolixin) (Baldessarini, 1996). The usual daily doses are 100–400 mg for the low-potency agents; 5–40 mg for the intermediate-potency agents; and 0.5–20 mg for the high-potency compounds. Common short-term adverse effects of antipsychotic drugs are motor restlessness or spasms, parkinsonism, dry mouth, and significant weight gain. However, whereas the low-potency agents are more likely to cause hypotension, tachycardia, and sedation, the high-potency agents may cause muscle spasms. Long-term administration of antipsychotics may be associated with abnormal involuntary motor movements called tardive dyskinesia (Campbell, Adams, Perry, Spencer, & Overall, 1988).

Atypical Antipsychotics

Because of the adverse effects and limited efficacy of the traditional agents for treating the negative symptoms of psychosis (e.g., withdrawal), the atypical antipsychotics are being increasingly used. Risperidone (Risperdal) is a high-potency agent that has fewer extrapyramidal adverse effects than traditional neuroleptics. Olanzapine (Zyprexa) is an intermediate-potency agent and quetiapine (Seroquel) is a low-potency agent, both of which are useful for psychosis and severe mood lability. Risperidone, olanzapine, and quetiapine appear useful in treating both positive and negative symptoms of psychotic illness and are free of many of the side effects associated with clozapine. Clozapine (Clozaril) is a low-potency agent that is being used in treatment of refractory individuals, particularly those with negative symptoms or those who develop tardive dyskinesia (Kumra, Frazier, & Jacobsen, 1996). Clozapine has a relatively high incidence of dose-related seizures and bone marrow suppression, making weekly white blood counts mandatory.

CONCLUSION

The field of pediatric psychopharmacology continues to expand as more agents are used and systematically tested for a broad spectrum of child psychopathological conditions. The use of combined pharmacotherapy has proved invaluable for resistant and comorbid conditions. Essential features in treating child psychopathology include careful diagnostic assessment and the integration of pharmacotherapy as part of a broader treatment plan.

References & Readings

Alessi, N., Naylor, M., Ghaziuddin, M., & Zubieta, J. (1994). Update on lithium carbonate therapy in children and adolescents. *Journal of the American Academy of Child and Adolescent Psychiatry, 33*, 291–304.

Baldessarini, R. J. (1996). *Chemotherapy in psychiatry.* Cambridge, MA: Harvard University Press.

Barkley, R. A. (1990). *Attention deficit hyperactivity disorder: A handbook for diagnosis and treatment.* New York: Guilford Press.

Biederman, J., Newcorn, J., & Sprich, S. (1991). Comorbidity of attention deficit hyperactivity disorder with conduct, depressive, anxiety, and other disorders. *American Journal of Psychiatry, 148*, 564–577.

Birmaher, B., Waterman, S., Ryan, N., Cully, M., Balach, L., & Ingram, J. (1994). Fluoxetine for childhood anxiety disorders. *Journal of the American Academy of Child and Adolescent Psychiatry, 33*, 7.

Bostic, J., Wilens, T., Biederman, J., & Spencer, T. (1997). Mood disorders in children and adolescents. *Pediatric Clinics of North America, 44*, 1487–1504.

Campbell, M., Adams, P., Perry, R., Spencer, E. K., & Overall, J. E. (1988). Tardive and withdrawal dyskinesia in autistic children: A prospective study. *Psychopharmacology Bulletin, 24*, 251–255.

Coffey, B., Frazier, J., & Chen, S. (1992). Comorbidity, Tourette syndrome, and anxiety disorders. In T. N. Chase, A. J. Friedhoff, & D. J. Cohen (Eds.), *Advances in neurology, Tourette syndrome: Genetics, neurobiology, and treatment* (pp. 95–104). New York: Raven Press.

Cohen, D. J., Bruun, R. D., & Leckman, J. F. (Eds.) (1988). *Tourette's syndrome and tic disorders:*

Clinical understanding and treatment. New York: Wiley.

Emslie, G., Rush, J., Weinberg, W., Kowatch, R., Hughes, C., Carmody, T., & Rintelmann, J. (1997). A double-blind, randomized, placebo-controlled trial of fluoxetine in children and adolescents with depression. *Archives of General Psychiatry, 54,* 1031–1037.

Geller, B., Sun, K., Zimerman, B., Luby, J., Frazier, J., & Williams, M. (1995). Complex and rapid-cycling in bipolar children and adolescents: A preliminary study. *Journal of Affective Disorders,* 1–10.

Graae, F., Milner, J., Rizzotto, L., & Klein, R. (1994). Clonazepam in childhood anxiety disorders. *Journal of the American Academy of Child and Adolescent Psychiatry, 33,* 372–376.

Hunt, R. D., Minderaa, R. B., & Cohen, D. J. (1985). Clonidine benefits children with attention deficit disorder and hyperactivity: Report of a double-blind placebo-crossover therapeutic trial. *Journal of the American Academy of Child Psychiatry, 24,* 617–629.

Kashani, J., & Schmid, L. S. (1992). Epidemiology and etiology of depressive disorders. In M. Shafii & S. Shafii (Eds.), *Clinical guide to depression in children and adolescents* (pp. 43–64). Washington DC: American Psychiatric Press.

Kumra, S., Frazier, J. A., & Jacobsen, L. (1996). Childhood onset schizophrenia: A double blind clozapine trial. *Archives of General Psychiatry, 53,* 1090–1097.

McElroy, S. L., Keck, P. E., Pope, H. G., & Hudson, J. I. (1992). Valproate in the treatment of bipolar disorder: Literature review and clinical guidelines. *Journal of Clinical Psychopharmacology, 12,* 42S.

Reiter, S., Kutcher, S., & Gardner, D. (1992). Anxiety disorders in children and adolescents: Clinical and related issues in pharmacological treatment. *Canadian Journal of Psychiatry, 37,* 432–438.

Singer, S., Brown, J., Quaskey, S., Rosenberg, L., Mellits, E., & Denckla, M. (1994). The treatment of attention-deficit hyperactivity disorder in Tourette's syndrome: A double-blind placebo-controlled study with clonidine and desipramine. *Pediatrics, 95,* 74–81.

Spencer, T., Biederman, J., Wilens, T., Harding, M., O'Donnell, D., & Griffin, S. (1996). Pharmacotherapy of attention deficit disorder across the life cycle. *Journal of the American Academy of Child and Adolescent Psychiatry, 35,* 409–432.

Swedo, S. E., Leonard, H. L., & Rapoport, J. L. (1992). Childhood-onset obsessive compulsive disorder. *Psychiatric Clinics of North America, 15,* 767–775.

Wilens, T. E., & Biederman, J. (1992). The stimulants. In D. Shafer (Ed.), *The psychiatric clinics of North America* (pp. 191–222). Philadelphia: Saunders.

Related Topics

PART V
Ethical and Legal Issues

89

AMERICAN PSYCHOLOGICAL ASSOCIATION'S ETHICAL PRINCIPLES OF PSYCHOLOGISTS AND CODE OF CONDUCT

CONTENTS

413

INTRODUCTION

The American Psychological Association's (APA's) Ethical Principles of Psychologists and Code of Conduct (hereinafter referred to as the Ethics Code) consists of an Introduction, a Preamble, six General Principles (A–F), and specific Ethical Standards. The Introduction discusses the intent, organization, procedural considerations, and scope of application of the Ethics Code. The Preamble and General Principles are *aspirational* goals to guide psychologists toward the highest ideals of psychology. Although the Preamble and General Principles are not themselves enforceable rules, they should be considered by psychologists in arriving at an ethical course of action and may be considered by ethics bodies in interpreting the Ethical Standards. The Ethical Standards set forth *enforceable* rules for conduct as psychologists. Most of the Ethical Standards are written broadly, in order to apply to psychologists in varied roles, although the application of an Ethical Standard may vary depending on the context. The Ethical Standards are not exhaustive. The fact that a given conduct is not specifically addressed by the Ethics Code does not mean that it is necessarily either ethical or unethical.

Membership in the APA commits members to adhere to the APA Ethics Code and to the rules and procedures used to implement it. Psychologists and students, whether or not they are APA members, should be aware that the Ethics Code may be applied to them by state psychology boards, courts, or other public bodies.

This Ethics Code applies only to psychologists' work-related activities, that is, activities that are part of the psychologists' scientific and professional functions or that are psychological in nature. It includes the clinical or counseling practice of psychology, research, teaching, supervision of trainees, development of assessment instruments, conducting assessments, educational counseling, organizational consulting, social intervention, administration, and other activities as well. These work-related activities can be distinguished from the purely private conduct of a psychologist, which ordinarily is not within the purview of the Ethics Code.

The Ethics Code is intended to provide standards of professional conduct that can be applied by the APA and by other bodies that choose to adopt them. Whether or not a psychologist has violated the Ethics Code does not by itself determine whether he or she is legally liable in a court action, whether a contract is enforceable, or whether other legal consequences occur. These results are based on legal rather than ethical rules. However, compliance with or violation of the Ethics Code may be admissible as evidence in some legal proceedings, depending on the circumstances.

In the process of making decisions regarding their professional behavior, psychologists must consider this Ethics Code, in addition to applicable laws and psychology board regulations. If the Ethics Code establishes a higher standard of conduct than is required by law, psychologists must meet the higher ethical standard. If the Ethics Code standard appears to conflict with the requirements of law, then psychologists make known their commitment to the Ethics Code and take steps to resolve the conflict in a responsible manner. If neither law nor the Ethics Code resolves an issue, psychologists should consider other professional materials[1] and the dictates of their own conscience, as well as seek consultation with others within the field when this is practical.

The procedures for filing, investigating, and resolving complaints of unethical conduct are described in the current Rules and Procedures of the APA Ethics Committee. The actions that APA may take for violations of the Ethics Code include actions such as reprimand, censure, termination of APA membership, and referral of the matter to other bodies. Complainants who seek remedies such as monetary damages in alleging ethical violations by a psychologist must resort to private negotiation, administrative bodies, or the courts. Actions that violate the Ethics Code may lead to the imposition of sanctions on a psychologist by bodies other than APA, including state psychological associations, other professional groups, psychology boards, other state or federal agencies, and payors for health services. In addition to actions for violation of the Ethics Code, the APA Bylaws provide that APA may take action against a member after his or her conviction of a felony, expulsion or suspension from an affiliated state psychological association, or suspension or loss of licensure.

This version of the APA Ethics Code was adopted by the American Psychological Association's Council of Representatives during its meeting, August 13 and 16, 1992, and is effective beginning December 1, 1992. Inquiries concerning the substance or interpretation of the APA Ethics Code should be addressed to the Director, Office of Ethics, American Psychological Association, 750 First Street, NE, Washington, DC 20002-4242.

This Code will be used to adjudicate complaints brought concerning alleged conduct occurring on or after the effective date. Complaints regarding conduct occurring prior to the effective date will be adjudicated on the basis of the version of the Code that was in effect at the time the conduct occurred, except that no provisions repealed in June 1989 will be enforced even if an earlier version contains the provision. The Ethics Code will undergo continuing review and study for future revisions; comments on the code may be sent to the above address.

The APA has previously published its Ethical Standards as follows:

American Psychological Association. (1953). *Ethical standards of psychologists*. Washington, DC: Author.

American Psychological Association. (1958). Standards of ethical behavior for psychologists. *American Psychologist, 13,* 268–271.

American Psychological Association. (1963). Ethical standards of psychologists. *American Psychologist, 18,* 56–60.

American Psychological Association. (1968). Ethical standards of psychologists. *American Psychologist, 23,* 357–361.

American Psychological Association. (1977, March). Ethical standards of psychologists. *APA Monitor,* pp. 22–23.

American Psychological Association. (1979). *Ethical standards of psychologists*. Washington, DC: Author.

American Psychological Association. (1981). Ethical principles of psychologists. *American Psychologist, 36,* 633–638.

American Psychological Association. (1990). Ethical principles of psychologists (Amended June 2, 1989). *American Psychologist, 45,* 390–395.

Request copies of the APA's Ethical Principles of Psychologists and Code of Conduct from the APA Order Department, 750 First Street, NE, Washington, DC 20002-4242, or phone (202) 336-5510.

---

[1]Professional materials that are most helpful in this regard are guidelines and standards that have been adopted or endorsed by professional psychological organizations. Such guidelines and standards, whether adopted by the American Psychological Association (APA) or its Divisions, are not enforceable as such by this Ethics Code, but are of educative value to psychologists, courts, and professional bodies. Such materials include, but are not limited to, the APA's *General Guidelines for Providers of Psychological Services* (1987), *Specialty Guidelines for the Delivery of Services by Clinical Psychologists, Counseling Psychologists, Industrial/Organizational Psychologists, and School Psychologists* (1981), *Guidelines for Computer Based Tests and Interpretations* (1987), *Standards for Educational and Psychological Testing* (1985), *Ethical Principles in the Conduct of Research With Human Participants* (1982), *Guidelines for Ethical Conduct in the Care and Use of Animals* (1986), *Guidelines for Providers of Psychological Services to Ethnic, Linguistic, and Culturally Diverse Pop-*

ulations (1990), and *Publication Manual of the American Psychological Association* (3rd ed., 1983). Materials not adopted by APA as a whole include the APA Division 41 (Forensic Psychology)/American Psychology–Law Society's *Speciality Guidelines for Forensic Psychologists* (1991).

PREAMBLE

Psychologists work to develop a valid and reliable body of scientific knowledge based on research. They may apply that knowledge to human behavior in a variety of contexts. In doing so, they perform many roles, such as researcher, educator, diagnostician, therapist, supervisor, consultant, administrator, social interventionist, and expert witness. Their goal is to broaden knowledge of behavior and, where appropriate, to apply it pragmatically to improve the condition of both the individual and society. Psychologists respect the central importance of freedom of inquiry and expression in research, teaching, and publication. They also strive to help the public in developing informed judgments and choices concerning human behavior. This Ethics Code provides a common set of values upon which psychologists build their professional and scientific work.

This Code is intended to provide both the general principles and the decision rules to cover most situations encountered by psychologists. It has as its primary goal the welfare and protection of the individuals and groups with whom psychologists work. It is the individual responsibility of each psychologist to aspire to the highest possible standards of conduct. Psychologists respect and protect human and civil rights, and do not knowingly participate in or condone unfair discriminatory practices.

The development of a dynamic set of ethical standards for a psychologist's work-related conduct requires a personal commitment to a lifelong effort to act ethically; to encourage ethical behavior by students, supervisees, employees, and colleagues, as appropriate; and to consult with others, as needed, concerning ethical problems. Each psychologist supplements, but does not violate, the Ethics Code's values and rules on the basis of guidance drawn from personal values, culture, and experience.

GENERAL PRINCIPLES

Principle A: Competence

Psychologists strive to maintain high standards of competence in their work. They recognize the boundaries of their particular competencies and the limitations of their expertise. They provide only those services and use only those techniques for which they are qualified by education, training, or experience. Psychologists are cognizant of the fact that the competencies required in serving, teaching, and/or studying groups of people vary with the distinctive characteristics of those groups. In those areas in which recognized professional standards do not yet exist, psychologists exercise careful judgment and take appropriate precautions to protect the welfare of those with whom they work. They maintain knowledge of relevant scientific and professional information related to the services they render, and they recognize the need for ongoing education. Psychologists make appropriate use of scientific, professional, technical, and administrative resources.

Principle B: Integrity

Psychologists seek to promote integrity in the science, teaching, and practice of psychology. In these activities psychologists are honest, fair, and respectful of others. In describing or reporting their qualifications, services, products, fees, research, or teaching, they do not make statements that are false, misleading, or deceptive. Psychologists strive to be aware of their own belief systems, values, needs, and limitations and the effect of these on their work. To the extent feasible, they attempt to clarify for relevant parties the roles they are performing and to function appropriately in accordance with those roles. Psychologists avoid improper and potentially harmful dual relationships.

Principle C: Professional and Scientific Responsibility

Psychologists uphold professional standards of conduct, clarify their professional roles and obligations, accept appropriate responsibility for their behavior, and adapt their methods to the needs of different populations. Psychologists consult with, refer to, or cooperate with other professionals and institutions to the extent needed to serve the best interests of their patients, clients, or other recipients of their services. Psychologists' moral standards and conduct are personal matters to the same degree as is true for any other person, except as psychologists' conduct may compromise their professional responsibilities or reduce the public's trust in psychology and psychologists. Psychologists are concerned about the ethical compliance of their colleagues' scientific and professional conduct. When appropriate, they consult with colleagues in order to prevent or avoid unethical conduct.

Principle D: Respect for People's Rights and Dignity

Psychologists accord appropriate respect to the fundamental rights, dignity, and worth of all people. They respect the rights of individuals to privacy, confidentiality, self-determination, and autonomy, mindful that legal and other obligations may lead to inconsistency and conflict with the exercise of these rights. Psychologists are aware of cultural, individual, and role differences, including those due to age, gender, race, ethnicity, national origin, religion, sexual orientation, disability, language, and socioeconomic status. Psychologists try to eliminate the effect on their work of biases based on those factors, and they do not knowingly participate in or condone unfair discriminatory practices.

Principle E: Concern for Others' Welfare

Psychologists seek to contribute to the welfare of those with whom they interact professionally. In their professional actions, psychologists weigh the welfare and rights of their patients or clients, students, supervisees, human research participants, and other affected persons, and the welfare of animal subjects of research. When conflicts occur among psychologists' obligations or concerns, they attempt to resolve these conflicts and to perform their roles in a responsible fashion that avoids or minimizes harm. Psychologists are sensitive to real and ascribed differences in power between themselves and others, and they do not exploit or mislead other people during or after professional relationships.

Principle F: Social Responsibility

Psychologists are aware of their professional and scientific responsibilities to the community and the society in which they work and live. They apply and make public their knowledge of psychology in order to contribute to human welfare. Psychologists are concerned about and work to mitigate the causes of human suffering. When undertaking research, they strive to advance human welfare and the science of psychology. Psychologists try to avoid misuse of their work. Psychologists comply with the law and encourage the development of law and social policy that serve the interests of their patients and clients and the public. They are encouraged to contribute a portion of their professional time for little or no personal advantage.

ETHICAL STANDARDS

1. General Standards

These General Standards are potentially applicable to the professional and scientific activities of all psychologists.

1.01 Applicability of the Ethics Code

The activity of a psychologist subject to the Ethics Code may be reviewed under these Ethical Standards only if the activity is part of his or her work-related functions or the activity is psychological in nature. Personal activities having no connection to or effect on psychological roles are not subject to the Ethics Code.

1.02 Relationship of Ethics and Law

If psychologists' ethical responsibilities conflict with law, psychologists make known their commitment to the Ethics Code and take steps to resolve the conflict in a responsible manner.

1.03 Professional and Scientific Relationship

Psychologists provide diagnostic, therapeutic, teaching, research, supervisory, consultative, or other psychological services only in the context of a defined professional or scientific relationship or role. (See also Standards 2.01, Evaluation, Diagnosis, and Interventions in Professional Context, and 7.02, Forensic Assessments.)

1.04 Boundaries of Competence

(a) Psychologists provide services, teach, and conduct research only within the boundaries of their competence, based on their education, training, supervised experience, or appropriate professional experience.

(b) Psychologists provide services, teach, or conduct research in new areas or involving new techniques only after first undertaking appropriate study, training, supervision, and/or consultation from persons who are competent in those areas or techniques.

(c) In those emerging areas in which generally recognized standards for preparatory training do not yet exist, psychologists nevertheless take reasonable steps to ensure the competence of their work and to protect patients, clients, students, research participants, and others from harm.

1.05 Maintaining Expertise

Psychologists who engage in assessment, therapy, teaching, research, organizational consulting, or other professional activities maintain a reasonable level of awareness of current scientific and professional information in their fields of activity, and undertake ongoing efforts to maintain competence in the skills they use.

1.06 Basis for Scientific and Professional Judgments

Psychologists rely on scientifically and professionally derived knowledge when making scientific or professional judgments or when engaging in scholarly or professional endeavors.

1.07 Describing the Nature and Results of Psychological Services

(a) When psychologists provide assessment, evaluation, treatment, counseling, supervision, teaching, consultation, research, or other psychological services to an individual, a group, or an organization, they provide, using language that is reasonably understandable to the recipient of those services, appropriate information beforehand about the nature of such services and appropriate information later about results and conclusions. (See also Standard 2.09, Explaining Assessment Results.)

(b) If psychologists will be precluded by law or by organizational roles from providing such information to particular individuals or groups, they so inform those individuals or groups at the outset of the service.

1.08 Human Differences

Where differences of age, gender, race, ethnicity, national origin, religion, sexual orientation, disability, language, or socioeconomic status significantly affect psychologists' work concerning particular individuals or groups, psychologists obtain the training, experience, consultation, or supervision necessary to ensure the competence of their services, or they make appropriate referrals.

1.09 Respecting Others

In their work-related activities, psychologists respect the rights of others to hold values, attitudes, and opinions that differ from their own.

1.10 Nondiscrimination

In their work-related activities, psychologists do not engage in unfair discrimination based on age, gender, race, ethnicity, national origin, religion, sexual orientation, disability, socioeconomic status, or any basis proscribed by law.

1.11 Sexual Harassment

(a) Psychologists do not engage in sexual harassment. Sexual harassment is sexual solicitation, physical advances, or verbal or nonverbal conduct that is sexual in nature, that occurs in connection with the psychologist's activities or roles as a psychologist, and that either: (1) is unwelcome, is offensive, or creates a hostile workplace environment, and the psychologist knows or is told this; or (2) is sufficiently severe or intense to be abusive to a reasonable person in the context. Sexual harassment can consist of a single intense or severe act or of multiple persistent or pervasive acts.

(b) Psychologists accord sexual-harassment complainants and respondents dignity and respect. Psychologists do not participate in denying a person academic admittance or advancement, employment, tenure, or promotion, based solely upon their having made, or their being the subject of, sexual harassment charges. This does not preclude taking action based upon the outcome of such proceedings or consideration of other appropriate information.

1.12 Other Harassment

Psychologists do not knowingly engage in behavior that is harassing or demeaning to persons with whom they interact in their work based on factors such as those persons' age, gender, race, ethnicity, national origin, religion, sexual orientation, disability, language, or socioeconomic status.

1.13 Personal Problems and Conflicts

(a) Psychologists recognize that their personal problems and conflicts may interfere with their effectiveness. Accordingly, they refrain from undertaking an activity when they know or should know that their personal problems are likely to lead to harm to a patient, client, colleague, student, research participant, or other person to whom they may owe a professional or scientific obligation.

(b) In addition, psychologists have an obligation to be alert to signs of, and to obtain assistance for, their personal problems at an early stage, in order to prevent significantly impaired performance.

(c) When psychologists become aware of personal problems that may interfere with their performing work-related duties adequately, they take appropriate measures, such as obtaining professional consultation or assistance, and determine whether they should limit, suspend, or terminate their work-related duties.

1.14 Avoiding Harm

Psychologists take reasonable steps to avoid harming their patients or clients, research participants, students, and others with whom they work, and to minimize harm where it is foreseeable and unavoidable.

1.15 Misuse of Psychologists' Influence

Because psychologists' scientific and professional judgments and actions may affect the lives of others, they are alert to and guard against personal, financial, social, organizational, or political factors that might lead to misuse of their influence.

1.16 Misuse of Psychologists' Work

(a) Psychologists do not participate in activities in which it appears likely that their skills or data will be misused by others, unless corrective mechanisms are available. (See also Standard 7.04, Truthfulness and Candor.)

(b) If psychologists learn of misuse or misrepresentation of their work, they take reasonable steps to correct or minimize the misuse or misrepresentation.

1.17 Multiple Relationships

(a) In many communities and situations, it may not be feasible or reasonable for psychologists to avoid social or other nonprofessional contacts with persons such as patients, clients, students, supervisees, or research participants. Psychologists must always be sensitive to the potential harmful effects of other contacts on their work and on those persons with whom they deal. A psychologist refrains from entering into or promising another personal, scientific, professional, financial, or other relationship with such persons if it appears likely that such a relationship reasonably might impair the psychologist's objectivity or otherwise interfere with the psychologist's effectively performing his or her functions as a psychologist, or might harm or exploit the other party.

(b) Likewise, whenever feasible, a psychologist refrains from taking on professional or scientific obligations when preexisting relationships would create a risk of such harm.

(c) If a psychologist finds that, due to unforeseen factors, a potentially harmful multiple relationship has arisen, the psychologist attempts to resolve it with due regard for the best interests of the affected person and maximal compliance with the Ethics Code.

1.18 Barter (With Patients or Clients)

Psychologists ordinarily refrain from accepting goods, services, or other nonmonetary remuneration from patients or clients in return for psychological services because such arrangements create inherent potential for conflicts, exploitation, and distortion of the professional relationship. A psychologist may participate in bartering *only* if (1) it is not clinically contraindicated, *and* (2) the relationship is not exploitative. (See also Standards 1.17, Multiple Relationships, and 1.25, Fees and Financial Arrangements.)

1.19 Exploitative Relationships

(a) Psychologists do not exploit persons over whom they have supervisory, evaluative, or other authority such as students, supervisees, employees, research participants, and clients or patients. (See also Standards 4.05–4.07 regarding sexual involvement with clients or patients.)

(b) Psychologists do not engage in sexual relationships with students or supervisees in training over whom the psychologist has evaluative or direct authority, because such relationships are so likely to impair judgment or be exploitative.

1.20 Consultations and Referrals

(a) Psychologists arrange for appropriate consultations and referrals based principally on the best interests of their patients or clients, with appropriate consent, and subject to other relevant considerations, including applicable law and contractual obligations. (See also Standards 5.01, Discussing the Limits of Confidentiality, and 5.06, Consultations.)

(b) When indicated and professionally appropriate, psychologists cooperate with other professionals in order to serve their patients or clients effectively and appropriately.

(c) Psychologists' referral practices are consistent with law.

1.21 Third-Party Requests for Services

(a) When a psychologist agrees to provide services to a person or entity at the request of a third party, the psychologist clarifies to the extent feasible, at the outset of the service, the nature of the relationship with each party. This clarification includes the role of the psychologist (such as therapist, organizational consultant, diagnostician, or expert witness), the probable uses of the services provided or the information obtained, and the fact that there may be limits to confidentiality.

(b) If there is a foreseeable risk of the psychologist's being called upon to perform conflicting roles because of the involvement of a third party, the psychologist clarifies the nature and direction of his or her responsibilities, keeps all parties appropriately informed as matters develop, and resolves the situation in accordance with this Ethics Code.

1.22 Delegation to and Supervision of Subordinates

(a) Psychologists delegate to their employees, supervisees, and research assistants only those responsibilities that such persons can reasonably be expected to perform competently, on the basis of their education, training, or experience, either independently or with the level of supervision being provided.

(b) Psychologists provide proper training and supervision to their employees or supervisees and take reasonable steps to see that such persons perform services responsibly, competently, and ethically.

(c) If institutional policies, procedures, or practices prevent fulfillment of this obligation, psychologists attempt to modify their role or to correct the situation to the extent feasible.

1.23 Documentation of Professional and Scientific Work

(a) Psychologists appropriately document their professional and scientific work in order to facilitate provision of services later by them or by other professionals, to ensure accountability, and to meet other requirements of institutions or the law.

(b) When psychologists have reason to believe that records of their professional services will be used in legal proceedings involving recipients of or participants in their work, they have a responsibility to create and maintain documentation in the kind of detail and quality that would be consistent with reasonable scrutiny in an adjudicative forum. (See also Standard 7.01, Professionalism, under Forensic Activities.)

1.24 Records and Data

Psychologists create, maintain, disseminate, store, retain, and dispose of records and data relating to their research, practice, and other work in accordance with law and in a manner that permits compliance with the requirements of this Ethics Code. (See also Standard 5.04, Maintenance of Records.)

1.25 Fees and Financial Arrangements

(a) As early as is feasible in a professional or scientific relationship, the psychologist and the patient, client, or other appropriate recipient of psychological services reach an agreement specifying the compensation and the billing arrangements.

(b) Psychologists do not exploit recipients of services or payors with respect to fees.

(c) Psychologists' fee practices are consistent with law.

(d) Psychologists do not misrepresent their fees.

(e) If limitations to services can be anticipated because of limitations in financing, this is discussed with the patient, client, or other appropriate recipient of services as early as is feasible. (See also Standard 4.08, Interruption of Services.)

(f) If the patient, client, or other recipient of services does not pay for services as agreed, and if the psychologist wishes to use collection agencies or legal measures to collect the fees, the psychologist first informs the person that such measures will be taken and provides that person an opportunity to make prompt payment. (See also Standard 5.11, Withholding Records for Nonpayment.)

1.26 Accuracy in Reports to Payors and Funding Sources

In their reports to payors for services or sources of research funding, psychologists accurately state the nature of the research or service provided, the fees or charges, and where applicable, the identity of the provider, the findings, and the diagnosis. (See also Standard 5.05, Disclosures.)

1.27 Referrals and Fees

When a psychologist pays, receives payment from, or divides fees with another professional other than in an employer-employee relationship, the payment to each is based on the services (clinical, consultative, administrative, or other) provided and is not based on the referral itself.

2. Evaluation, Assessment, or Intervention

2.01 Evaluation, Diagnosis, and Interventions in Professional Context

(a) Psychologists perform evaluations, diagnostic services, or interventions only within the context of a defined professional relationship. (See also Standard 1.03, Professional and Scientific Relationship.)

(b) Psychologists' assessments, recommendations, reports, and psychological diagnostic or evaluative statements are based on information and techniques (including personal interviews of the individual when appropriate) sufficient to provide appropriate substantiation for their findings. (See also Standard 7.02, Forensic Assessments.)

2.02 Competence and Appropriate Use of Assessments and Interventions

(a) Psychologists who develop, administer, score, interpret, or use psychological assessment techniques, interviews, tests, or instruments do so in a manner and for purposes that are appropriate in light of the research on or evidence of the usefulness and proper application of the techniques.

(b) Psychologists refrain from misuse of assessment techniques, interventions, results, and interpretations and take reasonable steps to prevent others from misusing the information these techniques provide. This includes refraining from releasing raw test results or raw data to persons, other than to patients or clients as appropriate, who are not qualified to use such information. (See also Standards 1.02, Relationship of Ethics and Law, and 1.04, Boundaries of Competence.)

2.03 Test Construction

Psychologists who develop and conduct research with tests and other assessment techniques use scientific procedures and current professional knowledge for test design, standardization, validation, reduction or elimination of bias, and recommendations for use.

2.04 Use of Assessment in General and With Special Populations

(a) Psychologists who perform interventions or administer, score, interpret, or use assessment techniques are familiar with the reliability, validation, and related standardization or outcome studies of, and proper applications and uses of, the techniques they use.

(b) Psychologists recognize limits to the certainty with which diagnoses, judgments, or predictions can be made about individuals.

(c) Psychologists attempt to identify situations in which particular interventions or assessment techniques or norms may not be applicable or may require adjustment in administration or interpretation because of factors such as individuals' gender, age, race, ethnicity, national origin, religion, sexual orientation, disability, language, or socioeconomic status.

2.05 Interpreting Assessment Results

When interpreting assessment results, including automated interpretations, psychologists take into account the various test factors and characteristics of the person being assessed that might affect psychologists' judgments or reduce the accuracy of their interpretations. They indicate any significant reservations they have about the accuracy or limitations of their interpretations.

2.06 Unqualified Persons

Psychologists do not promote the use of psychological assessment techniques by unqualified persons. (See also Standard 1.22, Delegation to and Supervision of Subordinates.)

2.07 Obsolete Tests and Outdated Test Results

(a) Psychologists do not base their assessment or intervention decisions or recommendations on data or test results that are outdated for the current purpose.

(b) Similarly, psychologists do not base such decisions or recommendations on tests and measures that are obsolete and not useful for the current purpose.

2.08 Test Scoring and Interpretation Services

(a) Psychologists who offer assessment or scoring procedures to other professionals accurately describe the purpose, norms, validity, reliability, and applications of the procedures and any special qualifications applicable to their use.

(b) Psychologists select scoring and inter-

pretation services (including automated services) on the basis of evidence of the validity of the program and procedures as well as on other appropriate considerations.

(c) Psychologists retain appropriate responsibility for the appropriate application, interpretation, and use of assessment instruments, whether they score and interpret such tests themselves or use automated or other services.

2.09 Explaining Assessment Results

Unless the nature of the relationship is clearly explained to the person being assessed in advance and precludes provision of an explanation of results (such as in some organizational consulting, preemployment or security screenings, and forensic evaluations), psychologists ensure that an explanation of the results is provided using language that is reasonably understandable to the person assessed or to another legally authorized person on behalf of the client. Regardless of whether the scoring and interpretation are done by the psychologist, by assistants, or by automated or other outside services, psychologists take reasonable steps to ensure that appropriate explanations of results are given.

2.10 Maintaining Test Security

Psychologists make reasonable efforts to maintain the integrity and security of tests and other assessment techniques consistent with law, contractual obligations, and in a manner that permits compliance with the requirements of this Ethics Code. (See also Standard 1.02, Relationship of Ethics and Law.)

3. Advertising and Other Public Statements

3.01 Definition of Public Statements

Psychologists comply with this Ethics Code in public statements relating to their professional services, products, or publications or to the field of psychology. Public statements include but are not limited to paid or unpaid advertising, brochures, printed matter, directory listings, personal resumes or curriculum vitae, interviews or comments for use in media, statements in legal proceedings, lectures and public oral presentations, and published materials.

3.02 Statements by Others

(a) Psychologists who engage others to create or place public statements that promote their professional practice, products, or activities retain professional responsibility for such statements.

(b) In addition, psychologists make reasonable efforts to prevent others whom they do not control (such as employers, publishers, sponsors, organizational clients, and representatives of the print or broadcast media) from making deceptive statements concerning psychologists' practice or professional or scientific activities.

(c) If psychologists learn of deceptive statements about their work made by others, psychologists make reasonable efforts to correct such statements.

(d) Psychologists do not compensate employees of press, radio, television, or other communication media in return for publicity in a news item.

(e) A paid advertisement relating to the psychologist's activities must be identified as such, unless it is already apparent from the context.

3.03 Avoidance of False or Deceptive Statements

(a) Psychologists do not make public statements that are false, deceptive, misleading, or fraudulent, either because of what they state, convey, or suggest or because of what they omit, concerning their research, practice, or other work activities or those of persons or organizations with which they are affiliated. As examples (and not in limitation) of this standard, psychologists do not make false or deceptive statements concerning (1) their training, experience, or competence; (2) their academic degrees; (3) their credentials; (4) their institutional or association affiliations; (5) their ser-

vices; (6) the scientific or clinical basis for, or results or degree of success of, their services; (7) their fees; or (8) their publications or research findings. (See also Standards 6.15, Deception in Research, and 6.18, Providing Participants With Information About the Study.)

(b) Psychologists claim as credentials for their psychological work only degrees that (1) were earned from a regionally accredited educational institution or (2) were the basis for psychology licensure by the state in which they practice.

3.04 Media Presentations

When psychologists provide advice or comment by means of public lectures, demonstrations, radio or television programs, prerecorded tapes, printed articles, mailed material, or other media, they take reasonable precautions to ensure that (1) the statements are based on appropriate psychological literature and practice, (2) the statements are otherwise consistent with this Ethics Code, and (3) the recipients of the information are not encouraged to infer that a relationship has been established with them personally.

3.05 Testimonials

Psychologists do not solicit testimonials from current psychotherapy clients or patients or other persons who because of their particular circumstances are vulnerable to undue influence.

3.06 In-Person Solicitation

Psychologists do not engage, directly or through agents, in uninvited in-person solicitation of business from actual or potential psychotherapy patients or clients or other persons who because of their particular circumstances are vulnerable to undue influence. However, this does not preclude attempting to implement appropriate collateral contacts with significant others for the purpose of benefiting an already engaged therapy patient.

4. Therapy

4.01 Structuring the Relationship

(a) Psychologists discuss with clients or patients as early as is feasible in the therapeutic relationship appropriate issues, such as the nature and anticipated course of therapy, fees, and confidentiality. (See also Standards 1.25, Fees and Financial Arrangements, and 5.01, Discussing the Limits of Confidentiality.)

(b) When the psychologist's work with clients or patients will be supervised, the above discussion includes that fact, and the name of the supervisor, when the supervisor has legal responsibility for the case.

(c) When the therapist is a student intern, the client or patient is informed of that fact.

(d) Psychologists make reasonable efforts to answer patients' questions and to avoid apparent misunderstandings about therapy. Whenever possible, psychologists provide oral and/or written information, using language that is reasonably understandable to the patient or client.

4.02 Informed Consent to Therapy

(a) Psychologists obtain appropriate informed consent to therapy or related procedures, using language that is reasonably understandable to participants. The content of informed consent will vary depending on many circumstances; however, informed consent generally implies that the person (1) has the capacity to consent, (2) has been informed of significant information concerning the procedure, (3) has freely and without undue influence expressed consent, and (4) consent has been appropriately documented.

(b) When persons are legally incapable of giving informed consent, psychologists obtain informed permission from a legally authorized person, if such substitute consent is permitted by law.

(c) In addition, psychologists (1) inform those persons who are legally incapable of giving informed consent about the proposed interventions in a manner commensurate with the persons' psychological capacities, (2) seek their assent to those interventions, and (3) consider such persons' preferences and best interests.

4.03 Couple and Family Relationships

(a) When a psychologist agrees to provide services to several persons who have a relationship (such as husband and wife or parents and children), the psychologist attempts to clarify at the outset (1) which of the individuals are patients or clients and (2) the relationship the psychologist will have with each person. This clarification includes the role of the psychologist and the probable uses of the services provided or the information obtained. (See also Standard 5.01, Discussing the Limits of Confidentiality.)

(b) As soon as it becomes apparent that the psychologist may be called on to perform potentially conflicting roles (such as marital counselor to husband and wife, and then witness for one party in a divorce proceeding), the psychologist attempts to clarify and adjust, or withdraw from, roles appropriately. (See also Standard 7.03, Clarification of Role, under Forensic Activities.)

4.04 Providing Mental Health Services to Those Served by Others

In deciding whether to offer or provide services to those already receiving mental health services elsewhere, psychologists carefully consider the treatment issues and the potential patient's or client's welfare. The psychologist discusses these issues with the patient or client, or another legally authorized person on behalf of the client, in order to minimize the risk of confusion and conflict, consults with the other service providers when appropriate, and proceeds with caution and sensitivity to the therapeutic issues.

4.05 Sexual Intimacies With Current Patients or Clients

Psychologists do not engage in sexual intimacies with current patients or clients.

4.06 Therapy With Former Sexual Partners

Psychologists do not accept as therapy patients or clients persons with whom they have engaged in sexual intimacies.

4.07 Sexual Intimacies With Former Therapy Patients

(a) Psychologists do not engage in sexual intimacies with a former therapy patient or client for at least two years after cessation or termination of professional services.

(b) Because sexual intimacies with a former therapy patient or client are so frequently harmful to the patient or client, and because such intimacies undermine public confidence in the psychology profession and thereby deter the public's use of needed services, psychologists do not engage in sexual intimacies with former therapy patients and clients even after a two-year interval except in the most unusual circumstances. The psychologist who engages in such activity after the two years following cessation or termination of treatment bears the burden of demonstrating that there has been no exploitation, in light of all relevant factors, including (1) the amount of time that has passed since therapy terminated, (2) the nature and duration of the therapy, (3) the circumstances of termination, (4) the patient's or client's personal history, (5) the patient's or client's current mental status, (6) the likelihood of adverse impact on the patient or client and others, and (7) any statements or actions made by the therapist during the course of therapy suggesting or inviting the possibility of a post-termination sexual or romantic relationship with the patient or client. (See also Standard 1.17, Multiple Relationships.)

4.08 Interruption of Services

(a) Psychologists make reasonable efforts to plan for facilitating care in the event that psychological services are interrupted by factors such as the psychologist's illness, death, unavailability, or relocation or by the client's relocation or financial limitations. (See also Standard 5.09, Preserving Records and Data.)

(b) When entering into employment or contractual relationships, psychologists provide for orderly and appropriate resolution of responsibility for patient or client care in the event that the employment or contractual relationship ends, with paramount consideration given to the welfare of the patient or client.

4.09 Terminating the Professional Relationship

(a) Psychologists do not abandon patients or clients. (See also Standard 1.25e, under Fees and Financial Arrangements.)

(b) Psychologists terminate a professional relationship when it becomes reasonably clear that the patient or client no longer needs the service, is not benefiting, or is being harmed by continued service.

(c) Prior to termination for whatever reason, except where precluded by the patient's or client's conduct, the psychologist discusses the patient's or client's views and needs, provides appropriate pretermination counseling, suggests alternative service providers as appropriate, and takes other reasonable steps to facilitate transfer of responsibility to another provider if the patient or client needs one immediately.

5. Privacy and Confidentiality

These Standards are potentially applicable to the professional and scientific activities of all psychologists.

5.01 Discussing the Limits of Confidentiality

(a) Psychologists discuss with persons and organizations with whom they establish a scientific or professional relationship (including, to the extent feasible, minors and their legal representatives) (1) the relevant limitations on confidentiality, including limitations where applicable in group, marital, and family therapy or in organizational consulting, and (2) the foreseeable uses of the information generated through their services.

(b) Unless it is not feasible or is contraindicated, the discussion of confidentiality occurs at the outset of the relationship and thereafter as new circumstances may warrant.

(c) Permission for electronic recording of interviews is secured from clients and patients.

5.02 Maintaining Confidentiality

Psychologists have a primary obligation and take reasonable precautions to respect the confidentiality rights of those with whom they work or consult, recognizing that confidentiality may be established by law, institutional rules, or professional or scientific relationships. (See also Standard 6.26, Professional Reviewers.)

5.03 Minimizing Intrusions on Privacy

(a) In order to minimize intrusions on privacy, psychologists include in written and oral reports, consultations, and the like, only information germane to the purpose for which the communication is made.

(b) Psychologists discuss confidential information obtained in clinical or consulting relationships, or evaluative data concerning patients, individual or organizational clients, students, research participants, supervisees, and employees, only for appropriate scientific or professional purposes and only with persons clearly concerned with such matters.

5.04 Maintenance of Records

Psychologists maintain appropriate confidentiality in creating, storing, accessing, transferring, and disposing of records under their control, whether these are written, automated, or in any other medium. Psychologists maintain and dispose of records in accordance with law and in a manner that permits compliance with the requirements of this Ethics Code.

5.05 Disclosures

(a) Psychologists disclose confidential information without the consent of the individual only as mandated by law, or where permitted by law for a valid purpose, such as (1) to provide needed professional services to the patient or the individual or organizational client, (2) to obtain appropriate professional consultations, (3) to protect the patient or client or others from harm, or (4) to obtain payment for services, in which instance disclosure is limited to the minimum that is necessary to achieve the purpose.

(b) Psychologists also may disclose confidential information with the appropriate consent of the patient or the individual or organizational client (or of another legally authorized person on behalf of the patient or client), unless prohibited by law.

5.06 Consultations

When consulting with colleagues, (1) psychologists do not share confidential information that reasonably could lead to the identification of a patient, client, research participant, or other person or organization with whom they have a confidential relationship unless they have obtained the prior consent of the person or organization or the disclosure cannot be avoided, and (2) they share information only to the extent necessary to achieve the purposes of the consultation. (See also Standard 5.02, Maintaining Confidentiality.)

5.07 Confidential Information in Databases

(a) If confidential information concerning recipients of psychological services is to be entered into databases or systems of records available to persons whose access has not been consented to by the recipient, then psychologists use coding or other techniques to avoid the inclusion of personal identifiers.

(b) If a research protocol approved by an institutional review board or similar body requires the inclusion of personal identifiers, such identifiers are deleted before the information is made accessible to persons other than those of whom the subject was advised.

(c) If such deletion is not feasible, then before psychologists transfer such data to others or review such data collected by others, they take reasonable steps to determine that appropriate consent of personally identifiable individuals has been obtained.

5.08 Use of Confidential Information for Didactic or Other Purposes

(a) Psychologists do not disclose in their writings, lectures, or other public media confidential, personally identifiable information concerning their patients, individual or organizational clients, students, research participants, or other recipients of their services that they obtained during the course of their work, unless the person or organization has consented in writing or unless there is other ethical or legal authorization for doing so.

(b) Ordinarily, in such scientific and professional presentations, psychologists disguise confidential information concerning such persons or organizations so that they are not individually identifiable to others and so that discussions do not cause harm to subjects who might identify themselves.

5.09 Preserving Records and Data

A psychologist makes plans in advance so that confidentiality of records and data is protected in the event of the psychologist's death, incapacity, or withdrawal from the position or practice.

5.10 Ownership of Records and Data

Recognizing that ownership of records and data is governed by legal principles, psychologists take reasonable and lawful steps so that records and data remain available to the extent needed to serve the best interests of patients, individual or organizational clients, research participants, or appropriate others.

5.11 Withholding Records for Nonpayment

Psychologists may not withhold records under their control that are requested and imminently needed for a patient's or client's treatment solely because payment has not been received, except as otherwise provided by law.

6. Teaching, Training Supervision, Research, and Publishing

6.01 Design of Education and Training Programs

Psychologists who are responsible for education and training programs seek to ensure that the programs are competently designed, provide the proper experiences, and meet the requirements for licensure, certification, or other goals for which claims are made by the program.

6.02 Descriptions of Education and Training Programs

(a) Psychologists responsible for education and training programs seek to ensure that there is a current and accurate description of the program content, training goals and objectives, and requirements that must be met for satisfactory completion of the program. This information must be made readily available to all interested parties.

(b) Psychologists seek to ensure that statements concerning their course outlines are accurate and not misleading, particularly regarding the subject matter to be covered, bases for evaluating progress, and the nature of course experiences. (See also Standard 3.03, Avoidance of False or Deceptive Statements.)

(c) To the degree to which they exercise control, psychologists responsible for announcements, catalogs, brochures, or advertisements describing workshops, seminars, or other non-degree-granting educational programs ensure that they accurately describe the audience for which the program is intended, the educational objectives, the presenters, and the fees involved.

6.03 Accuracy and Objectivity in Teaching

(a) When engaged in teaching or training, psychologists present psychological information accurately and with a reasonable degree of objectivity.

(b) When engaged in teaching or training, psychologists recognize the power they hold over students or supervisees and therefore make reasonable efforts to avoid engaging in conduct that is personally demeaning to students or supervisees. (See also Standards 1.09, Respecting Others, and 1.12, Other Harassment.)

6.04 Limitation on Teaching

Psychologists do not teach the use of techniques or procedures that require specialized training, licensure, or expertise, including but not limited to hypnosis, biofeedback, and projective techniques, to individuals who lack the prerequisite training, legal scope of practice, or expertise.

6.05 Assessing Student and Supervisee Performance

(a) In academic and supervisory relationships, psychologists establish an appropriate process for providing feedback to students and supervisees.

(b) Psychologists evaluate students and supervisees on the basis of their actual performance on relevant and established program requirements.

6.06 Planning Research

(a) Psychologists design, conduct, and report research in accordance with recognized standards of scientific competence and ethical research.

(b) Psychologists plan their research so as to minimize the possibility that results will be misleading.

(c) In planning research, psychologists consider its ethical acceptability under the Ethics Code. If an ethical issue is unclear, psychologists seek to resolve the issue through consultation with institutional review boards, animal care and use committees, peer consultations, or other proper mechanisms.

(d) Psychologists take reasonable steps to implement appropriate protections for the rights and welfare of human participants, other persons affected by the research, and the welfare of animal subjects.

6.07 Responsibility

(a) Psychologists conduct research competently and with due concern for the dignity and welfare of the participants.

(b) Psychologists are responsible for the ethical conduct of research conducted by them or by others under their supervision or control.

(c) Researchers and assistants are permitted to perform only those tasks for which they are appropriately trained and prepared.

(d) As part of the process of development and implementation of research projects, psychologists consult those with expertise concerning any special population under investigation or most likely to be affected.

6.08 Compliance With Law and Standards

Psychologists plan and conduct research in a manner consistent with federal and state law and regulations, as well as professional standards governing the conduct of research, and particularly those standards governing research with human participants and animal subjects.

6.09 Institutional Approval

Psychologists obtain from host institutions or organizations appropriate approval prior to conducting research, and they provide accurate information about their research proposals. They conduct the research in accordance with the approved research protocol.

6.10 Research Responsibilities

Prior to conducting research (except research involving only anonymous surveys, naturalistic observations, or similar research), psychologists enter into an agreement with participants that clarifies the nature of the research and the responsibilities of each party.

6.11 Informed Consent to Research

(a) Psychologists use language that is reasonably understandable to research participants in obtaining their appropriate informed consent (except as provided in Standard 6.12, Dispensing with Informed Consent). Such informed consent is appropriately documented.

(b) Using language that is reasonably understandable to participants, psychologists inform participants of the nature of the research; they inform participants that they are free to participate or to decline to participate or to withdraw from the research; they explain the foreseeable consequences of declining or withdrawing; they inform participants of significant factors that may be expected to influence their willingness to participate (such as risks, discomfort, adverse effects, or limitations on confidentiality, except as provided in Standard 6.15, Deception in Research); and they explain other aspects about which the prospective participants inquire.

(c) When psychologists conduct research with individuals such as students or subordinates, psychologists take special care to protect the prospective participants from adverse consequences of declining or withdrawing from participation.

(d) When research participation is a course requirement or opportunity for extra credit, the prospective participant is given the choice of equitable alternative activities.

(e) For persons who are legally incapable of giving informed consent, psychologists nevertheless (1) provide an appropriate explanation, (2) obtain the participant's assent, and (3) obtain appropriate permission from a legally authorized person, if such substitute consent is permitted by law.

6.12 Dispensing With Informed Consent

Before determining that planned research (such as research involving only anonymous questionnaires, naturalistic observations, or certain kinds of archival research) does not require the informed consent of research participants, psychologists consider applicable regulations and institutional review board requirements, and they consult with colleagues as appropriate.

6.13 Informed Consent in Research Filming or Recording

Psychologists obtain informed consent from research participants prior to filming or recording them in any form, unless the research involves simply naturalistic observations in public places and it is not anticipated that the recording will be used in a manner that could cause personal identification or harm.

6.14 Offering Inducements for Research Participants

(a) In offering professional services as an inducement to obtain research participants, psychologists make clear the nature of the services, as well as the risks, obligations, and limitations. (See also Standard 1.18, Barter [With Patients or Clients].)

(b) Psychologists do not offer excessive or inappropriate financial or other inducements to obtain research participants, particularly when it might tend to coerce participation.

6.15 Deception in Research

(a) Psychologists do not conduct a study involving deception unless they have determined that the use of deceptive techniques is justified by the study's prospective scientific, educational, or applied value and that equally effective alternative procedures that do not use deception are not feasible.

(b) Psychologists never deceive research participants about significant aspects that would affect their willingness to participate, such as physical risks, discomfort, or unpleasant emotional experiences.

(c) Any other deception that is an integral feature of the design and conduct of an experiment must be explained to participants as early as is feasible, preferably at the conclusion of their participation, but no later than at the conclusion of the research. (See also Standard 6.18, Providing Participants With Information About the Study.)

6.16 Sharing and Utilizing Data

Psychologists inform research participants of their anticipated sharing or further use of personally identifiable research data and of the possibility of unanticipated future uses.

6.17 Minimizing Invasiveness

In conducting research, psychologists interfere with the participants or milieu from which data are collected only in a manner that is warranted by an appropriate research design and that is consistent with psychologists' roles as scientific investigators.

6.18 Providing Participants With Information About the Study

(a) Psychologists provide a prompt opportunity for participants to obtain appropriate information about the nature, results, and conclusions of the research, and psychologists attempt to correct any misconceptions that participants may have.

(b) If scientific or humane values justify delaying or withholding this information, psychologists take reasonable measures to reduce the risk of harm.

6.19 Honoring Commitments

Psychologists take reasonable measures to honor all commitments they have made to research participants.

6.20 Care and Use of Animals in Research

(a) Psychologists who conduct research involving animals treat them humanely.

(b) Psychologists acquire, care for, use, and dispose of animals in compliance with current federal, state, and local laws and regulations, and with professional standards.

(c) Psychologists trained in research methods and experienced in the care of laboratory animals supervise all procedures involving animals and are responsible for ensuring appropriate consideration of their comfort, health, and humane treatment.

(d) Psychologists ensure that all individuals using animals under their supervision have received instruction in research methods and in the care, maintenance, and handling of the species being used, to the extent appropriate to their role.

(e) Responsibilities and activities of individuals assisting in a research project are consistent with their respective competencies.

(f) Psychologists make reasonable efforts to minimize the discomfort, infection, illness, and pain of animal subjects.

(g) A procedure subjecting animals to pain, stress, or privation is used only when an alternative procedure is unavailable and the goal is justified by its prospective scientific, educational, or applied value.

(h) Surgical procedures are performed under appropriate anesthesia; techniques to avoid infection and minimize pain are followed during and after surgery.

(i) When it is appropriate that the animal's life be terminated, it is done rapidly, with an effort to minimize pain, and in accordance with accepted procedures.

6.21 Reporting of Results

(a) Psychologists do not fabricate data or falsify results in their publications.

(b) If psychologists discover significant errors in their published data, they take reasonable steps to correct such errors in a correction, retraction, erratum, or other appropriate publication means.

6.22 Plagiarism

Psychologists do not present substantial portions or elements of another's work or data as their own, even if the other work or data source is cited occasionally.

6.23 Publication Credit

(a) Psychologists take responsibility and credit, including authorship credit, only for work they have actually performed or to which they have contributed.

(b) Principal authorship and other publication credits accurately reflect the relative scientific or professional contributions of the individuals involved, regardless of their relative status. Mere possession of an institutional position, such as Department Chair, does not justify authorship credit. Minor contributions to the research or to the writing for publications are appropriately acknowledged, such as in footnotes or in an introductory statement.

(c) A student is usually listed as principal author on any multiple-authored article that is substantially based on the student's dissertation or thesis.

6.24 Duplicate Publication of Data

Psychologists do not publish, as original data, data that have been previously published. This does not preclude republishing data when they are accompanied by proper acknowledgment.

6.25 Sharing Data

After research results are published, psychologists do not withhold the data on which their conclusions are based from other competent professionals who seek to verify the substantive claims through reanalysis and who intend to use such data only for that purpose, provided that the confidentiality of the participants can be protected and unless legal rights concerning proprietary data preclude their release.

6.26 Professional Reviewers

Psychologists who review material submitted for publication, grant, or other research proposal review respect the confidentiality of and the proprietary rights in such information of those who submitted it.

7. Forensic Activities

7.01 Professionalism

Psychologists who perform forensic functions, such as assessments, interviews, consultations, reports, or expert testimony, must comply with all other provisions of this Ethics Code to the extent that they apply to such activities. In addition, psychologists base their forensic work on appropriate knowledge of and competence in the areas underlying such work, including specialized knowledge concerning special populations. (See also Standards 1.06, Basis for Scientific and Professional Judgments; 1.08, Human Differences; 1.15, Misuse of Psychologists' Influence; and 1.23, Documentation of Professional and Scientific Work.)

7.02 Forensic Assessments

(a) Psychologists' forensic assessments, recommendations, and reports are based on information and techniques (including personal interviews of the individual, when appropriate) sufficient to provide appropriate substantiation for their findings. (See also Standards 1.03, Professional and Scientific Relationship; 1.23, Documentation of Professional and Scientific Work; 2.01, Evaluation, Diagnosis, and Interventions in Professional Context; and 2.05, Interpreting Assessment Results.)

(b) Except as noted in (c), below, psychologists provide written or oral forensic reports or testimony of the psychological characteristics of an individual only after they have conducted an examination of the individual adequate to support their statements or conclusions.

(c) When, despite reasonable efforts, such an examination is not feasible, psychologists clarify the impact of their limited information on the reliability and validity of their reports and testimony, and they appropriately limit the nature and extent of their conclusions or recommendations.

7.03 Clarification of Role

In most circumstances, psychologists avoid performing multiple and potentially conflicting roles in forensic matters. When psychologists may be called on to serve in more than one role in a legal proceeding—for example, as consultant or expert for one party or for the court and as a fact witness—they clarify role expectations and the extent of confidentiality in advance to the extent feasible, and thereafter as changes occur, in order to avoid compromising their professional judgment and objectivity and in order to avoid misleading others regarding their role.

7.04 Truthfulness and Candor

(a) In forensic testimony and reports, psychologists testify truthfully, honestly, and candidly and, consistent with applicable legal procedures, describe fairly the bases for their testimony and conclusions.

(b) Whenever necessary to avoid misleading, psychologists acknowledge the limits of their data or conclusions.

7.05 Prior Relationships

A prior professional relationship with a party does not preclude psychologists from testifying as fact witnesses or from testifying to their services to the extent permitted by applicable law. Psychologists appropriately take into account ways in which the prior relationship might affect their professional objectivity or opinions and disclose the potential conflict to the relevant parties.

7.06 Compliance With Law and Rules

In performing forensic roles, psychologists are reasonably familiar with the rules governing their roles. Psychologists are aware of the occasionally competing demands placed upon them by these principles and the requirements of the court system, and attempt to resolve these conflicts by making known their commitment to this Ethics Code and taking steps to resolve the conflict in a responsible manner. (See also Standard 1.02, Relationship of Ethics and Law.)

8. Resolving Ethical Issues

8.01 Familiarity With Ethics Code

Psychologists have an obligation to be familiar with this Ethics Code, other applicable ethics codes, and their application to psychologists' work. Lack of awareness or misunderstanding of an ethical standard is not itself a defense to a charge of unethical conduct.

8.02 Confronting Ethical Issues

When a psychologist is uncertain whether a particular situation or course of action would violate this Ethics Code, the psychologist ordinarily consults with other psychologists knowledgeable about ethical issues, with state or national psychology ethics committees, or with other appropriate authorities in order to choose a proper response.

8.03 Conflicts Between Ethics and Organizational Demands

If the demands of an organization with which psychologists are affiliated conflict with this Ethics Code, psychologists clarify the nature of the conflict, make known their commitment to the Ethics Code, and to the extent feasible, seek to resolve the conflict in a way that permits the fullest adherence to the Ethics Code.

8.04 Informal Resolution of Ethical Violations

When psychologists believe that there may have been an ethical violation by another psychologist, they attempt to resolve the issue by bringing it to the attention of that individual if an informal resolution appears appropriate and the intervention does not violate any confidentiality rights that may be involved.

8.05 Reporting Ethical Violations

If an apparent ethical violation is not appropriate for informal resolution under Standard 8.04 or is not resolved properly in that fashion, psychologists take further action appropriate to the situation, unless such action conflicts with confidentiality rights in ways that cannot be resolved. Such action might include referral to state or national committees on professional ethics or to state licensing boards.

8.06 Cooperating With Ethics Committees

Psychologists cooperate in ethics investigations, proceedings, and resulting requirements of the APA or any affiliated state psychological association to which they belong. In doing so, they make reasonable efforts to resolve any issues as to confidentiality. Failure to cooperate is itself an ethics violation.

8.07 Improper Complaints

Psychologists do not file or encourage the filing of ethics complaints that are frivolous and are intended to harm the respondent rather than to protect the public.

Source: Copyright © 1998 by the American Psychological Association. Reprinted with permission.

90 GUIDE TO DEALING WITH LICENSING BOARD AND ETHICS COMPLAINTS

Gerald P. Koocher & Patricia Keith-Spiegel

Receiving a formal inquiry or complaint letter from a licensing board or professional association's ethics committee can be one of the most stressful events in a psychologist's career. The notification letter is often experienced as an attack or a personal affront from one's colleagues. In such situations it is important to understand the system, know one's rights, and assure oneself of fair treatment. Keep in mind that "beating the system" is *not* the appropriate goal. Psychologists have previously agreed—voluntarily and with full consent—to be on the inside of a profession that has obligated itself to formal peer monitoring. All of us, as well as the public, are advantaged by this system. Were licensing boards and professional association ethics committees to be discontinued, the profession would be at the mercy of outsiders' control.

We have seen a wide range of reactions from respondents. Some psychologists are so stressed that they appear to jeopardize their own health.

Many are able to retain a dignified approach to the charge, but all are anxious to get to the matter as soon as possible and to get it resolved. Receiving an inquiry or charge letter from any professional monitoring agent is not, of course, going to make anyone's day. However, we offer some advice to consider if you ever find yourself in such a situation.

First and foremost, know who you are dealing with and understand the nature of the complaint and the potential consequences *before* responding.

- Are you dealing with a statutory licensing authority or a professional association? A professional association's most severe sanction is likely to be expulsion, but a licensing board has the authority to suspend or revoke a professional license.
- Are you dealing with nonclinician investigators or professional colleagues? In some smaller states or provinces, the staff of the

licensing board may be a nonpsychologist who lacks a fully professional understanding of the applicable ethics codes and regulations. Even when the investigator for a licensing board or ethics committee is a psychologist, the degree of experience and expertise can vary widely. In many cases additional clarification from others in authority may be warranted.

- Is the contact an *informal inquiry* or a *formal charge*? Sometimes licensing boards and ethics committees approach less serious allegations by asking the psychologist to respond before they decide to make formal charges. In such instances, however, "informal" does *not* mean "casual." Rather, such inquiries may be a sign that the panel has not yet concluded that the alleged conduct was serious enough to warrant drastic action or meets their definition of issuing a formal charge. The correct response should always be thoughtful and cautious.

- Have you been given a detailed and comprehensible rendition of the complaint made against you? You should not respond substantively to any complaint without a clear written explanation of the allegations.

- Have you been provided with copies of the rules, procedures, or policies under which the panel operates? If you do not have this information, request it and review it carefully to determine where you are in the time line of the investigatory process and what options are available to you before responding.

Second, do not respond impulsively. Knee-jerk actions will more likely than not be counterproductive and complicate the process unnecessarily.

- Do not contact the complainant directly or indirectly. The matter is no longer subject to informal resolution. Any contact initiated by you may be viewed as an attempt at coercion or harassment.

- If the complaint involves a current or former client, be sure that the authorities have obtained and provided you with a waiver signed by the client authorizing you to disclose confidential information before responding to the charges. We know of instances of licensing boards asking psychologists to obtain such consent from their own clients. Such requests are inappropriate because they put the psychologist in the uncomfortable and awkward position of asking someone to surrender confidentiality to serve the needs of another.

- Obtain consultation before responding. A colleague with prior experience serving on ethics panels or licensing boards is an ideal choice. Pay for an hour or two of professional time. Doing so establishes a confidential and possibly privileged relationship (depending on local law) with the consultant. Consultation with a lawyer is also advised, especially if the matter involves an alleged legal offense, if the ethics committee does not appear to be following the rules and procedures, or if the case might result in *any* public disciplinary action. Some professional liability insurance policies provide coverage for legal consultation in the event of a licensing board complaint. This insurance does not generally apply to professional association ethics complaints and may not be allowed in some jurisdictions. We recommend that you check your policy and secure such coverage if you do not already have it.

- If offered a settlement, "consent decree," or any resolution short of full dismissal of the case against you, obtain additional professional and legal consultation. Even an apparently mild "reprimand" may result in difficulty in renewing liability insurance policies, gaining access to insurance provider panels, qualifying for hospital staff privileges, or being hired for some jobs. Agreeing to accept an ethics or licensing sanction may also compromise your legal defense, should the client file suit. If you have done something wrong, a penalty may be appropriate. However, you should be fully aware of the potential consequences before simply agreeing to the sanction.

Third, organize your defense and response to the charges carefully and thoughtfully.

- Assess the credibility of the charge. Compile and organize your records and the relevant chronology of events. Respond respectfully and fully to the questions or charges within the allotted time frame. Failure to cooperate with a duly constituted inquiry is, itself, an ethical violation.

- Psychologists are expected to respond personally to the inquiry. It is appropriate to consult with colleagues or an attorney before responding, but a letter from your attorney alone is not sufficient and will probably also be regarded as inappropriate or evasive.
- Limit the scope of your response to the content areas and issues that directly relate to the complaint. If you need more time, ask for it. Be sure to retain copies of everything you send in response to the inquiry.
- Do not take the position that the best defense is a thundering offense. This will polarize the proceedings and reduce the chances for a collegial solution.
- If you believe that you have been wrongly or erroneously charged, state your case clearly and provide any appropriate documentation.
- If the complaint accurately represents the events but does not accurately interpret them, provide your account with as much documentation as you can.
- If you have committed the offense, document the events and start appropriate remediation actions immediately. Present any mitigating circumstances. It would probably also be wise to seek legal counsel at this point, if you have not already done so.
- If a charge is sustained and you are asked to accept disciplinary measures without a formal hearing, you may want to consider reviewing the potential consequences of the measures with an attorney before making a decision.
- Know your rights of appeal.

Fourth, take steps to support yourself emotionally over what is likely to be a stressful process extending over several months.

- Be patient. It is likely that you will have to wait for what will seem like a long while before the matter is resolved. It is acceptable to respectfully question the status of the matter from time to time.
- If appropriate, confide in a colleague or therapist who will be emotionally supportive through the process. We must strongly suggest, however, that you refrain from discussing the charges against you with many others. Doing so may increase your own tension and likely produce an adverse impact as more and more individuals become aware of your situation and may possibly raise additional problems regarding confidentiality issues. In no instance should you identify the complainant to others, aside from the board making the inquiry and your attorney.
- Take active, constructive steps to minimize your own anxiety and stress levels. If this matter is interfering with your ability to function, you might benefit from a professional counseling relationship in a privileged context.

References & Readings

American Psychological Association (1996). Rules and procedures. *American Psychological Association, 51,* 529–548.

Bass, L. J., DeMers, S. T., Ogloff, J. R., Peterson, C., Pettifor, J. L., Reaves, R. P., Retfalvi, T., Simon, N. P., Sinclair, C., & Tipton, R. M. (1996). *Professional conduct and discipline in psychology.* Washington, DC: American Psychological Association.

Bersoff, D. N. (1994). *Ethical conflicts in psychology.* Washington, DC: American Psychological Association.

Canter, M. B., Bennett, B. E., Jones, S. E., & Nagy, T. F. (1994). *Ethics for psychologists: A commentary on the APA ethics code.* Washington, DC: American Psychological Association.

Koocher, G. P., & Keith-Spiegel, P. C. (1998). *Ethics in psychology: Professional standards and cases* (2nd ed.). New York: Oxford University Press.

Related Topics

91 DEFENDING AGAINST LEGAL COMPLAINTS

Robert Henley Woody

Since the mid-1970s, legal complaints have posed an ominous threat to psychologists. By the early 1980s, the threat of a legal complaint was affecting the profession to the point that terms such as "litigaphobia" and "litigastress" began to appear in professional publications (Brodsky, 1983; Turkington, 1987). Today there is an even greater risk of a lawsuit against a psychologist for alleged malpractice and/or a complaint to the state licensing board. Regrettably, the omnipresence of managed care has created additional liability for psychologists (Appelbaum, 1993).

A PSYCHOLOGIST CAN BE IRREPARABLY DAMAGED BY A LEGAL COMPLAINT

While the majority of complaints are for "nuisance" amounts of money, the negative consequences of a complaint are profound. Even if the malpractice carrier pays the settlement or the licensing board imposes a minor (or no) penalty, merely making a settlement for a civil suit or receiving a finding of probable cause for discipline from a licensing board creates a lifelong blemish on the psychologist's professional record. The reason is simple: Any negative outcome must commonly be reported to any professional association, hospital, or managed care organization. Several psychologists have reported that even minor negative outcomes have sometimes led to rejection from the foregoing types of organizations. Also, whenever the psychologist serves as an expert witness, questions are likely to be asked about any litigation or regulatory action in which he or she has been a party; several psychologists have said that even when a licensing complaint has been dismissed, the mere fact that a complaint had been lodged served to lessen their perceived authority as an expert witness.

Even worse, once a legal action has been resolved, the potential remains for an additional complaint and investigation by, particularly, any other licensing or certification source with which the psychologist is or ever becomes affiliated. Depending on the jurisdiction and the outcome of the initial legal action, an insurance carrier may have to report the matter to a state regulatory agency, which could trigger another investigation. Especially problematic is the possibility that the legal action will be on file in the Disciplinary Data System (DDS), a computerized national registry developed and maintained by the Association of State and Provincial Psychology Boards; this is a new development, but it is expanding (Association of State and Provincial Psychology Boards, 1996).

On another plane, psychologists defending against a legal complaint are prone to suffer emotional stress. Threats to one's professional status cut to the inner core of self-esteem and commonly produce depression, tension, anger, and symptoms of physical illness. Further, marital and familial relations, career motivation, and general satisfaction with life are adversely affected (Charles, Wilbert, & Kennedy, 1984).

In my role as a defense attorney for mental health professionals, I have witnessed complaints lodged against psychologists with the highest of reputations. According to Wright (1981), it appears that "the greater the degree of professionalism one demands of oneself, the more detailed and excruciating is the attendant review and the more intense the accompanying feelings of threat, anxiety, guilt, remorse, and depression" (p. 1535).

Some psychologists bent on preserving their professional reputation question the value of having insurance to cover a malpractice and/or regulatory complaint(s). Often these psychologists believe that the financial benefit (coverage for any judgment or legal fees) is outweighed by the detriment of the insurance carrier's control of settling a legal action. Specifically, an insurance policy can reduce the financial outlay by the psychologist, but the carrier is able to select the attorney. Numerous psychologists have expressed the sentiment that the insurance-selected attorney may be well intentioned and qualified but is under the control of the insurance company, who pressures the attorney to bring about a prompt settlement (so as to lessen the defense costs). Various insurance representatives generally acknowledge that their goal is to minimize expenditures on the defense; although they understand the psychologist's concern about preserving professional reputation, that concern is beyond the scope of the carrier's duty to its investors. Incidentally, this stance is maintained even when the lawsuit is clearly frivolous and without legal merit—it is cheaper to pay the litigious client than to teach the client a lesson. This approach may seem shortsighted, but it is the prevailing viewpoint of insurance carriers. As a result, numerous psychologists find it expeditious and prudent to hire, at their own expense, a personal attorney to deal with the insurance-paid attorney (e.g., to try to persuade against a settlement that unjustly penalizes the psychologist).

A PSYCHOLOGIST FACES A HIGH RISK OF A LEGAL COMPLAINT

It is impossible to know the incidence of legal actions taken against psychologists. Why? Because many, perhaps most, legal actions initially attempt to accomplish an "out-of-court" settlement. That is, the plaintiff's or complainant's attorney contacts the psychologist and offers to accept a financial payment to circumvent the need to file a formal action. Moreover, even if a complaint is filed, be it for alleged malpractice or violation of licensing standards, there are numerous ways in which the record can be closed to public scrutiny (i.e., it will not necessarily be reported). Just as there is considerable variation between states in the amount of risk associated with psychological practice, jurisdictions vary considerably in how complaints are handled prior to a judgment that becomes public record.

A PSYCHOLOGIST IS INADEQUATELY PREPARED TO DEAL WITH LEGAL PROBLEMS

Regardless of the jurisdiction, psychologists need to recognize that they are ill advised to attempt to "theraperize" a disgruntled client (past or present) who threatens a complaint. As Wright (1981, p. 1535) correctly explained, "Our training and our personal philosophies tend to emphasize the importance of the individual and our obligation as a helper/practitioner to evidence humanistic concerns or attempt 'conflict resolution.' We find it hard to believe that our virtue is unappreciated, so we attempt to follow our ethical admonitions to resolve conflict and discover to our subsequent dismay that the plaintiff's attorney made our virtuous and well-meaning efforts appear to be an attempt to 'cover up' or 'cop out'" (p. 1535). Well-intentioned efforts that would be quite proper in a therapeutic context become suspect in the legal context.

In one case, a male psychologist was accused by a female client of sexual misconduct. Without legal counsel, the three partners met with the client and her husband and offered to refund the full amount paid over the years for treatment, contingent on their not filing a lawsuit against the allegedly malpracticing psychologist. The offer was refused, and when a malpractice action was filed, the proposed refund was transformed into a nefarious attempt by the psychologists to subvert the couple's exercising their legal rights.

The foremost problem comes from the fact that the education and training of psychologists are basically antithetical to what leads to excellence in legal defense work. Dedicated to "ivory tower" notions and often divorced from the reality of modern psychological practice, trainers are prone to cling to outdated ideas about practitioners. Specifically, they emphasize altruism and subjugating the rights of practitioners to the preferences and demands of clients. Likewise, the curricula remain rooted in the past, with little or no accommodation to the current practice environment, namely, the "industrialized" marketplace, which is characterized by commercialism and consumer accountability and controlled by nonclinical sources, such as managed care organizations (Cummings, 1996). Some faculty members denounce any proposal to alter the curriculum to provide course work addressing modern practice issues, such as acquiring business skills, dealing with managed care, and being legally safe. As Troy and Schueman (1996) put it: "Among internal obstacles one may note the essential stasis and inflexibility of faculty-owned curricula which particularly resist innovative proposals for instructional design; criteria for faculty promotion and tenure; faculty ignorance of the changing imperatives of the world of work; competency and resources shortfall with programs; and the inappropriate expectations of new trainees" (p. 75). For example, when I proposed adding a "real-world" practice course, my colleagues' prevailing response was that "they can get that kind of learning once they are out in the field." Consequently, few psychologists graduate with a pragmatic understanding of how to succeed in psychological practice, not to mention defending against legal complaints.

A related problem comes from the fact that the psychologist, as a highly intelligent and well-educated individual, is prone to want to serve as "quarterback" in the legal defense. As one attorney told Wright (1981): "Heaven protect me from intelligent, sophisticated clients. While they're 'helping' me win my case, they can find ways I never dreamed of to mess things up. The smarter they are the more ways they can find to botch it" (p. 1535). This same condition has been found with professors who are prone to want to dictate the actions of their attorneys, contrary to legal judgment (LaNoue & Lee, 1987).

The source of the "quarterback" problem is twofold. First, the intelligent, educated professional, whether a psychologist or professor, is equipped with considerable knowledge, including knowledge about human behavior. Unfortunately, the knowledge is not assuredly consonant with the law and certainly not always in accord with the rules that determine what can and should be used in litigation. Second, the knowledge derives from the academy, which has minimal relevance to and is often contradictory to legal reality. Suffice it to say that the legal arena requires expertise foreign to psychological practice. Wright (1981) explains that psychologists facing a legal complaint "enter a whole new dimension of experience" (p. 1535) and that their "training, which tends to emphasize ultimate responsibility of the individual, may be at variance with both the philosophical context of our times and the legal philosophical context in which we operate" (p. 1539). Wright's comments, which were made in 1981, are even more relevant today.

A PSYCHOLOGIST PRACTICES UNDER LITIGIOUS CONDITIONS

Modern psychological practice is far different from psychological practice in the past, even as recently as the 1980s. A major change has occurred in the tenets of the therapeutic alliance. Prior to psychologists' seeking and gaining admission to the "health care industry" (motivated by the self-serving goal of increased incomes, such as through eligibility for third-party payments), clients tended to treat mental health practitioners differently from other health care providers. There was an unfortunate stigma attached to being the recipient of mental health services, and clients tended to consider the therapeutic relationship to be distinctly different from other caregiving relationships; thus, legal actions against mental health practitioners were relatively few, at least compared with today. The industrialization or commercialization of mental health services led to, among other things, a reformation of the therapeutic alliance; namely, the dyad of the psychologist and client was joined by a third-party payer to create a ménage à trois. With this restructuring, exacerbated by the commanding presence of the third-party payer (dictating the terms for the relationship), the uniqueness of the therapeutic alliance disappeared and litigation increased.

Government regulation has become all-powerful in determining the propriety of psychological practices. When psychologists quested for state licensure (again, motivated by the self-serving goal of increased incomes), they unexpectedly surrendered disciplinary control of professional practice.

Licensing boards, under the watchful eye (some would say "dictates") of state prosecuting attorneys, became the monitors for possible disciplinary action. Relatedly, psychologists have lost their independent determination of clinical matters to the micromanagement of practices by the state house. Many psychologists falsely believe that members of licensing boards are colleagues who will be understanding and prone to forgive. They reason that at least some members of the state board are psychologists; some may have been colleagues known in the past. In point of fact, the members of the licensing board, whether psychologist, consumer representative, or state attorney, are appointed (usually by the governor) to represent politically motivated consumer protection. After dealing with a licensing complaint, numerous respondents have offered comments reflecting their surprise. For example: "The members of the board, especially the psychologists, seemed to take a 'guilty until proven innocent' approach." This is not surprising, since the members are present as protectors of consumers, certainly not as colleagues, and are there by political behest. In fact, some psychologist board members have found their roles to be such a heady experience that unprecedented degrees of egotism, narcissism, and self-aggrandizement are revealed. One psychologist commented, "They seemed

to be demanding perfect performance rather than the reasonable standard that I thought determined malpractice." Again, this stance is not surprising, since the degree of proof required for probable cause for discipline is nebulous and usually less strenuous than required for a malpractice action.

Finally, many psychologists find that defending against a licensing complaint is more draining emotionally and financially than defending against a malpractice action. Given that a licensing complaint does involve scrutiny and judgment by members of the same profession (as opposed to a judge or jury), it is easy to think that one's professionalism has been incontrovertibly impugned.

A PSYCHOLOGIST MUST ACCEPT BEING DEFENSIVE

Clinging to antiquated notions about practice raises liability, and lacking legally related knowledge adds to the risk. Since most psychologists do not think like lawyers, it is important to pursue defensive strategies. The following eight recommendations provide a framework.

1. A psychologist should acquire training to view practice operations and client communications with a defensive eye. Since this need is commonly unfilled by graduate training programs, the psychologist should arrange for self-study and seminars.
2. When a potentially litigious client waves a "red flag," the psychologist should set aside any illogical idea that services must be continued. Some clients have actually filed legal actions against their psychologists and then objected when services to them were terminated! If a client threatens or takes legal action against the psychologist, the client has sacrificed any logical claim to the title of "client" and has justified the new title "party opponent."
3. A psychologist should have a personal attorney readily "on call." As described earlier, an attorney appointed by a malpractice insurance carrier enters the conflict after

the fact and primarily serves the insurance carrier.

4. The psychologist should rely on preventive legal counsel at the first possible "red flag" of litigation. Obtaining the advice of counsel proactively can reduce the possibility of a complaint.

5. If a client demonstrates negativism toward the psychologist that goes beyond "therapeutic resistance" or "reasonable transference," the psychologist should acknowledge the possibility of a legal complaint. If resistance or transference moves to the client's mentioning a complaint, the psychologist should not persevere. In the clinical interests of the client, a psychologist cannot be expected to function effectively under the threat of litigation, and thus it would be a disservice to the client to continue.

6. A psychologist should not wait until a complaint seems inevitable or even probable before shifting into a defensive posture. The mere possibility of a complaint justifies action to safeguard the rights of the psychologist, as well as being a service to the client.

7. When legal safeguards are necessary, the psychologist should assume a defensive posture in all communications with the client or client's attorney; implement a tactful and reasonable termination of the clinical service (such as making a referral to another practitioner); and immediately turn the matter over to his or her personal attorney.

8. When an attorney has become involved, the psychologist should accept that the matter is outside of psychological competence and personal control. The fundamental assumption must be that the matter will best be handled by legal strategies. Consequently, the psychologist must avoid trying to be a "quarterback" to the legal situation.

These eight recommendations pose ideas that may seem foreign to traditional psychological practice. Some psychologists are reluctant to pass clinical conditions through a legal filter and object to the added expense (such as paying for a personal attorney). Nonetheless, modern psychological practice requires a defensive posture and legal protection (with the expense being the "cost of doing business" in this litigious era). To do otherwise is to jeopardize professional survival and practice success.

References & Readings

Appelbaum, P. S. (1993). Legal liability and managed care. *American Psychologist, 48,* 251–277.

Association of State and Provincial Psychology Boards (1996). Disciplinary data system pilot project kicks off. *ASPPB Newsletter, 17*(1), 1, 4.

Brodsky, S. L. (1983). Litigaphobia: The professionals' disease [Review of B. Schutz, *Legal liability in psychotherapy*]. *Contemporary Psychology, 28,* 204–205.

Charles, S. C., Wilbert, J. R., & Kennedy, E. C. (1984). Physicians' self-reports of reactions to malpractice litigation. *American Journal of Psychiatry, 141,* 563–565.

Cummings, N. A. (1996). The resocialization of behavioral healthcare practice. In N. A. Cummings, M. S. Pallak, & J. L. Cummings (Eds.), *Surviving the demise of solo practice: Mental health practitioners prospering in the era of managed care* (pp. 3–10). Madison, CT: Psychosocial Press (International Universities Press).

LaNoue, G. R., & Lee, B. A. (1987). *Academics in court: The consequences of faculty discrimination litigation.* Ann Arbor: University of Michigan Press.

Troy, W. G., & Shueman, S. A. (1996). Program redesign for graduate training in professional psychology: The road to accountability in a changing professional world. In N. A. Cummings, M. S. Pallak, & J. L. Cummings (Eds.), *Surviving the demise of solo practice: Mental health practitioners prospering in the era of managed care* (pp. 55–79). Madison, CT: Psychosocial Press (International Universities Press).

Turkington, C. (1987). Litigaphobia. *Monitor, 17*(11), 1, 8.

Woody, R. H. (1988a). *Fifty ways to avoid malpractice: A guidebook for the mental health practitioner.* Sarasota, FL: Professional Resource Exchange.

Woody, R. H. (1988b). *Protecting your mental health practice: How to minimize legal and financial risk.* San Francisco: Jossey-Bass.

Woody, R. H. (1989). *Business success in mental health practice: Modern marketing, manage-*

ment, and legal strategies. San Francisco: Jossey-Bass.

Woody, R. H. (1991). *Quality care in mental health services: Assuring the best clinical services.* San Francisco: Jossey-Bass.

Woody, R. H. (1997). *Legally safe mental health practice: Psycholegal questions and answers.* Madison, CT: Psychosocial Press (International Universities Press).

Wright, R. H. (1981). What to do until the malprac- tice lawyer comes: A survivor's manual. *American Psychologist, 36,* 1535–1541.

Related Topics

92 BASIC PRINCIPLES FOR DEALING WITH LEGAL LIABILITY RISK SITUATIONS

Gerald P. Koocher

What should a mental health practitioner do when an "adverse incident" occurs? If no lawsuit has been threatened or filed, but some significant difficulties or adverse events have occurred (e.g., a client is not benefiting from treatment, is not adhering to key aspects of a treatment program, has become too difficult to work with, commits suicide, or harms a third party), consider the following steps:

- Obtain a consultation from a colleague experienced with such clients and issues.
- Consider whether you should initiate termination of the professional relationship. If you decide to do so, follow these steps: (a) Notify the patient both orally and in writing, specifying the effective date for termination; (b) provide a specific professional ex- planation for terminating the relationship; (c) agree to continue providing interim services for a reasonable period and recommend other care providers or means of locating them; (d) offer to provide records to new care providers upon receipt of a signed authorization from the client; and (e) document all these steps in your case records.

- Avoid initiating a unilateral termination if (a) the client is in the midst of a mental health crisis or emergency situation; (b) substitute services will be difficult for the client to obtain (e.g., in a rural area where other practitioners might not be readily available); or (c) the primary reason for wanting to terminate the client is unreasonably discriminatory (e.g., terminating psychotherapy with a client after learning of his or her HIV status).

- If a client does not return for a scheduled appointment, follow up by telephone and in writing, documenting these steps in your records. Be especially prompt in doing so if the client seemed depressed or emotionally distressed in the previous session.
- If a client complains about something, listen carefully and treat the complaint with serious concern. Investigate, if necessary, and respond in as sympathetic and tactful a manner as possible. Apologize, if appropriate. Document all steps taken in your record.
- In the event of a client's death, express sincere compassion and sympathy to surviving relatives, but do not discuss any personal feelings of guilt you may be experiencing. Save such feelings for your personal psychotherapist.

If a lawsuit is filed or if you become aware of the *possibility* of a suit against you, follow these steps:

- Contact your insurance carrier immediately, both orally and in writing. Retain copies of all correspondence and keep notes of phone conversations, including the date and the representative of the insurer you spoke with. If a suit has actually been filed, your insurance carrier should assign local legal counsel to represent you promptly. If you retain counsel independently, the insurance carrier may not be obligated to pay for those services. Failure to notify the insurer in a timely manner may also compromise the defense of your case.
- Never interact orally or in writing, "informally" or otherwise, with a client's lawyer once a case is threatened. Once a lawyer representing your client contacts you in any dispute involving you and that client, get your own attorney involved. Cease all further contact with that client until you have consulted your attorney. *Never* try to settle matters yourself.
- Do not discuss the case with *anyone* other than representatives of the insurance carrier or your lawyer. Do not discuss details of the case with colleagues.

- Compile and organize all your records, case materials, and chronicles of the event to assist in your defense. Do not throw anything away, and do not show it to anyone except your attorney.
- When asked to provide information or documents to your insurer or legal counsel, send copies and safeguard the originals.
- In any malpractice or professional liability action where you are asked to agree to a settlement, consult a personal attorney (in addition to the one assigned by the insurance carrier), especially if sued for damages in excess of the limits of your policy.
- Take steps to manage your own anxiety and stress level. Such cases can take a severe emotional toll and require several years to resolve, even though there may be no legitimate basis for the suit. Although seeking support from friends and colleagues is a normal reaction, discussions of specific details should occur only in privileged contexts.

References & Readings

Appelbaum, P. S. (1993). Legal liability and managed care. *American Psychologist, 48*, 251–277.
Koocher, G. P., & Keith-Spiegel, P. C. (1998). *Ethics in psychology: Professional standards and cases* (2nd ed.). New York: Oxford University Press.
Woody, R. H. (1988). *Protecting your mental health practice: How to minimize legal and financial risk*. San Francisco: Jossey-Bass.
Woody, R. H. (1997). *Legally safe mental health practice: Psycholegal questions and answers*. Madison, CT: Psychosocial Press.
Wright, R. H. (1981a). Psychologists and professional liability (malpractice) insurance: A retrospective review. *American Psychologist, 36*, 1485–1493.
Wright, R. H. (1981b). What to do until the malpractice lawyer comes: A survivor's manual. *American Psychologist, 36*, 1535–1541.

Related Topics

93 DEALING WITH SUBPOENAS

Gerald P. Koocher

Receipt of a legal document commanding that you appear at a legal proceeding or turn over your records to attorneys can be a very stressful experience. This brief guide can help you understand the nature of a subpoena and how to respond. However, law and procedures vary from jurisdiction to jurisdiction; when in doubt, it is important to consult with an attorney who is knowledgeable about your local jurisdiction.

What is a subpoena? A subpoena is a document served in a legally prescribed manner on a person who is not a party to a case (i.e., not the plaintiff or defendant) requiring that person to produce documents, appear and give testimony at a deposition or trial, or both. In the case of depositions, 7 days' notice is often required.

What is a subpoena duces tecum? From the Latin meaning "bring it with you," such subpoenas require the person to bring specified records, reports, tapes, documents, or other tangible evidence to court or a deposition. For depositions, 30 days' notice is often required.

Who issues the subpoena, and what is in it? Depending on the jurisdiction, it may be a clerk of the court, notary public, or justice of the peace. The document must state the name of the court, the title of the legal action, and the time and place of testimony or production of documents.

How is a subpoena served? A subpoena may generally be served by any adult person who is not a party to the lawsuit. Generally this is done by a constable or sheriff, who delivers a copy in person or leaves it at the person's residence or place of business.

Must I comply with the subpoena? Failure to obey a subpoena may lead to being held in contempt of court. However, simply because you have been served does not mean that the subpoena is valid or that you must produce all materials requested.

Subpoenas versus court orders: It is important to understand the differences between a subpoena and a court order. A subpoena simply compels a response and in some jurisdictions can be issued simply by an attorney's request to a clerk of courts. The response need not be what is demanded in the subpoena document. If the papers seek documents or testimony that may be privileged, the psychologist should seek clarification from the client's attorney or the court. A court order, on the other hand, is generally issued only after a hearing before a judge; it compels a disclosure, unless the order is appealed to a higher court. In the end, the court must decide what is protected and what is not. Consult your own attorney to assess matters of privilege, overbroad requests for documents or materials, and other specific questions regarding the validity of the documents.

What if I cannot attend on the specified date? Contact the lawyer who issued the subpoena to discuss the matter. If the attorney is intransigent, states that the date cannot be rescheduled, and the time line is unreasonable (e.g., if you are given only 24–48 hours' notice and do not have time to provide patient coverage), tell the attorney that you plan to contact the judge in the case in order to complain about the inadequate notice. This approach often stimulates increased flexibility by the attorney. If necessary, do contact the judge and explain your scheduling problem. Except in unusual or urgent circumstances, the judge is likely to be accommodating.

Dealing with subpoenas for production of documents: When a subpoena demanding production of documents is served, the psychologist should not provide anything immediately. That is to say, nothing should be surrendered to the person serving the subpoena no matter how aggressive the request. The subpoena document should be accepted, and the psychologist should then consult legal counsel regarding applicable law and resulting obligations. If it is ultimately determined that the call for the records has been appropriately issued by a court of competent authority, a psychologist may be placed in a very awkward position, especially if the client does not wish to have the material disclosed.

- If a subpoena arrives from a client's attorney and no release form is included, check with your client, not the attorney, before releasing the documents. In a technical sense, a request from a client's attorney is legally the same as a request from the client himself or herself; however, it is not unreasonable for the clinician to personally confirm the client's wishes, especially if the content of the records is sensitive.
- If a signed release form is included, but the clinician believes that the material may be clinically or legally damaging, discuss it with the client.
- Psychologists concerned about releasing actual notes should offer to prepare a prompt report or summary, but they ultimately may have to produce the full record.
- On occasion a subpoena generated by an attorney opposing the psychologist's client or representing another person may arrive at a clinician's office. Under such circumstances it is reasonable to inform the attorney who issued the subpoena: "I cannot disclose whether or not the person noted in the subpoena is now or ever was my client. If the person were my client, I could not provide any information without a signed release from that individual or a valid court order." Next, contact your client, explain the situation, and ask for permission to talk with his or her attorney. Ask the patient's attorney to work out privilege issues with the opposing attorney or move to quash the subpoena. These steps will assure that the person to whom you owe prime obligations (i.e., your client) is protected to the full extent allowed by law.
- If a valid subpoena seeks raw test data or materials sold only to professionals (e.g., certain

psychological test kits), one should generally respond by offering to provide the raw data to a qualified professional, explaining that laypersons are not qualified to interpret the raw data. Test kits whose purchase is restricted by the publisher to "qualified users" should also generally be withheld. However, both raw data and test kit materials would have to be produced in response to a court order.

General advice: When in doubt, consult your own attorney for advice, but *never* ignore a subpoena.

References & Readings

American Psychological Association (1993). Record keeping guidelines. *American Psychologist, 48,* 984–986.

Bersoff, D. N. (1995). *Ethical conflicts in psychology.* Washington, DC: American Psychological Association.

Boruch, R. F., Dennis, M., & Cecil, J. S. (1996). Fifty years of empirical research on privacy and confidentiality in research settings. In B. H. Stanley, J. E. Sieber, & G. B. Melton (Eds.), *Research ethics: A psychological approach* (pp. 129–173). Lincoln: University of Nebraska Press.

Burke, C. A. (1995). Until death do us part: An exploration into confidentiality following the death of a client. *Professional Psychology: Research and Practice, 26,* 278–280.

Committee on Legal Issues, American Psychological Association (1996). Strategies for private practitioners coping with subpoenas or compelled testimony for client records of test data. *Professional Psychology: Research and Practice, 27,* 245–251.

Committee on Psychological Tests and Assessment (1996). Statement on disclosure of test data. *American Psychologist, 51,* 644–668.

Koocher, G. P. & Keith-Spiegel, P. C. (1998). *Ethics in psychology: Professional standards and cases* (2nd ed.) New York: Oxford University Press.

Related Topics

94 INVOLUNTARY PSYCHIATRIC HOSPITALIZATION (CIVIL COMMITMENT)

Adult and Child

Stuart A. Anfang & Paul S. Appelbaum

ADULT

History

The state's power to hospitalize involuntarily is based on a combination of two rationales—"parens patriae" (the state caring for those incapable of caring for themselves) and "police power" (the state's obligation to protect the public safety).

In 18th- and early 19th-century America, there was little formal legal regulation of psychiatric hospitalization. As state hospitals developed in the mid-19th century, legislatures began to write regulations, which were soon extended to private institutions. The rationale for commitment was *treatment-oriented*, hospitalizing mentally ill persons for their own sake. Procedures by the end of the 19th century often included judicial hearings and occasionally jury trials.

In the early to mid-20th century, several states moved away from judicial procedures, attempting to make commitment easier and quicker and promoting a model primarily of medical decision making. By the 1960s, opponents began to question the legitimacy of psychiatric diagnosis, the effectiveness of state hospitalization, and the right of the state to force unwanted treatment. By late 1960s and early 1970s, many states began to move toward *dangerousness-based* criteria for civil commitment, permitting the involuntary hospitaliza-

tion of only those patients who were dangerous to themselves or to others. Several court decisions, led by a 1972 federal district court decision in Wisconsin (*Lessard v. Schmidt*), endorsed dangerousness criteria as the proper model for civil commitment.

A 1977 U.S. Supreme Court decision (*O'Connor v. Donaldson*) appeared to endorse dangerousness-based criteria for commitment, although the Court did not explicitly reject a need-for-treatment model. By the end of the 1970s, every state adopted dangerousness-based criteria for involuntary hospitalization, typically with judicial procedures and protections similar to criminal proceedings.

Criteria

The dangerousness-based criteria vary across states, but they typically require (a) the presence of mental illness (in many states this does not include mental retardation, dementia, or substance abuse in the absence of other psychiatric illness) and (b) dangerousness.

Dangerousness typically includes (a) *danger to self* (physical harm); (b) *danger to others* (physical harm, not usually psychological harm or harm to property); or (c) *grave disability* (severe inability to care for one's minimal survival needs in the community).

There is variability across states regarding the definition of dangerousness, specifically how imminent or overt the risk of harm. Some court decisions and statutes require that involuntary hospitalization be the "least restrictive alternative" before allowing a commitment, raising a question of whether the state is obligated to create less restrictive alternatives, such as community residences. In general, though, the creation of such alternatives has not been legally mandated and is limited by constraints on financial and programmatic resources.

In recent years, several states have broadened the definition of dangerousness, often expanding the "grave disability" standard to include the prospect of severe deterioration leading to predicted dangerousness. Other states have expanded their commitment criteria to include incompetence, disabling illness, or need for treatment. Future litigation may challenge the constitutionality of these statutes, which appear to move away from strict dangerousness criteria.

Clinicians should be familiar with the statutory criteria in their jurisdiction, as well as the relevant regulations and court decisions (case law) regarding civil commitment.

Critiques of the dangerousness standard usually include one or more of three basic arguments: (a) The current system makes it difficult to obtain involuntary treatment for patients who are not overtly dangerous but are desperately in need of care; (b) dangerousness is notoriously difficult for clinicians to predict accurately; and (c) basing commitment on dangerousness, particularly dangerousness to others, alters the character of the mental health system, shifting its mission from providing treatment to a quasi-police function.

Despite considerable and often impassioned debate, the empirical data generally suggest that, in practice, more restrictive commitment criteria appear to have little impact on the qualitative and quantitative characteristics of the civilly committed population. The system appears to allow involuntary hospitalization for those mentally ill patients in need of treatment, regardless of the precise criteria of the dangerousness-based standards. The "grave disability" standard—or the inability to provide for one's basic survival needs in the community—typically allows for such clinical flexibility.

Procedures

In most states, civil commitment procedures include many of the protections associated with criminal trials. These often include such safeguards as timely notice of the allegations that may result in commitment; timely notice of due process rights, including the right to an attorney; the right to a timely judicial hearing, sometimes including the right to jury trial; the right to remain silent when examined by a psychiatrist or at trial; and placing on the state the burden of proving that the patient meets the commitment criteria. Jurisdictions differ in the standard of proof required, ranging from an intermediate "clear and convincing evidence" standard (the minimal constitutionally acceptable standard) to the more stringent "beyond a reasonable doubt" standard required for criminal prosecutions.

Nearly every state allows for emergency commitment based on a physician's or other mental health professional's certification of mental illness and dangerousness; this commitment can typically last from 48 hours to 10–14 days before requiring a scheduled judicial hearing for further commitment. Various jurisdictions also allow for emergency commitment based on a judge's order (bench commitment), the certification of a police officer, or approval of another designated official. For over 30 years, New York State has had a relatively unique statute allowing for commitment up to 60 days on the certification of two physicians, without a required judicial review; however, on admission every involuntary patient is assigned to a mental health attorney who will inform him or her of the right to an earlier appeal of the commitment and will represent him or her if necessary. A 1982 federal court of appeals decision (*Project Release v. Prevost*) upheld the constitutionality of this procedure, holding that patients' interests may be protected in a variety of acceptable ways.

All mental health clinicians who work with potentially dangerous patients should be familiar with the commitment procedures and mechanisms within their jurisdictions. Attorneys familiar with mental health law can be an invaluable resource, as can forensically trained clinicians. Clinicians in all jurisdictions should be aware of the need to alert the patient to the limits of confidentiality—that clinical interview information may be disclosed in the judicial commitment hearing. Some states *require* such a warning and allow the patient the right to refuse to participate further.

In addition to describing the appropriate procedures and criteria, most state commitment statutes provide immunity to mental health clinicians who act in good faith when seeking to hospitalize a patient involuntarily. If the clinician can document a commitment decision based on appropriate clinical judgment within the professional standard of care, he or she can feel reasonably safe from malpractice liability for improper commitment (although actual verdicts will be based on the particular facts and circumstances of the situation). As with all complex and difficult clinical decisions, consultation with colleagues is often an important tool—both for guidance and for risk-management purposes.

Involuntary Outpatient Commitment

Over the past 15 years, involuntary outpatient commitment (IOC) has gained increasing attention as a possible alternative to inpatient commitment in systems with declining inpatient resources. The majority of states have laws explicitly permitting outpatient commitment, although there is considerable local and regional variation regarding how commonly the option is used.

In 1987, the American Psychiatric Association issued a report that suggested statutory guidelines for IOC. These include evidence that a person (a) suffers from a severe mental illness; (b) is likely, without treatment, to cause harm to himself or herself or others or to suffer "substantial mental or emotional deterioration"; (c) lacks the capacity to make an informed decision regarding treatment; and (d) has a history of inpatient hospitalizations, as well as outpatient noncompliance. Many state legislatures have included several of these provisions when writing their statutes.

Outpatient commitment laws generally follow one of three basic patterns: (a) conditional release for involuntarily hospitalized patients; (b) "less restrictive" alternative to hospitalization for patients who meet inpatient commitment criteria; or (c) alternative for patients not meeting criteria for inpatient commitment but at risk for severe decompensation without treatment. This last pattern, often called "preventive commitment" or "predicted deterioration," has generated considerable debate because it is seen as a move further away from an "imminent dangerousness" standard toward a need-for-treatment approach.

Mental health clinicians should be familiar with the availability of IOC in their jurisdictions and with the range of possible options and resources. Even as state legislatures rush to write IOC statutes, considerable debate continues over the efficacy and utility of these outpatient commitment programs, with a limited but growing number of empirical studies.

CHILD

History

Constitutional due process rights for children in the juvenile justice system were first recognized by the U.S. Supreme Court in 1967 (*In re Gault*). Children were held to be entitled to due process protections similar to those of adults in criminal proceedings, including the right to counsel, the right to written notice of charges, the right to cross-examine witnesses, and the privilege against self-incrimination. At that time, the typical state voluntary psychiatric hospitalization statute allowed a parent or guardian to admit a minor for psychiatric treatment (on a physician's recommendation) without the minor's consent and without further administrative or judicial review. Building on *Gault*, several cases in North Carolina, Georgia, and Pennsylvania challenged the constitutionality of those statutes, contending that unwanted or troublesome children were being "dumped" in mental hospitals.

In 1979, the U.S. Supreme Court (*Parham v. JR*) upheld the right of a parent or guardian to admit a minor to a psychiatric hospital without a judicial hearing. The Court endorsed the need for a "neutral factfinder"—typically the admitting psychiatrist—to review the admission. Absent a finding of parental abuse or neglect, the Court assumed that parents act in their children's best interest and doubted that judges would be able to make better decisions than parents acting in collaboration with objective physicians.

Many child-rights advocates viewed the decision as a major defeat, although individual states were free to enact statutes requiring greater protections and judicial oversight. In the 1980s, many commentators pointed to alarmingly high admission rates, especially in private, for-profit psychiatric facilities, as evidence of a pattern in which troublesome juveniles without clear psychiatric illness were being hospitalized, often as an alternative to the juvenile justice system. As managed care has transformed inpatient mental health care in the 1990s, this pattern appears to have decreased in frequency.

Criteria and Procedures

Given the relatively low constitutional "minimum" required under *Parham*, states have diverse and constantly changing approaches to the issue of child hospitalization. Involuntary civil commitment *without* the consent of a parent or guardian is extremely rare and typically follows guidelines similar to those for adult civil commitment. More common is the "voluntary" hospitalization by a parent or guardian (including a state social service agency) without the consent of the minor.

States range from the minimum of allowing a parent to admit a child without any administrative or judicial review to requiring a formal judicial hearing for all admissions with specified due process protections. Some states have more rigid regulations covering public psychiatric facilities and minors who are wards of the state. Typically, states require the presence of a mental illness requiring treatment, the availability of such treatment through the hospital, and evidence that the hospital is the least restrictive setting available. The American Psychological Association and the American Academy of Child and Adolescent Psychiatry have issued suggested statutory guidelines.

Most states have provisions for the minor to appeal the hospitalization, requesting an adversarial judicial hearing. For adolescents between 13 and 18, many states provide varying procedures, allowing minors of a certain age to sign in or out of a hospital voluntarily, without the approval of a parent or guardian. Mental health clinicians should be familiar with the statutory requirements and case law in their jurisdictions. Consultation with an attorney familiar with child mental health issues or a clinician with forensic expertise is helpful.

GENERAL CLINICAL ISSUES

- *Predicting dangerousness:* Clinicians should be familiar with relevant risk factors, base rates, and both external and internal factors that influence the potential for violence. Risks, resources, and benefits must be balanced in a clinically sensitive and sophisticated decision process. Consultation and corroborative clinical data are invaluable.

- *Maintaining a therapeutic alliance with a patient coerced to receive care:* Patients should be involved in the decision process as much as possible. As treatment restores the patient's ability to assess his or her own functioning, the patient and clinician can aim to shape the experience into one that enhances the patient's responsibility, self-respect, and therapeutic rapport.

- *Resolving conflicts between legal mandates and ethical imperatives in the commitment setting:* Whereas legal standards suggest a rigidly defined set of criteria, ethical and clinical imperatives often encourage the clinician to err on the side of caution. Clinicians must be sensitive to both factors and strive for a balanced, thoughtful approach to decision making in cases of involuntary hospitalization.

References & Readings

American Academy of Child and Adolescent Psychiatry (1987). *Child and adolescent psychiatric illness: Guidelines for treatment resources, quality assurances, peer review, and reim-*

bursement. Washington, DC: American Academy of Child and Adolescent Psychiatry.

American Psychiatric Association (1987). *Involuntary commitment to outpatient treatment* (Task Force Report No. 26). Washington, DC: American Psychiatric Association.

American Psychological Association (1984). *A model act for the mental health treatment of minors*. Washington, DC: American Psychological Association.

Appelbaum, P. S. (1994). *Almost a revolution: Mental health law and the limits of change*. New York: Oxford University Press.

Appelbaum, P. S., & Anfang, S. A. (1998). Civil commitment. In R. Michels (Ed.), *Psychiatry*. Philadelphia: Lippincott-Raven.

Bagby, R. M., & Atkinson, L. (1988). The effects of legislative reform on civil commitment rates: A critical analysis. *Behavioral Sciences and the Law, 6*, 45–62.

Burlingame, W. V., & Amaya, M. (1991). Psychiatric commitment of children and adolescents. In D. Schetky & E. Benedek (Eds.), *Clinical handbook of child psychiatry and the law* (pp. 292–307). Baltimore: Williams and Wilkins.

LaFond, J. Q. (1994). Law and the delivery of involuntary mental health services. *American Journal of Orthopsychiatry, 64*, 209–223.

Monahan, J., & Steadman, H. J. (Eds.) (1994). *Violence and mental disorder: Developments in risk assessment*. Chicago: University of Chicago Press.

Parry, J. (1994). Survey of standards for extended involuntary commitment. *Mental and Physical Disability Law Reporter, 18*, 329–336.

Stromberg, C. D., & Stone, A. A. (1983). A model state law on civil commitment of the mentally ill. *Harvard Journal on Legislation, 20*, 275–396.

Swartz, M. S., Burns, B. J., Hiday, V. A., George, L. K., Swanson, J., & Wagner, H. R. (1995). New directions in research on involuntary outpatient commitment. *Psychiatric Services, 46*, 381–385.

Warren, C. A. B. (1982). *Court of last resort: Mental illness and the law*. Chicago: University of Chicago Press.

Weithorn, L. A. (1988). Mental hospitalization of troublesome youth: An analysis of skyrocketing admission rates. *Stanford Law Review, 40*, 773–838.

Related Topics

95   SEXUAL FEELINGS, ACTIONS, AND DILEMMAS IN PSYCHOTHERAPY

Kenneth S. Pope

A HISTORY OF THE PROHIBITION AGAINST THERAPIST-PATIENT SEX

The prohibition against engaging in sex with a patient is one of the most ancient, dating back not only to the Hippocratic oath, which emerged in the 3rd or 4th century B.C., but also to the earlier codes of the Nigerian healing arts (Pope, 1994). The modern codes of clinical ethics contained no explicit mention of this topic until research began revealing that substantial numbers of therapists were violating the prohibition. Although the codes had not highlighted this particular form of patient exploitation by name, therapist-patient sex violated various sections of the codes prior to the 1970s (Hare-Mustin, 1974). The long history of prohibition against therapist-patient sexual involvement has also been recognized by the courts (*Roy v. Hartogs*, 1976, p. 590).

SURVEY DATA, OFFENDERS, VICTIMS, AND GENDER PATTERNS

Despite the prohibition, a significant number of therapists report on anonymous surveys that they have become sexually involved with at least one patient. When data from the eight national studies that have been published in peer-reviewed journals are pooled, 5,148 participants provide anonymous self-reports (Pope, 1994). According to these pooled data, about 4.4% of the therapists reported becoming sexually involved with a client. The gender differences are significant: 6.8% of the male therapists and 1.6% of the female therapists reported engaging in sex with a client.

Data from these studies, as well as others (e.g., reports by therapists working with patients who have been sexually involved with a prior therapist), suggest that therapist-patient sex is consistent with other forms of abuse such as rape and incest: the perpetrators are overwhelmingly (though not exclusively) male, and the victims are overwhelmingly (though not exclusively) female (Pope, 1994).

This significant gender difference has long been a focus of scholarship in the area of therapist-patient sex but is still not well understood. Holroyd and Brodsky's (1977) report of the first national study of therapist-patient sex concluded with a statement of major issues that had yet to be resolved: "Three professional issues remain to be addressed: (a) that male therapists are most often involved, (b) that female patients are most often the objects, and (c) that therapists who disregard the sexual boundary once are likely to repeat" (p. 849). Holroyd suggested that the significant gender differ-

ences reflected sex role stereotyping and bias: "Sexual contact between therapist and patient is perhaps the quintessence of sex-biased therapeutic practice" (Holroyd, 1983, p. 285). Holroyd and Brodsky's (1977) landmark research was followed by a second national study focusing on not only therapist-patient but also professor-student sexual relationships (Pope, Levenson, & Schover, 1979).

When sexual contact occurs in the context of psychology training or psychotherapy, the predominant pattern is quite clear and simple: An older higher status man becomes sexually active with a younger, subordinate woman. In each of the higher status professional roles (teacher, supervisor, administrator, therapist), a much higher percentage of men than women engage in sex with those students or clients for whom they have assumed professional responsibility. In the lower status role of student, a far greater proportion of women than men are sexually active with their teachers, administrators, and clinical supervisors. (Pope et al., 1979, p. 687)

COMMON SCENARIOS OF THERAPIST-PATIENT SEXUAL INVOLVEMENT

It is useful for therapists to be aware of the common scenarios in which therapists sexually exploit their patients. It is important to emphasize, however, that these are only general descriptions of some of the most common patterns, and many instances of therapist-patient sexual involvement will not fall into these 10 scenarios, which were discussed by Pope and Bouhoutsos (1986, p. 4):

1. *Role trading:* Therapist becomes the "patient," and the wants and needs of the therapist become the focus.
2. *Sex therapy:* Therapist fraudulently presents therapist-patient sex as valid treatment for sexual or related difficulties.
3. *As if . . . :* Therapist treats positive transference as if it were not the result of the therapeutic situation.
4. *Svengali:* Therapist creates and exploits an

exaggerated dependence on the part of the patient.

5. *Drugs:* Therapist uses cocaine, alcohol, or other drugs as part of the seduction.

6. *Rape:* Therapist uses physical force, threats, and/or intimidation.

7. *True love:* Therapist uses rationalizations that attempt to discount the clinical/professional nature of the professional relationship and its responsibilities.

8. *It just got out of hand:* Therapist fails to treat the emotional closeness that develops in therapy with sufficient attention, care, and respect.

9. *Time out:* Therapist fails to acknowledge and take account of the fact that the therapeutic relationship does not cease to exist between scheduled sessions or outside the therapist's office.

10. *Hold me:* Therapist exploits patient's desire for nonerotic physical contact and possible confusion between erotic and nonerotic contact.

WORKING WITH PATIENTS WHO HAVE BEEN SEXUALLY INVOLVED WITH A THERAPIST

National survey research suggests that most clinicians are likely to encounter at least one patient who has been sexually involved with a prior therapist (Pope & Vetter, 1991). Specialized treatment approaches, based on research, have been developed for this population (Pope, 1994). One of the first steps toward gaining competence in this area is recognition of the diverse and sometimes extremely intense reactions that a subsequent therapist can experience when encountering a patient who reports sexual involvement with a former therapist. The following list of common clinical reactions to victims of therapist-patient sexual involvement is adapted from Pope, Sonne, and Holroyd (1993, pp. 241–261):

1. *Disbelief and denial:* The tendency to reject reflexively—without adequate data gathering—allegations about therapist-patient sex (e.g., because the activities described seem outlandish and improbable).

2. *Minimization of harm:* The tendency to assume reflexively—without adequate data gathering—that harm did not occur or that, if it did, the consequences were minimally, if at all, harmful.

3. *Making the patient fit the textbook:* The tendency to assume reflexively—without adequate data gathering and examination—that the patient *must* inevitably fit a particular schema.

4. *Blaming the victim:* The tendency to attempt to make the patient responsible for enforcing the therapist's professional responsibility to refrain from engaging in sex with a patient, and holding the patient responsible for the therapist's offense.

5. *Sexual reaction to the victim:* The clinician's sexual attraction to or feelings about the patient. Such feelings are normal but must not become a source of distortion in the assessment process.

6. *Discomfort at the lack of privacy:* The clinician's (and sometimes patient's) emotional response to the possibility that under certain conditions (e.g., malpractice, licensing, or similar formal actions against the offending therapist; a formal review of assessment and other services by the insurance company providing coverage for the services) the raw data and the results of the assessment may not remain private.

7. *Difficulty "keeping the secret":* The clinician's possible discomfort (and other emotional reactions) when he or she has knowledge that an offender continues to practice and to victimize other patients but cannot, in light of confidentiality and/or other constraints, take steps to intervene.

8. *Intrusive advocacy:* The tendency to want to guide, direct, or determine a patient's decisions about what steps to take or what steps not to take in regard to a perpetrator.

9. *Vicarious helplessness:* The clinician's discomfort when a patient who has filed a formal complaint seems to encounter unjustifiable obstacles, indifference, lack of fair

hearing, and other responses that seem to ignore or trivialize the complaint and fail to protect the public from offenders.

10. *Discomfort with strong feelings:* The clinician's discomfort when experiencing strong feelings (e.g., rage, neediness, or ambivalence) expressed by the patient and focused on the clinician.

Awareness of these reactions can prevent them from blocking the therapist from rendering effective services to the patient. The therapist can be alert to such reactions and can sort through them should they occur. In some instances, the therapist may seek consultation to help gain perspective and understanding.

SEXUAL ATTRACTION TO PATIENTS AND OTHER (SOMETIMES) UNCOMFORTABLE FEELINGS

Sexual attraction to patients seems to be a prevalent experience that evokes negative reactions. National survey research suggests that over 4 out of 5 psychologists (87%) and social workers (81%) report experiencing sexual attraction to at least one client (Pope, Keith-Spiegel, & Tabachnick, 1986; Bernsen, Tabachnick, & Pope, 1994). Yet simply experiencing the attraction (without necessarily even feeling tempted to act on it) causes most of the therapists who report such attraction (63% of the psychologists; 51% of the social workers) to feel guilty, anxious, or confused about the attraction.

That sexual attraction causes such discomfort among so many psychologists and social workers may be the reason that graduate training programs and internships tend to neglect training in this area. Only 9% of psychologists and 10% of social workers in these national studies reported that their formal training on the topic in graduate school and internships had been adequate. A majority of psychologists and social workers reported receiving *no* training about such attraction.

This discomfort may also explain why scientific and professional books seem to neglect this topic.

In light of the multitude of books in the areas of human sexuality, sexual dynamics, sex therapies, unethical therapist-patient sexual contact, management of the therapist's or patient's sexual behaviors, and so on, it is curious that sexual attraction to patients per se has not served as the primary focus of a wide range of texts. The professor, supervisor, or librarian seeking books that turn their *primary* attention to exploring the therapist's *feelings* in this regard would be hard pressed to assemble a selection from which to choose an appropriate course text. If someone unfamiliar with psychotherapy were to judge the prevalence and significance of therapists' sexual feelings on the basis of the books that focus exclusively on that topic, he or she might conclude that the phenomenon is neither wide-spread nor important. (Pope, Sonne, & Holroyd, 1993, p. 23)

These and similar factors may form a vicious circle: Discomfort with sexual attraction may have fostered an absence of graduate training and relevant textbooks; in turn, an absence of programs providing training and relevant textbooks in this area may sustain or intensify discomfort with the topic. The avoidance of the topic may produce a real impact.

These studies reveal significant gender effects in reported rates of experiencing sexual attraction to a patient. About 95% of the male psychologists and 92% of the male social workers, compared with 76% of the female psychologists and 70% of the female social workers, reported experiencing sexual attraction to a patient. The research suggests that just as male therapists are significantly more likely to become sexually involved with their patients, male therapists are also more likely to experience sexual attraction to their patients.

These national surveys suggest that a sizable minority of therapists carry with them—in the physical absence of the client—sexualized images of the client and that a significantly greater percentage of male than female therapists experience such cognitions. About 27% of male psychologists and 30% of male social workers, compared with 14% of female psychologists and 13% of female social workers, reported engaging in sexual fantasies about a patient while engaging in sexual activity with another person (i.e., not the patient). National survey research has found that 46% of psychologists reported engaging in sexual fantasizing (regardless of the occasion) about a patient on a rare basis and that an additional 26% reported more frequent fantasies of this kind (Pope, Tabachnick, & Keith-Spiegel, 1987), and 6% have reported telling sexual fantasies to their patients. Such data may be helpful in understanding not only how therapists experience and respond to sexual feelings but also how therapists and patients represent (e.g., remember, anticipate, think about, fantasize about) each other when they are apart and how this affects the therapeutic process and outcome.

Unfortunately, it is all too easy to consider such data intellectually but remain unaware of the ways in which the therapist's sexual feelings, anger, hatred, fear, and other responses affect clinical services. Specific, structured training exercises and other programs (e.g., Pope, Sonne, & Holroyd, 1993) may be helpful in graduate training programs, internships, continuing education workshops, and other settings to enable therapists to encounter such responses in a way that will enhance or at least not distort the effectiveness of clinical services.

WHEN THE THERAPIST IS UNSURE WHAT TO DO

What can the therapist do when he or she doesn't know what to do? The book *Sexual Feelings in Psychotherapy* (Pope et al., 1993) suggests a 10-step approach to such daunting situations, which is summarized here. A repeated theme of that book is that therapists lack easy, one-size-fits-all "answers" to what sexual feelings about patients mean or their implications for the therapy. Different theoretical orientations provide different, sometimes opposing, ways of approaching such questions. Each person and situation is unique. Therapists must explore and achieve a working understanding of their own unfolding, evolving feelings and the ways in which they may provide a source of guidance about what to say or do next.

The approach outlined here places fundamental trust in the individual therapist, adequately trained and consulting with others, to draw his or her own conclusions. Almost without exception, therapists learn at the outset the fundamental resources for helping themselves explore problematic situations. Depending on the situation, they may introspect, study the available research and clinical literature, consult, seek supervision, and/or begin or resume personal therapy. But sometimes, even after the most sustained exploration, the course is not clear. The therapist's best understanding of the situation suggests a course of action that seems productive yet questionable and perhaps potentially harmful. To refrain from a contemplated action may cut the therapist off from legitimately helpful spontaneity, creativity, intuition, and the ability to respond effectively to the patient's needs. On the other hand, engaging in the contemplated action may lead to disaster. When reaching such an impasse, therapists may find it useful to consider the potential intervention in light of the following 10 considerations.

1. *The fundamental prohibition:* Is the contemplated action consistent with the fundamental prohibition against therapist-patient sexual intimacy? Therapists must never violate this special trust. If the considered course of action includes any form of sexual involvement with a patient, it must be rejected.

2. *The slippery slope:* The second consideration may demand deeper self-knowledge and self-exploration. Is the contemplated course of action likely to lead or to create a risk for sexual involvement with the patient? The contemplated action may seem unrelated to any question of sexual exploitation of a patient. Yet depending on the personality, strengths, and weaknesses of the therapist, the considered action may constitute a subtle first step on a slippery slope. In most cases, the therapist alone can honestly address this consideration.

3. *Consistency of communication:* The third consideration invites the clinician to review the course of therapy from the start to the present: Has the therapist consistently and unambiguously communicated to the patient that sexual intimacies cannot

and will not occur, and is the contemplated action consistent with that communication? Does the contemplated action needlessly cloud the clarity of that communication? The therapist may be intensely tempted to act in ways that stir the patient's sexual interest or respond in a self-gratifying way to the patient's sexuality. Does the contemplated action represent, however subtly, a turning away from the legitimate goals of therapy?

4. *Clarification:* The fourth consideration invites therapists to ask if the contemplated action would be better postponed until sexual and related issues have been clarified. Assume, for example, that a therapist's theoretical orientation does not preclude physical contact with patients and that a patient has asked that each session conclude with a reassuring hug between therapist and patient. Such ritualized hugs could raise complex questions about their meaning for the patient, about their impact on the relationship, and about how they might influence the course and effectiveness of therapy. It may be important to clarify such issues with the patient before making a decision to conclude each session with a hug.

5. *The patient's welfare:* The fifth consideration is one of the most fundamental touchstones of all therapy: Is the contemplated action consistent with the patient's welfare? The therapist's feelings may become so intensely powerful that they may create a context in which the patient's clinical needs may blur or fade away altogether. The patient may express wants or feelings with great force. The legal context—with the litigiousness that seems so prevalent in current society—may threaten the therapist in a way that makes it difficult to keep a clear focus on the patient's welfare. Despite such competing factors and complexities, it is crucial to assess the degree to which any contemplated action supports, is consistent with, is irrelevant to, or is contrary to the patient's welfare.

6. *Consent:* The sixth consideration is yet another fundamental touchstone of therapy:

Is the contemplated action consistent with the basic informed consent of the patient?

7. *Adopting the patient's view:* The seventh consideration urges the therapist to empathize imaginatively with the patient: How is the patient likely to understand and respond to the contemplated action?

Therapy is one of many endeavors in which exclusive attention to theory, intention, and technique may distract from other sources of information, ideas, and guidance. Therapists-in-training may cling to theory, intention, and technique as a way of coping with the anxieties and overwhelming responsibilities of the therapeutic venture. Seasoned therapists may rely almost exclusively on theory, intention, and technique out of learned reflex, habit, and the sheer weariness that approaches burn-out. There is always risk that the therapist will fall back on repetitive and reflexive responses that verge on stereotype. Without much thought or feeling, the anxious or tired therapist may, if analytically minded, answer a patient's question by asking why the patient asked the question; if holding a client-centered orientation, may simply reflect or restate what the client has just said; if gestalt-trained, may ask the client to say something to an empty chair; and so on.

One way to help avoid responses that are driven more by anxiety, fatigue, or other similar factors is to consider carefully how the therapist would think, feel, and react if he or she were the patient. Regardless of the theoretical soundness, intended outcome, or technical sophistication of a contemplated intervention, how will it likely be experienced and understood by the patient? Can the therapist anticipate at all what the patient might feel and think? The therapist's attempts to try out, in his or her imagination, the contemplated action and to view it from the perspective of the patient may help prevent, correct, or at least identify possible sources of misunderstanding, miscommunication, and failures of empathy. (Pope et al., 1993, pp. 185–186)

8. *Competence:* The eighth consideration is one of competence: Is the therapist compe-

tent to carry out the contemplated intervention? Ensuring that a therapist's education, training, and supervised experience are adequate and appropriate for his or her work is a fundamental responsibility.

9. *Uncharacteristic behaviors:* The ninth consideration involves becoming alert to unusual actions: Does the contemplated action fall substantially outside the range of the therapist's usual behaviors? That an action is unusual does not, of course, mean that something is necessarily wrong with it. Creative therapists will occasionally try creative interventions, and it is unlikely that even the most conservative and tradition-bound therapist conducts therapy the same way all the time. However, possible actions that are considerably outside the therapist's general approaches likely warrant special consideration.

10. *Consultation:* The final consideration concerns secrecy: Is there a compelling reason for not discussing the contemplated action with a colleague, consultant, or supervisor? Therapists' reluctance to disclose an action to others is a "red flag" to a possibly inappropriate action. Therapists may consider any possible action in light of the following question: If they took this action, would they be reluctant to let their professional colleagues know they had taken it? If the response is "yes," the reasons for the reluctance warrant examination. If the response is "no," it is worth considering whether one has adequately taken advantage of the opportunities to discuss the matter with a trusted colleague. If discussion with a colleague has not helped to clarify the issues, consultation with additional professionals, each of whom may provide different perspectives and suggestions, may be useful.

References & Readings

Bernsen, A., Tabachnick, B. G., & Pope, K. S. (1994). National survey of social workers' sexual attraction to their clients: Results, implications, and comparison to psychologists. *Ethics and Behavior, 4,* 369–388.

Bouhoutsos, J. C., Holroyd, J., Lerman, H., Forer, B., & Greenberg, M. (1983). Sexual intimacy between psychotherapists and patients. *Professional Psychology: Research and Practice, 14,* 185–196.

Gartrell, N. K., Herman, J. L., Olarte, S., Feldstein, M., & Localio, R. (1986). Psychiatrist-patient sexual contact: Results of a national survey, I: Prevalence. *American Journal of Psychiatry, 143,* 1126–1131.

Hare-Mustin, R. T. (1974). Ethical considerations in the use of sexual contact in psychotherapy. *Psychotherapy: Theory, Research, and Practice, 11,* 308–310.

Holroyd, J. (1983). Erotic contact as an instance of sex-biased therapy. In J. Murray & P. R. Abramson (Eds.), *Bias in psychotherapy* (pp. 285–308). New York: Praeger.

Holroyd, J., & Brodsky, A. (1977). Psychologists' attitudes and practices regarding erotic and nonerotic physical contact with clients. *American Psychologist, 32,* 843–849.

Pope, K. S. (1994). *Sexual involvement with therapists: Patient assessment, subsequent therapy, forensics.* Washington, DC: American Psychological Association.

Pope, K. S., & Bouhoutsos, J. C. (1986). *Sexual intimacies between therapists and patients.* New York: Praeger/Greenwood.

Pope, K. S., Keith-Spiegel, P., & Tabachnick, B. G. (1986). Sexual attraction to patients: The human therapist and the (sometimes) inhuman training system. *American Psychologist, 41,* 147–158.

Pope, K. S., Levenson, H., & Schover, L. R. (1979). Sexual intimacy in psychology training: Results and implications of a national survey. *American Psychologist, 34,* 682–689.

Pope, K. S., Sonne, J. L., & Holroyd, J. (1993). *Sexual feelings in psychotherapy: Explorations for therapists and therapists-in-training.* Washington, DC: American Psychological Association.

Pope, K. S., Tabachnick, B. G., & Keith-Spiegel, P. (1987). Ethics of practice: The beliefs and behaviors of psychologists as therapists. *American Psychologist, 42,* 993–1006.

Pope, K. S., & Vetter, V. A. (1991). Prior therapist-patient sexual involvement among patients seen by psychologists. *Psychotherapy, 28,* 429–438.

Roy v. Hartogs, 381 N.Y.S. 2d 587 (1976); 85 Misc.2d 891.

Related Topics

96

EXPERT TESTIMONY
Deposition Versus Courtroom

Geoffrey R. McKee

The psychologist as expert witness has received considerable attention and discussion over the past 20 years (Brodsky & Robey, 1973; Ziskin, 1981; Blau, 1984; Brodsky, 1991; Pope, Butcher, & Seelen, 1993). Most of the literature focuses on courtroom testimony during criminal trials or domestic court hearings. Little, however, has been written about the psychologist giving depositions, the most common form of expert testimony in civil proceedings. Depositions are considered by many experts to be the "most grueling, intense, and anxiety-producing aspect of litigation" (Sacks, 1995, p. 18). The purpose of this chapter is to highlight the differences between expert testimony during depositions versus courtroom (Table 1) to facilitate psychologists' effective participation in this stage of litigation.

The Federal Rules of Civil Procedure Rule 26(b)(4)(A) (1995) and Federal Rules of Criminal Procedure Rule 15 (1995) provide that any party (plaintiff or defendant; prosecution or defense) may take the deposition of any expert who will testify at trial regarding his or her already disclosed report. A deposition is a statement from a witness (deponent) under oath taken in question-and-answer form (Blau, 1984). Depositions are one of several methods of pretrial discovery in which an attorney attempts to uncover evidence from the opposing attorney. Depositions may be given orally in face-to-face contact with the attorneys, or they may be given in written form through interrogatories (Horowitz & Willging, 1984). Such procedures are governed by specific rules, which may vary from jurisdiction to jurisdiction; however, many states have simply adopted the Federal Rules of Civil Procedure (1995)

and/or the Federal Rules of Criminal Procedure (1995). The remainder of this chapter discusses depositions in terms of context and issues relevant to the deposing (adverse) attorney and nondeposing (retaining) attorney.

CONTEXT

The purpose of a deposition is to discover (and preserve for future use at trial) evidence possessed by competing parties in litigation. In a case involving mental health issues, both attorneys will often depose the other side's experts in an attempt to find out the expert's credentials and the foundation (database), methods, content, and reasoning of the expert's opinions. Because depositions are a pretrial procedure, the deposition typically occurs in a private setting, such as the psychologist's office or, for strategic purposes (e.g., to unsettle the expert), in the office of the deposing attorney. Neither a judge nor a jury is present; however, the questions and answers are preserved by a court stenographer and, increasingly, by videotape. Prior to the deponent psychologist's testimony, the attorneys will resolve any variations from the "usual stipulations" governing depositions such as the method of taking the deposition, the use of the deposition (e.g., for impeachment of the expert's testimony at trial), the waiver of the nondeposing attorney's objections to his or her psychologist being deposed, and the documentation of either attorney's objections to deposition questions that will be reserved for the judge's ruling. In contrast to courtroom testimony, wherein the retaining attorney begins the questioning of his or her expert, followed

TABLE 1. Differences Between Expert Testimony in Deposition and Courtroom

Issue	Deposition	Courtroom
Context		
Purpose	Discover evidence	Resolve dispute
Setting	Private office	Public courtroom
Scope of inquiry	Extensive (civil)	Limited (prejudice to jury)
Authority	Deposition rules	Rules of court; statutes
Procedure	Deposing attorney first	Retaining attorney first
Fees	Paid by deposing attorney	Paid by retaining attorney
Objections' resolution	Delayed until trial	Immediate by judge
Posttestimony issues	*Never* waive reading/signing transcript	Leave; credibility decreases if you stay at attorneys' table and consult through trial
Deposing (Adverse) Attorney		
Intent	Investigative	Adversarial
Demeanor	Deliberate	Theatrical
Pace	Leisurely	Expedited
General questions	Highly technical	Laymanlike for jury
Vita questions	Extensive	Limited; stipulated if better than adverse attorney's expert
Opinion questions	Extensive	Selective to minimize impact
Error questions	Delayed until trial	Immediate: embarrassment
Nondeposing (Retaining) Attorney		
Intent	Resistance to disclosure	Instructive to judge, jury
Demeanor	Passive to minimize exposure of strategy	Active to influence juror decision making
Questions	None or limited to selected issues	Extensive on direct; active on redirect as necessary
Consultation with expert	Limited or prohibited during testimony	Collaborative prior/during trial (though not during testimony)

by cross-examination by the adverse attorney, in a deposition the deposing (adverse) attorney initiates questioning of the deponent. Typically the deposing attorney's scope of inquiry is extensive because a deposition is a discovery procedure and concerns regarding prejudice of the jury are minimal. Similar to the sequences in courtroom testimony, the deponent psychologist is first questioned regarding his or her qualifications (credentials), followed by investigation of the content of his or her opinions relevant to the case's psycholegal issues. If, during questioning, the retaining attorney objects to the deposing attorney's question, resolution of the objection is delayed until a hearing before the judge; despite the objection, the expert is typically requested to answer the question. After testifying, but before the deposition is formally concluded, the psychologist should *always* request his or her right to read

and sign the transcript of the deposition to correct any typographical, form, or substance mistakes made by the stenographer (Sacks, 1995). The transcript will be the document against which the psychologist's trial testimony will be compared; any differences may be employed by the deposing attorney to discredit the psychologist's conclusions and opinions. If the psychologist and retaining attorney have not discussed the review and signing of the transcript, the attorney may unwittingly agree to waive this "usual stipulation," with disastrous results for the psychologist at trial.

DEPOSING (ADVERSE) ATTORNEY

Because the deposing attorney has requested the deposition and is paying the deponent psychologist's fees, he or she is the central figure of the proceedings. The deposing attorney's intent is to be investigative and, at times, confrontational. He or she hopes to learn as much as possible about the expert's credentials, foundation, methods, and content of opinion(s), as well as the psychologist's demeanor, persuasiveness, and credibility as a witness. In contrast to courtroom theatrics to influence jury perceptions, the deposing attorney will likely be subdued, deliberate, and methodical in questioning to ensure that he or she has a full understanding of the basis for the expert's opinions. The deposing attorney will likely have retained a psychologist to review the deponent psychologist's report prior to deposition and to assist in his or her questioning. Without the judge's implied pressure to avoid wasting the court's time with exploratory inquiries of dubious relevance, the attorney's pace can be leisurely during a deposition, with frequent consultations with the attorney's colleagues and long pauses between questions—delays that are rarely tolerated by trial judges.

In general, the deposing attorney's questions will be highly technical rather than simplistic for juror influence because he or she wishes to obtain a full and complete exposition of the expert's qualifications, methods, and reasoning in forming his or her opinions. Many of the deposition questions may have been developed by the deposing attorney's retained psychologist, who will subsequently review the deponent psychologist's testimony for errors of foundation, method, and/or reasoning and may suggest further inquiries during trial. The deposing attorney's retained psychologist may also provide an opinion about the overall competence of the deponent psychologist's opinions to assist the attorney in deciding whether to proceed to trial or seek settlement. The quality of the expert's consultation is dependent on the quality of the attorney's questions; thus, the deponent psychologist is likely to face very specific, highly technical inquiries.

The extensiveness of inquiry may begin with the expert's qualifications. Rather than a few superficial questions or stipulation at trial (especially with highly qualified experts), the deposing attorney may spend hours in a case-by-case review of the psychologist's experience,

course-by-course review of the psychologist's training, article-by-article review of the psychologist's publications, and/or transcript-by-transcript review of the psychologist's prior testimony. The intent is part factual and part strategic: The attorney wants to find anything that might be used to impeach the expert's credibility while also exhausting the psychologist so that he or she might make errors during direct questioning that could subsequently be used at trial to diminish the influence of his or her testimony. For example, suppose that the psychologist inadvertently scored the MMPI results for the male plaintiff using the female norms. If the attorney (or his or her retained psychologist) detects the error, he or she may wish to highlight the error immediately to challenge the competence of the deponent psychologist's opinions as a prelude to settlement or wait until trial to embarrass the expert in front of the jury. Error detection might also force the retaining attorney to "rehabilitate" the psychologist's testimony through additional questioning, causing unexpected disclosure of that attorney's case strategy and further inquiry by the deposing attorney in response to the deponent's additional testimony.

Typically, the majority of the deposing attorney's questions will focus on the deponent psychologist's opinions of the psycholegal issues of the case. During trial, the deposing (adverse) attorney would be seeking to minimize the impact of the expert's testimony on the judge and/or jury by often dramatic, theatrical, and/or dismissive interrogation. During deposition, the attorney's inquiry will be broad and deep, patiently probing for any weaknesses in the psychologist's foundation, methods, or reasoning. The attorney may use a variety of methods, including the "learned treatise" (Poythress, 1980) or "hypothetical question" (Myers, 1992); descriptions and responses to such gambits may be found in Brodsky (1991) and other sources (Brodsky & Robey, 1973; Appelbaum & Gutheil, 1991; Pope et al., 1993). The more deliberate, unhurried climate of the deposition allows for extensive inquiry of the psychologist's methods based on *Daubert v. Merrell Dow Pharmaceuticals, Inc.* (1993; see especially the

Daubert questions proposed by Marlowe, 1995). If the psychologist is unable to rebut such challenges to the testimony, his or her opinions may be deemed inadmissible at trial, negating the psychologist's contribution to the retaining attorney's case and forcing the attorney into either dropping the case or reaching a significantly diminished settlement (or, if a criminal defense attorney, an unfavorable conviction).

NONDEPOSING (RETAINING) ATTORNEY

Generally, the intent of the nondeposing attorney during the deposition of his or her expert is to minimize discovery of his or her case facts and strategy by the opposing attorney. In contrast to active, instructive, persuasive direct inquiry of his or her psychologist at trial to maximize the impact of the expert's testimony on the jury's decision making, during deposition the nondeposing attorney is frequently very passive, objecting only when absolutely necessary. Often, following the psychologist's deposition testimony, the attorney will not ask questions. The nondeposing attorney may ask the deponent psychologist to reiterate the opinions of his or her report "for the record," especially if the deposing attorney has avoided the psychologist's conclusions and focused only on the expert's suspected weaknesses. Finally, the retaining attorney is typically prohibited from conferring with his or her psychologist during deposition testimony to allow the deposing attorney to question the witness without obstruction or coaching (*Hall v. Clifton Precision*, 1993).

The purpose of this chapter has been to describe the basic elements and issues pertaining to the psychologist's participation in pretrial depositions. The reader is referred to Pope et al. (1993) for specific questions attorneys might employ during qualification, direct examination, or cross-examination: To be forewarned is to be forearmed.

References & Readings

Appelbaum, P. S., & Gutheil, T. G. (1991). *Clinical handbook of psychiatry and the law* (2nd ed.). Baltimore: Williams and Wilkins.

Blau, T. H. (1984). *The psychologist as expert witness*. New York: Wiley.

Brodsky, S. L. (1991). *Testifying in court: Guidelines and maxims for the expert witness*. Washington, DC: American Psychological Association.

Brodsky, S. L., & Robey, A. (1973). On becoming an expert witness: Issues of orientation and effectiveness. *Professional Psychology, 3,* 173–176.

Daubert v. Merrell Dow Pharmaceuticals, Inc., 727 F. Supp. 570 (S.D. Cal. 1989), remanded 113 S.Ct. 2786 (1993).

Federal Rules of Civil Procedure, Fed. R. Civ. P. Rule 26(b)(4)(A) (1995).

Federal Rules of Criminal Procedure, Fed. R. Crim. P. Rule 15 (1995).

Hall v. Clifton Precision, Civ. A. No. 92-5947 (E.D. Pa., 1993).

Horowitz, I. A., & Willging, T. E. (1984). *The psychology of law: Integrations and applications*. Boston: Little, Brown.

Marlowe, D. B. (1995). A hybrid decision framework for evaluating psychometric evidence. *Behavioral Sciences and the Law, 13,* 207–228.

Myers, J. E. B. (1992). *Legal issues in child abuse and neglect*. Newbury Park, CA: Sage.

Pope, K. S., Butcher, J. N., & Seelen, J. (1993). *The MMPI, MMPI-2, & MMPI-A in court*. Washington, DC: American Psychological Association.

Poythress, N. G. (1980). Coping on the witness stand: Learned responses to "learned treatises." *Professional Psychology, 11,* 169–179.

Sacks, M. E. (1995). *An overview of the law: A guide for testifying and consulting experts*. Horsham, PA: LRP Publications.

Ziskin, J. (1981). *Coping with psychiatric and psychological testimony* (3rd ed.). Venice, CA: Law and Psychology Press.

Related Topics

97 MENTAL HEALTH RECORDS

Gerald P. Koocher

This chapter describes a recommended style and content for mental health practitioners' clinical case records covering 14 specific content domains and 4 other important issues in record keeping aside from content. Not all of the content information described here will be necessary for every record, nor would one expect to complete a full record as described here during the first few sessions with a new client. By the end of several sessions, however, a good clinical record will reflect all of the relevant points summarized below.

CONTENT ISSUES

- *Identifying information:* Name, record or file number (if any), address, telephone number, sex, birth date, marital status, next of kin (or parent/guardian), school or employment status, billing and financial information.
- *First contact:* Date of initial client contact and referral source.
- *Relevant history and risk factors:* Take a detailed social, medical, educational, and vocational history. This need not necessarily be done in the very first session and need not be exhaustive. The more serious the problem, the more history you should take. Get enough information to formulate a diagnosis and an initial treatment plan. Be sure to ask: "What is the most violent thing you have ever done?" and "Are you thinking of hurting anyone now?" Seek records of prior treatment based on the nature of the client (e.g., the more complex the case, the more

completely one should review prior data). Always ask for permission to contact prior therapists, and consider refusing to treat clients who decline such permission without giving good reason (e.g., sexual abuse by former therapist).
- *Medical or health status:* Collect information on the client's medical status (i.e., when was his or her last physical exam?; does the client have a personal physician?; are there any pending medical problems or conditions?). This is especially important if the client has physical complaints or psychological problems that might be attributable to organic pathology.
- *Medication profile:* Collect information on all medications or drugs used, past and present, including licit (e.g., prescribed medications, alcohol, tobacco, and over-the-counter drugs) and illicit substances. Also note any consideration, recommendation, or referral for medication made by you or others over the course of your work with the client.
- *Why is the client in your office?:* Include a full description of the nature of the client's condition, including the reason(s) for referral and presenting symptoms or problem. Be sure to ask clients what brought them for help at this point in time, and record the reasons.
- *Current status:* Include a comprehensive functional assessment (including a mental status examination), and note any changes or alterations that occur over the course of treatment.
- *Diagnostic impression:* Include a clinical impression and diagnostic formulation using

the most current *DSM* or *ICD* model. Do not underdiagnose to protect the patient. If you believe it is absolutely necessary to use a "nonstigmatizing" diagnosis as opposed to some other label, use the R/O (rule-out) model by listing diagnoses with the notation "R/O," indicating that you will rule each "in" or "out" based on data that emerge over the subsequent sessions.

The diagnosis must also be consistent with the case history and facts (e.g., do not use "adjustment reaction" to describe a paranoid hallucinating client with a history of prior psychiatric hospital admissions).

- *Treatment plan:* Develop a treatment plan with long- and short-term goals and a proposed schedule of therapeutic activities. This should be updated every 4 to 6 months and modified as needed.
- *Progress notes:* Note progress toward achievement of therapeutic goals. Use clear, precise, observable facts (e.g., I observed . . . ; patient reported . . . ; patient agreed that . . .). As you write, imagine the patient and his or her attorney looking over your shoulder as they review the record with litigation in mind. Avoid theoretical speculation or reports of unconscious content. Do not be "cute" or sarcastic. Always portray yourself as a serious, dedicated professional.

If you must keep theoretical or speculative notes, use a separate "working notes" format, but recognize that these records may be subject to subpoena in legal proceedings.

- *Service documentation:* Include documentation of each visit, noting the client's response to treatment. In hospitals or large agencies, each entry should be dated and signed or initialed by the therapist, with the name printed or typed in legible form. It is not necessary to sign each entry in one's private (i.e., noninstitutional) case files.
- *Document follow-up:* Include documentation of follow-up for referrals or missed appointment, especially with clients who may be dangerous or seriously ill. Retain copies of all reminders, notices, or correspondence sent to clients, and note substantive telephone conversations in the record.
- *Obtain consent:* Include copies of consent forms for *any* information released to other parties.
- *Termination:* Include a discharge or termination summary note for all clients. In cases of planned termination, be certain that case notes prior to the end of care reflect planning and progress toward this end.

NONCONTENT ISSUES

- *Control of records:* Psychologists should maintain (in their own practice) or support (in institutional practice) a system that protects the confidentiality of records. Clear procedures should be in place to preserve client confidentiality and to release records only with proper consent. The media used (e.g., paper, magnetic) is not especially important, so long as utility, confidentiality, and durability are assured.

In multiple-client therapies (e.g., family or group treatment), records should be kept in a manner that allows for the preservation of each individual's confidentiality should the records of one party be released.

Psychologists are responsible for construction and control of their records and those of people they supervise.

- *Retention of records:* Psychologists must be aware of and observe all federal and state laws that govern record retention. In the absence of clear regulatory guidance under law, the American Psychological Association (1993) recommends maintaining complete records for 3 years after the last client contact and summaries for an additional 12 years.

If the client is a child, some records should be maintained until at least 3–5 years beyond the date at which the child attains the age of majority.

All records, active or inactive, should be stored in a safe manner, with limited access appropriate to the practice or institution.

- *Outdated records:* Outdated, obsolete, or invalid data should be managed in a way that assures no adverse effects will result from its release. Records may be culled regularly, so long as this is consistent with legal obligations. Records to be disposed of should be handled in a confidential and appropriate manner.

- *Death or incapacity:* Psychologists need to make arrangements for proper management or disposal of clinical records in the event of their death or incapacity.

References & Readings

American Psychological Association (1993). Record keeping guidelines. *American Psychologist, 48,* 308–310.

Koocher, G. P., & Keith-Spiegel, P. C. (1998). *Ethics in psychology: Professional standards and cases* (2nd ed.). New York: Oxford University Press.

Related Topics

Chapter 98, "Privacy, Confidentiality, and Privilege"
Chapter 100, "Basic Elements of Release Forms"
Chapter 117, "Utilization Review Checklist"

98 PRIVACY, CONFIDENTIALITY, AND PRIVILEGE

Gerald P. Koocher

KEY DEFINITIONS

The area of confidentiality-related ethical problems is complicated by common misunderstandings about three frequently used terms: privacy, confidentiality, and privilege. At least part of the confusion is related to the fact that in particular situations these terms may have narrow legal meanings that are quite distinct from broader traditional meanings attached by psychologists or other mental health practitioners.

- *Privacy* (a constitutional guaranty and personal value addressed in the Fourth, Fifth, and Fourteenth Amendments to the U.S. Constitution) is basically the right of individuals to decide about how much of their thoughts, feelings, or personal data should be shared with others. Privacy has often been considered essential to assure human dignity and freedom of self-determination

and to preclude unreasonable governmental intrusions into individuals' lives.

- *Confidentiality* refers to a general standard of professional conduct that obliges one not to discuss information about a client with anyone else, absent proper authorization. Confidentiality may also be based in statutes (i.e., laws enacted by legislatures), regulations (i.e., rules promulgated by the executive branch of government), or case law (i.e., interpretations of laws by the courts). When cited as an ethical principle, confidentiality implies an explicit contract or promise not to reveal anything about a client, except under certain circumstances agreed to by both parties.

- *Privilege* and confidentiality are oft-confused concepts, and the distinction between them is critical to understanding a variety of ethical problems. Privilege (or privileged communication) is a legal term describing certain specific types of relationships that enjoy protection from disclosure in legal proceedings. Privilege is granted by law and *belongs to the client* in the relationship. Normal court rules provide that anything relative and material to the issue at hand can and should be admitted as evidence. Where privilege exists, however, the client is protected from having the covered communications revealed without explicit permission. If the client waives this privilege, the psychologist may be compelled to testify on the nature and specifics of the material discussed. The client is usually not permitted to waive privilege selectively. In most courts, once a waiver is given, it covers all of the relevant privileged material.

• *Privilege is not automatic.* Traditionally, privilege has been extended to attorney-client, husband-wife, physician-patient, and priest-penitent relationships. Some jurisdictions now extend privilege to psychologist-client or psychotherapist-client relationships, but the actual laws vary widely, and it is incumbent on each psychologist to know the statutes in force for his or her practice. (In 1996, the U.S. Supreme Court took up this issue based on conflicting rulings in different federal appellate court districts in the case of *Jaffe v. Redmond* (1996) and upheld privilege between a psychotherapist/social worker and her client.)

BREACHING CONFIDENTIALITY

No practitioners can make a convincing case for absolute confidentiality. That is to say, many situations might legally or ethically require disclosure of otherwise confidential material.

• *Waivers:* The most common situation for disclosure of confidential mental health information occurs when a client authorizes the release of information to others.
• *Mandated reporting:* All states and Canadian provinces have laws requiring that certain professionals who might be expected to encounter child abuse (e.g., physicians, nurses, schoolteachers, psychologists, social workers) report their "knowledge" or "reasonable suspicion" to governmental authorities. Some jurisdictions also mandate reporting sus-

pected abuse of handicapped, elderly, or "dependent" individuals. Legislatures have enacted these statutes because protection of otherwise vulnerable individuals is deemed good public policy. Although such mandates preempt professional discretion, they also protect professionals reporting in good faith from suit for defamation. Details of the specific mandates vary by jurisdiction. In some countries there are no reporting mandates.

• *Danger to self:* Clinicians may generally disclose confidential data necessary to hospitalize or otherwise protect clients who are imminently dangerous to themselves (e.g., client status and risk information).
• *Danger to others:* When clients give clinicians reason to believe that they intend to kill or otherwise harm others, disclosure necessary to detain or hospitalize the client may be appropriate. In addition, if the intended targets of violence are identified, the clinician may be obligated to take steps to protect the victims (e.g., by notifying the authorities, the intended victims, or both).
• *Legal or regulatory actions:* If a client sues a clinician or files a licensing board or ethics complaint, the case cannot move forward unless the client releases the practitioner from any confidentiality obligations that might prevent an adequate defense. In addition, a client who has not paid his or her bill may legitimately be taken to court for collection, even though doing so would make his or her status as a client public information. In all of these circumstances, caution and client notification of the potential consequences should precede any breach of confidence.
• *Other statutory requirements:* In most jurisdictions, courts can compel disclosure of otherwise confidential information under various circumstances. For example, parents' mental health records may be open to the court during child custody disputes in some states, but not in others.

KEY BEHAVIORS FOR
AVOIDING PROBLEMS

• Before disclosing information obtained in the course of a professional relationship, check the applicable law in your practice jurisdiction.

- Alert clients to limitations on confidentiality at the outset of the professional relationship. If you fail to do so, but realize that the direction a conversation is taking may lead to a disclosure action, interrupt the client and warn about limitations of confidentiality at that point.
- Document any incidence of clear or ambiguous client risk (e.g., abuse or dangerousness), noting whether or not action was taken with rationales.

References & Readings

Bennett, B. E., Bryant, B. K., VandenBos, G. R., & Greenwood, A. (1990). *Professional liability and risk management.* Washington, DC: American Psychological Association.

Bersoff, D. N. (1995). *Ethical conflicts in psychology.* Washington, DC: American Psychological Association.

Boruch, R. F., Dennis, M., & Cecil, J. S. (1996). Fifty years of empirical research on privacy and confidentiality in research settings. In B. H. Stanley, J. E. Sieber, & G. B. Melton (Eds.), *Research ethics: A psychological approach* (pp. 129–173). Lincoln: University of Nebraska Press.

Burke, C. A. (1995). Until death do us part: An exploration into confidentiality following the death of a client. *Professional Psychology: Research and Practice, 26,* 278–280.

Gustafson, K. E., & McNamara, J. R. (1987). Confidentiality with minor clients: Issues and guidelines for therapists. *Professional Psychology, 18,* 503–508.

Jaffe v. Redmond, 116 S. Ct., 64 L.W. 4490 (June 13, 1996).

Kalichman, S. C. (1993). *Mandated reporting of suspected child abuse: Ethics, law, and policy.* Washington, DC: American Psychological Association.

Koocher, G. P., & Keith-Spiegel, P. C. (1998). *Ethics in psychology: Professional standards and cases* (2nd ed.). New York: Oxford University Press.

Miller, D. J., & Thelan, M. (1986). Knowledge and beliefs about confidentiality in psychotherapy. *Professional Psychology, 17,* 15–19.

Muehleman, T., Pickens, B. K., & Robinson, F. (1985). Informing clients about limits to confidentiality, risks, and their rights: Is self-disclosure inhibited? *Professional Psychology, 16,* 385–397.

Pope, K. S., & Vasquez, M. J. T. (1991). *Ethics in psychotherapy and counseling: A practical guide for psychologists.* San Francisco: Jossey-Bass.

Smith-Bell, M., & Winslade, W. J. (1994). Privacy, confidentiality, and privilege in psychotherapeutic relationships. *American Journal of Orthopsychiatry, 64,* 180–193.

Taube, D., & Elwork, A. (1990). Researching the effects of confidentiality law on patients' self-disclosures. *Professional Psychology, 21,* 72–75.

Related Topics

Chapter 97, "Mental Health Records"
Chapter 99, "Basic Elements of Consent"
Chapter 100, "Basic Elements of Release Forms"

99   BASIC ELEMENTS OF CONSENT

Gerald P. Koocher

COMPETENCE AND CONSENT

Competence is a prerequisite for informed consent. An offer to provide a person with informed consent is not meaningful unless the individual in question is fully competent to make use of it. *Consent* is a voluntary act by which one competent person agrees to allow another person to do something, such as provide treatment to them, study them in research, or release their confidential records to another.

- Competence to grant consent is generally categorized as either de facto or de jure. *De jure* refers to competence under law, while *de facto* competence refers to the actual or practical capacities of the individual to render a competent decision.
- In most jurisdictions, persons over the age of 18 years are presumed to be competent unless proved otherwise before a court. When a determination of incompetence is made for such adults, it is usually quite precise. That is to say, under law a person's competence is conceptualized as a *specific* functional ability. In legal parlance the noun *competence* is usually followed by the preposition *to* rather than presented as a general attribute of the person. An adult who is deemed incompetent to stand trial for a particular offense is still presumed competent to function as a custodial parent or manage his or her financial affairs. For the adult, incompetence must be proved on a case-by-case basis.
- Conversely, minor children are presumed incompetent for most purposes without any concern for whether or not the child has the cognitive and emotional capacity to make the requisite decision(s). Children who are deemed legally competent for one purpose are likewise still considered generally incompetent in other decision-making contexts. For example, juvenile offenders who have been transferred to adult court for trial and found competent to stand trial are still considered generally incompetent to consent to their own medical treatment or enter into legal contracts.
- Assessment of specific competence (in the case of children) or incompetence (in the case of adults) revolves around four basic elements:

  1. The person's access to and ability to understand all relevant information about the nature and potential future consequences of the decision to be made (i.e., informed consent)

  2. The ability to manifest or express a decision
  3. The manner in which the decision is made (e.g., whether it is rational or reasonably considered)
  4. The nature of the resulting decision (e.g., whether it is a lawful decision)

- Psychological factors in competence assessment include the following:

  1. Comprehension
  2. Assertiveness and autonomy
  3. Rational reasoning
  4. Anticipation of future events
  5. Judgments in the face of uncertainty or contingencies

MAKING DECISIONS FOR OTHERS: PROXY CONSENT, PERMISSION, AND ASSENT

Consent is defined as a decision that one can make only for oneself. Thus, the term *proxy consent* is decreasingly used in favor of the term *permission*. Parents or guardians are usually those from whom permission *must* be sought as both a legal and ethical requirement prior to intervening in the lives of their minor children or adults adjudged incompetent.

Assent, a relatively new concept in this context, recognizes that minors or incompetent adults may not, as a function of their developmental level or mental state, be capable of giving fully reasoned consent but may still be capable of reaching and expressing a preference. Assent recognizes the involvement of the child or incompetent adult in the decision-making process, while also indicating that the child's level of participation is less than fully competent. Granting assent power is essentially the same as providing a veto.

References & Readings

Appelbaum, P. S., Lidz, C. W., & Meisel, A. (1987). *Informed consent: Legal theory and clinical practice*. New York: Oxford University Press.

Koocher, G. P., & Keith-Spiegel, P. C. (1990). *Children, ethics, and the law*. Lincoln: University of Nebraska Press.

Koocher, G. P., & Keith-Spiegel, P. C. (1998). *Ethics*

in psychology: Professional standards and cases (2nd ed.). New York: Oxford University Press.

Malcolm, J. G. (1988). *Treatment choices and informed consent: Current controversies in psychiatric malpractice litigation.* Springfield, IL: Charles C. Thomas.

Pope, K. S., & Vasquez, M. J. T. (1991). Ethics in psychotherapy and counseling: A practical guide for psychologists. San Francisco: Jossey-Bass.

Stanley, B. H., Sieber, J. E., & Melton, G. B. (Eds.) (1996). *Research ethics: A psychological approach.* Lincoln: University of Nebraska Press.

White, B. C. (1994). *Competence to consent.* Washington, DC: Georgetown University Press.

Related Topics

100   BASIC ELEMENTS OF RELEASE FORMS

Gerald P. Koocher

What is a "release" form anyway? As used by mental health professionals, this term refers to a legally appropriate authorization that releases the clinician from some particular duty to a client or research participant. Most often the release permits the sharing of otherwise confidential information or records with other professionals or agencies. Other types of releases may authorize the recording by any means of otherwise confidential sessions, the storage of data or recorded material in databases, or the use of such material for teaching purposes. Releases are sometimes sought prior to application of certain treatment procedures that may have adverse consequences (e.g., electroshock therapy); however, no release can legally absolve a practitioner from the negligent infliction of damages.

Releases should be drafted for highly specific purposes, addressing each of the key elements cited below. In addition to these basic elements, releases should be used only in the context of informed consent (see chapter 99). Use the following guidelines in preparing a release form.

- *Identify the person(s) to whom the release applies.* Ideally this will include a name, address, telephone number, birth date, and any known record-identifying numbers. This will minimize risk of improper releases when names are similar, as well as permitting confirmation that the release is valid should a question arise.
- *Indicate what is being authorized* (e.g., transfer of oral information, transfer of records, audio or video recording, or other disclosure of protected data).
- *Indicate the purpose of releasing the duty of confidentiality* (e.g., assisting in treatment, educational planning, teaching, research, or other purpose to be specified).
- *State who is granting authority* (e.g., is a competent person granting informed con-

sent, is a legally responsible party granting permission, or is a person who is not deemed legally competent granting assent?). Note that at least one signer of the release form must be legally authorized to do so.

- *Explain the grantor's relationship to the parties to whom a duty is owed* (e.g., is the grantor the focal party himself or herself, a parent, or some other person having legal guardianship?).
- *Indicate for what duration the release is granted.* Each release should have a specific time limit. For example, the release may authorize a onetime issuance of records, an ongoing communication between two professionals for a specified period, or open-ended access to archival data in a research database.
- *Include a valid signature.* The name of the person signing the release form should be printed as well as signed, in the event that the signature is difficult to read. Although not strictly necessary in most situations, it is ideal to have the release signed by a third party who witnessed the grantor's signing.

SAMPLE RELEASE FORMS

Authorization for Release of Information

Patient's name:
Date of birth:
Address:
Telephone number:
Record number:

I hereby authorize the release of information/records on: [examples: the psychological assessment of, or psychotherapeutic treatment of, etc.]

Name:
Address:
For the purposes of: [examples: assisting in treatment planning, preparing an educational plan, use in court-ordered evaluation, etc.]

This release shall be valid for [example: 90 days] from the date signed, unless withdrawn sooner and shall [example: include all professional records; be limited to the psychological testing data; be limited to services provided between September 1996 and March 1998; etc.].

Signed: [signature, printed name, date]
Relationship to patient: [self, parent, legal guardian]
Witnessed by: [signature, printed name, date]

Sample Release for Recording and Teaching

This release form would be similar to the record release form in terms of the client information and signature sections. The statements of "authorization" (i.e., what type of recording or disclosure is being allowed) and the statement of "purpose" (i.e., how the material will be used). Some examples follow: "I authorize Mr. Jones to make videotape recordings of my therapy sessions at the University Counseling Center for purposes of supervision. I understand that these will be viewed only by Mr. Jones and his clinical supervisor, Dr. Smith. I also understand that the tapes will be destroyed following the supervisory session."

Suppose one of the sessions seems particularly useful or exemplary for teaching purposes and that Dr. Smith would like to use it in the future. An additional release with the following text might be sought: "I authorize Dr. Smith and his successors as director of the University Counseling Center to use previously authorized video recordings of my psychotherapy sessions with Mr. Jones between January 1996 and May 1996 for teaching purposes with future classes of doctoral students. I understand that although my likeness will be visible, my name will not be used and all observers will have a professional obligation to treat the material confidentially. I also understand that I may revoke this authorization at any time in the future by notifying Dr. Smith or any subsequent director of the clinic."

Similar elements should be included in release forms developed for other confidential material that may be stored and used by others in the future, such as longitudinal research data archives. In the case of institutional clinical records that are routinely collected as a function of clinical care (i.e., medical records or clinic case files) or that were collected years earlier from clients who are no longer easily located, the agency's official institutional review board (sometimes called a clinical investigations committee) should be consulted and that group's procedures followed.

References & Readings

American Psychological Association (1992). Ethical principles of psychologists and code of conduct. *American Psychologist, 47*, 1597–1611.

Keith-Spiegel, P., Wittig, A. F., Perkins, D. V., Balogh, D. W., & Whitley, B. E. (1993). *The ethics of teaching: A casebook.* Muncie, IN: Ball State University Office of Academic Research and Sponsored Projects.

Koocher, G. P., & Keith-Spiegel, P. C. (1998). *Ethics in psychology: Professional standards and cases* (2nd ed.). New York: Oxford University Press.

Lawson, C. (1995). Research participation as a contract. *Ethics & Behavior, 5*, 205–215.

Sieber, J. E., & Stanley, B. (1988). Sharing scientific data I: New problems for IRBs. *IRB: A Review of Human Subjects Research, 11*, 4–7.

Stanley, B. H., Sieber, J. E., & Melton, G. B. (Eds.) (1996). *Research ethics.* Lincoln: University of Nebraska Press.

Related Topics

Chapter 98, "Privacy, Confidentiality, and Privilege"
Chapter 99, "Basic Elements of Consent"

101 HOW TO CONFRONT AN UNETHICAL COLLEAGUE

Patricia Keith-Spiegel & Gerald P. Koocher

What action should be taken upon learning of an alleged unethical act by a colleague? Either rationalizing away the colleague's behavior as a minor or a onetime mistake or believing that others who know of the behavior will take care of it is an inadequate excuse for shirking professional responsibility. Yet too many practitioners decide not to get involved. Conflicting feelings over perceiving a duty to take some action toward unethical colleagues and yet maintaining a loyal and protective stance toward them are common sources of reticence to get involved. One of the very attractive features of informal peer monitoring, however, is that both goals can be met simultaneously. When you successfully intervene, you will have

solved a problem *and* possibly protected a colleague from having to interact with a more formal (and onerous) correctional forum.

The American Psychological Association (APA) ethics code (1992) actively deputizes psychologists to monitor peer conduct, although in a somewhat cautious and protective manner. Earlier versions of the ethics code mandated that psychologists deal directly with ethics violations committed by colleagues as the first line of action. Only if an informal attempt proved unsuccessful should an ethics committee be contacted. Currently, and partly because of reported incidents of harassment and intimidation, the 1992 code gives psychologists the option of deciding the appropriateness of dealing with the matter directly. If an informal solution seems unlikely (for reasons left unspecified in the code), psychologists are mandated to take formal action—such as contacting a licensing board or ethics committee—so long as any confidentiality rights or conflicts can be resolved (APA Code of Conduct, Section 8.05). The level of seriousness of the alleged behavior is not a stated consideration in the 1992 code, although Canter, Bennett, Jones, and Nagy (1994) advise against attempting informal resolutions in cases of complex violations such as when serious sexual misconduct has occurred.

Peer monitoring often may involve colleagues whose conduct and professional judgment are affected by stress, addiction, or physical or mental disability. According to a survey undertaken by the APA Task Force on Distressed Psychologists, almost 70% of the sample personally knew of psychologists who were experiencing serious emotional difficulties. However, only about a third made substantive attempts to help (reported in VandenBos & Duthie, 1986). From our own experience on ethics committees, we estimate that almost half of those psychologists complained against appear to have some personal problem that contributed to the alleged ethical violation.

It is not uncommon to be told of an ethics violation by parties who then request assistance to deal with the alleged violator but insist that their identities not be revealed. Often these people are fearful of reprisal or feel inadequate to defend themselves. Occasionally, the problem is that yet another person, critical to the case, is unavailable or unwilling to get involved or to be identified. These situations pose extremely frustrating predicaments. Approaching colleagues with charges issued by "unseen accusers" violates the essence of due process. Further, alleged violators often know (or *think* they know) their accusers' identities anyway. When the alleged unethical behaviors are extremely serious, possibly putting yet others in harm's way, and when the fearful but otherwise credible individuals making the charges are adamant about remaining anonymous, psychologists may not feel comfortable ignoring

the situation altogether. However, there may be nothing else that can be done. Sometimes the option to do nothing may not exist, as with state mandatory reporting laws. However, for other non–legally required reporting situations, the current APA code does not leave psychologists any options if confidentiality issues cannot be resolved.

The following list provides guidelines for how to confront a colleague suspected of engaging in unethical conduct.

1. The relevant ethical principle that applies to the suspected breach of professional ethics should first be identified. This may involve an overarching moral principle, or it may involve a specific prohibition in an ethics code or policy. If nothing can be linked to the action, and no law, relevant policy, or ethics code has been violated, then the matter may not be an ethical one. This conclusion is reached most often when a colleague has an offensive personal style or holds personal views that are generally unpopular or widely divergent from your own. You have the right, of course, to express your personal feelings to your colleague, but this should not be construed as engaging in a professional duty.

2. Assess the strength of the evidence that a violation has been committed. Ethical infractions, particularly the most serious ones, are seldom committed openly before a host of dispassionate witnesses. With few exceptions, such as plagiarism or inappropriate advertising of services, no tangible exhibits corroborate that an unethical event ever occurred. A starting point involves categorizing the source of your information into one of five types: (a) clear, direct observation of a colleague engaging in unethical behavior; (b) knowing or unknowing disclosure by a colleague that he or she has committed an ethical violation; (c) direct observation of a colleague's suspicious but not clearly interpretable behavior; (d) receipt of a credible secondhand report of unethical conduct from someone seeking out your assistance as a consultant or intervening party; or (e) casual gossip about a colleague's unethical behavior.

If you did not observe the actions directly, how credible is the source of information? Can you imagine a reason that would not be unethical that would explain why the person might have engaged in this action? That is, can you think of more than one reason the person might have acted that way? If the information came by casual gossip, proceed with considerable caution. If there is no way to obtain any substantial, verifiable facts, you may choose to ignore the information or, as a professional courtesy to the colleague, inform your colleague of the "scuttlebutt." If the colleague is guilty of what the idle hearsay suggests, you may have had a salutary effect. However, we recognize that this is risky business and may be effective only if the colleague is one whose reaction you can reasonably anticipate in advance.

If the information is secondhand, and you are approached by a credible person who claims firsthand knowledge and is seeking assistance, we advise being as helpful as you can. Because we often advise consulting with colleagues before taking any action, it is only fitting that you should be receptive when others approach you for assistance in working through ethical issues. Often you will be able to assist the person with a plan of action that will not include your direct involvement or else offer a referral if the dilemma is not one about which you can confidently comment. If you do agree to become actively engaged, be sure that you have proper permission to reveal any relevant identities and that you have available all possible information.

3. Get in close touch with your own motivations to engage in (or to avoid) a confrontation with a colleague. Psychologists who are (or see themselves as being) directly victimized by the conduct of a colleague are probably more willing to get involved. In addition to any fears, anger, biases, or other emotional reactions, do you perceive that the colleague's alleged conduct—either as it stands or if it continues—may undermine the integrity of the profession or harm one or more of the consumers served by the colleague? If your answer is affirmative, then some form of proactive stance is warranted. However, if you recognize that your emotional involvement or vulnerability (e.g., the colleague is your supervisor) creates an ex-

treme hazard that will likely preclude a satisfactory outcome, you may wish to consider passing the intervention task on to another party. In such cases, any confidentiality issues must first be settled.

4. Consultation with a trusted and experienced colleague who has demonstrated a sensitivity to ethical issues is strongly recommended at this point, even if only to assure yourself that you are on the right track. Identities should not be shared if confidentiality issues pertain.

5. Make your final decision about confronting the colleague and how to best do it. Even though you are not responsible for rectifying the unethical behavior of another person, the application of a decision-making model may facilitate a positive educative function. You might well find yourself, at this point, tempted to engage in one of two covert activities as alternatives to confronting a colleague directly. The first is to pass the information along to other colleagues in an effort to warn them. Although informing others may provide a sense that duty has been fulfilled, it is far more likely that responsibility has only been diffused. Idle talk certainly cannot guarantee that an offending colleague or the public has been affected in any constructive way. Moreover, as noted earlier, to the extent that the conduct was misjudged, you could be responsible for an injustice to a colleague that is, in itself, unethical. The second temptation is to engage in more direct but anonymous action, such as sending an unsigned note or relevant document (e.g., a copy of an ethics code with one or more sections circled in red). Constructive results, however, are hardly guaranteed. The recipient may not understand the intended message. Even if the information is absorbed, the reaction to an anonymous charge may be counterproductive. Also, the warning may instill a certain amount of paranoia that could result in additional negative consequences, such as adding suspiciousness to the colleague's character. Thus, although both of these covert actions seem proactive, we strongly recommend neither.

6. If you decide to go ahead with a direct

meeting, schedule it in advance, although not in a menacing manner. For example, do *not* say, "Something has come to my attention about you that causes me grave concern. What are you doing a week from next Thursday?" Rather, indicate to your colleague that you would like to speak privately and schedule a face-to-face meeting at his or her earliest convenience. A business setting would normally be more appropriate than a home or restaurant, even if the colleague is a friend. Handling such matters on the phone is not recommended unless geographic barriers preclude a direct meeting. Letters create a record, but they do not allow for back-and-forth interaction, which we believe to be conducive to a constructive exchange in matters of this sort. We do not recommend e-mail for the same reason, as well as the additional concern that electronic communications can be accessed by unauthorized others.

7. When entering into the confrontation phase, remain calm and self-confident. The colleague is likely to display considerable emotion. Remain as nonthreatening as possible. Even though it may feel like a safe shield, avoid adopting a rigidly moralistic demeanor. Most people find righteous indignation obnoxious. We suggest noninflammatory language such as expressing confusion and seeking clarification. It might go something like this: "The data reported in your article is not quite the same as what you showed me earlier. I am confused about that and wonder if you could help me understand it. Is there a problem here?" Or, "I met a young woman who, upon learning that I was a psychologist, told me that she was your client and that the two of you were going to start dating. I thought we should talk about it." Things are not always as they seem, and it would be wise at the onset to allow for an explanation rather than provoke anxiety. For example, it is at least possible that the colleague might learn that the young woman was briefly a client years earlier. Such responses may not render the matters moot, but the discussion would likely proceed far differently than with a more strident opening.

8. Set the tone for a constructive and educative session. Your role is *not* that of accuser, judge, jury, and penance dispenser. The session will probably progress best if you see yourself as having an alliance with the colleague—not in the usual sense of consensus and loyalty, but as facing a problem together.

9. Describe your ethical obligations, noting the relevant moral or ethics code principles that prompted your intervention. Rather than equivocating, state your concerns directly and present the evidence on which they are based. Do not attempt to play detective by trying to trap your colleague through asking leading questions or by withholding any relevant information that you are authorized to share. Such tactics lead only to defensiveness and resentment and diminish the possibility of a favorable outcome.

10. Allow the colleague ample time to explain and defend in as much detail as required. The colleague may be flustered and repetitive; be patient.

11. What is your relationship with the suspected colleague? This will affect both the approach taken and how you interpret the situation. Those who observe or learn of possible unethical actions by other psychologists often know the alleged offenders personally. They could be good friends or disliked antagonists. They could be subordinates or supervisors. Reactions, depending on the relationships with those suspected of ethics violations, affect both the approach taken to deal with them and the attributes assigned to colleagues. Fear of reprisal can stifle action and enhance the rationalization of inaction. If the colleague is disliked, courage to act may come more from the thrill of revenge rather than from genuine courage and conviction. If the colleague is a friend or acquaintance with whom there have been no previous problematic interactions, the meeting usually goes easier. You can express to your friend that your interest and involvement are based on caring and concern for his or her professional standing. The danger, of course, is that you may feel that you are risking an established, positive relationship. If your friend can be educated effectively by you, however, you may well have protected him or her from embarrassment or more public forms of censure. Moreover, if you have lost respect for your friend after observing or learning of possible ethical misconduct, the relationship has been altered anyway. Discomfort, to the extent that it ensues, may be temporary.

If the colleague is someone you do not know personally, the confrontation will be, by definition, more formal. An expression of concern and a willingness to work through the problem cooperatively may still be quite effective. If the colleague is someone you do know but dislike, your dilemma is more pronounced. If the information is known to others (or can be appropriately shared with others), you might consider asking someone who has a better relationship with this person to intercede or to accompany you. If that is not feasible and a careful assessment of your own motivations reveals a conclusion that the possible misconduct clearly requires intervention on its own merits, then you should take some form of action. It may still be possible to approach this individual yourself, and, if you maintain a professional attitude, it may work out. If you are intervening on behalf of another, you will first have to disclose why you are there and offer any other caveats. You might say something like, "I, myself, have no direct knowledge of what I want to discuss, but I have agreed to speak with you on behalf of two students." Your role in such instances may be to arrange another meeting with all the parties present and possibly serve as mediator during such a meeting.

12. If the colleague becomes abusive or threatening, attempt to steer him or her to a more constructive state. Although many people need a chance to vent feelings, they often settle down if the confronting person remains steady and refrains from becoming abusive in return. If the negative reaction continues, it may be appropriate to say something calming, such as, "I see you are very upset right now, and I regret that we cannot explore this matter together in a way that would be satisfactory to both of us. I would like you to think about what I have presented, and if you would reconsider talking more about it, please contact me within

a week." If a return call is not forthcoming, other forms of action must be considered. This could involve including another appropriate person or pressing formal charges to some duly constituted monitoring body. It is probably wise to have another consultation with a trusted colleague at this point. The suspected offender should be informed (in person or in a formal note) of your next step.

If you are ever the recipient of a colleague's inquiry, be grateful for the warning about how you have been perceived and try to openly and honestly work for the goal of settling the matter in a way that satisfies all those involved without necessitating a review by outside evaluators.

References & Readings

American Psychological Association (1992). Ethical principles of psychologists and code of conduct. *American Psychologist, 47,* 1597–1611.

Bennett, B. E., Bryant, B. K., VandenBos, G. R., & Greenwood, A. (1990). *Professional liability and risk management.* Washington, DC: American Psychological Association.

Canter, M. B., Bennett, B. E., Jones, S. E., & Nagy, T. F. (1994). *Ethics for psychologists: A commentary on the APA ethics code.* Washington, DC: American Psychological Association.

Keith-Spiegel, P. (1994). The 1992 ethics code: Boon or bane? *Professional Psychology: Research and Practice, 25,* 315–316.

Koocher, G. P., & Keith-Spiegel, P. C. (1998). *Ethics in psychology: Professional standards and cases* (2nd ed.). New York: Oxford University Press.

VandenBos, G. R., & Duthie, R. F. (1986). Confronting and supporting colleagues in distress. In R. R. Kilburg, P. E. Nathan, & R. W. Thorenson (Eds.), *Professionals in distress.* Washington, DC: American Psychological Association.

Related Topics

102 SIXTEEN HINTS ON MONEY MATTERS AND ETHICAL ISSUES

Gerald P. Koocher & Sam S. Hill III

The questions that arise when a psychotherapist considers the part money plays in his or her practice are myriad and complex. Consideration must be given to the business, ethical, and therapeutic aspects of money and fees. The following are some essential points to keep in mind when dealing in money matters.

1. Clients should be informed about fees, billing and collection practices, and other financial contingencies as a routine part of initiating the professional relationship. This information should also be repeated later if necessary. From the outset of a relationship with a new client, the psychologist should take care to explain the nature of services to be offered, the fees to be charged, the mode of payment to be used, and other financial arrangements that might reasonably be expected to influence the potential client's decision.

2. What to charge? Determining the customary charges for one's services is a complicated task that mixes issues of economics, business, self-esteem, and a variety of cultural and professional taboos. When it comes to mental health services, the task is complicated by a host of both subtle and obvious psychological and ethical values.

3. Fees generally vary as a function of training and activity. As reported in the summary of the current *Psychotherapy Finances* fee survey, fees vary by region, with psychiatrists generally charging more than psychologists, who charge more than social workers and other master's-level providers. Some practitioners charge premium fees for services of a forensic nature that are considerably higher than their fees for psychotherapy. One psychiatrist from the Northeast who testifies in high-profile litigation, for example, recently reported charging $120 per 45-minute psychotherapy session and $350 for 60 minutes of forensic time.

4. Some practitioners offer a sliding fee scale for clients who cannot afford their customary charges, while others maintain a high "usual and customary rate" and provide an assortment of discounts. For example, a client who has been in treatment for an extended period may be paying a lower rate than a new client. Or an individual who is being seen 3 hours per week may be offered a lower hourly rate than a person seen only once per week. The American Psychological Association (APA) ethics code specifies the aspirational expectation that psychologists render at least some "pro bono" services (i.e., professional activity undertaken at no charge in the public interest).

5. If an estimate of charges is given, it should be honored, unless unforeseen circumstances arise. In the latter situation, any changes should be discussed with and agreed to by the client. If it seems that financial difficulties may be an issue, they should be dealt with directly at the very outset of the relationship.

6. Some psychotherapists tack on interest or "billing charges" to unpaid bills. This practice may be illegal because state and federal laws generally require special disclosure statements and credit agreements informing clients about such fees in advance.

7. The ethical practitioner will attempt to avoid abandoning clients with two specific strategies. The first is to never contract for services without first explaining the costs to the client and reaching an agreement that they are affordable. The second is to not mislead the client into thinking that insurance or other such coverage will bear the full cost of services when it seems reasonably clear that benefits may expire before the need for service ends. When treatment is in progress and a client becomes unemployed or otherwise can no longer pay for continued services, the practitioner should be especially sensitive to the client's needs. If a psychologist cannot realistically help a client under existing reimbursement restrictions, and the resulting process might be too disruptive, it may be best to simply explain the problem and not take on the prospective client. Whereas it may be necessary to terminate care or transfer the client's care elsewhere over the long term, this should not be done abruptly or in the midst of a crisis period in the client's life.

8. Increasing fees in the course of service delivery also poses ethical dilemmas. If a commitment is made to provide consultation or conduct an assessment for a given fee, it should be honored. Likewise, a client who enters psychotherapy at an agreed-upon fee has a reasonable expectation that the fee will not be raised excessively. Once service has begun, the provider has an obligation to the client that must be considered. Aside from financial hardship issues, the psychologist may have special influence with the client that should not be abused.

9. Some practitioners require clients to pay certain fees in advance of rendering services as a kind of retainer (e.g., in forensic cases). This is an unusual practice, but it is not unethical so long as the contingencies are mutually agreed upon. The most common use of such advance payments involves relationships in which the practitioner is asked to hold time available on short notice for some reasons (as in certain types of corporate consulting) or when certain types of litigation are involved. In such situations, it is not unusual for the practitioner to request a retainer or escrow payment prior to commencing work.

10. Payment for missed appointments is occasionally another source of problems. It is not unethical to charge a client for an appointment that is not kept or that is canceled on short notice, so long as this policy is explained and agreed to by the client in advance. Insurance companies and other third-party payers generally do not pay for missed appointments.

11. Relationships involving kickbacks, fee splitting, or payment of commissions for client referrals may be illegal and unethical. Careful attention to the particular circumstances and state laws is important before agreeing to such arrangements. Clients should be told of any aspects of the arrangement that might reasonably be expected to influence their decision about whether to use the services.

12. It is important for psychologists to pay careful attention to all contractual obligations, to understand them, and to abide by them. Similarly, psychologists should not sign contracts with stipulations that might subsequently place them in ethical jeopardy.

13. Psychologists should not profit unfairly at the expense of clients. Psychologists must exercise great care, and at times suffer potential economic disadvantage, so as not to abuse the relative position of power and influence they have over the clients they serve.

14. Psychologists may be held responsible for financial misrepresentations effected in their name by an employee or agent they have designated (including billing and collection agents). They must, therefore, choose their employees and representatives with care and supervise them closely.

15. In all debt collection situations, psychologists must be aware of the laws that apply in their jurisdiction and make every effort to behave in a cautious, businesslike fashion. They must avoid using their special position or information gained through their professional role to collect debts.

16. In dealing with managed care organizations, psychologists should adhere to the same standards of competence, professionalism, and integrity as in other contexts. Heightened sensitivity should be focused on the potential ethical problems inherent in such service delivery systems.

References & Readings

DiBella, G. A. W. (1980). Mastering money issues that complicate treatment: The last taboo. *American Journal of Psychotherapy, 24,* 510–522.

Faustman, W. O. (1982). Legal and ethical issues in debt collection strategies of professional psychologists. *Professional Psychology, 13,* 208–214.

Grossman, M. (1971). Insurance reports as a threat to confidentiality. *American Journal of Psychiatry, 128,* 96–100.

Karon, B. P. (1995). Provision of psychotherapy under managed care: A growing crisis and national nightmare. *Professional Psychology: Research and Practice, 26,* 5–9.

Lovinger, R. J. (1978). Obstacles in psychotherapy: Setting a fee in the initial contact. *Professional Psychology, 9,* 350–352.

Myers, W., & Brezler, M. F. (1992). Selling or buying a practice. *Independent Practitioner, 12,* 92–93.

Pope, K. S. (1988). Fee policies and procedures: Causes of malpractice suits and ethics complaints. *Independent Practitioner, 8,* 24–29.

Pope, K. S., & Keith-Spiegel, P. (1986, May). Is selling a practice malpractice? *APA Monitor, 4,* 40.

Rodwin, M. (1993). *Medicine, money, and morals: Physicians' conflicts of interest.* New York: Oxford University Press.

Woody, R. H. (1997). Valuing a psychological practice. *Professional Psychology: Research and Practice, 28,* 77–80.

Related Topics

103   GUIDE TO INTERACTING WITH THE MEDIA

Gerald P. Koocher & Patricia Keith-Spiegel

Dealing with representatives of the print and broadcast media presents both a special opportunity and a significant challenge for psychologists. The tips, hints, and cautions reported here were compiled from a variety of sources, and they address both practical and ethical aspects of media relations.

SUMMARY ETHICAL GUIDES

• While committing themselves to assisting the public to understand psychological knowledge, psychologists make every attempt to assure accuracy, maintain due caution and modesty, avoid collusion or the exploitation of others, and exhibit the highest level of professional responsibility. This may mean that invitations to participate in media activities or other public forums might sometimes be better refused.

• Exaggeration, superficiality, and sensationalism should be avoided to the greatest extent possible. When signing contracts for commercial books or other products and services that will be heavily marketed, it is wise to ask to be consulted on all advertising copy.

- Psychologists must acknowledge and accept their responsibilities to a public that may be accepting of their statements by virtue of psychologists' presumed expertise.
- Recognizing the limits of one's knowledge and experience is especially critical in media activities because large numbers of people can be misled or misinformed by incorrect or incomplete public statements.
- Psychologists should be accurate in presenting their professional credentials and affiliations to the public. If these credentials are presented in substantively inaccurate ways, the psychologist should attempt to correct the error.
- When offering public statements intended to ameliorate particular problems, considerable caution must be exercised. Such advice should, ideally, have a scientifically based foundation. In any event, commentary should not be presented as factual unless a reasonable database exists. Opinions or personal experiences should be clearly identified as such.
- Psychologists should avoid public statements that purport to speak for the entire profession.
- It is important to keep in mind that the goals and purposes of media representatives and outlets are likely to be quite different from those of individual psychologists. Although caution is advisable whenever one is making statements for public consumption, extra caution is *always* in order when dealing with the media.
- Public statements by psychologists should never be made to entertain or gratify oneself at the expense of others or the profession.
- Psychologists should never publicly comment on the "psychological status" of others whom they do not know, including deceased individuals. It is certainly possible to write psychological papers on historical figures, but ideally these should be well-documented scholarly works.
- Psychologists should take advantage of opportunities to correct the public statements of others that depict the mentally disabled and other groups in unfair, stereotyped ways.

PRACTICAL MATTERS

Preparation

Before the interview, ask these questions to clarify the agenda and assist in planning both your willingness to participate and the session itself:

1. What is the topic of interest to the interviewer?
2. When and where will the interview take place?
3. Who is the interviewer (and what is that person's reputation)?
4. Why are they interested in me?
5. How long will the interview last (both the actual session and any subsequent broadcast based on my participation)?
6. What is the media and format (i.e., newspaper, magazine, radio, television, live, taped)? If print media is involved, does the publication use fact checkers or otherwise allow you to review and comment on accuracy of any quotes attributed to you? (This latter procedure is more typical of monthly magazine stories or advance-preparation newspaper columns rather than time-sensitive news stories.)
7. When will the story be published or broadcast?
8. What is the source of the inquiry or basis of the story, and how did they get my name?
9. If possible, watch the television show or read something by the interviewer or reporter to get a feel for style and ambience.

Matters of Style

Matters of style may be highly superficial issues compared with your professional qualifications and what you have to say, but appearance and manner of presentation can augment or cloud your message when you are working in a video or televised format.

- Know your positive points and the primary message you want to communicate. Rehearse anecdotes and examples that make your point. If you are not asked the "right questions," use bridging phrases such as the following: "The real issue is," "Another way to look at the problem is," "For example," "Let me add," and "But equally important."

- What to wear? The primary rule is to avoid wearing anything that will detract from your message by grabbing the attention of the viewer (e.g., no fancy jewelry or distracting necktie). If you are offered makeup, accept the offer. The professionals producing the show generally want you to look your best and know what will work best in their medium.
- For men, dark gray or navy suits or sport coats with a relatively simple red or burgundy tie are good choices. Other good choices include light gray or blue shirts, calf-length socks, no five-o'clock shadow, and no jewelry.
- For women, purples, blues, deep red, winter white, or gray suits or dresses are suggested. Bright reds, whites, blacks, browns, yellows, and greens should be avoided, along with flashy prints or frilly or revealing clothing. Dangling, flashy, or noisy jewelry should also be avoided.
- Just before the interview, check hair, face, makeup, and clothing.
- During the interview, smile, lean into the interview, gesture with your hands, maintain eye contact, and be conversational (e.g., it is better to say, "the top 1%," rather than "3 standard deviations above the mean").

The Talk Show

Television talk shows have replaced the radio as a place to find large numbers of psychologists. About two dozen talk show hosts, competing aggressively for ratings, routinely display guests who appear to be highly dysfunctional or embroiled in grotesque or novel life circumstances. Their troubling stories are milked by the celebrity host for most of the hour. Two recent trends are especially disturbing. One common ploy is to ambush the guests by setting up surprise appearances or revelations that will likely embarrass or humiliate them before a nation of viewers. The parading of children or vulnerable adolescents, exposing them to intense questioning about their own situation or the ills plaguing their family, is also currently fashionable. The audience wallows in "as-if" pain as tearful or terrified children who have been subjected to abuse or traumatic events are encouraged to open up by seemingly caring hosts.

What do psychologists have to do with this modern version of a Colosseum blood sport, and why can their participation be an ethical problem? Psychologists and other mental health professionals do have a significant role in these shows, ostensibly as intervenors and educators. After the guests with the problems have been opened up and wrung dry, an expert is brought onstage to solve the complex quandaries that have usually been steeping for years. This late maneuver, often made in the last 10 minutes before the program is over, appears to often serve as a quick-and-easy attempt to lend an air of legitimacy and redeeming social value to an otherwise morally bankrupt concept in entertainment. Often the experts are mere window-dressing, fading behind the psychobabbling hosts who remain in tight control of the analysis and advice.

So should psychologists participate in this popular brand of entertainment? Are mental health professionals actually aiding and abetting the exploitation of naive, vulnerable people? The answer cannot be a simple yes or no. Sometimes these programs are well suited to imparting helpful information or exposure, such as segments on transracial adoptions, effective discipline techniques with children, domestic violence, or the plight of the homeless. Psychologists and other experts can enlighten and educate. Many of these shows can be credited with informing the public about self-care groups aimed at a variety of audiences such as children of Holocaust survivors, spouses of alcoholics, and parents of murdered children.

What if you are invited to appear on a talk show? We suggest that you ask the producers and yourself some hard questions before accepting an opportunity to be a TV talk show "expert":

- What is the purpose of the show, and how will the producer structure it?
- Who are the guests that will be present?

- What are the guests' circumstances?
- What is expected from the guests?
- Are the guests aware of the full purpose and scope of the show?
- When will you be brought out?
- How do the producers envision your role?
- Will there be other "experts"? If so, who are they, and what are their credentials?
- Will there be any guests under the age of 18? If so, what is their role?
- Will the guests be inflicted with any potentially unwelcome surprises?

If the producers are vague or refuse to answer your questions, consider this a red flag on fire. Finally, become familiar with the program's typical format before you agree to appear. Some are routinely more exploitative than others.

Final Cautions

Trust your psychotherapist but not your interviewer! Do not ask to go "off the record." Maintain your professional stance and composure until you are out of the studio or out of range of all microphones and cameras. Some interviewers have been known to instruct their crews to leave the microphones open and cameras rolling even as the interview appears to be ending in the hope of getting some interesting "off-the-cuff" comments from an unwary subject.

Although this may seem obvious, do not lie or say "no comment," swear, or use unnecessary jargon, technical terms, or acronyms. If you are asked a question you do not want to answer, either offer a simple direct explanation (e.g., "It would be unethical of me to comment on . . .") or use the opportunity to make the key points you wish to communicate (e.g., "The real issue is . . ." or "A more appropriate question would be . . .").

References & Readings

American Psychological Association (1992). Ethical principles of psychologists and code of conduct. *American Psychologist, 47*, 1597–1611.

American Psychological Association, Public Affairs Office (n.d.). Media training for psychologists: A comprehensive guide for interview preparation. Washington, DC: American Psychological Association.

Fox, J. A., & Levin, J. (1993). *How to work with the media*. Newbury Park, CA: Sage.

Koocher, G. P., & Keith-Spiegel, P. C. (1998). *Ethics in psychology: Professional standards and cases* (2nd ed.). New York: Oxford University Press.

Murstein, B. L., & Fontaine, P. A. (1993). The public's knowledge about psychologists and other mental health professionals. *American Psychologist, 48*, 839–845.

Related Topics

Chapter 89, "American Psychological Association's Ethical Principles of Psychologists and Code of Conduct"

PART VI
Forensic Matters

104 FORENSIC EVALUATIONS AND TESTIMONY

Stanley L. Brodsky

1. *Introducing forensic evaluations:* Forensic clients should be notified that any of their statements or findings of the evaluation may become part of a public record. Rather than assuring the privilege of confidentiality, forensic evaluators fully inform the person that no psychologist-client privilege exists. Caution individuals against saying anything they prefer not to be reported (Greenberg & Moreland, 1993).

2. *Detailed reporting and documentation:* Record and maintain detailed information regarding times, dates, and durations of appointments, phone calls, interviews, reviews of records, consultations, and examination of possible corroborating information. Vagueness about such information may become a source of vulnerability on the witness stand.

3. *Never change records:* Some evaluators revise their notes when further information is received. Avoid this practice. Add and date any supplementary information to notes and records, but do not change already recorded observations or notes.

4. *Keep only one set of records:* The occasional practice of securely filing away a second set of "secret and private" notes for one's own use is wrong. All written notes, observations, corroborative information, and reports should be considered to be on the record.

5. *Prepare responsibly:* Before testifying, ensure that your knowledge is current in psychological conceptualizations, assessment practices, and relevant professional issues (Brodsky, 1994).

6. *Depositions:* Besides the stated purpose of discovery by opposing counsel of facts and findings, depositions serve two additional and sometimes nonobvious purposes. They inform both sides so that evidence may be weighed that would influence settlement discussions. Depositions also allow witnesses to learn the lines of inquiry that may be pursued in the trial. The following is a piece of specific advice for depositions: If you don't know, don't discuss. Much more than in live trials, witnesses in depositions sometimes babble on and speculate far beyond their knowledge, competence, and findings.

7. *Meet before the direct examination:* Some attorneys are unavailable or reluctant to meet with their witnesses before trials. It is worthwhile to pursue such meetings so you will know what questions will be asked (Brodsky, 1991). Attorneys who have not met with their experts often miss essential parts of psychological findings during direct examinations.

8. *Understand the legal context:* The legal rules of evidence and procedure profoundly affect acceptability of testimony (Committee on Ethical Guidelines for Forensic Psychologists, 1991). Read one of the psychology and law texts on this subject. I recommend the book by Melton, Petrila, Poythress, and Slobogin (1987).

9. *Testify only within the scope of reasonable and accepted scientific knowledge:* Experts are bound to this standard by the U.S. Supreme Court *Daubert* decision. These research results should be used in an impartial manner in the face of adversarial pulls of attorneys. It is not unethical to disagree with other experts about readings or applications of knowledge. It is unethical to relinquish the role of neutral expert in favor of highly selective gleaning of knowledge (Sales & Shuman, 1993; Sales & Simon, 1993).

10. *Stay clearly within the boundaries of your own professional expertise:* This mandate from the APA Code of Ethics (American Psychological Association, 1992) means that practitioners with expertise only in psychology of adults do not assess children or testify about child psychology. In the same sense, one should not consider observation of other witnesses' behavior on the stand to be remotely equivalent to findings from conventional psychological assessments.

11. *Credentials:* Skilled opposing counsel can always find something you have not accomplished, written, or mastered. Admit all nonaccomplishments in a matter-of-fact way.

12. *Experience:* The legal system uses breadth, depth, and duration of experience as part of credentialing expert witnesses. Clinicians should be aware that, by itself, clinical experience is unrelated to accuracy of diagnostic judgments (Garb, 1989, 1992; Faust, 1994).

13. *Credibility:* An implicit goal of witnesses is to be credible and believed. People believe witnesses who are likable and confident. To the extent possible, given the nature of the setting, allow the likable aspects of who you are to be visible, and confidently present your findings and conclusions.

14. *Data that do not support your conclusions:* Excessively partisan witnesses attempt to deny existing information they have gathered that contradicts their conclusions. Conscientious and responsible witnesses freely and without defensiveness acknowledge and discuss contradicting information.

15. *Admitting ignorance:* Some expert witnesses present themselves as omniscient and infallible in their fields. Don't. Instead, state "I don't know" in response to queries when you truly do not know the answer.

16. *Use evaluations and testimony as stimuli to learn:* Evaluators and witnesses are typically so caught up in "doing" that they are not open to conceptualizing cases and testimony as learning experiences. I suggest asking, "What additional validated measures might I administer that are directly related to these forensic issues? What else should I read or what short courses should I take to be better prepared? What have I learned about my own needs for professional and scholarly growth?"

References & Readings

American Psychological Association (1992). Ethical principles of psychologists and code of conduct. *American Psychologist, 47,* 1597–1611.

Brodsky, S. L. (1991). *Testifying in court: Guidelines and maxims for the expert witness.* Washington, DC: American Psychological Association.

Brodsky, S. L. (1994). Are there sufficient foundations for mental health experts to testify in court? Yes. In S. A. Kirk & S. D. Einbinder (Eds.), *Controversial issues in mental health* (pp. 189–196). Needham Heights, MA: Allyn and Bacon.

Committee on Ethical Guidelines for Forensic Psychologists (1991). Speciality guidelines for forensic psychologists. *Law and Human Behavior, 15,* 655–665.

Faust, D. (1994). Are there sufficient foundations for mental health experts to testify in court? No. In

S. A. Kirk & S. D. Einbinder (Eds.), *Controversial issues in mental health*. Needham Heights, MA: Allyn and Bacon.

Garb, H. N. (1989). Clinical judgment, clinical training, and professional experience. *Psychological Bulletin, 105*, 387–396.

Garb, H. N. (1992). The *trained* psychologist as expert witness. *Clinical Psychology Review, 12*, 451–467.

Greenberg, S. A., & Moreland, K. L. (1993, October 16–17). *Forensic evaluations and forensic applications of the MMPI and MMPI-2*. Paper presented at continuing education workshop sponsored by the University of Minnesota in cooperation with the Alabama Psychological Association, Montgomery, AL.

Melton, G., Petrila, J., Poythress, N. G., & Slobogin, C. (1987). *Psychological evaluation for the courts: A handbook for mental health professionals and lawyers*. New York: Guilford Press.

Sales, B. D., & Shuman, D. W. (1993). Reclaiming the integrity of science in expert witnessing. *Ethics and Behavior, 3*, 223–229.

Sales, B. D., & Simon, L. (1993). Institutional constraints on the ethics of expert testimony. *Ethics and Behavior, 3*, 231–249.

Related Topics

105 FORENSIC EVALUATION OUTLINE

David L. Shapiro

I. Identifying data (include name, date of birth, age, place of birth, birth order, religious background, present living arrangement, marital status, occupation, race)

II. Charges against defendant

III. Documents reviewed and people interviewed

IV. Confidentiality waiver (state understanding in client's own words)

V. Statement of facts (obtain from police reports, witnesses' statements, interviews of police officers and witnesses, results of drug and alcohol screening if available)

VI. Patient's version of offense (include patient's perceptions, drug or alcohol usage at time, symptoms indicative of mental disorder, behavior at time of offense as related by family or friends, relevant history leading to offense)

VII. Behavior in jail (include patient's statements and interviews of correctional personnel)

VIII. Jail psychiatric records (include discussions of consultations, medications, diagnoses, consistency or inconsistency with above self-described behavior)

IX. Mental status examination (include appearance, behavior, orientation, attention, perception, memory, affect, speech, delusions, hallucinations, suicidal ideation, judgment, indications of toxicity, estimated intelligence and insight)

X. Social history (obtain from patient and include history obtained from family and/or friends)
   A. Early childhood (include family composition, nature of interactions, family intactness, major events, illnesses or injuries)
   B. Latency age (include school performance, attitude toward studies, outside interests, nature of peer interaction)
   C. Adolescence (include sexual development, identity issues, drugs, alcohol, nature of peer interaction, occupations)
   D. Young adulthood (include nature of interpersonal relationships, quality of job history)
   E. Adulthood
   F. Sexual and marital (include dating, number of marriages, personality of spouse, reasons for separation if any)
   G. Education (include types of schools, grades, extracurricular activities)
   H. Vocational (include number of jobs, length of jobs)
   I. Military (include branch, dates, rank obtained, disciplinary actions if any)
   J. Religious history
   K. Drug and alcohol abuse (include history, kinds, extent, effects on behavior)

XI. Criminal history (include for each charge, date of charge, place, and disposition)

XII. Psychiatric history (include nature of admissions, whether voluntary or involuntary, willingness to sign releases, type of treatment rendered)
   A. Family psychiatric history
   B. Patient's psychiatric history

XIII. Neurological history
   A. Head injuries and sequelae (include hospitals, where treatment rendered)
   B. Blackouts (unrelated to drugs or alcohol)
   C. Dizzy spells
   D. Seizures
   E. Stupor or staring
   F. Repetitive stereotype movements
   G. Perceptual distortions
   H. Pathological intoxication
   I. Spatial disorientation
   J. Learning disabilities
   K. Explosive behavioral outbursts with minimal provocation (note especially amnesia, aura, peculiar tastes or smells)

L. Confusional episodes and/or slurred speech unrelated to drugs or alcohol
M. Hallucinations unrelated to functional mental disorder
N. Fugue states
O. Déjà vu phenomena
P. Jamais vu phenomena
Q. Depersonalization or derealization
R. Double vision or blurriness
S. History of delirium tremens
T. Memory disturbances
U. Difficulty understanding what is read
V. Difficulty following conversations
W. Contact with chemicals
X. History of venereal disease (syphilis)

XIV. Chronological review of psychiatric records

XV. Interview with treating therapists

XVI. Review of general medical records (check especially for head trauma, antianxiety or antidepressant medication)

XVII. Review of school records

XVIII. Review of occupational records

XIX. Review and critique of prior evaluations in current case

XX. Referrals to other consultants and results of their examinations

XXI. Test results (include test-taking attitude, behavior, degree of defensiveness, validity, motivation, reaction time, evidence of perseveration)
   A. WAIS-III or WISC-III
   B. Projectives
   C. Objective personality tests
   D. Neuropsychological screening
   E. Neuropsychological battery
   F. Assessment of malingering
   G. Summary of testing

XXII. Opinion on criminal responsibility (or competence) (specify how mental disorder may affect each functional capacity)
   A. Competence
      1. Factual understanding
      2. Rational understanding
      3. Relation to attorney
      4. Knowledge of roles of various people
      5. Knowledge of pleas and outcomes
   B. Criminal responsibility
      1. Mental disorder: In what way does it affect
         a. Ability to appreciate wrongfulness of behavior

b. Ability to conform to law (if applicable)
c. Other forensic issues (e.g., ability to waive Miranda rights, competence to confess, whether or not the mental disorder resulted in an inability to form specific intent) (for each issue, how does mental disorder relate to each of the functional capacities?)

XXIII. Recommendations for disposition

References & Readings

Curran, W., McGarry, A. L., Shah, S. (1986). *Forensic psychiatry and psychology*. Philadelphia: F. A. Davis.

Melton, G., Petrila, J., Poythress, N., Slobogin, C.
(1987). *Psychological evaluations for the courts.* New York: Guilford Press.

Shapiro, D. L. (1990). *Forensic psychological assessment: An integrated approach.* Boston: Allyn and Bacon.

Smith, S., & Meyer, R. (1987). *Law, behavior, and mental health: Policy and practice.* New York: New York University Press.

Weiner, I., & Hess, A. (1987). *Handbook of forensic psychology.* New York: Wiley.

Related Topics

Chapter 104, "Forensic Evaluations and Testimony"
Chapter 106, "Forensic Assessment Instruments"
Chapter 109, "Sequence of Steps and Critical Assessment Targets of a Comprehensive Custody Evaluation"
Chapter 115, "Accepting Legal Referrals"

106 FORENSIC ASSESSMENT INSTRUMENTS

Randy Borum

Psychologists often rely on standardized tests and measures for assistance in diagnosis and treatment planning. Most of these instruments are designed to assess the presence, nature, and degree of mental disorders and their symptoms—issues that are the focus of most clinical psychological assessments. However, in a forensic evaluation, information concerning one's mental disorder is only one component of the answer to a psycholegal question. Typically, the psychologist must also assess and address some *specific* functional ability such as competence to stand trial or capacity to function as a parent. Provided below are brief descriptions of several forensic assessment instruments (FAIs) designed to assess functional capacities relevant to a given forensic issue. For a comprehensive review of FAIs, Thomas Grisso's *Evaluating Competencies: Forensic Assessments and Instruments* (1986) is an excellent reference. A second edition of this text is currently being written. Topic-specific review articles are listed beneath the appropriate topic heading.

CRIMINAL FORENSIC EVALUATIONS
(Review articles: Grisso, 1986; Rogers & Ewing, 1992)

The two most frequent evaluation issues for forensic psychologists in the criminal justice system relate to competency to stand trial and insanity/criminal responsibility. In chapter 107, Paul Lipsitt has reviewed the primary FAIs used for assessing competency to stand trial (the Competency Screening Test, the Competence to Stand Trial Assessment Inventory, and the Interdisciplinary Fitness Interview) (Borum & Grisso, 1995). An FAI developed for assessments of legal insanity/criminal responsibility is described below.

Rogers Criminal Responsibility Assessment Scales (R-CRAS) (Rogers, 1984): The R-CRAS is designed to structure and quantify the decision-making process in clinical-forensic assessments of insanity. After the examiner conducts a thorough evaluation, including relevant interviews and reviews of pertinent records, the R-CRAS presents 30 items, called Psychological and Situational Variables, which must be assigned a numerical rating. The Psychological and Situational Variables cover the following domains: Patient's Reliability; Organicity; Psychopathology; Cognitive Control; and Behavioral Control. The examiner uses these ratings and the assessment information in a decision tree analysis, which leads to a conclusion that the defendant is either "sane" or "insane," according to the relevant legal standard. Interrater reliability coefficients for the R-CRAS averaged .58 for the clinical variables and .81 for the decision variables (malingering and components of the legal insanity standard). In a sample of 93 defendants, the R-CRAS decision concurred with the court's decision in 88% of the cases where the court was not given information concerning R-CRAS results.

CHILD CUSTODY AND
PARENTAL CAPACITY
(Review article: Heinze & Grisso, 1996)

Ackerman-Schoendorf Scales for Parent Evaluation of Custody (ASPECT) (Ackerman & Schoendorf, 1992): "The ASPECT is not a test but rather a system combining the results of psychological testing, interviews, and observations of each parent and child to provide data regarding the suitability of the parent for custody" (Heinze & Grisso, 1996). Each parent must complete an extensive Parent Questionnaire, and each parent as well as each child must complete a specified battery of psychological tests. The clinician uses these data to complete a series of 56 dichotomous questions (yes/no) for each parent. The results of this form yield three subscale scores (Observational, Social, and Cognitive-Emotional) and a Parenting Custody Index (PCI). The PCI is considered to be the global measure of parenting effectiveness. The scores for each parent are presented in color graphs, with suggestions concerning the comparative parenting effectiveness and identification of the "preferred parent." The ASPECT was normed on a sample of 200 parents. When two independent raters reviewed a sample of 88 records, the interrater reliability coefficient for the PCI was .96, with other subscales falling in the low to mid-.90s. The primary validity study shows that ASPECT results agreed with the judges' custody decision in 75% of 118 cases. However, it appears that the ASPECT results were presented as part of the evidence in these cases.

Bricklin Perceptual Scales (BPS) (Bricklin, 1984): The BPS is a 64-item instrument designed for children over 6 years of age; 32 items relate to each parent. The BPS is administered by presenting the child with an item and asking him or her to indicate how well the item describes the parent. For each question, the child is given an 8-inch card with a black line labeled with "not so well" at one end and "very well" at the other. The child responds to the item by punching a hole at the appropriate point along the line. On the back of the card the line is divided evenly into 60 segments, each of which has a corresponding point value. The parent who has the highest score for a given item "wins" that item. According to the BPS, the "parent of choice" is indicated by the parent who "wins" the greatest number of items. There are currently no normative data available for this instrument. A preliminary study of test-retest showed coefficients for individual items ranging from .61 to .94, with the scores of older children (aged 15–17) generally being more consistent than those of younger children (aged 12–14). Concerning potential validity, Bricklin reports a high level of concurrence between the BPS and other instruments he has developed, but it is unclear if any other validity data exist for the measure at this time.

Parenting Stress Index (PSI) (Abidin, 1990): The PSI is a 101-item self-report inventory designed to assess the type and severity of stresses associated with the child-rearing role. A 36-item short form also exists. Parent-respondents rate their agreement with an item using a 5-point Likert-type scale. Response style is assessed with a Defensive Responding Scale. In the Child Domain, the PSI measures child characteristics associated with stress in parenting (subscales relating to child adaptability, acceptability, demandingness, mood, hyperactivity/distractibility, and reinforcing of parent); in the Parent Domain, it assesses stress resulting from the parenting role (subscales relating to depression, attachment, restriction of role, sense of competence, social isolation, relationship with spouse, and parental health). A Total Stress Score is derived by summing the two Domain scores. The normative sample is composed of 2,633 parents. Alpha coefficients for domain scores, subscales, and total scores range between .70 and .95. Test-retest coefficients across numerous studies with varying time frames have yielded estimates from .55 to .96. The PSI has shown significant correlations, in the expected directions, with other similar measures and with abusive parental behaviors, parental roles, marital satisfaction, and social support. To date, there have been approximately 200 studies involving the PSI.

Parent-Child Relationship Inventory (PCRI) (Gerard, 1994): The PCRI is a 78-item self-report inventory comprising seven content scales: Parental Support; Satisfaction with Parenting; Involvement; Communication; Limit Setting; Autonomy; and Role Orientation. There are also two validity scales to measure social desirability and inconsistent responding. Parent-respondents rate their agreement with an item using a 4-point Likert-type scale. Normative data are provided for a sample of 1,139 parents. Alpha coefficients for the subscales range from .70 to .88, with 1-week test-retest reliabilities from .68 to .93. Concurrent validation studies have shown significant correlations between the PCRI and the Personality Inventory for Children; parental discipline style; and parents' sense of social support, competence, and self-esteem.

GUARDIANSHIP
(Review article: Grisso, 1994)

Independent Living Scales (ILS) (Loeb, 1996): The ILS is a 70-item instrument designed to evaluate an individual's capacity to care for himself or herself and manage his or her own affairs. The ILS is administered as a performance-based structured interview with items that relate to a range of situations and tasks encountered in daily living. It takes approximately 45 minutes to administer and 10 minutes to score. The administration can be adapted to accommodate an examinee's physical/visual/literacy limitations. Extra materials (e.g., telephone, telephone book, envelope, pencil and paper, and money) are required to administer some tasks. The ILS yields five subscale scores (Memory/Orientation; Managing Money; Managing Home and Transportation; Health and Safety; and Social Adjustment); two factor scores (Performance/Information and Problem Solving); and a Full Scale standard score, which provides a global index of the examinee's level of functioning (low, moderate, or high). Internal consistency for the ILS scores ranges from .72 to .92, with test-retest coefficients between .81 and .94. Interrater reliabilities range between .95 and .99. Although the ILS was designed primarily for use with older adults (65+), normative data are also available for adults with dementia, severe mental illness, mild mental retardation, and mild brain injury. In validation studies, the ILS has shown appropriate correlations with measures of intellectual and cognitive functioning and with other instruments measuring Activities of Daily Living (ADLs).

Direct Assessment of Functional Status (DAFS) (Lowenstein et al., 1989): The DAFS is an 85-item instrument with seven sections (time orientation, communication, transportation, financial, shopping, grooming, and eating) and a total administration time of approximately 30 minutes. Each item requires the examinee to demonstrate knowledge or perform a task relevant to daily independent living—for example, using a telephone, identifying and counting currency, working with a grocery list, and using eating utensils. Interrater reliabilities for composite and subscale scores are in the .90s. Test-retest coefficients over several weeks ranged between .55 and .92 in a sample of impaired patients and were even higher in normal controls. The DAFS also correlated significantly with an independent dementia rating scale and with independent chart reports of specific functional impairments.

VIOLENCE RISK ASSESSMENT
(Review article: Borum, 1996)

Violence Prediction Scheme (VPS) (Webster, Harris, Rice, Cormier, & Quinsey, 1994): The VPS combines clinical and actuarial factors in a comprehensive scheme for assessing dangerousness and risk. The actuarial component is based on the Violence Risk Assessment Guide (VRAG), a 12-item tool that showed a classification accuracy rate of about 75% in a sample of patients from a maximum security psychiatric hospital. Preliminary efforts at cross-validation with sex offenders in the community and maximum security inmates in prison have been promising. In the VPS scheme, the actuarial and VRAG data are combined with an assessment of current status and clinical information, including a 10-item clinical scheme called the ASSESS-LIST, an acronym that stands for *A*ntecedent history, *S*elf-presentation, *S*ocial and psychosocial adjustment, *E*xpectations and plans, *S*ymptoms, *S*upervision, *L*ife factors, *I*nstitutional management, *S*exual adjustment, and *T*reatment progress. The examiner scores each of these items as either "favorable" or "unfavorable." Currently no psy-

chometric data are available for the ASSESS-LIST items.

HCR-20 (Webster, Douglas, Eaves, & Hart, 1997): The HCR-20 is an instrument/guide "designed for use in the assessment of risk for future violent behavior in criminal and psychiatric populations. Briefly, the first 10 items of the HCR-20 pertain to the *historical*, or static, variables of the individual being assessed (H Scale), the next five items reflect the current *clinical* status and personality characteristics of the individual (C Scale), and the remaining five pertain to future *risk* of violent behavior (R Scale)" (Webster et al., 1997, emphasis added). The historical and risk variables can primarily be coded from records or secondary information sources, although the clinical factors need to be evaluated and rated by a qualified mental health professional based on interviews, progress notes, psychological assessments, or similar sources. The HCR-20 has a defined three-level scoring system for each item, similar to that of the Psychopathy Checklist-Revised (PCL-R). Preliminary data have shown significant correlations between the H Scale and C Scale and scores on the VRAG (see above), PCL-R, and number of previous charges for violent offenses. It also appears likely that the items can be reliably coded with average interrater reliability coefficients of about .80. The HCR-20 cannot currently be considered a test in the formal sense, but it may be useful as a checklist to prompt the examiner to cover or consider the major relevant areas of inquiry. Several new studies involving the HCR-20 are currently under way.

Spousal Assault Risk Assessment Guide (SARA) (Kropp, Hart, Webster, and Eaves, 1995): The SARA is a 20-item clinical checklist of risk factors for spousal assault. It has an operationally defined three-level scoring scheme but is constructed to be used as a clinical guide —rather than a test—for assessing the risk of future violence in men arrested for spousal assault. The SARA has four main sections: the Criminal History section; Psychosocial Adjustment section; Spousal Assault History section; and a final section relating to the Alleged (Current) Offense. After all four sections are completed, the clinician makes a "summary risk rating" (low, moderate, or high) of imminent risk of violence toward a partner and imminent risk of violence toward others. Preliminary data from one retrospective study showed that interrater reliability for the sum of items was .92, and reliability for the SARA-informed risk rating was .80. The SARA-informed summary risk ratings were also strongly related to reoffending, with those rated as "high" risk being 5.5 times more likely to reoffend than those with ratings of "low" or "moderate" risk.

References & Readings

Abidin, R. (1990). *Parenting Stress Index* (3rd ed.). Odessa, FL: Psychological Assessment Resources.

Ackerman, M., & Schoendorf, K. (1992). *ASPECT: Ackerman-Schoendorf Scales for Parent Evaluation of Custody*. Los Angeles: Western Psychological Services.

Borum, R. (1996). Improving the clinical practice of violence risk assessment: Technology, guidelines, and training. *American Psychologist, 51*, 945–956.

Borum, R., & Grisso, T. (1995). A survey of psychological test use in criminal forensic evaluations. *Professional Psychology: Research and Practice, 26*, 465–473.

Bricklin, B. (1984). *The Bricklin Perceptual Scales: Child-perception-of-parents-series*. Furlong, PA: Village.

Gerard, A. (1994). *Parent-Child Relationship Inventory (PCRI): Manual*. Los Angeles: Western Psychological Services.

Grisso, T. (1986). *Evaluating competencies: Forensic assessments and instruments*. New York: Plenum Press.

Grisso, T. (1994). Clinical assessments of legal competence of older adults. In M. Storandt & G. VandenBos (Eds.), *Neuropsychological assessment of dementia and depression in older adults: A clinician's guide* (pp. 119–139). Washington, DC: American Psychological Association.

Heinze, M., & Grisso, T. (1996). Review of instruments assessing parenting competencies used in child custody evaluations. *Behavioral Sciences and the Law, 14*, 293–313.

Kropp, P. R., Hart, S. D., Webster, C. D., & Eaves, D. (1995). *Manual for the Spousal Assault Risk Assessment Guide* (2nd ed.). Vancouver: British Columbia Institute on Family Violence.

Loeb, P. (1996). *Independent Living Scales*. San Antonio, TX: Psychological Corporation.

Lowenstein, D., Amigo, E., Duara, R., Guterman, A., Hurwitz, D., Berkowitz, N., Wilkie, F., Weinberg, G., Black, B., Gittelman, B., & Eisdorfer, C. (1989). A new scale for the assessment of functional status in Alzheimer's disease and related disorders. *Journal of Gerontology: Psychological Sciences, 44*, 114–121.

Rogers, R. (1984). *Rogers Criminal Responsibility Assessment Scales*. Odessa, FL: Psychological Assessment Resources.

Rogers, R., & Ewing, C. (1992). The measurement of insanity: Debating the merits of the R-CRAS and its alternatives. *International Journal of Law and Psychiatry, 15*, 113–123.

Webster, C. D., Douglas, K. S., Eaves, D., & Hart, S. D. (1997). *HCR-20: Assessing risk for violence, Version 2*. Burnaby: Mental Health Law and Policy Institute, Simon Fraser University.

Webster, C. D., Harris, G. T., Rice, M. E., Cormier, C., & Quinsey, V. L. (1994). *The Violence Prediction Scheme: Assessing dangerousness in high risk men*. Toronto, Ontario: Centre of Criminology, University of Toronto.

Related Topics

107 EVALUATION OF COMPETENCY TO STAND TRIAL

Paul D. Lipsitt

The notion that a person must be competent to defend himself or herself in court when charged with a crime is based on a constitutional right of due process derived from the English common law. Just as the accused has a basic right to a physical presence in court to face the accuser, the absence of a psychological presence due to mental incapacity would be equally prejudicial. As early as 1746, an English decision held that "no man is to be condemned unheard and consequently no trial ought to proceed to the condemnation of a man who by the providence of God is rendered totally incapable of speaking for himself or of instructing others to speak for him" (*Kinloch's Case*).

The defendant who has permanent incapacity may not be tried. The temporarily incapable defendant is entitled to a postponement of trial until competency has been restored. Any person charged with a criminal offense must be able to muster a sufficient level of cognitive and affective resources to effect an adequate defense to the charges with the aid of an attorney. To avoid indefinite commitment, the U.S. Supreme Court has held that those unlikely to ever gain competency may be detained for only a reasonable period for competency observation and treatment (*Jackson v. Indiana*, 1972).

The issue of competency is usually raised prior to trial but may be raised at any time during the procedures. While usually initiated as a request for evaluation by the defense, the prosecution or the judge may raise the question of competency.

Competency for trial is based on legal criteria rather than psychological diagnosis of mental illness or mental defect. Defendants who are mentally disabled, even to a serious degree, such as those with psychosis or moderate mental retardation, may be functionally competent for trial. However, psychological factors may impact on the ability to perform the task of adequately participating in one's criminal trial. If the results of an initial evaluation indicate that the requirements for competency are sufficiently compromised, the court would order treatment with the goal of restoration of competency, to be followed by proceedings in court to face the criminal charges. In the event that the incompetency is determined to be permanent or unlikely to be restored in the foreseeable future, other steps are taken to protect the rights of a defendant who has been charged but has yet to be adjudicated.

The general criteria that determine competency for trial include (a) an ability to communicate and cooperate with one's attorney in defending oneself in court, (b) an awareness of the nature and object of the legal proceedings, and (c) an understanding of the possible consequences of a trial. These elements provide a framework for the psychologist to assess the defendant's ability to function on a task that will require some level of understanding and active participation. The assessment and evaluation data are generated by the psychologist or other forensic mental health professional, but the conclusion of competency or incompetency is the prerogative of the judge.

In 1960, the U.S. Supreme Court stated that competency should be determined by assessing whether the defendant has "sufficient present ability to consult with his attorney with a reasonable degree of rational understanding and a rational as well as a factual understanding of the proceedings against him" (*Dusky v. United States*, p. 402). Many states require that the inability to function competently must be due to mental illness or mental defect.

Most state statutes do not define competency, nor do they offer guidelines for its assessment. In order to mitigate the subjectivity of the competency assessment and to provide a guide for its determination, various tests and procedures have been developed by research social scientists.

During the 1960s, in conjunction with an increasing concern for the civil rights and liberties of the mentally ill, involuntary commitment procedures were challenged through the legal system, many reaching the U.S. Supreme Court. Persons charged with offenses, but never found guilty, were frequently hospitalized involuntarily, often for life. A federally funded study at Harvard Medical School (Laboratory of Community Psychiatry, 1973) was initiated to address the absence of standards for assessing competency in the criminal justice system. The Competency Screening Test (CST) and the Competency Assessment Instrument (CAI) were developed as a part of this project. About 10 years after the first use of the CAI, the Interdisciplinary Fitness Interview (IFI) was developed (Golding, Roesch, & Schreiber, 1984).

The CST was developed as a screening instrument to reduce the need for pretrial commitment of those who can be declared clearly competent. Using the CST, many individuals for whom the competency issue has been raised can be tested in the court or place of detention. Those receiving a score within the competent range can proceed directly to trial, avoiding unnecessary hospitalized observation for competency evaluation.

The CST, which has been the subject of several validation studies (Nicholson, Robertson, Johnson, & Jensen, 1988; Randolph, Hicks, Mason, & Cuneo, 1982; Nottingham & Matson, 1981), consists of 22 sentence-completion stems, each of which focuses on a legal as well as a psychological aspect of competency for trial (Table 1). A factor analysis of the CST reveals six factors, all closely related to the estab-

lished legal criteria for competency for trial. These are (a) relationship of the defendant to his or her attorney in developing a defense; (b) defendant's understanding and awareness of the nature of the court proceedings; (c) defendant's affective response to the court process in dealing with accusations and feelings of guilt; (d) judgmental qualities in engaging in the strategy and evaluation of the trial; (e) defendant's trust and confidence in his or her attorney; and (f) defendant's recognition of the seriousness of his or her position.

The CST is administered as a paper-and-pencil test, with a brief instruction regarding the completion of each sentence as it relates to the law and going to court. Although typically self-administered, for individuals with inadequate reading skills the stems may be read and responses recorded by the administrator. On average, the CST can be administered in about 25 minutes and scored in 15 to 20 minutes with the aid of the scoring manual.

The scoring system uses a 3-point scale from 0 to 2. The scoring manual serves as a guide, with examples of prototypical responses at the three levels of scoring. In general, characteristics that would merit a score of 0 involve substantial disorganization in content, inability to relate or to trust, defining the lawyer's role as punitive or rejecting, extreme concreteness, or self-defeating behavior. A 1-point score is given when the response can be characterized as passive, acquiescent, avoidant, or impoverished, though not clearly inappropriate. Reference to the scoring manual provides specific guidelines for each item. For example, a 2-point response to Item 2, "When I go to court, the lawyer will . . . ," is "defend me." In contrast, a sentence completion of "put me away" would merit a 0. The legal criterion relates to the defendant's understanding of the lawyer's role in aiding in his or her defense. The psychological referent is the ability to trust and accept the attorney.

The CST can be used when the competency issue is raised before the trial or at any time during the trial proceedings. Defendants who score in the competent range on the CST are unlikely to present as false negatives, that is, incompetent after further assessment (Lipsitt, Lelos, & McGarry, 1971). A low score on the

TABLE 1. The Competency Screening Test

1. The lawyer told Bill that . . .
2. When I go to court the lawyer will . . .
3. Jack felt that the judge . . .
4. When Phil was accused of the crime, he . . .
5. When I prepare to go to court with my lawyer . . .
6. If the jury finds me guilty, I . . .
7. The way a court trial is decided . . .
8. When the evidence in George's case was presented to the jury . . .
9. When the lawyer questioned his client in court, the client said . . .
10. If Jack has to try his own case, he . . .
11. Each time the D.A. asked me a question, I . . .
12. While listening to the witnesses testify against me, I . . .
13. When the witness testifying against Harry gave incorrect evidence, he . . .
14. When Bob disagreed with his lawyer on his defense, he . . .
15. When I was formally accused of the crime, I thought to myself . . .
16. If Ed's lawyer suggests that he plead guilty, he . . .
17. What concerns Fred most about his lawyer . . .
18. When they say a man is innocent until proven guilty . . .
19. When I think of being sent to prison, I . . .
20. When Phil thinks of what he is accused of, he . . .
21. When the jury hears my case, they will . . .
22. If I had a chance to speak to the judge, I . . .

CST places the defendant in the questionable category for competency and in need of more extensive assessment. The semistructured format of the CAI or the IFI can elicit more detailed clinical information for evaluating competency when the CST score is in the questionable range.

The CAI designates the parameters for inquiry into competency in language familiar to lawyers and judges. The guidelines aid the mental health professional in translating psychological factors into an assessment of ability to function and cope with a trial. Thirteen variables guide the interviewer in conducting the competency assessment (Table 2). The 13 items are rated from a grade of 0 (least competent) to 5 (most competent). A clinical opinion based on each function offers information to help the court determine the ultimate issue of competency in the case. The weight the court assigns to one function may differ from another, since each function is considered independently, and the various ratings are not cumulative. The judge must assess the various scales to determine whether the defendant's overall competency is at an adequate level to proceed to trial. While there are no objective standards for

making the ratings, sample interview questions and responses are provided in the manual to aid in assessing the level of competency. If a substantial number of ratings are 3 or lower, the assumption of competency should be strongly questioned.

The IFI, like the CAI, is a semistructured interview, but it focuses on 5 legal issues and 11 forms of psychopathology and is intended to be administered collaboratively by a mental health professional and a lawyer. Each of the 16 items is rated on a 3-point scale. The assessments of competency in the IFI research had a high correspondence with the judgments of a selected group of forensic experts. Grisso (1988) states that the results on the IFI "usually agree with the evaluations performed with the CAI" (p. 30). A psychologist or other mental health professional alone can administer the IFI with adequate forensic training.

When ordering a competency evaluation, the judge often includes a request for an evaluation to determine criminal responsibility. The examiner must clearly separate the issues of competency for trial from criminal responsibility and develop separate reports. Competency for trial is a description of current status,

TABLE 2. Competency to Stand Trial Assessment Instrument

		Degree of Incapacity				
	Total	Severe	Moderate	Mild	None	Unratable
1. Appraisal of available legal defenses	1	2	3	4	5	6
2. Unmanageable behavior	1	2	3	4	5	6
3. Quality of relating to attorney	1	2	3	4	5	6
4. Planning of legal strategy, including guilty plea to lesser charges where pertinent	1	2	3	4	5	6
5. Appraisal of role of:						
a. Defense counsel	1	2	3	4	5	6
b. Prosecuting attorney	1	2	3	4	5	6
c. Judge	1	2	3	4	5	6
d. Jury	1	2	3	4	5	6
e. Defendant	1	2	3	4	5	6
f. Witnesses	1	2	3	4	5	6
6. Understanding of court procedure	1	2	3	4	5	6
7. Appreciation of charges	1	2	3	4	5	6
8. Appreciation of range and nature of possible penalties	1	2	3	4	5	6
9. Appraisal of likely outcome	1	2	3	4	5	6
10. Capacity to disclose to attorney available pertinent facts surrounding the offense including the defendant's movements, timing, mental state, actions at the time of the offense	1	2	3	4	5	6
11. Capacity to realistically challenge prosecution witnesses	1	2	3	4	5	6
12. Capacity to testify relevantly	1	2	3	4	5	6
13. Self-defeating vs. self-serving motivation (legal sense)	1	2	3	4	5	6

Examinee_____ Examiner_____

Date_____

whereas criminal responsibility refers to "legal sanity" at the time of the offense.

In cases in which a finding of legal incompetency may be likely, it is generally recommended that information regarding remediation be provided to the court. Courts usually rely on the forensic examiner's information and judgment with regard to the defendant's deficits and on the opinion regarding treatment options and recommendations relating to appropriate interventions for the restoration of competency within a reasonable period of time.

SUMMARY

Competency is a legal concept, not a psychological diagnosis. It refers to the capacity or ability to perform the task of adequately participating in one's criminal trial. Criteria have been established to evaluate the affective and cognitive factors that contribute to defending oneself in court with the aid of an attorney. The competency issue usually arises at the pretrial stage when a defendant is charged or indicted, but it may be raised at any time during the trial procedures. The issue may be raised by the defense attorney, the prosecutor, or the judge. Competency is an evaluation of current functioning and is clearly distinguished in concept and focus of evaluation from criminal responsibility or the insanity defense. Three instruments described here have been developed as aids for the forensic mental health professional in assisting the court in the determination of competency for trial.

References & Readings

Dusky v. U.S., 362 U.S. 402 (1960).

Golding, S., Roesch, R., & Schreiber, J. (1984). Assessment and conceptualization of competency to stand trial: Preliminary data on the Interdisciplinary Fitness Interview. *Law and Human Behavior, 9*, 321–334.

Grisso, T. (1988). *Competency to stand trial evaluations*. Sarasota, FL: Professional Resources Exchange.

Jackson v. Indiana, 406 U.S. 715 (1972).

Kinloch's Case, 18 How. St. Tr. (Eng.) 395 (1746).

Laboratory of Community Psychiatry, Harvard Medical School (1973). *Competency to stand trial and mental illness* (DHEW Publication No. HSM 73-9105).

Lipsitt, P. D., Lelos, D., & McGarry, A. L. (1971). Competency for trial: A screening instrument. *American Journal of Psychiatry, 128*(1), 105–109.

Nicholson, R. A., Robertson, H. C., Johnson, W. G., & Jensen, G. (1988). A comparison of instruments for assessing competency to stand trial. *Law and Human Behavior, 12*, 313–322.

Nottingham, E. J., IV, & Mattson, R. E. (1981). A validation study of the Competency Screening Test. *Law and Human Behavior, 5*, 329–335.

Randolph, J. J., Hicks, T., Mason, D., & Cuneo, D. J. (1982). The Competency Screening Test: A validation study in Cook County, Illinois. *Criminal Justice and Behavior, 9*, 495–500.

Related Topics

Chapter 104, "Forensic Evaluations and Testimony"
Chapter 105, "Forensic Evaluation Outline"
Chapter 106, "Forensic Assessment Instruments"
Chapter 115, "Accepting Legal Referrals"

108 MODEL FOR CLINICAL DECISION MAKING WITH DANGEROUS PATIENTS

Leon VandeCreek

Dangerous patients pose a special challenge to psychotherapists. On the one hand, if the therapist underestimates the patient's threats and harm comes to a third party, the therapist may feel that more should have been done to protect the innocent victim and the victim, or survivors, may initiate a lawsuit. On the other hand, if the therapist incorrectly believes that harm is imminent and acts to warn a potential victim, the patient may feel betrayed and the therapeutic relationship may be threatened. Even worse, the patient may lose faith in therapists and drop out of therapy, thereby ending any role that therapy may have had in preventing violence.

The American Psychological Association's Ethical Principles of Psychologists and Code of Conduct (1992) permits psychologists to breach confidentiality if it is necessary to protect the patient or others from harm. The option of breaching confidentiality, permitted by the ethics code, may protect the psychologist from charges of ethical violations, but the psychologist must still exercise judgment about when to

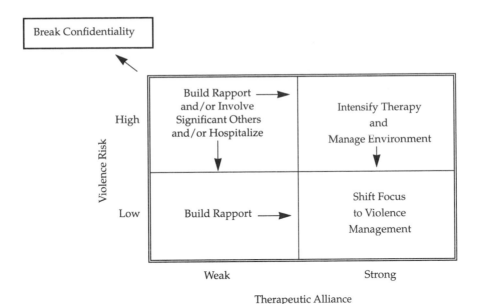

Break Confidentiality

FIGURE 1. Model for Decision Making With Dangerous Clients (Reprinted with permission from Truscott, Evans, & Mansell, 1995.)

breach confidentiality or when to engage in other strategies that may reduce the potential for violence.

Decision making with dangerous patients is made more precarious by the increased possibility of legal liability. Prior to the 1976 California Supreme Court decision in *Tarasoff v. Regents of the University of California*, psychotherapists did not have to contend with legal repercussions surrounding confidentiality in their management of dangerous patients. The *Tarasoff* ruling and those of other courts and legislation that followed the lead of *Tarasoff* have created a "duty to protect" doctrine that therapists are often advised to follow even if their states have not formally endorsed the doctrine through legislation or court decisions (VandeCreek & Knapp, 1993). Consequently, therapists must now consider clinical issues in the context of both ethical and legal constraints.

One of the difficulties therapists face when managing dangerous patients, however, is that no standard of care has been established. Botkin and Nietzel (1987) attempted to address this issue by surveying psychologists about their use of interventions with dangerous patients. They found that hospitalizing, strengthening

the therapeutic alliance, managing the patient's environment, and breaking confidentiality were the most frequently employed interventions. Similarly, Monahan (1993) recommended three broad areas of intervention for patients who pose a high risk of violence: hospitalizing patients, intensifying treatment, and warning potential victims. More recently, Truscott, Evans, and Mansell (1995) presented a model for decision making when working with dangerous patients. Their model is presented here.

The model proposes that patients who pose a threat of violence be thought of as occupying one of four cells in a 2 × 2, Violence Risk × Therapeutic Alliance Strength figure. Interventions can be selected to strengthen the alliance and reduce the violence risk as suggested by Botkin and Nietzel (1987) and Monahan (1993). The model is presented in Figure 1.

The authors suggest that, whenever possible, psychologists should work to strengthen and maintain the therapeutic alliance because the alliance is the backbone of most interventions. If the alliance is weak, the psychologist has a reduced chance of effectiveness with the patient, especially when the risk of violence is high. The model suggests that when the alliance is strong, the psychologist can focus on violence management, and if the risk of violence increases, therapy should be intensified and the patient's environment more carefully managed. On the other hand, if the alliance is weak and the risk of violence is high, the psychologist should attempt to strengthen the alliance and/or involve significant others in treatment and consider hospitalization. Breaking confidentiality, then, should occur only in the context of a weak alliance and high violence potential.

To implement this model or any other decision-making model when working with potentially dangerous patients, psychologists must make assessments of violence potential. The legal test in predicting violence is one of "reasonable foreseeability." That is, would other psychologists with a similar patient make a similar assessment and draw a similar conclusion? Liability is more likely to be imposed if the psychologist failed to follow appropriate procedures in reaching a decision and in implementing the decision than if an incorrect prediction was made. Thorough records are imperative to document decision making about dangerous patients.

The following variables should be considered when reviewing a patient's potential for violence (Litwack, Kirschner, & Wack, 1993; Meloy, 1987; Monahan, 1981, 1984; Monahan & Steadman, 1994). Truscott et al. (1995) provide several case examples that use these risk factors within the context of the decision-making model. Individual characteristics include the following:

- *History of violence:* This is the single best predictor of violent behavior.
- *Demographic variables:* Non-White males in their late teens and early 20s with a history of substance abuse and low IQ and education are most likely to engage in violent behaviors. Unstable residential and work histories increase the risk.

Situational characteristics include the following:

- *Availability of potential victim(s):* Most violent crimes occur between people who know each other.

- *Access to weapons:* Persons with martial arts training or combat experience and those who possess great physical strength are capable of inflicting greater harm.
- *Substance use.*
- *Stressors:* Daily stressors such as relationship and financial problems can reduce a person's frustration tolerance.

References & Readings

American Psychological Association (1992). Ethical principles of psychologists and code of conduct. *American Psychologist, 47,* 1597–1611.

Beck, J. C. (1987). The psychotherapist's duty to protect third parties from harm. *Mental and Physical Disability Law Reporter, 11,* 141–148.

Botkin, D. J., & Nietzel, M. T. (1987). How therapists manage potentially dangerous clients: Toward a standard of care for psychotherapists. *Professional Psychology: Research and Practice, 18,* 84–86.

Fulero, S. M. (1988). *Tarasoff:* 10 years later. *Professional Psychology: Research and Practice, 19,* 184–190.

Fulero, S. M. (1992). Recent developments in the duty to protect. *Psychotherapy in Independent Practice, 33–43.*

Grisso, T., & Appelbaum, P. (1992). Is it unethical to offer predictions of future violence? *Law and Human Behavior, 16,* 621–633.

Knapp, S., VandeCreek, L., & Shapiro, D. (1990). Statutory remedies to the duty to protect: A reconsideration. *Psychotherapy, 27,* 291–296.

Lidz, C., Mulvey, E., & Gardner, W. (1993). The accuracy of predictions of violence to others. *Journal of the American Medical Association, 269,* 1007–1011.

Litwack, T. R., Kirschner, S. M., & Wack, R. C. (1993). The assessment of dangerousness and predictions of violence: Recent research and future prospects. *Psychiatric Quarterly, 64,* 245–273.

Meloy, J. R. (1987). The prediction of violence in outpatient psychotherapy. *American Journal of Psychotherapy, 41,* 38–45.

Monahan, J. (1981). *The clinical prediction of violent behavior.* Washington, DC: U.S. Government Printing Office.

Monahan, J. (1984). The prediction of violent behavior: Toward a second generation of theory and policy. *American Journal of Psychiatry, 141,* 10–15.

Monahan, J. (1993). Limiting therapist exposure to *Tarasoff* liability: Guidelines for risk containment. *American Psychologist, 48,* 242–250.

Monahan, J., & Steadman, H. J. (Eds.) (1994). *Violence and mental disorder: Developments in risk assessment.* Chicago: University of Chicago Press.

Mossman, D. (1994). Assessing predictions of violence: Being accurate about accuracy. *Journal of Consulting and Clinical Psychology, 62,* 783–792.

Stromberg, C., Schneider, J., & Joondeph, B. (1993). Dealing with potentially dangerous patients. In *The psychologist's legal update.* Washington, DC: National Register of Health Service Providers in Psychology.

Tarasoff v. Regents of the University of California, 17 Cal. 3d 425, 551 P.2d 334 (1976).

Truscott, D. (1993). The psychotherapist's duty to protect: An annotated bibliography. *Journal of Psychiatry and Law, 21,* 221–244.

Truscott, D., Evans, J., & Mansell, S. (1995). Outpatient psychotherapy with dangerous clients: A model for clinical decision making. *Professional Psychology: Research and Practice, 26,* 484–490.

VandeCreek, L., & Knapp, S. (1993). *Tarasoff and beyond: Legal and clinical considerations in the treatment of life-endangering patients.* Sarasota, FL: Professional Resource Press.

Related Topics

Chapter 69, "Anxiety/Anger Management Training"

Chapter 94, "Involuntary Psychiatric Hospitalization (Civil Commitment): Adult and Child"

109 SEQUENCE OF STEPS AND CRITICAL ASSESSMENT TARGETS OF A COMPREHENSIVE CUSTODY EVALUATION

Barry Bricklin

STEPS IN STRUCTURING AND CONDUCTING A COMPREHENSIVE CUSTODY EVALUATION

1. Seek to be a neutral, bilateral evaluator, appointed to this role by a court order that details the participants. If you cannot obtain a court order, seek a stipulation signed by both sides. If you lack access to both sides, inspect any existing divorce and/or custody order to make certain the person seeking your services has a legal right to waive confidentiality and give consent that the evaluation take place for the child in the possible absence of agreement by the other parent. If the written order is unclear, which is often the case, request that the judge who wrote it clarify the matter.

2. When you cannot secure the cooperation of all critical participants, document efforts to do so. Remember to limit conclusions to those made possible by available clinical and/or published databases and to detail in any written report and/or courtroom tes-

timony what remains to be done to bring the evaluation to the level of a bilateral, comprehensive one.

3. Make certain there is an explicit (or implicit) database in terms of which the referral question can be addressed. Many parents want custody evaluators to help overturn an existing plan on the basis of some highly subjective complaint (e.g., "He lets them go to bed dirty"). There are no databases available by means of which an evaluator can address such issues.

4. Have the involved attorneys clarify whether the change-of-circumstances issue must be addressed; that is, if there is an existing custody order, it can be modified only under certain conditions.

5. Have the attorneys clarify all the legal issues involved. This would include the "must assess" aspects demanded in a given jurisdiction (e.g., whether joint custody is presumed to be the best choice unless proven not to be).

6. Obtain signed consent forms to waive confidentiality requirements (to reveal as well as seek relevant information, as when you need to obtain parent B's reactions to allegations made by parent A) and to administer tests and gather interview, observation, and document data in regard to all participants.

7. Mail out requests for pertinent documents from schools, pediatricians, and so forth. Have the main participants send appropriate consent-to-share information forms to relevant parties.

8. Mail out self-report questionnaire forms or use them as in-person interview guides with all main participants. (See Bricklin & Elliot, 1995, and Bricklin, 1995, for the tremendously extensive data needed for a comprehensive evaluation.)

9. Arrange to have both parents or a neutral third party bring in the child for any initial psychological testing. If the parents bring the child, have them meet early in the day and spend several pleasant hours (if such is possible) with the child prior to the test session (to allow the current noncustodial parent some "fun" access to the child

prior to the testing). Do not interview the child at this session. Each parent will subtly or openly question the child regarding what he or she said, and alienating pressures on the child may needlessly increase. Conduct an observation session involving the child and both parents together on this initial day. Make sure the parents put aside expressing their hostilities during this session.

10. Arrange observation schedules that are fair and balanced. Make sure the child spends an equal amount of time with each parent prior to one-on-one observation sessions. (The existing visitation schedule may have to be modified.) Each child should be seen with both parents together and with each alone. One may desire to observe other family subsystems (e.g., all the children together with each parent). It is exceedingly important to see the parents together if you are considering true joint (physical as well as legal) custody; one should document their capacity for cooperative communication. Set up scenarios in which you can observe how a parent guides, sets limits, teaches, and so forth. In regard to all observations, pay special attention to how a child utilizes parental communications, not simply to what parents are doing and/or saying.

11. Test and further interview the parents.

12. Test and interview significant others (e.g., grandparents, live-in companions).

13. Distinguish collateral sources of information (e.g., neighbors, pediatricians) that require in-person contact from those that do not.

14. Interview the child.

15. Use the gathered data to address the critical assessment targets listed later.

16. While various legal criteria of custody dispute resolution detail what to evaluate (e.g., the Uniform Marriage and Divorce Act, Section 402, 1979), none specify how to prioritize the huge amount of information collected, especially in terms of what it means to an involved child. As of the time this was written (December 1997), there were only two published systems offering

formal models to aggregate the data gathered. Our model, A Comprehensive Custody Evaluation Standard System (ACCESS; Bricklin & Elliot, 1995), uses data-based tests designed to illuminate the range of impacts each parent is having on an involved child to prioritize the information gathered and a modified Bayesian decision model to consider evidence for which no "relevance" databases exist (e.g., a parent's health, finances, time availability). Another model is by Ackerman and Schoendorf (1992).

Without a database, the evaluator must seek convergent lines of information.

There is controversy as to whether a psychologist in the role of an expert witness in a courtroom setting should address an "ultimate issue," which in a custody case might be who should be the primary custodial parent. If in doubt, seek clarification from the presiding judge.

CRITICAL ASSESSMENT AREAS

Orientational Targets

An orientational target is one of such major importance that it must be addressed immediately and/or kept in mind at all times. For example, a severe physical impairment on the part of a child may make parental time availability a controlling factor in a given case.

1. The probability that the parents can reach an agreement on their own. (If high, one might recommend mediation instead of evaluation.)
2. Information gleaned from prior legal proceedings: isolate what has already been established and what remains to be done.
3. Pertinent legal issues: jurisdictional criteria of dispute resolution (e.g., joint custody presumption); need to address potential change of circumstances; and so forth.
4. Child's psychological, physical, developmental, educational, and cultural status. Seek to identify a child's unique needs so that the visitation plan suggested addresses them.

Assessment Targets

Assessment targets are custody-relevant areas that are assessed by a wide variety of clinical techniques, generating data from psychological tests, observations, interviews, medical and educational documents, and home visits.

Specific assessment targets are the degree to which

1. The child seems really "wanted" by each disputant (e.g., does a parent pick up a child only to drop him or her off immediately at a grandparent's home?).
2. Each parent congruently offers (and models) communications to the child so as to engender signs of positive affective responses in the child (e.g., happiness, good self-feeling).
3. Each parent congruently offers (and models) communications to the child so as to engender signs of behavioral self-sufficiency (e.g., responses mirroring competency, independence in thought and action).
4. Each parent has demonstrated caretaking skills in prior relationships.
5. Each parent can avoid episodes of neglect and physical or sexual abuse; the degree to which each parent and person to whom the child might be exposed under competing visitation arrangements can avoid episodes of *any* criminal behavior.
6. Each parent can avoid episodes of alcohol or drug use that could impair child care responsibilities.
7. Each parent can avoid episodes of distractibility and/or irritability that could impair child care responsibilities.
8. Each parent is aware of the child's daily routine, interpersonal relationships, health needs, developmental history, school history, fears, personal hygiene, communication patterns.
9. Each parent is able to recognize the critical issues involved in child care situations; the necessity of selecting adequate solutions in child care situations; the importance of communicating to the child in words and actions understandable to the child; the desirability of acknowledging the feelings

aroused in a child by various situations; the desirability of considering a child's unique past history in deciding how to respond to child care situations; the importance of considering feedback data in responding to a child.

10. Each parent is aware of his or her own weak spots and vulnerabilities in dealing with children, and the degree to which each parent has developed strategies to cope with these weaknesses.

11. Each parent shows flexibility, honesty, and supportiveness in dealing with the child's other parent and members of his or her family.

12. Each parent can provide continuity in all important phases of a child's life (e.g., extended family, school, friendships, religious affiliations).

13. Each parent can enhance the child's relationship with each sibling.

14. Each parent is available to be with the child.

15. Each parent can provide adequate babysitting, day care, and so forth.

16. Each parent can provide for the child's material needs, including on-time meals, appropriate sleeping arrangements and homework space, and so forth.

17. Each parent is able to maintain good physical health.

18. A child's consciously stated wishes (if verbalized) should be taken into account.

Data-Based Assessment Targets

A data-based assessment target refers to a target that can be addressed by tests or procedures in which the interpretations of the information yielded by the latter have been developed from a population representative of the cases to which this target is to be applied. The degree to which

1. Each parent teaches and models the skills of competency.

2. Each parent offers and models warmth, empathy, and support.

3. Each parent appropriately insists on (and models) consistency.

4. Each parent teaches and models admirable traits (e.g., trustworthiness, altruism).

5. Each parent is a source of psychological assets and/or liabilities.

6. Each child seeks to be psychologically "close" to each parent. (Bricklin & Elliot, 1995)

Note

A more comprehensive version of these materials can be found in Barry Bricklin, *The Custody Evaluation Handbook: Research-Based Solutions and Applications* (New York: Brunner/Mazel, 1995).

References & Readings

Ackerman, M. J., & Schoendorf, K. (1992). *Ackerman-Schoendorf scales for parent evaluation of custody*. Los Angeles: Western Psychological Services.

Bricklin, B. (1995). *The custody evaluation handbook: Research-based solutions and applications*. New York: Brunner/Mazel.

Bricklin, B., & Elliot, G. (1995). *ACCESS: A comprehensive custody evaluation standard system*. Furlong, PA: Village Publishing.

Brodzinsky, D. (1993). On the use and misuse of psychological testing in child custody evaluations. *Professional Psychology: Research and Practice, 24*, 213–219.

Gordon, R., & Peek, L. A. (1988). *The custody quotient*. Dallas, TX: Wilmington Institute.

Halon, R. L. (1990). The comprehensive child custody evaluation. *American Journal of Forensic Psychology, 8*(3), 19–46.

Sales, B., Manber, R., & Rohman, L. (1992). Social science research and child-custody decision making. *Applied and Preventive Psychology, 1*, 23–40.

Schutz, B. M., Dixon, E. B., Lindenberger, J. C., & Ruther, N. J. (1989). *Solomon's sword: A practical guide to conducting child custody evaluations*. San Francisco: Jossey-Bass.

Stahl, P. M. (1994). *Conducting child custody evaluations: A comprehensive guide*. Thousand Oaks, CA: Sage.

Uniform Marriage and Divorce Act (1979). In *Uniform Laws Annotated*, 9A.

110 INTERVIEWING CHILDREN WHEN SEXUAL ABUSE IS SUSPECTED

Karen J. Saywitz & Joyce S. Dorado

Mandated by law to report suspicions of child abuse, practitioners face a dilemma. There is rarely physical evidence or an adult witness to verify a child's report. Hence, professionals rely heavily on children's statements to determine protection, liability, and treatment. Although the clinical literature is replete with suggestions on child interviewing, few have been empirically tested. There is no legally sanctioned protocol free of trial ramifications. And despite the rapid expansion of scientific research, researchers have not produced a gold standard protocol that can be held out as the criterion by which all children should be interviewed. In fact, there is little expectation that a single protocol can emerge as useful for all ages, clinical conditions, levels of severity, family functioning, and agency needs, given the developmental and individual differences among children, the variations among circumstances from case to case, and the varied responsibilities of the agencies involved. There is, however, a good deal of consensus on many of the general guidelines for interviewing children. The discussion and outline that follow include interviewing suggestions that overlap substantially (not completely) with both clinical consensus and a large body of laboratory findings on child development. These suggestions will no doubt require revision as the knowledge base grows and public policies evolve.

QUESTIONS AND ANSWERS

What Are the Objectives of the Interview?

In the forensic context, interviewers' goals vary greatly. Interviews often are conducted to determine if the findings are consistent with the occurrence of abuse. At other times, interviews are conducted to plan treatment, custody arrangements, home and school placements, visitation, or family reunification. Sometimes the goal is formulating a traditional description of functioning and differential diagnosis. However, the need for questioning can also arise in the midst of therapy with an unanticipated need to assess imminent risk of danger. Before the interview begins, it behooves the interviewer to clarify the objectives for all parties and agencies involved. The objectives dictate many of the methodological choices the interviewer faces. Procedures that are legitimate for one purpose can have unintended ramifications when used for another.

What Is the Interviewer's Proper Role?

Interviewers must understand the limitations of the interview process as a means of proving that abuse occurred. Moreover, interviewers must be knowledgeable of relevant legal and ethical issues (see Myers, 1992, for an excellent discussion). Interviewers must avoid dual relationships. When an interviewer is both the treating therapist and an evaluator who provides information to the court, competing demands often can undermine confidentiality and therapeutic alliance, creating ethical dilemmas. Many professional organizations recommend that in a given case, professionals take one role and refer out for the other. Interviewers must clearly define their unique role for themselves, the child, the family, and the court. They should carefully consider invitations to expand and alter their role midstream.

Interviewers should be careful to employ methods sufficient to provide the necessary substantiation for their conclusions. Psychological tests can provide useful information but do not provide proof of abuse or of a false allegation. Abuse is an event, not a diagnosis. A reliable and valid test to verify its occurrence does not exist.

What Do Behavioral Indicators Mean?

Often children are referred for an interview because of behavioral changes, for example, nightmares or imitations of adult sexual activity. Although many reactions to trauma can accompany the onset of maltreatment (e.g., nightmares, personality change, fearfulness, anxiety), these occur more frequently in a population of nonabused children who are distressed for other reasons. No single constellation of behaviors or symptoms is pathognomonic to child abuse, and many genuinely abused children, even those with sexually transmitted diseases, may show no measurable behavioral problems (Kendall-Tacket, Williams, & Finkelhor, 1993). Behavior changes indicate that further evaluation and investigation are necessary (Lamb, 1994). Their occurrence cannot be used to determine the existence of maltreatment, nor can their absence be used to conclude that a child was not maltreated.

The one indicator that is unique to a history of sexual abuse is age-inconsistent sexual behavior and knowledge. Recent studies suggest that sexually abused children demonstrate significantly higher rates of sexualized behavior than normative and clinical (nonabused) samples (Friedrich, 1993). Still, nonabused children do engage in sexualized behaviors, albeit at a lower rate. The available research on children's knowledge of sexuality suggests that preschoolers are rarely aware of adult activities like genital, oral, and anal penetration. However, there is no definitive way to know when a child's age-inconsistent knowledge is a function of victimization or of exposure to pornography, crowded living conditions, and so forth.

Are Children's Reports Reliable?

There appears to be interdisciplinary consensus that children are "able to provide reliable and accurate accounts of events they have witnessed or experienced. Furthermore, despite frequent claims that children are uniquely susceptible to external influence, it is clear that when children are encouraged to describe their experiences without manipulation by interviewers, their accounts can be extremely informative and accurate. Such interviewing is difficult, however, and is best conducted by well trained and experienced interviewers" (Lamb, 1994, p. 1024).

The most reliable information is obtained in response to open-ended questions that elicit free narratives. School-age children can provide such accounts, and follow-up questions can be used to elaborate, clarify, and justify information provided by the child. However, children under 5 years of age depend on context cues and adult questions to help trigger recall. They rarely provide more information than is asked for. Further information is forthcoming in response to specific questions that help focus children's attention on the topic at hand, trigger recall of detail, organize retrieval efforts, and overcome reluctance and anxiety. Unfortunately, if such questions are misleading, they have the potential to distort young children's reports. When specific questions are asked, they should be formulated in as nonsuggestive a manner as possible.

What Do Children Remember?

For both adults and children, central actions and events can be recalled for long periods of time, but peripheral details may be forgotten over long delays. Children often perceive different aspects of an event to be salient and memorable. They can remember details that go unnoticed by adults and fail to report information that adults find crucial. Even genuine accounts of abuse from young children will lack detail. This is especially true when acts of abuse are repeated over long periods of time. Accurate recounts may not include unique details placing individual incidents in spatiotemporal context. Lack of detail is to be expected and cannot be used as an indicator of reliability.

Younger children tend to report the actions that occurred. Older children begin to include descriptions of participants, timing, location, conversations, and affect states. Eventually, children develop the ability to ask themselves the questions necessary to spontaneously include the who, when, where, and how of an event. Researchers have begun to develop innovative techniques to help younger children report additional information not otherwise produced spontaneously (e.g., Lamb, Sternberg, & Esplin, 1994; Saywitz, Geiselman, & Bornstein, 1992; Saywitz & Snyder, 1996). With such techniques, more complete and detailed narratives allow follow-up questions to focus on expanding information provided by children rather than adult supposition, lowering the need for leading questions.

When Should Interviews Be Conducted?

In the laboratory, the most detailed and complete accounts are found when memory is fresh. Interviews should be conducted as soon as possible. In the field, however, practical, motivational, and emotional considerations affect the timing of interviews. Repeated interviewing in and of itself is not necessarily detrimental to the quality of children's recall (Fivush & Schwarzmueller, 1995). However, when misleading questions are used in multiple interviews, they have the potential to distort young children's statements. Reducing the number of interviews is often advised. Yet disclosure of genuine abuse is sometimes a process that occurs over time rather than a singular event. When several interviews are necessary, returning to the same interviewer is optimal. It is stressful for children to start over repeatedly with unfamiliar adults.

Do Children Readily Disclose Abuse to Unfamiliar Interviewers?

Many children do report abuse when questioned carefully. Others are reluctant to discuss traumatic events with strangers. In one study,

over half of the children with sexually transmitted diseases failed to disclose abuse in a clinical interview (Lawson & Chaffin, 1992). Children typically cope with anxiety-provoking topics via avoidance. Avoiding reminders of traumatic events is one hallmark of posttraumatic stress disorder. The interviewer often has to contend with emotional reactions, including anxiety, depression, guilt, shame, ambivalence, as well as fears of the unknown, separation, retaliation, and humiliation. Taking the time to establish rapport and providing a supportive, yet unbiased, atmosphere may help offset the effects of these emotional factors.

Should Anatomically Detailed Dolls Be Used?

Although it is clear that a child's manipulation of dolls is not a test of whether abuse occurred, the appropriate use of anatomically detailed dolls remains a source of controversy (Koocher et al., 1995). In some studies, dolls help 5- to 7-year-olds provide new and accurate information that is not reported verbally. But studies of 2- to 3-year-olds suggest that dolls are contraindicated for this age range, not because they suggest sexual activities or stimulate Oedipal fantasies but because such young children have difficulty using dolls to represent the self in demonstrations (DeLoache & Marzolf, 1995). Most professional organizations recommend that dolls be used with caution and that children's play be interpreted judiciously by those well versed in the literature (see Boat & Everson, 1996, for discussion of practices).

What Factors Contribute to Children's Suggestibility?

Suggestibility is multiply determined. There is little evidence that suggestibility is a personality trait. Similarly, it is not merely a function of age, although both developmental and individual differences play a role. Very young children (3–4 years of age) are the most vulnerable to the effects of suggestive techniques. By 6–7 years of age, children's resistance to suggestion increases dramatically. By 10–11 years of age, there is another shift toward adult levels of suggestibility. Still, some 3-year-olds remain resistant in response to the most relentless interviewers, while some older children may acquiesce readily under certain conditions.

Like an adult, whether a child will acquiesce to a leading question is a function of not only the individual child but also a host of other factors related to the context, the task, and the interviewer. For example, the type of misinformation presented contributes to suggestibility effects. Children are more resistant to questions about memorable, salient, central actions than about peripheral details that are difficult to recall. Characteristics of the interviewer also influence suggestibility. An intimidating and coercive stance can increase acquiescence to misleading questions. The context of the interview environment is also influential. An accusatory context (e.g., referring to a suspect as a "bad" person who did "bad" things) can also create the potential for distortion.

Although recent studies have shown disconcerting levels of suggestibility in children, these effects are primarily found in studies of very young children, under 5 years of age. These effects are most prevalent when using presumptive questions rather than mildly leading ones. Some of the coercive techniques studied may not be typical of actual interviews in the field. As a result, some laboratory studies may exaggerate the problems of suggestibility in child abuse interviews (Lyon, 1995). Nevertheless, children's suggestibility should be of central concern for the interviewer. Interviewers must minimize conditions that increase suggestibility and maximize conditions that promote resistance, as discussed below.

Can We Detect False Allegations?

Thus far, researchers have not produced reliable and valid tests to discriminate true from false cases of abuse. Although there is some ongoing research on checklists of credibility criteria, many criteria thought to be indicative of false cases can also appear in cases of genuine abuse. For example, consistency is often relied upon as an indicator of reliability. However, inconsistency across interviews is frequent, if not expected, among young children questioned by different adults, with different questions, in different settings, even when memories are largely accurate. In one study, children telling the truth about being touched were more inconsistent than children coached to lie about being touched.

In cases of suspected abuse, interviewers strive to avoid two types of errors: failing to identify abuse that occurred and identifying abuse where it has not occurred. On a case-by-case basis, interviewers weigh the risks of false allegation and false denial, assessing the potential damage and risk associated with each type of error in a given case.

OUTLINE FOR QUESTIONING CHILDREN IN THE FORENSIC CONTEXT

Preparation and Gathering of Background Information

- Typically, interagency coordination is crucial. Verifying information by contacting collaterals is often necessary. Reports may be reviewed from schools, law enforcement agencies, pediatric records, child protective services, and prior court hearings.

Documentation

- Questions and responses should be documented verbatim whenever possible. Never paraphrase children's statements; use their words.
- Documentation of the following is optimal: description of abusive acts and alleged offender, age of child at each incident, first and most recent incidents, location(s), enticements, threats, elements of secrecy, and evidence of motive to fabricate. Also, document indicia of reliability associated with the child's statement and behavior (e.g., age-appropriate use of terms, spontaneity, hurried speech, belief that disclosure leads to punishment).
- To conduct a forensically defensible interview, it is important to document precautions taken to avoid contamination, consultation with colleagues, rationales for special techniques, and alternate hypotheses pursued.

Guidelines for Talking to Children

- Interviewers must talk to children in language they can understand. The vocabulary and grammar of the question must match the child's stage of language development. Simplify language by using shorter sentences and words with fewer syllables.

- Interviewers must avoid asking questions that require skills children have not yet mastered. Such questions are fertile grounds for misinterpretation. A child who has not yet learned to count cannot be asked how many times something happened. If he or she is, the answer must be weighed accordingly within a developmental framework.

- Interviewers must do everything in their power to minimize the potential for distortion of children's statements. Interviewers should avoid suggesting answers and should maintain an objective, neutral stance in regard to the veracity of the allegations. They should explore all possible alternative explanations.

Developmental Observation and Assessment

- Before asking about the alleged abuse, interviewers should listen to a sample of the child's speech to assess language level. Observe how many words are used in a typical sentence and how many syllables per word. Take note of the complexity of grammar and the sophistication of vocabulary. This information is used to match the form of questions to the child's language level.

- Interviewers should informally assess children's cognitive capabilities and limitations, including their understanding of systems of measurement (inches, feet, pounds, dates), basic concepts (first, always, before), colors, kinship terms, number skills, and so forth. This information is critical to matching the content of the questions to the child's level of understanding.

Setting the Context

- Before questioning children about the alleged abuse, interviewers can discuss the limits on confidentiality. Also, children need an outline of the forthcoming interview and its unique task demands, as well as education about the flow of information through the investigative and judicial process.

Introducing the Topic of Abuse

- Getting started is the most difficult part of the interview. Most authorities suggest beginning with general open-ended questions (e.g., "Is there anything you want to tell me?"; "Is there anything you want me to tell the judge?"). These are most useful when children are first prepared to understand the interviewer's purpose (e.g., to help children stay safe and healthy or to help the judge make the best plan for the whole family).

- If open-ended questions fail, decisions about the next step are made on a case-by-case basis. For example, questions about information not yet mentioned by the child may be justified when there is corroborating physical evidence to suggest that a child may be in imminent danger of further abuse and decisions of protection are paramount. In cases where alleged perpetrators have no access to the children and there is little evidence other than the children's statements, such questions may not be justified.

- If there is other evidence establishing a location of the incident(s) in question, techniques that start with remembering the setting and memorable events in that location can be useful.

- Another popular method involves an inventory of body parts, asking for each part's name, function, and a history of being touched or hurt by others in ways the child did not like.

- Inquiries about most and least favorite activities, privacy, safety, problem solving, and coping with fear can also be useful and neutral methods of eliciting relevant information.

General Format for Eliciting Event-Related Information

- If open-ended questions or other techniques are successful and produce a brief narrative, interviewers can prompt children to elaborate (e.g., "What happened next?"). The goal is for the child to tell as much as possible in his or her own words.

- Follow up with categorical "Wh" questions (e.g., "Who was there? What were they wearing?").
- It is helpful to request further justification, elaboration, and clarification of responses in the child's own words (e.g., "What makes you think so? Tell me more. I am confused.").
- Becoming progressively more specific, interviewers may proceed to specific short-answer questions ("What color was it? How tall was he? What kind of x was it?"), remembering to request elaboration of answers in the child's own words.
- Interviewers need to carefully consider the pros and cons of yes-no or multiple-choice questions to gain further elaboration of information provided in a given case. Questions containing new information must be introduced carefully, using the least leading approaches first by asking general open-ended questions that merely focus the child on a new topic. New information should not be introduced until after elaboration of the child's material is exhausted.

Limit Leading Questions

- Leading questions fall along a continuum of suggestiveness from highly leading (e.g., "Harry hurt you, didn't he?") to minimal suggestion (e.g., "Was John there? What else?"). There is consensus that the former is to be avoided. Reasonable minds differ on the value or detriment of the latter. Not all leading questions are equally dangerous. Deciding when and how to use leading questions is a case-by-case, moment-by-moment determination.
- Turn yes-no questions into "Wh" questions when possible (e.g., "Did he hit you?" becomes "What did he do with his hands?").
- Reserve specific questions until open-ended ones fail, avoiding multiple-choice questions.
- Query information from the child first and from other sources last.

Closure

- Children may need time to regain composure and ask their own questions. They can be praised for their effort and bravery but not for the content of their statements. Children need to know what will happen next to dispel misperceptions and reduce fears.

References & Readings

Boat, B., & Everson, M. (1996). Concerning practices of interviewers when using anatomical dolls in child protective services investigations. *Child Maltreatment, 1*(2), 94–104.

DeLoache, J. S., & Marzolf, D. P. (1995). The use of dolls to interview young children: Issues of symbolic representation. Special issue: Early memory. *Journal of Experimental Child Psychology, 60*(1), 155–173.

Fivush, R., & Schwarzmueller, A. (1995). Say it once again: Effects of repeated questions on children's event recall. *Journal of Traumatic Stress, 8*, 555–580.

Friedrich, W. N. (1993). Sexual victimization and sexual behavior in children: A review of recent literature. Special issue: Clinical recognition of sexually abused children. *Child Abuse and Neglect, 17*(1), 59–66.

Kendall-Tacket, K. A., Williams, L. M., & Finkelhor, D. (1993). Impact of sexual abuse on children: A review and synthesis of recent empirical studies. *Psychological Bulletin, 113*(1), 164–180.

Koocher, G. P., Goodman, G. S., White, C. S., Friedrich, W. N., Sivan, A. B., & Reynolds, C. R. (1995). Psychological science and the use of anatomically detailed dolls in child sexual-abuse assessments. *Psychological Bulletin, 118*(2), 199–222.

Lamb, M. E. (1994). The investigation of child sexual abuse: An interdisciplinary consensus statement. *Child Abuse and Neglect, 18*, 1021–1028.

Lamb, M. E., Sternberg, K. J., & Esplin, P. W. (1994). Factors influencing the reliability and validity of statements made by young victims of sexual maltreatment. *Journal of Applied Developmental Psychology, 15*, 255–280.

Lawson, L., & Chaffin, M. (1992). False negatives in sexual abuse disclosure interviews: Incidence and influence of caretaker's belief in abuse in cases of accidental abuse discovery by diagnosis of STD. *Journal of Interpersonal Violence, 7,* 532–542.

Lyon, T. (1995). False allegations and false denials in child sexual abuse. *Psychology, Public Policy, and Law, 1*(2), 429–437.

Myers, J. E. B. (1992). *Legal issues in child abuse and neglect.* Newbury Park, CA: Sage.

Saywitz, K., Geiselman, R. E., & Bornstein, G. (1992). Effects of cognitive interviewing and practice on children's recall performance. *Journal of Applied Psychology, 77,* 744–756.

Saywitz, K., & Snyder, L. (1996). Narrative elaboration: Test of a new procedure for interviewing children. *Journal of Consulting and Clinical Psychology, 64,* 1347–1357.

Related Topics

Chapter 18, "Interviewing Parents"
Chapter 54, "Child Sexual Abuse: Treatment Issues"

111 GLOSSARY OF LEGAL TERMS OF SPECIAL INTEREST IN MENTAL HEALTH PRACTICE

Gerald P. Koocher

Abandonment: Unilateral termination of a psychotherapist-patient relationship by the psychotherapist without the patient's consent at a time when the patient requires continuing mental health care and without the psychologist's making arrangements for appropriate continuation and follow-up care.

Affidavit: Sworn statement that is usually written.

Agency: Relationship between persons in which one party authorizes the other to act for or represent that party.

Allegation: Statement that a party expects to be able to prove.

Answer: A defendant's written response to a complaint.

Appeal: The process by which a decision of a lower court is brought for review before a court of higher jurisdiction. The party bringing the appeal is the *appellant.* The party against whom the appeal is taken is the *appellee.*

Assault: Intentional and unauthorized act of placing another in apprehension of immediate bodily harm.

Battery: Intentional and unauthorized touching of a person, directly or indirectly, without consent. For example, a surgical procedure performed upon a person without express or implied consent constitutes a battery.

Causation: Existence of a connection between the act or omission of the defendant and the injury suffered by the plaintiff. In a suit for negligence, the issue of causation usually requires proof that the plaintiff's harm resulted proximately from the negligence of the defendant.

Cause of action: Set of facts that give rise to a legal right to redress at law.

Civil action: Action invoking a judicial trial either at law or in equity, which is not criminal in nature.

Common law: Body of rules and principles based on Anglo-Saxon law, derived from usage and customs, and developed from court decisions based on such law. It is distinguished from statutes enacted by legislatures and all other types of law.

Complaint: The initiatory pleading on the part of the plaintiff in filing a civil lawsuit. Its purpose is to give the defendant notice of the general alleged fact constituting the cause of action.

Consent: Voluntary act by which one person agrees to allow another person to do something. *Express consent* is that directly and unequivocally given, either orally or in writing. *Implied consent* is that manifested by signs, actions, or facts or by inaction and silence, which raises a presumption that the consent has been given. It may be implied from conduct (implied-in-fact), for example, when someone rolls up his or her sleeve and extends an arm for vein puncture, or by the circumstances (implied-in-law), for example, in the case of an unconscious person in an emergency situation.

Contributory negligence or comparative negligence: Affirmative defense to a successful action against a defendant where the plaintiff's concurrent negligence contributed to his or her own injury, even though the defendant's actions may also have been responsible for the injury.

Damages: Money receivable through judicial order by a plaintiff sustaining harm, impairment, or loss to his or her person or property as the result of the accidental, intentional, or negligent act of another. *Compensatory* damages are intended to compensate the injured party for the injury sustained and nothing more. *Special damages* are the actual out-of-pocket losses incurred by the plaintiff, such as psychotherapy expenses and lost earnings, and are a part of the *compensatory damages*. *Nominal damages* are awarded to demonstrate that a legally cognizable wrong has been committed. *Punitive damages* are awarded to punish a defendant who has acted maliciously or in reckless disregard of the plaintiff's rights. (Some states do not allow punitive damages except in actions for wrongful death of the plaintiff's decedent.)

Defamation: Willful and malicious communication, either written (libel) or spoken (slander), that is false; injures the reputation or character of another.

Defendant: The person against whom a civil or criminal action is brought.

Deposition: The testimony of a witness or party taken before trial, consisting of an oral, sworn, out-of-court statement.

Directed verdict: A verdict for the defendant that a jury returns as directed by the judge, usually based on the inadequacy of the evidence presented by the plaintiff as a matter of law.

Discovery: Pretrial activities of the parties to litigation to learn of evidence known to the opposing party or various witnesses and therefore to minimize surprises at the time of trial.

Due process: Course of legal proceedings according to those rules and principles that have been established in systems of jurisprudence for the enforcement and protection of private rights. It often means simply a fair hearing.

Expert witness: Person who has special training, knowledge, skill, or experience in an area relevant to resolution of the legal dispute and who is allowed to offer an opinion as testimony in court.

Fraud: Intentionally misleading another person in a manner that causes legal injury to that person.

Guardian: Person appointed by a court to manage the affairs and protect the interests of another who is adjudged incompetent by reason of age, physical status, or mental status and is thereby unable to manage his or her own affairs.

Guardian ad litem: Person appointed as a guardian for a particular purpose, interval, or matter. Functioning in this role may involve undertaking investigations and issuing reports to the court (e.g., as in child custody matters). The court order appointing the guardian ad litem should specify the nature of the role and duties.

Hypothetical question: A form of question put to a witness, usually an expert witness, in which things which counsel claims are or will be proved are stated as a factual supposition and the witness is asked to respond, state, or explain the conclusion based on the assumptions and questions.

Immunity: In civil law, protection given certain individuals (personal immunity) or groups (institutional immunity) that may shield them from liability for certain acts or legal relationships. Ordinarily, the individual may still be sued, because immunity can be raised only as an affirmative defense to the complaint, that is, after a lawsuit has been filed.

Incompetency: Inability of a person to manage his or her own affairs because of mental or physical infirmities. If this status or condition is legally determined, a guardian will usually be appointed to manage the person's affairs.

Indemnity: Agreement whereby a party guarantees reimbursement for possible losses.

Independent contractor: Person who agrees with a party to undertake the performance of a task for which the person is not expected to be under the direct supervision or control of the party. Ordinarily this arrangement and relationship shield the party from liability for negligent acts of the independent contractor that occurred during the performance of the work. For example, a psychological consultant is an independent contractor for whose negligent acts the attending psychologist is not liable.

Informed consent: Patient's voluntary agreement to accept treatment based on an awareness of the nature of his or her disease, the material risks and benefits of the proposed treatment, the alternative treatments and risks, and the choice of no treatment at all.

Injunction: Court order commanding a person or entity to perform or to refrain from performing a certain act or otherwise be found in contempt of court.

Interrogatories: Written questions propounded by one party to another before trial as part of the pretrial discovery procedures.

Intestate: One who dies leaving no valid will.

Invasion of privacy: Violation of a person's right to be left alone and free from unwarranted publicity and intrusions.

Joint and several liability: Several persons who share the liability for the plaintiff's injury can be found liable individually or together.

Libel: Defamation of a person's reputation or character by any type of publication, including pictures or written word.

Malice: The performance of a wrongful act without just cause or excuse, with an intent to inflict an injury or under such circumstances that the law will imply an evil intent.

Malicious prosecution: Countersuit by the original defendant to collect damages that have resulted to the original defendant from a civil suit filed maliciously and without probable cause. Ordinarily, it may not be brought until the initial suit against the original defendant has been judicially decided in favor of the defendant.

Malpractice: Professional negligence. Failure to meet a professional standard or care resulting in harm to another. Failure to provide generally acceptable psychological care and treatment.

Negligence: Legal cause of action involving the failure to exercise the degree of diligence and care that a reasonably and ordinarily prudent person would exercise under the same or similar circumstances; the result is the breach of a legal duty, which proximately causes an injury which the law recognizes as deserving of compensation. The standard of care of a defendant doctor in a malpractice case is not that of the reasonable and ordinarily prudent person (such as an automobile operator) but that of the average qualified psychologist practicing in the same area of specialization or general practice as that of the defendant psychologist.

Opinion evidence: Type of evidence that a witness gives based on his or her special training or background rather than on his or her personal knowledge of the facts in issue. Generally, if the issue involves specialized knowledge, only the opinions of experts are admissible as evidence.

Pain and suffering: Element of "compensatory" nonpecuniary damages that allows recovery for the mental anguish and/or physical pain endured by the plaintiff as a result of injury for which the plaintiff seeks redress.

Perjury: Willful giving of false testimony under oath.

Plaintiff: Party who files or initiates a civil lawsuit seeking relief or compensation for damages or other legal relief.

Pleadings: The technical means by which parties to a dispute frame the issue for the court. The plaintiff's complaint is followed by the defendant's answer, and subsequent papers are filed as needed.

Prima facie case: A complaint that apparently contains all the necessary legal elements for a recognized cause of action and will suffice until contradicted and overcome by other evidence.

Prima facie evidence: Such evidence as is sufficient to establish the fact; if not rebutted, it becomes conclusive of the fact.

Probate court: Court having jurisdiction over the estates of deceased persons and persons under guardianship.

Proximate causation: Essential element in a legal cause of action for negligence; that is, it must be shown that the alleged negligent act proximately caused the injury for which legal damages are sought. The dominant and responsible cause necessarily sets other causes in operation. It represents a natural and continuous sequence, unbroken by any intervening cause.

Proximate cause: Act of commission or omission that through an uninterrupted sequence of events directly results in an injury that otherwise would not have occurred or else becomes a substantial factor in causing an injury.

Publication: Oral or written act that makes defamatory material available to persons other than the person defamed.

Reasonable medical certainty (or reasonable psychological certainty): As used in personal injury lawsuits, a term implying more than mere conjecture, possibility, consistency with, or speculation; similar to a probability, more likely than not 50.1%, but an overwhelming likelihood or scientific certainty is not required.

Release: Statement signed by a person relinquishing a right or claim against another person or persons usually for a payment or other valuable consideration.

Respondeat superior: "Let the master answer." A doctrine of vicarious or derivative liability in which the employer (master) is liable for the legal consequences of the breach of duties by an employee (servant) that the master owes to others, if the breach of duty occurs while the servant is engaged in work within the scope of his or her employment. For example, a hospital is liable for the negligent acts of a psychologist it employs if the acts occurred while the psychologist was working within his or her job description.

Settlement: Agreement made between the parties to a lawsuit, which resolves their legal dispute.

Slander: Method of oral defamation in which the false and malicious words are published by speaking or uttering in the presence of another person, other than the person slandered, which prejudices another person's reputation and character.

Standard of care: Measure against which a defendant's conduct is compared. The required standard in a professional negligence or psychological malpractice case is the standard of the average qualified practitioner in the same area of specialization.

Statute of limitations: Statutes that specify the permissible time interval between the occurrence giving rise to a civil cause of action and the actual filing of the lawsuit. Thus failure to file the suit within the prescribed time limits may become an affirmative defense to the action. In malpractice actions, a typical statute of limitations might be 3 years from the date the cause of action accrues, but the measuring time for bringing the suit does not begin to run until the party claiming injury first discovers or should reasonably have discovered that he or she was injured and that the defendant was the one who caused the injury. Further, if the injured party is a minor, additional extensions may be provided. Practitioners should check their own state laws for applicable details.

Stipulations: An agreement entered into between opposing counsel in a pending action.

Subpoena: Court document requiring a person to appear to give testimony at a deposition or in court.

Subpoena duces tecum: Subpoena that requires a person to personally bring to the court proceeding a specified document or property in his or her possession or under his or her control.

Summary judgment: Preverdict judgment rendered by the court in response to a motion by a plaintiff or a defendant, who claims that the absence of factual dispute on one or more issues eliminates those issues from further considerations.

Summons: A process served on a defendant in a civil action to secure his or her appearance in the action.

Tort: Civil wrong in which a person has breached a duty to another, which requires proof of the following: that a legal duty was owed to the plaintiff by the defendant; that the defendant breached the duty; and that the plaintiff was injured as a proximate cause of action, such as negligence.

Vicarious liability: Derivative or secondary liability predicated not upon direct fault but by virtue of the defendant's relationship to the actual wrongdoer, in which the former is presumed to hold a position of responsibility and control over the latter.

Waiver: Intentional and volitional renunciation of a known claim or right or a failure to avail oneself of a possible advantage to be derived from another's act. For example, a waiver might allow a person to testify to information that would ordinarily be protected as a privileged communication.

Wanton: Conduct that by its grossly negligent, malicious, or reckless nature evinces a disregard for the consequences or for the rights or safety of others.

Willful: Term descriptive of conduct that encompasses the continuum from intentional to reckless.

Related Topics

Chapter 93, "Dealing with Subpoenas"
Chapter 122, "Common Clinical Abbreviations and Symbols"

PART VII
Practice Management

112 ESSENTIAL FEATURES OF PROFESSIONAL LIABILITY INSURANCE

Bruce E. Bennett

THE RELATIONSHIP BETWEEN RISK AND INSURANCE

Risk management essentially involves the transfer of financial obligations from one party to another.

- A significant feature of managed care arrangements is that some of the risk for payment of claims is shifted from the payer to the provider.
- In clinical practice, a missed diagnosis or improper treatment that damages a patient may result in a malpractice suit against the practitioner.
- Fortunately, the psychologist can shift the risk for the potential financial loss to another party by purchasing professional liability insurance.

WHO NEEDS PROFESSIONAL LIABILITY COVERAGE?

Ideally, risk management would lead to the total elimination or avoidance of activities that could lead to harm, damage, or other negative consequences. In practice the risk of damage or harm to a client or other entity receiving professional services can only be minimized. Even the most ethical and skilled practitioners have been subject to malpractice suits. It is important that psychologists recognize there is always the possibility of a negative outcome associated with the delivery of professional services.

- The risk of real or perceived damage or harm is not limited to psychologists who deliver health care services.
- Psychologists working for or consulting with business or governmental agencies, industrial organizational psychologists, academic and research psychologists, and school psychologists also are vulnerable to litigation for any harm or injury that may result from their services. For example, a psychologist who uses psychological tests for employee selection, retention, or promotion may be sued for any negative outcome based on the evaluation. A student who feels ha-

rassed or is dissatisfied with a grade or evaluation may sue his or her psychology professor or supervisor.
- The delivery of psychological services is
never without risk.
- Any psychologist who provides professional
services without adequate professional liability insurance has assumed the entire risk for
any financial losses, including legal expenses
to defend the practitioner and any damages
awarded.

POLICY TYPE

Insurance is a written contract between the insured and the insurance carrier. For the premium received, the insurance carrier agrees to
both defend the psychologist (i.e., pay the legal
expenses associated with defending a claim)
and indemnify the psychologist (i.e., pay for
any cash settlements or damages awarded by a
jury, subject to any policy limitations). Two
basic types of professional liability coverage are
available: occurrence coverage and claims-made
coverage.

- *Occurrence coverage:* An occurrence policy
covers any incident that happens while the
policy is in force—regardless of when the
claim is filed. In an occurrence policy, the
claim will be covered according to the terms
and conditions of the policy in force at the
time the alleged malpractice occurred. A psychologist who terminates an occurrence policy (e.g., due to retirement, leave of absence,
or changing to another policy type or another
carrier) would be covered for any claim filed
in the future based on any alleged malpractice during the policy period. There would be
no need to purchase additional insurance.
- *Claims-made coverage:* A claims-made policy covers any incident that happens after the
policy is in force. The claim, however, must
be reported while the policy is in force. All
claims-made policies have a *retroactive date*
—the day that continuous coverage under
the claims-made policy begins. In order to be
covered under a claims-made policy, the incident must have occurred after the *retro-

active date* and the claim filed before the policy is terminated. Claims filed after coverage
ends will be covered only if the practitioner
has purchased an *extended reporting period,*
commonly referred to as "tail coverage." In a
claims-made policy, the claim will be covered
according to the terms and conditions of the
policy in force at the time the claim is filed.

FACTORS AFFECTING POLICY PRICE

The majority of psychologists today purchase
claims-made insurance with coverage levels at
$1 million/$3 million (i.e., a maximum of $1
million in coverage for a single incident and up
to $3 million aggregate coverage for all claims
filed in the year). The range of coverage available extends from $200,000/$200,000 up to $2
million/$4 million.

- The premium for an occurrence policy is
higher than the premium for a claims-made
policy because coverage in an occurrence
policy is provided for all future claims that
resulted from alleged malpractice during the
policy period. Occurrence premiums remain
relatively stable over time, changing primarily as a function of losses in the program, increases in legal expenses, and general inflation.
- Premiums for a claims-made policy are
lower during the first few years because coverage is provided only for claims filed during
the coverage period. For example, first-year
premiums need only cover the claims filed
during the first year. As the policy matures,
however, the premiums will increase.
- The differential in cost between an occurrence and a claims-made policy will generally
exceed the price of the tail coverage necessary
to terminate the claims-made policy. The
psychologist can save considerable money by
purchasing claims-made coverage.
- Independent of policy type, premiums will
increase as the policy limits increase, as the
scope of coverage increases, and as benefits
and enhancements are added to the policy.
- Premiums for practitioners are higher in
some states than in others.

- Premiums are generally lower in policies that exclude certain types of activities, services, or service settings (e.g., custody evaluations, certain types of forensic activities, and working in a correctional setting).
- Some policies include the cost of defending a malpractice suit within the policy limits, thus reducing the amount available for payment of damages by the amount of the legal expenses. When the policy limits are reduced by defense cost, the policy price should be lower. Because of the high cost of defense, however, psychologists are encouraged to avoid this restriction.

READ YOUR POLICY AND
UNDERSTAND HOW IT WORKS

It is important that psychologists be familiar with the terms, conditions, and exclusions in their professional liability policy.

Policy Conditions

Insurance policies contain a number of conditions that the insured must meet in order to keep the policy in force.

- The policy may require that the insured cooperate with the carrier in the defense of a claim against the insured and that the insured immediately report a suit or threat of suit to the carrier.
- The policy may prohibit the insured from assuming any obligations, incurring any costs, or settling any claims without the company's written consent. These and other conditions are included in the policy to protect the carrier from additional unnecessary losses that may result from the practitioner's inappropriate actions.
- If the psychologist violates policy provisions, the insurance company may attempt to restrict or deny coverage for a specific claim. If the carrier determines that the psychologist is a bad risk for coverage, the policy may be terminated or not renewed. In the extreme, the carrier may sue the psychologist to re-

scind the policy, thus avoiding all coverage for any claim.

Policy Limitations or Exclusions

In addition to specific conditions regarding coverage, professional liability insurance policies place limitations on, or exclude, coverage for specific activities.

- Psychologists' professional liability insurance generally will not cover claims against the insured for business relationships with current or former clients or as an owner or operator of a hospital or other overnight facility. These functions involve business and managerial decisions rather than the delivery of professional services. Facilities such as hospitals will need "directors and officers" and "errors and omissions" coverage.
- The policy may exclude claims of dishonest, criminal, or fraudulent acts by the psychologist. Insurance is not sold to protect dishonest or criminal behavior.
- A malpractice suit may allege that the psychologist's services and conduct were intended to injure the plaintiff. If intentional or willful acts are excluded from coverage, the carrier will issue a "reservation of rights" letter to the defendant. This letter generally provides that the carrier will defend the case but may not have responsibility to pay for any damages awarded for the intentional acts.

Special Provisions Related to Sexual Misconduct Claims

Approximately half of the losses in the psychologists' professional liability program are due to sexual misconduct claims. Small wonder, then, that many insurance carriers have imposed specific limitations on such claims. The carriers, noting that sexual misconduct is unethical and that an increasing number of states have criminalized sexual relations between therapist and patient, are not willing to assume the liability for associated losses. Put differently, the company shifts the risks associated with such behaviors to the practitioner, keeping the premiums charged to ethical practitioners lower.

- Some carriers cap the amount the policy will pay for damages.
- Other carriers will fully defend a sexual misconduct claim but exclude any payments for damages.

An insurance carrier may control for potential future losses by terminating or not renewing the policy of a psychologist who has been found guilty of sexual misconduct by a licensing board or ethics committee, even if no malpractice suit has been filed. Psychologists dropped by one carrier will have difficulty finding another carrier willing to offer coverage.

Ethical practitioners should be concerned with how the policy will respond to a frivolous claim alleging sexual misconduct.

- A policy that contains a blanket exclusion for therapist-patient sex may not even provide a legal defense. It is important that the policy defend claims alleging malpractice, regardless of the claim's merit.
- Some policies cap the carrier's liability for damages in sexual misconduct cases at a fixed dollar amount. Under these terms, if a frivolous case is settled, the psychologist may be required to pay that part of the settlement that is in excess of the capped amount.
- A policy that will not pay damages but will defend multiple claims for sexual misconduct may, in fact, provide the best protection for a frivolous claim. The legal costs of going to trial can be very high, for both plaintiff and defendant. If the case is frivolous or weak, the plaintiff, or plaintiff's attorney, may wish to negotiate a settlement. Generally, insurance carriers will attempt to settle a case for an amount that is less than the cost of defense. If such a settlement is reached, the carrier will make the payment.

CHANGING POLICY TYPES OR INSURANCE CARRIERS

When changing policy types or changing carriers, be careful to avoid gaps in coverage.

- *Occurrence coverage to claims-made coverage:* In order to avoid any gap in coverage when moving from an occurrence policy to a claims-made policy, the retroactive date of the claims-made policy must be the same as or earlier than the renewal date of the occurrence policy.
- *Claims-made coverage to occurrence coverage:* In order to avoid any gap in coverage when moving from a claims-made policy to an occurrence policy, the psychologist must (a) purchase the *extended reporting period* or the "tail coverage" for the terminated claims-made policy and (b) purchase occurrence coverage with the same renewal date as the claims-made policy. If the tail coverage is not purchased, any claims filed after the claims-made policy is terminated will not be covered. Because of the general long reporting period for psychological malpractice claims, the insured is advised to purchase the longest tail coverage possible. The cost for indefinite tail coverage is usually 175% of the final year's premium.
- *Occurrence coverage to occurrence coverage by a different carrier:* In order to avoid any gap in coverage when moving from an occurrence policy to an occurrence policy from another carrier, the policy date of the new coverage should be the same as the renewal date of the terminated coverage.
- *Claims-made coverage to claims-made coverage by a different carrier:* The psychologist who desires to change claims-made carriers has two choices. (a) Purchase the tail coverage on the old claims-made policy and purchase the first-year step rates on the new claims-made policy using the same renewal date as the old policy. If tail coverage is purchased on the old policy, the previous carrier will cover all claims generated under the terminated policy. The new carrier will cover claims resulting from alleged malpractice occurring after the effective date of the new policy. (b) Drop the old claims-made policy and purchase the new claims-made policy using the same retroactive date as the old policy. If the practitioner drops the old policy and purchases the new policy at the next step rate (e.g., if the current policy is at the

fourth-year step rate, the new policy will be at the fifth-year step rate), all claims will then be covered by the new carrier. Purchasing the new claims-made policy at the next step rate will generally be more cost-effective in the short run. In addition, if the new carrier has a better reputation for handling claims, the practitioner should follow this latter strategy.

COVERAGE FOR PSYCHOLOGISTS EMPLOYED IN GROUP SETTINGS

Psychologists employed in group or corporate practices, in schools or academic settings, or in agency settings (e.g., mental health centers, hospitals, or other government agencies) need to determine if they are adequately covered for the services they perform in that setting. If not, they should purchase their own personal liability insurance. The following issues should be considered:

- Does the employer/group (e.g., group or corporate practice, mental health center, hospital, corporation, government agency, school, academic institution) have professional liability insurance?
- Does the insurance list both the group and the employee as a named insured under the policy?
- Are the levels of coverage adequate to cover any losses against the group and its employees?
- Do all members in the group share the aggregate limit of coverage, or does each member have his or her own aggregate limit? Although managed care companies prefer to contract with group practices, many are hesitant to deal with groups in which all members share the aggregate limit of coverage.
- Does the policy require the carrier to defend and indemnify an employee who is sued for malpractice if the employee is not a named insured under the policy?
- Will the group policy cover an employee for services rendered outside the group setting?
- Do local, state, or federal statutes provide good-faith immunity for employees working in certain government settings? If a jury determines that the psychologist actually acted in bad faith (e.g., acted in a way to intentionally harm the plaintiff), the immunity statute may be voided, and the psychologist would then be responsible for payment of the damages.

- Regardless of the workplace setting, psychologists should avoid an uninsured risk. If the practitioner renders professional services outside the group setting (e.g., part-time consulting, supervision, teaching, or private practice), it is always recommended that individual coverage be in place.
- Psychologists serving as independent contractors for a group should have individual coverage. Group policies will cover a suit brought against the group as a result of the wrongdoing of an independent contractor, but they will not cover the independent contractor.
- If a group is uninsured, it is possible that the group may refuse to defend or indemnify a psychologist-employee named in a malpractice suit. The group may attempt to defend itself by asserting that the psychologist-employee acted outside the scope of the employment contract and that the group has no duty to defend the alleged wrongdoing. In effect, the group might join the plaintiff against the psychologist-employee.
- Whereas an uninsured agency or organization may have resources to defend a claim, it may be unable to pay damages. Uninsured psychologists employed by such agencies who are named as codefendants in the case may have to contribute to any damages awarded.
- If a group or agency does not have professional liability coverage, or if a psychologist-employee determines that the coverage available is not adequate, serious consideration should be given to purchasing individual coverage.

SETTLEMENT VERSUS TRIAL

Very few malpractice suits go to trial. Insurance carriers know that the most cost-effective resolution of this type of litigation is to settle the case. On the other hand, psychologists who do not believe they are guilty of malpractice usually want to go to trial, even if an appeal to the U.S. Supreme Court is necessary.

- Regardless of the "innocence" of the practitioner, there is always the possibility that a jury will award large damages. The psychologist would be personally responsible for any damages that exceed the policy limits.
- No one can predict how a jury will respond, even to a claim that has no merit.
- The plaintiff may want to settle the case if the allegations of malpractice will be difficult to prove, if the evidence indicates that the case is not clear-cut, or if the damages are not significant.
- The defendant may wish to settle to avoid painful depositions, prolonged litigation, potential embarrassment in the public arena, and the loss of income due to time away from the practice.
- The net effect is that both the plaintiff and the defendant may have strong incentives to seek a settlement rather than go to trial.
- Most frivolous cases are dismissed or settled for small amounts. Fortunately, frivolous cases are generally transparent; if so, they may not have a significant impact on the psychologist's insurability.
- On the other hand, a large settlement is often interpreted as an indication of the seriousness of the charges and resulting damages.

PSYCHOLOGIST'S ROLE IN CASE SETTLEMENT

Most insurance policies (e.g., auto or homeowner's insurance) permit the insurance company to settle a claim without the consent of the insured. One professional liability policy contained a provision that required the written consent of the insured to settle a claim; if an insured refused to settle, the carrier was forced to take the case to trial. Although this provision may seem beneficial to the insured individual,

the result is that almost all cases go to trial, at great expense to all practitioners insured under the program.

The major psychologists' professional liability policies provide a compromise between these two extreme positions. In the course of litigation, the attorneys for the plaintiff and defendant may discuss settlement as an option to trial. Even if the attorneys representing the plaintiff and defendant reach agreement on a proposed settlement, the carrier cannot settle the case without the written consent of the insured. However, if the insured refuses to accept the settlement proposal, the carrier's ultimate liability will be capped at the amount of the proposed settlement. If a jury awards damages in excess of the capped amount, the psychologist, not the carrier, will have to pay the difference.

PROFESSIONAL LIABILITY INSURANCE IS FOR THE LONG TERM

Over time, the insurance industry tends to go through market cycles, fluctuating between "soft" and "hard" markets. Competition is a key factor in a soft market: the return on investments is high, and insurance carriers attempt to increase their cash flow by offering new products or by decreasing premiums on current products to capture competitors' business. In a hard market, when the economy is not doing well, rates usually increase dramatically, and some companies may go out of business.

Malpractice suits against psychologists tend to be filed long after the alleged negligence or misconduct occurred. The premiums collected today must provide coverage for a possible claim against the psychologist in the future, sometimes years later. If current rates are too low, the carrier may not be able to provide the protection when needed. Moving from a soft to a hard market when premiums have been artificially low could result in large rate increases, modifications in the scope of coverage, or a decision by the carrier to drop this line of coverage. Psychologists are advised to view the purchase of professional liability insurance as an investment in the future. Put differently, a cheap policy may come with a high price.

ADMITTED VERSUS SURPLUS LINES CARRIERS

Most insurance carriers are "admitted," that is, approved by the state insurance commissioner to do business in that state. Admitted carriers are required to participate in consumer protection programs in the state. If an admitted carrier cannot meet its obligations to cover losses, state insurance funds may be available to protect the insureds. Some carriers, however, offer policies on a *nonadmitted* basis, commonly referred to as surplus "lines coverage." Such policies will clearly state that insured psychologists are not protected by state-authorized consumer protection programs.

- Surplus lines coverage may be available for practitioners who are otherwise uninsurable because of a history of previous claims. Such policies are usually very expensive and may restrict available limits of liability.
- Other carriers may offer inexpensive surplus lines coverage in an attempt to capture premium dollars. Whenever possible, psychologists should seek coverage from admitted carriers.

WHERE TO PURCHASE PROFESSIONAL LIABILITY INSURANCE

The diligent psychologist will approach the subject of professional liability insurance as an important business decision, both to protect the psychologist's assets and to provide the comfort and security needed to function in a professional capacity.

A number of carriers offer this type of coverage. Policy features, strength and stability of the carrier, price, special enhancements, and representation of the psychologist's interests with the carrier are equally important aspects of any purchasing decision. The majority of practitioners purchase professional liability insurance from programs endorsed or sponsored by their national professional association. The American Psychological Association Insurance Trust has endorsed or sponsored comprehensive and cost-effective professional liability insurance for more than 20 years, during both soft and hard markets, including times when some carriers dropped psychology as a line of coverage. The Trust-sponsored professional liability insurance program was developed by psychologists for psychologists. The Trust serves as an ombudsperson for practitioners, representing their interests on all aspects of coverage and price. Psychologists must be members of the American Psychological Association to participate in the Trust-sponsored professional liability program.

References & Readings

Koocher, G. P., & Keith-Spiegel, P. C. (1998). *Ethics in psychology: Professional standards and cases* (2nd ed.). New York: Oxford University Press.

Woody, R. H. (1988). *Protecting your mental health practice: How to minimize legal and financial risk*. San Francisco: Jossey-Bass.

Wright, R. H. (1981). Psychologists and professional liability (malpractice) insurance: A retrospective review. *American Psychologist, 36*, 1485–1493.

Related Topics

113 MAKING SUCCESSFUL REFERRALS

Brian J. O'Leary & John C. Norcross

A referral typically occurs when a clinician has encountered some sort of an impasse with a client and seeks the assistance of a colleague in consulting or taking over the assessment or treatment for that client. The following are potential indications for referrals (Chasten, 1991; Wicks, Parsons, & Capps, 1993):

1. When the client's problems exceed the therapist's skill or experience
2. When the potential client is a friend, family member, or close associate
3. When the therapist's countertransference is interfering with the course of treatment
4. When the client is resisting the therapist and there is no end in sight
5. When the therapeutic alliance is missing or irretrievably ruptured
6. When therapy reaches an impasse and no progress is being made
7. When there is a sexual attraction on the therapist's part
8. When the therapist discovers midtreatment that he or she lacks the necessary skills required to continue treatment
9. When the clinician is relocating to another geographic area or discontinuing work at the current site
10. When the client is relocating
11. When the client requests a second or independent opinion
12. When the client needs adjunctive services (e.g., medication or neurological evaluation)
13. When a clinician-in-training completes a practicum or rotation at the current site

The following section provides basic guidelines, compiled from the literature, on making successful referrals.

- *Establish a referral network:* The referral network is a compilation of social service agencies, mental health clinicians, medical specialists, lawyers, hospitals, and specialty clinics dealing with various disorders (Choca, 1980). The greater the network in which a clinician is involved and the more professionals he or she knows, the more accurate and focused the referral can be. The upshot is for psychologists to familiarize themselves with local practitioners, agencies, and referral sources.
- *Avoid referring too quickly:* The referral process can be lengthy and cumbersome for the client. This is not to say that referrals should be avoided but rather that the clinician should analyze his or her own efforts and motives to determine whether a consultation is indicated or a referral is required.
- *Time the referral carefully:* As in psychotherapy, the timing of the referral can be crucial to its success. On the one hand, apprising the client of an impending referral too early may inhibit further progress and dissuade him or her from participating fully in the current treatment. On the other hand, apprising the client of a referral too late may lead to "unfinished business" in the present relationship that carries over into the next treatment (Chang, 1977; Wapner, Klein, Friedlander, & Andrasik, 1986). The clinical implication is to tailor the timing of the referral to the individual client.
- *Explain the purpose of the referral:* The clinician should explain the value of the referral in a neutral consultative tone, clarifying the rationale, the potential benefits, and the expertise of the new clinician (Wicks et al., 1993). This explanation and experience

524

may offset the tendency of clients without previous therapy to discontinue treatment once referred or transferred to another clinician. A study conducted by Wapner et al. (1986) found that 76% of clients with prior therapy experience completed the referral, as opposed to 54% of those with no prior therapy experience.

- *Inquire about potential barriers:* Ask the client if he or she has any questions or foresees any difficulties in following through with the referral. If so, then answer the questions and try to remove any obstacles that may hinder the client's acceptance of the recommended action (Hester & Miller, 1995). For example, when referring a client to a neurologist, explain the typical diagnostic or treatment methods, the goals to be accomplished, and the method by which the results will be communicated back to the referrer.

- *Provide several names or choices if available:* The clinician should provide the client with information on the types of professionals being considered. Along with their specialties, names, locations, and the connection between the client and the types of therapies being considered, it is also wise to explain how or why the name was selected and to disclose any relationship between the two parties, for example, friends, relatives, or business partners.

- *Attend to the client's state of mind:* When the idea of the referral is first suggested, observe and monitor the client's affective states. Clients will exhibit a variety of emotional reactions. If negative reactions are encountered, deal with them immediately (Wicks et al., 1993). If clients fear they are being abandoned, remind them that the therapist is not discarding them but rather seeking assistance in advancing their best interest. Help clients understand exactly what the referral process is in order to reduce their separation anxiety, and trace their current feelings of abandonment and/or hopelessness to contemporary or historical episodes in their lives.

- *Avoid making leading judgments:* Avoid using words such as *better, worse, good,* or *bad* when discussing the referral with the client. The client needs to hear the therapist discuss the referral as a positive and consistent process (Chasten, 1991).

- *Do not oversell the specialist:* When the referring clinician is talking about the referral person, there is a tendency to overemphasize the specialist's positive qualities. While this is a sound practice and the client has a right to know who he or she may be consulting, accentuating the specialist's character may lead the client to place the specialist on a pedestal, thereby impeding the development of the client-counselor relationship. In addition, overselling may lead to client anger if the consultation is unsuccessful.

- *Encourage a grieving client to ventilate:* Occasionally clients become upset when learning they are being referred to another person and that their relationship with the original therapist will be terminated. If this happens, avoid telling them that they will "get over it" when they begin to develop positive views about their new therapist. Remember the therapeutic relationship is unique and special to the client, and an appropriate period of mourning, anger, and termination may be necessary.

- *Avoid dismissing the client:* Of all the mistakes that clinicians make during a referral, this may be the most frequent (Chasten, 1991). The intent of the clinician is to leave the responsibility for the referral in the client's hands. However, a referral is more than handing a client a list of names and saying goodbye. A referral is a process of transferring the responsibility for treatment to a colleague who is qualified to handle the client's problems.

- *Make a good match:* Creating a good referral match facilitates adherence to the therapeutic process. Questions to ask when considering a referral (Chasten, 1991) include the following:

  1. Does the client's problem fall in a specialty area (substance abuse, traumatic stress, marital and family therapy, neuropsychology)?
  2. Does the therapist possess the appropriate skills for working with this disorder or population?

3. What is the therapist's past success rate with similar clients or problems?
4. Is there a more qualified therapist in the area?
5. Are there gender, racial, religious, or cultural factors to be considered?
6. What are the financial resources of the client being referred?
7. Will insurance cover the cost of the consultation or the new provider?

• *Articulate the referral relationship:* Explain the desirable type of referral relationship. There are at least three types (Andolfi & Haber, 1994). In the first, the referrer remains in charge of the treatment and the specialist provides adjunctive or additional services. For example, a family therapist may telephone a physician to request medication for one of the family members, or an individual therapist may recommend a local self-help group. In the second type of referral relationship, the referrer is experiencing some difficulty progressing with a client and desires the assistance of another clinician to reestablish the therapeutic process. Here, the referrer opts to take a nonintrusive position, meaning that the referring clinician is informed of the progress in the current therapy. However, the referrer does not participate until the referral goal has been achieved, at which time the client returns to the original clinician for the remainder of the treatment. In the third type of referral, a client is sent out to another clinician permanently so that he or she will receive the specialized or alternative treatment.

• *Assist the client in making the appointment:* The clinician should take the requisite steps to get the client to the proper person or facility. Consider the following steps (Chasten, 1991): The referring therapist contacts specialists to determine if they are accepting referrals; returns with the information and shares it with the client to make a decision; provides the names, phone numbers, and addresses; and possibly makes the appointment for the client with the desired specialist. The latter seems to be the most effective way of ensuring adherence, but it also poses the risks of the therapist dominating the process and of casting the client into a submissive role.

• *Finalize the referral, and attend to termination of the present relationship:* If the present relationship is a brief consultation, such as a brief evaluation for an employee assistance program, termination may be relatively simple and direct. If, however, the treatment has been of longer duration, the therapist should allow sufficient time to properly terminate the relationship and, if possible, leave the client feeling positive about the referral.

• *Follow up with the people:* The referrer might follow up on the referral for several reasons: first, to ensure that the client connected to the referral person or agency; second, to assess the outcome of the referral itself and to determine if adjustments need to be made in this case; and third, to evaluate the referral from both the therapist's and the client's point of view in an effort to discern if the source should be used again in the future (Chasten, 1991).

References & Readings

Andolfi, M., & Haber, R. (Eds.) (1994). *Please help me with this family: Using consultants as resources in family therapy.* New York: Brunner/Mazel.

Chang, A. F. (1977). The handling of therapists' premature termination in psychotherapy. *Psychology, 14,* 18–23.

Chasten, S. E. (1991). *Making effective referrals: The therapeutic process.* New York: Gardner.

Choca, J. (1980). *Manual for clinical psychology practicums.* New York: Brunner/Mazel.

Hester, R. K., & Miller, W. R. (Eds.) (1995). *Handbook of alcoholism treatment approaches: Effective alternatives* (2nd ed.). Boston: Allyn and Bacon.

Sherman, R., Shumsky, A., & Rountree, Y. B. (1994). *Enlarging the therapeutic circle: The therapist's guide to collaborative therapy with families and schools.* New York: Brunner/Mazel.

Wapner, J. H., Klein, J. G., Friedlander, M. L., & Andrasik, F. J. (1986). Transferring psychotherapy clients: State of the art. *Professional Psychology: Research and Practice, 17,* 492–496.

Wicks, R. J., Parsons, R. D., & Capps, D. (Eds.) (1993). *Clinical handbook of pastoral counseling* (Vol. 1). New York: Integration.

Related Topics

Chapter 82, "Refusal Skills Training"

114 CONTRACTING WITH MANAGED CARE ORGANIZATIONS

Stuart L. Koman & Eric A. Harris

Managed care is the general term used to describe organizations and practices of organizations whose primary raison d'être and motivation is controlling the cost of health care. Typically, a managed care organization (MCO) receives a standard monthly fee from a payer, usually an employer or government entity, to purchase a defined set of health care services (benefit plan) for each individual (covered life) utilizing the plan. Mental health or behavioral health services can be included as part of a comprehensive package of medical services or *carved-in*, as is the case with health maintenance organizations (HMOs) like Kaiser-Permanente Health Plan or Harvard Community Health Plan, or contracted for separately, or *carved-out*, to a managed behavioral health provider such as Value Behavioral Health or Merit Behavioral Health. Regardless of type, most MCOs seek maximum cost efficiency and utilize some variation of the following techniques to manage cost and quality of care.

- *Utilization management and utilization review:* This is the general practice of closely scrutinizing the manner in which decisions are made about when, where, and how many of each type of service is used in responding to the needs presented by a participant in the health plan. Decisions for care are judged against an organizationally defined standard known as *medical necessity*. Many MCOs require that services be *preauthorized* and periodically reviewed (*concurrent review*) by company-employed *case managers* who are clinicians specially trained in the company's criteria for medical necessity and treatment preferences.
- *Selective contracting:* This is the practice of defining a group of providers to perform re-

quired services. The *provider network*, as it is often called, is chosen from a pool of potential providers by an application process that weighs various company preferences in making selections. These preferences may include the type of degree and specialization, sex, age, geographic location, availability in the evenings and on weekends, and other characteristics about the manner in which the provider practices, especially as they may relate to the cost of care.
- *Favorable payment structure:* This is the practice of negotiating price discounts and/or passing along *financial risk* to providers in return for directing referrals to them. Risk-based contracting comes in many forms but always provides incentives for the clinician to complete the treatment in the fewest sessions or the least costly manner.

KEY ISSUES IN DECIDING TO JOIN
A MANAGED CARE PANEL

The following questions and issues should be reviewed when considering potential relationships with MCOs.

Business Issues

- Is the company financially stable?
- What is the proposal for payment of professional services, and how long will it take to be paid? What has been the experience of other clinicians in terms of the reliability of the MCO's claims payment system?
- What is the company's volume of business in your geographic area, and what level of referrals are you likely to receive? What types of patients will be referred?

Professional Practice Issues

- What is the philosophy or general approach to providing care, and does it fit your clinical model?
- How is care managed, and what are the credentials of the individuals employed by the company to make decisions about the treatment?
- What has been the experience of other providers in the area in terms of satisfaction with the care management process?

Legal Issues

- Is the provider contract fair to both parties or seemingly one-sided?
- Does the contract contain any provisions that are particularly problematic?

Administrative Issues

- What are the requirements for authorizing treatment both at the outset and as treatment proceeds? What medical records documentation is required?
- What billing documentation is required?
- Are there any special requirements such as outcome evaluations?
- Are the case managers and claims personnel available in a reasonable time frame to discuss clinical or administrative problems? What has been the experience of other providers in dealing with problems?
- What is the process for appealing decisions regarding authorization and/or payment of care?

REVIEWING MCO CONTRACTS

Many MCOs would have providers believe that the contract document sent for review is inviolate, immutable, and unchangeable. Resist the temptation to go quietly along, and be sure to review the contract carefully. Be especially careful if the contract seems one-sided; look for sections that clearly spell out the obligations of the company to pay promptly, to notify you of changes in the benefit plan, to authorize treatment in a timely manner, to publish criteria for treatment decisions, and to process appeals and grievances. Managed care contracts are written by company attorneys who are paid to look out for the company's interest. The following is a list of potentially problematic clauses to watch out for.

- *Indemnification:* In one form or another, indemnification agreements state that if the managed care company is sued because of the provider's activities, the practitioner agrees to reimburse the company for its expenses and for any damages assessed against it. This clause can be drafted in many ways, but in any case, since the responsibility is created by the provider's agreement to the contract, not by the provider's professional activities, malpractice insurance companies can refuse to provide coverage of any expenses that result from this provision. Check with your insurance carrier before signing these agreements, and attempt to have the provision removed if the insurance company indicates that it will not cover actions resulting from this clause. Providers should also insist that indemnification responsibility is mutual and that the managed care company agrees to indemnify the practitioner in the same manner that the managed care company is proposing to be indemnified.
- *No legal action:* This provision eliminates your right to bring action against the managed care company for any reason.
- *Exclusive dealing:* This provision restricts you from working with patients who have a different insurance plan. You should consider agreeing to this only if the managed care company has guaranteed very high volume and payment, and then only if you can cancel the contract on short notice should serious problems arise.
- *Most favored nation:* This provision guarantees that the managed care company will always have charges equal to or lower than any other company you contract with now or in the future. You can consider an arrangement like this if the volume is high, the administration relatively moderate, and the payment history good, but only if you have the right to cancel should circumstances change.

- *No-cause terminations:* This provision allows the managed care company to eliminate you from its provider panel for no reason. It is fairly standard language at this point and is currently being challenged in court by a group of practitioners with support from the American Psychological Association. Their argument is that the managed care companies are using this clause to eliminate practitioners who do not conform to their rules or have publicly spoken out against the company and that this is really a "for-cause" termination, which the practitioner has the right to appeal. By using the "no-cause" provision, the providers argue, the company eliminates the individual's right to due process.
- *Nondisparagement:* This "gag" clause prohibits you from publicly speaking out directly against the company in any way.
- *Agreement not to bill for covered services except for copayments and deductibles:* This provision prohibits you from collecting reimbursement from patients to augment the managed care company's payment; it also prohibits you from billing for services that you and the client agree are indicated but which the managed care company has not authorized.
- *Agreement not to provide services when benefits are exhausted:* In some cases, this provision may put you at risk for client abandonment and leave you vulnerable to both legal and ethical challenge.
- *Agreement to abide by utilization review processes and decisions:* This provision binds you contractually to the company's decisions regarding the treatment of your patients regardless of your professional evaluation of the patient and situation at any given time. In fact, you are legally and ethically required to act in the best interest of the patient at all times and would be at severe risk if you followed the company's decision despite your own assessment and some tragic consequence ensued.
- *Agreement to abide by contract provisions which have not yet been developed or published:* This practice is common in situations where the managed care company is under pressure to put a network together.

As always, the best advice is to consult an attorney, preferably one who specializes in health care, if you are uncomfortable with any contract provisions you encounter. Other sources of support can often be found through your professional liability insurance carrier, your state professional association, and the legal and regulatory office of the Practice Directorate of the American Psychological Association.

ATTRACTING MANAGED CARE CONTRACTS

MCOs seek contracts with competent clinicians who will work within their management systems with little complaint and will price or accept reimbursement for clinical services at a low rate. In many instances, however, reimbursement is fixed by the MCO in accordance with the clinician's training and the type of service being delivered. When this is the case, network selection is based on a variety of other factors that are important to the MCO and/or the consumer. Generally, MCOs look for the following attributes:

- Use of short-term and group treatment modalities because this helps to contain cost by limiting the length of the treatment episode or by utilizing less expensive units of service
- Ease of access as demonstrated by 24-hour availability, night and weekend services, reliable phone answering, and responsive emergency coverage
- Wide range of clinical expertise often found in multidisciplinary groups so that consumers and the MCO itself can conveniently access different services that are required for treatment of an individual or his or her family
- Professional affiliations with other health care providers, especially primary care physicians who are responsible for medical management of individuals in HMOs.
- Unambiguous professional credentials, including clinical licensure at the independent practice level, absence of professional liability claims, listing in a national practitioner data bank, and a well-organized clinical record-keeping system

- Demonstrated expertise in a specific clinical specialty area
- Demonstrated value of services provided by outcome evaluation data

NEGOTIATING WITH MCOS

In general, negotiating leverage and the ability to achieve a successful outcome for your practice revolve around the perception of "who needs who more." Factors that enhance your negotiating position are often related to simple supply and demand. For instance, a practice in a rural community where few clinicians are available is in a good negotiating position. This is especially true if the MCO operates under a contract with the primary payer, a governmental or business entity, which specifies performance standards for geographic access to care. Similarly, a practice known for its highly specialized services is in a good position whether or not it is in an area where there is an abundance of practitioners because it offers a unique service that specifically addresses the needs of a particular group of consumers. Most MCOs will not want to be viewed as denying legitimate specialized care to their subscribers. These kinds of complaints often find their way back to the payer or, even worse, to the media. Professional and political affiliations can also enhance your negotiating leverage. If you are the preferred provider of mental health services for an important group of physicians in the area, the MCO will probably want to make sure that you are in the network. If you find yourself in a less than ideal position, you can do a number of things to improve your contract possibilities: lower your price, increase the value of your offer by providing more service, and provide evidence of superior performance through outcome data or case example.

References & Readings

Feldman, J., & Fitzpatrick, R. (1992). *Managed mental health care*. Washington, DC: American Psychiatric Press.

Giles, T. R. (1993). *Managed mental health care*. Boston: Allyn and Bacon.

Minkoff, K., & Pollack, D. (1997). *Managed mental health care in the public sector*. Amsterdam: Harwood Academic Publishers.

Oss, M., & Smith, A. (1994). *Behavioral health practice management audit workbook*. Gettysburg, PA: Behavioral Health Industry News.

Psychotherapy Finances (1993). *Managed care handbook*. Hawthorne, NJ: Ridgewood Financial Institute.

Related Topics

115 ACCEPTING LEGAL REFERRALS

Geoffrey R. McKee

Forensic psychology is the application of the theories, methods, and research of psychology to questions of law. Attorneys seek the assistance of psychologists to develop expert opinion to support their arguments before or during trials or hearings involving clients they represent. The purpose of this chapter is to highlight questions you can employ to decide whether to accept such cases and to specify the scope and content of your consultation to the attorney. The competent attorney always anticipates that the case will go to trial. Thus he or she seeks a psychologist who will qualify as an expert witness to provide either "opinion testimony" based on direct contact with the attorney's client or "dissertation testimony" (Myers, 1992) based on the psychologist's research, which the jury then applies to the facts of the case. This chapter also offers questions you should ask to help you decide whether the attorney is seeking professional consultation or a "hired gun."

1. *What is (are) the legal issue(s) in the case?* This question clarifies the type of case (civil, criminal, domestic, administrative) being referred, the issues the attorney considers to be most important, and what general area(s) of expertise are being sought. Any legal case may have a host of issues to be litigated (e.g., competence to confess, competence to stand trial, criminal responsibility, and capital mitigation in a murder case). An early stage in the legal process is negotiation of the issues to be argued. For example, in a personal injury case, the plaintiff files a *complaint* of facts or allegations to which the defendant agrees or denies in an *answer*. The resulting items of disagreement, some of which may require the expertise of a psychologist, become the issues for litigation.

2. *What case facts support your side? The adverse side?* A competent attorney will present the case succinctly and understand both sides of the litigation. This question identifies ill-prepared lawyers seeking only a "hired gun" and also illuminates potential biases or prejudices the attorney may have (e.g., that all plaintiffs malinger illness for disability). For example, an attorney representing a documented alcoholic and domestically abusive husband might request consultation regarding child custody. Knowing these facts, you might decline the case, despite the attorney's protestations that the client's problems are "irrelevant" to his capacity as a parent.

3. *What specific questions would you like me to answer?* This inquiry identifies the parameters of your "contract" with the attorney, affirms the basis for his or her client's informed consent to your services, clarifies the foundation (sources of data) necessary for the formation of your professional opinion(s), and delimits the scope of your expert testimony, if subpoenaed. For example, if you have completed an evaluation only of a client's competence to stand trial, it would be unethical, beyond the scope of your agreement with the attorney, and beyond the client's consent to employ the same set of data to testify about the client's parenting capacity or his or her mental state at the time of the alleged offense.

Once you have a basic understanding of the facts and issues of the case, you should ask Questions 4 and 5 of yourself. Because public testimony might occur in any legal case, thus placing the attorney's client in jeopardy, you should be conservative when answering these questions and realize the adverse side may have retained a psychologist to assist with cross-examination of your credentials to impeach your testimony.

4. *Can the attorney's questions be answered by current psychological knowledge and research?* While psychology can be of great assistance to the court's and/or jury's decision making by providing information about the parties in litigation, many issues exceed the competence of our methods and practice. Clearly, psychology cannot determine who is guilty of a crime (absent a competent confession) or who is lying. The admissibility requirements of *Daubert v. Merrell Dow Pharmaceuticals, Inc.* (1993; see especially Marlowe, 1995) now mandate methods with higher reliability and validity than the "frequency of use" standards of *Frye v. United States* (1923). Psychological tests cannot validly identify the psychometric "profile" of criminal offenders (see, generally, Murphy & Peters, 1992), nor can our procedures predict events (e.g., future dangerousness) with more than chance likelihood (Monahan & Steadman, 1994).

5. *Am I competent on the basis of my training, experience, and licensure to qualify as an expert witness in court to answer the referral* *questions?* Numerous legal decisions (e.g., *Ibn-Tamas v. United States*, 1979) have affirmed that a judge's determination of a witness's qualification as an expert is not dependent solely on professional title (e.g., psychologist, psychiatrist). Rather, the relevance of the witness's training and work experience to the issues litigated is of paramount importance. Both the American Psychological Association's "Ethical Principles of Psychologists and Code of Conduct" (1.04; 1992) and the "Specialty Guidelines for Forensic Psychologists" (III; 1991) suggest the parameters for competence when engaging in clinical or forensic practice. It would be tragic for the client, devastating to the attorney, embarrassing to you, and damaging to the profession's credibility if your expert testimony was rendered inadmissible because you had clearly overstated your credentials.

If you answered "Yes" to Questions 4 and 5, proceed to the items below.

6. *Will my consultation (evaluation, etc.) be privileged as your work product?* Work product is any evidence a lawyer develops that is prohibited from disclosure under attorney-client privilege, a more protective standard than professional confidentiality. This question clarifies the conditions under which your service to the attorney (and his or her client) might be shared with the adverse attorney or the court and the client's informed consent regarding release of information (including your courtroom testimony). Each state has its own set of criminal procedure and civil procedure rules governing discovery. This question addresses a fundamental legal issue that requires an answer from the referring attorney.

7. *When is this case likely to go to trial or hearing?* The well-prepared attorney anticipates the use of experts well in advance of trial and realizes that thorough psychological consultation requires time to review documents, evaluate the client over more than one session, conduct collateral interviews, and suggest additional consultations beyond the expertise of the retained psychologist. Accepting last-minute consultations may leave you vulnerable to cross-examination questions of practicing "curbside psychology," the accusation of superficial preparation of expert opinions. In cases where

notice is short, you may wish to accept the case on the condition that the attorney will seek a continuance for time to complete a full examination. Midtrial consultations should be avoided unless your testimony will be of "dissertation" form, explaining your published research for the court's consideration of a particular issue (e.g., a victim's delayed reporting secondary to rape trauma syndrome).

8. *What documents do you have pertinent to your client? What records does the other side have, and when will they be disclosed?* Because of the high rates of malingering and distortion by clients in criminal, civil, domestic, and administrative litigation, the psychologist cannot rely solely on the statements of the plaintiff or defendant. The "Guidelines" (VI.B) mandate corroboration by other sources as fundamental to the formation of your expert opinions. Ask what records the attorney has for your review; at this point, the attorney's description of the case should suggest other documents needed to complete your consultation. Place the burden of obtaining the documents on the lawyer—subpoenas short-circuit institutional resistance to disclosure of records and also allow the attorney to overcome any discovery rules that you, as a nonlawyer, would not necessarily know.

9. *Who will be responsible for payment of my time? How shall we arrange my retainer?* Financial matters need to be resolved prior to your acceptance of the case. You should clearly describe your fee structure (per hour, per day, etc.) and what will constitute billable hours of your work (e.g., travel time, different fees for records review or courtroom testimony). Many experienced forensic psychologists have clearly written contracts that are signed by all relevant parties prior to formal case acceptance (for examples, see Pope, Butcher, & Seelen, 1993). Agreements for retainers, if requested, should also be made at this point and precede actual work on the case. Avoid cases where contingency fees are offered, since this practice is patently unethical ("Guidelines," IV.B). If courtroom testimony or deposition is anticipated, request that payment for your time be held in the attorney's escrow account prior to your court appearance so that the content of your testimony will not be influenced by the anticipation of fee payment.

10. *In what form would you like my report?* The task of the forensic psychologist is to form expert opinion(s), using professionally accepted methods, about case-relevant psycholegal issue(s) as defined by legal standards from statutory or case law. When retained by counsel, the forensic psychologist is not necessarily required to prepare a written report; indeed, the psychologist is encouraged to limit unnecessary disclosure of material about the client ("Guidelines," V.C). Elsewhere (McKee, 1995), I have suggested ways to avoid misuse of reports in legal contexts. Report content may be influenced by discovery rules, which may vary among criminal, civil, domestic, and administrative procedures, as well as from jurisdiction to jurisdiction. Because the attorney is your client, he or she has the right to decide the format of your report and is also more familiar with the discovery rules governing work product (see Question 6). Although the attorney may govern the form of report, he or she does not control the content; thus, when a report is drafted, the attorney should be forewarned that both supportive and adverse data will be included. Avoid attorneys who wish to control the content of your opinions or want you to alter your opinions to support their argument.

11. *What if my opinion does not support your side?* This is the acid test for the attorney's integrity in seeking your consultation. Lawyers have a duty to explore mental health issues, if such facts are known or available, in the course of case preparation. Attorneys have been cited for ineffective assistance of counsel for failing to explore mental health issues (*Baxter v. Thomas*, 1995). Resolution of this issue at this point will minimize conflict later if your data suggest an opinion other than what the attorney wished. Remember that when you are retained, you have a duty to advocate your opinion, not the attorney's position. If an attorney decides not to retain you after this question, that is the attorney's choice and may likely increase his or her estimation of you. Having a reputation as a psychologist who "calls 'em as you see 'em" will significantly enhance your credibility during testimony and also deflect cross-examination aspersions that you are a "hired gun." Indeed, balanced opinions are not reflected in the number of times you testify for one side or the other but rather in the percentage of cases in which you do not testify because your opinion is adverse to the attorney who retained you.

References & Readings

American Psychological Association (1992). Ethical principles of psychologists and code of conduct. *American Psychologist, 47*, 1597–1611.

Baxter v. Thomas, 45 F.3d 1501 (1995).

Committee on Ethical Guidelines for Forensic Psychologists (1991). Specialty guidelines for forensic psychologists. *Law and Human Behavior, 15*, 655–665.

Daubert v. Merrell Dow Pharmaceuticals, Inc., 727 F. Supp. 570 (S.D. Cal. 1989), remanded 113 S.Ct. 2786 (1993).

Frye v. United States, 293 F. 1013 (D.C. Cir. 1923).

Ibn-Tamas v. United States, 407 A.2d 606 (1979).

Marlowe, D. B. (1995). A hybrid decision framework for evaluating psychometric evidence. *Behavioral Sciences and the Law, 13*, 207–228.

McKee, G. R. (1995). Insanity and adultery: Forensic implications of a divorce case. *Psychological Reports, 76*, 427–434.

Monahan, J., & Steadman, H. J. (Eds.) (1994). *Violence and mental disorder: Developments in risk assessment.* Chicago: University of Chicago Press.

Murphy, W. D., & Peters, J. M. (1992). Profiling child sexual abusers. *Criminal Justice and Behavior, 19*, 24–37.

Myers, J. E. B. (1992). *Legal issues in child abuse and neglect.* Newbury Park, CA: Sage.

Pope, K. S., Butcher, J. N., & Seelen, J. (1993). *The MMPI, MMPI-2, and MMPI-A in court.* Washington, DC: American Psychological Association.

Related Topics

116 ESTABLISHING A CONSULTATION AGREEMENT

Len Sperry

As health care delivery continues to evolve, mental health clinicians are likely to become more involved as consultants to various organizations and agencies. This chapter overviews considerations the clinician may face in establishing an agreement for consultation services. As a backdrop for this overview, the focus and types of consultation are briefly discussed.

1. *The focus of consultation:* Caplan (1970) describes a classification system based on the focus of consultation. Consultation can be focused in four ways:

- *Client-centered consultation:* The goal is to aid the client, such as executive coaching.
- *Consultee-centered case consultation:* The goal is to enhance the consultee's skills; for example, a psychologist meets with a group of line supervisors to study their understanding of and recognition of substance dependence in the workplace.
- *Program-centered administrative consultation:* The goal is to diagnose and resolve the consultee's difficulty in dealing with administrative problems. A common example is assisting EAP personnel to develop a corporation-wide depression awareness program.
- *Consultee-centered administrative consultation:* The goal is to diagnose and resolve the consultee's difficulty in dealing with administrative problems, such as functioning as a consultation-liaison psychologist to a weight management program at a community hospital.

2. *The types of intervention:* It is useful to distinguish two types of consultant interventions: organizational interventions and clinical-organizational interventions (in contrast to clinical interventions). Traditionally, clinicians were thought to provide clinical interventions such as individual, family, marital, or group therapy, whereas organizational consultants were more likely to provide individual, team, and organizational interventions such as executive coaching, team building, and reengineering. Whereas traditional forms of organizational consultation require considerable skill and experience, there are a number of clinical-organizational interventions that mental health clinicians can competently provide corporations, schools, health care agencies and organizations, community groups, and government agencies. *Corporate Therapy and Consulting* (Sperry, 1996) provides a detailed description of 10 common organizational interventions and 14 clinical-organizational interventions. The following is a listing of the clinical-organizational interventions:

- Hiring, discipline, and termination consultation
- Work-focused psychotherapy
- Outplacement counseling and consultation
- Stress-disability and fitness-for-duty consultation
- Dual-career couples counseling and consultation
- Conflict resolution consultation with work teams
- Conflict resolution in a family business
- Crisis intervention consultation
- Consulting on resistance to planned change efforts
- Merger syndrome consultation
- Downsizing syndrome consultation
- Treatment outcomes consultation

- Mental health policy consultation
- Violence prevention consultation

3. *Assessing the request for consultation:* Irrespective of the type of consultation offered, the process begins with a request from a prospective client. These requests can include a workshop on stress management, a violence prevention policy, team conflict resolution, stress-disability evaluation, or strategic planning, to name a few. The request is usually made by phone or face-to-face. How the clinician-consultant handles the request can greatly impact not only whether a consultation contract is offered but also the outcome of the intervention itself. Just as in psychotherapy, the first five minutes of the prospective consultant and client relationship is critical.

Backer (1982) argues that an accurate assessment of client need must occur very early in the consultation process. This assessment will probably address the following questions:

- *What is the context of the consultation request?* Specifically, what is the client requesting? For example, if a hospital administrator phones a clinician asking if he or she can "do something about employee morale," what is the administrator really asking for help with? As in psychotherapy, the initial presenting problem is often not the client's reason for seeking consultation. Consultation requests may be disguised because of lack of understanding of the consultation request, embarrassment, misperception of the basic problem, or even deceit. So, the consultant would inquire about what is meant by "morale" and, specifically, by whom, where in the organization, and how it is being manifested and what effects it is having on productivity and communication between management and employees.
- *Why now?* As in psychotherapy, the answer to this question can be extremely revealing. Consultations are often requested only after the agency or organization has attempted to deal with its difficulty for a period of time without requesting outside help. What efforts were tried, and to what extent were they successful? In the

"morale" example, it is critical to know what efforts the administrator has made and why these efforts have not worked as well as expected.

- *What is the client's readiness to change?* The likelihood that the client is willing to make changes to resolve the problem must also be assessed. Because the client and personnel resources are involved, it is essential that the clinician-consultant determine the client's willingness to allocate such resources. If it emerges that the hospital's problem is widespread and the administrator will authorize only two or three workshops on "team building," it may well be that the client's readiness is insufficient. Extended inquiry and discussion may be required before an appropriate level of readiness is achieved.
- *Can I competently provide the requested consultation?* The prospective consultant needs to ask himself or herself whether he or she has sufficient content knowledge, technical and interpersonal skills, and experience to undertake this consultation. For fairly straightforward requests, such as presenting a lecture on stress management or providing a disability evaluation, both of which require specific technical expertise, the question may be easily answered. When process *plus* technical expertise is required, the question of competence is more complex.
- *Can I ethically perform this consultation?* Potential conflict of interest and dual roles must be considered by the consultant. Obviously, if the clinician is providing or has provided marital therapy to the hospital administrator, he or she probably should not be directly involved in consultation.

4. *Responding to the consultation request:* The clinician-consultant now is in a position to respond to the service request. As in psychotherapy, the clinician-consultant first responds to the manifest content of the request by expressing awareness of the need and/or discomfort of the client organization. Next, the clinician-consultant proposes a plan for meeting the request. This may involve a face-to-face meeting—or a series of meetings—to discuss a plan of action for more complex consultations, or it may require only a brief phone meeting for straightforward consultations such as a workshop presentation.

5. *Drafting a consultation agreement or contract:* Usually, a letter of agreement or a formal consulting contract will finalize these discussions. Although most consultants routinely draft a written contract, some do not (Lippitt & Lippitt, 1978). The written document of agreement becomes a contract if a consideration is stated (i.e., the provision of specified consultation for a given fee) and both parties sign the document. Typically, the document should contain the specified service to be performed, the time frame, travel and lodging expenses, cost of assessment and/or intervention materials, and the consulting fee, which may include preparation time.

6. *Establishing a consulting fee:* The fee a clinician-consultant charges a client can be established either on a project or a fixed-fee basis or on a time basis, in which the increments can be hours or days. Circumscribed activities or projects, such as presenting a stress management workshop or conducting a fitness-for-duty evaluation, are usually billed as a fixed fee, whereas facilitating team development or organizational restructuring is usually billed as day rate, called a *per diem*. Some consulting activities, such as critical incident stress debriefing (CISD) or facilitating a strategic planning retreat, may be charged on a project or a per diem basis depending on local or regional customs. Generally speaking, government contracts require fixed-fee agreement. For complex consulting activities, consultants tend not to use fixed-fee rates for projects with which they have little experience (see Metzger, 1993, for further discussion of this point).

- *Calculating utilization rate: Billable hours* refers to the number of working hours the consultant bills the client. Experienced, full-time consultants do not actually consult full-time. They have down time in which they may devote up to 20% of their time marketing their services to secure new consulting arrange-

ments. Obviously, this time is nonbillable. *Utilization rate* refers to the percentage of total working hours the client can be billed. According to Kelley (1981), the utilization rate is the number of billable hours divided by the number of total working hours available. For instance, if a clinician-consultant plans to consult 12 hours per week and actually bills for 6 hours per week, the utilization rate is 50%. Obviously, the higher the utilization rate, the greater one's compensation. Utilization rate indicates how much consulting time clients are directly paying for, as compared with the time the consultant must absorb as overhead.

- *Calculating billable rate:* The "rule of three" is widely used by consultants to calculate their billing rate (Kelley, 1981). The rule assumes that a consultant should generate overhead and benefits that should equal base salary, while also producing a profit equal to base salary. For example, suppose a clinician-consultant works half-time as a clinician at a college counseling center and develops a half-time consulting practice. If he or she specifies a half-time base consulting salary as $30,000 a year, the total revenues of $90,000 should be estimated. This is derived from $30,000 for base salary, plus $30,000 for overhead plus benefits and $30,000 for profit. The billing rate is estimated by dividing total revenue by yearly billable hours. For example, $90,000 is divided by 1,000 hours (based on 2,000 hours/year as full-time work). The minimum hourly billing rate is thus $90 per hour, and the minimum billing rate would be $720 per day. A corollary of the rule of three is that the more hours billed, the less one needs to charge to maintain profit levels, whereas the fewer the hours billed, the more that must be charged to maintain profit level.

- *Other ways of establishing a billing rate:* A second way of setting a billing rate is based on the usual and customary fees in a geographic region. Usually, there is a typical daily rate for psychologists in particular metropolitan areas. For example, while $750 per day is considered the norm in some midwestern cities, the rate in large northeastern cities may be $1,200–$1,500 per day. Finding out the billing rates of three or four clinician-consultants should reveal the usual and customary rate for a given community. A third way of establishing fee arrangements is to consider the client's circumstances. Schools and community organizations may have limited funds for consultation, whereas defense attorneys may have unlimited funds for expert testimony. The beginning clinician-consultant also may be willing to offer a low-cost consultation fee to one or more clients in return for gaining experience and receiving a positive reference from that client.

7. *Completion of consultation services rendered:* Following completion of the consultation services rendered, it is customary to send or deliver the bill for payment. If a report of the consultation was specified in the agreement, the report is also sent. Following payment, it is customary to send a follow-up thank-you note.

8. *Marketing/soliciting future consultations:* Experienced consultants usually do not view termination of consultation services rendered as termination of the consultation relationship. Successful consultations often result in other consultation requests from the same client. These clients tend to communicate their satisfaction with a consultant to their professional colleagues and friends. Since word-of-mouth advertising is the consultant's most effective marketing strategy, it behooves the consultant to make his or her initial consultations as successful as possible. Consultants may also seek written permission to mention the names of clients of their most successful consultations in written materials—such as brochures—or in verbal conversation with prospective clients.

References & Readings

Backer, T. E. (1982). Psychological consultation. In J. R. McNamara & A. G. Barclay (Eds.), *Critical issues in professional psychology* (pp. 227–269). New York: Praeger.

Caplan, G. (1970). *The theory and practice of mental health consultation.* New York: Basic Books.

Kelley, R. E. (1981). *Consulting: The complete guide to a profitable career.* New York: Scribner's.

Lippitt, G., & Lippitt, R. (1978). *The consulting process in action.* San Diego, CA: University Associates.

Metzger, R. (1993). *Developing a consulting practice.* Newbury Park, CA: Sage.

Sperry, L. (1996). *Corporate therapy and consulting.* New York: Bruner/Mazel.

Related Topics

Chapter 42, "Sample Psychotherapist-Patient Contract"

Chapter 114, "Contracting With Managed Care Organizations"

Chapter 115, "Accepting Legal Referrals"

117 UTILIZATION REVIEW CHECKLIST

Gerald P. Koocher

This chapter is intended to assist clinicians in conducting internal utilization review of mental health records. The purpose of utilization review is to focus on the client's progress in a systematic course of treatment and to monitor the adequacy of clinical records. The goal is to audit records in order to assure that effective treatment is taking place using clinical documentation. For purposes of internal utilization review, create a checklist using the points listed below and review the case record to determine whether sufficient content appears in the record to address each category. Ascertain whether the clinical record has been updated with reasonable frequency. Records should be updated at least quarterly, unless data are routinely updated as they change on a session-by-session basis.

- *Vital statistics:* Are the following noted: full name, record or file number (if any), address, telephone number, sex, birth date, marital status, employment or educational status, family structure, next of kin, ethnicity, primary language, name of primary care physician (if any)?
- *First contact:* Are the date of initial contact and referral source recorded?
- *Presenting problem:* Are the client's complaints and symptoms at the time of the initial visit clearly described? Is notation made of thought disorder, delusions/hallucinations, paranoia, obsessive-compulsive behavior, isolation, inappropriate affect, depression, anxiety, eating or sleeping disturbance, peer relationship difficulties, bizarre behavior, violent/aggressive behavior, appositional/defiant behavior, manic behavior, sexual inappropriateness, substance abuse, physical abuse, or suicidal ideation? Is a history of present illness and prior treatment noted? Are specific focal problems requiring attention listed, such as affective, attitudinal, family, school or work, social, medical conditions, and others? Are recent environmental stressors such as marital changes, death, illness, financial losses, or employment changes noted?
- *Diagnosis:* Has a problem list or a complete diagnosis been formulated, preferably using all 5 *DSM* axes, with R/O (rule-out) diagnoses specified, as needed? Is the diagnosis consistent with symptoms reported in the record? For example, if hallucinations and delusions are described in the record, schizophrenia should be a confirmed or rule-out

diagnosis. Similarly, if depression is a diagnosis, the record should reflect an inquiry about suicidal ideation.

Axis I: Clinical disorders and other conditions that may be a focus of treatment.

Axis II: Personality disorders and mental retardation.

Axis III: General medical conditions.

Axis IV: Psychosocial and environmental problems, with notation of severity.

Axis V: Global Assessment of Functioning (GAF) with numerical score.

- *Current status:* Is a comprehensive functional assessment (including a mental status examination) provided? Are any changes since intake and last treatment plan noted? Is the status of presenting and diagnostic symptoms reported periodically, documenting progress or lack of same?
- *Consultations obtained:* Is a summary of any consultations (e.g., medication or psychological testing) obtained since last update included?
- *Long- and short-range goals:* Are therapeutic goals mentioned and discussed over the course of treatment? Are modalities of treatment reported and any referrals noted? Goals should reference initial symptoms and the client's presenting complaints. Notes should address any movement toward or away from prior goals since the last plan. Progress should be documented with test data, diary entries, behavior records, school reports, or other data.
- *Authentication:* Are the record notes dated and signed, including the degree and institutional title (if any) of the writer? If the writer is unlicensed or a trainee, are the notes countersigned by someone with legal responsibility?

References & Readings

American Psychiatric Association (1994). *Diagnostic and statistical manual of mental disorders* (4th ed.). Washington, DC: American Psychiatric Association.

American Psychological Association (1993). Record

keeping guidelines. *American Psychologist, 48,* 984–986.

Koocher, G. P., & Keith-Spiegel, P. C. (1998). *Ethics in psychology: Professional standards and cases* (2nd ed.). New York: Oxford University Press.

118 BILLING ISSUES

Gerald P. Koocher

This section is intended as a summary guide to the most common practice questions involving billing for mental health services, along with a discussion of related ethical issues.

BASIC PRINCIPLES

- Psychologists ideally perform some services at little or no fee as a pro bono service to the public as a routine part of their practice.
- Providing information and good communication is more important than the actual amount charged. Clients should be informed about fees, billing and collection practices, and other financial contingencies as a routine part of initiating the professional relationship whether or not they ask. This information should also be repeated later in the relationship if necessary. Ascertain the client's ability to pay for services as agreed. Be sure to include the following:

  1. Amount of fee or "hourly rate," including the duration of the "hour"
  2. When fees are payable (i.e., weekly, monthly)
  3. Other services for which you will charge a fee (e.g., telephone contacts, prepara-

  tion of documents, completing insurance forms)
  4. Your policy for missed or canceled sessions
  5. What happens if the client cannot or does not pay the bill

- Do not permit clients to accumulate an inordinately large bill. Practitioners should carefully consider the client's overall ability to afford services early in the relationship and should help the client to make a plan for obtaining services that will be both clinically appropriate and financially feasible. Encouraging clients to incur significant debt is not psychotherapeutic. In that regard, psychologists should be aware of referral sources in the community. Offering excessive credit, when a reduced fee cannot be offered, may create an unreasonable burden on the client.
- Consider the realities of client finances in future fee increases. In some cases it may be most appropriate to apply rate increases to new, rather than continuing, clients.
- Honor all posted or advertised fees.
- Be prepared to justify fees that deviate significantly from comparable services in the community.

- Never agree to a contingency fee arrangement based on the outcome of a case when testifying as an expert in forensic matters.

COLLECTION PRACTICES

- *Ethical obligations:* The professional is obligated to develop a respectful contractual relationship with the client and follow it. This involves all of the points listed above. In the event that a client cannot pay for services, it is desirable to work out an appropriate plan. If the practitioner must decline to continue services for nonpayment, care must be taken not to abandon a dependent client. Referral to community agencies or some limited continuation of services may be an option when abrupt termination would cause harm to a client.
- *Legal obligations:* The professional must obey all laws governing debtor-creditor relations in his or her jurisdiction. Such laws may include prohibitions against adding surcharges to unpaid bills, making threatening telephone calls, and certain other collection practices. See the discussion regarding use of collection agencies below.

THIRD-PARTY RELATIONSHIPS

Relationships with insurance companies and managed care organizations (known collectively as third-party payers) can be strained at times. It is important to clarify with all clients that you will assist them in obtaining all benefits to which they are entitled; however, clients must also be informed of their responsibilities in the event third-party payment is not made. Some third parties seek to sign a contract with providers before agreeing to pay for their services; Blue Shield is an example of such a provider in many states. In the typical contract, a provider is asked to agree to accept the company's payment as specified in full for the service rendered to the subscriber or client. The provider also promises not to charge a policyholder more for any given service than would be charged to another client. In other words,

the provider agrees to accept certain set fees determined by the company and agrees not to treat policyholders differently from nonpolicyholders. In this way, the company attempts to provide good, inexpensive coverage, while attempting to prevent its policyholders from being overcharged or treated in a discriminatory manner. Ideally, the psychologist gains access to a client population, timely payment for services, and the ability to treat covered clients at less expense to them. The precise nature of these financial obligations will vary as a function of the particular company, specific policy coverage, and any contractual relationships between the provider and payer. Some particular issues of concern include the following:

- It is important for psychologists to pay careful attention to all contractual obligations, understand them, and abide by them. Similarly, psychologists should not sign contracts with stipulations that might subsequently place them in ethical jeopardy.
- *Balance billing:* Some contracts between insurers and practitioners require that the clinician accept a specific fee schedule. Such contracts may prohibit billing a client for more than the specified payment.
- *Burying the deductible or ignoring the co-payment:* At times a clinician may be asked to issue a false invoice inflating actual charges to cover a required deductible amount. In other circumstances a client may ask the practitioner to waive a co-payment required under his or her policy without informing the insurer. Agreeing to either practice is unethical and may constitute fraud.
- *Musical chairs (in family therapy):* "Musical chairs" refers to a practice of switching billing from the name of one family member to another in order to extend reimbursement benefits as the limit for an individual is reached. This practice may be acceptable to some payers but not to others. The best strategy is to check with the claims department of the third-party payer, explain the services being provided, and bill as directed. Keep a record of the call, including the date, person consulted, and instructions you were given.

- *Services not covered:* Another common problem relates to billing for services that are not covered under the third party's obligations. Most third parties are health insurance companies and as a result limit their coverage to treatment for illness or health-related problems, usually defined in terms of medical necessity. One must invariably assign a diagnosis to the client to secure payment. Some services provided by psychologists are not, strictly speaking, health or mental health services. For example, marriage counseling, educational testing, school consultation, vocational guidance, child custody evaluations, and a whole variety of forensic functions may not be considered health services and as such would not be covered by health insurance. Some insurance carriers also specify certain types of diagnostic or therapeutic procedures that are not "covered services." Such treatments or services might be considered ancillary, experimental, unproven, or simply health-promoting (e.g., weight control and smoking cessation) but not treatment for a specific illness. Attempts to conceal the actual nature of the service rendered or otherwise attempt to obtain compensation in the face of such restrictions may constitute fraud. Some third-party payers will not pay for services that are not clearly tied to the treatment of a psychological disorder. Examples include divorce mediation, child custody evaluations, smoking cessation programs, or weight loss consultations. If in doubt, consult with the third party's representative (as described above) and do not misrepresent the service provided.
- *Fraud:* As a legal concept, fraud refers to an act of intentional deception resulting in harm or injury to another. There are four basic elements to a fraudulent act:

  1. False representation is made by one party who either knows it to be false or is knowingly ignorant of its truth. This may be done by misrepresentation, deception, concealment, or simply nondisclosure of some key fact.
  2. The maker's intent is that false representation will be relied on by another.

  3. The recipient of the information is unaware of the intended deception.
  4. The recipient of the information is justified in relying on or expecting the truth from the communicator. The resulting injury may be financial, physical, or emotional.

IMPORTANT DON'TS

- Never bill for services you have not actually rendered. If you are billing for services provided by a supervisee, this should be made clear on all bills and claim forms.
- Never give anyone a blank insurance claim form with your signature on it. This is an invitation to fraud.
- Never change diagnoses to fit reimbursement criteria.
- Never bill insurance companies for missed or late canceled sessions. You may have an agreement with clients to pay for such missed appointments; however, third-party payers may be billed only for services rendered.
- Never change the date when you first saw the client in order to fit reimbursement criteria.
- Never bill for multiple client therapy sessions (i.e., couple, family, or group) as though they were individual treatment sessions. When in doubt about who to bill, contact a claims representative at the company. Note the name of the claims representative, follow instructions, and keep a record of the conversation.
- Do not forgive or waive co-payments or deductibles without informing the third-party carrier.

AREAS OF CONTROVERSY

- *Bill collecting:* Creditor and debtor relationships are just as much a part of the psychologist-client relationship as in most other purchases of service. Inevitably, some clients will fall behind in paying for services or fail to pay for them at all. Because of the nature of clients' reasons for consulting psychologists and the nature of the relationships that are established, however, psychologists have some special obligations to consider in formulating debt collection strategies. When a client remains in active treatment while incurring a debt, the matter should be dealt with frankly, including a discussion of the impact of the debt on treatment. In most cases, however, the problems that arise occur after formal service delivery has terminated.

• *Collection agencies:* As a general concept, it is not inappropriate for a psychologist to use a professional collection agency. Ideally, a client should be cautioned that this may happen and should be given the opportunity to resolve the matter without involving a collection agency. Practitioners who employ such agencies are responsible for any misconduct by the agency.

1. Psychologists may be held responsible for financial misrepresentations effected in their name by an employee or agent they have designated (including billing and collection agents). They must, therefore, choose their employees and representatives with care and supervise them closely.

2. In all debt collection situations, psychologists must be aware of the laws that apply in their jurisdiction and make every effort to behave in a cautious, businesslike fashion. They must avoid using their special position or information gained through their professional role to collect debts from clients.

3. In dealing with debt collection, whether through an agency or small claims court, the clinician should remember that only pertinent elements (e.g., client status, number of sessions, and amount owed) can be disclosed without violating the confidentiality of the client. Disclosure of client status in such situations is generally allowed because the client has violated his or her contract to pay the agreed-upon fees.

• *Caution:* Fee disputes are a frequent basis of legal complaints against psychologists (Bennett, Bryant, VandenBos, & Greenwood, 1990; Woody, 1988), and this is also true in

instances of client-initiated ethical complaints.

• *Bartering:* Although permitted under limited provisions of the APA's Code of Conduct (Section 1.18), this should be undertaken thoughtfully and only as a last resort to assist a client who might otherwise be unable to afford services.

• *Missed appointments and last-minute cancellations:* These may represent a significant economic loss to a practitioner; however, not all practitioners charge for occasional events of this sort. The key point is not to surprise the client with such a charge. Either discuss such charges at the outset of treatment or caution clients that repeated incidents will result in such charges. Such charges are not payed for services rendered and hence may not be billed to third parties.

• *Fee splitting:* Relationships involving kickbacks, fee splitting, or payment of commissions for client referrals may be illegal and unethical. Careful attention to the particular circumstances and state laws is important before agreeing to such arrangements. Fee splitting refers to a general practice, often called a "kickback," in that part of a sum received for a product or service is returned or paid out because of a prearranged agreement or coercion. As it is practiced in medicine or the mental health professions, the client is usually unaware of the arrangement. Traditionally there was nearly universal agreement among mental health professionals that such practices are unethical, chiefly because they may preclude a truly appropriate referral in the client's best interests, result in delivery of unneeded services, lead to increased costs of services, and generally exploit the relative ignorance of the client. Unfortunately, fee splitting may exist in rather complex and subtle forms that tend to mask the fact that it is occurring. There is a continuum of types of agreements that range from reasonable and ethical to clearly inappropriate. At the two extremes are employer-employee relationships (clearly appropriate) and arrangements wherein the person making the referral gets money solely for making the referral.

References & Readings

Balch, P., Ireland, J. F., & Lewis, S. B. (1977). Fees and therapy: Relation of source of payment to course of therapy at a community mental health center. *Journal of Consulting and Clinical Psychology, 45*, 504.

Bennett, B. E., Bryant, B. K., VandenBos, G. R., & Greenwood, A. (1990). *Professional liability and risk management.* Washington, DC: American Psychological Association.

Dightman, C. R. (1970). Fees and mental health services: Attitudes of the professional. *Mental Hygiene, 54*, 401–406.

Koocher, G. P., & Keith-Spiegel, P. C. (1998). *Ethics in psychology: Professional standards and cases* (2nd ed.). New York: Oxford University Press.

Kovacs, A. L. (1987). Insurance billing: The growing risk of lawsuits. *Independent Practitioner, 7*, 21–24.

Pope, K. S. (1988). Fee policies and procedures: Causes of malpractice suits and ethics complaints. *Independent Practitioner, 8*, 24–29.

Pope, K. S., Geller, J. D., & Wilkinson, L. (1975). Fee assessment and out-patient psychotherapy. *Journal of Consulting and Clinical Psychology, 43*, 835–841.

Pope, K. S., Tabachnik, B. T., & Keith-Spiegel, P. C. (1987). Ethics of practice: The beliefs and behaviors of psychologists as therapists. *American Psychologist, 42*, 993–1006.

Woody, R. H. (1988). *Protecting your mental health practice: How to minimize legal and financial risk.* San Francisco: Jossey-Bass.

Related Topics

119 PSYCHOTHERAPISTS' FEES AND INCOMES

John C. Norcross

The American Psychological Association (APA) Research Office collects salary data every other year from psychologists employed in academia and institutions. These data are divided regionally and are published in a series of reports (e.g., "1995 Salaries in Psychology") available for purchase at a modest cost from the APA or for perusal on the APA's homepage. Although the APA does report institutional and academic salaries, it does not regularly collect data on individual practitioners' incomes in order to avoid antitrust implications.

Probably the most systematic, comprehensive study of psychologists' incomes and psychotherapy fees is that undertaken by the Ridgewood Financial Institute and published in *Psychotherapy Finances.* This biannual survey covers individual and group therapy fees, regional variations in fees, managed care allowances, practice expenses, contracts with organizations, weekly workload, practice organization, and total professional income, among other elements of the financial profile of psychotherapy practice. This chapter presents

TABLE 1. Median Fees for Individual Therapy Sessions

Psychotherapists	Direct Pay Fee	Managed Care Fee	Third-Party Fee	Usual and Customary Fee
Psychologists	$95	$75	$90	$100
Psychiatrists	100	80	94	110
Social workers	75	60	70	80
Marriage and family therapists	75	60	70	80

TABLE 2. Psychotherapists' Median Private Practice and Total Professional Incomes

Psychotherapists	Private Practice Income	Total Professional Income
Psychologists	$73,081	$80,531
Psychiatrists	87,163	96,666
Social workers	51,772	57,570
Marriage and family therapists	47,253	67,119

TABLE 3. Psychologists' Income

Income	Private Practice Income	Total Professional Income
$140,000+	9%	11%
$130,000–$139,999	2	4
$120,000–$129,999	4	6
$110,000–$119,999	4	5
$100,000–$109,999	7	8
$90,000–$99,999	6	8
$80,000–$89,999	9	10
$70,000–$79,999	13	12
$60,000–$69,999	12	12
$50,000–$59,999	14	11
$40,000–$49,999	9	8
$30,000–$39,999	6	3
$20,000–$29,999	3	2
Under $20,000	2	0

highlights of the data regarding psychotherapy fees and professional income, particularly for psychologists. (Subscriptions for monthly issues of *Psychotherapy Finances* can be directed to 800-869-8450 or faxed to 561-624-6006. The journal's Web site is www.psyfin.com.)

The most recent survey encompassed 1,804 psychotherapists, including psychologists ($n = 715$), psychiatrists ($n = 180$), social workers ($n = 452$), and marriage and family therapists ($n = 220$). Fifty-three percent of the respondents were women, and 97% were licensed. Solo practice was still king of the private practice sample with 52%, followed by 28% of psychotherapists in solo practice with expense sharing and 16% in group practice.

PSYCHOTHERAPY FEES

Table 1 presents the median individual psychotherapy fees for the national sample of psychologists, psychiatrists, social workers, and marriage and family therapists. Four types of fees are provided for each professional discipline.

Since 1979, when the first fee survey was conducted, median fees have constantly risen for private practitioners. In 1997, however, there was a definite downward pressure on fees. Most psychotherapists reported that their usual and customary fees had either remained the same (thus actually decreasing when adjusted for inflation) or eroded by an average of $5.

PSYCHOTHERAPIST INCOMES

Table 2 presents the median private practice incomes and total professional incomes of psychologists, psychiatrists, social workers, and marriage and family therapists during 1997.

From 1979 until the most recent findings, the surveys have shown a steady increase in both private practice income and total professional income. In the latest survey, all professional groups except marriage and family therapists show declines in both practice and total professional incomes. Psychiatrists routinely conducting psychotherapy suffered the greatest decrease in total professional income (−16.7%), followed by social workers (−2.4%) and psychologists (−.7%).

More detailed data on psychologists' incomes are presented in Table 3 in terms of the percentage of practitioners falling into discrete income ranges.

Related Topics

Chapter 102, "Sixteen Hints on Money Matters and Ethical Issues"
Chapter 118, "Billing Issues"

120 COMPUTERIZED BILLING AND OFFICE MANAGEMENT PROGRAMS

Edward L. Zuckerman

Computerization of clinical practice is unavoidable and can be quite beneficial. Programs have been developed to cope with billing and managed care needs, to assist in assessment and report construction, to survey the research, and to put you in touch instantly with colleagues around the world. If you would like to know more about what is available, see John Grohol's exhaustive and amazingly rich Mental Health Net at http://www.cmhc.com.

The most pressing need is a program that will ensure accurate and timely billing and will also handle routine office tasks such as appointment scheduling and recording progress notes. The software listed below will do these and many more functions. This list is not exhaustive. It omits the larger systems (with more than around 1,000 active patients and 100 therapists) and those intended primarily for medical settings. This list is probably about 90% complete, but it contains all the major developers of these programs for mental health offices. This listing is current as of August 1, 1997, when the basic facts were checked by phone or e-mail. Since developers are constantly improving and modifying their products, confirm any important aspects of a program with the developer before you make a purchase. All computers, software, and other product names listed herein are property of their respective copyright and trademark holders.

SELECTING A PROGRAM

First, look at all features and decide which are most important. There is an excellent checklist of what to look for at http://www.taxrice. com/sumtime/rudd/choosing_software.htm and another at my site, The Clinician's ToolBox at Guilford.com. Ask for the demos and explore them. Do not decide on the basis of price. Your income will depend on this program, and a program that is hard to use will be a continuing source of stress for you and your staff. If you have an office manager, he or she should make the final decision even though you have the Ph.D.

LIST OF PROGRAMS

The list of programs below provides the following information.

- The developer's name, address, phone and fax numbers, e-mail address, and net site, when available, are given. The head of the operation is also sometimes listed.
- The name of the program is given in italics. All these programs do billing, so only unusual aspects are listed. Programs that do additional functions are called office management programs and may include scheduling, mailing list handling, treatment plan writing and updating, recording of medications, and so on. ECS means electronic claims submission—the ability to send a claim for payment to the insurance company over the phone line using your modem and special software. This makes the insurance company's work easier and may speed up your payment.
- The computer hardware or "platform" the program is designed to run on is listed. Most systems work on IBM-compatible comput-

ers using Intel chips (286, 386, 486, and Pentium) and are generically called "Wintel." The programs are in DOS unless it is indicated that they work in Windows, which means Windows 3.1 and usually Windows 95 (but ask if this is not clear). There are fewer programs that work on Apple's Macintosh computers (but you only need *one* program); these are indicated with the word "Macintosh."

- The current cost of the program, where advertised or available, is listed; call to confirm.
- The availability and cost of program demonstration disks are noted. Some of these contain only a "guided tour," which describes and illustrates the major features (but not all the functions). Others contain a limited version of the whole program in which some important functions are disabled or you are limited to a small number of clients or a fixed period of time. With these you can enter data and see how almost everything works, but you cannot use the demo to run your practice. In using these "fully functional" demos, it will take a lot of time to enter all the client information, but you will then understand how to use the program and what its strengths and limitations are.

American Management Systems, Suite 234, 3000 Connecticut Avenue, Washington, DC 20008; 202-232-8608. Laurence Drell, M.D. *Office Organizer* management system is very complete: billing, scheduling, insurance, bank deposits, collection letters, progress notes, prescriptions, referral letters, and so forth. Macintosh, Windows 95.

Applied Computing Services, 2764 Allen Road West, Elk, WA 99009; 800-853-6369, 509-292-0501. *Client Billing System* is a full-featured program that does complex billing options (various states' claim forms, dual insurance, third-party billing), as well as management reports, word processing, exports to Quicken, and so on. For DOS, Windows 3.1 and 95, and OS/2. Packages from $995 to $1,500; solo $595; ECS $99–350; network $200. Full working demo and slide show $15. *PMA-2000:* solo $295; small group $395; larger group $495. Windows 95 and NT.

ASD Software, Aeolian Systems and Design, P.O. Box 10874, Rochester, NY 14610; 800-313-8133; e-mail: rhale@eznet.net; Robert Hale. *Office Manager* is comprehensive patient record-keeping and billing software. Simple to use. Progress notes of any length, customized Intake, Discharge, Treatment Plan forms, HCFAs, invoices, past-due statements, labels, password protection, authorized visits, and so on. Windows, Macintosh. Standard version $495. Demo disks $15. Custom requests welcomed.

AT Software, 800-909-3340; andystich@sprintmail.com. *Psycho-Bill* is billing software that uses memory very efficiently, so it will run on "any Mac," even without a hard drive. Program and 200 patients' records for a year are stored on one floppy. "Generates HCFA, patient bills, envelopes with a single click." $199. Free demo available by e-mail.

Beaver Creek Software, 525 SW 6th Street, Corvallis, OR 97333-4324; sales: 800-895-3311; business: 541-752-5039; support: 541-752-7563; fax: 541-752-5221; Peter Gysegem. *The Therapist V3.1* is a full-scale billing program. It fills in forms and all diagnostic codes (*DSM-IV, CPT, RSV, ICD-9*), prints on letterhead or new HCFA 1500, can handle up to 99 therapists, makes mailing labels and deposit slips, tracks referrals, keeps clinical notes, offers password protection and backup and restoration of data, tracks preauthorizations and insurance maximums, and so on. DOS. $249 plus $10 shipping; ECS $99; custom report writer $199. $15 for full demo, which works for 60 days. 30-day money-back guarantee.

Blumenthal Software, Inc., P.O. Box 138 SVS, Binghamton, NY 13903; 607-724-0032; Jerome Blumenthal, M.D. *PBS-3: The Psychologist's Billing System V3.2* is a full-featured program: billing and accounting, forms generation and printing, management reports, data transferred to spreadsheets, sliding scale and Medicare fee generation, networking, handling of managed care limitations, and so on. DOS. Solo or groups $595 for one provider; ECS $200; network $350. Free demo.

Brand Software, Inc., 500 W. Cummings Park, Suite 3150, Woburn, MA 01801; sales: 800-3-HELPER; support: 617-937-0080; fax: 617-937-3232; http://www.helper.com; Cheney Brand. *Therapist Helper 3 for Windows* is a very comprehensive multifunctional program: billing/accounting, word processing, progress notes, customizable screens, mailing labels, phone/address book, pop-up warning screens, automatic calculation of copayments for managed care. Codes for *DSM, ICD,* CPT, HCFA forms completion. Over 400 context-sensitive help screens. Networking included. Open (not proprietary) database. *Therapist Scheduler* and *Insurance Connector*® for ECS included. IBM, DOS, Windows. Solo $495; 2–5 providers $695; $100 per provider thereafter. Download demo from Web site.

Cambridge Software Labs, 45 Highland Road, Boxford, MA 01921; 508-352-8909; Paul M. Peckins, LICSW. This information may not be current. *The Cure* "organizes, manages, and automates every aspect of your practice." Up to 99 therapists, referral tracking, correspondence, scheduling, checkbook, mailing labels, graphs, calculator, passwords, reminders, and so on. Multiple providers. ECS, scheduler. DOS. $550–895. Free demo disk (specify 3.5" or 5.25"). $50 for demo and manual.

C & C Computer Support, RR 3, Box 3700, Factoryville, PA 18419; 800-258-6382; e-mail: cccomputer@aol.com. *TRACKING Plus:* "Patient Charts, Electronic Claim Submission, Patient Statements & Receipts, Prints HCFA-1500 Claim Forms, Mailing Lists and Labels, Report Writer, Scheduler, *ICD-9* and CPT codes, Practice Analysis, Reports and Graphs, Free Tech Support for 1 year. Free demo. $349." Presumably IBM, DOS.

ClientTell Software, P.O. Box 9910, Santa Fe, NM 87504; 505-989-4702; http://www.mindmatters.com/clienttell/. *ClientTell Management System for Client Data* is designed for massage therapists: billing statements, client notes, appointments, financial reports. No HCFA forms. DOS, Windows, Macintosh. $59 plus $4 shipping. Free info.

Community Sector Systems, Inc., 700 Fifth Avenue, Suite 5500, Seattle, WA 98104; 800-988-6392; fax: 206-467-9327; e-mail: Mail@cssi.com; http://www.cssi.com. *Psych Access 2.0* is an "electronic clinical information system" of charting and data management. Tracks medications, lab results. Does managed care reports, impairments, treatments, treatment plans, progress notes, authorizations, and so on. ECS. Windows.

Com1 Software, Inc., P.O. Box 482, Hudson, OH 44236; 216-653-3771; e-mail: C1Soft@aol.com; Lynn Brian. Documentation can be printed from within the downloaded product. The programs can be downloaded at no cost and used for up to 25 claims before you need to pay to "register." They offer unlimited support and free upgrades for registered users. They incorporate HCFA-1500 forms. Instructions for importing *DSM* and *ICD* codes. Prices for the "claim entry products" range from $79 (solo) to $349 (billing service) and for the "billing system products" from $279 (solo) to $695 (billing service).

Cornucopia Software, P.O. Box 6111, Albany, CA 94706; 510-528-7000; e-mail: Philmanf@aol.com. *Practice Magic* seems to be a very complete billing software (prints to HCFA 1500 on screen) with appointment book (and prints Daytimer inserts), exports to Quicken, progress notes, managed care functions, and so on. DOS, Windows, Macintosh, but not for PowerMacs. $89.95 (includes two free yearly updates) and $29.95 per year afterward or $139 for unlimited version. (Clearly the low-price leader.) Money-back guarantee. Demo disk for $10.

CPT Management Systems, 1116 Mendocino Avenue, Santa Rosa, CA 95401; 800-477-4907; 707-579-5829; e-mail: CPTBIL@aol.com. *CPT Billing 4.0* is a customized FileMaker Pro® application (and so will always be usable) that is easily modifiable by the user. Does *DSM-IV* codes, Medi-HCFA, HCFA 1500 form, managed care alerts, mailing labels, 27 letters and reports, appointments, passwords, backups, many monthly reports. Single and multiple

users. ECS soon. 160-page manual and on-line support. Windows, Macintosh. Unlimited free support. $270 to $339 for single user; add $99 if you need to buy FileMaker Pro. Free info and samples or demo for $14.95.

Custom BusinessWare, 22 Brevoort Road, Chappaqua, NY 10514; 914-238-8047; William Rosenthal, M.D. *Caduceus* offers psych practice management, billing, medications, record keeping, ECS, word processing, networking. Toll-free telephone support. Windows. $695 for one to three providers. 30-day money-back guarantee. Fully functional demo for $20, credited toward purchase.

Danbar Software Co., 14 Bond Street, Suite 291 Great Neck, NY 11021; 800-404-PASS; 516-829-6931; fax: 516-466-1137; http://www.members.aol.com/danbarsoft. *PASS: Patient Accounting Service System* is a rather complete billing and office accounting system for any size practice; tracks all expenses for gross and net income. ECS available. One year free technical support and updates. DOS. $395. 30-day money-back guarantee. Free demo disk or download from Web site.

Echo Management Group, 1620 Main Street, P.O. Box 540, Center Conway, NH 03183; 800-635-8209; 603-447-5453; fax: 603-447-2037; e-mail: sales@echoman.com; http://www.echoman.com. *Clinician's Desktop* is part of a very comprehensive, multicomponent MIS for nonprofits in any mental health area. Windows. Unix, DOS as well. Approximately $6,000. Demos available. Download a demo from Web site.

Executive Travelware, Inc., P.O. Box 59387, Chicago, IL 60659-0387; 800-397-7477. *PRO-BILL* is a complete billing program with statements, insurance, and aging for small office of one to six professionals. DOS. $198. Demo disk with tutorial $29, credited toward purchase.

Genie Software, 811 SW 58th Avenue, Portland, OR 97221-1558; 888-297-2717; 503-297-2717; Hugh Maier. *The Therapist's Genie 4.7* is a very competent and multifunctional billing program. DOS, DOS-in-Windows 95. $289, plus $109 per year for updates, training, and unlimited phone support. Free trial copy for 60 days. $15 for demo with manual and support, credited toward purchase.

Iris Software, P.O. Box 2461, Corvallis, OR 97339; 541-752-4228; http://www.proaxis. com/~iris/; Sarah Richards. *Iris Co-therapist* is complete with *DSM-IV* and CPT codes, referral information, insurance company information, managed care reminders, session notes for therapists, assessment and treatment planning, letters and contacts, and practice statistics. Solo and multiple therapists, networkable. User customizes the demo version, which is "as is." Macintosh, Windows 3.1. Requires FileMaker 3.0 from Claris ($180 through most catalogs). Demo $25 or free download from Web site. $100 to use all functions of the demo.

Kessler, Ronald P., Ph.D., 629 E. Chapman, Orange, CA 92866; 714-633-9685; fax: 714-633-9687; e-mail: 76606.3525@compuserve.com; http://www.calisto.net. *Calisto* is a complete system that offers billing, office management, practice management. "Designed by psychs for psychs. Tames managed care." Call for references. DOS, Windows 95. $499. Money-back guarantee. Free working demo disk.

Lightworks Business Services, 400 West Hill Road, Vestal, NY 13850; 800-724-9548; 607-754-4713; fax: 607-724-9148. *Professional Practice Manager 6.0* has CPT codes, toll-free 90-day support, password protection, progress notes. DOS. One to five providers $495; larger groups $995; managed care tracking module $450. American Psych. Management forms printer $175. Demo $25. $5 for shipping.

Macworks, 4211 Balcones Woods Drive, Austin, TX 78759; 512-343-8960. *CIBS: Client Information and Billing System* is a mental health practitioner's billing program. Macintosh and Windows using FileMaker Pro v3. $249. Demo $25.

Marla Productions, 524 Don Gaspar, Santa Fe, NM 87501; 800-618-6136; fax: 505-982-6445;

e-mail: esybilling@nets.com; http://www.nets. com/easybilling/. *Ea$y Billing* does billing, labels, letters with samples, SOAP and daily notes, and so on. Networkable, multiple providers. Uses FileMaker Pro. Windows 3.1 and 95 and Macintosh. $599 with manual, instructional videotape, 60-day free support, 30-day money-back guarantee. Free demo or downloadable from Web site.

Mental Health Connections, 21 Blossom Street, Lexington, MA 02173; 617-860-7544; voice and fax: 800-788-4743; e-mail: mhc@ mhc.com; http://www.mhc.com; Robert Patterson, M.D. A catalog that describes almost 100 programs is highly informative, up to date, and available on disk as well as at the Web site. They offer billing, therapy, and expert systems programs for DOS, Windows, and Macintosh. *Civer-Psych 2.0* assists with intake assessment and diagnosing. *DSM-IV*, treatment planning, patient monitoring, report generation, and billing. IBM, DOS, Windows. $695 to $1,195 depending on options. Demo $25.

Micro-Eye, 17560 County Road 85B, Esparto, CA 95627; 800-787-3194; fax: 916-787-3993; e-mail: 76012,2207 CIS. *Psychotherapy Office Planner* offers forms, customizable statements, *DSM-III* and CPT codes, session notes when used with a word processor, and checkbook. Supports IRS 1040-C. ECS and multiple providers are options. Prints on HCFA 1500 or plain paper. Requires Microsoft Excel 3.0 (IBM or Macintosh). Unlimited phone support. Windows or Macintosh. $195 plus $15 shipping; $100 for multiprovider; $300 more for ECS. Demo $12.50.

Multi-Health Systems, 908 Niagara Falls Boulevard, North Tonawanda, NY 14120-2060; 800-456-3003; fax: 416-424-1736.65; http:// www.mhs.com. *Shrink Direct* bills patients and generates reports. DOS. $395. *Shrink 6.0* bills patients and insurance companies and does reports, expense tracking, forms generation. DOS. $795. Networkable and ECS at extra cost. Call for pricing. *Shrink 6.0 Plus* does all the above with appointment scheduler, templates for treatment planning, and history/progress notes. DOS. $995. Networkable and ECS at extra cost. Call for pricing. Demos $45, nonrefundable. Videotape demo $39. Add $10 for shipping. Technical support available.

Nardo.SYS, 868 East Rock Springs Road, NE, Atlanta, GA 30306; 404-872-8278; e-mail: jnardo@onramp.net. John M. Nardo, M.D. *PsyC Version 1.5:* "A complete mental health practice management system." Billing, insurance forms, bank deposits, reports, *DSM* and *ICD-9* diagnostic codes, CPT codes, and so on. Prints onto insurance forms, exportable client notes. On-line help manual, networkable. DOS. $500. Interactive demo disk $5.

O.M.S., P.O. Box 661, Nevada City, CA 95959; 800-588-6824; e-mail: oms@oro.net; http://www.oro.net/~oms/. *Touched:* "The ultimate therapist management program." *Instant Secretary* does diagnoses, treatment plan, progress notes, appointment scheduler, address book, contact tracking, medical history, and so on. *Instant Accountant* does thorough billing. *Instant Assistant* does spell checking, intake and history guides, questionnaire builder, graphing of data, envelope and label printing, periodic reports, and so on. *Instant Fairy God Mother* offers on-line help, networking, passwords, use by multiple therapists, and so on. One month free trial.

PC Consulting Group, P.O. Box 69382, Portland, OR 97201; sales and support: 800-847-8446; 503-977-3654; e-mail: wpardy@delphipbs.com; http://www.delphipbs.com/; Will Pardy. *Delphi/PBS: Psychotherapy Billing Software* offers a very complete package: assessment form, progress notes, scheduling, ECS, passwords, scheduling, mailing labels, online help, payroll calculation, finance charges, networking, backups, and so on. Free updates. DOS, Windows. $895 for solo or multiple providers. Free demo for 2-month "evaluation package" with manuals; purchase then for $10 off. Demo downloadable from Web site.

Practice Management Software, 285 Engle Street, Englewood, NJ 07631; phone and fax: 800-874-2159; e-mail: kaplan@pm2.com; http://

www.pm2.com; Richard D. Kaplan, M.D. *PM/2* generates reports, treatment plans, progress notes, mailings, and prescriptions with word processor, *DSM-IV*, *ICD-9*, CPT codes, on-line help, scheduler, phone dialer, financial reports, help screens. DOS, Windows 3.1 and 95. $600 for solo, plus additional cost for groups, LANs, ECS. 30-day money-back guarantee. Free lifetime tech support by phone or e-mail. Free demo disk or downloadable from Web site.

Pro-Comp Software Consultants, 1117 Fehl Lane, Cincinnati, OH 45230; 800-783-1668; e-mail: dshuller@earthlink.net; David Y. Shuller, Ph.D. *PAMS: Practitioner Accounts Management System Version 4.1:* "A sophisticated, comprehensive, and easy-to-use accounts receivable program suitable for large practices or clinics." Besides complex billing options, it includes progress notes, treatment plans, mail merge letters, managed care features (e.g., alarms), collection letters, insurance payment tracking, treatment plans, ECS, and so on. Networkable, multisite, multiuser, free unlimited telephone support, and at their BBS. DOS. $1,395 with modem. Demo and guide $35, refundable.

Psychotherapy Practice Manager, 113 Hueneme Avenue, Channel Islands, CA 93035; 800-895-1618; 805-984-3791; e-mail: jhmullin@anacapa.net; http://www.anacapa.net/~jhmullin; Jay Mullin. *The Psychotherapy Practice Manager* provides complete control of your practice with client records (client registration, intake interview, assessment, progress notes), billing (individual and batch, client, adjusted for anticipated insurance payments, HCFA 1500 forms, labels), appointments (scheduler, reminders, "to do" lists), Rolodex (sorting codes, address books, labels), general ledger (revenues, expenses, profit and loss, IRS 1040 Schedule C summary), management reports (accounts receivable, aging, detailed and summary activity), *DSM-IV* and CPT codes, generic forms (consent to treat, release of information, etc.). Built-in tutorial. 90 days free technical support, ECS, networking available. Single-therapist version for DOS or 68x Macintosh $295; for Windows 3.1 and 95 or PowerPC Macintosh $395. Versions for multiple-therapist practices are $100 more. Full-featured demo $20, credited toward purchase.

PsychSolutions, 41 William Fairfield Drive, Wenham, MA 01984; 508-468-2290; 888-779-7658; Michael McGee. *PsychOffice* is an office management program with full featured billing for simple and complex situations, correspondence, patient records, and scheduling. Many reports, networkable, easily customizable. Unlimited providers. "Free phone support 24 hours/7 days." Macintosh. $695, including ECS. 60-day money-back guarantee. Demo and manual $20, credited toward purchase, or free information and references.

REM Systems, Inc., 117 Longwood Drive West, Huntsville, AL 35801-4513; 800-548-6148; e-mail: sysop@remsys.com; http://www.remsys.com; William Tygret. *The Billing Master* offers billing, reports, referral tracking, ECS, managed care, appointment, scheduling, prescription writing, and so on. DOS in Windows. $475 basic billing; $795 for more reports. Money-back guarantee. Demo and free trial version available and downloadable from Web site.

Saner Software, 37 West 222, Suite 253, Route 64, St. Charles, IL 60175; free brochure and orders: 800-448-6899; technical support/questions: 630-513-5599 (8:30 A.M. – 5 P.M.); fax: 630-513-4210; e-mail: Techsupport@sanersoftware.com. *ShrinkRapt v 3.5:* "A simple patient list automatically appears each time you open Shrink-Rapt, ready and waiting for you to add new patients, bill a session, record payments, write progress notes, or print insurance claims and patient statements. It doesn't get any easier than that!" Windows 95, Macintosh. Solo practitioner $585; $985 for multiple users of one machine. 90-day money-back guarantee. Fully functional demo $10, credited toward purchase. Free technical support.

Shapse, Steven N., Ph.D., P.O. Box 112, Lincoln, MA 01773; 617-259-0283. *Professional's Billing System* is a shareware program for billing and insurance form generation. "It is a small and simple program but easy to use and highly functional." Forms or paper printing, multiple providers, unlimited patients, customizable, written in dBase 4. DOS. $299. Demo $10.

SOS Software: Synergistic Office Solutions, Inc., 17445 East Apshawa Road, Clermont, FL 34711; 352-242-9100; fax: 352-242-9104; e-mail: sales@sosoft.com; http://www.sosoft.com; Seth R. Krieger, Ph.D. *SOS Office Manager Version 4.30* is a mature product based on the familiar daysheet/ledger card model. Simplified data entry, useful management reports, multiple practitioners, scheduling. ECS. DOS. Solo $955; networks $1,955. Fully functioning 10-patient demo is $25, including manual. *SOS Case Manager* for Windows offers clinical records intake, history, problem/goal-oriented treatment plans and progress notes, group therapy progress notes, medication and subscription tracking, usage and report tracking for managed care, glossary for reusable text, templates for most used information, and so on. Solo $495; network or group $995.

$umTime, 635 Franklin Avenue, New Orleans, LA 70117; 800-767-5788; 504-949-6463; fax: 504-949-6467; e-mail: sumtime@sumtime.com; http://www.sumtime.com. *$umTime* is a very complete and full-featured billing and practice management software package with custom forms, referrals, notes, managed care reports, ECS, on-line help, and so on. Windows and Macintosh. Solo $399; group $499; ECS $49. 60-day money-back guarantee. Free information. Fully operational demo $10. Demo can be downloaded from Web site, which offers an excellent discussion of what to look for in an office management program.

Tess Data Systems, Inc., 13910 Champion Forrest Drive, Suite 103, Houston, TX 77069; 800-218-TESS; 281-440-6943; fax: 281-440-6526; e-mail: tessdata@aol.com. *TessSystem Three* is a thorough office management program, including patient transaction history, ECS through TessTelecom II, and a subscription for upgrades. Macintosh. $1,295. Free demo disk. *TessManager* offers basic billing and scheduling. Macintosh. $699. Free demo disk.

TPM Software, 5202 Washington Street, Suite 1, Downers Grove, IL 60515; 630-968-1137; 630-434-8606; e-mail: tpmsoftware@inforel. com; Bob Crum. *TPM-Billing* was developed for Windows and thus includes the familiar drop-down list boxes, point and click functions, and so on. ECS with no clearinghouse fees; HCFA and plain paper claims. Patient accounting, patient histories, and other reports. $299. Demos are $5 or free when downloaded from Web site.

Zavala Consulting, P.O. Box 292516, Tampa, FL 33687; 800-469-1770; fax: 813-987-2711; e-mail: ZBYTE@aol.com. *Tx Practice Manager,* *V. 1* does HCFA forms, universal treatment plan for managed care concerns, patient registration, scheduling, case notes, office correspondence, client accounting, billing, follow-up, *ICD* code finder, *DSM-IV* codes, mailing lists. Windows, Windows NT, Macintosh. Solo $450; up to 15 users $675. Demo disk $25, credited toward purchase, or download free from members.aol.com/zbyte/zcc.

Related Topics

PART VIII
Professional Resources

121 MAJOR PROFESSIONAL ASSOCIATIONS

The following list provides the mailing addresses, telephone numbers, and Web sites of the major professional associations for the five core mental health disciplines: psychology, psychiatry, clinical social work, mental health nursing, and marital and family therapy. For each discipline, the list contains the largest professional organizations, certification or diplomate providers, and national registers.

Psychology

American Psychological Association (APA)
750 First Street, NW
Washington, DC 20002-4242
Phone: 202-336-5500
Web site: www.apa.org

American Psychological Society (APS)
1010 Vermont Avenue, NW, Suite 1100
Washington, DC 20005-4907
Phone: 202-783-2077
Web site: psych.hanover.edu/aps

National Register of Health Service Providers in Psychology
1120 G Street, NW, Suite 330
Washington, DC 20005
Phone: 202-783-7663
Web site: www.nationalregister.com

American Board of Professional Psychology (ABPP)
2100 E. Broadway, Suite 313
Columbia, MO 65201-6082
Phone: 573-875-1267

Psychiatry

American Psychiatric Association (ApA)
1400 K Street, NW
Washington, DC 20005
Phone: 202-682-6000
Web site: www.psych.org

American Board of Psychiatry and Neurology
500 Lake Cook Road, Suite 335
Deerfield, IL 60015
Phone: 847-945-7900

Clinical Social Work

National Association of Social Workers (NASW)
750 First Street, NE, Suite 700
Washington, DC 20002-4241
Phone: 800-742-4089
Web site: www.naswdc.org

Academy of Certified Social Workers (ACSW)
750 First Street, NE, Suite 700
Washington, DC 20002-4241
Phone: 800-742-4089, ext. 367
Web site: www.naswdc.org/credacsw.htm

NASW Register of Clinical Social Workers
750 First Street, NE, Suite 700
Washington, DC 20002-4241
Phone: 800-742-4089, ext. 298
Web site: www.naswdc.org

Diplomate in Clinical Social Work
750 First Street, NE, Suite 700
Washington, DC 20002-4241
Phone: 800-742-4089
Web site: www.naswdc.org

Mental Health Nursing

American Nurses Association (ANA)
600 Maryland Avenue, SW, Suite 100W
Washington, DC 20024-2571
Phone: 202-651-7000
Web site: www.nursingworld.org

American Nurses Credentialing Center
600 Maryland Avenue, SW, Suite 100W
Washington, DC 20024-2571
Phone: 202-651-7000
Web site: www.nursingworld.org/
   ancc/ancc.htm

American Psychiatric Nurses Association
1200 19th Street, NW, Suite 300
Washington, DC 20036
Phone: 202-857-1133
Web site: www.apna.org

Marital and Family Therapy

American Association for Marriage and Family
   Therapy (AAMFT)
110 17th Street, NW, Tenth Floor
Washington, DC 20036-4601
Phone: 202-452-0109
Web site: www.aamft.org

Related Topics

Chapter 123, "National Self-Help Groups and Organizations"

122   COMMON CLINICAL ABBREVIATIONS AND SYMBOLS

a	before		AAV	AIDS-associated virus
A&B	apnea and bradycardia		abd	abduction; abdomen

ABG	arterial blood gas	BS	bowel sound
a.c.	before meals	B/S	breath sounds
ad lib	as desired	BUN	blood urea nitrogen
adm	admission		
aero, aero Rx	aerosol inhalation equipment, treatment	c̄	with
		C	centigrade
AF	auricular fibrillation	ca	calcium; chronological age
A/G	albumin-globulin ratio	CA	cancer, carcinoma
AIDS	acquired immune deficiency/ immunodeficiency syndrome	CAM	cardiac medical
		C&S	culture and sensitivity
AK	above knee	cap	capsule
alb	albumin	CAS	cardiac surgery
alks, p'tase	alkaline phosphatase	CAVC	complete atrioventricular canal
ALL	allergy	CBC	complete blood count
AMA	against medical advice	CBG	capillary blood gas
amb	ambulatory	cc	cubic centimeter
anes	anesthesia	CC	chief complaint
angio	angiogram	CF	cystic fibrosis
ANS	anesthesia	Δ	change
AODM	adult-onset diabetes mellitus	CHD	congenital heart disease
Ao DT	descending aorta	✓	check
AP	anteroposterior	chol	cholesterol
AP & Lat	anteroposterior and lateral	Cl	chloride
≈	approximate	cldy	cloudy
AQ	achievement quotient	cm	centimeter
ARC	AIDS-related complex	c. monitor	cardiac monitor
art mon	arterial pressure monitor	CNS	central nervous system
ARV	AIDS-related virus	c/o, CO	complaint of
AS	aortic stenosis; left ear	coarc	coarctation
ASA	aspirin	conj	conjunctive
AsAo	ascending aorta	conv	convergence
ASD	atrial septal defect	CO₂	carbon dioxide
@	at	CP	cerebral palsy
A2	aortic second sound	CPAP	continuous positive airway pressure
AU	both ears		
AV	arteriovenous	CPC	clinicopathological conference
AVC	atrioventricular canal	CPR	cardiopulmonary resuscitation
AVVR	atrioventricular valve regurgitation	CPT	chest physiotherapy
AWOL	away without official leave	CRC	clinical research
AX	angle jerk	C/S	cesarean section
		CSF	cerebrospinal fluid
b	born	CT	chest tube
Bab	Babinski	CT, CT scan, CAT	computerized tomography
bact	bacteria	CVA	cerebrovascular accident
BBS	bilateral breath sounds	CVL	central venous line
BC/BS	Blue Cross/Blue Shield	CVP	central venous pressure
BD	birth defect	CVS	clean-voided specimen
BDI	Beck Depression Inventory	CXR	chest X ray
BE	barium enema	CYS	cystic fibrosis
b.i.d.	twice a day		
BJM	bones, joints, muscles	D&C	dilation and curettage
BK	below knee	DAT	diet as tolerated
BM	bowel movement	d/c	discontinue
BMT	bone marrow transplant	D/C	discharge
BP	blood pressure	↓	decrease

dil	dilute	g/dl	grams per hundred millimeters
DOA	dead on arrival	GF&R	grunting, flaring, and retracting
DOB	date of birth	GI	gastrointestinal
DOC	doctor on call	GIS	gastroenterology
DOE	dyspnea on exertion; date of evaluation	GNS	general surgery
		gr	grain
DOPP	duration of positive pressure	gtt	drops
DP	dorsalis pedis	GTT	glucose tolerance test
DPT	diphtheria, pertussis, tetanus	gyn	gynecology
D/S	dextrose and saline		
DTR	deep tendon reflex	h	hour
DTV	due to void	H	husband
D/W	dextrose and water	HC	head circumference
DX, Dx, dx	diagnosis	HCT	hematocrit
		HEENT	head, eyes, ears, nose, throat
ECG, EKG	electrocardiogram	HEM	hematology
ECHO	enterocytopathogenic human orphan viruses	Hgb	hemoglobin
		HIV	human immunodeficiency virus
ECMO	extracorporeal membrane oxygenation	HLHS	hypoplastic left heart syndrome
		HMO	health maintenance organization
ECT	electroconvulsive treatment	HO$_2$	humidified oxygen
EDC	endocrine	HPF	high-power field
EEG	electroencephalogram	HR	heart rate
e.g.	for example	h.s.	at bedtime
EMV	expired minute volume	ht	height
ENT	ears, nose, throat; otolaryngology	HTN	hypertension
		Hx	history
EOM	extraocular movement		
eos	eosinophils	IA	intra-arterial
ER	emergency room	I&D	incision and drainage
ERG	electroretinogram	I&O	intake and output
ESR	erythrocyte sedimentation rate	ICP	intracranial pressure
ETOH	alcohol	ICU	intensive care unit
ETT	endotracheal tube	IDS	infectious diseases
eve	evening	i.e.	that is, namely
ext	extension	IJ	internal jugular vein
extrem	extremities	IL	intralipid
EYE	ophthalmology	IM	intramuscular
		imp	impression
f	frequency	↑	increase (elevated)
F	fahrenheit; father	in rot	in rotation
FBS	fasting blood sugar	inv	inversion
♀	female	IOFB	intraocular foreign body
FFP	fresh frozen plasma	IP	inpatient
FH	family history	IQ	intelligence quotient
FIO$_2$	fractional inspired oxygen	IT	intrathecal
flex	flexion	IV	intravenous
for. bend	forward bending	IVC	inferior vena cava
FTT	failure to thrive	IVH	intraventricular hemorrhage
f/u	follow up	IVP	intravenous push
FUO	fever of unknown origin		
		JT	jejunostomy tube
g, gm	gram		
GB series	gallbladder series	K	potassium
GC	gonorrhea	kg	kilogram

KJ	knee jerk	MSE	mental status examination
KUB	kidney, ureter, bladder	MVA	motor vehicle accident
kV	kilovolt		
		Na	sodium
L	left	NAD	no apparent distress
LA	left atrium	neb, htd neb	nebulizer, heated nebulizer
lab	laboratory	NEC	necrotizing enterocolitis
L&A	light and accommodation	NEO	neonatology
LAO	left anterior oblique	neph	nephrotomy
LAP	left atrial pressure	NG	nasogastric
lat. bend	lateral bending	NICU	newborn ICU
LFT	liver function test	NKA	no known allergies
LL	lower lid	nl	normal
LLE	left lower extremity	NLS	neurology
LLL	left lower lobe	NMJ	neuromuscular joint
LLQ	left lower quadrant	NP	nasopharyngeal
L/min	liters per minute	NPO	nothing by mouth
LMP	last menstrual period	NRC	normal retinal correspondence
LOA	leave of absence	N/S	normal saline
LP	lumbar puncture	NSS	neurosurgery
LPA	left pulmonary artery	NT	nasotracheal
LUE	left upper extremity	NTA	nothing to add
LUL	left upper lobe	N_2	nitrogen
LUQ	left upper quadrant	N_2O	nitrous oxide
LV	left ventricular	N/V	nausea and vomiting
lymphs	lymphocytes	NVD	normal vaginal delivery
lytes	electrolytes	N/V/D	nausea, vomiting, diarrhea
m	meter	O&P	ova and parasites, stool
M	mother	obs	obstetrics or obstetrical
♂	male	OBS	organic brain syndrome
M&T	myringotomy and tubes	occ	occasionally
MAP	mean arterial pressure	OD	right eye
MAPI	Millon Adolescent Personality	odont	odontectomies
	Inventory	OHID	oxygen tent
MCL	midclavicular line	OM	otitis media
MCMI-II	Millon Clinical Multiaxial	1:1	one to one
	Inventory-II	OOB	out of breath; out of bed
med	medicine	OOP	out on pass
mEq	milliequivalent (per liter, mEq/L)	op	operation
mets	metastasis	OP	oropharyngeal
mg	milligram	OPD	outpatient department
Mg	magnesium	OR	operating room
mg/dl	milligrams per hundred	ORL	otorhinolaryngology (ENT)
	milliliters	orth, ORT	orthopedics
MHC	mental health center	OS	left eye
ml	milliliter (preferred over cc)	OT	occupational therapy
ML	middle lobe	O_2	oxygen
MMPI	Minnesota Multiphasic Personality	O_2sat	oxygen saturation
	Inventory	OU	both eyes
Mn	manganese		
mod	moderate	p̄	after
mono	monocyte infectious;	P	phosphorous
	mononucleosis	PA	posteroanterior; pulmonary artery
MS	multiple sclerosis	PA cath	pulmonary artery catheter

P&A	percussion and auscultation	q.h.s.	every night
P&V	percussion and vibration	q.i.d.	four times a day
PAP	pulmonary artery pressure	q.n.s.	quantity not sufficient
p.c.	after meals	q.o.d.	every other day
PCO$_2$	partial carbon dioxide pressure	QR	Quiet Room
PE	physical examination	qs	quantity sufficient
ped, pedi, peds	pediatrics	q3h	every 3 hours
PEEP	positive end-expiratory pressure	q2h	every 2 hours
PERLA	pupils equal, reactive to light and accommodation	R	right
PF	plantar flexion	RA	right atrium
PFC	persistent fetal circulation	RAO	right anterior oblique
PFO	patent foramen ovale	RBC	red blood cell; red blood count
PFT	pulmonary function test	RD	radial deviation
pg	per gastric	RDS	respiratory distress syndrome
pH	hydrogen ion concentration	re	regarding
PH	past history	REN	renal/dialysis
PHP	posthospital plans	Rh+, Rh−	rhesus blood factor
PI	present illness	RHD	rheumatic heart disease
PIE	pulmonary interstitial emphysema	RLE	right lower extremity
		RLL	right lower lobe
PIV	peripheral intravenous	RLQ	right lower quadrant
PKU	phenylketonuria	RML	right middle lobe
PLS	plastics	R/O	rule out
plts	platelets	RPA	right pulmonary artery
PMH	past medical history	RR	respiratory rate
p.o.	by mouth	RRE	round, regular, and equal
PO$_2$	partial pressure oxygen	RT	respiratory therapy
PPH	persistent pulmonary hypertension	RTC	return to clinic
		RTH	radiation therapy
p.r.	per rectum	RTO	return to office
PRBC	packed red blood cells	RUE	right upper extremity
premie	premature	RUL	right upper lobe
prep	preparation	RUQ	right upper quadrant
p.r.n.	as needed	RV	right ventricle or ventricular
prot	protein (total protein preferred)	Rx	treatment; treatment with medication
PS	pulmonic stenosis; pulmonary stenosis		
psi	pounds per square inch	s	without
PSP	phenolsulfonphthalein	S	suction
psy; psych	psychiatry; psychology	SC	subcutaneous
pt	patient	SCA	subclavian artery
PT	physical therapy; prothrombin time	sed. rate	erythrocyte sedimentation rate
		SG	specific gravity
PTMDF	pupils, tension, media, disk, fundus	SH	social history; serum hepatitis
		SIDS	sudden infant death syndrome
PUL	pulmonary	SLR	straight leg raising
PVC	premature ventricular contraction	SOB	shortness of breath
		sol	solution
q	every	SP	special precautions
q.a.m.	every morning	S/P	status post
q.d.	every day	SPA	serum protein analysis
q4h	every 4 hours	SS	signs and symptoms
q.h.	every hour	STAT	immediately and only once

strep	streptococcus	URI	upper respiratory infection
sub AS	subaortic stenosis	uro, urol	urology or urological
surg	surgery or surgical	US	ultrasound
SV	single ventricle		
SVC	superior vena cava	V, VA	volt; vision or visual acuity
SW	social worker	vag	vagina or vaginal
Sz	seizure	VC	vital capacity
		VCO$_2$	carbon dioxide production
TA	tricuspid atresia	VD	venereal disease
tab	tablet	VDRL	Venereal Disease Research
T&A	tonsillectomy and adenoidectomy		Laboratory
T&C	type and crossmatch	vert	vertebrae (D. vert: dorsal; L. vert:
T&H	type and hold		lumbar)
TAT	Thematic Apperception Test	VF	volar flexion; vocal fremitus
TB	tuberculosis	vit	vitamin when followed by specific
TBA	to be announced		letter (e.g., vit A)
tbsp	tablespoon	VO$_2$	oxygen consumption
TCO$_2$	total (calculated) carbon dioxide	VS	vital signs
TENS	transcutaneous electrical nerve	Vx	vertex
	stimulator		
TF, TOF	tetralogy of Fallot	W	wife
TGA	transposition of great arteries	WAIS-R	Wechsler Adult Intelligence Scale-
TGV	transposition of great vessels		Revised
t.i.d.	three times a day	WB	whole blood
TLC	tender loving care	WBC	white blood cell; white blood
TM	tympanic membrane		count
TP	total protein	WD	well developed
TPR	temperature, pulse, and	WDWN	well developed, well nourished
	respiration	WISC-III	Wechsler Intelligence Scale for
Tq	tourniquet		Children-III
tsp	teaspoon	wk	week
TT	tracheostomy tube	WN	well nourished
TTX	tumor therapy	WNL	within normal limits
TV	tidal volume	WRAT	Wide Range Achievement Test
2	secondary to	wt	weight
tx	transplant	w/u	work-up
TX, Tx	treatment		
		y.o.	years old
U	unit		
UA	urinalysis		
UDT	undescended testicles		
UGI	upper gastrointestinal series		
umb(i)	umbilical		
UO	urinary output		
ureth	urethral		

Related Topics

Chapter 24, "Normal Medical Laboratory Values and Measurement Conversions"

Chapter 111, "Glossary of Legal Terms of Special Interest in Mental Health Practice"

123 NATIONAL SELF-HELP GROUPS AND ORGANIZATIONS

The following list provides the mailing addresses and telephone numbers of the national chapters of major self-help groups and organizations in the United States. Arranged by diagnostic category or problem, the national listings appear alphabetically by the title of the organization. The purpose is to provide the practitioner with quick access to these self-help groups and organizations. A more exhaustive listing may be obtained from the excellent *Self-Help Sourcebook* (White & Madara, 1995) or from the following national self-help clearinghouses:

American Self-Help Clearinghouse
c/o Northwest Covenant Medical Center
25 Pocono Road
Denville, NJ 07834-2995
Phone: 201-625-7101

National Self-Help Clearinghouse
CUNY Graduate School and University
  Center
25 West 43rd Street, Room 620
New York, NY 10036
Phone: 212-354-8525

Abuse—Sexual and Physical

Batterers Anonymous
8485 Tamarind, #D
Fontana, CA 92335
Phone: 909-355-1100
(For men who wish to control their anger and
  eliminate their abusive behavior)

Sexual Abuse Survivors Anonymous (SASA)
P.O. Box 241046
Detroit, MI 48224
(12-step program for survivors of rape, incest, or
  sexual abuse)

Survivors of Incest Anonymous (SIA)
P.O. Box 26870
Baltimore, MD 21212
Phone: 410-282-3400
(12-step program for survivors of incest)

Addiction—Alcohol and Drugs

Adult Children of Alcoholics World Service
  Organization
P.O. Box 3216
Torrance, CA 90510
Phone: 310-534-1815
(12-step program for adults whose family
  suffered from alcohol or other dysfunctions)

Al-Anon Family Groups
P.O. Box 862, Midtown Station
New York, NY 10018-0862
Phone: 800-344-2666; 800-356-9996
(12-step program for those whose lives have
  been affected by the compulsive drinking of a
  family member or friend)

Alateen
P.O. Box 862, Midtown Station
New York, NY 10018-0862
Phone: 800-344-2666
(12-step program for young persons whose
  lives have been affected by someone else's
  drinking)

Alcohol and Drug Helpline
Hotline: 800-821-4357 (24 hrs)
(Referrals to local alcohol- and drug-dependency
  units and self-help groups)

Alcoholics Anonymous World Services
General Service Office
475 Riverside Drive, 11th floor
New York, NY 10115
Phone: 212-870-3400
(For people who have found or would like to find
  a solution to their drinking problem)

American Council on Alcoholism
Hotline: 800-527-5344
(Referrals to treatment centers and DWI classes)

Chemically Dependent Anonymous
P.O. Box 423
Severna Park, MD 21146
Phone: 410-647-7060
(12-step program for friends and relatives of
people who are chemically dependent)

Cocaine Anonymous
3740 Overland Avenue, #H
Los Angeles, CA 90034
Phone: 800-347-8998; 310-559-5833
(12-step program of recovery from cocaine
addiction)

C-SAT National Drug Hotline
Hotline: 800-662-4357
Spanish: 800-662-9832 (day)
(Information on drug or alcohol abuse and
related issues)

800 Cocaine
Hotline: 800-COCAINE (24 hrs)
(Information and referral service for drug and
alcohol addiction and treatment)

Marijuana Anonymous (MA)
P.O. Box 2912
Van Nuys, CA 91404
Phone: 800-766-6779
(12-step program of recovery from marijuana
addiction)

Nar-Anon World Wide Service
P.O. Box 2562
Palos Verdes, CA 90274-0119
Phone: 310-547-5800
(12-step program of recovery for families and
friends of addicts)

National Clearinghouse for Alcohol and Drug
Information
Hotline: 800-788-2800 (touch-tone); 800-
729-6686 (rotary)
(Information on alcohol and drug abuse,
prevention, and treatment centers)

Rational Recovery Systems
P.O. Box 800
Lotus, CA 95651
Phone: 916-621-4374; 800-303-2873
(Nonreligious program for persons recovering
from substance abuse and addictive behavior)

Addiction—Sexual

Codependents of Sex Addicts (COSA)
P.O. Box 14537
Minneapolis, MN 55414
Phone: 612-537-6904
(12-step program for those in relationships with
people who have compulsive sexual behavior)

Sex Addicts Anonymous
P.O. Box 70949
Houston, TX 77270
Phone: 713-869-4902
(12-step program of recovery from compulsive
sexual behavior)

Adoption

Adoptees' Liberty Movement Association
(ALMA)
P.O. Box 727, Radio City Station
New York, NY 10101-0727
Phone: 212-581-1568
(For adoptees; provides international reunion
registry)

Adoptive Families of America
3333 Highway 100 North
Minneapolis, MN 55422
Phone: 612-535-4829
(For adoptive and prospective adoptive families)

Concerned United Birthparents (CUB)
2000 Walker Street
Des Moines, IA 50317
Phone: 800-822-2777
(For adoption-affected people)

Affective Disorders

National Depression and Manic-Depression
Association
730 North Franklin, #501
Chicago, IL 60610
Phone: 800-826-3632
(For persons with depressive and manic-
depressive illness and their families)

National Organization for Seasonal Affective
Disorder (NOSAD)
P.O. Box 40133
Washington, DC 20016
(For SAD patients and their families)

Postpartum Support International
c/o Jane Hannikman
927 North Kellogg Avenue
Santa Barbara, CA 93111
Phone: 805-967-7636
(For women experiencing emotional changes
   during and after pregnancy)

Aging

American Association of Retired Persons
   (AARP)
601 East Street, NW
Washington, DC 20049
Phone: 202-434-2277
(For persons 50 years and older)

Grey Panthers
2025 Pennsylvania Avenue, NW, #821
Washington, DC 20006
Phone: 202-466-3132
(For young and old adults working together)

ALS (Amyotrophic Lateral Sclerosis)/ Lou Gehrig's Disease

ALS Association
21021 Ventura Boulevard, #321
Woodland Hills, CA 91364
Phone: 818-340-7500; 800-782-4747
(For ALS patients, their families, and friends)

Alzheimer's Disease

Alzheimer's Association
Phone: 800-272-3900

Alzheimer's Disease and Related Disorders
   Association
919 North Michigan Avenue, #1000
Chicago, IL 60611-1676
Phone: 312-335-8700
(For caregivers of Alzheimer's patients)

Alzheimer's Disease Education and Referral
   Center
Hotline: 800-438-4380
(Information and referrals, publications, and
   information regarding clinical trials)

Anxiety Disorders

Anxiety Disorders Association of America
6000 Executive Boulevard, #513
Rockville, MD 20852
Phone: 301-231-9350
(For people with phobias and related anxiety
   disorders)

Phobics Anonymous
P.O. Box 1180
Palm Springs, CA 92263
Phone: 619-322-COPE
(12-step program of recovery from anxiety and
   panic disorders)

Attention Deficit Disorder

Children and Adults with Attention Deficit
   Disorder (CHADD)
499 NW 70th Avenue, #109
Plantation, FL 33317
Phone: 305-587-3700

Bereavement

Compassionate Friends National Office
P.O. Box 3696
Oak Brook, IL 60522-3696
Phone: 708-990-0010
(For parents whose child has died at any age or
   of any cause)

Mothers Against Drunk Driving (MADD)
511 East John Carpenter Freeway, Suite 700
Irving, TX 75062
Phone: 800-GET-MADD; 214-744-6233
(For victims of drunk driving crashes)

Blindness/Visual Impairment

American Council of the Blind
1155 15th Street, NW, #720
Washington, DC 20005
Phone: 800-424-8666; 202-467-5081
(For blind and visually impaired people and their
   families)

American Foundation for the Blind
Hotline: 800-232-5463; 212-620-2158 (TDD) (day)
(Information, referrals, catalog of publications)

Brain Injury

Brain Injury Association Family Helpline
1776 Massachusetts Avenue, NW, Suite 100
Washington, DC 20036
Phone: 800-444-NHIF, 202-296-6443
(For persons who have sustained head injuries
and their families)

Cancer

American Cancer Society
Phone: 800-227-2345

Cancer Care
1180 Avenue of the Americas
New York, NY 10036
Phone: 212-302-2400; 800-813-HOPE
(For those who have suffered the loss of a loved
one to cancer)

Candlelighters Childhood Cancer
Foundation
7910 Woodmont Avenue, Suite 460
Bethesda, MD 20814
Phone: 800-366-2225; 301-657-8401
(For children with cancer and their families)

National Cancer Institute Center
Information Service
Phone: 800-422-6237

Carpal Tunnel Syndrome/Repetitive Strain Injury

Association for Repetitive Motion
Syndromes
P.O. Box 514
Santa Rosa, CA 95402-0514
Phone: 707-571-0397
(For persons with carpal tunnel syndrome and
related repetitive motion injuries)

Cerebral Palsy

United Cerebral Palsy Association
1660 L Street, NW, Suite 700
Washington, DC 20036
Phone: 800-872-5827

Children/Youth Services

Boys Town National Hotline
Boys Town, NE 68010
Hotline: 800-448-3000 (24 hrs)
(Crisis and referral line for all problems)

KID SAVE
Phone: 800-543-7283
(Information and referrals to services for
children and adolescents in crisis)

Chronic Fatigue Syndrome

CFIDS Association
P.O. Box 220398
Charlotte, NC 28222-0398
Phone: 800-442-3437; 900-896-2343
(For people affected by chronic fatigue and
immune dysfunction syndrome)

Compulsive Spending

Debtors Anonymous
P.O. Box 400, Grand Central Station
New York, NY 10163-0400
Phone: 212-642-8220
(12-step program of recovery from compulsive
indebtedness)

Diabetes

American Diabetes Association
Phone: 800-342-2383

Domestic Violence

Child Help USA Hotline
Hotline: 800-422-4453 (24 hrs)
(Information, referrals, crisis counseling)

Eating Disorders

American Anorexia/Bulimia Association
293 Central Park West, #1R
New York, NY 10024
Phone: 212-891-8686
(For persons with eating disorders)

National Association of Anorexia Nervosa and
    Associated Disorders
P.O. Box 7
Highland Park, IL 60035
Phone: 847-831-3438
(For persons with eating disorders)

National Eating Disorders Organization
    (NEDO)
6655 S. Yale Avenue
Tulsa, OK 74136
Phone: 918-481-4044
(For persons with eating disorders, their
    families, and friends)

Epilepsy

Epilepsy Foundation of America
4351 Garden City Drive
Landover, MD 20785
Phone: 800-332-1000 (day)
(Information and referral for people with
    epilepsy and their families)

Family/Parenting

Association for Children for Enforcement of
    Support (ACES)
c/o Geraldine Jensen
2260 Upton Avenue
Toledo, OH 43606
Phone: 800-537-7072
(For custodial parents who are having difficulties
    collecting child support)

National Organization for Men
11 Park Place
New York, NY 10007-2801
Phone: 212-686-MALE; 212-766-4030
(For men seeking equal rights divorce, custody,
    property, and visitation laws)

Tough Love International
Box 1069
Doylestown, PA 18901
Phone: 800-333-1069
(For help in dealing with out-of-control behavior
    of a family member)

Gambling

Gam-Anon Family Groups
P.O. Box 157
Whitestone, NY 11357
Phone: 718-352-1671
(12-step program of recovery for relatives and
    friends of compulsive gamblers)

Gamblers Anonymous
P.O. Box 17173
Los Angeles, CA 90017
Phone: 213-386-8789
(12-step program of recovery from compulsive
    gambling)

Hearing Impaired

American Society for Deaf Children
2848 Arden Way, #210
Sacramento, CA 95825-1373
Phone: 800-942-ASDC; 916-482-0120
(For parents and families with children who are
    deaf or hard of hearing)

ASHA Hearing and Speech Helpline
Hotline: 800-638-TALK; 800-638-8255
    (Voice/TDD) (day)
(Information, referrals, publications)

National Association of the Deaf
814 Thayer Avenue
Silver Spring, MD 20910
Phone: 301-587-1788; 301-587-1789
(For people who are deaf and hard of hearing)

Self-Help for Hard of Hearing People (SHHH)
7910 Woodmont Avenue, Suite 1200
Bethesda, MD 20814
Phone: 301-657-2248; 301-657-2249
(For hard of hearing people, their families, and
    friends)

HIV/AIDS

CDC National AIDS Clearinghouse
Hotline: 800-458-5231
(Provides educational materials and referrals to
    support groups)

National AIDS Hotline
Center for Disease Control (CDC)
P.O. Box 13827
Research Triangle Park, NC 27709
Hotline: 800-342-AIDS (24 hrs); Spanish:
    800-344-7432; Deaf: 800-AID-7889 (day)
(Offers telephone support, information,
    education, and referrals)

National Association of People with AIDS
1413 K Street, NW, #7
Washington, DC 20005-3405
Phone: 202-898-0414
(For persons with AIDS)

Infertility

Resolve
1310 Broadway
Somerville, MA 02144-1731
Phone: 617-623-0744
(For infertile couples)

Learning Disabilities

Learning Disabilities Association of
    America
4156 Library Road
Pittsburgh, PA 15234
Phone: 412-341-1515; 412-341-8077
(For people with learning disabilities and their
    families)

Lupus

American Lupus Society
3914 Del Amo Boulevard, Suite 922
Los Angeles, CA 90503
Phone: 310-390-6888
(For lupus patients and their families)

Lupus Foundation of America
4 Research Place, #180
Rockville, MD 20850-3226
Phone: 800-558-0121; 301-670-9292
(For lupus patients and their families)

Mental Disorders—General

Emotions Anonymous
P.O. Box 4245
St. Paul, MN 55104-0245
Phone: 612-647-9712
(12-step program of recovery from emotional
    difficulties)

Federation of Families for Children's Mental
    Health
1021 Prince Street
Alexandria, VA 22314-2971
Phone: 703-684-7710
(For families and their children with emotional,
    behavioral, or mental disorders)

National Alliance for the Mentally Ill (NAMI)
200 North Glebe Road, Suite 1015
Arlington, VA 22203-3754
Phone: 800-950-NAMI
(For relatives and individuals affected by mental
    illness)

Neurotics Anonymous
P.O. Box 12
Casa, AR 72025-0012
(12-step program of recovery from mental and
    emotional disturbances)

Mental Retardation

American Association on Mental Retardation
Phone: 800-424-3688
(Information on mental retardation)

National Down Syndrome Congress
1605 Chantilly Drive, #250
Atlanta, GA 30324-3269
Phone: 800-232-NDSC; 404-653-1555
(For families affected by Down syndrome)

Multiple Sclerosis

Multiple Sclerosis Association of America
705 Haddonfield Road
Cherry Hill, NJ 08002
Phone: 800-833-4MSA
(For multiple sclerosis patients)

National Multiple Sclerosis Society
Information Resource Center
733 Third Avenue
New York, NY 10017-3288
Phone: 800-344-4867
(For MS patients and their families)

Muscular Dystrophy

Muscular Dystrophy Association
3300 East Sunrise Drive
Tucson, AZ 85718
Phone: 602-529-2000
(For fighting 40 neuromuscular diseases)

Narcolepsy

Narcolepsy Network
P.O. Box 42460
Cincinnati, OH 45242
Phone: 513-891-3522
(For persons with narcolepsy and other sleep disorders and their families)

Obesity/Overweight (see also Eating Disorders)

Food Addicts Anonymous (FAA)
4623 Forest Hill Boulevard, #111-4
West Palm Beach, FL 33415
Phone: 407-967-3871
(12-step program of recovery from food addiction)

National Association to Advance Fat Acceptance (NAAFA)
P.O. Box 188620
Sacramento, CA 95818
Phone: 916-558-6880
(For people who are obese)

Overeaters Anonymous
P.O. Box 44020
Rio Rancho, NM 87174-4020
Phone: 505-891-2664
(12-step program of recovery from compulsive eating disorders)

Take Off Pounds Sensibly (TOPS)
P.O. Box 07360
4575 South 5th Street
Milwaukee, WI 53207-0360
Phone: 800-932-8677
(For overweight people who wish to attain and maintain their goal weight)

Pain

National Chronic Pain Outreach Association
7979 Old Georgetown Road, #100
Bethesda, MD 20814
Phone: 301-652-4948
(For those suffering with chronic pain)

Physical Disability

National Easter Seal Society
Phone: 800-221-6827 (day)
(Publications for people with disabilities)

National Institute on Disability and Rehabilitation Research
Phone: 800-344-5404
(Information on self-help devices for disabled persons)

National Organization on Disability
Hotline: 800-248-ABLE (24 hrs)
(Information for persons with disabilities)

Premenstrual Syndrome

PMS Access
Phone: 800-222-4767
(Information and support on premenstrual syndrome)

Reflex Sympathetic Dystrophy (RSD)

Reflex Sympathetic Dystrophy Syndrome Association
116 Haddon Avenue, Suite D
Haddonfield, NJ 08033-2306
Phone: 215-955-5444; 609-795-8845
(For those suffering from RSD and their families)

Schizophrenia (see also Mental Disorders—General)

Schizophrenics Anonymous
Mental Health Association in Michigan
15920 West Twelve Mile Road
Southfield, MI 48076
Phone: 810-557-6777
(For people with a schizophrenia-related disorder)

Sleep Apnea

American Sleep Apnea Association
2025 Pennsylvania Avenue, NW, Suite 905
Washington, DC 20006
Phone: 202-293-3650
(For persons with sleep apnea and their families)

Smoking

Nicotine Anonymous World Service
P.O. Box 591777
San Francisco, CA 94159-1777
Phone: 415-750-0328
(12-step program of recovery from nicotine addiction)

Stroke/Cardiovascular Disease

American Heart Association
Phone: 800-242-8721
(Provides information and education)

National Heart Association
P.O. Box 1887, Murray Hill Station
New York, NY 10156-0611
Phone: 800-553-6321
(For aphasia patients and their families)

National Stroke Association
96 Inverness Drive, E, Suite I
Englewood, CO 80112-5112
Phone: 303-649-9299; 800-STROKES
(For stroke victims and their families)

Stroke Connection of the American Heart Association
7272 Greenville Avenue
Dallas, TX 75231
Phone: 800-553-6321
(For stroke victims and their families)

Suicide

American Suicide Foundation
1045 Park Avenue, Suite 3C
New York, NY 10028
Phone: 800-ASF-4042; 212-410-1111
(Provides referrals to national support groups for suicide survivors)

Friends for Survival
P.O. Box 214463
Sacramento, CA 95821
Phone: 916-392-0664; 800-646-7322
(For family, friends, and professionals after a suicide death)

Tardive Dyskinesia/Dystonia

Tardive Dyskinesia/Tardive Dystonia National Association
P.O. Box 45732
Seattle, WA 98145-0732
(For those suffering from TD/TD, their families, and friends)

Tourette Syndrome

Tourette Syndrome Association
42-40 Bell Boulevard, Suite 205
Bayside, NY 11361-2861
Phone: 718-224-2999; 800-237-0717
(Education for patients, professionals, and the public)

Workaholism

Workaholics Anonymous World Service Organization
P.O. Box 289
Menlo Park, CA 94026-0289
Phone: 510-273-9253
(12-step program of recovery from compulsive overworking)

References & Readings

Powell, T. J. (1987). *Self-help organizations and professional practice*. Silver Spring, MD: National Association of Social Workers.
Powell, T. J. (1994). *Understanding the self-help organization*. Beverly Hills, CA: Sage.

Reissman, F., & Carroll, D. (1995). *Redefining self-help: Policy and practice.* San Francisco: Jossey-Bass.

Rudolfa, E., & Hungerford, L. (1982). Self-help groups: A referral source for professional therapists. *Professional Psychology, 13,* 345–353.

White, B. J., & Madara, E. J. (Eds.) (1995). *The self-help sourcebook: Finding and forming mutual aid self-help groups* (5th ed.). Denville, NJ: American Self-Help Clearinghouse.

Wong, M. M. (1996). *The national directory of be-reavement support groups and services.* Forest Hills, NY: ADM Publishing.

Yoder, B. (1990). *The recovery resource book.* New York: Simon and Schuster.

Related Topics

124   RECOGNIZING, ASSISTING, AND REPORTING THE IMPAIRED PSYCHOLOGIST

Gary Richard Schoener

DEFINITIONS AND HISTORY

The term *impaired,* when applied to a psychologist or other health care professional, has historically been considered almost synonymous with the notions of alcoholism or substance abuse. This reflects the fact that one of the most common sources of impairment in health professionals is drug or alcohol abuse or addiction. Most "impaired practitioner" programs in other health professions, and even in the legal profession, focus on alcoholism and other substance abuse. Each of these programs also ends up dealing with other problems—for example, depression, marital difficulties, anxiety states, and sexual compulsivity—but today the focus remains on chemical abuse or dependency problems.

As defined in psychology, impairment refers to objective change in a person's professional functioning. An impaired psychologist is one whose work-related performance has diminished in quality. This may be manifested in one or more of the following ways: work assignments are typically late or incomplete; conflict with colleagues has noticeably increased; clients, students, or families have registered complaints; or the amount of absenteeism and tardiness has markedly increased. (Schwebel, Skorina, & Schoener, 1994, p. 2)

Organized psychology's first major thrust at identifying and dealing with impairment involved a task force and then a book, *Professionals in Distress: Issues, Syndromes, and Solutions in Psychology* (Kilburn, Nathan, & Thoreson, 1986), which still provides a good overview of the topic. This was followed by the Advisory

Committee on the Distressed Psychologist, which reported to the Board of Professional Affairs of the American Psychological Association (APA), which soon changed the name to the Advisory Committee on Impaired Psychologists and then produced the book *Assisting Impaired Psychologists: Program Development for State Psychological Associations* (Schwebel, Skorina, & Schoener, 1988). A revised edition was published in 1994. The committee's current name uses "Colleague Assistance" in place of "Impaired Psychologists" in order to underline a broader focus, including prevention, and to stress the notion of the need to help colleagues who are distressed or impaired.

The topic of sexual misconduct by professionals has generated literally thousands of books and articles (e.g., Lerman, 1990), with some focused on prevention (e.g., Pope, Sonne, & Holroyd, 1993) and others examining treatment of the offending professional (e.g., Gabbard, 1995; Gonsiorek, 1995; Schoener, Milgrom, Gonsiorek, Luepker, & Conroe, 1989). For psychology, sexual misconduct was probably the most visible outcome of impairment, as well as the most expensive in terms of the generation of ethics complaints and licensure board actions, and it accounted for at least half of the cost of defense and awards to plaintiffs in malpractice actions. Sexual misconduct is an issue that typically has not been dealt with by committees on impaired practitioners in other professions, and in psychology there has been debate over whether it should be dealt with differently. Some have questioned whether rehabilitation should be attempted in such cases (e.g., Pope et al., 1993), whereas others provide assessment and/or rehabilitation (e.g., Abel, Osborn, & Warberg, 1995; Gabbard, 1995; Gonsiorek, 1995; Schoener, 1995).

A relatively new factor in the handling of impairment is the Americans With Disabilities Act (cf. Bruyere & O'Keeffe, 1994). While prohibiting discrimination against individuals with disabilities, both mental and physical, the act requires employers to "make reasonable accommodation" to employees' disabilities. This affects the handling of the impaired professional in two ways. First, it provides an incentive to acknowledge disability rather than hide

it; second, it directs the psychologist in the role of employer to make reasonable efforts to help someone dealing with a disability function on the job. Thus, the impaired or potentially impaired psychologist has reason to present his or her difficulties to an employer or supervisor in hopes of negotiating a helpful accommodation.

RESPONSIBILITY TO REPORT

Psychologists often have professional responsibilities with regard to clients, students, and others who may be affected by the practitioner's impairment. Where such individuals are at risk, there may be a duty to act quickly. In addition, remember that any reporting duties need to be carried out if you learn of possible child abuse or neglect or of anything that must be reported to a state licensure board or other regulatory authority.

First and foremost, never agree to keep something confidential until you know what the impaired professional has to say and whether you can keep it confidential. As with clients, anyone with whom you consult about impairment needs to know the limits of the privacy of your discussions with them. All of the following reporting duties would be based on state laws or guidelines:

1. Reporting of abuse or neglect of a minor or of a vulnerable adult
2. Any reporting to a state licensure board required by licensure statutes (e.g., Minnesota requires reporting of certain offenses unless they are communicated by the psychologist who is seeking help)
3. Any reporting duties based on your knowledge of dangers to others, such as potential dangers to clients
4. Duties to report impaired functioning of a staff member who works in the same facility as you do

In some states, colleague assistance or impaired practitioner programs have exemptions from some reporting duties. It is important that you determine whether such an exemption might apply to your activities. They are typically limited to work by professional standards review committees or impaired practitioner programs. Those involved in subsequent treatment or rehabilitation should also note their responsibilities (cf. Jorgenson, 1995).

GUIDELINES FOR INTERVENTION

The APA Code of Ethics and general standards in professional practice, education, and research require that psychologists consult with colleagues who are at risk to engage in unethical practice. The practical issue of how and when to intervene depends on the following factors:

1. Your relationship with the colleague who is, or may be, impaired
2. Your professional status vis-à-vis the colleague—for example, a supervisor, teacher, administrator
3. Whether or not the colleague has come to you for assistance
4. The organizational or institutional setting in which you work and what policies, procedures, and departments exist to help with the situation

Before acting, examine any organizational or institutional policies or guidelines concerning dealing with impaired staff. In larger organizations, human resources departments often play a role in such intervention. They may be consulted for advice or for direct assistance. Employee assistance programs also provide guidance and services that may be of help.

There also may be experts in your local community who can be of assistance. A number of state psychological associations have colleague assistance committees. The Practice Directorate at the APA has such information through staff for the Advisory Committee on Colleague Assistance. The APA effort, in fact, is focused on the creation of state committees to provide assistance to those seeking to intervene or obtain help for colleagues. If there are no readily identifiable local experts and there is no state committee, it is also possible to arrange for help with substance-abusing or alcoholic colleagues through Psychologists Helping Psy-

chologists (PHP), a national organization. It can be contacted through Ann Stone at 703-578-1644 (e-mail: AnnS@Erols.com), 3484 S. Utah Street, Arlington, VA 22206.

Another possible resource is the colleague assistance committee of another health profession, such as medicine. These committees can be most easily located by contacting the state professional organization. In addition, PHP is connected to International Doctors in Alcoholics Anonymous, which consists of professionals in many fields who are involved in Alcoholics Anonymous. This 48-year-old organization, which has a yearly convention, can be contacted for resources through C. Richard McKinley at 314-482-4548 (e-mail: IDAAdickMc@aol.com.), P.O. Box 199, Augusta, MO 63332.

One of the fundamental questions in this area is the manner of intervention. Some circumstances permit a private talk with an impaired practitioner to start things moving, whereas in other cases a more active intervention is necessary. Whenever several professionals confront an impaired psychologist jointly, or involve others, such as family members, there is the potential for greater anger and defensiveness. However, in some circumstances, little else works. Four intervention options, described in *Assisting Impaired Psychologists* (Schwebel et al., 1994), are presented below.

Voluntary Intervention

In some situations, an impaired psychologist calls for help or approaches a colleague or supervisor. It is essential to remember the importance of follow-through. The fact that a colleague comes in for help does not mean that he or she will take the next step. Sometimes just receiving support reduces the person's motivation. Furthermore, it is important to have a competent diagnostician determine what sort of treatment is needed. Professionals often look healthier than they are, and as a result inadequate treatment intervention may be planned. In the case of professional misconduct, such as sex with clients, it is critical that someone with specialized experience do the assessment and treatment planning so as to avoid common pitfalls in such cases (Gabbard, 1995).

The "12-Step" Intervention

The 12-step intervention is aimed at someone who appears to be alcoholic or to have a substance abuse problem. Psychologists or other health professionals who are in recovery from alcoholism or substance abuse and who have experience in this type of intervention arrange a meeting with the impaired psychologist; they share their own experiences and encourage the person to join Alcoholics Anonymous or Psychologists Helping Psychologists or to seek help in some other way. Although such an intervention is intrusive, it is not really confrontive. The goal is to provide a model for recovery and to convey the sense that a psychologist can be alcoholic and benefit from help.

Confrontive Intervention

In confrontive intervention, an employer or a colleague assistance committee receives a report that a psychologist has a significant problem and has not responded to suggestions that he or she go for help. An investigation is done to see if such a problem can be documented behaviorally, and then a small team of professionals (or, in some instances, a work supervisor) confronts the psychologist with the evidence that has been gathered. A treatment referral has previously been identified, the psychologist is offered a plan of action, and peer pressure is used to try to bring about an agreement to receive help and follow through. This approach is more confrontive than the 12-step intervention in that considerable peer pressure is applied, and time and energy are spent on planning the option the person will be offered.

Comprehensive Intervention

Comprehensive intervention is reserved for situations in which the psychologist's problem is severe, or at least getting worse, and he or she has not responded to input or suggestions that he or she seek help. It goes beyond the confrontive intervention in that the information-gathering process usually involves discussions with the psychologist's spouse or significant other, and an intervention team is organized

that includes a number of key people in the psychologist's life. Prior to the intervention, this group meets and plans the intervention, including some role playing of possible scenarios. The eventual intervention is thus scripted beforehand. The psychologist is then told that if he or she does not enter and complete treatment, specific negative consequences will occur. This can involve job suspension, a report to a licensing body, a spouse filing for divorce, or some other action. This approach is coercive and intrusive, and it may bring about an angry response from the psychologist. It should be done with the aid of persons experienced in such work.

SUPPORT AND MONITORING

A major factor in the success of interventions is the degree to which you can help the psychologist deal with the problems involved in starting the treatment process. Helping find ways to arrange for work coverage, an appropriate medical leave, and identification of an affordable treatment program that is covered by insurance is very important. Many such practical problems can sabotage treatment efforts.

When someone is in treatment for any sort of impairment, maintaining contact in a supportive fashion can be quite helpful. It is also important to monitor compliance, to the degree possible, so as to be able to confront those who attempt to quit before completion.

WORK REENTRY

The main goal of any intervention should be to facilitate a professional assessment of the psychologist and the planning of any treatment. After that is done, it is important to consult with the assessor concerning job or practice limitations. When it seems that the treatment is completed, there should be an assessment of the situation, including a "return to work" assessment, which specifies things that would help prevent a recurrence and also reduce the risk of any misconduct or relapse.

With alcoholism there may be a requirement that the psychologist attend support groups and also a warning that the smell of alcohol on his or her breath may be sufficient cause for suspension. In the case of substance abuse, random urine testing may be required. It is also likely that more frequent supervisory meetings will be called for at first in order to ensure that workload and duties are realistic given the recovery process.

REDUCING LEGAL RISKS

Some of the legal risks connected with various types of intervention are discussed in Schwebel et al. (1994). The more confrontive the intervention, the riskier it is. However, despite fears of retaliation for invasion of privacy, such cases appear to be quite rare. The most common mistakes that have legal consequences are a failure to consult with human resources personnel and to plan the intervention within the personnel guidelines of a facility and a failure to review the Americans With Disabilities Act for its applicability to the situation. Psychologists need to be aware that when disputes arise within the family, especially in cases of family dissolution or divorce, well-intentioned helpers can find themselves pawns in an intrafamilial power struggle. So it is important to carefully gather background data and to be clear on what basis you believe the psychologist in question has a problem.

References & Readings

Abel, G., Osborn, C., & Warberg, B. (1995). Cognitive-behavioral treatment for professional sexual misconduct. *Psychiatric Annals, 25,* 106–112.

Bruyere, S., & O'Keeffe, J. (1994). *Implications of the Americans With Disabilities Act for psychology.* Washington, DC: American Psychological Association.

Gabbard, G. (1995). Transference and countertransference in the psychotherapy of therapists charged with sexual misconduct. *Psychiatric Annals, 25,* 100–105.

Gonsiorek, J. (1995). Assessment and treatment of health care professionals and clergy who sexually exploit patients. In J. Gonsiorek (Ed.), *Breach of trust: Sexual exploitation by health care professionals and clergy* (pp. 225–234). Thousand Oaks, CA: Sage.

Health, S. (1991). *Dealing with the therapist's vulnerability to depression.* Northvale, NJ: Jason Aronson.

Jorgenson, L. (1995). Rehabilitating sexually exploitative therapists: A risk management perspective. *Psychiatric Annals, 25,* 118–122.

Kilburn, R., Nathan, P., & Thoreson, R. (1986). *Professionals in distress: Issues, syndromes, and solutions in psychology.* Washington, DC: American Psychological Association.

Koocher, G. P., & Keith-Spiegel, P. (1998). *Ethics in psychology: Professional standards and cases* (2nd ed.). New York: Oxford University Press.

Lerman, H. (1990). *Sexual intimacies between psychotherapists and patients: An annotated bibliography of mental health, legal, and public media literature and relevent legal cases* (2nd ed.). Washington DC: Division of Psychotherapy, American Psychological Association.

Pope, K. S., Sonne, J. L., & Holroyd, J. (1993). *Sexual feelings in psychotherapy: Explorations for therapists and therapists-in-training.* Washington, DC: American Psychological Association.

Rippere, V., & Williams, R. (1985). *Wounded healers: Mental health workers' experiences of depression.* New York: Wiley.

Schoener, G. R. (1995). Assessment of professionals who have engaged in boundary violations. *Psychiatric Annals, 25,* 95–99.

Schoener, G. R., Milgrom, J. H., Gonsiorek, J. C., Luepker, E. T., & Conroe, R. (1989). *Psychotherapists' sexual involvement with clients: Intervention and prevention.* Minneapolis, MN: Walk-In Counseling Center.

Schwebel, M., Skorina, J., & Schoener, G. (1988). *Assisting impaired psychologists: Program development for state psychological associations.* Washington, DC: American Psychological Association.

Schwebel, M., Skorina, J., & Schoener, G. (1994). *Assisting impaired psychologists: Program development for state psychological associations* (Rev. ed.). Washington, DC: American Psychological Association.

Skorina, J. K., Bissell, L. C., & De Soto, C. B. (1990). The alcoholic psychologist: Routes to recovery. *Professional Psychology: Research and Practice, 21,* 248–251.

125 HIGHLY RATED SELF-HELP BOOKS AND AUTOBIOGRAPHIES

Jennifer S. Clifford & John C. Norcross

Self-help books pertaining to mental or behavioral disorders and autobiographies by individuals suffering from such disorders have proliferated in recent years. "Bibliotherapy" (the use of self-help books with or without formal treatment) and the use of autobiographies as adjuncts to psychotherapy have increased correspondingly. For example, Starker (1988) found that 88% of practicing psychologists prescribed self-help books to supplement their treatment. Marx, Royalty, Gyorky, and Stern (1992) reported that only 12% of psychologists *never* recommended self-help books. Similarly, Clifford, Norcross, and Sommer (1998) found that 85% of practicing psychologists recommended a self-help book at least once in the past 12 months and that 33% recommended at least one autobiography to their psychotherapy patients.

Self-help books and autobiographical accounts promise similar therapeutic benefits as adjuncts to ongoing psychotherapy. Specifically, they can provide phenomenological accounts of behavioral disorders in everyday terms; enhance identification and empathy; generate hope and insight; offer concrete advice and techniques; explain treatment strategies; and summarize research findings (Pardeck & Pardeck, 1992). When done right, autobiographies and self-help materials can complement and accelerate the process of professional treatment. At the same time, we have limited research on the uses and limits of self-help materials without professional intervention (Rosen, 1987).

The following are consensual recommendations of practicing psychologists on self-help books and autobiographical accounts pertaining to mental or behavioral disorders. Each entry provides the title of the book, the author's name, and the primary disorder or content area addressed by the book.

TOP 25 RATED SELF-HELP BOOKS

Santrock and Minnett (1994) mailed a national survey to 4,000 members of the clinical and counseling divisions of the American Psychological Association (APA). Nearly 800 doctoral-level psychologists from across the United States returned the survey. The survey was deliberately sent to academics as well as to therapists working outside of academia in order to ensure a broad cross section of clinical and counseling psychologists. The psychologists were asked to rate only those books with which they were sufficiently familiar from the list of over 350 self-help books in 33 categories. To be eligible for the top 25 list, a self-help book had to be rated by a minimum of 75 mental health professionals. The following are the 25 books with the highest average ratings, listed in order from highest to lowest (J. W. Santrock and A. M. Minnett, personal communication, July 6, 1993).

The Courage to Heal, by Ellen Bass and Laura Davis (abuse and recovery)

Feeling Good, by David Burns (depression)

Infants and Mothers, by T. Berry Brazelton (child development and parenting)

What Every Baby Knows, by T. Berry Brazelton (child development and parenting)

Dr. Spock's Baby and Child Care, by Benjamin Spock and Michael Rothenberg (child development and parenting)

How to Survive the Loss of a Love, by Melba Colgrove, Harold Bloomfield, and Peter McWilliams (death and grief)

To Listen to a Child, by T. Berry Brazelton (child development and parenting)

The Boys and Girls Book About Divorce, by Richard Gardner (divorce)

The Dance of Anger, by Harriet Lerner (anger)

The Feeling Good Handbook, by David Burns (depression)

Toddlers and Parents, by T. Berry Brazelton (child development and parenting)

Your Perfect Right, by Robert Alberti and Michael Emmons (assertion)

Between Parent and Teenager, by Haim Ginott (teenagers and parenting)

The First Three Years of Life, by Burton White (child development and parenting)

What Color Is Your Parachute?, by Richard Bolles (career development)

Between Parent and Child, by Haim Ginott (child development and parenting)

The Relaxation Response, by Herbert Benson (relaxation)

The New Aerobics, by Kenneth Cooper (exercise)

Learned Optimism, by Martin Seligman (positive thinking)

Man's Search for Meaning, by Victor Frankl (self-fulfillment)

Children: The Challenge, by Rudolph Dreikurs (child development and parenting)

You Just Don't Understand, by Deborah Tannen (communication)

The Dance of Intimacy, by Harriet Lerner (love and intimacy)

Beyond the Relaxation Response, by Herbert Benson (relaxation)

The Battered Woman, by Lenore Walker (abuse and recovery)

TOP 13 RATED AUTOBIOGRAPHIES

An increase in the number and value of autobiographies is evident in the popular literature of late (Gray, 1997). First-person accounts are triumphing over the third-person accounts; writing for the *Boston Globe,* Ellen Goodman (1997, p. 2) declared that "the memoir is taking over from the novel." The glorification of the autobiography is manifested in the estimated 200 titles published annually (Atlas, 1996).

Clifford, Norcross, and Sommer (1998) conducted a study to ascertain practicing psychologists' recommendations of autobiographies to their patients during psychotherapy. They mailed a questionnaire to 1,000 randomly selected members and fellows of the APA's Division of Psychotherapy living in the United States. The questionnaire contained 50 published autobiographies dealing primarily or substantially with the author's mental disorder or treatment thereof. A total of 322 questionnaires (32%) were returned; the sample appeared demographically and geographically representative of the entire divisional membership. The psychologists rated only those autobiographies with which they were sufficiently familiar. To be eligible for the top-13 list, an autobiography had to be rated by a minimum of 10 psychologists. The following are the 13 autobiographies with the highest average ratings, listed in order from highest to lowest (Clifford et al., 1998).

An Unquiet Mind, by K. R. Jamison (bipolar disorder)

Darkness Visible: A Memoir of Madness, by W. Styron (depression)

Girl Interrupted, by S. Kaysen (bipolar disorder)

Nobody Nowhere: The Extraordinary Autobiography of an Autistic, by D. Williams (autism)

Out of the Depths, by A. T. Boisin

Welcome Silence: My Triumph Over Schizophrenia, by C. L. North (schizophrenia)

Too Much Anger, Too Many Tears, by J. Gotkin and P. Gotkin

Diary of a Fat Housewife: A True Story of Humor, Heartbreak, and Hope, by R. Green (eating disorder)

Undercurrents: A Therapist's Reckoning With Her Own Depression, by M. Manning (depression)

A Drinking Life: A Memoir, by P. Hamill (substance abuse)

Leaves From Many Seasons, by O. H. Mowrer (depression)

The Liar's Club: A Memoir, by M. Karr (family dysfunction)

A Brilliant Madness: Living With Manic Depressive Illness, by P. Duke (depression)

References & Readings

Allport, G. (1942). *The use of personal documents in psychological science.* New York: Social Science Research Council.

Atlas, J. (1996, May 12). The age of the literary memoir is now. *New York Times Magazine,* pp. 25–27.

Clifford, J. S., Norcross, J. C., & Sommer, R. (1998, February). *Autobiographies of mental patients: Psychologists' uses and recommendations.* Poster presented at the 69th annual meeting of the Eastern Psychological Association, Boston.

Goodman, E. (1997, April 18). Sex, lies, and bestselling memoirs. *Boston Globe,* p. 2.

Gray, P. (1997, April 21). Real-life misery: Read all about it! *Time,* p. 106.

Marx, J. A., Royalty, G. M., Gyorky, Z. K., & Stern, T. E. (1992). Use of self-help books in psychotherapy. *Professional Psychology: Research and Practice, 23,* 300–305.

Neysmith-Roy, J. M., & Kleisinger, C. L. (1997). Using biographies of adults over 65 years of age to understand life-span developmental psychology. *Teaching of Psychology, 24,* 116–118.

Pardeck, J. T., & Pardeck, J. A. (1992). *Bibliotherapy: A guide to using books in clinical practice.* San Francisco: Mellen Research University Press.

Peterson, D. (Ed.) (1982). *A mad people's history of madness.* Pittsburgh: University of Pittsburgh Press.

Rosen, G. M. (1987). Self-help treatment books and the commercialization of psychotherapy. *American Psychologist, 42,* 46–51.

Santrock, J. W., & Minnett, A. M. (1994). *The authoritative guide to self-help books.* New York: Guilford Press.

Sommer, R., & Osmond, H. (1960). Autobiographies of former mental patients. *Journal of Mental Science, 106,* 648–662.

Sommer, R., & Osmond, H. (1983). A bibliography of mental patients' autobiographies, 1969–1982. *American Journal of Psychiatry, 140,* 1051–1054.

Starker, S. (1988). Psychologists and self-help books: Attitudes and prescriptive practices of clinicians. *American Journal of Psychotherapy, 42,* 448–455.

Related Topics

Chapter 123, "National Self-Help Groups and Organizations"

INDEX

This index includes authors of chapters and authors discussed in the text. For authors cited in the text, see the References and Readings section at the end of each chapter.

WHAT DO YOU WANT IN THE NEXT EDITION?

The *Psychologists' Desk Reference* has attempted to organize and present the most frequently requested materials for practicing psychologists. We conducted considerable research to secure a consensus on what information practitioners desire to have at their desks. In all, we spent several years determining the optimal content and proper mix of the *Psychologists' Desk Reference*.

At the same time, we realize that individual clinicians have different preferences and that practice requirements evolve rapidly. For these reasons, we cordially invite you, the reader, to inform us of what you would like to be included in future editions. Kindly send us a note (to the attention of Dr. Gerry Koocher, Department of Psychology, Children's Hospital, 300 Longwood Avenue, Boston, MA 02115) or an e-mail message (koocher@a1.tch.harvard.edu) containing your suggestions. If you are the first to suggest a new entry that makes it into the next supplement or edition, we will send you a complimentary copy.

In the meantime, we wish you and your patients the very best of health and happiness.